Richard Greene is professor of English at the University of Toronto. He is the author of three volumes of poetry and a biographical and critical study of the eighteenth-century poet Mary Leapor. He is also the critically acclaimed editor of *Selected Letters of Edith Sitwell* and *Graham Greene: A Life in Letters*.

'. . . a model of its craft: quietly subversive, unexpected and rescuing a poet of incomparable but not always consistent skill from the mocking hands of the "pipsqueakery", as Sitwell called her critics'

Nicholas Shakespeare, *Daily Telegraph*

'Greene writes with conviction and sensitivity, and he nicely balances a no-nonsense approach with a capacity to be held in thrall'

Alexandra Harris, *Guardian*

'. . . brilliant, wise, funny and affectionate. It is perfection, actually'

Roger Lewis, *Daily Mail*

'Greene takes pains to show us the private Sitwell, her loyalty and sympathy, her gentleness and generosity, her loneliness and vulnerability'

Deborah Longworth, *Times Higher Education*

'. . . an excellent biography, particularly in its analysis of Edith's poetry and her literary relationships. Greene quotes lavishly from her wonderfully entertaining letters'

Sarah Bradford, *Literary Review*

'Richard Greene's excellent biography of Edith Sitwell is informative, witty and entertaining. It is a timely reminder of a writer exotic in appearance and character'

The Economist

Also by Richard Greene

The Selected Letters of Edith Sitwell

Graham Greene: A Life in Letters

EDITH SITWELL

Avant-Garde Poet, English Genius

Richard Greene

virago

VIRAGO

First published in Great Britain in 2011 by Virago
This paperback edition published in 2012 by Virago

A CIP catalogue record for this book
is available from the British Library.

ISBN 978-1-86049-968-5

Typeset in Goudy by M Rules
Printed and bound in Great Britain by
Clays Ltd, St Ives plc

Papers used by Virago are from well-managed forests
and other responsible sources.

MIX
Paper from
responsible sources
FSC
www.fsc.org   FSC® C104740

Virago
An imprint of
Little, Brown Book Group
100 Victoria Embankment
London EC4Y 0DY

An Hachette UK Company
www.hachette.co.uk

www.virago.co.uk

For Marianne

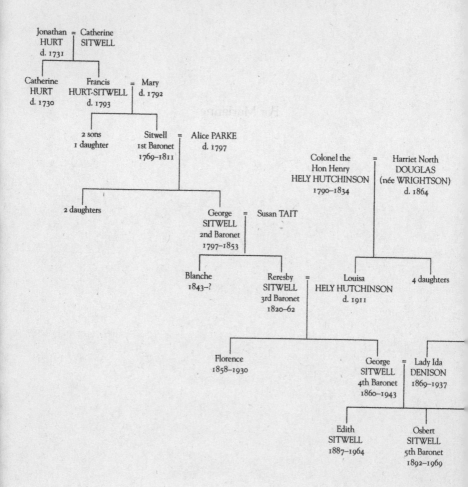

Simplified Family Tree

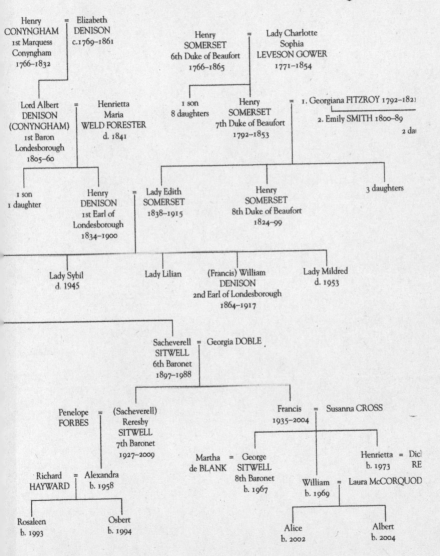

Henry CONYNGHAM
1st Marquess Conyngham
1766–1832
= Elizabeth DENISON
c.1769–1861

Henry SOMERSET
6th Duke of Beaufort
1766–1865
= Lady Charlotte Sophia LEVESON GOWER
1771–1854

Lord Albert DENISON (CONYNGHAM)
1st Baron Londesborough
1805–60
= Henrietta Maria WELD FORESTER
d. 1841

1 son
8 daughters

Henry SOMERSET
7th Duke of Beaufort
1792–1853
= 1. Georgiana FITZROY 1792–182?
2. Emily SMITH 1800–89
2 da?

1 son
1 daughter

Henry DENISON
1st Earl of Londesborough
1834–1900
= Lady Edith SOMERSET
1838–1915

Henry SOMERSET
8th Duke of Beaufort
1824–99

3 daughters

Lady Sybil
d. 1945

Lady Lilian

(Francis) William DENISON
2nd Earl of Londesborough
1864–1917

Lady Mildred
d. 1953

Sacheverell SITWELL
6th Baronet
1897–1988
= Georgia DOBLE

Penelope FORBES
= (Sacheverell) Reresby SITWELL
7th Baronet
1927–2009

Francis
1935–2004
= Susanna CROSS

Richard HAYWARD
= Alexandra
b. 1958

Martha de BLANK
= George SITWELL
8th Baronet
b. 1967

William
b. 1969
= Laura McCORQUOD

Henrietta
b. 1973
= Dic?
RE?

Rosaleen
b. 1993

Osbert
b. 1994

Alice
b. 2002

Albert
b. 2004

Contents

Edith Sitwell in Her Own Words

I am fundamentally kind, if you discount my conversation, which is very often not . . .

On cats: They never say anything silly, you see, and that's something.

I have always been in bad taste – and glory in it. Good taste, I think, belongs to the world of advertisements – 'Persil' etc, and fussing about what the neighbours think.

On being asked if she was a handful for her parents: My parents were a handful for me. They weren't parents I would recommend to anybody.

Why *is* it that every man who possesses genius in his head and love in his heart, every man who can think and dares speak against abuses, everybody who pleads the cause of mercy and who champions the unfortunate, is called a crank by all the half-wits of his time?

On hostile reviewers: All the Pipsqueakery are after me in full squeak.

Yes. I believe. I believe in people – and I believe. Anyway, it's better with all banners flying – isn't it?

On being asked, at seventy-five, how she was: Dying, but apart from that I'm all right.

Still falls the Rain

Light and Dawn: December ... at
December ...

Still falls the Rain,
Dark as the world of man, black as our loss,
Blind as the nineteen hundred and forty nails
Upon the Cross.

Still falls the Rain
With a sound like the pulse of the heart that is
changed to the hammer beat
In the Potter's Field, and the sound of the
impious feet

On the Tomb....
In the Field of Blood where the small hopes
breed and the human brain
nurtures its greed, that worm with the brow of Cain

Still falls the Rain
Upon the flesh and soul of the world ... black are
these flails
as the pain of the suffering soul that each hour nails
To the suffering flesh, its cross,

Still falls the Rain —
Then O Ile leape up to my God: who pulles me
downe—
See see where Christs blood streames in the firmament

A manuscript of 'Still Falls the Rain', Edith Sitwell's most famous poem. It was inspired
by the bombing of Sheffield in December 1940

WHY?

On the night of 12 December 1940, three hundred aeroplanes operating under the light of a full moon struck Sheffield. They blasted factories, shops, and houses, and for those hours the city was turned into a hell of dust, flame, and flying glass. At 11.44 p.m. a high-explosive bomb demolished the seven-storey Marples Hotel in Fitzalan Square; seventy people inside, many of them sheltering in the cellars, were killed. The next day, a handful of survivors were pulled from the heap of bricks and girders. It is said that one man, though physically unharmed, was so shocked that he eventually hanged himself. In the years to come, the site of the hotel was treated with the fear and reverence that New Yorkers feel for the site of the World Trade Center. Sheffield was attacked again on 15 December, and between the two raids over six hundred people were killed. In the following week, there was yet more bombing.

Renishaw Hall stands about eight miles from the heart of Sheffield. It was relatively safe, though stray bombs fell in the neighbourhood. Edith Sitwell heard the planes overhead and the repeated explosions. She wrote to her brother Sacheverell, 'one thought every second or so would be our last'.[1] A few days later, she wrote to the painter Pavel Tchelitchew: 'How wonderful was the experience, when I went into the town; work-girls, shop-girls, men assistants whom I knew, – as we clasped each other by the hand, each said to the other, I to them and they to me: "Thank God you are safe." They are utterly unmoved, and resolute.'[2]

Although she had been one of Britain's leading poets in the 1920s, Sitwell had spent most of the following decade grinding out prose works to pay other people's bills. The coming of the war rekindled her poetry. In late 1939, she had written 'Lullaby' and its companion 'Serenade: Any Man to Any Woman' – two visionary poems that captured, as well as any of the time, the calamity of Europe's return to slaughter. Sitwell herself, often flippant, often snobbish, was now unable to turn her eyes from the war and from the pity of war. The challenge for a poet, she thought, was to meet the sheer magnitude of events. At the time of Dunkirk, she wrote: 'The last fortnight has been on such a gigantic scale, that everything in history since the Crucifixion seems dwarfed – only Shakespeare could do justice to it.'[3] A year later she wrote: 'after those two terrible raids [on Sheffield] in December one could not write about them straight away, and how, immediately after such an experience, *could* one write about anything else in one's own life?'[4] By then, she had written the quintessential poem of the Blitz:

> Still falls the Rain –
> Dark as the world of man, black as our loss –
> Blind as the nineteen hundred and forty nails
> Upon the Cross.

> Still falls the Rain
> With a sound like the pulse of the heart that is changed to the
> 	hammer-beat
> In the Potter's Field, and the sound of the impious feet

> On the Tomb:
> Still falls the Rain
> In the Field of Blood where the small hopes breed and the
> 	human brain
> Nurtures its greed, that worm with the brow of Cain.

> Still falls the Rain
> At the feet of the Starved Man hung upon the Cross.
> Christ that each day, each night, nails there, have mercy on us –
> On Dives and on Lazarus:
> Under the Rain the sore and the gold are as one.

Still falls the Rain –
Still falls the Blood from the Starved Man's wounded Side:
He bears in His Heart all wounds, – those of the light that died,
The last faint spark

In the self-murdered heart, the wounds of the sad
    uncomprehending dark,
The wounds of the baited bear, –
The blind and weeping bear whom the keepers beat
On his helpless flesh . . . the tears of the hunted hare.

Still falls the Rain –
Then – O Ile leape up to my God: who pulles me doune –
See, see where Christ's blood streames in the firmament:
It flows from the Brow we nailed upon the tree
Deep to the dying, to the thirsting heart
That holds the fires of the world, – dark-smirched with pain
As Caesar's laurel crown.

Then sounds the voice of One who like the heart of man
Was once a child who among beasts has lain –
'Still do I love, still shed my innocent light, my Blood, for thee.'

Sitwell believed that much of the meaning of a poem is in the sound it makes. Twenty-five years earlier, she had told a cousin that she was experimenting with rhythms that were like a heartbeat.[5] Here she goes much further, tying together the sounds of falling rain, the hammering of nails, a pulse, the sound of feet on a tomb, the dropping of blood, and (never explicit except in a headnote) the thudding of bombs. All this is performed in the poem's rhythm, which changes death into a solemn music and offers at the level of form the hope of a greater change. At the end of the poem there are two voices, Marlowe's Faustus pleading in his last hour before damnation, and Christ offering Blood, 'my innocent light'. In Sitwell's view, there is as much chance that hell will take us as that we will accept the grace that is offered.

'Still Falls the Rain' is an extraordinary poem. It is not necessarily her best, but it was here that a poet of incomparable skill spoke most directly to the agonies of her time. However, her time is no longer our time. She died in 1964, and her reputation crashed soon after. To some degree, she created the conditions for such a reaction. For five decades, she had been brawling with her critics, whom she dubbed the 'pip-squeakery'. Once she was gone, they were free to savage her work, even as she had savaged them. But tit for tat is not the whole story.

Edith Sitwell's particular kind of modernism – her refusal to be trapped by ancestral memory and her desire to overturn conventional ideas of the self – was rooted in the desolation of her family life. Her search for vision and greatness in poetry was partly an attempt to move beyond what she saw as the blindness and the smallness of the exis-tence she was born to. As a woman, she lacked confidence in her gifts, and took many years to pass through an apprenticeship, so she came to the party just as other guests were leaving. It is common, even for sym-pathetic critics, to dodge Sitwell's later poems and say that she was at her best in the 1920s – in the years of *Façade*, her playful and ingenious collaboration with the composer William Walton. That evasion hap-pens because we do not yet have the nerve to say that the generation of Philip Larkin imposed as orthodoxy a painfully narrow, indeed inco-herent, account of where poetry comes from.

It is commonly observed that the 'Movement' poets of the 1950s were influenced by logical positivism – a philosophical stance that held, among other things, that knowledge must be strictly empirical, and that metaphysics and theology are meaningless. That view still has its adherents, not least among them Richard Dawkins. But the position hardly bears a second glance. An empiricist's trust in the data of the senses will always be a matter of faith. It is undoubtedly right to believe in facts, but there is no way to get to that belief empirically. These philosophers refused to admit that beyond what we see and beyond the structures of language, we assume (as they silently assumed) another metaphysical authority for knowing. Under the influence of logical pos-itivism, many critics spoke of Sitwell's expansive rhetoric and religious claims as 'unearned' – a notion that has dogged her reputation for sixty years. They insisted that good poetry lay in small gestures and close observation. A taste for empiricism can indeed produce some won-derful poetry, but it can also lead to an obtuseness among reviewers and critics – it promotes an impoverished conception of the real to which poetry may speak. And so our recent literary history still echoes with the donnish cry, 'It just won't do!'

Of the great poets of her generation, Sitwell was the easiest to knock off the pedestal. She was a flamboyant, combative aristocrat and, better still, she was a woman; therefore, she served as a critical soft target. Attacking her was a way of attacking the influence of Yeats, Pound, and Eliot without taking on their more fortified reputations. She remarked at the end of her life: 'I am resigned to the fact that people who don't know me loathe me. Perhaps it is because I am a woman who dares to write poetry. It must be awfully annoying to a man who wants to write and can't to see this horrid old lady who *can* write poetry.'⁶

However, Edith Sitwell has continued to have some shrewd admirers. One of her earlier biographers, Victoria Glendinning, believed that Sitwell published more poems than she needed and that this has clouded her legacy, but she added, 'I believe that if the world of literary criticism knew nothing but, say, her twelve finest poems, she would have an unquestioned, uncategorized place on anyone's Parnassus.'⁷

In the pages that follow, I have taken the view that Sitwell is a writer who matters – enormously. Although she was eccentric and savagely amusing, I do not want to settle for a portrait of quirks or a compilation of quips. I have dwelt not just on her odd family and childhood, but on her friends Helen Rootham, Siegfried Sassoon, and Pavel Tchelitchew as key influences. I have spent some time accounting for her reading – not least because she is often portrayed, even by friends like Stephen Spender, as amazingly talented with the sounds of language but devoid of ideas.⁸ Finally, I have tried to explain the evolution of her technique. For a poet such as Sitwell, the most important events in her life were the poems. This book would therefore be pointless if the reader came away without some understanding of how to read her work.

Of course, Edith Sitwell is also keenly interesting on other fronts. Just as a personality, she was a strange combination of kindness and cruelty, courage and duplicity, simplicity and artifice. She could be funny and generous, as well as sometimes pompous and mean-spirited. She nurtured any number of rising talents, and slapped down others. She was by turns compassionate and cutting; she inspired devotion among most of those who knew her, but a few, legitimately, resented her.

In the thirty years since a biography of Edith Sitwell last appeared, much new evidence has become available. Long gaps in her life can now be filled. There are many new documents pertaining to her early years. Her vast correspondence with Pavel Tchelitchew has been released from embargo, and many other collections of letters have come to light. New biographies of her brothers Osbert and Sacheverell have been written. It is time to look again at Edith Sitwell. Part of the challenge, of course, is how to do justice, both to the seriousness of her life and work, and to her playfulness. She wrote: 'It is terrible to find oneself a solitary, highly unpopular electric eel in a pool peopled by worthy, slightly somnolent flat-fish.'[9] Shame on the biographer who does no better for Edith Sitwell than the flatfish might. Her conversation and her letters ring with an anarchic laughter, which will be heard in the later chapters of this book.

Any life worth writing about is strange. While we may observe blandly that her life and sensibility were only possible in a certain time, class, and culture, Edith Sitwell achieved a dazzling degree of originality in life and in art. There is a mystery about this individuality – how to explain a woman, who, at the last, will not submit to comparison? The idea of the definitive biography is often self-deceiving – the subject of such a book will keep many secrets, then vanish across a closed border. We would expect no less of Edith Sitwell. Her first escape was from the life that was expected of her as a young woman. Then, as the years passed, she put together a literary career unlike any other, repeatedly breaking from common paths into unexplored territory. Her themes were endurance, flight, compassion, courage. What follows is the story of that difference, that fugitive impulse towards greatness.

1

FACTS OF LIFE

There is no more important fact in Edith Sitwell's early life than that
her mother did not want her. The Honourable Ida Denison's marriage
to Sir George Sitwell in November 1886 was arranged by their omnipo-
tent mothers. The courtship consisted of two luncheons. Knowing
practically nothing about sex, the beautiful seventeen-year-old found
the experience shocking. She fled from her new husband, but her
mother sent her straight back to him. She soon became pregnant, and
gave birth to Edith Louisa Sitwell at Wood End, her mother-in-law's
house in Scarborough, on 7 September 1887. Ida's second child,
Osbert, born five years later, remembered his mother as affectionate to
him, but given to 'ungovernable, singularly terrifying rages' with his
sister.[1] He believed she saw in Edith 'a living embodiment of some past
unhappiness of her own. These and other things made her cruel.'[2]

In 1938, Edith Sitwell spoke of her childhood as 'so unhappy that
even now I can hardly bear to think about it'.[3] She does not give many
details about the troubles of her earliest years, so we have to work
around the edges and try to reason out what happened between Edith
Sitwell and her mother. In 1941, she told the novelist 'Bryher'
(Winifred Ellerman) that her mother would unleash 'rages so violent
that they would lead to a sort of cataleptic state, – first a tornado of fury,
and then an immobility which was terrifying. These happened, literally, every day, and I can't think how she lived till she was well over
sixty.'[4]

She wrote in 1945 to Pavel Tchelitchew that all her life she had
been 'bound hand and foot. First by my frightful mother, and then
afterwards by affection, pity, and duty.'[5] The language of bondage, slav-
ery and release often comes into her stories of childhood. Although she

could not pardon her parents, she could see that their lives were never free. She wrote at the end of her own life: 'I do not wish to be cruel about a poor dead woman. I have forgiven the unhappiness long ago, and now write of it only because otherwise, after my death, much in me will be misunderstood. I now feel only pity for my mother, a poor young creature, married against her will into a kind of slave-bondage to an equally unfortunate and pitiable young man.'[6] This was for public consumption; in truth, she never forgave them, especially, 'my admirable mother, – who, each day expressed herself, though without particular meaning, in prose that might have been called Elizabethan – to her daughter, and to her helpless servants'.[7]

Ida Sitwell (1869–1937) came from a wealthy family. Her grandfather, Albert Denison Conyngham, created the first Baron Londesborough in 1850, inherited £2,300,000.[8] Her father, William Henry Denison, second Lord Londesborough, did his very best to spend this fortune and failed. Liking musical theatre, he backed lavish productions, and slept with actresses and girls from the music halls. He kept up a good many houses that he occupied at different times of the year: Londesborough Lodge in Scarborough, an estate at Londesborough Park in Yorkshire's East Riding, a house in the New Forest; others at Blankney and Grimston, and, for a time, the largest house in Berkeley Square, then another in Grosvenor Square. He was created first Earl of Londesborough in the Jubilee honours of June 1887. This meant new courtesy titles for his children, among them Lady Ida Sitwell.

Lady Ida's mother, Edith Sitwell's grandmother, was born Lady Edith Somerset. Her father, the seventh Duke of Beaufort, traced his ancestry back to John of Gaunt. On her mother's side, she was the niece of the Duke of Wellington and it is said that Napoleon III once wanted to marry her. She loved music, especially opera, and had grown up in a house where great singers and musicians performed, including Franz Liszt who played for her parents in 1840.[9] She and Lord Londesborough had four daughters, Ida, Sybil, Mildred and Lilian, and one son, Francis.

Edith Sitwell grew to hate her grandmother but knew that she was somewhat like her: 'I had, I regret to say, inherited my grandmother Londesborough's violent temper – but not her passion for making rows about trivial subjects.'[10] Much of Sitwell's personal style would be modelled on this countess and her distant forebears. Sitwell carved out an authoritative persona, donned medieval gowns and jewellery, and learnt to crush 'impertinence': 'I inherit my appearance from the family of my maternal grandmother. And therefore that same appearance can be seen in the effigies of the Plantagenets in Westminster Abbey.'[11] Although she made a stand against conventional standards of beauty, Sitwell lamented that she was 'plain'. The one part of her body she thought beautiful were her much-photographed hands, an inheritance from her grandmother: 'She had exceedingly beautiful hands, which remained like those of a young woman until she died; these beauties were nearly always hidden by black suede gloves to preserve their whiteness (which was like that of privet flowers).'[12] The Countess required Lady Ida and her other children, including her son, to wear such gloves even indoors. Those gloves became, in Edith's eyes, a symbol of their way of life – protected, pretty, and useless.

Lady Ida's upbringing was at once privileged and curiously disabling. Her youngest child, Sacheverell Sitwell (b. 1897), always known as 'Sachie', wrote: 'Her character, when I first remember her, was [a] compound of natural high spirits and a sort of palace-bred or aristocratic helplessness.'[13] She was taught deportment by the eighty-year-old Marie Taglioni, who in her youth had been one of the world's leading ballerinas.[14] She also learnt some French and music, but her education had no rigour. Sacheverell thought her 'entirely uneducated, having, as I say, left the schoolroom and the nurses and governesses at the age of seventeen when her allowance of pocket money had been eighteen pence a week; she could not add up, could very decidedly not subtract, and I think had only the mistiest notion of who Julius Caesar was, or the meaning of the Napoleonic Wars'.[15] As we will see, there were legal reasons to speak in later years of Lady Ida's lack of brains and her ignorance.

Although frivolous, Lady Ida was by no means stupid. She was a constant though not a wide reader, and possessed an actress's gift of mimicry and an amusing, if hurtful, tongue. Osbert maintained that the Londesboroughs were devoted to 'fun'.[16] There were shooting parties at Londesborough Park, the cricket festival at Scarborough, coaching meets where the Earl drove his own team, receptions for politicians, gatherings of actors and actresses. In 1871, the Prince of Wales nearly died of typhus after visiting the Londesboroughs in Scarborough.

Another guest, the Earl of Chesterfield, did die of it, along with his groom.[17] However, the atmosphere soon revived, and Ida's childhood passed as a succession of house parties.

She absorbed her father's attitude towards money and her mother's attitude towards her inferiors. Edith remembered,

> My mother was slightly too insistent on her social position – (those were the days when an Earl was regarded as a being on the highest mountain peaks, to be venerated, but not approached, by ordinary mortals). She was in the habit of saying, (no doubt with my father in mind) 'A Baronet is the lowest thing on God's earth' – lower, presumably, than a black beetle. And when she was in a rage with me – this being a constant state with her – she would say to me, 'I am better-born than you are.' This puzzled me slightly.[18]

Since Lady Ida became an alcoholic, it is possible that these comments fell from her lips after a few drinks, but Edith Sitwell was perfectly capable of merely inventing them or giving them a false context.

One of Sitwell's anecdotes demonstrates how unreliable her evidence is: 'And I remember, too, driving every afternoon with my great grandmother, the very aged Dowager Duchess of Beaufort, the original of the Dowager Queen in my poem "The Sleeping Beauty" and of the old woman in "Colonel Fantock" . . . She never discovered – nodding into a sleep that would soon be eternal, that we drove on the same route every afternoon.'[19] The Duchess died on 2 October 1889, when Edith was barely two. Her brother Osbert gives the story a more likely provenance: 'my mother used to describe her, a formidable figure still, but rather vague mentally, taking her pet parrot out for a drive in the New Forest. She always wished to go for a new drive, but the coachman invariably took her the same way; she was too old to be aware of the deception. The parrot, too, had long been dead and stuffed so as to give an illusion of life.'[20]

In old age, Edith Sitwell would scarcely admit to having received anything from her parents, not even an anecdote; nonetheless, she seems to have recycled a good many of Lady Ida's stories. Around 1930, she remarked, 'It has always been one of the pleasures of my life to hear my mother describe her childhood among these splendours.'[21] Sitwell's relationship with her mother was more complicated than she was willing to explain at the end of her life. She seems to have seen her early years through the lens of an appalling adolescence, and to have erased any warmth her mother ever displayed towards her. Indeed, we do not know what particular things Lady Ida did to her daughter in childhood, and it is hard to know when the suffering began. In 1922, Sitwell wrote under a persona:

> Alas, in what remote life of the spirit and the body, I had my home; and these are lost to me. Only sometimes in the heart of music and on the brink of sleep, can I find them now, and become a little child again. Then everything seems familiar to me, yet fresh and sweet and most infinitely beloved. – My mother saying goodnight . . . her pink gown and her perfume that reminds me of a tune by Mozart . . . Her fingers that are like honeysuckle. Ah, that was before I had grown wise.[22]

Lady Ida was sometimes affectionate towards her daughter, which made her rages all the more bewildering. Sitwell concluded over time that these shows of affection were just a trick – and any sense of her mother's love wishful thinking.

As the years passed, Sitwell came to represent her early life in mythic terms. She portrayed herself as a child destined for greatness and a 'changeling':

> My parents were strangers to me from the moment of my birth. I do not forget that I must have been a most exasperating child, living with violence each moment of my day. I was rather a fat little girl: my moon-round face, which was surrounded by green-gold curls, had, strangely for so small a child – indeed for any child, the eyes of someone who had witnessed and foretold all the tragedy of the world. Perhaps I, at four years old, knew the incipient anguish of the poet I was to become.[23]

She tells of being asked by a friend of her mother's, 'What are you going to be when you are grown up, little E?', to which she replied, 'A genius.' She says she was then swept from the drawing room and put to bed.

'But my disgrace was not forgotten, and was frequently referred to, in after years, in a disgusted whisper.'[24] In an earlier version of this story deleted from Osbert's memoir, Edith was six or seven, and she did not propose to be 'a genius' but 'a Great Woman'.[25]

The young Sitwells spent a good deal of time with Lady Ida's relatives. Edith remembered with some pleasure her childhood visits to Londesborough Park. The 11 a.m. breakfasts with her otherwise difficult grandmother were 'languid feasts'. They sat in a dining room 'surrounded by green trees, in which the sun fluttered like a bird, and seemed to be singing'. The table was laid out with cutlets, partridges, peaches, and hot-house grapes. More pleasant still was the time she spent with her grandfather. A very tall man with a glass eye from a shooting accident, he was roguish and good-natured towards the children, and his oaths were clever. Edith wrote, 'He was a singularly delightful grandfather and all the children adored him, for he made us seem important, and he turned everything into an adventure.' They rode with him across the fields in a light carriage pulled by four horses, 'our small faces just peering over the rugs and the leather apron, and with my grandfather, tall and dark and with a foreign look, talking to us and to the horses'.[26] In the spring of 1900, the Earl visited a warehouse full of tropical birds, where he caught psittacosis, a form of pneumonia contracted from parrots.[27] Lady Ida was devoted to her father. As she had already lost her sister Lilian in 1897, his death came as a hard blow.

Lady Ida's brother Francis Denison succeeded as the second Earl of Londesborough. For several years, the Sitwells came at Christmas to his house at Blankney in Lincolnshire. Edith claimed that although she disliked 'Ye ancient Boar's Head kind of jollity', she enjoyed Christmas in a country house, 'even if it means quarrelling with all my favourite relations'.[28] Among her many cousins Edith found a close friend in Veronica Codrington, a girl close to her own age, the daughter of her mother's sister Sybil. At much the same time, Edith was compared, disadvantageously, to her charming and beautiful cousin, Irene Denison. The daughter of the new earl, she became, later, Marchioness of Carisbrooke.

The adults loved practical jokes such as placing a pail of water above a door, tethering a hen beneath a bed, or placing a live lobster between the sheets. Lady Ida's relatives spent most of their days shooting at birds and animals. If targets ran short, the gamekeepers released rabbits from sacks to be shot or beaten with sticks. *In extremis*, they would go 'ratting' in the house. Sir George Sitwell was bored by these antics and Edith Sitwell actively repulsed. Lady Ida pressed her to join in or at least to watch the hunt. Instead, she came to hate blood sports and campaigned against them throughout her life.[29]

If conflict with a charismatic but embittered mother was the key fact of Edith Sitwell's childhood, another fact was nearly as important: she was 'in disgrace for being a female'[30] – her father would have preferred a boy. Sitwell wrote of her father with anger and contempt, but felt less injured by him: 'It was my mother, and not my father, who made my childhood and youth a living hell.'[31] Sir George Sitwell was of a background and temperament utterly unlike his wife's. A shrewd businessman, he kept up to date with the latest developments in science, while another part of him lived, quite happily, in the Middle Ages.

The village of Renishaw, just south of Sheffield, had been the home of the Sitwells, or 'Cytewels', since the beginning of the fourteenth century. Renishaw Hall was built by the first George Sitwell, who took up residence in 1625. This H-shaped manor house, with gables and battlements, provided the nucleus for a dwelling that would later be enlarged, especially in the late eighteenth and early nineteenth centuries. The first George Sitwell also took the family into the iron business, and by the end of the seventeenth century the Sitwells were the world's largest makers of iron nails. However, by the eighteenth century the family consisted mainly of uncles; the male line died out with the merchant and philanthropist William Sitwell in 1776. His nephew, Francis Hurt, inherited an estate valued at about half a million pounds, and decided the surname should be his as well. His son, christened Sitwell Hurt, thus became Sitwell Sitwell (1769–1811).[32] In 1961, Evelyn Waugh wrote in his diary that the 'hypersensitive' Osbert should take back the old name and call himself 'Sir Hurt Hurt'.[33]

Sitwell Sitwell spent recklessly on the house, adding a private racecourse and classical stables for his fighting cocks and for his hounds, which chased a tiger that had escaped from a Sheffield menagerie. He built a new dining room, a large drawing room, and a ballroom, where in 1806 he gave a rout for the Prince of Wales, who afterwards made him a baronet.[34] The prodigal son of a prodigal father, Sir George Sitwell (1797–1853), succeeded as second Baronet in 1811 with an inheritance half what his father had received; the Napoleonic Wars then wiped out much of the value of his land by driving down farm rents. He lost yet more money in a bank failure and a fraud. In 1846, Renishaw was shut up and many of its contents sold.[35] Sir George Sitwell did not return there except for two nights in the winter before he died.[36]

Sir Reresby Sitwell (1820–62), third Baronet, having inherited the mess that his grandfather and father had made, also had to provide for many relatives while taking on his father's debts. An amateur watercolourist and friend of Ruskin, Sir Reresby apparently had a sensitive nature. Once a cornet in the First Life Guards, he was ground down by fatigue and worry, dying at forty-one. He left behind a widow, Louisa Lucy, and two children, Florence (1858–1930) and George (1860–1943), who as a toddler became fourth Baronet. A central figure in Edith's early life, Lady Sitwell, her paternal grandmother, was one of five daughters of Colonel Henry Hely-Hutchinson of Weston, Northamptonshire. She was careful with money, and the discovery of a large coal deposit at Renishaw allowed her to set things right by the mid-1870s.[37]

Lady Sitwell made a home for herself and the children in Scarborough, which was cheaper than Renishaw. In Scarborough she had many friends and relatives, among them her husband's unmarried sister Blanche, who lived there until about 1896, when she moved to London. A great favourite of the younger Sitwells and a friend of the reforming Rowntrees of Yorkshire, Blanche was an activist for almost any progressive cause. For years, she badgered her old friend and kinsman Archbishop Randall Davidson over penal reform and then the Boer War.[38] Some of her political sympathies rubbed off on Edith Sitwell.

Louisa Sitwell found Scarborough a good place for church work. As a young woman she had been swept up in the religious ferment that followed the Crimean War. Sacheverell would speak of her views as 'nearly maniacal',[39] and Edith, who had actually been very close to her grandmother, would remark to a friend in the early 1940s: 'I've also had a letter from obviously a very old gentleman enquiring the *whereabouts* of my grandmother (who died in 1910 [*sic*]). It is rather difficult to answer, as my idea and hers of her ultimate home didn't tally!'[40]

Louisa Sitwell supported low-church missionaries, and her house was said to be infested with curates. Her main project was a home for 'Magdalens' in Scarborough. She and a suffragan bishop would make evening 'sorties together in her barouche, driven by her old coachman [George] Hill. Encircling the town they would capture any young woman who appeared to them to be unsuitably dressed and in a deplorable "state of joyosity" as John Knox called it.' The matron, Sister Edith Woods, 'a bursting woman like an advertisement for tomatoes on a railway station', would bathe the girls, clothe them in navy-blue uniforms, and set them to work in a laundry. It is said that on one occasion a slim young man with a grudge against the bishop disguised himself as a prostitute, was captured, refused the bath, and then impregnated all the Magdalens.[41]

This set-piece Sitwellian anecdote captures the domineering side of Louisa Sitwell's religious work. However, when viewed from her daughter Florence's perspective it all looks more sympathetic. Her mother's collaborator, she remained unmarried, and seems always to have lived on the edge of other, more powerful lives. Osbert, who thought that in another age she would have been a saint, published selections from her journals.[42] She describes a conversion experience when she was fifteen: '*Sunday, May* 3 [1874]. A year ago to-day, that Sunday evening on which Kate Swinton and I went to St Martin's church to hear Mr. Parr preach, and he spoke so beautifully of God's great love to us! I never knew before how very, very much Christ has loved us. And I remember the quiet time afterwards, when it was nearly dark in my room, and I knelt down and asked Christ to take me for His own.'[43]

Florence was a considerable presence in Edith's imagination, appearing under various guises in poems and autobiographical pieces, as in this scene from around 1905:

Outside a stuffy bookshop, two maiden ladies were on the pavement lost in speculation. The elder of these wore a long dress which burst

into a thousand leaves and waterfalls and branches and minor worries. She had hair of the costliest gold thread, bright as the gold in
a fourteenth-century missal, and this, when undone, fell in a water-
fall till it nearly reached her feet. But at this moment, it was
crammed beneath a hat which seemed to have been decorated with
all the exports of our colonies – ostrich feathers, fruits, furs, and
heaven knows what besides. Her eyes were blue as a saint's eyes, and
were mild as a spring wind.[44]

The hat, of course, is telling. Edith herself feared the life of the maiden
aunt and believed that the spiritual potential of a woman like Florence
was wasted in a modern age obsessed with buying and selling.

Sir George Sitwell had a holy upbringing, driving him to become an
atheist, at least until his later years, when he remarked: 'no one who
has reached the age of reason will be the worse for possessing a second
line of defence.'[45] His great-uncle Archbishop Tait became his guardian
after the death of Sir Reresby. Although Sir George recoiled from his
teaching, he remained fond of the Archbishop. Edith described Louisa
and Florence as 'Lambeth Palace lounge-lizards'. Sir George spent most
of his holidays at Lambeth until Tait's death in 1882.[46] His son-in-law
Randall Davidson, who became Archbishop in 1903, regarded Sir
George as a tiresome eccentric, while Sir George regarded him as a
meddler.

After a grim school in Hertfordshire, Sir George went in 1873 to
Eton, where he remained until 1878. Information about this portion of
his life is surprisingly scant. He played the Field Game (one of Eton's
forms of football) for his house. However, he did not belong to any
school teams and won no major prizes.[47] Nevertheless, while at Eton
he is supposed to have invented a toothbrush that played 'Annie
Laurie' and a tiny revolver for killing wasps.[48]

He went up to Christ Church, Oxford, in January 1879 and
remained there until 1883. Despite extraordinary gifts, his performance
was mediocre, and he left without a degree.[49] Perhaps he was distracted
by coming into his fortune and by some offbeat adventures. In his
second year at Oxford, he and a friend attended a seance at the head-
quarters of the British National Association of Spiritualists.[50] They
took the precaution of tying up the medium with ropes, as a result of

which there were no manifestations. Soon, they returned for another seance, but this time an official of the organisation tied the knots. The shade of a twelve-year-old girl called Marie appeared. Her face was veiled and she was dressed in white, but they saw that under her robes she was wearing stays, and concluded that real ghosts probably do not have underwear. On their third visit, accompanied by two more witnesses, they heard undressing behind a curtain during the seance. When Marie appeared, Sir George seized her wrist. The curtain was pulled back, to reveal the scattered garments the medium had been wearing. The lights were suddenly put out, and the meeting broke up in yelling and abuse. Sir George and his friends appeared in the press as having exposed a fraud.[51]

Sir George Sitwell had his own way of contacting ghosts, perhaps trying to substitute many dead fathers for a single living one. As a boy, he had studied ancient documents in the muniment room at Renishaw and taught himself to read black-letter; in time, he became an expert on genealogy and local history. Seeking an outlet for his writings, he purchased the chairmanship of the board of directors of the *Saturday Review*, while Shaw and Wells were regular contributors, but he fell out with the editor Frank Harris.[52] He purchased the *Scarborough Post* and, with it, the press that printed his first book in 1889. The full title requires at least three breaths: *The Barons of Pulford In the Eleventh and Twelfth Centuries and Their Descendants The Reresbys of Thrybegh and Ashover, the Ormesbys of South Ormesby, and the Pulfords of Pulford Castle, Being An Historical Account of the Lost Baronies of Pulford and Dodleston in Cheshire, of Seven Knights' Fees in Lincolnshire Attached to them, and of Many Manors, Townships and Families in Both Counties.* Oddly enough, Sir George thought this study of local governance after the Conquest had a modern relevance: 'Home Rule' caused these counties 'to be divorced from national progress and popular reforms, and to be a perpetual danger and menace, first to the Crown, and then, after the Crown had absorbed it, to the liberties of England'.[53]

Sir George Sitwell stood, unsuccessfully, for the riding of Scarborough at two by-elections in November and December 1884, and was elected in 1885, holding the seat until the general election of the following year, when he was defeated. He won the seat back in 1892, lost it again in 1895, and was defeated for the last time in 1900.

A moderate Conservative and a good constituency man, he served a
total of five years in Parliament, during which time he rose to speak on
only four occasions.[54] For all his gifts, Sir George was an unlikely politician, as he had no instinct for public relations. Towards the end of her
life, Edith told Muriel Spark that her father had once received an
anonymous letter accusing him of having an affair with a notorious
woman in the village; he wanted to find out who had written the letter,
so had it displayed in the window of the village post office with the
promise of a five-pound reward. Sitwell claimed that she and her brothers delighted in going down to the post office in order to read 'the
salacious letter' in the window.[55]

In the mid-1880s, Sir George was an eligible young man, with a
baronetcy, an estate, a large income, a seat in Parliament, and a family
connection with Lambeth Palace. In a peculiar phrase, Edith Sitwell
described her father in youth as 'good-looking in an insipid way, the
insipidity being largely the result of his blinking with pink eyelids'. She
thought that in later years, when he had retired to an estate near
Florence, he looked 'very handsome and noble-looking; with his
strange, pale, wild, lonely-looking eyes, and his red beard, he resembled
a portrait of one of the Borgias, or some other early Italian tyrant'.[56]

Most of what we know of Sir George Sitwell is from Osbert's memoir
Left Hand, Right Hand!, which, though truthful in matters of detail,
presents only a sly caricature of a man whom many thought more
intelligent than Osbert himself. While extremely funny, Osbert's
memoir is an act of revenge against the father with whom he had
always quarrelled about money. Osbert's problem was that, whereas he
wanted a princely life, he was obliged by his father to settle for mere
privilege.

Edith had a much more authentic grievance against Sir George than
Osbert ever had, even if what she wrote was incoherent and sometimes deceptive. Pursuing his own scholarly and aesthetic interests, Sir
George left Edith to be abused by Lady Ida. He sentimentalised the
situation and provided little of the protection to which she was entitled. As an old woman, she could point to few episodes where he had
actively done her harm, so she attempted to read perversity or self-
delusion into any act of his that she could remember:

My father had only one comfort. In my earliest childhood, before he had retired into a Trappist seclusion within himself, he had seen himself always as the apex of one of those hierarchical family pyramids favoured by photographers. Then, when I was just able to walk, he saw this imaginary photograph labelled 'Charming photograph of a young father with his child.' And under the spell of this fantasy, he would bowl me over with a cushion, pinning my forehead to the iron fender.[57]

While this and other attempts to read her father's inner life (also a favoured approach of Osbert's) are absurd, the anecdote shows her father as both playful and interested in her. It should be remembered that this particular passage was written in her old age when years of physical pain, depression, and heavy drinking made her an unreliable witness to her own life.

2

A SENSE OF PLACE

Scratch the surface of Edith Sitwell's poetry and you will find Scarborough and its contradictions. Divided into North and South Bays, the harbour is overhung by a cliff that looks far out into the North Sea. That view could be a terrible one – at least in the days of sail. It is believed that, since 1500, about fifty thousand ships have been wrecked on the Yorkshire coast. Between 1855 and 1880, there are records of 51,841 shipwrecks around the shores of the United Kingdom, a great number of them occurring in the North Sea. In a single gale in late October 1880, there were nine wrecks just outside Scarborough, and many more ships were lost further out. The lifeboat made five forays in that storm, rescuing twenty-eight people, but still the coast was littered with ships and bodies.[1] Nature's menace was openly displayed in Scarborough, and yet this was a popular seaside resort. After the discovery of spa waters in the seventeenth century, people went there for their health as well as for their ease. The railways connected Scarborough to London in the late 1840s, bringing enough visitors to justify the construction of the twelve-storey, turreted Grand Hotel – one of the largest in the world when it opened in 1867. In this seaport, fashion and frivolity formed a thin façade beyond which lay grief and catastrophe.

In summer, the seafront at Scarborough was filled with minstrels, bathing machines, contortionists, clowns, acrobats, and pierrots. Sitwell remembered having been fearful of Punch and Judy shows, the 'unconscious cruelty' in the puppet's fate, being subject in every way to 'the mechanical actions of that ragged hunger, the showman'.[2] One of her earliest memories, she said, was of seeing 'jockey carriages' racing on the sand.

The carriages were open and held two people; and instead of being driven in the ordinary way, the horses were ridden by persons dressed as jockeys. On they would rush, against the gold-freckled dancing summer seas, in airs that were like great rainbows, with their parti-coloured clothes, of chattering-white satin striped with all the colours of those rainbows. This was one of the first strange sights that I remember, and often, thinking of those carriages rushing past in the summer weather, I have seen them as a symbol of fleeting fashion, coming from nowhere and going nowhere.[3]

These recollections are continually at play in her poetry of the 1910s and 1920s, where she often writes of elegant and empty-headed people at the seaside, a world where

> Daisy and Lily,
> Lazy and silly,
> Walk by the shore of the wan grassy sea.[4]

This was one face of Scarborough. In autumn, the town resumed a traditional character, which brought with it a different set of impressions. On Martinmas (11 November), ploughmen and maidservants came in from the farms and walked about the market in search of work; it was also a favoured date for weddings among farm people, making processions a common sight. However, agriculture meant less to Scarborough than fishing. Each morning, the fleet returned under sail with holds full of fish to be smoked and dried. The harbour was a sway-ing thicket of masts and yards, the air thick with smells of fish, salt and tar, the paving stones slick with crushed herring. By December, great storms came in and the lifeboat would make foray after foray into the massive waves. The Sitwell children revered its heroic skipper John Owston, a white-bearded fisherman who taught Osbert to dance the hornpipe.[5] There is doubtless a memory of him at the root of Edith Sitwell's playful poem by that title.

In the 1890s, the Sitwells occupied Belvoir House, a tall stone struc-ture that backed on an alley frequented by tramps. The children watched them and listened to their conversations from the night nursery. There was Snowball, a black man who dragged his leg and sold flowers; Lousy Peter, mentally disabled and tortured by gangs of boys; and the Cat Man, who mewed to himself on the sands. There were hurdy-gurdy players with their monkeys, to whom the children threw down pennies wrapped in bits of paper. Osbert claimed that his own first words mimicked the cry of a man who pushed a barrow in the alley, 'Rags and bones, rags and bones!'[6]

Edith Sitwell saw poverty in Scarborough. She said she had a friend named Tommy, aged twelve. He sold rides on his donkey Jacko to earn some money for his mother, who sold poisonous lemonade from a booth. They lived in a street of sagging roofs and stinking drains, where drunks lurched from door to door. One day Tommy rushed past his mother, sheltered from her by the donkey. He explained to Edith, 'The old woman's been having one. I'll get the stick.' Edith asked why his mother was always angry with him, and he answered, 'Because I'm a bastard, Miss Dish.' Edith urged him to share her father, but this only made him more unhappy. Then, his mother, 'breasts shaking in a kind of dreadful bacchic dance, advanced upon him . . . but seeing me, stopped'.[7] Throughout her life, Edith Sitwell was sensitive to the desperation of the slums, but it is not certain whether this anecdote records an actual event, or, like others, serves as a parable to explain something in herself. The story grants to the child Edith, simply by virtue of rank, the opportunity to protect the defenceless. It was a notion of herself and her place in the world that she would cherish as an adult. The story also grants to the child Edith the ability to control a drunken and abusive mother.

It was in Scarborough that the Sitwells had most contact with their extended family. Louisa Sitwell had closed up Wood End, where Edith had been born, and taken another house, Hay Brow, just outside town. She spent most of the year at Gosden in Surrey, but while in Scarborough she was close to her son and grandchildren, as well as to her sisters who congregated there. Each summer, the Londesboroughs and the Sitwells came together at Scarborough to 'form a kind of Laocoon group on the shores of the sea, [with] my grandmothers as the serpent'. There were quiet conflicts, especially over religion. The Countess, Edith's maternal grandmother, looked on heaven as her aristocratic birthright and so did not speak of it, whereas Lady Sitwell was conscious of having to work for salvation. The matriarchs found themselves a little at odds, 'one lady complaining subtly of lack of breeding, the other lady complaining a little less subtly, of lack of piety'. When the Countess was cross, a common occurrence according to Edith, she would round up the household and head to church and there attempt to intimidate the Almighty with her 'snarling prayers'. She also found ways to assert rank, and 'by a kind of freemasonry of the fan' indicated how little she thought of some of Louisa's relatives.[8]

Just after the turn of the century, Sir George took over the unoccupied Wood End, where Edith would now spend much of her adolescence. Lady Sitwell had bought the house in 1870. It was situated on the Crescent, overlooking on the east the gardens of Londesborough Lodge. She added a large conservatory, which gave to her house a tropical atmosphere, with exotic birds flying among creepers and flowering trees. As a boy, Sir George was enchanted by them: Peking nightingales, zebra finches and a Virginian nightingale: 'The Whydah Birds are blue-black with silvery breasts and a touch of orange at the throat and have long sheaf-shaped tails. They are attracted by music, and when there was dancing would sometimes fly in and out of the arches to the further end of the drawing-room, passing over the heads of the dancers.'[9] Renovated in 2006–8, this house has become the Woodend Creative Workspace, providing offices, conference rooms and artists' studios. Andrew Clay, the director, reports that the builders disturbed many ghosts, among them Lady Ida's. It appears that the various spirits now make noises in the kitchens, set off sensor lights, and show up on CCTV.[10] Sadly, none of the ghosts has consented to an interview.

In the summer and early autumn the Sitwells stayed at Renishaw Hall, the other place that shaped Edith Sitwell's poetry. Like her brothers, she was struck by the darkness of its shuttered rooms and by its antiquity. She described it as seen by a child:

The house is dark and forgotten and a little precious, like an unopened seventeenth century first edition in a library. I must creep away silently, for the whole of existence in that dark house has the curious, sweet, musty smell and the remoteness of such a book; the great trees outside are motionless and dark and unliving as a library lined with dusty and uncared for meanings, and the sunrays lying

upon the floor smile as dimly as the chapel's smiling cherubim. Here
we cease living and the house is filled with other and darker exis-
tences; we put on their lives and go clothed in them.[11]

The child's discovery of herself hardly matters among memories of the
dead, and the growth of her perceptions counts for little where the very
walls are marked with 'uncared for meanings'. Each of the Sitwell children regarded the house with fascination and sadness. It was, as Sachie
put it, 'the house of tragic memories'.[12]

Renishaw Hall was thought to harbour many ghosts – even more
than Wood End. Although Sir George forbade such talk, the children
soon learnt about them from their mother and from the servants.
According to tradition, Sitwell Sitwell had twice been seen after his
death, once in the streets of Sheffield, and once at the door of
Renishaw while his body was lying in the library.[13] He could still be
heard, from time to time, calling for his wife. The ghost of a boy who
had drowned in 1724 was said to wake sleepers with a cold kiss.[14] This
curious image, reminiscent of Poe, made its way into Edith's later
poetry, where the kiss from the grave is an image she returns to almost
obsessively. Sacheverell thought it 'terrifying' merely to walk through
the enormous, unused drawing room and ballroom. In the dining
room, the eyes of wigged ancestors followed him from their portraits
and their heads seemed to be turned in his direction wherever he
stood.[15] Osbert remembered that when, as a child, he asked his mother
how she had slept, she would often give the answer, 'Oh, fairly well,
but the ghosts were about again.'[16] Lady Ida had an easygoing interest in the macabre and kept a piece of hangman's rope knotted at the
head of her bed: 'Nothing's so lucky! It cost eight pounds – they're
very difficult to get now.'[17]

Although the weight of the past was oppressive, Edith and her
brothers found much in the house that was inspiring – above all, the
five great panels of Brussels tapestry, purchased by an ancestor from the
Philippe Égalité collection in London. Despite being unable to discover
who designed them, Sachie believed them 'some of the most beautiful
products of human genius'.[18] The tapestries in their setting evoked a
rhapsody from Edith in 1929:

The ballroom at Renishaw is immensely long, and shines like the water of a kingfisher's lake in the deep afternoon of a dream; the windows are tall as waterfalls. And the dark pomp and splendour of those tapestries which are, to my brothers and myself, more a part of our spiritual and imaginative life than anything else which is material, these hang upon the walls like some mournful and eternal music. Those processions of queens, – blackened with age, beneath their many-coloured plumaged helmets and turbans, those long and mournful red trains, those cascades of crackling pearls, echoed in the mirrors and in many pools, those elephants rearing their trunks in homage to a reed-crowned water-god sitting beside his forest-shadowed waterfalls – (the forest is deep as that in Hyperion) – these blackened nymphs, crowned with strange head-dresses of feathers, gazing at themselves in mirrors beside many fountains, (echoing the long windows of a far-off house that is like our house) – these imaginations, the unheard sound that haunts that silence, is a part of our life.[19]

Renishaw had the air of a melancholy dream, but there was also a good deal of building, digging, and planting. About the time of Edith's birth, Sir George began the landscaping project that became, according to Sachie, his 'life work', laying out the full plan in 1895. He was interested in lines and perspectives, and not at all in flowers. Sachie could not remember his ever admiring one and thought he rather resented them because they took attention away from garden design.[20] Although Sir George's attitude became a joke within the family, especially as Lady Ida surrounded herself with cut roses, it is interesting that in this quirky and expensive art form he was a formalist. Had he been a stranger, Edith might have applauded his sensibility. As it was, Osbert teased him by nurturing a rhododendron within sight of his study so that it produced fiery purple blossoms.[21]

Sir George cut a strange figure as he created his views. Edith and her brothers had only to look up to see their father perched like a stylite on one of the wooden platforms he placed about the estate. Shaded from the sun by a floppy hat or an umbrella, with a lunch of cold roast chicken beside him, he sat on these platforms for hours, confronting his huge canvas through a telescope. Over many years, he planted hedges and lines of trees, created a garden, raised and lowered hills. He installed a pair of marble fountains and various statues, and he turned a ruined aviary into a Gothic temple. He placed a lake in the middle of the property and, nearer the house, two formal ponds.[22]

The family's annual journeys to the continent, usually in the spring, allowed him to study the gardens of France and, especially, of Italy, a project that bore fruit in a remarkable book, On the Making of Gardens (1909). In it he said that he had visited two hundred Italian gardens – this allows us a glimpse of how the Sitwell children spent some of their time abroad. Sir George at work on his landscape was Edith's first experience of an artist consumed with his craft. His gardens were not companionable places: 'The garden, in every language, speaks of seclusion . . . No sound of the outer world should break the enchantment; no turret-clock should toll the passing hours; nor, could one silence it, should there vibrate through the garden the menacing voice of the church bell, with its muttered curse on nature and on man, lest it beat down the petals of the pagan roses.'[23] His taste was in some ways Pre-Raphaelite, but it was also the expression of an aloof personality. He created spaces for solitude; the grounds at Renishaw are marked with his sense of separateness.

There were, nonetheless, simple pleasures to be had in the grounds of Renishaw and in the surrounding countryside. Edith Sitwell could remember picking mushrooms as a child, and Sacheverell described encounters with miners' children on blackberrying expeditions. The three Sitwells, being very tall and thin, could reach the highest berries, while the miners' children had to lift one another to grasp the same branches.[24] Osbert recalled donkey rides with Edith to a disused canal. Some afternoons they sailed on the lake with their nurse, Eliza Davis, in a wide flat-bottomed boat, while Sir George took out a canoe. On the heels of a footman carrying a hamper, Lady Ida and her friends would, if they remembered, come down for a picnic.[25]

One of the attractions of Renishaw was the animals. Sitwell's early years fairly swarmed with pets, and rarely in her life was she without at least a cat. She said that when she was about five she became enraptured with a peacock at Renishaw. 'Peaky' would greet her in the mornings with a shriek from the leads outside her mother's bedroom (adjoining her own), and then fly down to the gardens: 'We walked round these, with my arm round his lovely neck that shone like tears in a dark forest.' Asked by her nurse why she loved Peaky so much, she gave the Blakean answer, 'Because he is beautiful and wears a Heavenly Crown.' When Sir George bought Peaky a mate, Edith found herself discarded. The bird now spent his time teaching his offspring to unfurl their tails. 'I do not think it was the injury to my pride at being jilted by a peacock that I minded. It was the injury to my affection. It was my first experience of faithlessness.'[26]

3

SERVANTS AND SURGEONS

'Most English gentlemen at this time believed that they had a particular aptitude for endearing themselves to the lower classes.' So wrote Evelyn Waugh in *Men at Arms*.[1] The Sitwells fit the description even more closely than do the officers in the regiment of Halberdiers. Osbert wrote: 'I have never experienced that sensation of being separate from the working classes, in the way in which the city-bred, middle-class poets of the proletarian movement continually proclaim themselves to feel cut off.'[2] The Sitwells believed that, unlike the despised middle classes, labouring people had a bond with old aristocrats and at the level of instinct understood them; the permanently poor, in their view, had a soft spot for the permanently rich. Perhaps they weren't entirely wrong – as the manorial connections were still strong enough in 1969 for one of the tenants at Renishaw to give a warm address at Osbert's memorial service, praising him as a good landlord.[3] The claims of being at home with the lower classes now seem naive, but the Sitwell children did have a bond with one group of working people – the servants.

Most of these people are found only at the edge of the historical records – no more than a name in the census or a comment in *Left Hand, Right Hand!*[4] Yet they were key figures in Edith Sitwell's life. There was Jones, once Sir George's scout, who became his butler. Under him, there was old Stephen Pare who went blind after being struck by lightning, and who lit the candles in the evening even though he could not see the flames. His niece, Rose, worked for the Sitwells as a maid around 1900 when she was in her late teens. As an old woman, she wrote to Edith Sitwell about how she had run afoul of her mistress: 'Lady Ida asked me one day to take Master Sacheverell down the steps to shew him the lakes and coming to the small one at the top he put his foot in the water. Oh dear I did get a scolding from Lady Ida. But Sir George came to the rescue, but I never forgot it.'[5] Rose left service when her aunt was sent to a mental hospital. Stephen Pare himself soon died of liver cancer. There were others: Eliza Knowles, the laundress Mrs Westerley, and the coachman, jolly James Broadbent, as well as an array of untraceable maids and footmen. These lives pass like shadows below the stairs.

But then there was Henry Moat (1871–1940), whose quips and shenanigans Osbert made famous – he now has his own article in the *ODNB*. Moat worked for the Sitwells, with some long interruptions, over a period of forty-three years, beginning as a footman and succeeding Jones as the butler. Edith described Henry as 'an enormous purple man like a benevolent hippopotamus'. Born into a family of whalers from Whitby, he had eighteen brothers and one sister, not to mention a tame seal.[6] He and Sir George were inseparable, but often separated. Repeatedly, Henry walked out or was sacked and then taken, perhaps cajoled, back. Osbert recalls that his attitude towards his master was a mixture of profound disrespect and veneration. In time, Moat took to calling the red-bearded Sir George 'Ginger' behind his back. He had acquired this nickname in a dispute with a taxi driver about his fare: 'After the war, Ginger, I'll get even with you!'[7] (It was a name that Edith would later use for him herself.) Sir George always referred to Moat as 'The Great Man'. Pancho to Sir George's Don Quixote, he exploded his master's many scientific schemes for domestic improvement, or as Moat called them, 'his fads'. Osbert writes, '"Henry," he called one day to the great man, "I've a new idea! Knife-handles should always be made of condensed milk!" (I must explain that a substance derived from milk, a sort of paste in various colours, had lately made its appearance.) Henry looked particularly disgusted at the idea and very worried at its application. Then, with emphasis, and with an unusual air of correctitude, he countered, "Yes, Sir George . . . But what if the cat gets at them?"'[8]

Edith Sitwell remembered Moat as a protector: 'I think of him as if at any moment, his living being might come through a door, and say to me, "You'd better run, Miss Edith. Her ladyship is in one of her states and is looking for you."' On the night of Henry Moat's death,

Osbert thought he heard his ghost in the pantry at Renishaw. Edith commented, 'I believe – I like to think – that he was looking for the three children, now two grown men and a grown woman, whom he had befriended through the sad years.'[9] Perhaps, Moat's real gift to the younger Sitwells was a no-nonsense kind of wisdom – a counterweight to their imaginings. Once Edith found him contemplating the stars, but he remarked, 'All the same, miss, let's stick to the eggs and bacon.'[10]

In the past, wealthy families usually delegated the love of small children to the servants. The figure of Nanny Hawkins in *Brideshead Revisited* stands for countless female servants who entered more deeply into the affections of their charges than did their parents. The care of the Sitwell children was entrusted to their nurse Eliza Davis and to the maids who worked under her. Born in 1852,[11] she was the daughter of a cobbler from Newbury, Berkshire, and she had once been Lady Ida's own nursery maid.[12]

Osbert remembered Davis typically in a grey alpaca dress, with a look of puzzlement and patience on her face.[13] In winter she wore black bonnets, and she could often be seen working at an already outdated sewing machine, attaching ribbons to white lace to make the high caps she wore indoors. A conservative woman, she deplored the changes she saw in the world around her.[14] When the children bruised themselves, she applied, from its distinctive green box shaped like a metronome, Butler & Crisp's Pomade Divine, a compound that had been passing for medicine since the time of Napoleon.[15] She was in the habit of taking Edith and Osbert for long walks in Scarborough's municipal cemetery. Had Sir George, the rationalist, known of this morbid recreation he would have been annoyed,[16] but Davis's taste for such places was shared by most Victorians. Osbert later described similar strolls in his novel *Before the Bombardment* (1926).[17]

Osbert believed that although Davis loved Sachie and himself, the best part of her affection was reserved for Edith, who remembered her as 'my dear old nurse'. Mysteriously, she saw in Davis an image from Gertrude Stein's *Geography and Plays*: 'a shadow, a white shadow, is a mountain'. However, there was nothing mysterious in the remark, 'her real name was comfort.'[18] Davis disapproved of Sir George's cleverness as unbecoming a gentleman, and she did not mind criticising him in front of the children. In 1902, she argued 'violently' with Sir George, gave in her notice, and, to her surprise, he let her go.[19] The children, horrified, kept in touch with her. Indeed, about a decade later Edith took her to see the Dowager Countess of Londesborough, who had been her first employer. By that time Davis was back in Newbury, working for a vicar, her existence made lonely as most of her family had emigrated.[20]

One type of servant gets rough treatment at the hands of Edith and Osbert – governesses. Osbert describes how at family gatherings at Christmas, retired governesses would appear and exert their waspish authority over the young women who had succeeded them. This species of dictator is represented by a woman to whom Edith gives the names 'Mademoiselle Blanchatte' and 'Mademoiselle Richarde' and whom Osbert calls 'Dickie'. In her prose memoir of the 'Dukes of Troy', Edith describes her as crushing Colonel Fantock over his claim to have advised Napoleon III.[21] Colonel Fantock was based on Major A. B. Brockwell or 'Brockie', a sometime tutor to Osbert and Sacheverell, but essentially a defeated old man whom Sir George helped out. Edith's poem 'Colonel Fantock' depicts him slipping into senility.

When Edith Sitwell was about eleven years old, her education was handed over to a governess, Lydia King-Church (1868–1963),[22] who stayed with the family for five years. Sitwell referred to her as 'Maum' and occasionally as 'Kingie'. When Sachie was five, he offered her sixpence to allow him to use her Christian name and was gently refused.[23] Davis waged a proxy war with King-Church, seeing her as the agent of Sir George. Nonetheless, Osbert recalled happy days with the governess, when she read Rider Haggard aloud in the schoolroom and helped them construct a house of twigs; he spoke of her as someone 'whom we so much loved and revered'.[24] Edith herself seems to have enjoyed her company and found her entertaining. She wrote to Sir George on 17 March 1903 (she was fifteen then): 'Last night, Maum and I had several games of "draughts"; she is a splendid player, and usually sweeps me off the board in less than no time, but what was the matter with her yesterday, I can't think, for I actually managed to beat her twice! But at the end we were quits, as I was forced to withdraw twice; we are going to play again this evening.'[25]

In later years Sitwell recalled the schoolroom where Miss King-Church instructed them as resembling 'a billiard-room, because of its system of backboards covered with green baize, of rods and poles used for pointing out flat places on a map in which Italy, Greece, China, India, and all the romance of the world was reduced to small pieces of inexpressive paper that you could hold in your hand'.[26] She said she was once punished for refusing to memorise 'The Boy Stood on the Burning Deck'; in her eyes, the boy was 'the epitome of idiocy, because, as everybody else had left the Burning Deck, and he was doing no conceivable good by remaining there, why in heck didn't he get off it!'[27]

Sitwell believed that the education she received was 'a devoted, loving, peering, inquisitive, interfering, stultifying, middle-class suffocation, on the chance that I would become "just like everybody else"'.[28] Be that as it may, she became well read in English literature and history, functional in French, and had smatterings of German and Italian. She wrote to Sir George on 12 February 1903:

> I have been having some particularly interesting lessons lately; Auntie Floss has very kindly lent me some books, and I have been getting some ideas on Political Economy (which interests me very much) and also upon Greek Literature. While I rest in the afternoon Maum reads me Macauley's essay on Frederick the Great, and I am studying a great deal of English Literature. Grannie has got some charming music for the Angelus, among which are Tchaikowsky's 'Symphonie Pathetique', and the same composer's 'Chant sans Paroles', one of the daintiest and most fascinating small pieces I have ever heard. The list also includes several of Mme Chaminade's charming little dances, and various music by Chopin and Liszt. There are also some of Sousa's Marches, which Sachie loves.[29]

The curriculum for a girl at the turn of the century, even Sir George Sitwell's daughter, had some gaps; she wrote to the poet Demetrios Capetanakis in 1943: 'I cannot forgive the fact that I wasn't taught Greek. I know one should start as a child. It is terrible what I have missed.'[30] At one point, Sir George thought that she should acquire office skills and prepare for a career in business, but Edith was disinclined and her mother thought the plan too middle class.

One door was definitely closed. Upon receiving an honorary degree from Leeds in 1948, Edith Sitwell said in her address:

It was my strong ambition as a girl, to be sent to a University. But this was not allowed – and for the oddest reason . . . My father was under the sway of Lord Tennyson's longer poems . . . Instead of seeing 'The Princess' as a farrago of condescending nonsense, interspersed by some of the most wonderful, the most heavenly, lyrics in the English language, he gained from that poem the impression that for a woman to become an undergraduate in a university would result in her becoming unwomanly. He did not seize the point that Tennyson made – that the segregation of women was a mistake – as indeed it most certainly is – rather, he concentrated on the false assumption that *learning* makes women unfeminine.[31]

Miss King-Church kept a schoolroom diary of the children's, especially Edith's, activities, through 1901 and 1902.[32] It indicates that while staying at Lancaster Gate in London, Miss King-Church took Edith to museums, galleries, and concerts. For example, in October 1901 they went to the Wallace Collection, the Royal School of Art Needlework, the National Gallery, the Donaldson Museum to see old musical instruments, the Royal College of Music, the British Museum, and the aquarium, also taking in a 'symphony concert' as well as two concerts of John Philip Sousa at the Albert Hall. As the family travelled on the continent, Sitwell learnt about European art; she wrote to Tchelitchew in the 1930s: 'I know the Michael Angelo, da Vinci, Raphael, and Rembrandt drawings at the Uffizi by heart. When I was a girl I used to visit them every day.'[33]

Edith Sitwell took art lessons from a Scarborough watercolourist named Ellen Edwards; this 'tea-addicted elderly maiden' noticed that the young Sitwells' favourite game was composing limericks. Sometimes Edwards came to the schoolroom, and sometimes Edith went to her studio at nearby Westborough; a photograph survives of a group of girls at work there, among them Sitwell with her spaniel stretched out on a mat.[34] For several years, Edith and Osbert took dancing lessons twice a week, laboriously acquiring the steps of quadrilles, minuets, gavottes, lancers, and waltzes.[35]

Miss King-Church was Edith's main piano teacher; they played duets together and performed Grieg's 'Morgenstemning' from *Peer Gynt* at a concert in Scarborough on 24 April 1902 in support of the Primrose League, a large organisation that promoted Tory principles. Miss King-Church's instruction was supplemented by lessons from leading musicians. Sheffield had a rich musical culture at the time, and at some point Edith received piano lessons at Renishaw from Frederick Dawson (1868–1940). A student of Anton Rubinstein and Edvard Grieg, and highly regarded as a concert pianist in Vienna and Berlin, he continued to live in Yorkshire where he had been born.[36] At Sir George's insistence, she also took lessons on the cello from the Spanish master Agustín Rubio (1856–1940). She made little of the instrument, and her refusal to practise – Sachie remembers her preferring to read and copy out poetry – led to trouble with Sir George.[37] It seems she also worked at the harp.

Part of Miss King-Church's task was to make sure that Edith followed her doctor's orders and carefully alternated periods of rest and exercise. The diaries note long walks and games of ping-pong. The governess played hockey on the sands at Scarborough, encouraging Edith and Osbert to take up the game. It did not come naturally to Edith, who wrote to Sir George on 2 February 1903 from Louisa Sitwell's house at Gosden in Surrey: 'People round about here seem to be very fond of hockey, and spend as many afternoons in the week as possible hitting about in a field just outside Grannie's garden, a lot of lovely ladies in mustard coloured blouses and black skirts (they look just like wasps) are playing there now!'

Miss King-Church became engaged to Osbert's tutor, Herbert Keigwin, who may be related to the Cornish family, noted, charmingly, in *Burke's Landed Gentry* as Keigwin of Mousehole. He appears briefly in the diaries, but not after 6 August 1902, which Miss King-Church records with a hint of sadness: 'very wet day – HSK left at 11:10 a.m.' He went on to Rhodesia, with the governess to follow the next spring. Edith was caught up in the excitement of planning for the wedding, writing to Sir George on 2 February 1903: 'Maum has just heard from Mr. Keigwin, he has changed from the Mines Office, to the Native

Commissioner's Office, which Maum says is a very good thing, and he hopes soon to write to you and tell you all about everything. I believe he is getting on splendidly.'[38] In other letters, Edith described the wedding presents: cutlery, prints of famous paintings, and a sun umbrella with an owl dangling from the handle. Miss King-Church left the Sitwells and sailed for Rhodesia on 18 April 1903, where she and Keigwin were married the following month. It is impossible to believe that Edith did not admire and miss her.

In later life, Sitwell wrote of Miss King-Church as a gaoler. It is necessary to quote at length Sitwell's story of the 'Bastille' as it became a standard anecdote, repeated countless times, and then formed part of the various versions of her autobiography:

> When I was between eleven and twelve years old, it was noticed that my thin body stooped slightly, in a deprecating and rather frightened way; and this was due to curvature of the spine. Also my ankles, because of the delicacy of their structure, were weak.
>
> My family, with their usual thoroughness, took the matter in hand. I was taken to a surgeon, who, in turn, placed me in the hands of an orthopaedic manufacturer, (I believe that is the correct term,) – an immensely fat gentleman, the colour of a November fog, his eyes, and all the expression they may have held, were shrouded behind black glasses . . . Mr. E. constructed for me a prison of iron, which reached from under my arms to below my hips; under my arms were thick pads of leather, rather reminiscent of saddlery, so that my arms could never hang to my side, and were constantly always numbed. My feet were incased in boots with steel linings, which pressed on my bones. And at night, when I went to bed, although the prison enclosing my body was removed, my legs and feet were immured in a contraption of steel, so that I could not move. The bones of my legs were tightly walled into a cage, which ran on either side of them, and my feet were strapped down onto a kind of sandal with a most complicated lock and key system of steel, about four inches deep under the soles, Miss H had charge of the key to this prison, and before she went down to dinner every night, she would lock up my feet. Sometimes she screwed them into a position pointing downwards, and the discomfort,

amounting to pain, kept me awake all night. Sometimes they
pointed heavenward, and then the same pain happened. It would
have been impossible for me to leave my bed, even if the room was
on fire.[39]

In *Taken Care Of*, Edith dubs the surgeon Dr Stout and the
manufacturer Mr Steinberg. The schoolroom diary indicates that these
names stand for Mr Tubby[40] and Mr Ernst. Alfred Herbert Tubby was
one of Britain's pioneering orthopaedic surgeons; F. Gustav Ernst constructed orthopaedic braces for an array of purposes and made
important improvements in the designs of artificial limbs. Both men
wrote textbooks on their specialities.

Presumably, Lady Ida or one of her deportment-obsessed family
noticed that Edith could not stand up straight. Sir George sent her to
the most eminent specialist Britain had to offer, who would have confirmed, by flexibility and rotation tests and by measurement with a
plumbline, that her spine was curved. Tubby held the orthodox view
of the day: 'Scoliosis is not a disease, but an alteration in the position,
shape and texture of the spinal structures, dependent on long-contin-
ued pressure in an abnormal direction.'[41] Although he made allowance
for congenital curvatures and rickets, he generally looked for the causes
in muscular weakness owing to general poor health and unsuitable
occupations. Although modern research has disproved this idea,[42]
Tubby believed that posture was a great villain: 'Certain attitudes are
very likely to be followed by scoliosis, e.g. standing on one leg and sitting cross-legged. These cause twisting of the pelvis and rotation of the
lumbar spine; so does excessive horse-exercise by girls without a
reversible saddle. The exceedingly faulty arrangement of music-stools
and school-desks is responsible for many cases of scoliosis.'[43] Tubby goes
on at length about desks and piano stools – and his opinions, which
now seem silly, created nothing but trouble for a young woman who
was both studious and devoted to the keyboard.

Tubby believed that children suffering from adenoids should be
placed under early treatment, as this could lead to general poor health,
loss of muscle tone, and subsequent curvature.[44] Sitwell says that her
adenoids were removed in the spring of 1900;[45] however, it was not
uncommon for this to be done in stages. The schoolroom diaries

FIG. 44.—Piano-practice in
a bad position.

FIG. 45.—Piano-practice in a correct
position.

From Tubby's *Deformities*

indicate that she was cauterised, and underwent procedures involving bougies and cocaine (as an anaesthetic) as late as 1902. The problem with her adenoids would have singled her out in Tubby's view as a patient likely to have trouble with her spine: the nose-bone, it seems, was connected to the backbone.

On Tubby's advice, Edith Sitwell embarked on a regime that would shape her daily life for several years. He recommended treatments to improve general health, as well as a combination of exercises and 'recumbency'. Apart from strengthening the body, he thought it necessary for the patient to take some of the weight of the head, neck and upper extremities off the back by lying down for up to six hours per day, a restful practice that he judged 'more efficient than suspending the head by means of a jury-mast'.[46]

He recommended, as in some cases specialists still do, a back-brace, which she remembered as a 'prison of iron'. Tubby sent her to the 'orthopædic mechanician' F. Gustav Ernst for two fittings in March 1901. On 13 April, the schoolroom diary notes: 'E's boots & spinal stays arrd. from Ernst's.' While it is difficult to know which therapeutic boot she was wearing, it is likely that her brace followed a design by the surgeon William Adams, favoured by both Tubby and Ernst. It was constructed mostly of fabric, some leather padding, thin steel supports and shoulder straps with elastic inserts. One of the advantages of this design was its weight, usually less than five pounds.[47] The apparatus must have been wearisome and limiting. It apparently did not produce great pain, but, as she put it, 'discomfort amounting to pain'. That remembered discomfort and constraint became for her in later years a symbol of how her parents tried to reshape her personality.

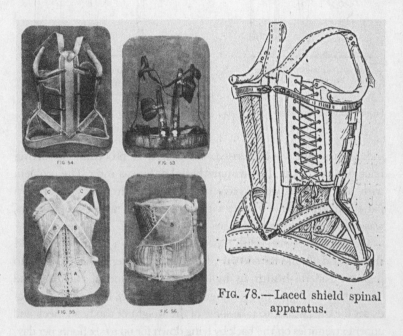

FIG. 78.—Laced shield spinal apparatus.

However grim the episode was for a girl of thirteen, the retrospective vilification of all those involved seems unfair. There can be no doubt that Sir George was trying to get the best care possible for his daughter. Tubby and Ernst, who spent their working lives restoring capacity to broken bodies, were hardly the monsters that she depicted. In October 1901, at Tubby's behest, she began a programme of massage. She enjoyed this part of her treatment, but it is not mentioned in her accounts of 'my Bastille'.

There was more to the story of the boots and back-brace. She wrote of Lydia King-Church:

Although she slept in my very large room, I was never released when she went to bed. My only happiness, at this time, was that at one moment or another during the day I was able to secrete a book of poems in the fastnesses of my bed, before I was locked up for the night – for some reason she never found these. By the time I was thirteen, I knew the whole of the Rape of the Lock by heart – learnt while she was at dinner, and by the time I was fourteen, I was enriched, further, by knowing nearly all Shelley's poems, and, a little later, most of the greatest passages in Shakespeare's plays, and all his Sonnets by heart. These were the only poets I knew, for I lived in a very solitary world. I learned these poems in a profound secrecy, hurriedly and guiltily, sometimes by the light of a single brightly-feathered candle, whilst outside, the seas of beauty, the wildness of the spring, broke upon a magical shore.[48]

That her governess deprived her of books is nonsense, although she did require her charge to keep regular hours. Sitwell was encouraged to read widely, and her letters to her father are full of comments on what interested or impressed her. Sachie disputed her claim to have memorised *The Rape of the Lock* at fourteen, claiming that he introduced her to Pope's works much later.[49] Nonetheless, the reference to Alexander Pope is revealing. He suffered from extreme curvature of the spine as a consequence of Pott's disease, and relied on heavy linen stays in order to move about. Sitwell's biography of Pope, published in 1930 (just before she wrote the passages above), presents him as a supreme craftsman and formalist. Moreover, the curvature of his spine, compared by Lady Mary Wortley Montagu and Lord Hervey to the mark of Cain, set him apart from ordinary society. In her account of the 'Bastille', Sitwell is not so much recounting facts as creating a myth of herself as a poet. Her genius and her suffering are comparable to those of Alexander Pope. As a celebrated woman who was rejected by the men she loved, Sitwell had other grounds for her sense of kinship with Pope: 'Though he was deformed, people with beautiful shapes surrounded him, were proud of knowing him – if he did not make love to them.'[50]

Undoubtedly, Edith Sitwell was an outsider in her family. Sir George preferred boys, as a general rule. Her mother, a great beauty, had little

time for a plain daughter. Early on, Sitwell became conscious of her long
body as awkward and inadequate. At the age of fifteen she wrote to her
father about a cousin who had a parrot named 'Wee Poll': 'the boys have
insultingly named *me* Wee Poll, partly from my size and partly from the
shape of my nose!'[51] One element of her Bastille, she said later, was a
brace worn on her nose while she was in the schoolroom: 'a band of elastic surrounded my forehead, from which two pieces of steel (regulated
by a lock and key system) descended on each side of the organ in question, with thick upholstered pads at the nostrils, turning my nose firmly
to the opposite way which Nature had intended, and blocking one nos-
tril, so that breathing was difficult.'[52] Among Ernst's designs were a
number of strange devices, such as an 'ear spring' for fixing ears made
prominent by sleeping on them or 'the careless adjustment of the hat or
bonnet'. He also made a 'nose-truss' intended for use when a broken
nose healed badly. After an operation to rebreak it, the truss would
ensure that the septum grew straight again. The device had no lock and

Fig. 28.

A nose-truss of the sort Edith Sitwell was forced to wear: 'There are … cartilaginous
deformities which affect the personal appearance alone, and which by a perserverance
in the use of an apparatus at night might easily be corrected.' (F. Gustav Ernst)

key mechanism (indeed, none of his designs did). The removal of her adenoids indicates that Sitwell did have difficulty with her breathing passages and the truss may have been prescribed as part of her treatment, but Ernst believed that it could be used for cosmetic purposes: 'There are, however, a large number of cartilaginous deformities which affect the personal appearance alone, and which by a perseverance in the use of an apparatus at night may easily be corrected.'[53] Some of Lady Ida's friends came to the schoolroom to peer at Sitwell in her nose-truss – an experience she never forgave or forgot.[54]

When Lydia King-Church left the Sitwells in April 1903, she wrote Sir George a letter about Edith Sitwell and her brothers. About half of it was devoted to medical questions. At a recent examination, Mr Tubby had observed an improvement in Edith's back, which had grown broader and taller. Her feet were 'better, but far from well yet: & are scarcely strong enough to support her weight and height'. Miss King-Church's own opinion was that Edith's health was much improved, but that she must not overtire herself and must keep regular hours. She urged that 'great care be taken by everyone about her that she sits, stands and walks *straight*: her tendency is to develop the *right* shoulder & side altogether to the detriment of the left'.[55] Having thanked Sir George for his kindness through the five years of her employment, she left for Rhodesia, little knowing what seeds of anger had been planted in Edith.

Louisa Sitwell took charge of finding a new governess, allowing Osbert to sit in on the interviews.[56] Eventually she chose Helen Rootham, a musician who would become Sitwell's close friend for the next thirty-five years. Her full name was Helene Edith Rootham, but for the first few years she worked for the Sitwells she went by the name Edith – making her the third by that name in the extended family, along with Edith Sitwell and the Dowager Countess of Londesborough. Born in 1875 in Bristol, she was the eighth of nine children. Her mother, Frances (née Ross), died when Helen was about ten. Her father was Samuel Rootham, a music teacher. Her uncle Daniel, who lived with his family in the house next door,[57] was director of the Bristol Festival Chorus. He was also an extremely successful voice teacher, who included among his students the contralto Dame Clara Butt and the soprano Dame Eva Turner, leading singers in the first half of the twentieth century. One of Daniel's children was Cyril Bradley Rootham, who, like Helen, was born in 1875 and died in 1938; he was the organist at St John's College, Cambridge, and a prolific composer in the tradition of Sir Charles Stanford, under whom he studied. Cyril Rootham organised the first English performances of Kodály and Pizzetti.[58] By the time Helen was fifteen, she was living in South Kensington with her eldest sister Kate,[59] whose husband, Hartmann Just, rose in the civil service to become Assistant Under-Secretary of State for the Colonies from 1907 to 1916 and was knighted in 1911.[60] Sitwell came to know Kate Just fairly well and regarded her as one of the more sensible members of a difficult family. Another of Helen's sisters, Ethel, was mentally ill and sometimes tried to kill people.[61]

Osbert believed that Helen Rootham misunderstood her own talents; she thought of herself primarily as a singer, whereas he described her as the best female pianist he had ever heard.[62] Sacheverell was less admiring: he felt that Edith was too influenced by Helen, with too much emphasis on Swinburne and Brahms, and he noted that Edith found Debussy on her own.[63] However, his recollections of Helen's earliest years with the family are not very reliable, as she was hired when he was only five years old. Certainly, her abilities spread in several directions. Apart from music she was a translator of Rimbaud, of Serbo-Croat ballads, and of the Russian mystic Vladimir Solovyev;[64] she wrote some poetry and short stories of her own, as well as criticism of music and literature. By the 1930s, Edith sensed a kind of jealousy or competitiveness from Helen, which may have arisen from her failure to develop a single talent to the full. She remained an artistic jack of all trades.

However, in 1903, Helen brought a fervour for the arts that would transform Sitwell's life. Without Helen, Edith's existence might have mirrored that of her Aunt Florence, dependent on her father and brothers for a roof over her head and for the meals she ate. She would not have gone beyond 'talent' to expertise in either poetry or music. This is an important point as the education of upper-class women sought to make them 'accomplished' – that is, capable of ordering in a Paris restaurant, painting a watercolour, discussing a recent book without sounding highbrow, or playing an instrument in company. The idea was not to give a young woman a profession but to make her marriageable.

Sitwell's parents would probably have sorted out a marriage for her, either to a young man of a family with whom they had connections or, conceivably, to some clergyman of Louisa Sitwell's choosing. That she would become a successful professional writer was hardly to be imagined; that by the 1940s she would be thought one of the great poets of the age was beyond all possibility.

4

GROWING EYEBROWS

'I can never equal that,' said John Singer Sargent in August 1899.[1]
He was looking at Copley's *The Sitwell Children*, a conversation-piece
from 1787 hanging in the Great Drawing Room at Renishaw Hall.
Commissioned by Francis Hurt Sitwell, it portrays his four children,
Frank, Mary, Hurt, and Sitwell Sitwell.[2] Sir George wanted a painting of his own family to hang as a companion. His cousin George
Swinton and his wife Elsie (an important figure in Edith Sitwell's
youth) brought Sargent to Renishaw. An artist in demand, he was
paid £1500 by Sir George and insisted that he do the work in his
studio in London.

The Sitwells took a house at 25 Chesham Place that belonged to
Clarita Frewen (née Jerome), whose younger sister Jennie married
Randolph Churchill. The children studied in Frewen's boudoir,
whose walls were lined with photographs of her nephew, Winston,
who had recently effected his escape from Pretoria to Durban. His
eyes seemed to fill the room; several times Edith screened them with
newspapers and exercise books so that they could get on with their
lessons.[3]

Every second day for five or six weeks, beginning on 1 March 1900,
the family gathered at the studio. Sargent tried to keep the two-year-
old Sachie's attention by reciting:

> There was a young lady of Spain
> Who always was sick in the train –
> Not once and again,
> Or again and again,
> But again and again and again.[4]

Although Edith Sitwell respected Sargent as a craftsman, she could never think well of the painting he produced:

> My father was portrayed in riding-dress (he never rode), my mother in a white-spangled low evening gown and a hat with feathers, arranging, with one prettily shaped, flaccid, entirely useless hand, red anemones in a silver bowl (she never arranged flowers, and in any case it would have been a curious occupation for one wearing a ball-dress, even if, at the same time, she wore a hat). The colour of the anemones was repeated in my scarlet dress. I was white with fury and contempt, and indignant that my father held me in what he thought was a tender paternal embrace.[5]

Osbert says that Sargent was incensed when Sir George 'pointed out that my sister's nose deviated slightly from the perpendicular, and hoped that he would emphasise this flaw'. In retaliation, Sargent made Edith's nose straight and Sir George's crooked, refusing to alter them however much he protested.[6] Sir George's exact words are not quoted, or else Osbert was an unusual seven-year-old who knew what it meant to deviate from the perpendicular. More likely, Edith told him of this putative exchange long afterwards and he included it in his account, but it is a very odd thing for Sir George to have said. If Edith would soon be wearing, at his instigation, a brace to straighten her nose, why would he want the artist to make the defect perpetual by adding it to a portrait? One accusation of cruelty is at odds with the other. In any event, Sir George nagged the painter with suggestions and instructions. Sargent growled to George Swinton, 'Never again!'[7]

The conversation-piece presented a family stable and at ease, but this was hardly the case. Worried about lawsuits over mining leases, Sir George decided it was time for austerity at home. Christmas and birthday presents for the children were to be useful things such as soap and hairbrushes. Nearing the end of her employment, Davis denounced this as 'downright mean' – not least because they were told of it by her enemy, Miss King-Church.[8] More importantly, from about May 1901, Sir George was himself falling apart. He experienced extreme restlessness and irritability mixed with depression. His thoughts often racing, he could not sleep and felt unable even to stay consecutive nights in

the same house. It was then that Louisa Sitwell gave the unoccupied
Wood End to 'the dear invalid'.[9] Sir George put his illness down to
'over-work'.[10] It is just possible that he suffered from manic depression
or bipolar illness, but great caution is necessary in making retrospective
diagnoses. In old age, Sachie suggested to John Pearson that the problem arose from a disastrous marriage and that Sir George might have
sorted himself out with a few affairs if he had not been such a prude[11] –
it is hard to believe that a bad marriage would have been improved by
adultery.

Sir George's life changed abruptly in the first years of the century.
Finished as a parliamentary candidate, he took very long journeys to
France, Germany, and especially Italy, where, under the eye of Henry
Moat, he sought peace of mind by visiting ancient gardens. The children might not see their father for many months at a time, and when
they did see him he was unresponsive. Edith's letters to him over several years typically open as on 28 December 1902: 'I am so glad to hear
you are so much better and hope you are enjoying yourself very much
abroad. We do wish you could have been with us at Christmas.'[12] How
bad things were in 1902 is suggested from a letter to her Aunt Florence
of 26 May 1903: 'Dear Father seems so very much better and stronger,
is able to walk, and is, I think, so different to last year.'[13] It seems that
there were phases when he could not sleep and others when he could
not even get out of bed. Sir George was not that much better in May
1903, though his daughter wanted to believe otherwise. His mother
noted in her diary the arrival of 'George looking nervous & ill, having
a return of disturbing symptoms, through eating (it is supposed) some
tinned food in Paris'.[14]

During his long illness, Lady Sitwell did her best to help out with the
children and was especially watchful of Edith: 'On the 11th August
[1903], my dear granddaughter Edith Louisa Sitwell, was confirmed at
Hackness Church [Whitby], by the Bishop of Hull, a sweet & peaceful
service in the lovely little church.' A week later, on 18 August, came
a sign that things might be coming right: 'by 8.35 a.m. train, George &
the three children started for Renishaw, with their governess Miss
Rootham, nurse, & 4 other servants, the children so intensely happy,
at going to their old home again, if only for a week.' Sir George's
mental state was improving, but now Lady Ida was sick. She returned

from a visit to Scotland on 21 September 'overwrought & overtired & ill from internal catarrh. Dr. Salter attended & she had to keep to her bed for many days.' By mid-January, she had broken a rib from coughing. Undeterred, she went to parties in London when she was supposed to be convalescing in Gosden. Lady Sitwell complained of her 'callousness about her own health, & about the wishes of her husband & her Doctors'.[15] Lady Ida was suffering from the tuberculosis prevalent among the Londesboroughs, and it cost her a lung.[16]

In her adolescence, Edith learnt to play hide-and-seek in her relationships, as she tried not to upset the unstable Sir George or provoke the ill and bad-tempered Lady Ida. Her letters to her father are unfailingly polite, deferential, and warm-hearted, although her conversations about him with Helen and her brothers developed a very different tone. Indeed, throughout her life Edith treated friends, relatives, and even strangers, with a heroic kindness in person, but then, sometimes, with mockery or bitterness in their absence. I am reluctant to use the term 'real' feelings to describe the behind-the-back comments. Edith Sitwell developed an extraordinary ability to perceive suffering; its accompanying harshness was partly a way of pulling herself back from the abyss of other people's troubles. She was defending herself against the things she had seen. This combination of kindness and cruelty is mysterious; her finest and worst qualities grew inseparable.

Some letters to Sir George hint at her emerging skill as a writer. From Gosden House on 2 February 1903, she describes

> the village watch-maker – the quaintest old man, quite a Dickens
> character, very eccentric, and supposed to be unapproachable; at one
> time he refused to speak to anyone (he comes weekly to wind
> Grannie's clocks,) however we were very amiable to him, and in
> return he showed us a very queer collection of old watches, mostly
> gold ones, and beautifully chased, some 200 years old or more, which
> he has picked up in various places. Other customers came in, but he
> was so interested in showing us his collection that he was quite
> oblivious to their needs. The musical watches and old repeaters were
> specially wonderful.[17]

A sharp eye was matched by a sharp ear; she wrote on 26 November 1903: 'I am learning an Etude of Chopin's, my first thing of his, it is rather difficult and has to be played fast. I hope you will like it. Miss Rootham is playing now, a most beautiful thing of Rubinstein's, she has also got Schubert-Liszt's "Erl-King" which is quite ghastly, and she plays it so well.'[18]

Edith Sitwell had come to a point where, in her class, a period of 'finishing' was usual, although in later years she spoke often of having been 'finished off'. Sitwell's cousin Veronica Gilliat (née Codrington) spoke in 1962 on *This Is Your Life* of how Sitwell ran away from home when she was seventeen.[19] Sitwell may have felt as if she were making an escape, but it was all done with her parents' encouragement. She and Helen Rootham spent the latter part of 1904 in Paris, staying in a *pension* run by a Mademoiselle de Vérey at 16 Quai de Passy, near a house once occupied by Jean-Jacques Rousseau. Sitwell was pleased with her room and decorated it with picture postcards. Then came a personal make-over: 'I have got my hair done up now, and I should like you to see it; it looks much better done up than it did hanging down,' she told her father on 6 October. 'I am growing eyebrows. One can see them distinctly.' In November, Helen sent a bill for 64 francs to cover hairdressing lessons, for which were required 'pads which were especially made to match her hair'.[20] Sitwell complained in later years that a fashionably frizzed look was forced on her, but at the time she liked it. She was also taking lessons from a French cook: 'all sorts of strange foreign receipts, for dishes that one *never* gets in England; for instance, she is teaching me to make a grape tart, (it is a peculiarly delicious open tart, with white grapes, and some people put whipped cream.)' She tried this one on Sir George at Christmas to good effect. There were a number of visits to the Louvre, where she was especially drawn to Corot's *The Matinée*, *L'Étang*, and *Paysage*. She was reading about the history of the revolution, as well as Racine's *Andromaque* and Rostand's *Cyrano de Bergerac*. Still something of a little girl, she signed off: 'With very best love, ever your loving "Dish" aged 17.'[21]

In Paris, Edith Sitwell became friends with another of Helen's sisters. Born in 1877, Ella Evelyn Rootham was two years younger than Helen and, like her, was known by different Christian names in different contexts. To her family, she was Ella, while to Sitwell she was, through a friendship of sixty years, always Evelyn. During the First World War, she served as a nurse and was decorated for remaining with liquid-fire victims in a hospital that was being bombed.[22] She married Truels Wiel, the Norwegian vice-consul in Paris, and for a time enjoyed the glamour of the diplomatic service. However, the marriage failed, her husband left Paris, and she had to take secretarial jobs to make ends meet. Edith Sitwell and the ailing Helen came to live with her in the French capital in the 1930s, and she was very glad to have them there to share expenses. Indeed, Evelyn's dependence on Sitwell when they were both old became a cause of exasperation, although in 1905 Sitwell thought her 'so charming . . . she is very amusing, and so very pretty'.[23]

With the Rootham sisters, Sitwell was strictly chaperoned, but it was hardly needed. Though quirky, Edith was pious and straitlaced. Later, there were men in her life whom she would gladly have married, but there is no solid evidence that she ever had sex with a man – or a woman for that matter. Helen was prudish – Osbert called her 'censorious'[24] – and there is no sign, apart from friendship and shared lodgings, that she and Sitwell ever became lovers. However, Helen was possessive of her younger friend and over the years got in the way of Sitwell's relations with men. Helen herself had a failed engagement in the 1920s, but beyond that it is impossible to judge whether she might also have entertained a passion for Sitwell. There is, by the same token, no evidence of a sexual relationship between Sitwell and Evelyn Rootham.

The Sitwells came together for Christmas 1904 in San Remo, where Lady Ida could have easy access to the roulette tables at Monte Carlo. Osbert had not seen Edith for six months: 'I found my sister a changed person . . . Still more, though, did I notice an alteration in her way of looking at things, for her absence from home – and, as a result, the discontinuance of the perpetual nagging to which for years she had been obliged to submit – had lifted the whole range of her spirits. She knew now, she would be going away again before long.'[25]

Edith Sitwell met a number of people at San Remo, among them the Princess Salm-Salm.[26] An American woman born Agnes Joy, she had married a Prussian nobleman, tended the wounded on the battlefields of the American Civil War, attempted to save the life of Emperor

Maximilian, and tended the wounded again in the Franco-Prussian War. She wrote a memoir and became a figure almost of legend in the late nineteenth century.[27]

Sitwell's return to Paris was complicated by one of Sir George's sudden outbreaks of cheapness. At the end of January he disputed the bill at the *pension*, and Helen had to pacify the landlady. Sir George wanted to make weekly rather than monthly payments, and threatened to take his daughter out of the house altogether. Lady Ida proposed that Helen remove Edith at once to rooms elsewhere, but that was impossible: 'Naturally Mdlle de Vérey would keep our luggage until the bill is paid.'[28] Helen refused to take up Sir George's argument with de Vérey, writing to him: 'She has not been disagreeable to us, on the contrary she has acted with much delicacy and showed real kindness to Edith. But our position was none the less most humiliating and painful. I should be much obliged if you would send some money for our train-fares and our tea.'

By 12 February, things had settled down; Sir George accepted the existing arrangements. However, the episode offers a further, unexpected glimpse into the world of Edith Sitwell and the Roothams. Sir George backed off because of a letter written by Evelyn at the urging of a prominent surgeon named Henri Albert Hartmann, who was actually treating Edith. Evelyn pleaded with Sir George not to put Helen under any strain because of its likely medical consequences. Helen followed with a letter of her own, explaining the situation. While treating Edith, Hartmann had decided that Helen Rootham was in danger of a relapse of neurasthenia, for which she had received the Mitchell treatment some years earlier.[29]

Neurasthenia was first described by doctors around 1870, after which it became a common diagnosis throughout Europe and North America; Sir George himself was sometimes referred to as a neurasthenic. According to the medical historian David Schuster, it was thought to be caused by the depletion of a nervous energy produced by the digestive system and distributed throughout the body by the nervous system.[30] Symptoms included insomnia, depression', fatigue, indigestion, muscle pain, headaches, inability to concentrate, and general anxiety. A basket diagnosis, neurasthenia included what would now be seen as separate conditions – chronic fatigue syndrome, fibromyalgia, clinical depression, bipolar disorder, post-traumatic stress disorder, and post-partum depression. A neurologist and novelist, Dr Weir Mitchell contrived a treatment for the illness that became known as the 'rest-cure': six to eight weeks of complete bedrest, isolation from family and friends, a diet of fattening foods, massage, and sometimes electric shocks to prevent muscular atrophy.

Helen Rootham may have suffered from a mental illness. On the other hand, Dr Weir Mitchell's ideas were more pernicious and constraining than any back-brace, nose-truss, or ear-spring that Mr Ernst could come up with. Mitchell argued that women were by nature less intelligent than men and should not compete with them for fear of over-exertion; this meant that they should not think deeply, enter colleges, or join professions because of the danger of depleting their nervous energy. He botched the treatment of Charlotte Perkins Gilman, an American author best known for her short story 'The Yellow Wallpaper', for what would now be thought post-partum depression. His prescription to her is notorious: 'live as domestic a life as possible. Have your child with you all the time . . . Lie down an hour after each meal. Have but two hours' intellectual life a day. And never touch pen, brush or pencil as long as you live.'[31] Rootham may have been the sane patient of mad doctors. For Edith Sitwell, fear of neurasthenia dovetailed with Tubby's insistence that she spend a great portion of her day horizontal. She later interpreted the troubles of her youth as leading directly to neurasthenia. She wrote in 1944: 'My nerves were completely broken, and my nervous system ruined for life before I was ten years old. This was perfectly well known to the doctors who attended me then, and to the doctors who have attended me since.'[32]

Gradually taking over from Tubby, Hartmann would be involved in Sitwell's and Rootham's lives for many years. For the time being, Sitwell's back was growing stronger and straighter. In January 1904, she reported to her father: 'I have been to see Mr Tubby again, and he is delighted with my back and says it is nearly straight.'[33] In late 1904 and 1905, Hartmann was similarly encouraging, at a time when she was drawing great benefit from a masseur named Arcier. Helen wrote on 2 March 1905: 'The progress she has made since her return from San Remo is quite extraordinary, and her right shoulder is slowly but quite steadily getting on a level with the left. It's a real happiness to watch the improvement.' Echoing an appeal from Helen, Sitwell wrote two days later to ask Sir George 'if I may have a month extra here so as to continue the massage, and have two months less in Germany, so as to pay the extra massage and pension'.[34] Sir George sent money for another month in Paris, but pressed Helen to keep expenses down. In May, Edith reported her back 'quite cured';[35] however, Hartmann continued the regime of braces, and a new set of 'corsets' was fitted in May.[36] It is not known when Sitwell finally laid them aside, but if her back was so much better they cannot have been necessary for long.

Despite the flap over the rent, these months in Paris were some of the happiest of her life. She wrote to Florence, 'I am so busy nearly all day here practising and learning French, but I lie down a lot, too, and my back is most wonderfully better.'[37] She attended many concerts, including one in April by the acclaimed Jan Kubelík, a twenty-four-year-old Czech 'otherwise known as "the Violin-Cello Man"! he played very wonderfully, and did impossible feats on his violin.'[38] Helen was stretching Sitwell's own talent on the piano as far as it would go. On 6 February she asked Sir George to give permission for extra music-lessons. 'If I were only giving her one or two lessons a week I should not think it necessary, but as I work with her every day at the piano I think it better for her that she should have another influence besides mine. I should like to choose a teacher of the German school.'[39] Rootham believed Edith Sitwell had a considerable talent and could achieve a professional standard.

On 18 May, Sitwell and Rootham joined Sir George and Lady Ida at Bad Nauheim, a spa town near Frankfurt. From there, Sitwell and Rootham went on to Berlin in June, where they took rooms from Fräulein von Versen (a name that serendipitously means 'of verses') in Altonaer Strasse 3, near the Tiergarten and the zoological gardens. Sitwell took lessons from a master pianist named Berkovitch, and set to work on the language, although it ultimately defeated her. The city itself fascinated her: she was charmed by designs traced above the door-ways of old houses, especially one of Phoebus and his chariot, and she delighted in the balconies full of geraniums and hydrangeas. Berlin offered many galleries and museums; Sitwell especially admired an exhibit of landscapes and seascapes by the Symbolist painter Arnold Böcklin, who is now mainly remembered as an allegorist. Nonetheless some artwork was incomprehensible, as she told her father: 'One after-noon we went to see an exhibition of Impressionist paintings; they were really funny, and at first we didn't know that they weren't intended to be.'[40] The word 'we' indicates that Helen, too, was strug-gling to understand modern art.

They returned to England to spend the last of the summer at Renishaw. Sitwell took long walks with her father each afternoon. She was enthusiastic about his most recent Italian purchases, three foun-tains and 'some "new" "old" furniture', remarking to Florence that they 'do improve the place so'. Lady Ida was upbeat and busy: 'Mother has been doing quite a lot of gardening, and takes such an interest in it. She gardens nearly every day.'[41]

On 6 September 1905, the day before her eighteenth birthday, Sitwell and Rootham took the night train back to Berlin. They stayed there, with some breaks, through the following year and possibly into the first months of 1907. Edith wrote to Sir George on 4 November 1905 to report on her reading and her dancing lessons. She added whimsically: 'How lovely it must be at Venice. Please don't let your uncertainty as to the quantity that would be needed, prevent your sending us some figs. I think we could manage to consume as many as you could send through the post. You need not be afraid of sending too many.'[42] She and Helen appear to have remained in Germany until the late spring of 1906, before returning, for a time, to England.

In August 1906 at Renishaw, Sir George announced that Edith's sojourns in Germany would have to end soon. Disappointed, Helen told him that she would be staying on in Germany to continue her own training as a singer and would support herself as a music teacher, effec-tively giving in her notice. However, once Edith returned to Germany, Sir George acquiesced and offered to keep paying their costs for at least another four months and perhaps beyond that, if Helen were able to cover more of her own expenses as a music teacher.

Once Sir George gave way in the autumn of 1906, Helen wrote to him:

perhaps you will forgive me if I take a little of your time to talk about myself. Mr Griswold, my singing master, told me before I left Berlin last spring, that in three months – studying with him and taking into consideration what I had already learnt – I could learn sufficient to enable me to teach, but that if I could stay for a year or eighteen months I had a career before me as a concert singer. The first is of course useful, but the latter is something more, and means more than anyone but my sisters could realise for it would mean our having a house together. As I have no pupils yet, if I accept your very generous offer it means that I can stay at any rate for four months, and in that fourth month I might perhaps get just the very teaching I need . . . So if I ever do attain to being a singer, it will be owing to you, who helped me over the first rough ground.[43]

Two weeks later, Helen had more to say – her thoughts going back, possibly, to February 1905 when Sir George had disputed the rent in Paris, or perhaps to some more recent quarrel:

There is something I must tell you because I feel so dreadfully badly about it and you are so good to me. When that unpleasantness happened in Paris I did not say very nice things about you. I was very miserable and very angry, and – oh everything I said seems to rise up and hit me in the face. Of course it does not make any difference to you what I said, but it makes a big difference to me, and it isn't good to feel as mean as I feel now. I was obliged to confess to you; it is not possible that I should let you be so good to me and pretend I had nothing to be ashamed of. You will probably think very badly of me, but not nearly so badly as I think of myself. I feel so small I hardly like even to thank you, but perhaps someday I shall be able to do something to show how grateful I am.[44]

No other letters have come to light that show us so much of Helen's personality: intensely ambitious, generous, hot-tempered, self-dramatising, honest to a fault. It is conceivable that Helen's exchange with Sir George actually occurred in 1905, when the rent incident, if that is what she means by the 'unpleasantness', was still fresh in her mind. Her letters bear a day and month but no year, while his letters have not come to light. However, letters by Edith Sitwell from the autumn of 1905 are all addressed from Fräulein von Versen's – whereas these by Helen to Sir George are from the house of Mrs A. V. Reitze in

Apostel Paulus Strasse 1, in the Schöneberg district, where she and Sitwell were certainly living in late 1906.

On 18 October 1906, Sitwell described their accommodation to her father as though it were still a novelty: 'This is such a charming flat in one of the nicest parts of Berlin, and Mrs Reitze is the happy possessor of some wonderful Chinese embroideries. A relation of hers was in China at the time of Boxer troubles, and took these. The colours and the gold work are gorgeous. There are also some lovely pieces of work in ivory and bronze.'[45] As for herself, she wrote shortly afterwards: 'I am getting on with my voice to a wonderful extent: I don't want to sing to anyone just yet, because I really think I shall be able to do something at singing, so does Mme. Mara, who is teaching me.' With Christmas looming, she proposed a medieval feast of swan and noted, 'There is a very savage swan at Foxton Dam that might well be spared.'[46]

5

BRINGING OUT

Luckily for the swan, the Sitwells went for Christmas to Ingleborough in the Yorkshire Dales. This was the home of Sir George's second cousin Elizabeth Farrer, known as 'Cousin Bessie' – a woman as churchified as Louisa or Florence. Edith Sitwell often visited Ingleborough and was close to Bessie's son Reginald Farrer. A very short man with a cleft palate and a harelip disguised by a moustache, he is described by the *ODNB* as 'a rare example of a Yorkshireman with an inferiority complex'. He wrote a number of indifferent plays and novels but became famous as a traveller and a horticulturalist. His book *My Rock Garden* (1907) was popular for many years. Once, he loaded a shotgun with seeds gathered in his travels and, from a boat, blasted them into a cliff near his home, with the result that Alpine plants bloomed there.

Farrer had a sceptical turn of mind and disappointed Lady Sitwell, Florence, and his mother by his unbelief. However, their prayers for him were eventually answered in a way that may prove God has a sense of humour: 'In 1903 Farrer went on his first long journey, reaching Peking, briefly visiting Korea, and spending about eight months in Japan, where he had an affair with a geisha girl and his drift to vegetarianism was hastened by the discovery that he had eaten his pet kitten, served as fricassée of chicken.'[1] In time, he became a Buddhist; this horrified most of the family, but Sir George found it entertaining.[2] In 1913, Reginald Farrer stood for Parliament in Kent but disbursed the thousand pounds his father gave him for his campaign on the purchase of bulbs.[3] On his last journey in 1920, he caught diphtheria and died at the age of forty in a hut in northern Burma, where his gravestone bears the inscription, 'He died for love and duty in search of rare plants.'[4]

A pleasant Christmas with Reginald Farrer probably gave Sitwell a brief respite from a new round of troubles with Lady Ida. For most of the past few years, Sitwell had successfully interposed the North Sea and a considerable landmass between herself and her mother. Sir George always preferred to save money, but he knew that his daughter was prospering in Berlin, and he could be talked into a degree of indulgence. Lady Ida wanted to rein her in, yet did not want to take time away from her own friends to be with her daughter. From Lady Ida's perspective, this period of finishing was turning into a way of life.

In mid-November 1906, it was learnt that Lady Ida needed surgery, so Edith dutifully volunteered to make an early return to England. Writing to Sir George, Lady Ida dismissed the suggestion: 'That tiresome Edith is fussing, she is such a worry, suggests coming home all sorts of nonsense, if she was worried about me she ought not to have gone abroad when she did.' Lady Ida wrote that she was going from Londesborough to Scarborough, where she would need bedrest. She was expecting a friend to visit and asked Sir George to delay his and Edith's return by a few days: 'I hope darling you won't think I don't want you, it will be [illegible] having you back. I shall have a miserable winter as am to do nothing.'[5]

During that 'miserable winter', Lady Ida appears to have insisted upon Edith's 'coming out', but when Edith refused to do it on her mother's terms, a serious quarrel ensued. On 16 May 1907, Lady Ida wrote to Sir George as 'My darling Duddy': 'Edith is anxious to stay with Miss Lane, I think she might do so, I don't know her, I should think it would be all right. So cold here.'[6] Her handwriting is at times unreadable, and her style in letters is to jump suddenly from thought to thought with just a peppering of commas. In the following week, she wrote: 'I am so glad you are enjoying yourself. However I do feel it *very* very much the way you & your Mother allow Edith to treat me, she has never been near my Mother, I think it very unkind, you would feel the same if she did it to your Mother.' At the bottom of the page for three lines the handwriting degenerates; it seems that Lady Ida is taking comfort in 'the two darling boys'. On the next page her outburst continues: 'We can never really be happy together when you allow it as it makes me very very bitter, however I won't say any more . . . Is Edith coming home? Or what are you & Lady Sitwell arranging about her. I should simply love an umbrella handle it is so kind of you thinking of me.'[7]

It seems that Edith refused to be 'brought out' by the autocratic dowager. This letter reveals some of what Edith faced in the early months of 1907 – Lady Ida sick, depressed, probably drunk, and lashing out. Sir George and Lady Sitwell had decided to do their best for Edith and get her away from Lady Ida. Where Lady Sitwell was concerned, the solution to any significant problem usually had an ecclesiastical dimension. Accordingly, Edith was sent to Adela Lane, a clergyman's widow who lived in Hemel Hempstead in Hertfordshire. Her house was near Ashridge, the estate of the Earls of Brownlow to whom the Lanes were related. She was bringing out her daughter Constance that year, so Sir George hired her to bring out Edith as well.

Constance Lane, known as 'Cooie', was a talented young woman, about a year younger than Sitwell.[8] She became a professional artist, and collaborated on some frescoes with her friend Dora Carrington. In a memoir published sixty years after her death, she describes Edith Sitwell's arrival at her home around the end of May 1907:

> I went to meet her at Berkhamsted station, and driving up the hill to the common in a one-horse fly Edith said, 'Are you keen on poetry?' A tall slender figure, stepping on long narrow feet she had a curiously distinguished and enigmatic air. She wore a floppy hat and pale suede gloves. Soon after her arrival she brought sheets of music down to our drawing room and played, exceedingly well, Chopin, Brahms and Debussy. It was early summer and we used to wander about the fields and watch the wind brushing across the tops of the young barley, and as it whitened the field in waves Edith said, 'It's as if these are all people who will come into one's life.'[9]

Sitwell spent much of that summer with Constance Lane, who sketched her in her studio, and with Lane's cousin, also, somewhat confusingly, named Constance; her last name was Talbot and she was generally called 'Contie'. She lived at nearby Marchmont House and often came to visit in a dog cart. Sitwell stayed several times subsequently at Marchmont House, and Talbot stayed several times with the

Sitwells. She eventually married one of their distant relatives. Under her married name, Constance Sitwell, she became a memoirist and travel writer. By the 1940s, Edith Sitwell felt she was 'muscling in' on the family's fame and that many of her reminiscences were just nasty.[10] However, despite an undercurrent of rivalry, she found her 'perfectly charming' when they were nineteen.[11]

Sir George set up the Lane family for the London season in a house at 6 Sloane Court next door to that of Lord Monteagle. His son Tom Spring-Rice (later third Baron Monteagle) was a diplomat and an expert pianist. He often visited in the evenings and sometimes played Brahms's *Variations on a Theme by Handel* for them. Reginald Farrer also came by and entertained them with what Constance Lane called his 'curious humour'. Another family that lived near by – all good-looking and in Constance's term 'Londony' – were baffled by Sitwell: 'Why does she always read Swinburne? Is she in love?' they asked.[12]

Adela Lane, 'a mixture of nervousness and ready wit', held dinner parties for Edith and Constance. They dressed in long full dresses, done up at the back – Adela in black, Constance in pink, and Edith in pale green or white. Edith attended a number of balls, including, as she told her father, one given by a woman named Bowens, whose daughter was spooked beyond the tolerance even of a Sitwell: 'The daughter is pretty, but is marred by the attraction she has for ghosts!!! Whatever house she lives in, she is followed by ghosts, and quite prosaic people see them.' Sitwell even confessed to enjoying a garden party held by the Bishop of Southwark, whose family she liked because of their 'huge sense of humour'. Lady Ida arranged for Edith to attend court on 5 July, though Edith was 'not the least bit keen on it'.[13] She was presented by a 'Mrs Tom Gurney',[14] apparently a Scarborough friend of Lady Ida's.

For Edith Sitwell, entering society was a bit like learning German: she memorised a few declensions and then accepted defeat. She told Sir George: 'I am studying the heavy art of light conversation. I think the best plan is to try and look terribly interested in everything that is being said to one, and then the other person goes on talking.'[15] She used the same strategy for dealing with bores for the next six decades. At Lord's, Sitwell walked about dreamily, oblivious to the cricket, with a white feather boa flapping in the wind.[16]

Sitwell teased Constance Lane as being interested only in ploughed fields and porridge, but begged her to do impressions of cockney accents. Lane wrote:

> We were serious pleasure seekers, Edith and I, Edith reading poetry, Swinburne, Verlaine and Baudelaire, and practising Brahms, and I going to art school in Chelsea . . . Sometimes one of our relations gave a party to which we went, Edith dressed in white brocade with golden lily woven in it. She generally looked aloof and amused. It might be a musical party at which the fellow guests were not as seri-ous about the music as we could have wished – 'Philistines,' Edith called them; I suppose they were.

Lane understood Sitwell fairly deeply: 'There was a softness and poignant sympathy in her as well as the strong personal prejudice that sharpened her angle of vision.'[17]

Lane's cousin Talbot wrote about some of the same things in her diary with a good deal less sympathy:

> Later, I went for tea at the Lanes, where Edith Sitwell is staying; she plays the piano all day, very well too, very literary and artistic, of course, but always laughing at the uneducated in her special fashion, – rather boring. The next day was Sunday. A London Sunday . . . We went to Holy Trinity, Sloane Square, and heard Canon Beeching, who slanged the decadent sort of Swinburne poetry, and this I passed on to Edith without any softening at luncheon, and she was rather angry over it. But later she and I went to St. Paul's, and heard a sermon about peace and the serious way Christians ought to look on the conference going on at the Hague. It was lovely sitting under the Dome, when thousands of voices sang 'Oh, happy band of pilgrims'.[18]

Back in Hemel Hempstead, there were debates about poetry and religion:

> The protégée, Edith Sitwell, was there – a fine specimen, railing and raging against the smart 'fast' set, in the heated middle of which she seems to have passed her days. It poured in torrents the whole

afternoon. I sat in the window in the schoolroom, and Cooie painted the blue forget-me-knots [sic], and the blue distance, and Miss Sitwell raved over the Greenery-Yellerys, and kept declaiming Swinburne at us. We replied as staunch Chestertonians, and tried to advance our theory that it is not the beautiful and the wonderful we have to like, but the stupid, the unlovely, and the squalid; that Swinburne and his like did not look at life as a whole, but divided poetry from mankind, instead of having it as a help. We had great and fascinating arguments – very heated and exhilarating.[19]

Sitwell's coming-out had its low moments. There are at least two versions of the story of her biggest disaster. In one she refers to a time when she was 'seventeen'. Her Aunt Grace, the Countess of Londesborough, held a dinner and carefully seated Edith beside an eligible baronet. Edith talked about Brahms, he complained, and she was sent packing.[20] A more plausible version of the story is Osbert's; he places it c.1908. At a relative's, presumably the Londesboroughs', Edith was seated next to the ageing politician and huntsman, Lord Chaplin, whose family had once owned Blankney. She asked whether he preferred Bach to Mozart and was hastily 'withdrawn from circulation'.[21]

Cooie Lane stayed with Louisa Sitwell in London in mid-February 1908, presumably as Edith's guest. Her mother, Adela Lane, wrote to express thanks and to comment on Edith:

Last year, after Edith had been with us, I intended – but somehow it never came off – to write to tell you how very glad we were to have had her with us & how really fond of her we became. She has such a good heart & she has noble impulses & a sweet disposition. She was exceedingly nice to me in all ways & very patient under quite a plethora of good advice wch I fear I poured upon her. I feel her intense love of music makes life difficult for her, for it seems to make her unable to really care for anything else & in a way to unsettle her. My girl has rather a healthy way of looking at things & being about Edith's age can sometimes help her to feel young & amused, wch I think is good for Edith. But I am afraid there will be too much music![22]

The Sitwells admired musicians – even Lady Ida conducted a correspondence with the singer and composer Lawrence Kellie between
1898 and 1910.[23] Although Sir George pressed Edith to play the cello,
he was certainly aware of her talent at the keyboard and years later
lamented: 'Such a mistake that Edith gave up her music; at one time
she had quite a pretty touch on the pianoforte.'[24] By then, of course,
she was a knuckledusting modernist poet, and the days of her passion
for the keyboard may have seemed idyllic to him. Edith was discour-
aged from playing, not because the Sitwells and the Denisons despised
music, but because young women of her class did not normally pursue
a profession. Earning a living was best left to those who had no money.
There was also the memory of Mr Tubby: 'One of the most prolific
causes of scoliosis in girls is prolonged piano-practice on the ordinary
pattern of music-stool.'[25] Thus were the prejudices of class fortified by
science.

While her family nattered about her music, Sitwell lived a quiet and
respectable life, surrounded by elderly aunts and cousins and a horde
of clerics. In late June 1908, for example, writing from Sloane Gardens,
she reported to Florence that she had enjoyed the Lambeth Palace
garden party 'hugely', and that 'Cousin Edie Davidson' (wife of the
Archbishop) was anxious to know about Lady Sitwell's health. The
garden itself was 'positively soaked with memories'. Modern clothing
seemed wrong for the Palace, but the bishops who had assembled that
month for the immense Pan-Anglican Congress seemed to get it right,
especially the blacks and the Japanese. She attended the Chelsea and
the Winchester historical pageants and particularly enjoyed the
Winchester: 'Queen Elizabeth didn't come into it, which was such a
boon. I am tired of the good lady, and I don't care about her gowns.'
She changed her mind, as she later wrote two books about the Virgin
Queen, even taking up her style of dress. Sitwell went to the Academy
with Constance Lane where she spotted the popular painter Marcus
Stone, who specialised in romantic and sentimental scenes: 'I didn't
shoot him, but I hadn't thought of bringing a gun.'[26] On the whole, it
seems a tame existence enlivened chiefly by a tongue growing ever
sharper.

In early September 1908, Sir George, an unlikely master of revels,
threw a twenty-first birthday party for his daughter at Renishaw. Cars

were hired to ferry the thirty house-guests to the St Leger Stakes at Doncaster and, for those who did not trust the new technology, special trains were laid on. There was an invasion of chefs, footmen, and other temporary additions to the staff. Silver plate, unused for many years, was brought out of the bank. Hired for a ten-day engagement, a blue-uniformed band of Hungarian Hussars played at meals. Renishaw Hall had just one bathroom; Osbert recalls the maids and footmen labouring on the stairs with tin baths, hip baths, and cans of hot water. Although the party was in honour of Edith, there were few young guests apart from Veronica Codrington and a solitary young man, an American courting one of Edith's cousins. Lady Ida had a taste for hubbub in almost any form, and even Sir George, who hated parties and horse races, seems to have had a moderately good time.[27] Disliking the races, Edith turned her back to them.[28]

By 1908 and 1909 Lady Ida was becoming more and more unreasonable. Although Edith spent as much time as possible abroad, Osbert says that she was more often with their parents than was he or Sachie, and so bore the brunt of the quarrels. A wedge had been driven between Sir George and Lady Ida, who believed that he and his mother were encouraging Edith in her rebellion. Moreover, she had seriously outspent her income and Sir George was unwilling to make up the difference. 'I never hear from Father,' she wrote to Osbert in October 1908. 'I suppose he is cross with me. He generally is.'[29]

The less Lady Ida had to do, the more she spent, gave, or gambled away. Edith's friends were invited to Renishaw and to Italy, in order to create an air of vitality and to surround Lady Ida with pleasant people who would not take advantage of her. Both Lane and Talbot came away with strong physical impressions of the Sitwells' world. Lane wrote:

When I went to stay at Renishaw I saw the background that explained [Edith]. The house itself, long, battlemented and brooding, the beautiful terraced garden sloping to the valley below, the Italian fountains and terraces made a strong contrast to its setting, a coal-mining country with blast furnaces that flared up at night. The house was haunted. Inside, it had a solemn luxury about it, but the great ballroom was full of light and held it like a bubble between the high ceiling and the polished parquet floor. Large pieces of

Italian and French furniture were beautifully placed in that room. I remember their shadows reflected in the parquet floor; a fine Sargent family group hung up at one end. Edith, in white, swaying slightly, played sometimes Scarlatti and Corelli (to please me), or Brahms and Debussy to please herself, the Indian queens and Roman captains of the tapestries seeming part of the music.[30]

On one of her visits, Talbot engaged Lady Ida:

I remember feeling rather awkward and out-of-place in Lady Ida's boudoir, which had a mixed smell of cigarettes and the tube-roses [sic] which she always had there; it was full of novels, magazines, and large photographs of women in Edwardian evening dress, their hair piled on the top of their heads and wearing tiaras, which stood about on little tables in silver photograph frames, as was the fashion then. A bridge table was set out ready for players, and one always felt boredom was just round the corner with her; the day had to be filled up as best it could with bridge, talking, meals, and jokes which were repeated many times in her lazy, rather random fashion. She has an air of great distinction with her height and small dark head held high. She used to wear dark tweeds in those days, with a silk handkerchief knotted round her neck, gypsy-fashion.[31]

Easily bored himself, Sir George was always casting about for worthy projects, and he was about to do something startling. Around the beginning of October 1909 he was riding in a car from Florence to Siena when the driver took the wrong road. The car broke down beneath the walls of the Castello di Montegufoni. Sir George ambled about in the company of two friends, watching the peasants treading grapes, and inspecting the ancient statues that had been brought there from Greece. He fell in love with the place, writing to Osbert soon afterwards: 'You will be interested to hear that I am buying in your name the Castle of Acciaiuoli (pronounced Accheeyawly) between Florence and Siena . . . The castle is split up between many poor families, and has an air of forlorn grandeur . . . There is a great tower, a picture-gallery with frescoed portraits of the owners, from a very early period, and a chapel full of relics of the Saints . . . We shall be able to grow our own fruit, wine, oil – even champagne!'[32] There was something wild, almost visionary, in the purchase of the *castello*. He saw a new enterprise lying before him – the restoration of a great piece of a lost world and the building of a garden. Perhaps there was a glint in his eye.

6

BECOMING A POET

According to Osbert, the clergymen who sprang up around Lady Sitwell like 'inedible fungi' thought there was something wicked in his sister's taste for Swinburne. According to Edith herself, her grandmother, under the advice of a Reverend Losey, burnt her copy of the poems. In retaliation, Edith rose early on a September morning and boarded the boat that connected Bournemouth and Ventnor on the Isle of Wight. She took with her a disapproving lady's maid of about thirty whose face turned green during the crossing. They went to the churchyard at Bonchurch, where, after an argument with the sexton, Sitwell poured a jug of milk and placed bay leaves, honeycomb and red roses on Swinburne's grave. They returned to Bournemouth, where, according to Osbert, 'An appalling storm broke and long raged round her head, alternating with calm patches of religious resignation.'[1]

As usual, Sitwell herself assigned this episode to her seventeenth year[2] – which would be September 1904 when she was actually in Paris. Moreover, Lady Sitwell was living mainly in Surrey until 23 January 1907, when she gave up Gosden House.[3] It was only later that she made her home in Bournemouth. However, the really awkward point is that Swinburne did not actually occupy his grave until 15 April 1909. The most likely date, then, is September 1909, when Edith Sitwell was twenty-two. In the preceding months there was a controversy over whether the rector of Bonchurch had defied Swinburne's wishes by reading parts of the Anglican service at his burial. Though Christian herself, Sitwell was providing classical obsequies for the poet who wrote so warily of the 'pale Galilean'. Half a century later she wrote in her selection of his work: 'It is my firm belief that Swinburne, for all his defiance, for all his raging blasphemies, was born a believer. It was his tragedy that he dreamed mankind had been abandoned.'[4]

As with many of Sitwell's stories of her youth, the visit to Bonchurch may be invented or embellished as part of a personal myth. Swinburne was at the foundation of her sense of poetry and of a poetic vocation. In her introduction to his poems she quotes his remarks on Blake: 'Now on his own ground, no man was ever more sane or more reverent. His outcries on various matters of art or morals were in effect the mere expression, not of reasonable dissent, but of violent belief . . . Indifference was impossible to him.'[5] She says that this might have served as Swinburne's own epitaph, but she was probably thinking of herself.

Some of Sitwell's behaviour was like another generation's Beatlemania. She said that in her 'adolescence' she had a passion for Yeats: 'I once left red roses on his doorstep. I ran away quickly before anyone opened the door but I think he knew who had left them.'[6] If he could guess who had left the roses, then she had done things like it before. Twenty years on, she would count Yeats among her friends, and *his* extravagant behaviour would cause mild embarrassment to *her*.

Sitwell's real introduction to the artistic and literary scene in London came through her 'cousin-by-marriage' Elsie Swinton, née Ebsworth (1874–1966), who had a celebrated career as a singer beginning in 1906 but lasting only about a decade when her husband and mother pressured her to retire.[7] She had been brought up in St Petersburg and later wrote vividly about the Russia she had known as a child. She was an attractive and charismatic woman, of whom Sitwell wrote: 'Elsie Swinton turned all days to glamour: in her presence the thought of dullness could not exist: all the lights and colours and excitement of summer entered a room with her.'[8] Elsie was the subject of one of the most famous of John Singer Sargent's portraits, and it was she who recommended him to Sir George for the commission of his family portrait. Sitwell described the Swintons:

> Elsie was married to my father's first cousin, George Swinton, a
> member of one of the most ancient untitled Scottish families, a mag-
> nificent looking being, immensely tall, and with a 15th century type
> of face. He was Lion King of Arms, and looked as if he should be

wearing, always, Herald's costume. George was interested in *things*, Elsie in vital people, in life. She took no interest in things, and regarded dull people as furniture. There they were in a room, and were, perhaps, necessary . . . she did as much to awaken my mind as anyone in my youth. She introduced me to Dostoievsky, to Balzac, and to Russian Songs.[9]

In such a passage, Sitwell is glossing over trouble in Elsie's life. On 30 April 1895, she had married Captain George Swinton; the eight-year-old Sitwell was a bridesmaid.[10] Though pleasant and handsome, Captain Swinton was fifteen years older than Elsie. He shared Sir George Sitwell's fascination with genealogy and was a talented painter; otherwise, he had little to do after retiring from the army and lived off Elsie's rich family. When she became a professional singer in 1906, it reinforced the impression that she was the provider and he the dependent spouse. He did become an important figure in the London County Council, and also worked with Lutyens on the design of the new imperial capital in Delhi, but he was generally outshone by his wife.[11]

The passion of Elsie's life was the British Impressionist painter Walter Sickert. In February 1905, Sickert took part in a retrospective of the works of his teacher James McNeill Whistler. Rodin made the trip to London to open the exhibition, and a large reception was held for him by Mrs Mary Hunter, a flamboyant hostess who was the model for another of Sargent's best-known portraits; she was also a distant cousin of the Sitwells. Among those who performed at the reception was Elsie Swinton; her mezzo-soprano rendition of Russian songs caught Sickert's attention: 'I must know that superb Russian,' he said to Mary Hunter. Though not actually Russian, Elsie Swinton's mastery of the language was such that once, when she forgot the words to a song, she merely listed with great emphasis what she expected to eat at supper – to the amusement of one Russian speaker in the audience. She sat for Sickert on many occasions and a relationship developed.[12] Their biographers are not certain whether it was a sexual affair, though it is likely. Sickert got on well with George Swinton and their children, often visiting their house in Pont Street. When Elsie said she was prepared to leave her husband for him, Sickert asked what George had done to deserve such treatment.[13]

Edith Sitwell described her introduction to Sickert: 'When Elsie took me to his studio, I was an unimaginably shy young girl. Elsie said to him "This woman admires your La Vecchia" (a picture being shown at that time in a London gallery). "Well, then, she must be a very intelligent woman, or else she is mad. Which are you?" turning on me suddenly. I was almost too awed to reply. "Mad" I said. Enchanted by this answer, he gave me a drawing of the Bedford Music Hall.'[14]

There are several versions of this story, some set in Elsie's house, some in Sickert's studio. As ever, Sitwell says that it occurred when she was seventeen. That date, 1904, is apparently confirmed by her saying that Sickert (1860–1942) was forty-four at the time, but he was mainly living in Dieppe until 1905.[15] Osbert recalls that he was on holiday from Eton when Edith acquired the picture and brought it to Renishaw. Since he first went to the school in autumn 1905,[16] the meeting with Sickert could not have happened before the summer of 1906. In the last version of *Taken Care Of*, Sitwell drops the title *La Vecchia* and has Elsie say merely, 'This woman admires your pictures.'[17] Presumably between drafts she had checked and discovered that *La Vecchia* was not exhibited until the summer of 1907.[18] She evidently wanted to continue to portray her seventeenth year as the time of her rebellions and illuminations, so made the necessary adjustments.

Sickert's gift did not go down well in Bournemouth. Edith wrote to Osbert: 'I want you to see the drawing Mr. Sickert has given me . . . Aunt Floss is such a fool about it. She doesn't think it "pretty". And she doesn't think it quite "Right" to draw four women watching at a music-hall. Church of England Saints are the only really suitable subjects for art. She says one ought not to have any character or individuality. It is the devil trying to get hold of one.'[19] Perhaps Florence had heard that the Byronic Sickert had got hold of Elsie Swinton. Like his sister, Osbert became devoted to Sickert, eventually editing a volume of his essays and writing about their long friendship in *Left Hand, Right Hand!*.

Elsie Swinton belonged to a professional community somewhat different from Sickert's although they overlapped. At her house, Edith Sitwell met singers, musicians, composers, and writers. From the late 1890s Gabriel Fauré often visited, and he conducted an effusive correspondence with Swinton, describing himself, with a pun on his name, as her 'fallen archangel'. Among the other composers who visited were

Ethel Smyth (Mary Hunter's sister), Maude Valérie White, Percy
Grainger, Cyril Scott, and Roger Quilter. The harpsichordist Violet
Gordon Woodhouse and the tenor Gervase Elwes were both guests, as
were George Moore and Max Beerbohm. One night in early 1913, with
the composer Karol Szymanowski listening, Sergei Prokofiev and
Arthur Rubinstein played the piano, Paul Kochanski performed on the
violin, and Ruth Draper acted out one of her monologues, while Igor
Stravinsky lay on the hearthrug.[20]

We cannot know precisely whom Sitwell met through Elsie Swinton
or when the introductions occurred, but she did meet some of these
people, and she seems to have been taken seriously by Swinton's circle.
For example, Roger Quilter.

A writer of songs and stage musicals, he was, with Grainger and
Scott, a member of the Frankfurt Group of composers.[21] He was working on an opera, apparently never performed, based on a Chinese story
in which the emperor is obliged to have a woman strangled to prevent
an uprising among his troops. In September 1910, Sitwell wrote to
Quilter from Ingleborough, where she and Reginald Farrer had been
discussing A Lute of Jade (L. Cranmer-Byng's anthology of classical
Chinese poetry), and the work of Lafcadio Hearn, a translator and
scholar of Oriental literature. She passed on Farrer's observations on
the poems from which the story of the strangling is drawn. Quilter later
showed her a draft of his opera, and on 16 May 1911 she wrote a more
assured letter, suggesting revisions and even proposing some poetic
images to Quilter:

> I have just been seized with an expression to describe the peach-
> blossoms; it is rather unmeaning, but I have never, from being a
> child, seen very delicate flowers, without thinking of it: 'like blown
> spray from the fountain of dreams'. I suppose peach-blossoms would
> be very faint-coloured by moon-light. What a bore it is that every-
> one reads Sappho, for how lovely it would be if you could use 'And
> round about, the breeze murmurs cool through apple-branches, and
> sleep flows down upon us in the rustling leaves.' One of the most
> divinely beautiful things in the world, and I think the feeling would
> be just right for your opera.

Sitwell was at this time reading Henry Wharton's very popular *Sappho* (1885), containing a biography and translations by himself and other hands. She has improved Wharton's version of Fragment 4, substituting 'branches' for 'boughs', 'sleep' for 'slumber', and 'rustling' for 'quivering'.[22] Probably based on another translation by Palgrave also included in the book, these choices pull the English towards common speech. She goes on to remark to Quilter how difficult it must be to keep the words subdued enough for music: 'it is a great temptation to over-elaborate' and, rather revealingly, she says that she envies him for having this subject to write about.

Elsie Swinton's career, and her role in Sitwell's life, ended around the beginning of the First World War as rumours of another affair reached her mother and husband. It was said that she was sleeping with her accompanist, Hamilton Harty, later famous as a conductor and composer. Swinton and her husband left London, and she eventually became a follower of Gurdjieff and Ouspensky, dedicating her life to mysticism and good works.[23] However, between 1907 and 1914 her influence on Edith Sitwell was pivotal. She was an example of a woman who defied expectation and became a serious artist.

Walter Sickert was an enormously influential figure, who in 1910 urged artists 'to avoid the drawing-room and stick to the kitchen'.[24] The student of Whistler, he was first famous for his music-hall drawings, which reflect the influence of Degas. His gift to Sitwell was from this series which he revived after his return to England.[25] He had worked for a time on paintings of Venetian prostitutes, including nudes and semi-nudes in a seedy bedroom. Back in London (as Sitwell came to know him), his career took a new turn with his Camden Town paintings of fleshy naked women lying on iron bedsteads with clothed male figures near by. Several bear the title *The Camden Town Murder*, of which the best known portrays a man sitting in despair on the edge of the bed with the corpse of a woman behind him. Patricia Cornwell used the paintings as evidence that Sickert was Jack the Ripper. Her argument involved a failed hunt for DNA samples on stamps and envelopes, and an assumption that an artistic interest in violence indicates guilt. Muriel Spark once remarked of this kind of argument, 'There's a lot of people think they can take my books and analyse me from them. On that principle Agatha Christie would be a serial killer.'[26] Sitwell shared Sickert's interest in the Ripper murders. Many years later, she also went to look at 10 Rillington Place where the serial killer John Christie committed his crimes and decided that it must be haunted.[27]

Extremely quirky himself, Sickert defended artists and their maligned temperament against a misunderstanding world: 'Haberdashers have been known to be regrettably irregular in their domestic and financial relations. Yet I have never heard invectives against the "haberdashing temperament".'[28] Edith Sitwell was influenced by his grittiness, which shows through in her taste for toughness, even ferocity, in art. For example, she could never fully settle into the Bloomsbury scene in the 1920s: 'They've civilised all their instincts away. They don't any longer know the difference between one object and another. They've civilised their senses away, too.'[29] Sickert's writing and conversation dwelt constantly on problems of technique, how to lay a brush on canvas to greater effect. Sitwell had spent much of her own life thus far attempting to achieve an effective technique at the keyboard. That such technical standards should exist for poetry made perfect sense to her. The essays she wrote years later on 'vowel-technique' are sometimes subjective and hard to follow, but she was trying to address the refinements of sound in language that lie deeper than scansion, as well as attempting to articulate her own sense of the medium. She was doing her best to explain something that was happening in her ear just as Sickert had so often attempted to explain what his hand had to do for his eye.

In 1907, Sickert established a studio at 19 Fitzroy Street, where he and his friends exhibited their works through the year under the formula, 'Mr Sickert at Home'. His original partners in this enterprise were Spencer Gore, William Rothenstein, Albert Rothenstein, Harold Gilman, Walter Russell, Nan Hudson, and Ethel Sands. They were soon joined by Lucien Pissarro, the son of Camille Pissarro. Sitwell must have attended some of these 'at homes' with Swinton. She may also have gone to them with Constance Lane, then a student at the Slade, where her tutors included Henry Tonks and William Orpen,[30] both associates of Sickert's. In fact, like Sickert and Sargent, Orpen had painted a portrait of Elsie Swinton. Augustus John was a friend of Sickert's, and whether she met him then or not Sitwell attended an exhibit of his work at the Chenil Gallery, bringing young Sacheverell with her.[31] In due course, Fitzroy Street became a haunt of Edith's

future friend, suitor, and finally arch-enemy, Wyndham Lewis. The art
critic Clive Bell became an occasional visitor, as did his wife, Virginia
Woolf's sister Vanessa Bell, whose paintings had won Sickert's admiration when exhibited at the New English Art Club (NEAC) in 1909.
Later, Nina Hamnett, a particular friend of the Sitwells, was a regular
exhibitor at Fitzroy Street.[32]

A sketch of Osbert Sitwell from the 1920s. The artist is thought to be Nina Hamnett

How often Edith Sitwell attended the 'at homes' is not certain, and,
since she was often on the continent, there were stretches when she did
not attend at all. Something of the sort is implied in an invitation
Sickert issued to her c. May 1913. She had brought Inez Chandos-Pole,
a distant relative, to the Carfax Gallery where, like a 'cuckoo', she
began talking big to Sickert. Edith wrote to Osbert: 'I found he had
been much amused. He said the atmosphere was much too rarefied for
him to live in, so he left – as he found Inez knew so much more about
pictures than he did!! He then said he thought people who talked so

grandly about pictures, generally knew very little, for, as William Morris once said to him: "A picture is well drawn, or it is badly drawn – that is all there is to say.'" Nevertheless, Sickert was always glad to see a Sitwell: 'he hopes we will come to look upon Fitzroy Street as an institution, to which we can always go when we have nothing better to do. So you and I will go together, some time. I must say my nerves were fairly shattered by not finding him there on Saturday, and being left to the mercy of what he calls the "jeunesse." He says they have turned him into an academician!!!'

The suggestion here is that Edith had little to do with the younger artists; however, she had certainly made a friend of Albert Rothenstein, soon to anglicise his name to Rutherston. In the same letter to Osbert, she describes a lunch with him: 'He was wearing a new pair of trousers, which were the cause of much excitement to Mrs. Hutchinson, who watched him coming along the street, and called out of the window: "Oh, Albert, you are smart. What a lovely new pair of trousers!" Mr. Rothenstein was rather disgusted with Isadora Duncan about her children's funeral. He said he thought that at the back of her mind was the germ of a thought: "What a feather in my cap!"'[33] An outgoing and dandyish figure, Rutherston remained a friend, and he did some illustration for the Sitwells in the 1920s. His nephew, John Rothenstein, later served as director of the Tate Gallery.[34]

'Mrs Hutchinson' is Mary Hutchinson, a writer herself and a cousin of Lytton Strachey's; she had affairs with Clive Bell and with both Aldous and Maria Huxley. While at the Slade School, Constance Lane became a friend of Dora Carrington, which may have been how Sitwell became acquainted with Hutchinson. Oddly enough, Edith Sitwell's and Mary Hutchinson's faces would both eventually appear in the Boris Anrep mosaics at the National Gallery: Hutchinson on the halfway landing in the *Awakening of the Muses*, and Edith Sitwell as *The Sixth Sense* in the North Vestibule where she walks across a tree branch over a ravine, reading a book of poems, unconcerned by the dragon, swooping raven, and blowing winds.[35] Friendship with Mary Hutchinson indicates that by 1913 Sitwell knew her way around the artistic circles of London.

Roger Fry was an old friend of Sickert and a leading figure in Bloomsbury. It is not clear when Sitwell made his acquaintance, but she was reading his essays from the beginning of 1911. He had recently organised the landmark exhibition *Manet and the Post-Impressionists* at the Grafton Gallery between November 1910 and January 1911. Attended by over twenty-five thousand people, this show and its successor in 1912 introduced to England the works of Cézanne, Van Gogh, Gauguin, Picasso, Matisse, and Rouault – doing so over the howls of many art experts and journalists. Most of Sickert's younger associates were enthusiastic, while he himself remained politely unsurprised about artists well established in Paris. In fact, Cézanne, Van Gogh, and Gauguin were already dead.[36]

Unlike the girl who had found the Berlin exhibition of Impressionists in June 1905 'funny', Edith Sitwell now took modern art very seriously. She made notes from Sickert's article on the exhibition in January 1911, which contained the remarkable dictum: 'Deformation or distortion in drawing is a necessary quality in hand-made art. Not only is this deformation or distortion not a defect. It is one of the sources of pleasure and interest. But it is so on one condition: that it result from the effort for accuracy of an accomplished hand, and the inevitable degree of human error in the result.'[37] She took notes on an essay by Manet's friend and biographer Théodore Duret. From Fry's article on 'Post-Impressionism' in the *Fortnightly Review* (1 May 1911), she copied out a key passage: '[the problem for painters] is to discover the visual language of the imagination. To discover, that is, what arrangements of form and colour are calculated to stir the imagination most deeply through the stimulus given to the sense of sight. This is exactly analogous to the problem of music, which is to find what arrangements of sound will have the greatest evocative power.' Many years later, she returned to this paragraph and underscored it.

On the surface, it is odd that a musician should be learning from painters how to become a poet, but the ideas underlying Impressionist and Post-Impressionist art are bound up with the Symbolist movement in the arts, with which Sitwell had had her first serious contact in the works of Debussy. In this particular notebook,[38] she seems to be struggling towards a theory of Symbolism. Among the eighty-eight pages of transcribed poems and essays by Yeats, she includes this comment of his on Blake's 'Jerusalem': 'So when man's desire to rest from spiritual labour, and his thirst to fill his art with mere sensation and memory, seem upon the point of triumph, some miracle transforms them to a new inspiration; and here and there among the pictures born of sensation and memory is the murmuring of a new ritual, the *glimmering of new talismans and symbols* [her emphasis]'. There are also notes from Arthur Symons, the poet whose critical works introduced British readers to the French Symbolist poets. There are transcriptions of twenty-seven poems by Baudelaire and notes on her reading of many more Symbolist poets, among them Albert Samain, Gustave Kahn, Maurice Maeterlinck, Villiers de l'Isle-Adam, Rémy de Gourmont, and André Fontainas. This is the sort of reading that was having a decisive effect on Pound and Eliot at much the same time.[39]

Sitwell's immersion in French poetry taught her to seek out images that are fragmentary, sometimes dreamlike, suggestive rather than representative, and synaesthetic (that is, crossing the usual borders of sensory experience). It encouraged her to regard the poet or the artist as isolated from normal society and often burdened by genius. It led her to believe that the relation of one sound to another had an enormous power to evoke meanings beyond any direct statement a poem might make. In that sense, she regarded the writing of a poem rather like an expert performance of music, requiring, in Sachie's phrase, 'the attack and entry of a virtuoso pianist'.[40] Towards the end of her career, this sense of her work put her very much at odds with younger critics who felt she was repeating herself by returning to a limited group of images and symbols, while she understood her poetry of that period, with its highly individual explorations of rhythm and sound, as going from strength to strength.

In 1911 and 1912, Edith Sitwell was hardly in danger of repeating herself – she had written almost nothing. To understand her early efforts it is necessary to introduce yet another scholarly and eccentric cousin on Sir George's side of the family. Joan Wake (1884–1974), daughter of the robustly named Sir Herwald Craufurd Wake of Courteenhall, Northamptonshire, was essentially the founder of the Northamptonshire Record Society in 1920, and she made a large contribution to its publications over the next forty years. 'She was stockily and heavily built, with a determined jaw. Clothes were of little interest to her, though she always carried her best hat in a box on her motorcycle.' She was eventually granted honorary degrees by Oxford and Leicester and was made a CBE in recognition of her historical research,[41] which, of course, belonged more to the world of Sir George Sitwell and Captain George Swinton than to that of Edith Sitwell.

Family visits threw the two barely acquainted cousins together:

> In January 1913, Edith came to stay at Courteenhall – Bad Weather, what to do with her? I found out she was musical. I thought I was at that time so we played a great many duets. Then I dragged her out for a walk . . . We started to talk about poetry and she started to quote it – line after line, verse after verse, poem after poem poured from her lips. At last I said: 'Edith! I don't believe *music* is your line of country – I think it's *poetry*. Have you ever written any?' 'One line!' she said dramatically. 'Out with it!' said I – and out it came. I haven't the slightest recollection of it, but I approved, and told her so, and said she had better go on – she did – and apparently that day – anyhow before her visit came to an end, for one of her early poems which I have in *her handwriting* is written on Courteenhall note-paper.[42]

Sitwell was being shy when she said she had written only one line of poetry. In one of her early notebooks is a short poem marked 'Nocturne by myself 16 June: 1912':

> The tremulous gold of stars within your hair
> Are golden bees flown from the hive of night
> Finding the blossoms of your eyes more fair
> Than all the pale flowers folded from the light.
> And in your voice more fresh than roses, sing
> The vanished flute-songs of the withered spring.[43]

This alone of Edith Sitwell's earliest poems is included in her *Collected Poems* of 1957 – perhaps it was her first poem or the first that showed any skill. In its final form the poem is entitled 'Serenade'; the word 'golden' in line two is switched to yellow, and the last two lines are replaced with much more vigorous ones:

> Then, Sweet, awake, and ope your dreaming eyes
> Ere those bright bees have flown and darkness dies.[44]

The poem is followed in the notebook by two others in a similar vein, dated 18 and 21 June 1912, as well as transcriptions from Sappho, Swinburne and Poe, all of whose influence is obvious in these poems of dreamy eroticism. The notebook also contains transcriptions from Walter de la Mare, the Homeric Hymns translated by Andrew Lang, the poems of Richard Middleton, and the plays of Massinger and Ford. Pasted into the notebook is a Tennysonian piece, 'In Fancy's Tower', which contains the following stanza:

> As in a mirror one may spy
> The world's great pageant rolling by,
> Or, turning to the past, may know
> The lives that men lived long ago:
> A scytheless Time sets back the hour
> In Fancy's Tower.

This poem, so characteristic of its author, is marked 'by my Father'. This was perhaps the last time Edith Sitwell would write or speak of him with uncomplicated pride.

7

THE GREAT WARS

'When I am told by the left-wing boys that I can't write poetry because
I have not proletarian experiences, I often wonder how many of them,
at the age of 17, have been sent to pawn false teeth – parental false
teeth!!!!! You get 10/5 on them. And whisky was then 12/6d.'[1] Edith
Sitwell's dismal family life was proceeding in parallel to the rich artistic one described in the last chapter. As a story, it is hard to credit that
of the false teeth but Sacheverell confirms, for example, that Lady Ida
sent Edith to the golf course near Renishaw Hall to buy brandy.[2]

Drinking was only one problem. Lady Ida was also a gambler, and
her expenses exceeded her personal income of five hundred pounds,
which included an allowance from Sir George. According to one of her
lawyers, Sir George had cleared her debts 'over and over again', most
recently in 1903 when he arranged a loan for her secured by an insurance policy on her life. The premiums came to a hefty £330 per year for
ten years.[3] With that loan not nearly paid off, Lady Ida's bills mounted
to about two thousand pounds, and she was in debt to the servants. She
was afraid to tell Sir George as he had made it clear he would not
rescue her again. Indeed, they had reached a point where in another
generation divorce would be the sole solution. She wrote: 'It seems as
if Fate is against me. Naturally, George is very angry with me, and
rightly so.'[4]

As their family life turned poisonous, a few pleasures were still pos-
sible, especially during visits to Italy, which included time at
Montégufoni but also a memorable trip to Sicily in March 1910, where
Edith and Osbert watched again and again plays performed in a disused
church by a member of the then-famous Grasso family of actors. Sir
George and Lady Ida were back at the hotel, playing bridge with an

amicable Polish count and his wife who later became visitors at
Scarborough and Renishaw. According to Osbert, Sir George was easier
to get along with when travelling, as his mind was free of worries.
Osbert recalled a particular moment of benevolence in Sicily when he
clumsily dropped and broke a piece of amber his father had just bought,
but there was no reproach.[5]

These were at best happy interludes. London was an exciting place
for her, but Edith felt imprisoned during her long spells in Scarborough.
She wrote to Sachie on 15 November 1910: 'I do wish Osbert wouldn't
write Mother cross letters. At least, I think it would be better not. I am
so terrified of Father turning round, and saying we are not to go to
London at all. And after all, he *is* extravagant. I wouldn't say so for
worlds, for you know I'm devoted to him, but he *is*. And we are all
being punished for it more than he is, for I at any rate, will have to be
here for two months! It is hard.'[6] Sudden changes of plan and being
stuck in Scarborough became a grievance for her over a number of
years. She wrote to Osbert on 13 February 1912 from a boarding house
at 18 Langham Street in London: 'Do you suppose I have been allowed
to go in peace to Miss Rootham's? – No, bless you! I was just standing
at the door in my hat and new sealskin-rabbit coat of ravishing beauty,
when a telegram was thrust into my hand: "Father wants you to stay in
home till Thursday, then come to Curzon [Hotel]." I suppose that
means Scarborough. I wish someone would heave half a brickbat at
both of them. I wish I had given them the measles.'[7]

Visits to her grandmother had at least offered peace and quiet,
but that world was winding down. First, Edith's 'Aunt Puss' (Lady
Hamner – one of Lady Sitwell's sisters) died on 17 May 1911. Edith
wrote to Osbert from Bournemouth: 'Auntie Puss died suddenly early
yesterday morning. It was a shock to Grannie and Auntie Georgie
[Georgiana Thomas, another of Lady Sitwell's sisters]. Father is being
pompous, and coming home for the funeral. Poor Auntie Puss! But still,
she was 84, which after all, is a great age. Of course, as you can well
imagine, Auntie Floss had a field-day yesterday, with prayers and tracts,
and Bible readings.'[8] Childless herself, Aunt Puss had always made a
quarterly gift to Osbert and Sachie of a gold sovereign wrapped in tissue
paper. At her death, she left everything to Sir George and the boys
including 1500 such sovereigns, all wrapped, inside a cabinet: as Osbert

noted, enough for quarterly gifts for the next 350 years. Edith was left nothing.[9]

Lady Sitwell herself was failing. Osbert recalled, 'it was sad for those who loved her to see one on whom so many had depended, now dependent on others. Her firm will and able brain had not failed her, but an immense fatigue assailed her. Though her hair was white now, she did not look older, but the passage of the last few years had made her finer, had given a sense of transparency and had deepened her expression of resignation and sweetness.'[10] Her death on 2 November 1911 took from Edith one of her chief protectors. Moreover, Sir George had listened to his mother's advice as he listened to that of no one else. Her counsels of patience and moderation might have helped him protect his family from the storm that was gathering.

Edith Sitwell did her best to avoid her parents, spending as much time as she could among artists and writers in London. Also, she saw something of her friend, Tom Spring-Rice, the diplomat and pianist who had come for musical evenings with the Lanes in 1907. We glimpse the connection through Sacheverell's letters to Osbert. On 3 March 1912 he describes a museum visit in London: 'Father whilst climbing the steps in front of the door, tripped in the door-mat, hurtling through the swing-doors, fell down the steps, & knocked over 3 priceless Italian cabinets, the best in the Museum . . . Father, Edith, & I had tea here [the Curzon Hotel], after which Edith drove me to Grannie's [Lady Londesborough's] in a taxi, & then went herself to tea with the Spring-Rices.'[11] In another letter, also from the first half of 1912, he writes that he has been out shopping with Edith and Tom for a wedding present for a friend; they went to a Japanese shop in Bond Street and bought a green glass pendant that looked like jade. 'Edith liked it so much that she doesn't think she can give it after all, but will keep it herself.'[12] Nothing came of her relationship with the cultured and sympathetic Spring-Rice. Having been third secretary in St Petersburg, he was sent to Washington in 1913; he eventually acceded to a peerage and died in 1934.[13] However, it is pleasant to imagine that in other circumstances Britain's outstanding woman poet of the twentieth century might have been styled 'Lady Monteagle'.

That summer, Edith, Sachie and Sir George went to Florence, staying at the Grand Hotel Baglioni, while making forays to the *castello*,

although the atmosphere was distressing. The Italians had seized from
the decaying Ottoman Empire the territories that now comprise Libya
in a short but bloody campaign that involved for the first time the use
of aeroplanes and other technology that would figure in the First World
War. On their way back from the *castello* one evening the Sitwells were
unable to get to their hotel; the streets were crowded with conscripts
returning from Tripoli, being carried shoulder-high, and covered with
flowers and confetti.[14]

Meanwhile, the private troubles of the Sitwells were coming to a
crisis. Part of the problem was Osbert, who was spending his way
through a large allowance and expected his father to keep writing
cheques. In 1909, Sir George had decided that his son needed the army
for discipline, so sent him to a crammer near Camberley to prepare for
his examinations.[15] There he became friends with a young man named
Willie Martin.[16] In the summer of 1911, Osbert invited Martin to stay
with the Sitwell family – possibly presenting him as someone with a
bright idea. As was her habit, Lady Ida laid out her woes to this brand-
new acquaintance. He gave her the name of a financial wizard – Julian
Osgood Field – who could fix her debts.

At first glance, Field was a respectable figure, the son of an important American family, educated at Harrow and Oxford, and an
acquaintance of Victor Hugo, Maupassant, Swinburne, and Walter
Besant. He had produced several books, wrote short stories, and was the
editor and translator of an eighteenth-century work on the spiritual
life. In fact, he was a crook and a moneylender's tout. He had been
imprisoned for forgery, and when Lady Ida met him he was living in
ease at the Grosvenor Hotel, even though he was an undischarged
bankrupt pursued by many creditors.[17]

Lady Ida explained her needs. In the next year and a half she seems
to have signed almost any paper Field laid in front of her; taken
together, Osbert says, they made her responsible for thirty thousand
pounds.[18] Her strict liability seems to have been closer to twelve thousand – still a very large sum. Field took her signed bills of exchange for
specific amounts, which other people, some of them strangers, accepted
and signed as guarantors. He arranged for the bills to be discounted,
that is, purchased at a greatly reduced value for immediate cash, by
a private moneylender. The transactions were to be further secured by a

life insurance policy of eight thousand pounds, which she found herself unable to obtain once the claims for repayment started. Nowadays
a woman with one lung would hardly be insurable at all. At one point,
Field promised Lady Ida 25 per cent of the profits of a non-existent
yeast business.[19] In the end, she received six hundred pounds to apply
to her original debts.[20] Field and his associates pocketed the rest.

Along the way, Lady Ida tried to turn her social connections to her
advantage and volunteered to introduce those who backed her bills
into social circles normally closed to them. This was the inducement
offered to Frances Bennett Dobbs, an elderly eccentric in Streatham
with a good deal of money and few friends. Field contacted David
Herbert, a 'private inquiry agent' who maintained a second,
professional identity as 'Oliver Herbert' and worked mainly as a rent-
collector – a man with the business ethics of Uriah Heep. He was
managing Dobbs's money and offered to marry her, despite already
having a wife, not to mention a girlfriend with whom he was living at
a second address. He arranged for Dobbs to back a note of Lady Ida's for
three thousand pounds and then to sign another, which she later
claimed was presented to her merely as a duplicate of the first. The two
notes totalling six thousand pounds were then discounted for £4450 by
a lender named Charles Owles.[21] They came due in July 1912, but Lady
Ida could not pay.

On 8 August, Herbert wrote to Sir George: 'I have something very
urgent to convey to you re your wife – Lady Ida Sitwell. She got me
to obtain the signature of a lady client of mine to a bill. My client
threatens serious proceedings unless paid, so please let me know what
is to be done. Am quite unable to get reply from Lady Ida.' Much the
same letter was sent on the same day to her brother, the Earl of
Londesborough. Herbert soon afterwards threatened to denounce her
at a ball to be held in Scarborough in aid of the Lady Ida Sitwell
Convalescent Home for Children, but he backed off once six hundred
pounds was paid to his solicitor.[22] The moneylender Owles, who held
the dishonoured bills, brought the matter to court in October and
obtained a default judgment against Lady Ida. Having backed the
notes, Dobbs was also on the hook.

Osbert, now in the 11th Hussars, had something of a nervous breakdown in August 1912. He was unhappy in the cavalry, and Sir George

accepted that he should seek a more congenial regiment,[23] but Osbert's worries went much deeper. In the preceding year, Lady Ida had asked him to find backers for her notes among his fellow subalterns. Although his biographer concludes that he made no money from his mother's borrowings, he was certainly involved in them from the beginning. She kept to herself the full details of her involvement with Field, but it is difficult to believe Osbert's claim: 'She told us nothing.'[24] He had his mother's confidence to a degree and was willing to act as her agent.

Osbert was desperate about the situation of Willie Martin, who had not only introduced them to Field but had himself backed at least one bill for Lady Ida. When she did not pay by November 1912, the money-lender R. Leslie Limited demanded from Martin the amount of £825 6s then due. Martin was served with a bankruptcy order, so he put the matter in the hands of a solicitor. Martin appealed to Osbert, 'you know my whole life is ruined if I become a bankrupt. What am I to do? I am so worried.'[25] On 20 November 1912, that solicitor demanded a meeting with Osbert.[26] The immediate danger was that Osbert, who would be commissioned a second lieutenant in the Grenadier Guards on 7 December 1912 and posted to the Tower of London, would be revealed as a swindler willing to prey on his brother officers. Although Martin's debt was dealt with, Lady Ida's letters on the subject would haunt Osbert.

The stress worsened Lady Ida's tuberculosis. Sachie reported to Osbert from Scarborough on 26 December 1912: 'Mother is still very ill. I never knew how really seriously ill she has been. She has had lots of blood & congestion of the brain, & very nearly became off her head . . . Every day after dinner Mother goes to get her medicine, and you know what that means. Before she undresses she has a glass of hot whiskey.'[27]

No longer Edith's governess but still an emeritus member of the household, Helen Rootham took Edith's fight on to herself and confronted Lady Ida. Edith had to be got clear of the scandal. Sachie wrote to Osbert: 'Mother is now at daggers drawn with Miss Rootham. Please warn [Edith], & tell her how things are happening.' Sir George agreed that there was a practical reason to keep Edith and Lady Ida apart. Edith had been with her mother a great deal in 1911, and the fraudsters swarming around Lady Ida might 'get at' Edith[28] and induce her to say something that would have to be repeated in court: she could even be subpoenaed. 'I escaped from them for a short while, as a Ticket-of-Leave Woman.'[29] A ticket-of-leave was granted to a convict who wanted to live abroad and was a reward for good behaviour. Abroad for Edith Sitwell meant London. She took a flat with Helen Rootham, who would serve as chaperone.

This was a crucial time. At twenty-five, Edith Sitwell had been granted, under hideous circumstances, the opportunity to make her own life. Fifteen-year-old Sachie sounds a note of self-pity in a letter to Osbert on 20 February 1913: 'As Edith has, I do sincerely hope, escaped from home for good, I shall be left from now till I am 19 or so alone with *them* during the holidays. Neither of them are really fond of me neither is Edith. I am hated here, consequently you are the only person who could be fond of me.'[30] Edith did love him, but this was not the moment for her to turn back. She spent most of 1913 at a rooming house run by a Miss Fussell at 14 Pitt Street in Kensington. Helen covered her own expenses, while Sir George paid for Edith and provided a servant. In many ways, it was a continuation of the life they had led together on and off in London, Paris, and Berlin since 1905. Lady Ida believed they were in league against her. Writing to Sachie from Italy on 9 June, she raged against Sir George, who had as allies 'Miss Rootham & Edith who I hate. I do hope you will persuade him that I never want to see Edith again, Miss Rootham was detestable since when I was ill not a word, she is the only person I know who never did. I know you like her but I hope some day you will find out what a deceitful liar she is.'[31]

Bad news kept coming. A Yorkshire cricketer named John Philip Wilson had guaranteed a note for four thousand pounds with a mortgage on his reversion – a matter that threatened to destroy the young man and to become a scandal in their own county. Sir George and the Earl paid off this amount.[32] However, the case of Frances Dobbs would not go away. Once judgment was granted by default against Lady Ida, Dobbs disputed the claim against herself on the grounds that she had been the victim of a fraud. Her efforts to prove this point were stymied when Lady Ida dodged service of a subpoena. Justice Horridge adjourned the case, urging Lady Ida 'for her credit's sake' to come forward. Her barrister said that she had been very surprised to read of these things in the newspaper, to which opposing counsel drily responded that her solicitors had received twenty-three letters concerning the matter.

Lady Ida was a poor witness, and when asked about her husband's wealth remarked vaguely that he owned some collieries. She confirmed that she had written, as dictated by Field, a letter to Herbert that included this sentence: 'You who have known me for so long and known my people know that Miss Dobbs will be running no kind of risk.' She did not know Herbert and he did not know her family; the deceptive letter was intended for Herbert's use in persuading Dobbs to sign the bills. Although Horridge concluded that Dobbs was indeed liable to Owles for both bills, he described this letter as 'most improper'. Observing that a 'horrible fraud' had been committed against Dobbs, he urged the Sitwells to settle the matter if there was an appeal of his judgment.[33]

Lady Ida herself now appeared in the press as a swindler, and it seemed that Edith Sitwell would soon have to go into the witness box. Helen was trying to prevent that. She wrote to Osbert on 1 November: 'I have just received the enclosed telegram. If you meant to say in it that Edith should take no part in the case that is coming on, you may rest assured that she never would with my approval.'[34] There was no going back to the old arrangements. By the beginning of 1914, Edith and Helen needed a new place to live permanently. Edith wrote to her father in measured terms that conceal how important this negotiation was for her:

You understand I was only able to be at Miss Fussell's for nine months in the year, at the price arranged. So the whole year would have worked out at £120 – plus extra food . . . When Helen is able to pay exactly half of the entire expenditure you will be paying about £20 a year more for me than you were doing at Miss Fussell's, and that is probably what we should have had to pay her if we had stopped. At present, as Helen has already told you, she is only able to pay for herself, to the exclusion of the servant. I don't think you will find that a heavy drain. We will see if we can find someone else like Miss Fussell, but if not, a flat is undoubtedly cheaper than rooms.[35]

It was no time to put pricey propositions to her father, but having a separate home (along the lines of Virginia Woolf's *A Room of One's Own*) was essential. In May 1914, Edith Sitwell and Helen Rootham took a flat at 22 Pembridge Mansions, Moscow Road, in Bayswater. This was a poor but lively spot where their neighbours included the Greek Orthodox Cathedral and the New West End Synagogue. They were surrounded by dozens of small businesses, among them a school of dance, a button maker, a chiropodist, a cigarette maker, and a depot of the Aerated Bread Company.[36] Pembridge Mansions was a working-class block of flats, with little to recommend it but a fine view of the trees in Kensington Gardens. It had no lift, and Edith's and Helen's flat was approached by five flights of bare stone stairs; since they were not properly marked it was always possible to go up the wrong stairwell. Inside the flat were naked light bulbs and doors without knobs. Some years later, Sitwell sent directions to Joe Ackerley: 'half way up Queen's Road, on the right hand side, you will find Moscow Road. This is not the rich Jewish red-brick block of flats, but the untidy, dingy, badly lighted block of flats just past the garage clock; and my name is on the board in the hall.'[37]

There was a difference between Sir George's desire to get Edith out of the way of subpoenas and Edith's desire to live permanently as a writer in London. Her father was surprised and unhappy that she was making such a break. Though accustomed to rows with her mother, Edith tried to avoid them with her father – not least because he was impossible to push around. As they moved into the new flat, Edith gathered that Lady Sitwell had left her a diamond pendant, which could be sold for furnishings. She wrote to Osbert: 'don't tell the wife of the Red Death *or* the Red Death itself, about the pendant, what I told you about today. I don't want them to know. This *is* not the atmosphere. Don't on any account let on, or I am lost. Burn this letter.' Soon enough, she asked Sir George to have the pendant released to her but it turned out that she had confused the pendant to which she was entitled with another of greater value. Her father wrote: 'In the entailed list in the box of diamonds, the diamond link at the top of the locket is mentioned, & there was never anything of the kind attached to the star I handed over to you. This I think identifies the locket.'[38] In a twist of property law, the most valuable women's jewellery in the Sitwell family had to be handed down in the male line. As a consolation, he offered her carpets and curtains from Lady Sitwell's properties in Bournemouth, but it was not what she wanted.

While Sir George never liked spending money, something happened in 1913 that may have darkened his view of Edith. Among his mother's papers he found letters written by his crusading aunt Blanche Sitwell – his father's sister to whom Edith was especially close. In those letters Blanche had criticised him severely, and despite his normal reserve he thought it worth quarrelling with her. About a year and half later, she told Archbishop Davidson what had happened, and his reply to her, contemptuous of Sir George as 'a queer person', survives among correspondence transcribed by Joan Wake. We do not know exactly what Blanche said about Sir George that so stung him, but in a handwritten note Wake suggests that Blanche had 'naughtily' listened to the young Sitwells' complaints against their father and passed them on to Lady Sitwell. If so, Sir George now had some idea what his children were saying about him.[39]

On 28 June 1914, Archduke Franz Ferdinand was shot in Sarajevo, bringing on the July crisis. Doubtless listening to sad talk of soldiers making their wills, Edith decided to try to secure Helen's future, so on 28 July she wrote a letter 'To my brother Osbert Sitwell. To be opened in the event of my decease before 15th November 1918'. It read:

> This letter is being placed with my will, for you to read when I die. There are some things I should like to happen, and I think you will do them for my sake, if I should die before you. Do you remember the letter in *The Way of All Flesh* – well, this isn't that kind of letter. It is because we are bound up as brother and sister much more than most brothers and sisters, on account of having had such a terrible childhood, and such an appalling home. I don't believe there is another family in England who have had parents like ours.

In a surge of emotion, she committed herself to providing for Helen whose steadfastness in recent times had enabled her to break free of her parents:

Well, if I should die, I leave Helen Rootham to your care; I know you will do what you can for her – because she has been so good to me – such a good friend to me, as you know. The £5000 which will one day be mine if I live till Sachie is of age (twenty-one) I have left to her. But if I die before that sum becomes mine – then Osbert, for my sake, I implore you to make her an allowance, that allowance that would have been mine. For my sake, give her, or see that she gets £200 a year. Otherwise, she is quite unprovided for, and it is too dreadful to contemplate. I think I shouldn't be able to rest in my grave.

The letter was moot – Sitwell lived another half-century – but in 1914 she decided to care for Helen Rootham as long as she lived. That arrangement actually went long past Rootham's death in 1938 as Sitwell then assumed her sister Evelyn as a dependant on the same terms. She remarked in 1945: 'I should have been lost if it had not been for them.'[40] However, in the 1950s and early 1960s, Sitwell felt burdened by this obligation, believing that her early gratitude to Helen Rootham had been overblown and then exploited.

From July to mid-September, with Helen in Paris for a time visiting Evelyn, Sitwell was chiefly in Renishaw, with two breaks in nearby Harrogate, where she stayed with Inez Chandos-Pole. Edith wrote to Osbert: 'Dear old boy, how I hope and pray you won't have to go. I think I shall go mad if you do.' Meanwhile, there was constant family trouble. She asked him: 'Did you have an odious letter from Mother? She is drunk all the time now, and I think has really come to imagine that she has done the right thing and covered herself with glory. She says only middle-class people look down on her! . . . Mother is more than incoherent with 'emotion' and whisky. Oh, it's been a *lovely* summer.'[41]

On 20 July, Sir George recalled Osbert from his regiment to prepare for a career in the Town Clerk's office in Scarborough. He was drilled in penmanship and taught to form better pothooks, a lesson he soon forgot. In his autobiography Osbert suggests that this was an act of spite on his father's part, since he was prospering in the army.[42] From Edith's account, however, it seems that he had had another emotional collapse and needed time to pull himself together: 'Osbert left to rejoin his regiment, the Grenadier Guards, the middle of the night before the war broke out. He was convalescing after a serious illness. For this reason he had to undergo a month's training before he could be sent to the Front. I must always be grateful to that illness, for all his young friends, with the exception of two, were killed in the first month of the war.'[43]

Those summer weeks in Renishaw in 1914 had their bizarre moments. Among the guests at the Hall was Louisa Sitwell's old crony, Sister Edith Woods, whom Edith Sitwell called 'Little Dimple'. Sacheverell wrote to Osbert on 18 August: 'We played a game of consequences in the "Ball Room" last night, & the following sentence appeared, "The Fish-faced negress Edith Sitwell, met the flat-footed sister Edith in the Chamber of Horrors." You can imagine what a dreadful lull in the conversation ensued. Father came out as "pig-faced & obstinate & pompous."'[44]

In early September, Sir George quarrelled with the solicitor, Sir George Lewis, and with the Londesboroughs over whether to go ahead with a suit that would make Field responsible for losses in the Frances Dobbs case. Apart from the large sum of money involved, Sir George Sitwell thought the new action would clear his wife's name in a very public way. He was opposed to just settling the case as it involved so much criminal misrepresentation, and he maintained that if she was not cleared in a civil case, she could expect to be arrested and tried as a criminal. For a time, though, it appeared that the suit would have to be called off. Sachie commented: 'Of course it is playing into Field's hands, but at the same time Father says Lewis declares Mother will be arrested now whatever happens, & so perhaps we are well out of the case, as there is now no room for it in the papers, owing to the war, which was the whole point of having the case at all.'[45]

Nevertheless, the suit finally went ahead, and Field brandished his only weapon when he subpoenaed Osbert in October. The implication was that if the matter was not dropped, Osbert would be cross-examined and his reputation blasted. As it played out, Field put up no defence when the case was heard in November. He was bankrupt so another judgment against him hardly mattered; he did not contest the claim of 'fraudulent misrepresentation'.[46] It looked even to Sir George Lewis that Lady Ida was in the clear. He wrote to Osbert on 6 November: 'I am delighted to think how satisfactorily the case went, and only trust that your mother will now be free from trouble.'[47] At Lambeth, Davidson remarked: 'I am glad it has ended thus and I suppose that Lady Ida will realise that she has been making a mess of things.'[48]

Still, trouble had a way of falling out of the sky. Around 8:10 a.m. on 16 December 1914 three German warships appeared out of the fog and discharged five hundred shells on Scarborough. A coastguard station on Castle Hill was hit, and new holes were blown in the old castle itself. In the town below, seventeen people were killed, and dozens of houses damaged or destroyed.[49] Part of a shell came through the front door at Wood End, and shrapnel penetrated deep into the house. Sir George took refuge in the cellar with the servants, while Lady Ida remained in bed. After it was it over, she got up and boarded a train for London. She appeared at Edith's flat bearing a heavy shell fragment for Osbert: 'Here you are, darling! I've brought it with me specially, for you to take to France. I'm sure it'll bring you luck!'[50]

No luck from this grisly object rubbed off on Lady Ida herself. The moneylender Charles Owles had died, but his executors still expected payment for the bills of exchange. The judgment in favour of Lady Ida meant they could pursue only Field, who had no money, so the one way forward was to allege that Lady Ida was part of a criminal conspiracy to commit fraud. Edith Sitwell always claimed that her father could not face facts; whether this was strictly true or a case of the pot calling the kettle black, in late 1914 he failed to see that the evidence against Lady Ida was strong and that she was still in trouble. If the matter was not quickly put to rest, she could be imprisoned.

At the instigation of Owles's executors, Lady Ida, Julian Field, and David Herbert were prosecuted for conspiring to cheat and defraud Frances Dobbs of six thousand pounds. When served with his summons, Field said, 'What! Conspiracy with Lady Ida Sitwell. I never heard of such a thing. This is very pleasant. I must go and see my solicitor about this.'[51] In a hearing at Marlborough Street Police Court on 22 January 1915, Lady Ida declared, 'I am absolutely innocent.'[52] On 12 February, the three were committed for trial at the Central Criminal Court, with Field and Herbert released on bail and Lady Ida on her own recognisance.[53]

Early 1915 was a bad time for her to be tried. On 30 January, the *Daily Mail* reported on the defence case at Marlborough Street on the same page as it listed the names of the three hundred men drowned, including a group of gallant Newfoundlanders, in the sinking of HMS *Viknor* off the coast of Ireland. On 8 February, Prime Minister Asquith rose in the House of Commons to announce that casualties in the British Expeditionary Force in Western Europe had reached 104,000 of all ranks. Often enough, law reports were framed by long lists of the dead, wounded and missing, each name representing heartbreak to some family. In a time of national sacrifice, stories of Lady Ida's spending and borrowing could only stir distaste and resentment among prospective jurors.

In all of this, Edith Sitwell was worried not about her mother but about Osbert. Field's lawyer hinted again that if Lady Ida tried to shift the blame to their client, he would have to ask questions about Osbert. He knew that at one point in the scandal Lady Ida had said that some of the money was borrowed to cover Osbert's debts, and he was willing to probe the point. Edith was certain that this and any other imputation against her brother must be lies. Moreover, she believed Lady Ida's vigorous defence strategy was a piece of treachery in that it exposed Osbert to disgrace in order to keep herself out of prison. Evidently at Blanche Sitwell's suggestion, Edith put this view to Archbishop Davidson before the trial to see whether he might be able to control Lady Ida. He wrote to Blanche on 8 February 1915: 'Ida S. is a problem which I can't solve! Edith was very nice about it all when she dined here the other day, and I feel intensely for her. But I fear Ida has lost all sense of self respect if she is ready to give away Osbert by a lying story.'[54]

On 8 March 1915, the scene shifted to the Old Bailey. As ever, Sir George hired good help, replacing the barrister Sir Frederick Low, who had been elevated to the bench, with Gordon Hewart, KC, who went on to become Lord Chief Justice.[55] The judge, Charles John Darling, had also heard the case in November, which was decided by a special jury. Darling had once served in Parliament with Sir George Sitwell and had no obvious prejudice against Lady Ida. After the criminal trial started he realised he had some social connections with her, yet heard the case through.[56] While an intelligent man, he was not a first-rate

Lady Ida's spending and borrowing landed her in a criminal case for fraud. The *News of the World* (14 March 1915) and other newspapers gleefully reported the Sitwells' humiliation.

judge. A former journalist, he was inclined to show off his wit in the courtroom and was criticised for 'levity'.[57]

The first day offered prime opportunities for judicial mirth, which aided the defence. When called, Frances Dobbs described Herbert's handling of her business, their short engagement, and the presentation of the two bills for signature. She claimed that since her mother died she had been surrounded by swindlers, 'the robbery and murder gang . . . You can never get out of it once you are marked down. You can never free yourself in this world. They "do you in" in the end.' Under Hewart's questioning, Dobbs, once unhappily engaged to a clergyman, said the gang was connected with the clergy of the Church of England. Darling intervened: 'With regard to your marriage, did you propose to be married by a clergyman?' With the court laughing, she said she did not want a clergyman, 'but we did not get so far as that'.[58] At the end of her testimony, Dobbs, chief witness for the prosecution, appeared mad.

Field offered no evidence in his own defence; presumably, cross-examination would have revealed him as a career swindler and made his inevitable sentence all the harder. Herbert came to the witness box on 9 March, and gave evasive testimony about his bigamous engagement to Dobbs. Cross-examining him, Hewart dwelt on the double life Herbert led – two names, two houses, two telephone numbers, very nearly two wives. The accounts are not clear on this point, but it appears that Hewart tried to show collusion between Herbert and Dobbs. The Sitwells believed that Frances Dobbs was part of the original scheme to entrap Lady Ida. His line of questioning indicates that the Sitwells had them investigated but could not find enough evidence to clinch the point. For all his skill, Hewart could do no more than insinuate the connection and hope to plant a doubt in the jurors' minds. He also asked Herbert about his letters to Sir George and the Earl of Londesborough, as well as his threat to denounce Lady Ida at the ball in Scarborough in 1912, representing these as attempts at blackmail.[59]

When Lady Ida was called on 11 March, she appeared fragile. Thin and tired-looking, she wore a black cape and Cossack cap. Her testimony took almost two days to complete. Led by Hewart, she described her money troubles and her introduction to Field. She said she had written letters at the dictation of Field, and was questioned especially about one of 6 April 1912 in which she made a gift to him of the proceeds from the Dobbs transaction, apart from a thousand pounds owing to Herbert as a fee.[60] The letter showed that she was gullible and that she had not profited from the bills. Her answers confirmed to some degree the claim Hewart had made in his opening statement that she was a 'child' in matters of business.[61]

Under cross-examination another impression emerged. Opposing counsel questioned her over a series of letters in which she appeared frantic for money and was actively pursuing backers for her bills. In one she said she was willing to explain the transactions to potential backers, which made short work of the claim that she had no understanding of business. She was presented with other letters that revealed the worst of her personality, as she spoke bitterly of servants who had paid her tradesmen's bills. In one, she referred to Henry Moat (who walked out on the Sitwells in 1913 and stayed away for a decade): 'I owe my butler £145. I want to get out of his clutches, the brute!'[62] When asked whether this was how she spoke of someone who had advanced her money, she could only nod her head.

Field's lawyer read out a letter that Osbert had long feared becoming public: it showed that she was looking for dupes among young officers and that Osbert was helping her. On 29 December 1911 she had referred to the search for another backer in the transaction that involved Willie Martin: 'I find Glass is only twenty. My boy thinks that if he were with him for a few days he could get hold of him; and he quite hopes that if he joins the 11th Hussars there must be some boy he can get hold of.' The judge demanded to see the letter and asked, 'Do you say that your boy really said these things?' Having been fairly sympathetic towards her, Darling was shocked. During the rest of her testimony he intervened repeatedly and with increasing scepticism.

On 12 March, with the preceding day's testimony widely reported, Edith wrote to Sachie who was still at Eton: 'I know how painful all this is for you, but try not to worry too much about it, my poor old darling. A notice will be put in the paper after the case is over, that Osbert *never* did any of these foul things. I saw Osbert today, and he was quite calm, though naturally *awfully* upset, as I am, and as you must be. She is a *monster*. There is no other word for it . . . Osbert is well again, and goes back to the front, I am afraid, on Sunday.'[63]

On the second day of Lady Ida's testimony, Hewart attempted to repair the damage. He led her to say that it was only at Field's suggestion that she sought young officers to back the bills. This had the unintended effect of giving the judge another chance to intervene:

> 'Do you mean to say you did not realise what you were doing by asking your son to get "some boy" to back a bill for you?'
> 'I did not mean boys. I meant officers.'
> 'Do you really wish me to believe you thought your son could get hold of the Colonel?'
> 'No.'
> 'You knew that was absurd?'
> 'Yes.'
> 'One of the majors?'
> 'No.'
> 'Did you think about the captains?'
> 'I was not sure about the captains.'
> 'Then, lieutenants, second lieutenants, and probationers?'
> 'Not a probationer.'
> 'Why did you exclude probationers?'
> 'Because they were too young.'
> 'Yes.'[64]

This exchange must have had an effect on the jurors, some of whom would have had sons or brothers in uniform.

In his summary of the evidence, Darling dwelt upon the vulnerability of young men in the army, away from home and without their parents – quietly painting Lady Ida as a predator. He noted that although the letter about the Hussars was not related to the Dobbs transaction, Lady Ida and Osbert Sitwell could have been charged with a crime if the letter had been acted upon.[65] He instructed the jury to remember that the case rested on intent to commit fraud, and that they could consider 'that Lady Ida was a person so weak, so easily influenced, that when she did a thing which an ordinary person would say showed intent to defraud she did not realise what she was doing and did not have any intent'. However, such a defence, he said, was hard to make where the person went about the world, wrote letters when Field was not present, and had no recognisable mental illness. Nearly an instruction to convict, his words stand as a rebuttal to the efforts of Osbert and Sachie over the years to excuse their mother on such grounds as poor education and the inability to do arithmetic; Osbert even proposed menopause as an explanation for the scandal.[66] It is reasonable to speak up for a parent, and in Osbert's case he was scrubbing at stains on his own reputation, but it remains a form of special pleading.

After an hour and twenty minutes, the jury returned, convicting Lady Ida and Julian Osgood Field while, mysteriously, acquitting David Herbert. In sentencing, Justice Darling told Lady Ida that he accepted that she was greatly influenced by Field and that he had dictated many of the letters, 'but for all that you must have known, from your knowledge of the world and your education, that you were doing something dishonest. You copied the letters without a word of question, careless what happened or who suffered so long as you got money.' Taking into consideration her poor health, he sentenced her to three months, and she was taken to Holloway Prison.

The conviction came as such a shock that no one in the family thought to tell Sacheverell, who, Sarah Bradford tells us, learnt of it at school from the *Sunday Express*.[67] Osbert returned to the Front, where, with lieutenants in short supply, the Grenadiers overlooked the scandal. According to Edith, Sachie's housemaster at Eton said, 'It is a good thing a war is on, so that your brother can fight for his King and country – otherwise nobody would ever speak to him again.'[68] Cruel words, but Osbert did serve competently and honourably in the trenches.

Sir George Sitwell believed that his wife, though foolish, was the victim of a miscarriage of justice. He worked all day for the last two weeks of April, writing a petition to the Home Secretary to have the sentence overturned. The Archbishop saw the 'immense' document – but what he really wanted, he told Blanche Sitwell, was to sit down and have 'a conversation with that strangely constructed nephew of yours!' Three times Sir George refused his invitation to have a pious talk and told Davidson to put his thoughts in writing.[69] Davidson visited Lady Ida, and he later told Joan Wake: 'She cried a little, and it was so pathetic to see her wiping her eyes with a large coarse prison pocket-handkerchief.'[70]

In the midst of all this, the Dowager Countess of Londesborough was gravely ill. According to Edith, she had been weak for a very long time and now faced the amputation of a foot. Before that could happen, she died on 15 May 1915.[71] In a last general rebuke to her other daughters and granddaughters, she left all her money and jewellery to Lady Ida's sister Mildred Cooke. The Home Secretary was kinder. Lady Ida was given an early release. Edith wrote to Sachie from Pembridge Mansions on 19 May: 'Mother came out yesterday, and I went to see her at Aunt Millie's. She seems absolutely unchanged; rather nervous, it is true, but she actually made jokes about the life in there. Of course, she is hardly believable, isn't she? However, Osbert says she is amiably disposed. Isn't it *heavenly*?'[72]

8

I DO HOPE IT ISN'T LADYLIKE

'I thought Edith's poem quite lovely in rhythm, & feeling, but it was rather a comedown to publish it in the "Daily Mirror" wasn't it? Is she going to publish any more?'[1] Sachie wrote, having seen 'Drowned Suns', printed on 13 March 1913:

> The swans more white than those forgotten fair
> Who ruled the kingdoms that of old-time were,
> Within the sunset water deeply gaze
> As though they sought some beautiful dim face,
> The youth of all the world; or pale lost gems
> And crystal shimmering diadems,
> The moon for ever seeks in woodland streams
> To deck her cool, faint beauty; thus in dreams
> Belov'd, I seek lost suns within your eyes
> And find but wrecks of love's gold argosies.

This was her first publication and it typified the verses she had written in her first year as a poet – languid dreams of failed love addressed, apparently, to no one in particular. The rhythms and moods of Swinburne are here, but the vigour of Sitwell's mature work is hinted at only in the last four lines.

Nevertheless, it was a debut. Even Lady Ida paused from fury to praise it.[2] Sachie may have thought a publication in the *Daily Mirror* odd, but it had been founded in 1903 as a ladies' newspaper and still had about it a whiff of gentility. Edith Sitwell made a friend in the newspaper's literary editor Richard Jennings. Her only venue until late 1915, the newspaper published ten more of her poems, and in 1916

Jennings arranged for the first of Osbert's poems to be published in *The Times*. Jennings was an unusual man, writing highbrow leaders for the *Daily Mirror*, as well as light-hearted columns on such things as money from Eldorado and aluminium Christmas trees. A book-lover, he hated noise and inveighed more than once against whistling boys. His political views took on great importance from about 1932, when he was among the first to identify Hitler as a threat to England.[3] Although Sitwell did not publish poetry in the *Daily Mirror* after 1915, she and Richard Jennings remained friends for many years.

That first published poem, 'Drowned Suns', survives on Courteenhall stationery and is likely the one she wrote while visiting Joan Wake in Northamptonshire in January 1913. For the next two years she relied, to a surprising degree, on Wake's advice. In late 1913, Sitwell wrote: 'I have been working at my ballad-thing, and think it is about finished, so am sending it to you. I am in two minds about it. Sometimes I think it absolutely contradictory, and awful doggerel. At other moments it seems to me really rather good of its kind, and for someone who has had only eighteen months experience of writing. But oh, I do hope it isn't ladylike. I wish you would criticise it.'[4]

Wake's advice cannot have helped much:

> Your nature poems are good for their beauty of form – & your delight in the music of words – not for the underlying ideas. Your ballad is good for the extreme beauty of the idea, which more than redeems the ugliness of the form – & in that respect is better art than the nature poems – certainly a much more ambitious form of art. Don't make yourself write. Rather refrain from it till you feel obliged to write (except for practice of technique) – but study good classical models – say, a course of Robert Bridges.[5]

That last suggestion was lost on Sitwell. It took almost a quarter of a century for her to find much to admire in Bridges, who was appointed Poet Laureate in 1913.[6]

By July 1914, Sitwell had assembled enough work to propose a short book to the publisher Elkin Mathews. She asked how much it would cost her to publish a volume of thirty pages with a paper cover, following a format used by one of her favourite contemporary poets,

Wilfrid Gibson.[7] Perhaps they were not interested or the price was too
high, for the volume was not published. In the meantime, she tried for
some new effects in her poetry. 'The Drunkard', written after she
moved to Pembridge Mansions in the early summer of 1914, is an enig-
matic poem in which a knife-wielding drunkard approaches an
apparently sleeping woman. She told Wake: 'I don't care what people
write about, as long as they write properly.' In this poem, she was interested not in ideas, but in atmosphere and sound:

> Now in 'The Drunkard', I simply set out to give an impression of
> horror; I think I have done that. It is also an experiment in rhythm;
> I have tried to get the beat of a terrified heart; also the drunken reel
> of the murderer. In judging it, remember, the man is dazed and stupid.
> Since sending it to you, I have added some more verses, I want you
> to like it, because I believe it is one of the best things I have done . . .
> I am going in for writing horrors, as it is obvious I do that better than
> anything else.[8]

By the end of the year she had completed a new 'horror', 'The
Mother', an ambitious poem about a woman whose beloved son murders her in her bed to get money for a prostitute. Even if from time to
time Edith Sitwell thought of doing in Lady Ida, this poem, despite its
title, has nothing to do with her own mother; indeed, women murdered
in their beds was a theme of Walter Sickert's. Like 'The Drunkard' this
poem is too melodramatic, but its conclusion anticipates the language
and rhythms of the poetry she wrote after 1940. In a touch of the
macabre, the ghostly mother is left to suckle worms, who taunt her:

> The child she bore with bloody sweat
> And agony has paid his debt.
> Through that bleak face the stark winds play;
> The crows have chased his soul away.
>
> 'His body is a blackened rag
> Upon the tree – a monstrous flag.'
> Thus one worm to the other saith.
> Those slow mean servitors of Death,

> They chuckling said: 'Your soul, grown blind
> With anguish, is the shrieking Wind
> That blows the flame that never dies
> About his empty lidless eyes.[9]

Though overwrought, this poem was pointing to Sitwell's future. Ghostly speakers reappeared in some of her best-known works, as did the mythic figure of the worm; even the flags reappear in 'The Shadow of Cain' (1946). 'The Mother', for all its flaws, had a grip on her. She wrote to Constance Lane in December 1914: 'I want badly to know what you think of "The Mother". I think it is horribly true – I am quite sure it is. Anyhow, it makes me quite ill, and if I try to read it aloud, I always cry, and so does everyone else.'[10]

These poems would never have been written, and Sitwell would never have learnt her craft, had she continued to live with her parents. And yet, apart from a quiet atmosphere in which to work, there were few luxuries at Pembridge Mansions. Possessing little chinaware, she often greeted her guests at the door carrying an ordinary kitchen teapot, revealing behind her a bare room with a lamp, many books, a bedroom divan, and a piano.[11] Osbert provided green and silver hangings for Helen's sitting room, and red and gold for Edith's. 'The furniture of my flat was poor, – it was not, (being unfashionable,) made of tin, ostrich feathers did not trail on my floor, I had never hit anybody with a bottle, and I avoided those circles in which this was regarded as a sign of mental superiority.'[12]

She claimed that when the war started she took a job for twenty-five shillings a week and two shillings' war bonus in the Chelsea pensions office, where about four hundred people worked.[13] She breakfasted on porridge, home-made scones, and *café au lait*, before signing in at nine – an early hour for her. For luncheon, she avoided the canteen, which was noisy and smelt overwhelmingly of fat. She went instead to a large dress shop nearby where she bought a cup of coffee with milk and two rolls and butter. In the evening, 'released from servitude',[14] she took the tube back home from Sloane Square, and for her supper had soup made of meat-bones and white haricot beans. She claimed she was undernourished but never hungry because Helen was a good manager.

In old age, Sacheverell expressed doubt about this account, and probably saw in it a sly way of slandering Sir George. He told Geoffrey Elborn, one of Edith's biographers, that she did no more than a week of war work.[15] The job cannot have lasted for long; when Sir George heard that Edith was working at a desk, he immediately feared for her back and insisted that she quit. This detail is so much in character for Sir George that it provides a degree of confirmation for the story.[16] Mr Tubby had made an impression on him. Edith says that her father offered her instead a job in a photographer's shop in Bond Street, which he was financing. He promised her the same pay but she could come in to work at ten o'clock – presumably allowing more rest for her back. She refused since he was asking her to spy on the people who worked there, a detail intended to demonstrate that she was nobody's class enemy, whatever left-wing critics might say. Osbert also refers to the incident of the photographer's shop, but places it around 1912.[17]

Sitwell maintained that Moscow Road opened her eyes: 'I had lived the kind of life known to families like mine, and therefore the experience of hammering coal, laying fires, etc was new to me.'[18] Sacheverell doubted this story too, observing that Edith always had a servant and never lit the fires.[19] Her char at this time was small, plump and lazy, but willing to oblige. Edith and Helen found her cockney wit sufficient reason to keep her on; an aficionado of funerals, she once remarked: 'It's your last chance, Miss, an 'alf the time it's bin' your first one, so why act begrudgin'?'[20] Whether Edith Sitwell lit many coal fires seems a small point, but having to do domestic chores made a difference for her writing: 'When I came to London, I was unused to household work, but this ineptitude on my part was, gradually, cured. I am the crane-tall Jane of my poem "Aubade" [1920].' She said that she changed her situation to that of a country servant, perhaps resembling one in a painting by Modigliani that Osbert owned.[21] In that poem, 'Jane, Jane, tall as a crane' rises in the first light and goes down the creaking stairs:

In the kitchen you must light
Flames as staring, red and white,

As carrots or as turnips, shining
Where the cold dawn light lies whining.[22]

With her height and ungovernable hair, Jane resembles Sitwell. It is, however, just possible that Sitwell was also thinking of a woman who once worked for Lady Sitwell. Osbert wrote: 'Jane, who had been there twenty years, the delightful lanky housemaid from Suffolk, so kind and rustic, with a bump on her head.' This may be the Jane Fenwick who shows up in the census report for 1901 as part of Lady Sitwell's household.[23] However much housework Edith Sitwell did at Pembridge Mansions, it was enough to stir her interest and sympathy for those whose lives were spent laying fires and scrubbing floors.

On 14 October 1915, Sitwell's first book, *The Mother and Other Poems* appeared. It was a pamphlet of twenty pages in brown wrappers, printed by B. H. Blackwell, who charged her £5 10s for a print run of five hundred. Each copy sold for 6d – a far cry from the £1500 that Bertram Rota would seek for a fine copy in 2009.[24] It contained just five poems; 'Drowned Suns' and 'Serenade' had already appeared in the *Daily Mirror*; 'The Web of Eros', 'The Drunkard', and 'The Mother' were published here for the first time.

For such a slight production, it was extremely well received, especially by the *Times Literary Supplement*, which ran a short review on 4 November 1915, remarking on her 'glowing fancy', followed on 9 December by something much longer:

There are only ten pages in Miss Sitwell's book, but it justifies an economy that would alone be proof enough of a rare poetic ideal . . . The Elizabethans wrote scores of lyrics like this 'Serenade' and with a less literary tinge. But it is not merely derivative. It, too, tells of experience, imaginative experience; and its music, its none too lucid or logical fantasy, evoke an answer from that Orient of the mind from which come our strongest dreams. Miss Sitwell's two longer poems, 'The Drunkard' and 'The Mother', are nightmares. The one records the half-insane gropings of a consciousness in the toils of an unbelievable horror that is reality. With hideously acute but still bemused senses the murderer looks down upon his victim, listless, voiceless, freed at one stroke even from her fear. 'The Mother', in which this theme is reversed – the ghost of the murdered passionately taking upon itself the guilt of the beloved – is less sure. But in all these poems one thing is clear. They come from within. Miss

Sitwell does not describe, she lives in her verse. This very little therefore points a long way, into silence again, for one thing, which is what poetry always does.

Edith described this to Sachie as 'a long and, it seems, extraordinarily enthusiastic notice. Helen says she doesn't see how I could possibly have got a better one.'[25] One aspect of her triumph was invisible. In the days of unsigned reviews, she probably had no idea that these encouraging words came from Walter de la Mare.[26]

Public acclaim mattered, but Sitwell still found herself bludgeoned by other people's opinions. She wrote to Sachie:

I spent the morning with the Young-and-Pretty-Married-Woman, with a skin-like-a-magnolia-flower-and-ah-such-an arrogant-mouse! So if this letter should prove dull, well, you will understand why; for she sucked my brains as your grandmother was taught to suck eggs, and the result is that vacuum abhorred by nature. If the Y. and P. M. W. would only profit by her powers of suction, I shouldn't mind, but she doesn't, all being as it was in the beginning, with the exception of my mind. And she has now taken to reading poetry, partly to dazzle the Aged Peer, and partly so as to lay down the law to me on my own subject. She is always making discoveries; she has just discovered quite a good new man called John Keats. No, Ediss, you really should read him . . .

It is just possible that this woman was Osbert's friend the poet Nancy Cunard, with whom Edith would collaborate briefly and then come to hate. However, it is more likely that she was the former Constance Talbot, now, by marriage, a Sitwell. With Lady Ida in prison, she had told one of Edith's great-aunts, probably Blanche, that because of the scandal she could not very well ask Edith to her mother's house.[27] Edith despised her ever after, even if as a member of the family she could not escape her. More regrettably, that episode appears also to have marked the end of Sitwell's friendship with Constance Lane, who disappears from Sitwell's story at about the same time; she is glimpsed only once more – in a list of mourners at Lady Ida's memorial service in 1937.[28]

Sacheverell was still at Eton and in a bad way. His mother's conviction, Osbert's peril at the Front, and simple isolation left him
anguished, and his letters to Edith often plead for her attention. In
February 1916, she promised to visit on his first whole holiday and also
expressed the hope that he would come to live with them: 'We are
longing for it to happen.'[29] This invitation is a sign that Edith and
Helen were not lovers, as a younger brother living in the flat would
have been extremely awkward. In any event, he did not move in.

Sachie did not much like Helen Rootham. A few years earlier he
had spoken dismissively of her as 'Helen of Troy' and complained to
Osbert: 'Her conversation was centred on the White Slaves, the
Inquisition, & the Putamayo Atrocities. So cheerful, & elevating.'[30]
His need for affection put Edith in a difficult position. She had to refuse
to accompany him to Renishaw in March: 'Helen can't get away; and
both she and I realise that Ginger [Sir George] is in the sort of state that
it would be most dangerous for me to go down alone. I don't see how
I would ever get away again. My darling it *isn't* a lack of love for you.
Only I *have* to think of the future, when you get away for good. It would
be fatal if I once let them get a grip on me again. You *know* I love
you.'[31]

Often enough, Edith answered the summons from her family and
went to Renishaw or Montegufoni. However, she usually wanted Helen
to stand between herself and her parents and, in a surprisingly literal
way, to fend off the ghosts. Sitwell claimed that a visit to Renishaw in
1915 involved the exorcism of an 'elemental'. This term for a particular kind of spirit comes from Madame Blavatsky, in whom Rootham,
though a Catholic, developed a great interest.[32] Edith's story portrays
Helen as a hero and a mystic.

The elemental inhabited the 'ghost passage' in an unused wing of
the house. The family once laughed at the Welsh caretaker's stories of
encounters with it. Then, around 1905, Sitwell herself heard something – a clanging footstep followed by a lame dragging footstep. In the
company of a cousin in a bedroom adjacent to her own, she saw the
handle turn three times before the door burst open. She stepped into
the passage with a candle, 'but though I felt something unutterably
menacing watching me, I could see nothing . . . The footsteps went
away.'

Others encountered it over the years, until Helen Rootham consulted a priest who said she should say prayers for the dead. So Helen,
Edith, and a 'near relative' (probably Osbert, one of whose poems seems
to describe the event[33]) made the circuit of the house. Standing at the
bottom of a stairway, Helen said, 'It is coming.' They heard the heavy
footstep followed by the dragging footstep as it made its way along the
top corridor and start slowly down until it was three steps above where
she stood, still reciting prayers for its repose. 'Nobody could imagine
such a horrible suggestion of the very soul of evil as that presence con-
veyed.' It had come in opposition to the prayers. Helen decided she had
two courses open to her – to go up the stairs past it or turn her back on
it and join Edith and Osbert. She chose to turn her back and the elemental followed her. Osbert said, 'It is coming for us.'

There were no more footsteps, but, Edith recalled, 'we were aware
of a sound that was half unheard, and only somewhere in the consciousness, if you know what I mean, – rather like the sound in our
head when we are being given gas, or like the swishing of a sea.' They
were aware of a black floating mist, shapeless, and detached from the
floor, drifting down the stairs. 'It seemed as though my brain was
divided into two halves. The half that was nearest to the Elemental was
completely black and silent. The other half seemed clattering and shattering with jumping lights.' It floated past them and went out a door.
'That night, the ghost sought out the human being who had prayed
over it, and, after a battle the details of which are known only to
Miss . . . the ghost was beaten, and has never been seen or heard again
in the house.'[34]

The dead were everywhere that year, and the sudden ramping-up of
concern about spirits reflects that anxiety. Osbert was back at the front
from August 1915, and took part in the Battle of Loos, which began on
25 September. This especially tragic battle – it came very close to a
war-ending breakthrough – produced sixty thousand casualties, most on
the first day.[35] Among the dead were the poet Charles Sorley, Rudyard
Kipling's son John, and Fergus Bowes-Lyon, brother of Elizabeth Bowes-
Lyon, the future Queen Consort. When the fighting began, Osbert's
battalion was held in reserve, but was eventually called forward to
occupy a portion of the former German front line, coming under heavy
fire as the Germans tried to take it back.[36] On the first day of the battle,

Osbert spoke to an old friend from Eton, Peter Lycett Green, who within a few hours took a wound that cost him his leg. Another friend, Ivo Charteris, the younger brother of Lady Cynthia Asquith, was killed in action in the aftermath of the main battle.[37] In total, Osbert spent about ten months at or near the trenches, during which time he saw many men shot. As Philip Ziegler observes, there were at least a dozen occasions when Osbert might himself have been killed.

Upon the death of another officer, he was promoted acting captain and given a company to command. Enlisted men liked him for his courage and intelligence, and because he made sure they were well fed. At Christmas he paid for them to have a good turkey dinner. An infected cut sent him back to England in May 1916. He was hospitalised and underwent a further convalescence in Renishaw before returning to the regiment in the late summer. To Edith's relief, he was not sent back to the Front and instead spent much of the rest of the war in London. When diagnosed with a heart ailment in 1943, he wondered whether the doctors had known about it during the First World War, since after the summer of 1916 his requests for service abroad were consistently refused.[38] It is just as likely that, because of the scandal, his superiors decided that doubts about his character outweighed his record of service.

For many years, the poetry of the Great War was seen as a closed shop – women need not apply. Indeed, the one woman poet most likely to be remembered earned her reputation the hard way. Jesse Pope, a regular contributor of patriotic verse to the *Daily Mail* and author of *Jesse Pope's War Poems* (1915), was blasted in some of Wilfred Owen's best-known lines:

> If you could hear, at every jolt, the blood
> Come gargling from the froth-corrupted lungs,
> Obscene as cancer, bitter as the cud
> Of vile, incurable sores on innocent tongues, –
>
> My friend you would not tell with such high zest
> To children ardent for some desperate glory,
> The old Lie: Dulce et decorum est
> Pro patria mori.

Soldier poets in the second half of the war often insisted that civilians had no idea what was being suffered in the trenches. Siegfried Sassoon could imagine in 'Blighters' a tank rolling into a music hall, where 'prancing ranks / Of harlots shrill the chorus'. The anger against the Home Front was, partly, an anger against women as the stupid accomplices of the politicians, bishops, and journalists who sent young men to their deaths. In the face of such rage, it was difficult for women poets to be taken seriously when they wrote about the war. Until the 1990s, women poets of the First World War were overlooked, something feminist scholars and anthologists have tried to set right.[39]

Edith Sitwell knew that the entertainments of civilian life could offer a terrible insult to the men in uniform. Her poem 'The Dancers' was written 'During a great battle, 1916' – that is, the Battle of the Somme, which stretched from 1 July – the worst day in the history of the British Expeditionary Force with fifty-seven thousand dead, wounded, and missing – into November, when the number reached 420,000:

> The floors are slippery with blood:
> The world gyrates too. God is good
> That while His wind blows out the light
> For those who hourly die for us –
> We still can dance, each night.
>
> The music has grown numb with death –
> But we will suck their dying breath,
> The whispered name they breathed to chance,
> To swell our music, make it loud
> That we may dance, – may dance.
>
> We are the dull blind carrion-fly
> That dance and batten. Though God die
> Mad from the horror of the light –
> The light is mad, too, flecked with blood, –
> We dance, we dance, each night.[40]

Through Osbert, Edith met many soldier poets. Among the first was Edward Wyndham Tennant, known as 'Bimbo'. Eldest brother of the aesthete Stephen Tennant (a bright young thing and favoured subject of Cecil Beaton), Bimbo Tennant was Osbert's closest friend and a first cousin of Ivo Charteris, with whom he joined the Grenadiers. He was killed in action in September 1916, leaving behind a number of poems that showed promise. His death came as a blow to the Sitwells and their circle, especially to Osbert for whom it was one of the most terrible events of his life.

In June 1916, Edith and Osbert put out a twenty-eight-page volume of verses, which took its title from one of Osbert's contributions, 'Twentieth Century Harlequinade'. Watching the slaughter in France, Osbert had begun to think of himself as a poet. Never in Edith's or Sachie's league, Osbert was competent in verse but discovered in time that his greater talent lay in prose. In 1915 and 1916 he wrote a number of satires against the war, which capture the sense of waste and disgust to which his friends Siegfried Sassoon and Wilfred Owen gave a finer voice. Edith's contributions to *Twentieth Century Harlequinade* are considerably more important than her brother's. She was, however, uncertain how the book would be received, writing to Richard Jennings: 'I am trembling with fright: I am sure that the poem called "The Spider" will infuriate everyone. When I brought out my last book, an old lady said to me: she hoped I wouldn't mind, but would I tell her, was it *meant* to be *Poetry?*'[41] 'The Spider' was another horror: in an unspecified way, a father forces his will on his son, just as a spider ropes a fly. The son turns into a drunkard and his personality is erased. Whether an allegory of Osbert and Sir George, or of the conflict of generations that supposedly produced the war, the poem had the potential to make someone angry. Sir George was soon complaining, 'Edith's poems make *me* look ridiculous!'[42]

Edith had been mulling over one poem in the volume for at least a year. She had described 'The Fair' to Joan Wake as 'bosh' since the subject did not possess her.[43] Nevertheless, she could not walk away from it easily; she revised and renamed it 'Clowns' Houses'. A departure from the 'horrors', it was the most important of all her early works. Here she discovered the kinds of images – fragmented, synaesthetic, fantastical, macabre, jangling – that became her trademark in the 1920s:

> Beneath the flat and paper sky,
> The sun, a demon's eye,
> Glowed through the air, that mask of glass;
> All wand'ring sounds that pass
>
> Seemed out of tune, as if the light
> Were fiddle-strings pulled tight.
> The market square with spire and bell
> Clanged out the hour in Hell [. . .][44]

Over the next seven or eight years Edith Sitwell would enlarge on such images in dozens of poems. The culmination of that impulse was the sequence *Façade* (1922), which incorporates 'Clowns' Houses' and had a much longer genesis than is commonly understood. As early as 1914, she had struck upon one of the central themes of her life's work: that the self we know is a mask or puppet, and that our normal reality is a false floor over hell:

> Then underneath the veilèd eyes
> Of houses, darkness lies.
> Tall houses; like a hopeless prayer
> They cleave the sly dumb air;
>
> Blind are those houses, paper-thin;
> Old shadows hid therein
> With sly and crazy movements creep
> Like marionettes, and weep.

It is easy and useful to think of Sitwell's career as dividing into an early satiric phase and a later visionary one. However, most of her early satires are visionary in the manner of Pope's *Dunciad*, which in its last lines speaks of the triumph of Dulness as 'Universal Darkness buries all'. She was propounding a vision of hell as camouflaged by the accustomed surfaces of life, describing how Time the Clown conjures

> . . . star-bright masks for youth to wear,
> Lest any dream that fare

– Bright pilgrim – past our ken, should see
Hints of Reality.

The poet's work, to her mind, was to unsettle or subvert the lethal nor-
malcy of our perceptions and to clear a path for such 'hints'. She said
a few years later that a poet must 'show this dwindling world in all its
triviality. He can speak of nobility, also, but he would not be doing his
duty if he spoke only of nobility. He must show how, through fear of
life, some souls have become part of the stocks and stones.'[45]

Edith Sitwell was becoming increasingly well known to artists and
poets, who often gathered at Oscar Wilde's old haunt in the Café Royal
and at the Eiffel Tower – a restaurant at 1 Percy Street decorated by
Wyndham Lewis's Vorticist murals. By 1915, she was sought out by
artists and portrait painters. She sat to the ebullient Nina Hamnett several times, most famously for a portrait, now lost, in which she was
given 'kaleidoscopic breasts'.[46] She admired Hamnett's free spirit and
identified with her open-handedness: 'If she had money she invited her
friends to share it with her. If she had no money she had no food, unless
friends were equally generous towards her.'[47]

Nina Hamnett's portrait of Edith Sitwell, 1915

Sitwell sat to Roger Fry on a number of occasions, perhaps with Nina Hamnett in attendance,[48] but only two portraits survive. For one of these Sitwell wore a green evening dress; after sitting to him in the mornings, she and Fry, whose long grey hair floated out from under a sombrero, walked through Fitzroy Square from his studio to his house for lunch. The local children asked, 'perhaps not unnaturally', whether their mothers knew they were out. Sitwell found Fry delightful but absent-minded. She says that once when they went for lunch he could not find his slippers – 'a game of hunt-the-slipper ensued'. A crash interrupted them and a hoarse voice announcing, '"Coal, sir!" "Put it

Cecil Beaton's sketch of the three Sitwells in a characteristic mock-gothic pose, c.1931

my good man," said Mr. Fry, whirling round and round like a kitten chasing its tail, losing his spectacles, and speaking in a voice weak from fatigue – "Oh, well, put it on the bed." At this point I found the slippers in the milk-jug and the fun stopped.'[49]

Sitwell adopted Walter Sickert's practice of 'at homes'. On Saturdays she held a literary gathering, and on Wednesdays Helen held one for musicians. The Saturdays were by far the more important. They had begun by 1916 and continued until about 1932. In the dinginess of

Pembridge Mansions, Sitwell found herself presiding over one of the most important literary salons of the time. William Butler Yeats, T. S. Eliot, Siegfried Sassoon, Virginia Woolf, Arnold Bennett, Robert Graves, Gertrude Stein, E. M. Forster, Aldous Huxley, Graham Greene, and dozens of others made the long ascent to her flat, where they read poems and stories, exchanged compliments and insults, sipped strong tea, and ate halfpenny buns. The crowds that gathered in the flat were sometimes ill-assorted; apart from the writers, musicians and artists, there were Londesborough relatives, who regarded the other guests as something of a mystery.[50] Sitwell invited some people simply because she felt sorry for them.

One of the earliest regulars at Moscow Road was the Welsh poet W. H. Davies, who had spent his youth as a tramp and fruit-picker in the United States. On his way to the Klondike, he lost a leg jumping on a freight train in Ontario. Undaunted, he went on walking tours back in Britain, peddling laces, pins and needles. At times, he preached on street corners. With his wooden leg and angelic demeanour, he came across as a sanctified Long John Silver. When Sitwell met him in early 1917 he was living on a civil-list pension in a room in Great Russell Street overrun with mice. His neighbour was a Belgian prostitute with whom he conducted a feud through the wall that separated them; she tried to wake him at night with her national anthem and he retaliated with 'The Men of Harlech'.[51] He often appeared at Pembridge Mansions unexpectedly and, despite his wooden leg, would leap from behind the door to surprise Sitwell when she opened it. During the 'at homes', relatives found their worst suspicions of the company confirmed when Davies showed up. On one occasion he apologised for his lateness with the comment that 'there were a lot of police about'. When Sitwell failed to grasp his point, he repeated what to a former vagabond seemed a perfectly reasonable decision: 'You see, Oxford Street was full of them, so I had to come here by side streets.'[52]

Davies's *Autobiography of a Super-Tramp* (1908) was often reprinted, but serious writers admired his poetry even more. In the early 1920s Sitwell named him as one of the five greatest poets of the age, along with Ralph Hodgson, Thomas Hardy, Walter de la Mare, and W. B. Yeats.[53] Davies's reputation has diminished over the years, but Sitwell's view of him was not unique – Davies's poetry was fervently admired by George Bernard Shaw,

D. H. Lawrence, and Arnold Bennett. Edward Thomas promoted his work, and for a time paid for his rent, coal and light.[54] He was prolific and uneven, but his finest works stand up very well, among them 'The Inquest', about an infanticide, and 'My Old Acquaintance' about a ninety-year-old who believes that when she dies her elderly daughters will fight over her false teeth, which cost her five pounds. Davies had a great affection for the Sitwells, and once remarked, 'Edith is always as fine as a queen.'[55]

Osbert's social connections brought him into the orbit of Maud (later called Emerald) Cunard, the American who had married Sir Bache Cunard, grandson of the shipping magnate. Their daughter Nancy was beautiful and charismatic, and had no difficulty persuading people that she was a poet. She struck up a brief friendship with the Sitwells, having in common with them the loss of Bimbo Tennant, who had been a close friend of hers. She and Edith Sitwell conceived a new anthology, which would put an elbow in the ribs of Edward Marsh's staid but immensely popular *Georgian Poetry* series that had dominated the literary scene since 1912. At first, Sitwell overrated Cunard's talents and allowed a strikingly bad poem to become the signature work of the new anthology:

> Now in the scented gardens of the night,
> Where we are scattered like a pack of cards,
> Our words are turned to spokes that thoughts may roll
> And form a jangling chain around the world,
> (Itself a fabulous wheel controlled by Time
> Over the slow incline of centuries).
> [. . .][56]

Cunard had little to do with the editing of the anthology as she was getting married in November 1916,[57] but as a darling of the gossip columnists she brought publicity to the project that even the Sitwells could not match at that time. The first 'Cycle' of *Wheels* appeared on 13 December 1916,[58] an eighty-four-page production in yellow boards illustrated with a line-drawing of a woman pushing a pram. There were ten poems by Osbert, and one by Sacheverell, the first of his ever to be published, 'Li-Tai-Pé Drinks and Drowns', a polished short poem reminiscent of Pound's Rihaku phase. Giving pride of place to Nancy Cunard's work created an impression of flippancy, but this was con-

Geoffrey Gunther's cartoon (1918) portrays Osbert as both a Grenadier Guard and a contributor to Edith's anthology *Wheels*

trasted by the work of her friend Iris Tree, a daughter of the actor Herbert Beerbohm Tree, whose poems were unremittingly glum: 'The long road unto nothing I will sing, / Sing on one note, monotonous and dry.'[59] In fact, the tone of the volume was, with a few exceptions, sorrowful. There were three poems by Bimbo Tennant, as well as Helen's poem on his death. Edith Sitwell contributed nine of her own works, including 'The Mother', 'The Drunkard', and 'A Lamentation'.

Wheels brought together work of different kinds that ranged from Helen Rootham's translations of Rimbaud to Osbert's 'The Lament of the Mole-Catcher', a poem very much in the Georgian manner. Reviewers were divided. The *Pall Mall Gazette* said it was 'conceived in morbid eccentricity and executed in fierce factitious gloom'. The *Morning Post* predicted that in fifty years this publication would be 'remembered as a notable event in the inner history of English Literature'.[60] The latter judgment is closer to the mark. In the six 'Cycles' of the anthology, Sitwell brought forward works by Wyndham Lewis, Aldous Huxley, and Wilfred Owen, none of whom was at that time well known. It was the beginning of her heroic efforts to promote the work of rising talents; she was still doing it on her deathbed. At the same time, the anthology gave Sitwell a new heft in the literary world. Henceforth, she would be known as 'The Editor of *Wheels*'.

9

THE TANGO

Álvaro de Guevara (1894–1951) was a man of extremes. Described in the *ODNB* as an 'artist and boxer', he hated quarrels and loved fist-fights.[1] His childhood in Chile was divided between a house in Valparaiso that was flattened in an earthquake and a country estate that sat peacefully beside a volcano in Arauca. His father made a great deal of money in the woollen trade and was an Anglophile even though one of his sons had gone mad in England in 1902: convinced of a plot against King Edward VII, the young man had stabbed himself repeatedly, then leapt to his death from a house in South Kensington, clutching an umbrella as a parachute.[2] In 1910, Álvaro de Guevara was sent to Bradford Technical College to prepare to enter the family business. He was desolate there, but Albert and William Rothenstein, whose family was in the same business, spotted his artistic gifts and encouraged him to get training. He won a scholarship to the Slade School in London in 1912 and stood out in a group that included Dora Carrington, Mark Gertler, Paul and John Nash, and Stanley and Gilbert Spencer. Known as 'Chile', he soon came to the notice of Walter Sickert, C. R. W. Nevinson, and Augustus John. His most admired early works included a series of paintings of swimming baths in the manner of Matisse. He also produced impressive restaurant and theatre scenes. In 1917, he had his first one-man exhibition at the Chenil Galleries.

His biographer, Diana Holman-Hunt, believes that Guevara met Edith Sitwell by early 1914 and that she made an 'extraordinary impression' on him.[3] She says that he much preferred the romantic qualities of her early poetry to the violence of Wyndham Lewis and the Vorticists. Moreover, he found her personally captivating. I have not found evidence to confirm such an early date for their meeting, but it is possible, as Edith Sitwell had met a good many artists by then, some of them through Sickert, and some through Constance Lane, who, like Guevara, was a student at the Slade School before the war.

Guevara was a handsome man with a muscled physique often displayed in the ring – he became the champion of all weights in South America in 1924. An accomplished dancer, he probably tried to teach Edith Sitwell to tango. It is hard to imagine such a thing, as it brings to mind a scene from *Addams Family Values*. However, it was one of Guevara's passions. He wrote plays and poetry, and a few of his translations appeared in *Wheels*, as did his illustrations. He came often to Pembridge Mansions, and in the summer of 1916 painted her portrait there. *The Editor of Wheels* is remarkable not least for its perspective; it looks down to its subject, seated on an Omega Studio dining chair. Sitwell wears a long green dress in a medieval mode, and the rough boards beneath her feet are partly covered by chequered mats. Guevara seems to have been the first of many artists fascinated by her long hands, which, resting on her lap, lend to the image a strange serenity.[4]

Edith Sitwell fell in love with Álvaro de Guevara. She told Allanah Harper, whom she met in 1925, that they had actually been engaged until someone warned her that he suffered from a serious venereal disease. This claim is always dismissed as Sitwell's wishful thinking. Harold Acton, who believed her the one true genius in her family, described Edith Sitwell to John Pearson as 'a sex-starved spinster all her life. She really desperately needed someone to take her to bed, but I'm sure that no one ever did. Certainly if it did happen – which I doubt – he was an extremely courageous gentleman . . . dear Edith wasn't exactly what you might call cuddly.'[5] Acton knew her well and honoured her as a poet, although one hesitates to rely on his idea of what is 'cuddly'. Moreover, the 'sex-starved spinster' is a stereotype that is not much help in understanding her.

It is essential to be cautious in dealing with Sitwell's claims about her personal history, but it is another thing to be casually dismissive. No letters, diaries, or other contemporary evidence about this relationship have come to light. No one knows what passed between

Edith Sitwell and Álvaro de Guevara. When she was about seventy, she wept before her secretary Elizabeth Salter because, she said, she had never had a passionate relationship and felt that she was built for it.[6] Nevertheless, that does not preclude an engagement or fleeting sexual experiences. According to Holman-Hunt, Guevara was a man of machismo; he tended to divide women into two categories: those you could have easy sex with (many) and 'ladies' you might consider marrying (few). He was very anxious to find a wife; virginity would have been in Edith's favour. Writing nearly sixty years after the events, Holman-Hunt gives no source to back up her unqualified assertion that he did not propose to Edith Sitwell. Indeed, Holman-Hunt's readiness to distinguish a 'rare and exalted friendship' from romantic love invites scepticism. She insists that the story of the venereal disease was someone making mischief between them.[7] However, when he eventually married Meraud Guinness in 1929, it was after a secret engagement. It is not impossible that there was once a private understanding between himself and Sitwell that soon came unravelled.

A marriage would have been disastrous. Chile was promiscuous, with a taste for prostitutes of both sexes. Despite his gentle ways in conversation, he could be thuggish. Examples of brawling abound, including an apparent attempt in Paris to throw the admittedly provoking Brian Howard – the writer and aesthete upon whom Waugh's Anthony Blanche is modelled – from a hotel window. He survived (so it is said) by holding the curtains and crawled back in. Guevara threw him a second time and he clung to the sill. Holman-Hunt remarks cheerfully of Guevara, 'At least he had avoided prosecution for manslaughter or attempted murder.'[8] In addition to his violent nature, Guevara had a taste for opium, about which he later had a row with Sachie.[9] He was hardly a boy to take home, especially to such a mother as Lady Ida.

Sitwell looked on bitterly when Chile became involved with Nancy Cunard. He had known her since about 1914, when her friends Iris Tree and Lady Diana Manners were both studying at the Slade. Along with Osbert and others, they formed what was called 'the corrupt coterie'. Nancy and Chile were sleeping together around the end of 1915 but seem to have drifted apart. Nancy had affairs with a number of young men who were headed for the Front; one romance, with Peter Broughton Adderley, lasted just five days before he went back to France and was killed.[10] In November 1916, she married a Grenadier Guard from Australia named Sydney Fairbairn, and went on to spend about twenty unhappy months with him. In the autumn of 1919, Guevara began a portrait of Nancy and fell in love with her. He asked her to marry him, but she refused. When pressed, she explained that she was sleeping with various men. Her answer, a jolt to his Latin pride, shamed him. He thought little of his own promiscuity but was horrified by the same conduct in a woman. Some part of this story got back to Edith Sitwell and confirmed that as a lover Chile was lost to her; however, as late as 1927 she recommended him to Gertrude Stein as a 'real genius' and 'one of my greatest friends'.[11] On the other hand, Sitwell never lost an opportunity to speak ill of Cunard.

Edith Sitwell first met with Aldous Huxley at the Isola Bella restaurant in Soho – a haunt of many writers including the Imagist poet Hilda Doolittle ('H.D.') – on a June day in 1917: 'The air was like white wine, spangled with great stars of dew and sun motes.' In the cool of the restaurant, she sat with the tall, thin Huxley, whose 'silences seemed to spread for miles, extinguishing life when they occurred, as a snuffer extinguishes a candle'. She had come to solicit work for *Wheels* and in the process began a lasting friendship. Though daunting, he was friendly, and, once started, an accomplished talker. She met often with him and his first wife Maria. He would speak of animals and minerals as if they possessed a human lewdness. One of his monologues concerned the sex life of melons, so carnal, even incestuous, that gardeners kept them under glass. Once, in the tube station at Sloane Square, he held other travellers spellbound as he talked about the sexual dexterity of the octopus.[12]

Huxley was not sure at first what he was getting involved in and was doubtful of the *Wheels* coterie. In a letter to his brother Julian in August, he referred first to *The Egoist*, a modernist journal which published portions of Joyce's *A Portrait of the Artist as a Young Man* and *Ulysses*, as a 'horrid little paper' and then looked further down his nose:

I am also contributing to the well-known Society Anthology, *Wheels*,
in company with illustrious young persons like Miss Nancy Cunard,
Miss Iris Tree and the kindred spirits who figure in the gossip page
of the *Daily Mirror*. This year, containing as it does, selections from
me and Mr. Sherard Vines, it should be quite a bright production.
The folk who run it are a family called Sitwell, alias Shufflebottom,
one sister and two brothers, Edith, Osbert and Sacheverell – isn't
that superb – each of them larger and whiter than the other. I like
Edith, but Ozzy and Sachy are still rather too large to swallow. Their
great object is to REBEL, which sounds quite charming; only one
finds that the steps they are prepared to take, the lengths they will
go are so small as to be hardly perceptible to the naked eye. But they
are so earnest and humble . . . these dear solid people who have suddenly discovered intellect and begin to get drunk on it . . . it is a
charming type.[13]

The Second Cycle of *Wheels*, when it appeared in December, contained nine of his poems and none of Nancy's; the gossip page receded.
Huxley's view that real rebellion called for more than some members
of the *Wheels* coterie were doing in 1917 is hard to dispute, but his
comments do not hold up in relation to Edith Sitwell herself, who was
developing into a daring and inventive poet. Before long, he changed
his mind and decided he liked *Wheels* for its combativeness. For her
part, Edith Sitwell was quickly convinced of Aldous Huxley's genius,
and throughout her life preferred his work to that of most of their contemporaries, including Virginia Woolf.

At the same time that her friendship with Huxley was developing,
another even more important one was taking root. In April 1917,
Siegfried Sassoon was shot through the shoulder at the Battle of Arras
and returned home from the Front. He had won the Military Cross for
rescuing a wounded soldier in 1916, and was then recommended for
the Victoria Cross in another action. His diaries show him both disgusted with war and, paradoxically, anxious to prove his valour.
Having begun as a lyrical poet in the Georgian mode, he abandoned
the patriotic assurances of Rupert Brooke, describing the trenches and
battlefields with revulsion. The publication of *The Old Huntsman* in
May 1917 established him as one of the most important younger poets.

While in England he was a frequent visitor at Garsington Manor where Lady Ottoline Morrell had surrounded herself with conscientious objectors. He also kept the company of Robert Ross, the old friend of Oscar Wilde. Until his sudden death on 5 October 1918, Ross was a mentor to many literary homosexuals including Osbert Sitwell. Holding strong anti-war opinions, he carried about photographs of dead and wounded soldiers for the inspection of anyone who spoke too complacently of sacrifice. Ross introduced Sassoon and Osbert Sitwell.

The young Sassoon was bold: on one occasion he had driven forty Germans out of a trench single-handedly. Now he intended to take 'Independent Action' to stop the war. Encouraged by Morrell, the philosopher Bertrand Russell, H. W. Massingham (editor of *The Nation*), the writer John Middleton Murry, and others, he composed his well-known public protest: 'I am making this statement as an act of wilful defiance of military authority, because I believe that the War is being deliberately prolonged by those who have the power to end it.' He claimed that the original war aims could now be achieved by negotiation and that the suffering of soldiers was being prolonged for other ends which were 'evil and unjust'.[14] That summer, his protest was published in *The Times* and a dozen other newspapers, and it was read out in the House of Commons. The army and the government had no desire to try a gallant officer for mutiny. Robert Graves persuaded Sassoon to stand before a medical board, which concluded that he was suffering from shell-shock and hospitalised him. Sassoon's actions were honourable and idealistic, although after the Second World War he concluded that a negotiated peace in 1917 would have been unrealistic, as nothing could have prevented a recurrence of German aggression.[15] Desperation for the war to end gave force to the claim, however naive, that the British government was wickedly prolonging the slaughter.

At the beginning of the year Sacheverell had joined Osbert in the Grenadiers. The family had done their best to keep him out of service altogether, with Lady Ida's physician providing a certificate declaring him unfit. Sacheverell never saw combat, and it is thought that Osbert used his influence to keep him stationed at Chelsea Barracks. It is also possible that the Grenadiers were slow to trust Osbert Sitwell's brother.

Sachie, who had nothing to do with the scandal, may have been viewed with undeserved scepticism by his commanders.

In the meantime, Edith Sitwell, anxious for the safety of her brothers, was dazzled by Sassoon's protest. Through Robert Ross, she tracked him to Craiglockhart Hospital near Edinburgh, where he had recently met another patient, the younger soldier-poet Wilfred Owen. On 30 August 1917 she wrote a letter to him on behalf of herself and her brothers: 'we wish to write and tell you with what great sympathy – and envy – we regard your courage. It is very difficult to write a letter like this without appearing very stilted and lacking in a sense of humour . . . I expect all the old gentlemen are ever so pleased that you are a poet; it gives them the opportunity of jumping on two vices at the same time.'[16]

That the war was something old men inflicted on young men made sense to the Sitwells, who were so disillusioned with their own parents. After the death of his son at Loos, even Kipling wrote among his 'Epitaphs of the War' (1919): 'If any question why we died, / Tell them, because our fathers lied.' Yet the idea that by 1917 the war was animated by 'evil and unjust' aims led to a somewhat distasteful search for villains. Sassoon believed, as did many others, that the war continued because of a conspiracy among politicians, generals, and profiteers. His father's family were Sephardic, but even Sassoon complained of 'Jew profiteers'.[17] For many 'progressive' thinkers the collocation seemed natural; for them, the epitome of the profiteer was the international arms salesman Basil Zaharoff of Vickers Ltd, makers of the Maxim machine gun. In a portrait of him, Osbert reminds the reader that he is a Jew and then writes of 'the beaky face, the hooded eye, the wrinkled neck, the full body, the impression of physical power and of the capacity to wait, the sombre alertness' of a vulture.[18] This description of Zaharoff is quoted without demur by the ODNB in its most recent revision. Graham Greene based a character on Zaharoff in A Gun for Sale, and later revised the portrait to remove traces of anti-Semitism. He explained that before the Holocaust 'one regarded the word Jew as almost a synonym for capitalist. Big business seemed our enemy and such men who happened to be Jewish as Zaharoff who indulged in the private sale of arms.'[19]

Edith Sitwell ventured into this territory in 1917 or early 1918 with her poem 'Plutocracy at Play'. It is an obscure piece about the rich attending concerts, where 'Eyes glitter like the scales of fish / With some half-formed Hebraic wish'. She continues:

> ... pastoral life befits their rank
> With field of commerce, marbled bank,
> Where seated the Eternal Nose
> Finds out the worm within their rose:
>
> 'Let those exalted be brought low' –
> And noses follow suit you know [. . .][20]

While large noses were a sensitive point for Sitwell, this is a disparagement not just of wealth and power but of a race. Published in 1918, 'Plutocracy at Play' was not reprinted. Indeed, Edith Sitwell's poems about the war otherwise stay out of the bog of anti-Semitism.

Not all of Sitwell's new friends shared her pacifism or, indeed, her opinions about poetry. Edmund Gosse was a disappointed poet who became the most influential critic and literary historian of his time. He was knighted in 1925.[21] As a young man, he had been a friend of Tennyson, Rossetti, Stevenson, and Swinburne. Osbert first met Gosse through Robbie Ross in 1916. Gosse invited the Sitwells to his Sunday-afternoon tea parties. A knock at his door would be answered by Parker, the parlourmaid, whose authority in the house was second only to that of Buchanan, the cat, whom Gosse summoned to family meals with a bell. Edith Sitwell recalled that the cat had his own writing paper and envelopes, and that when Gosse was travelling he would dictate gossipy letters to him.[22]

Gosse had a ferocious style of conversation: like Samuel Johnson, he talked to win. Osbert compared him to a boxer or a fencer.[23] He was also touchy; when he and his wife paid a visit to the Sitwells in January 1918, he brought a set of his new edition of Swinburne. Sachie expressed delight that the poems were now available in a cheap edition, to which he responded, 'NOT SO CHEAP AS ALL THAT.'[24] Edith described his conversation as a 'treasure' but never 'was any treasure-seeking in the world more fraught with danger'.[25] He was nevertheless supportive of young writers and easily charmed. Osbert says that they

were invited to Gosse's house for dinner one evening, when bombs
began falling in the first big raid of the war. (Zeppelins had been bombing London since 1915, but Osbert may be referring to the first massive
raid by Gotha bombers on 13 June 1917.) Edith did not appear, and
Parker eventually announced: 'Miss Sitwell has telephoned. She sends
her compliments, but says she refuses to be an Aunt Sally for the
Germans, so she is not coming to dinner.'²⁶ The Gosses found the
message enchanting. On another occasion, the Sitwells left after a
bruising afternoon of debate. Gosse saw them to the door himself and
called after them with a wave, '"Good-bye, you delightful but deleterious trio!"'²⁷

For at least a year or so, Gosse had scant idea of what the Sitwells
were really up to as writers, and appears to have been less conscious of
their acquaintance than they were of his. He wrote to Edward Marsh
on 20 November 1917:

I have been dragged into promising to preside at a reading of poets
got up by Mrs Coalbox and Madam Fan-the-Devil, who would talk
any human being into anything. I don't know what I have let myself
in for, but at all events some sound 'Georgians' will be represented –
Nichols, Graves, Sassoon. But the protagonists are Edith and Osbert
Sitwell, of whom I know nothing. I pray Apollo that they be not
pacifists. I told the two fiery ladies that I would leave the house, not
to say the chair, if the names of Alfred Douglas or Ezra Pound are
mentioned, but they swear their poets are perfectly respectable. (I
nearly wrote 'respectful'; I am sure they are not that!)²⁸

At the same time, the little-known T. S. Eliot wrote to Pound: 'I
have been invited by female VANDERVELDE to contribute to a reading of POETS: big wigs, OSWALD and EDITH Shitwell, Graves
(query, George?) Nichols, and OTHERS.'²⁹ The reading was held on
12 December at the house in Onslow Square of the veteran lion-
catcher Sybil Colefax. It was organised by Robbie Ross and Lalla
Vandervelde, the wife of a Belgian politician. She was able to get
what she wanted from Gosse because in 1917 affection for Belgians
was still a great motivator. One hundred and fifty people attended,
paying 10s 6d for their tickets as a fund-raiser for the Red Cross. As

it turned out, the 'sound "Georgians'" were under-represented: Sassoon did not show, and Graves walked straight past the house while proposing marriage to Nancy Nicholson. As chairman, Gosse wasted no time: recitations started promptly at five since he had a dinner engagement at a quarter past six. T. S. Eliot hurried from his job at Lloyd's Bank, but was unavoidably late, earning a public rebuke from Gosse when he took his place on the platform. Osbert was struck by Eliot's courtesy, his features like an Aztec carving, and his eyes like those 'of one of the greater cats'.[30] Aldous Huxley thought that only he and Eliot read with dignity, that the Sitwells were nervous, and that Nichols was all too 'thrusting' in his efforts to be the leader among the young poets.[31]

Edith Sitwell's friendship with Eliot grew quickly. She also won the confidence of his unstable wife Vivienne, who was then reaching the conclusion of her affair with Bertrand Russell, begun in the summer of 1915 during the first weeks of her marriage to Eliot. Sitwell certainly found her engaging and did her best to be sympathetic over the years, even when Vivienne was utterly irrational. His biographers show that Tom Eliot was not much of a husband. Psychologically fragile himself, he had a streak of misogyny in his thinking that separated spirit and flesh, and then associated women negatively with the flesh. However, only a few people had such a close view of the Eliots' marriage as Edith Sitwell did, and she had no doubt that Eliot behaved well towards Vivienne in appalling circumstances. As she put it years later, 'What that great man has suffered, nobody knows.'[32] In the early days of their friendship, she felt a bond with Eliot and afterwards maintained that the 'hyacinth girl' passage of *The Waste Land* was based on her.[33]

Other women had similar reactions to Eliot. Virginia Woolf and, later, even Helen Gardner found him enthralling. However, Lyndall Gordon, one of his biographers, wonders about Eliot's view of Sitwell in light of his misogyny: 'Does hatred come from sexual failures, or suppressed affinities, or resentful envy? Another woman writer is called "Shitwell" – a reward for the affability which the eccentric aristocrats, Edith Sitwell and her brothers, offered Eliot when, a newcomer in London, he used to sit with them in dank tea-rooms that seemed to be papered with their tea-leaves.'[34] It should be noted, in

Eliot's defence, that the schoolboy pun on the Sitwells' name was
by Eliot, Pound, and Wyndham Lewis also at the expense of her brot
ers, so it cannot be a pure indication of revulsion for female flesh, ever
though there is ample evidence elsewhere that these three men took
a dim view of women. Gordon rightly observes a 'coterie misogyny'
among them that led to harsh comments on Lady Ottoline Morrell
and others.[35]

Literary associations were important, but Sitwell needed to get
her work out. Now thirty years old, she had to her credit one pamphlet of poems, another shared with Osbert, and various pieces in
the *Daily Mirror* and *Wheels*. It was time for more substantial collections. The first of these was *Clowns' Houses*, published by
Blackwell on 9 June 1918. At forty pages it was still a 'slim volume',
but at least it was a book. Moreover, she had found her way to the
'glittering' style. The first poem, 'Fireworks', announces the effect
she is looking for:

. . . the night

Will weld this dust of bright Infinity
To forms that we may touch and call and see . . .
[. . .]
And, 'gainst the silk pavilions of the sea
I watch the people move incessantly

Vibrating, petals blown from flower-hued stars
Beneath the music-fireworks' waving bars;

So all seems indivisible, at one:
The flow of hair, the flowers, the seas that run, –

A coloured floating music of the night
Through the pavilions of the Infinite.[36]

The theme of this poem is actually very traditional; though compris-
ing oddly sorted images, it is still a search for a metaphysical unity. It
is a mixture of Baudelaire and William Blake. The pavilions beside the

sea are an evocation of Scarborough in her childhood, but she has gone
for the effect of a kaleidoscope. In much of her poetry of the 1910s and
1920s she describes provincial towns and villages, squires and bump-
kins, country fairs and parish churches, as in 'Weathercocks':

> Like wooden bumpkin's sun-round stare
> Clocks seem, in new-washed air:
> Bucolic round-faced clocks
> That laugh at pirouettes
> Of glittering weathercocks
> Each preening as he sets
> Clouds tumbling like striped coloured clowns
> Through all the far blue towns
> With thunder drumming after.
> A coloured bubble is the world –
> A glassy ball that clowns have hurled
> Through the rainbow space of laughter.[37]

The fascination with clowns and acrobats and, elsewhere, harlequins
and the stock characters of *commedia dell'arte* may indicate a debt to
Picasso. Indeed, in her fascination with surfaces and with a multiplic-
ity of viewpoints, Sitwell may be attempting a Cubism in words. Her
refusal to offer a reliable, even comforting, persona seems to have bothered some critics. The poem 'Acrobats' opens with a quotation from
the journal *The Literary World*: 'Edith Sitwell tries all manner of spiritual contortions with no great success. We suggest it is because she is
too self-conscious.' Her poem debunks the kind of 'sincerity' that had
been expected of poets since the days of the Romantics:

> O world! Fat woman ambling, with your hair
> Blond as the locks of Fortune, or the stare
>
> Of opulent suns, – your tights are thought to be
> Pink flesh itself, and youth's simplicity.

The key phrase here is 'thought to be'. At the poem's end Edith Sitwell
returns to this image and asks bluntly:

Yet why should poets be constrained to bare
Mock souls, fat Acrobatics at a Fair,

In pink tights, imitative flesh; their goal
To be admired for fatted weight of Soul?[38]

Even though a special degree of earnestness was often expected of
female poets, Sitwell seems to have grasped a point that eluded many
poets and reviewers of the day: that the self in a poem is a performance,
at times a tumbling act. To make a similar point, Pound used the
metaphor of the persona and Eliot spoke of the flight from personality.
Sitwell offered no philosophical account for her view, but she is in the
mainstream of literary modernism. Even in the phrase 'fatted weight of
Soul' she refuses the sort of quick transcendence served up by the minor
heirs of the romantic tradition – what T. E. Hulme dismissed as 'spilt
religion'.

Edith Sitwell's own ambitions as a poet were always matched by a
search for genius in others. On 3 July 1918, Sassoon wrote to Osbert
Sitwell: 'Have you met Wilfred Owen, my little friend, whose verses
were in The Nation recently? He is so nice, & shy, & fervent about
poetry, which he is quite good at, & will do *very well* some day.'[39]
Osbert had, in fact, met him the previous September through Robert
Ross, who asked the larger-than-life Sitwell 'not to frighten him'.[40] In
July 1918, Owen was stationed at Scarborough, where books by the
Sitwells were not popular. He wrote to Osbert about his tangles with
the seaside booksellers:

Last week I broke out of camp to order *Wheels*, 1917. Canning
refused to stock copies. I persisted so long that the Young Lady loudly
declared she knew all along I was 'Osbert himself'. This caused a
consternation throughout the crowded shop; but I got the last laugh
by – 'No madam; the book is by a friend of mine, Miss Sitwell.'

Rigby's people would not order a single copy without deposit!

Is the 1918 vol. designed to go on the caterpillar wheels of
Siegfried's Music Hall Tank? If so I might help with the ammunition.
Would you like some short war poems, or what? Please give me a
final date for submitting them to you.[41]

Although Owen refers to Edith as 'a friend of mine', the two never met. He was returned to the Front in September and soon led troops in a storming of enemy positions at the village of Joncourt. On 4 November, a week before the war's end, he was killed at the Sambre–Oise Canal and was posthumously awarded the Military Cross for his valour at Joncourt.

Over the next two years, Edith Sitwell regarded it as almost a religious mission to get his poems into print. In February 1919, Osbert obtained the manuscripts from Owen's mother, Susan Owen, with whom Edith exchanged a number of letters: 'I write with the kind of reverence and humility with which I should have written to Dante's mother.'[42] With Sachie's help, she transcribed the various poems, which still had on them the mud of the trenches, and she expected to have a final manuscript ready by October: 'You cannot *think* what it means to me that you should allow me to see to his book; I think it is the greatest and most sacred honour. I have to copy out the poems one by one and slowly, as frankly they upset me so terribly I often have to stop.'[43] She wrote to Sassoon for help unravelling the texts of the last two poems; he appeared at Moscow Road, insisting that as Owen's friend he should take over the publication. She told Susan Owen, 'In those circumstances I could do nothing but offer to hand them over to him; though it has cost me more to relinquish them than I can tell you.'[44]

On the eve of the anniversary of Owen's death she wrote to Susan Owen again: 'All my thoughts are with you today, and will be tomorrow, unceasingly. If only one could express what one feels, ever. My heart aches for you. I am dumb when I think what not only you, his mother, but we all, have lost. I shall keep the 4th of November always, as long as I live, as a day of mourning. I know you are broken-hearted, but oh, you are just the mother for such a son. Tomorrow, his first poems in book form will be with you – the immortality of his great soul.'[45] Sitwell was referring to the Fourth Cycle of *Wheels* which, dedicated to Owen, contained 'Strange Meeting', 'A Terre', 'The Sentry', 'Disabled', 'The Dead-Beat', and 'The Chances'. Only four of his poems had been published in his lifetime. In the months following his death, the Sitwells had arranged publications of some individual poems, but this was the first time that Owen's work appeared in bulk. John

Middleton Murry observed in the *Athenæum* (5 December 1919) that by including 'Strange Meeting' 'the editor of "Wheels" has done a great service to English letters'.

In January 1919, Sassoon headed off to the United States for an eight-month reading tour. He returned the manuscripts to Edith Sitwell to be

In the fourth cycle of *Wheels* (1919), Edith Sitwell published a group of poems by Wilfred Owen, who had been killed in action in the last days of the war

made ready for delivery by 1 February. According to Sitwell's report to Susan Owen, he had done nothing with them in the interim apart from finding a publisher.[46] She got the last of the editing done (Susan Owen had sent more poems since September) and delivered the manuscript to Frank Swinnerton at Chatto & Windus. The volume of Owen's work that appeared in the autumn contained Sassoon's introduction and an acknowledgment: 'For the preparation of this book thanks are primarily due to Miss Edith Sitwell.'[47] Although this note appeared as the first thing in the book after the half-title, Sitwell remained unhappy that her role as Owen's first editor was generally overlooked.

For a time, Sitwell shared Edmund Gosse's view that the poet Robert Nichols was a sure thing. A friend of Sassoon and Graves, Nichols served briefly at the Front, and his volume *Ardours and Endurances* (1917) was widely praised. He wrote a series of episodes from the trenches, which, raw and memorable, suffer by comparison only with the best poetry the war produced. Although Sitwell and Gosse hoped his development would continue, Nichols turned out to be a poet of authentic but not extraordinary gifts, briefly galvanised by a terrible subject. A few years after the war, he was essentially finished as a poet, though he continued to write drama and fiction. W. H. Davies once remarked in a penetrating way: 'Robert Nichols wants me to give him lessons in writing *sonnets* . . . But you know, you can't *teach* a mun to write sonnets.'[48]

Nichols first came to Pembridge Mansions in October 1917. He and Edith Sitwell had a close friendship for about two years, and she wrote him fulsome letters: 'Why do you say you will "only attempt side glances"? The only Prometheus we have got, pretending he is frightened of fire.' Apart from such earnestness, one hears emerging Sitwell's characteristic voice as a letter-writer: 'God, I am so bored with nearly everything; have had a horrible week, pursued by virtuous female cousins like very large empty omnibuses on very small wheels, who live in drawing rooms like railway carriages – only one never gets anywhere, even to a terminus.' In August 1918, she complained to Nichols from Renishaw that she was surrounded by her mother, her father, and her duty, 'rather an uncomfortable ménage à trois'. The food was bad and she was afflicted by the attentions of a pony:

> I sustain a nymph-like existence by splashing among the muddy streams of watered coffee which flow at breakfast time. My mother has a pony which thinks it is a Pekinese and tries to sit on one's lap; it has a glassy eye, and I am absolutely terrified of it; and, though no athlete, fly for miles pursued by its affections and cries of 'Your grandfather was such a *sportsman*! I can't imagine what makes you like this.'

In her next letter, she spoke of a living toad that had been found in a coal seam a few years earlier. It was thought to have been there for two or three million years 'with nothing to look at and nobody to talk to. As Sachie remarks, the first million years must have seemed a bit long. Well, only that toad could even attempt to enter into my agonies, though with only partial success, as at least he had silence. With his advantage in that direction, I should have written better poems.' Meanwhile, her father was 'too marvellously fantastic, so Italian

Comedy, I expect him to break into tail-feathers at any moment'. She tried to play the piano, but 'jellified females would melt over me'. Ginger wept over her music and offered the back-handed compliment, 'Oh, my darling, every girl should have *some* talent or other.' Meanwhile she noticed among his books one intended for her, titled 'How to be Pleasing, though Plain'.[49] This is all great fun, but it is well to remember that Sitwell's letters are often a kind of comic fiction. Although there were books with similar titles, the one she mentions never made its way to Britain's copyright libraries.

On Boxing Day 1918, she wrote to Nichols from Scarborough and said that she had been discussing religion with Margaret Nevinson, a writer and suffragette, and the mother of the painter C. R. W. Nevinson: 'It makes me feel more and more as though one day I shall become a Roman Catholic. (It is the only creed for someone like myself, I do feel that more and more.)'[50] Pious but disaffected from the Church of England, Edith Sitwell was influenced by Helen Rootham (whose interest in the esoteric may have complicated the issue) and even perhaps by Robert Ross, another Catholic. Although the theology of her work is indisputably Catholic from about 1940 – explicit allusions to Thomas Aquinas can be traced in the notes to her *Collected Poems* – she did not finally enter the Church until 1955. She usually tried to deflect talk about her personal faith, and some of her wisecracks encouraged friends to think the conversion either a passing fancy or a failed attempt to contain her bad temper by submission to higher authority. In fact, she had pondered conversion for almost forty years, and once she did convert she remained a communicant until her death in 1964.

Nichols took a professorship in Japan in 1921 and then went to Hollywood where he advised Douglas Fairbanks, Senior, on the finer points of swashbuckling. In 1930, he read Osbert's short story 'Alive – Alive O' and assumed that he was being satirised in the figure of a war poet who fakes his own death to achieve a Keatsian fame. Eddie Marsh thought that if the character named 'Bundle' resembled anyone, it was Edmund Blunden, but Nichols was offended and started a feud with Osbert.[51] Afterwards Edith thought him fit only for teasing.

10

ALICE IN HELL

I often see your photo in the Daily Mail; I think how wonderful you look. Do you remember me when you & Miss Rootham lived in Pembridge Mansions, Bayswater? & I supplied you with coal at Stubbs in Queen's Rd. If you remember, you were the first two ladies to come along & shake hands with me when the Armistice was signed in the 'First World War'. They were such happy days to me ... If you are able to answer this letter, [I] should so much like to know how you are, & if you still see Miss Rootham.[1]

So wrote the seventy-three-year-old Ethel Grant in August 1964 to Dame Edith Sitwell, who was by then in the last months of her life. Helen Rootham had been dead for a quarter of a century. For almost everyone of their generation, 11 November 1918 had been a day of rejoicing. Sitwell and Rootham were on their way to the Eiffel Tower restaurant that afternoon, joining Osbert, Nina Hamnett, Aldous and Julian Huxley, and Dora Carrington.[2] Then came a dinner party at Osbert's house in Swan Walk, where Sachie joined them, with Lalla Vandervelde, Ethel Sands, the Russian impresario Sergei Diaghilev, and the dancer and choreographer Léonide Massine. They made their way to Trafalgar Square where thousands danced and sang. In Whitehall, Nina Hamnett saw a man perched on a ladder, scraping the black paint from an arc light. Peace meant the relighting of the city.[3]

The Sitwells went to a party that night at the Adelphi, hosted by Monty Shearman and attended by the most of the Bloomsbury set: Hamnett, Clive Bell, Roger Fry, Lytton Strachey, Mark Gertler, Lady Ottoline Morrell, D. H. Lawrence, John Maynard Keynes, Duncan Grant, and David Garnett. Diaghilev and Massine were joined by the ballerina Lydia Lopokova. After an evening of pianola music and dancing, one of the party-goers, on his way home, tried to set fire to Nelson's plinth. Going back to Aldershot, Sachie saw drunken women rolled like milk cans along the platform at Waterloo Station and stowed in the guard's van.[4] The reign of peace began the next morning with a hangover and some bruises.

After the armistice, Edith Sitwell headed north to Scarborough, where Osbert, then an admirer of the Bolsheviks, was standing as an Asquith Liberal in his father's old constituency in the general election of 14 December. Edith wrote to Robert Nichols:

> The horror of Scarborough has, however, acted like electricity upon me. What a strange place – partly a clownish bright-coloured tragic hell, partly a flatness where streets crawl sluggishly, and one drop of rain (no more) drops on one's face half way down the street, and there are no inhabitants, or so it seems, but boys so indistinguishable in their worm-white faces that they have to wear coloured caps with initials that one may be known from another. Osbert didn't 'get in'. I suppose they found out he is a poet.

It can be assumed that on the hustings Edith Sitwell lacked the common touch.

Back in London, she described for Nichols a 'very depressing evening' organised by Alida Klemantaski, 'a very nice girl' later married to Harold Monro of the Poetry Bookshop. She brought together at the beginning of 1919 a group of women poets with a particular view to introducing Edith Sitwell and Charlotte Mew, who, though she had published only one collection by that time, was probably the leading woman poet in Britain. Poems like 'The Farmer's Bride' and 'In Nunhead Cemetery' continue today to hold a deserved place in anthologies. Sitwell admired Mew's writings, but found her reserve and her state of mind impenetrable: 'What a grey tragic woman – about sixty in point of age, and sucked dry of blood (though not of spirit) by poverty and an arachnoid mother. I tried to get her to come and see me, but she is a hermit, inhabited by a terrible bitterness, and though she was very nice to me, she wouldn't come.'[5] Two years later, Sitwell wrote of an expanded edition of Mew's poems: 'she is utterly un-selfconscious, and she never spares herself; there is no self-protective weakness in her.'[6] Sitwell wrote several more times in praise of Charlotte Mew, whose personal life grew ever more sorrowful. Following the death of a beloved sister, she committed suicide in 1928 by drinking Lysol. By the 1950s, Sitwell changed her mind about Mew and said she had been 'trying to be nice' when she praised her.[7] Sitwell's tastes in poetry became much more definite in later years, but she also became more defensive of her own position as Britain's leading woman poet of the twentieth century.

The pre-eminent woman novelist of Sitwell's generation was, of course, Virginia Woolf. She wrote a review of *Clowns' Houses*, com-plimenting Sitwell for the honesty of her images and for not caring if they seemed outlandish, but she also criticised her for repeating favourite adjectives and similes. Woolf remarked: 'Miss Sitwell owes a great deal to modern painters and until her optic nerve has ceased to be dazzled it is difficult to say how interesting her vision is.' The review appeared, unsigned, in the *Times Literary Supplement* on 10 October 1918. By chance, Woolf had just met Osbert and Sachie, and they invited her to a dinner party at Osbert's house at Swan Walk on the very day the review appeared. It is not certain whether Edith knew she had written it, but this seems to be their first meeting.

Woolf noted in her diary: 'Edith Sitwell is a very tall young woman, wearing a permanently startled expression, and curiously finished off with a high green silk head-dress, concealing her hair, so that it is not known whether she has any.'[8] At the end of her life, Sitwell recalled Woolf's appearance more poetically: 'Virginia Woolf had a moonlit transparent beauty. She was exquisitely carved, with large thoughtful eyes that held no foreshadowing of that tragic end which was a grief to everyone who had ever known her. To be in her company was delight-ful. She enjoyed each butterfly aspect of the world and of the moment, and would chase the lovely creatures, but without damaging the dust on their wings.'[9]

On the evening they met, Woolf got straight to the point: '"Why do you live where you do?" "Because I have not much money." "How much money a year have you?" I told her. "Oh well, I think we can do better for you than that."'[10] Woolf thought Sitwell interesting enough to deserve the sort of project that eventually lifted T. S. Eliot out of Lloyd's Bank and into the job of poetry editor at Faber & Faber. Nothing like that happened for Edith Sitwell, but she did establish a complicated friendship with Woolf, at once intimate and competitive.

Few of Sitwell's statements have been so widely quoted as one to the critic Geoffrey Singleton in 1955: 'Virginia Woolf, I enjoyed talking to her, but thought nothing of her writing. I considered her "a beautiful little knitter"'[11] – an odd expression to the effect that Woolf's fiction was precious and on a small scale. Sitwell once boasted of herself to Robert Graves: 'though I shouldn't say so, I'm a very good knitter.'[12] It was the one domestic task she mastered – so perhaps the term had other resonances for her. Nonetheless, in the description of Woolf's 'moonlit' beauty quoted above she makes no comment on her fiction. In 1930, Sitwell had written: 'you are one of the only living writers whom I can read with joy and perpetual astonishment and satisfaction, and the fact that you like my poems makes me proud and happy'.[13] In the mid-1930s she wrote in a newspaper article: 'The fool is out of fashion, and now we have women succeeding in practically every profession . . . We have numerous admirable, witty, and incisive novelists, headed by that great stylist, Mrs. Virginia Woolf.'[14] On another occasion, she wrote, 'It is silly . . . to underrate Mrs. Woolf because she does not bellow like a bull.'[15] It is possible that throughout the earlier years she had been trying to make herself believe in a friend's gifts and finally gave up on the effort in old age. She may even have been influenced in this by her younger friends Evelyn Waugh and Graham Greene who thought little of Woolf. Yet as seems also to have happened with her views of Charlotte Mew, Sitwell probably grew tired of sharing honours. As we shall see, there were changes in Sitwell's outlook in her last decade that force us to take her opinions and recollections with an extra grain of salt.

In late 1918, Osbert Sitwell became co-editor, with Herbert Read, of the short-lived quarterly *Arts and Letters*, a venture in which he had the backing of Arnold Bennett and Sydney Schiff, a wealthy translator and novelist who wrote under the pseudonym Stephen Hudson. Herbert Read was a poet, an art critic, and a socialist. Edith Sitwell was charmed by him. A frequent visitor to Moscow Road, Read remembered making omelettes for her.[16] It is suggested that Sitwell had a crush on Read and that she received the news of his marriage in August 1919 with stony silence – perhaps. Yet a close friendship with Read was probably never on the cards. Although he was much loved by his male friends, his biographer says that he 'saw women as controlling and punitive'.[17] The sculptor and painter John Skeaping, who made some of Sitwell's amber jewellery, described a conversation with her in the late 1920s: 'about intellectualism in art, one of my pet hates, I mentioned the name of Herbert Read. "That crashing bore," she said, and went on, "Sachie and I went to dinner with him some weeks ago, passing a long and tiresome evening. Finally, I said to Herbert, 'We really must be going now, our last bus goes at 12.30 and we daren't miss it', whereupon Herbert looked at his watch and said: 'But Edith, it's only 9.15'".'[18] A few years later, Read managed to irritate Sitwell with his book reviews at much the same time as she was tangling with F. R. Leavis, prompting her to write: 'The attitude shown by some of the newer critics of poetry towards that art is deeply reminiscent of a dear old country clergyman preaching a sermon on the Woman Taken in Adultery. Now Professor Herbert Read will never be a dear old clergyman, but I do perceive ominous signs that he may, if he is not very careful, become a young curate.'[19] Nevertheless, over many years she maintained an affection and respect for him.

From the beginning of 1919, Edith Sitwell spent a great deal of time with Marguerite Bennett (née Soulié), the wife of Arnold Bennett. Born in Paris in 1874, and thus close in age to Helen Rootham, she had carved out an odd niche in literary London as a professional reciter of French poetry. Sitwell was enthralled by her performances and invited her to a musical evening at Pembridge Mansions on 11 February – one of Helen's Wednesdays. Sitwell said that Helen would be singing 'some marvellous Van Dieren songs, also some by a new (and very good) composer called de Mérey. It would be such a great pleasure if you and Mr. Bennett would come.'[20]

Sitwell received an invitation to give a lecture on 17 March to the 'Lend a Hand Guild' at Lady Baring's House in Cadogan Square. She proposed to speak on modern English poetry and the influence on it of French poetry. She asked Marguerite Bennett to recite in illustration of the lecture, and so began a three-year collaboration. Soon they established the Anglo-French Poetry Society. Arnold Bennett was the nominal president, and the managing committee consisted of Marguerite Bennett, Edith Sitwell, and Helen Rootham. The plan was to hold meetings about once a month in whatever drawing room Edith could lay hold of and from time to time to rent a large hall. A form letter declared their intention to 'combine recitals of poetry (both English and French) and causeries, which will be varied by music of the period. There will be occasional readings at which poets will read their own verses.' An indication of how seriously Bennett and Sitwell took the art of recitation is found in this statement: 'All reciters will be trained, as the object of the Society is to make the recital of poetry a pleasure both to the reciter and to the audience.'[21]

An inaugural meeting was held at Bennett's house at 12B George Street, Hanover Square, and a preliminary list of members included Siegfried Sassoon, Mrs Bernard Shaw, H. Granville Barker, Gordon Bottomley, Marie Belloc Lowndes, W. H. Davies, Frederick Delius, André Gide, John Galsworthy, Ralph Hodgson, Gustav Holst, Valery Larbaud, Walter de la Mare, Vita Sackville-West, Francis Poulenc, Maurice Ravel, and Hugh Walpole.[22] Doubtless some of these paid their guinea's subscription and lent their names just to help a good cause. However, for a time the Society was a going concern. Sitwell and Bennett found several young women, mainly actresses, willing to declaim in the approved manner. Meanwhile, they simply bore with the unimproved reading styles of Robert Graves and W. H. Davies, who were among the poets invited to read their own works.

Sitwell and Bennett became a double act. Sitwell said in one of her lectures to the Society:

Whenever I am asked to speak about English poetry, I have to speak about French poetry too, so that I can worry Mrs. Arnold Bennett to recite. When I first met Mrs. Bennett I was under the impression (quite well-founded) that I was absolutely steeped in the magic of French poetry. So I was . . . But . . . well the things Mrs. Bennett's recitations have taught me about rhythm, to speak only of the technical side of her wonderful art; the things I have learnt about the elasticity of dactylic measures, (the Alexandrine, for instance). This measure can spread itself like a peacock's tail, can have the deadly

suavity and curl of [a] rattlesnake, or can move with the pomp of a
wave that is just going to break into spray. I believe if Mrs. Bennett
were English instead of French and were to recite Byron's poor old
'The Assyrian came down like a wolf on the fold' we might even find
out there was something to be said for the poem.[23]

The Fifth Cycle of *Wheels* appeared in October 1920, dedicated to
Mrs Arnold Bennett, 'Poetry's Greatest Interpretative Artist'. The
friendship continued happily through 1921. In August, Sitwell invited
the Bennetts to join her family and Siegfried Sassoon at Renishaw:
'This is a lovely house, (and what a perfect place to hear you recite in:
it is absolutely made for Samain's "Silence"); we have got rid of the
ghosts; since Helen's encounter with them, we've not heard a sound or
seen anything of them.' The Bennetts could not come, so in December
Sitwell proposed that she and Marguerite travel to Paris at Easter, closing the letter, *'Je vous embrasse.'*

By April, however, the tone had changed. One of the reciters chosen
by Bennett, Marjorie Gabain of the Old Vic, had complained about a
programme that included some of Helen's translations of Rimbaud.
Sitwell wrote to Bennett that Gabain had made herself 'ridiculous'.

A caricature of Edith Sitwell by Siegfried Sassoon. They had a close friendship in the
1920s and 1930s, and the critic Sir Edmund Gosse suggested they should marry

Bennett then complained about Rootham's notions of art. Sitwell
retorted: 'I don't know why you thought you dared write such a letter
about Helen to me. Your spiteful impertinence merely throws a most
unpleasant light upon yourself. Conceit about any form of art is really
the last thing Helen can be accused of! As for her art, I do not choose
to discuss Helen's art with you.'

Things were patched up enough for the Society to limp on for a
few more meetings, but it was soon disbanded. From time to time Edith
Sitwell was genuinely reconciled to friends with whom she quarrelled,
but on this occasion the circumstances were against it. Marguerite
and Arnold Bennett had recently separated, and Marguerite passed
out of the Sitwells' world. Though Edith Sitwell saw much less of
him, Arnold Bennett was unshaken in his view of her poetry. He wrote
in April 1922: 'Valery Larbaud once astonished and delighted me
by stating, quite on his own, that the most accomplished of all the
younger British poets was Edith Sitwell; a true saying, though I had
said it before him.'[24] In 1930, Bennett grouped Edith Sitwell with James
Joyce and William Faulkner as 'originators' in literature (Evening Standard,
12 June 1930).

Domestic life was taking a sad turn in the last years of the decade.
In 1914, Helen Rootham had pulled Sitwell out of the water. However,
by the end of the war it was harder for them to live together. As an old
woman (and, we have to remember, a cantankerous one), Sitwell
recalled that 'suddenly, life rotted. Helen, a wonderful friend to me
when I was a child and young girl, seemed to become semi-poisoned by
the smell of money, and a silly wish to "get into society".' She wrote a
pen-portrait of Helen, then tore the pages from a draft of her memoir,
but she missed one telling phrase intended as an insertion: 'as she
always believed, (she used to cry when any coarse person said she had
been my governess.)'[25] If true, this makes it easier to understand Helen's
position. Among aristocrats, artists, and intellectuals, she was touchy
because she did not want to be thought of as a servant. But Sitwell felt
that Rootham actually became 'more and more the governess and less
and less of a friend'. She criticised Sitwell for being untidy – a reasonable complaint since her music students came to the flat – and she
policed Sitwell's dealings with men.

Part of the problem was that Helen never fulfilled her great ambitions as a singer. On 1 April 1914, she appeared at Steinway Hall in a programme sponsored by the Society of Women Musicians.[26] On 9 November 1916, she sang pieces by Ravel, Duparc, and Debussy at the Aeolian Hall, as well as old English tunes arranged by Cyril Scott, which a critic thought over-elaborated: 'But some people enjoy the unexpected; in fact, they seem to be prepared to stand anything by way of harmonic combination. It is a mark of superiority.'[27] On 13 November 1917, she sang a programme of songs by Roger Quilter and her cousin Cyril Rootham at the Aeolian Hall; *The Times* (14 November 1917) remarked on her 'stately style of singing'. In October 1918, she was to sing Serbian folk songs in a benefit for the Serbian Red Cross; this may be the occasion when she had a bout of nerves and could not perform, leaving the pianist to carry the whole concert.[28] On 21 April 1920 she appeared in Nottingham with the pianist Eric Paul May; she sang traditional airs such as 'O Death, Rock Me to Sleep' and won the reviewer's faint praise: 'An appropriate simplicity of style distinguished the vocalist's contributions.'[29] There were doubtless other performances, but this was not the level of success she had once hoped for. It is likely that she was frustrated.

The unravelling of a close friendship can be every bit as complicated as a divorce, and in this case most of the evidence comes from one side, with the effect that Helen Rootham is always seen as a pill. She was unpopular among Sitwell's friends. When Richard Aldington asked T. S. Eliot in November 1921 whether Sitwell could help start his sister's musical career, he responded that the only way to get that help would be for his sister to take lessons from Rootham, 'an appalling woman who trains and launches young singers'.[30] Aldington decided to give it a try. Sitwell wrote to Robert Graves not long after, 'Richard Aldington's sister is shouting scales at the top of her voice next door. It is a lovely voice, and she has got a small part in the Rosenkavalier, (she is a pupil of Helen's).'[31]

When Harold Acton spoke to the biographer John Pearson, he tried to do justice to Helen Rootham's memory: 'True she was rather dreary and intense – the essential hysterical intellectual spinster, don't you know, – but she was something of a rebel. She believed in the modern movement. She had read Verlaine and Rimbaud, and she was just what Edith needed to be able to make the break from Renishaw. She'd never,

never have done it on her own.'[32] Yet this places the benefit to Sitwell in the early period of the relationship, leaving just dreariness for the later years. And his notions of hysteria and spinsterhood still muddy the waters.

Even by Sitwellian standards of eccentricity Helen was an odd person. The exorcism she performed at Renishaw was part of a deepening involvement with spirits. Sitwell recalled Rootham being obsessed by dreams and visions: 'There was one that interested her profoundly. She saw two Beings, lying side by side. Suddenly, out of one Being, issued something that might have been a huge leaf, or might have been a great flame of fire, and this deliberately entered the other Being.' She thought it must have a meaning, so she described it to 'all the young males of my acquaintance, and enquired, "Do you know what it means?" They said they did.'

Although Catholic, Helen Rootham was drawn to esoteric religion, especially anthroposophy. A movement led by Rudolf Steiner, it had recently broken with the main Theosophical movement largely over the role of the young Jiddu Krishnamurti, whom Annie Besant and C. W. Leadbetter were grooming as a 'world teacher'. Years later, Sitwell described Rootham's interest in anthroposophy to, of all people, Marilyn Monroe:

> We talked mainly, as far as I remember, about Rudolf Steiner, whose works [Monroe] had just been reading. At one time Helen Rootham was most interested in Steiner, with the result that I found myself, one evening, watching what I believe was known as a Nature-Dance (something uniting one, I expect, with Mother Earth) in which ladies of only too certain an age galloped with large bare dusty feet over an uncarpeted floor. I do not know that this exhibition could be ascribed to Dr. Steiner, but it seemed to have something to do with Higher Thought, and I am afraid that Miss Monroe and I could not resist laughing about it.[33]

Presumably, Sitwell had attended a session of eurythmy, the movement art promoted by Steiner for its spiritual, educational, and curative powers. Although she mocks this dance, she avoids mocking Steiner himself, whose ideas had some impact on her poetry.

Towards the end of the war Rootham made friends with some refugees from what was later known as Yugoslavia. According to Sitwell, they convinced her that in a former life she had been their Princess Yelena 'who, singlehanded, had thrown the Turks out of wherever they happened to be at the moment'. Rootham became absorbed with the plight of the South Slavs, as many people were. Readers of *Brideshead Revisited* will recall that Charles Ryder's mother went as a nurse to Bosnia and died there. Helen Rootham translated traditional ballads describing the Battle of Kosovo in 1389 in which Serbia lost its freedom. The poems present the heroic figures of Tsar Lazar and Jug Bogdan, and his nine sons the Jugovitch, all slaughtered in the name of Christ and Serbia in an epic struggle against the Turks. In the 1990s, these same poems were seized upon by some Serbian nationalists to justify a programme of ethnic cleansing in Kosovo.

Rootham's interest in them likely derived from the Croat Ivan Meštrović, a friend of Rodin. His monumental carvings of warriors from the Kosovo cycle appeared in an exhibition at the Victoria and Albert Museum in the summer of 1915. Although criticised by Pound and Wyndham Lewis, Meštrović's work won many admirers, including Robert Ross, who nonetheless remarked that one carving added 'incest to injury'.[34] There were other exhibitions of his work at the Grafton Gallery, Twenty-One Gallery, and the City Art Gallery in Leeds.[35] The sculptures created a demand for a new English version of the ballads. Helen Rootham was probably guided by Janko Lavrin, a Slovene who became Professor of Slavonic Studies at the University of Nottingham. Lavrin provided a historical preface for the volume that appeared from Blackwell's in 1920.[36]

Rootham also came under the influence of the poet and pseudo-mystic Dimitrije Mitrinović, who, his friend Lavrin thought, had 'a home-made messiah-complex' and relished the role of saviour.[37] The poet Edwin Muir described him as 'a tall, dark, bullet-headed Serbian with the lips of a Roman soldier and an erratic, soaring mind'.[38] Indeed, he may well have been the religious teacher to whom Helen was engaged from about 1920, but no document confirms this. He appeared in England at the right time and was unmarried. Sitwell described the fiancé as a friend of the poet Alan Porter, a stalwart of the Adler Society for the promotion of individual psychology, an outfit actually founded by Mitrinović in the mid-1920s. Sitwell also called him a 'bad painter'; while there is no record of Mitrinović being a painter, he was constantly in the company of artists and probably dabbled. He certainly wrote about painting.[39] Although he was primarily Helen's find, Edith Sitwell too fell under his sway, although she later thought him a fraud. She inscribed a copy of her *Bucolic Comedies* (1923): 'For Mr. D. Mitrinović with hommage [sic] and with unending gratitude from his pupil Edith Sitwell.'[40]

Before the war, Mitrinović had inspired and organised South Slav nationalists in their struggles against the Austro-Hungarian empire. It is claimed that he opposed violence, but his ideas contributed materially to the outbreak of war. In 1910, one of his associates proposed to assassinate Emperor Franz Josef; a second tried to kill General Marijan Varesanin and had to shoot himself with his last bullet. In 1912, a soon-to-be-famous man enthusiastically endorsed Mitrinović's revolutionary programme: Gavrilo Princeps, who killed the Archduke Franz Ferdinand and his wife on 28 June 1914.[41]

In 1913, Mitrinović went as a student to Munich where he befriended the painter Wassily Kandinski, who theorised on abstract art. They both became part of the 'Blutbund' or blood brotherhood, a short-lived organisation of cultural leaders, among them the philosopher Martin Buber and the novelist Upton Sinclair. Their modest objective was to unify the human race and to lift it out of materialism. When war broke out, Mitrinović hurried to London and took a position in the Serbian legation. He championed the work of Meštrović, and came to be regarded as a fashionable guru. His chief British disciple and collaborator was Philippe Mairet, the draughtsman and critic to whom Eliot dedicated 'Notes towards the Definition of Culture' (1948).[42] Mairet was also a friend of Rootham's.[43] In the mid-1920s, Mitrinović founded the Adler Society, and at different times advocated Social Credit, guild socialism, and communal living.[44]

Mitrinović's ways of thinking were messy by choice, and his obsession was to show synthesis, a spiritual unity underlying all reality: 'We require only a philosophy that sings its own system, a science that wishes us good, a plasticity that is symphony, a portrait that is a novel; and we need a great music that is a performed religion, a poetry that is metaphysics, a dancing that is a philosophical thesis, and an acting that is social revolution . . . For whoever has anything to say to us moderns must speak not with the intellect but with song, with symbol, with paradox and intuition. To think in concepts is altogether too academic.'[45] He happily collapses one category into another on his way to Utopia.

By early 1916, Rootham was working on a translation of Rimbaud that she hoped to have published as a book in the autumn of that year. It did not appear in its entirety until 1932, although selections appeared before that. It is believed by some that Sitwell collaborated on this work without taking credit.[46] In addition to her contributions to *Wheels* and the translations of Serbian ballads, Rootham tried her hand at short fiction, producing a glum tale about a puppet-like woman dying on a park bench.[47] In December 1918, she contributed a poem, 'The Two Old Beggars of Bayswater Road', to the *New Age*, a journal that featured most of the important modernist writers at one time or another. Its editor, the charismatic A. R. Orage, was a Nietzschean, a socialist, and (like Ezra Pound) an advocate for Social Credit. He published essays by Steiner and Mitrinović, and was himself influenced, at different times, by P. D. Ouspensky and Gurdjieff. Though cranky, the journal was receptive to new ideas, and it suited Helen Rootham perfectly.

Orage published some of her Serbian translations, including five poems by the contemporary Symbolist poet Jovan Dučić.[48] In late 1921, she became the journal's music critic. Apart from displaying her expertise, these columns are the only evidence that she had a sense of humour. She remarked that 'the Albert Hall is not a place calculated to inspire noble feelings on any subject whatsoever.'[49] Of Stravinsky's bleak *Symphonies d'instruments à vent*, intended to be played without expression or inflection, she wrote: 'The result is a cold, acrid blare of sound, with edges as jagged as a split iceberg, and a rhythm which is as comfortable and reassuring as the swaying of a polar bear. Indeed, Monday's performance rather resembled an attempt to brighten up the North Pole with a very big megaphone and a gas fire.'[50]

Edith Sitwell followed Rootham into the *New Age* as the result of a row. In a review of the Fifth Cycle of *Wheels* in April 1921, Edwin Muir described Osbert's poems as the work of a craftsman but not an artist, and Sacheverell's as those of an artist but not a craftsman – actually an astute judgment. Osbert's poems are always ably cobbled together – and forgettable. Sacheverell, at his best, is luminous, but he is uneven to a startling degree. As Muir put it, Sacheverell's poems can alternate between 'incompetence' and 'the grace of nature itself'. That judgment remained true. Over a long career, Sacheverell Sitwell failed to select among his work, so that a superb talent lies unnoticed among the rubble of many poems – a situation that might yet be remedied by a short selected volume of his best work.

Muir wrote: 'Miss Edith Sitwell is more tantalising and more prolific in good lines than ever. Her apparent perversity of expression is really a form of wit; a cross between Meredith and the Queen of Spades. She appears to be writing more and more a sort of "Alice in Hell".'[51] However, he preferred her 'limpid and crystalline images' to those he thought 'overcharged'. Unable to see Edwin Muir as a plain-spoken friend to their work, the three Sitwells appeared at Orage's office, Edith threatening a libel suit. Orage countered that she should write for him. The libel suit evaporated, and by June she was contributing prose and verse to the magazine.[52] Muir remained the poetry reviewer, and continued to speak his mind, especially about Sacheverell, whom he later called 'the poet most gifted by nature and by art that has appeared since Mr. W. B. Yeats'.[53]

Helen Rootham left the *New Age* in August 1923. She continued to write about music, but never again with humour. In her lethal book, *Fundamentals of Music and their Relation to Modern Life* (1925), she offered theories about 'That Something, the spiritual and convincing Something – the touch, the breath, the quality of psychic presence, of divinity, in the works of genuine art'. As an anthroposophist, she attempted to show a literal convergence of art, science and the sacred. She could also collapse categories just as Mitrinović did in his quest for synthesis: 'I feel intuitively certain that the impression of sound upon the heart – and the heart is the psychic receiver and judge within all human beings – is an impression equivalent to the calorific impression . . . of heat and cold upon the sense of feeling.'[54] Edith Sitwell, always a synaesthetic poet, later absorbed some of Rootham's ideas into 'The Song of the Cold' and other works. Whereas Rootham sees heat and cold as literally connected to spiritual states, Sitwell makes them

into symbols and manages them with an elegance her friend could not
approach:

> But the great sins and fires break out of me
> Like the terrible leaves from the bough in the violent spring . . .
> I am a walking fire, I am all leaves –
> I will cry to the Spring to give me the birds' and the serpents'
>   speech
> That I may weep for those who die of the cold –
> The ultimate cold within the heart of man.[55]

11

TOO FANTASTIC FOR FAT-HEADS

The world grows furry, grunts with sleep . . .
But I must on the surface keep.
The jolting of the train to me
Seems some primeval vertebrae
Attached by life-nerves to my brain –
Reactionary once again,
So that I see shapes crude and new
And ordered, – with some end in view,
No longer with the horny eyes
Of other people's memories.
Through highly varnished yellow heat,
As through a lens that does not fit,
The faces jolt in cubes, and I
Perceive their odd solidity
And lack of meaning absolute [. . .][1]

Published by Basil Blackwell on 26 June 1920, *The Wooden Pegasus*,
a collection of poems mainly from the preceding two years but with
some earlier pieces, was a pivotal book for Edith Sitwell. By now, she
had sharply defined the theme of her poetry: deceived by customary or
inherited ways of seeing the world, most of us have no identity at all
and live, rather, in a hellish puppet show. Human beings and landscapes are repeatedly described as 'wooden' to emphasise their role in
the 'Comedy for Marionettes'. Her poetry is centred on a puppeteer's
booth on the Scarborough sands – a world made with hammer and
nails:

> I, painted like the wooden sun,
> Must hand-in-hand with angels run –
> The tinsel angels of the booth.[2]

Jules Laforgue wrote about puppets, and his work is one of the inspirations for this phase of Sitwell's poetry. Stock characters of *commedia dell'arte* also appear frequently in the collection, among them, the farcical Scaramouche who figures also in Punch and Judy shows, the miser Pantalone and the pedantic Il Dottore, both *vecchi* or old ones who stand opposed to the happiness of the young lovers or *innamorati*. The image of a generation frustrated or betrayed by its elders captured Sitwell's sense of the Great War and of her own family's disasters. The power of the elders lay in shaping the perceptions of the young, making them see the world as they do. For Sitwell, the object is to disorganise these inherited perceptions, so in two poems she writes from the perspective of one of the fairground animals – an observant ape. A sequence of 'Seven Nursery Songs' attempts, however ironically, to capture the spiritual vitality of the child and oppose it to the notions of the elders. Among these poems is one of her most popular:

> The King of China's daughter,
> She never would love me
> Though I hung my cap and bells upon
> Her nutmeg tree.
> For oranges and lemons,
> The stars in bright blue air,
> (I stole them long ago, my dear)
> Were dangling there.
> The Moon did give me silver pence,
> The Sun did give me gold,
> And both together softly blew
> And made my porridge cold;
> But the King of China's daughter
> Pretended not to see
> When I hung my cap and bells upon
> Her nutmeg tree.[3]

Given the drift of the whole collection, it would be a mistake to regard
this poem as merely 'pretty' – a condescending term that Geoffrey
Grigson applied to Sitwell's early work, having dismissed all the later
poems.[4] The point Sitwell is making about youth, age, and culture
needs at times to be shouted – as in 'Solo for Ear-Trumpet', where she
visits a rich relation who remains impervious even to the Second
Coming:

> Down the horn
> Of her ear-trumpet I convey
> The news that: 'It is Judgment Day!'
> 'Speak louder; I don't catch, my dear.'
> I roared: 'It is the Trump we hear!'
> 'The What?' – 'The TRUMP!' . . . 'I shall complain –
> The boy-scouts practising again!'[5]

Aldous Huxley was thrilled by *The Wooden Pegasus*. He wrote in the
Athenæum (9 July 1920): 'Fixedly, intently she focuses the figures on
the stage until they assume a peculiar significance, not their own, but
derived from the very intentness with which they are viewed. Reality
takes on the strange nightmarish qualities of hallucination.' He
believed that her methods produced 'interesting and often fantastically
beautiful results'.

As she was writing some of the poems that appeared in this book,
Edith Sitwell became swept up in Sacheverell's devotion to the Ballets
Russes, which had returned to London in September 1918. He became
a friend of Sergei Diaghilev, the impresario who commissioned works
by Rimsky-Korsakov, Debussy, Prokofiev, and Stravinsky, and was the
close friend of Nijinsky through his best years until they had a falling-
out in 1913. When she was old, Edith Sitwell claimed that ballet bored
the pants off her,[6] but that was not always the case.

Her short book *Children's Tales (From the Russian Ballet)* appeared in
November 1920, hailing the arrival of Russian ballet in England, but
it also took readers, incidentally, on a tour of the imagery of her recent
poems. Her rhapsodic introduction remarks on how the British had
been galvanised by music halls: 'we move somnambulantly through this
mirror-bright world, and cling into some mournful patterning; while

the harsh mordant music strips off our flesh and shows us, marionettes that we are, clothed only in our primal lust. Performing animals mimic our tricks, our poor impertinences against the Infinite, much as we mimic those of a higher order of being.'[7]

The Russian ballet offers something different, which Sitwell calls a 'philosophy': 'Seen with the clearness of a dream, these bright magical movements have, now the intense vitality of the heart of life, now the rigidity of death; and for speech they have the more universal and larger language of music, interpreting still more clearly these strange beings whose life is so intense, yet to whom living, seen from the outside, is but a brief and tragic happiness upon the greenest grass, in some unknown flashing summer weather.' Above all, she is absorbed in *Petrouchka* (1911), the ballet Igor Stravinsky wrote for the Ballets Russes about a puppet that comes to life: here 'in the loneliness of identity' we watch the images and ideas of Laforgue acted out 'as the puppets move somnambulantly through the dark of our hearts. For this ballet, alone among them all, shatters our glass house about our ears and leaves us terrified, haunted by its tragedy. The music, harsh crackling rags of laughter, shrieks at us like some brightly painted Punch and Judy show.'[8]

Following the British debut of *Le Sacre du Printemps* at the Queen's Hall on 7 June 1921, Sitwell returned to these ideas in an essay about Igor Stravinsky for the *New Age*: 'He is, I honestly believe, the most important living artist of any kind whatsoever . . . he knows that every sight, touch, sound, smell, of the world we live in, has its meaning – is the result of a spiritual state (as a great philosopher said to me), is, in short, a kind of psycho-analysis. And he can interpret those meanings to us.' The great philosopher is Mitrinović and Sitwell is praising Stravinsky for his approach to 'synthesis'. She describes *Petrouchka* in language that anticipates her poetry after 1940, as 'a warning of the ultimate darkness. How well this piercing and undeceivable genius knows that the modern world is but a thin matchboard flooring spread over a shallow hell. For to him Dante's hell has faded, and Lucifer, son of the morning, is dead. Hell is no vastness; there are no more devils who weep, or who laugh – only the maimed dwarfs of this life, terrible straining mechanisms, crouching in trivial sands, and laughing at the giants' crumbling.'[9]

Though ten years younger than Edith, Sachie was her guide to the ballet. Even as a young man, he was extraordinarily perceptive about the arts. Demobbed, he went up to Balliol College, Oxford, in early 1919 and stayed for just two terms among serious-minded ex-soldiers. While there, he made the friendship of the sixteen-year-old William Walton and became convinced of his genius. Before long, Walton, who kept failing examinations at Oxford, became a regular visitor at the brothers' house at Swan Walk. Osbert and Sacheverell brought him to Italy in the spring of 1920, after which he settled in as a kind of third brother in a house in Carlyle Square that Osbert took on a long lease. The Sitwells fended off all advice that Walton should study at the Royal Conservatory. Instead, he made his own way as a composer, and in late 1921 became Edith's collaborator.

As she recalled, Façade began as a dare: 'Willie gave me certain rhythms and said, "There you are, Edith, see what you can do with that."' Walton's recollection was somewhat different. He told John Pearson that the idea for a collaboration came entirely from Edith. Although her poems cried out to be set, he did not want to take them on. Osbert and Sacheverell said they would bring in Constant Lambert, then a student at the Royal College of Music, to do the job if he refused, so of course he capitulated. As he recalled, Edith had already written a good number of the poems, including 'Hornpipe'; 'Popular Song' was the only one he could remember having started her on. It is commonly thought that most of Façade was written between 1921 and 1923. In fact, the first performed version contained sixteen poems, of which ten had already been published. Façade grew not just by the addition of new poems, but by the inclusion of old ones, among them 'Clowns' Houses', of which she wrote the first version in 1914. By the time her Collected Poems of 1930 came out, the sequence had twenty-seven poems, and she continued to fold early poems into the sequence. A version from 1950 has thirty-three, and another, in her final Collected Poems of 1957, thirty-seven. Sitwell's work on Façade went on for more than forty years.[10]

Nevertheless, the years 1921–23 were an extraordinary time for Edith Sitwell's poetry. When he was himself about to turn eighty, Sacheverell remembered those days:

How Max Beerbohm saw Osbert and Sacheverell Sitwell in 1923

Let me hear the barrel-organ
      that played on Saturday afternoons in Moscow Road,
It matters not how banal the tune:
Let it be 'When Irish eyes are smiling',
      and I am back with you
On a blazing June evening in 1921 or 1922.
There seemed to be a new poem of yours
      to read to us,
Almost every time we came to see you,
And climbed the four double-flights of stone stairs
      up to your flat: –
Poems in a vein of fantasy
      invented for yourself,
And all your own,
      like nothing before or since.
[. . .]
They make for themselves a little niche in time
      that I have tried to halt for a moment
On a hot June evening in Bayswater all those years ago,

So that you can hear her happy laughter in her poems,
    and see her as I have often written of her,
Long and thin and tall and aquiline,
    like no one we will ever see again: –
Before we throw down a coin
    from the window
And the barrel-organ moves on
    into receding time[11]

When she came to explain the poems she wrote in this period, Edith
Sitwell spoke of them as a musician would, as 'virtuoso exercises in technique of an extreme difficulty'. She had little to say about the meaning
of the marionettes, the fairgrounds, the glimpses of hell, but she did
want to explain that the poems in *Façade* were 'abstract' in that they
were 'patterns of sound' – her comments lean in the direction of pure
formalism. The rhythms of poetry had gone dead in the preceding generation and needed reviving: 'My experiments in *Façade* consist of
inquiries into the effect on rhythm and on speed of the use of rhymes,
assonances, and dissonances, placed at the beginning and in the middle
of lines, as well as at the end, and in most elaborate patterns. I experimented, too, with the effect upon speed of the use of equivalent
syllables – a system that produces great variation.'[12] What she was talking about is perhaps best seen in the concluding poem of the sequence:

When
Sir
Beelzebub called for his syllabub in the hotel in Hell
Where Proserpine first fell,
Blue as the gendarmerie were the waves of the sea,
(Rocking and shocking the bar-maid).
Nobody comes to give him his rum but the
Rim of the sky hippopotamus-glum
Enhances the chances to bless with a benison
Alfred Lord Tennyson crossing the bar laid
With cold vegetation from pale deputations
Of temperance workers (all signed In Memoriam)
Hoping with glory to trip up the Laureate's feet,

(Moving in classical metres) . . .
Like Balaclava, the lava came down from the
Roof, and the sea's blue wooden gendarmerie
Took them in charge while Beelzebub, roared for his rum.
. . . None of them come!

This glimpse of hell in a hotel and Beelzebub in a baronet takes up the
imagery of *The Wooden Pegasus* and adds a comical slap at Georgian
poets, who in their devotion to Tennyson have become literary tee-
totallers, signing *In Memoriam* like a pledge against modern excess – but
they are led off, presumably in cuffs, for making a tangle of Tennyson's
feet. In this deliberate tour de force, Sitwell is showing off as she treats
prosody like a keyboard. She is aiming for an effect that Sachie wrote of
in one of his biographies: 'The secret of the power and the spell of Liszt
lay in the new system that he had invented. His attack and brilliance, his
speed and his exquisite arpeggios and runs, together with the extraordinary quality of his touch, these things gave him an unfair advantage over
pianists of the old classical school.'[13] Edith Sitwell was not Liszt, but in
poems like this she was making her claim to a new kind of virtuosity.

Osbert recalls that Edith and Willie would work together in sessions
of two or three hours, reading carefully over the poems. Walton would
make note of stresses and points of special emphasis, as well as inflec-
tions. His score drew on music halls, jazz, cabaret tunes, foxtrots, the
Charleston and other popular music; he produced instrumental paro-
dies and pastiches that matched the strange ironies of Sitwell's verse.

Osbert arranged for Frank Dobson to paint a curtain, behind which
Edith would stand while reciting. It depicted three arches, and in the
centre arch was a formalised mask with fair hair and an open mouth for
the sound to pass through. There was a smaller black mask in the left
arch for Osbert, the master of ceremonies, to speak through. Since the
curtain would still muffle Edith's voice, Sachie contacted an ageing
opera singer named Senger who had patented a megaphone which,
since it was made of compressed grass, had more resonance than metal
versions; it covered the nose and mouth, making it responsive to techniques of voice production. In performance, Edith would bury her face
in the Sengerphone and poems would emerge out of the cone that protruded beyond Dobson's curtain. Osbert explained that the object was

to eliminate the personalities of the speaker and the musicians, as well as any 'constricting self-consciousness . . . We had, in short, discovered an abstract method of presenting poetry to an audience.'[14] Eventually, the availability of microphones allowed productions of *Façade* to forgo this comic touch.

POETRY THROUGH A MEGAPHONE.

ONE-NOTE CONCERT BY MISS SITWELL.

If Miss Edith Sitwell considers that the best way to recite her poems is through a megaphone in a tragic voice on one note, that is her affair. She wrote them, and ought to know best. The Æolian Hall was half filled yesterday to hear her do it.

Across the platform was stretched a curtain representing, chiefly, a piebald face, one half red, the other white. Mr. Osbert Sitwell introduced this as "Venus." Where the mouth should have been a gaping megaphone protruded. Miss Sitwell called it a sengerphone.

There were twenty-eight items on the programme, but only one note came

MISS EDITH SITWELL.

'It was Edith's char-lady who gave it the name Façade,' Walton remembered. 'She said to Edith one day – all this carry on is just one big façade, isn't it? And Edith liked it so much that she used it.'[15] Osbert put a similar comment in the mouth of a painter. In any event, as a title it captured Edith's characteristic view that our normal reality is not much more than a veneer. Moreover, the title reminded the audience, just as the curtain did, that a poem is a thing of irony and does not offer easy access to the poet's soul.

The first performance took place at Carlyle Square on the evening of 24 January 1922. As a conductor, William Walton resembled, in Osbert's eyes, a boxing kangaroo then popular in the music halls. When they saw the music on the day before, the musicians were irate. One asked in rehearsal, 'Excuse me, Mr. Walton, has a clarinet player ever done you an injury?'[16] Osbert recalled in 1949 that there had been six instruments, but he must have been thinking of the public performances of 1923. In 1976, Walton told John Pearson that the work was originally scored for three instruments, but a year later he said on the BBC that the number was four. As Neil Ritchie points out, Edith Sitwell's letters from early 1922 say that the band consisted of trumpet, clarinet, flute, drum, and cello.[17] Eighteen numbers (including the overture and interlude) were performed, of which only six were included in Walton's definitive score of 1951; however, five more reappeared in his *Façade Revived* (1977) or *Façade 2* (1979).[18]

The musicians sat under windows that reflected a world of snow outside, while the room itself was filled with light thrown back from mirrors and from the many glass objects that Osbert collected. The curtain was placed in front of a set of double doors. The audience sat tightly packed in rows of narrow gold chairs. In this small space, the sound was overwhelming. Osbert recalls that the poets and artists received the new work enthusiastically but the more orthodox guests were 'perturbed' – they settled down when the rum punch was served. Eva Mathias, a patron of the Ballets Russes, was excited by the whole performance and invited them to give another at her house in Montagu Square on 7 February; the music was less daunting in the larger space, but it is likely that few of those present grasped what Edith Sitwell and William Walton were up to. When she had finished her reciting at Mathias's house, Sitwell, overcome by nerves, nearly fainted.[19]

A volume of the poems was printed by the Favril Press in February, and won a war-whoop from Siegfried Sassoon, who reviewed it in the *Daily Herald* (24 May 1922) under the title, 'Too Fantastic for Fat-Heads': 'As a composer of fantastical verse Miss Sitwell is fully aware of her own limitations. This is only another way

of saying that she is a first-class writer.' Sassoon then took a shot at
cowardly anthologists:

> If after reading the following lines ['Herodiade'] you disagree with
> me, I recommend you to wait thirty years and peruse the poem in Sir
> Joshua Jebb's Anthology [published in 1951]. You will then be safe
> to enjoy it automatically, unless you have passed into coffin or cre-
> matorium . . . All fantastic art is 'nonsense' until we have got over
> our astonishment. Miss Sitwell's originality has affinities with
> Aubrey Beardsley. 'But Beardsley was an obscene artist!' shrieks some
> fat-headed critic of Miss Sitwell's 'asylum poetry.' The answer is that
> Aubrey Beardsley was a great artist, and, as such, has triumphed over
> all the fat-heads of his day. Miss Sitwell will do the same.

There was still a great deal of work to do on *Façade*, and Sitwell was
short of time and money. The Anglo-French Poetry Society was about
to disintegrate, and *Wheels* had made its last turn in November 1921.
The first four Cycles had been published by Blackwell, and the fifth by
Leonard Parsons. However, at the beginning of August, Parsons
dropped the anthology. Working through an agent named Moore
(probably Leonard Moore, who later represented George Orwell), she
was able to get C. W. Daniel to publish the Sixth.[20] She blamed J. C.
Squire, a Georgian poet and the editor of the *London Mercury*, for
Wheels' ultimate demise. She wrote to the French poet and translator
Valery Larbaud on 10 March 1922: 'I have been having a *terrible* time,
what with the boycott on the part of the Squire-controlled press, and
the insults on the part of the press which is not so controlled. Publishers
will no longer take my work unless I pay for it; and I shall be obliged to
discontinue "Wheels." It is so irritating for I *know* Squire is no good as
a writer; one has only to compare him with the poets whom he imitates.
Meanwhile, he is preventing any new work obtaining a hearing in
England!'[21] It is worth noting that Sitwell, who admired W. B. Yeats,
Thomas Hardy, W. H. Davies, and Ralph Hodgson, was not against
Squire on the grounds that he was a traditional poet, but because he was
a bad one. He is best known nowadays for his dismissal of *The Waste
Land*. It has become normal for scholars to strut their fair-mindedness
by defending Squire on various small points – for example, to say that

he was a good parodist – but his obtuseness and partisanship are amply demonstrated by his anthology *A Book of Women's Verse* (1921), in which there is no poem by Edith Sitwell.

Squire was only an opponent. The year 1921 saw the arrival of a proper Enemy – Percy Wyndham Lewis, whom Sitwell called 'Perks'. She had already met him casually among the artists of the Slade School, the Camden Town Group, and the Omega Workshop, and was present with her brothers at a dinner at Verrey's restaurant in Regent Street in the summer of 1919 when Lewis, with a cigarette butt hanging from his upper lip, squinted in the drifting smoke, pencilled some numbers on a matchbox, then issued his command: 'I'm thirty-seven till I pass the word round! D'you understand?' A biographer suggests that since Lewis felt the war had ripped at least two years out of his life, he was declaring a moratorium on birthdays and planned to make his thirty-seventh the last for some time.[22] Thinking Lewis took himself a bit seriously, Sitwell wrote: 'This got on my nerves to such an extent that when told by a doctor to say "ninety-nine" I responded, invariably, "thirty-seven".' To calculate his age properly, she believed that you had to count the rings on his collar.[23]

Unstable and hard-up, Lewis counted on handouts from the Sitwells, the Schiffs, and other patrons, and was usually dodging creditors. At some point, Lewis was invited to Renishaw, where he appeared with no suitcase and his clothes in a bundle. Lady Ida remarked to Osbert: 'Your friend is a charming man, but he will have to have a pill.'[24] At the end of 1921, Lewis took a very cheap studio, with an exterior of corrugated iron, in Adam and Eve Mews in Kensington. Edith Sitwell sat to him there for several drawings and a painting. She remembered it as situated in waste ground 'haunted by pallid hens squawking desolately and prophetically'. The floor of the studio was hidden under newspapers, books, pots, pans, kettles, a teapot, tins of milk, and Lewis's discarded underwear.[25] Sitwell recalled that he believed Roger Fry and Clive Bell were always perched on the roof watching him and that there were rats lurking in the mess.

'D'you mind rats?' he asked her one day.

She said she did.

'Well, they're here all right . . . Night and day. Day and night. But I'll try to keep them off.'

He then brandished his brush and returned to the canvas. Sitwell
suggested that a Gargantuism in his way of thinking caused him to see
rats where there were only mice – in fact, there were so many mice that
he would strike a gong in front of their hole to make them retreat.
Sitwell says that she sat to him every day except Sundays for ten
months. More likely their sessions drew to an end around May, but
Lewis continued to work on the painting from time to time until about
1935. The canvas shared some of his escapades; one night in 1923, he
carried it down Adam and Eve Mews, following a route that would
avoid his landlady's window as he skipped out on the rent for his
studio.[26]

In an emerald jacket and cap, Sitwell, eyelids almost closed, sits
beside a shelf of books in the picture. Regarded as a central work of
modern portraiture, it now hangs in the Tate Gallery. However, it was
never finished: 'he was, unfortunately, seized with a kind of
Schwärmerei [mad enthusiasm, literally a swarming as of bees] for me.
I did not respond. It did not get very far, but was a nuisance as he
would follow me about, staring in a most trying manner and telling our
acquaintances about the *Schwärmerei*. So, eventually, I stopped sitting
to him (the reason why the portrait has no hands).'[27] In *Taken Care
Of*, Sitwell refers to his 'threatening behaviour' during sittings as the
reason for her ending them. It seems that he became demanding and
that she feared a sexual assault. While ostensibly still a friend, Lewis
now had a grudge against Sitwell and her brothers, and he would take
his revenge.

Though it seems she spent much of her time sitting for Lewis and
other artists, Sitwell was actually working hard at her writing. Probably
through a connection of Helen's, Sitwell began to review poetry for the
musical journal, the *Sackbut*. In December 1921, she wrote of Marianne
Moore's *Poems*, published by 'H.D.' at the Egoist Press: 'These curious
and difficult poems are almost invariably interesting, being, as they are,
the product of a real and individual intellect . . . The poems are thick
and uncouth, blocks of meaning; they have the unconscious gait of that
elephant who is the protagonist of "Black Earth." They are strange and
I believe them to be entirely new; I can see no trace of any influence.'
Not unreasonably, she complained of some of Moore's 'tricks' such as
ending a line in the middle of a word: 'Miss Moore is too good a poet

to do that kind of thing. This book should be studied; for certainly she is among the most interesting American poets of the day.'[28] Sitwell's admiration would grow over the years, and among women poets of her own generation Marianne Moore was the one she most consistently praised.

In the summer of 1922, Edith Sitwell took on the 'Readers and Writers' column of the *New Age*, formerly written by Orage himself, who had given it for a time to Herbert Read. Although she was not paid, the column gave her a much better platform to discuss new works, among them the poems of Isaac Rosenberg: 'strong and rank as marvellous jungle animals, they terrify by their crouch and spring; the fire in them is acrid and terrible.'[29] Although she had not yet laid hands on a copy of Joyce's newly published *Ulysses*, she ragged on those who accused him of indecency by offering a mock review of the Song of Solomon: 'A mass of senseless and obscure sensuality . . . far-fetched images.' And the Book of Job got the same notice once given to *Wheels*: 'Conceived in morbid eccentricity and executed in fierce factitious gloom.' At the end of that piece, she baited her detractors: 'In spite of the general belief that I am a woman of incalculable savagery, with only one end in view, that of burning the Library of the British Museum, it is a fact that I have read and know intimately practically all the poetry written in the English tongue since the time of Chaucer.'[30] Given that she means to provoke, this is still a striking statement as she always downplayed her education when talking to her male contemporaries who had studied Latin and Greek. Yet she knew the English literary tradition as well as any of them and her knowledge of French literature was, in most instances, better.

For some time, Sitwell's poetry had been making the case that what seems to us a personal identity is, in fact, other people's memories – a sense of the cultural and family past that shackles love, daring, and originality. What, then, was she to make of the myth she had herself inherited? Doubts about the whole question of personal identity led to her first and most interesting attempt at autobiography; the others were written when she was depressed and had scores to settle. Portions of this first memoir appeared in 'Readers and Writers', and I have quoted from it in earlier chapters of this book.[31] She wrote about her family as the Dukes of Troy, but Sitwell's Troy is unlike Homer's. She explained to Robert Graves: 'I had a Chinoiserie grandmother who came of a family which owned an old castle called "Troy Castle" in Wales . . . it was called after a game people played in the time of Elizabeth.'³² Perfectly suited for a mock epic, Troy House, near Monmouth, was the seat of her maternal ancestors the Dukes of Beaufort. The sword Henry V used at Agincourt was said to have been deposited there.³³

The name of the house likely derives from a corruption of the name of the River Trothy,³⁴ but it is better that Sitwell was mistaken. The game of Troy, which had nearly vanished by the nineteenth century, involved ceremonial movements in a maze³⁵ – a fitting background for her narrative. Sitwell absorbs into her Troy Castle aspects of Renishaw. She honours the heroic past of ancestors going back to the Angevin kings, but finds that their heritage has little to do with modern life. The boldness one might learn from those otherwise barbaric figures is just the thing that gets stamped out in our own time. She wants to explode a kind of snobbery – '"Yesterday I lunched with Lady B . . ."' – and instead assert an aristocracy of the spirit, and of intellect, and of authentic tradition.

In the first of her columns, she allows a ghostly version of herself to speak: 'As a member of a family whose tradition is hunting (of the rare and of the unattainable), whose skill in falconry was used indiscriminately on the smallest song-birds and on a winged and blinded Fate, my grandmother insisted on the pursuit of health.' The anticlimaxes remind the reader what has become of the tradition. The ghost never fully inhabits the life she is born to and grows more separate with the passage of time: '"everything seemed to hold some promise, I do not know of what; life seemed less a stranger than at any other time in my existence . . . I have always been a little outside life, and the things one could touch comforted me; for I am like a ghost, a dead person."' If she lived in the present, this woman would be chased into corners by 'dwarfs on stilts . . . they would squeak like guinea pigs'.³⁶

Unable to find a proper shape for the memoir, Sitwell had to give up on it; she told Robert Graves, 'prose is not for me. I'm terrified of it as a medium.'³⁷ Nevertheless she reworked some passages into poems, among them one of her best, 'Colonel Fantock', published in 1924:

Thus spoke the lady underneath the trees:
I was a member of a family
Whose legend was of hunting – (all the rare
And unattainable brightness of the air) –
A race whose fabled skill in falconry
Was used on the small song-birds and a winged
And blinded Destiny . . . I think that only
Winged ones know the highest eyrie is so lonely.
There in a land, austere and elegant,
The castle seemed an arabesque in music;
We moved in an hallucination born
Of silence, which like music gave us lotus
To eat . . .

Having eaten the lotus, children discover a delusive hope:

But Dagobert, Peregrine and I
Were children then; we walked like shy gazelles
Among the music of the thin flower-bells.
And life still held some promise, – never ask
Of what, – but life seemed less a stranger, then,
Than ever after in this cold existence.
I always was a little outside life –
And so the things we touch could comfort me;
I loved the shy dreams we could hear and see –
For I was like one dead, like a small ghost,
A little cold air wandering and lost.

A mother's kiss in the prose memoir becomes in the poem that of a great-grandmother (skipping back over both Lady Ida and the Countess of Londesborough to a woman Sitwell hardly remembered and could not resent), and in that woman's shadow appears Colonel Fantock, a character based on Sir George's retainer Major A. B. Brockwell. Like the woman under the trees he is 'outside life forever'; he boasts of old exploits, and 'For us defended Troy from the top stair / Outside the nursery.' In the prose memoir, his claims are punctured by the old governess Mademoiselle Blanchatte, but in the poem there is less venom and more sorrow:

> But then came one cruel day in deepest June,
> When pink flowers seemed a sweet Mozartian tune,
> And Colonel Fantock pondered o'er a book.
> A gay voice like a honeysuckle nook –
> So sweet, – said, 'It is Colonel Fantock's age
> Which makes him babble' . . . Blown by winter's rage
> The poor old man then knew his creeping fate,
> The darkening shadow that would take his sight
> And hearing; and he thought of his saved pence
> Which scarce would rent a grave . . . That youthful voice
> Was a dark bell which ever clanged 'Too late' –
> A creeping shadow that would steal from him
> Even the little boys who would not spell –
> His only prisoners . . . On that June day
> Cold Death had taken his first citadel.[38]

Both the woman under the trees and Colonel Fantock have seen past a façade of stories; on the other side are littleness and death. The wisdom of this poem was hard won for Edith Sitwell, for she often took refuge in just the kind of snobbery that is debunked here – and, as an old woman, she fell into Fantock's trap of using tall tales to fend off a sense of diminishment.

Edith Sitwell left the *New Age* much as she had come in – complaining about a review of *Wheels*. A former contributor to the anthology, the poet and translator Paul Selver, found much to praise in the preceding Cycles, but found the sixth unnecessarily obscure. His review came out on 19 October 1922; Sitwell immediately sent in a letter saying she would not write again for the magazine.[39] However, it had been nearly a month since her last piece had appeared. During that time Orage had handed over the *New Age* to a new editor, Major Arthur Moore, who perhaps did not want her back. Sitwell probably seized on the Selver review as an opportunity to retreat with covering fire.

After his appearance at the Anglo-French Poetry Society in April 1922, Robert Graves became, for a few years, a friend of Edith Sitwell's. He and his wife, Nancy Nicholson, were then living in tight circumstances at Islip, north-east of Oxford, following the failure of Nancy's shop at Boar's Hill. In Sitwell's account of one particular visit, Graves rode his bicycle to the station to meet her. With his arm injured from rugby, he could not carry her suitcase, which contained books, manuscripts, and an eighteenth-century brocade coat. They tried to prop it on the bicycle, but it came crashing down, and Sitwell was obliged to lug it herself. Graves remarked that it was nice to see a 'fine strapping woman who could carry her own suitcase'. She was not pleased.

Along the way Graves cleared his throat and said, '"Look here, Edith (pause), you leave Nancy alone and she'll leave you alone. *See*. She'll be alright if you are alright. But don't try anything on with her, because she won't stand for it. D'you understand?"' Quaking, she continued with him to the house where Nancy greeted her pleasantly but timidly. Before going to the station, Graves had said to his wife, '"Look here, Nancy, you leave Edith alone and she'll leave you alone. *See*. She'll be alright if you are alright. But don't try anything on with her, because she won't stand for it. D'you understand?"' Although Sitwell hardly took a traditional view of the role of women, she was not at ease with Nancy: 'She was intensely anxious that no woman, however tiresome, should be quelled . . . What did a man's art, his work, matter, if his hand could rock the cradle.' Sitwell liked to quell tiresome women and much preferred art to cradles.

Nancy and Robert produced four babies in five years, and Sitwell seems to have visited them after the birth of the third, Catherine. Graves wrote: 'It was a surprise, after reading her poems, to find her gentle, domesticated, and even devout. When she came to stay with us she spent her time sitting on the sofa and hemming handkerchiefs.'[40] Graves struck Sitwell as something of a 'high wind . . . With one hand he made up the kitchen fire, with the other he played with the children, or fried the eggs, or made the toast' and all the while he chatted about how the ideas of Freud could explain Shakespeare. When the noise of the children interrupted the flow of his ideas, he put his hands to his head and screamed at them. With Nancy out of the house, he carried two of them up the stairs, 'much as a fox carries chickens'. Sitwell heard sounds of 'tribulation' and when Robert came down again, he said, 'There is no need to worry Nancy with things like that.'[41] Sitwell enjoyed the friendship of Robert Graves while it lasted, and she admired his work: 'When I read your poems, I so often think of a very clear lake, and looking down through the lake to some shining beauty very far below, but most clearly seen.'[42]

12

GERTRUDE

By the mid-1920s, Edith Sitwell had gripped the imaginations of many young writers, among them the eighteen-year-old Graham Greene, who declared himself converted to Sitwellism in March 1923. In April he invited her to read poems to the Balliol College Society of Modern Poetry and Drama. She turned him down, since she had to give other lectures and was getting ready for a performance of *Façade* at the Aeolian Hall, but a friendship was begun.[1]

Greene then read her new collection, *Bucolic Comedies*, published on 24 April 1923, and told his mother it was absolutely 'out middle stump'. He wrote an essay on Sitwell's work and sent it to the *Weekly Westminster Gazette*. The editor told him they had run enough on Edith Sitwell lately, but sent the piece directly on to her.[2] She wrote to Greene on 15 June: 'I am not used to people understanding anything whatever about my poetry, excepting perhaps an occasional image, and that only partially, as they do not understand the spiritual impulse behind the image. You have understood it all. Your comprehension appears to be absolutely complete. And this has given me the greatest possible pleasure.'[3] By 29 June, Graham Greene was drinking tea at Pembridge Mansions.

Bucolic Comedies, the book that so excited Greene, contained a nineteen-poem version of *Façade* and other recent compositions. In the autumn of 1921, Sitwell had finally found a mainstream publisher. Gerald Duckworth (Virginia Woolf's half-brother) ran a conservative firm, but Sitwell, soon joined by her brothers, added spark to their list. Her editor was Duckworth's new partner, Thomas Balston. He stayed with the firm until 1934, and Sitwell regarded him as a close friend. Also in the early 1920s Sitwell threw in her lot with agents at Curtis

Brown – first an old man named Henry Bounds, then his apprentice David Higham, whom she followed in 1935 into the breakaway firm of Pearn, Pollinger and Higham.[4]

A pugilist for the modern movement in the arts, Sitwell was often in demand as a speaker, and she could fill a room. On 8 May 1923, she debated with the poet Alfred Noyes at the London School of Economics to raise money for the Hospitals of London Appeal. Sitwell associated Noyes with J. C. Squire and once remarked that his work was like cheap linoleum: 'they have the same kind of smoothness.'[5] Edmund Gosse, the chairman, asked Noyes beforehand to take it easy: '"Do not, I beg of you, use a weaver's beam on the head of poor Edith."' Noyes did win the opening round. Sitwell, wearing gold laurels, asked if she could bring her supporters to the platform; Noyes agreed on the condition that he could bring his. When asked who they were, he answered blandly, '"Oh, Virgil, Horace, Dante, Chaucer, Shakespeare, Milton, Wordsworth, and a few others."' Sitwell opened her lecture, 'In their day, Keats and Shelley were the most persecuted of poets, and Tom Moore was the most popular. In our days, my brothers and I are the most persecuted of poets, and,' pointing an accusing finger at her opponent, 'Mr Noyes . . .' At that point laughter drowned out her words. She went on to deliver a scripted talk on how all great poets are innovators in their time and that she was glad to join them in the asylum to which their contemporaries assigned them. Noyes ad-libbed a rebuttal that true poetry is contemporary in all ages. Once they were finished, Gosse said, 'Come along, Edith. I have no doubt that in his day Shakespeare was thought to be mad.'[6]

On 12 June, the revised *Façade* was given a public performance. Osbert took the stage at the Aeolian Hall in New Bond Street at 3.15 to explain to the audience the novel aspects of the work, especially how the curtain was intended to remove the reciter's personality from the performance. However, to the audience clutching programmes headed 'Osbert Sitwell Presents Miss Edith Sitwell in "Façade"', the personalities were inescapable. This version had twenty-seven numbers, and the orchestra now included a saxophone.[7] Osbert recalled some applause but also hissing – mainly from the front rows. At the end, Edith was told to remain behind the curtain until the hostile crowd dispersed.[8] She remembered that she was pursued by a 'sex maniac', whom Sachie tried to drive off with a good kick, and that there was an old woman with an umbrella, ready to thump and poke the artists.[9] William Walton said that the concert nearly led to fisticuffs,[10] but his friend, the pianist Angus Morrison, thought that their recollections were exaggerated and that not much happened apart from Noël Coward ostentatiously walking out.[11]

For the Sitwells, the concert was a perfect demonstration of philistinism. Walton thought rather that they had brought it on themselves: the event was disorganised and the music poorly performed.[12] Virginia Woolf sat 'dazed', listening to Edith Sitwell 'vociferating through the megaphone'. She continued, 'I should be describing Edith Sitwell's poems, but I kept saying to myself "I don't really understand . . . I don't really admire."'[13] Others, though, had a different reaction. Constant Lambert was in the audience and found the work intriguing. He soon met Walton, and became an indispensable part of the enterprise. He collaborated with Walton on the music for 'Four in the Morning', and soon became Façade's most accomplished reciter. On many occasions, he was the conductor of Frederick Ashton's ballet of Façade (1931), a work with which Sitwell herself was not involved.

The press for the Aeolian Hall performance was bad. 'Drivel They Paid to Hear' was the headline to one review, which went on to congratulate Coward on his walk-out and to report the fireman's opinion that he had seen nothing like it in his twenty years at the hall.[14] Most of the other reviews repaid the efforts of Sitwell and Walton with a harrumph. One exception was Gerald Cumberland, writing in Vogue: 'To this hour I am by no means certain what some of her poems mean, but if I do not understand their beauty, I divine it, and for that reason am all the more attracted, drawn, seduced.'[15]

Coward lampooned the Sitwells as the Swiss Family Whittlebot and Edith, in particular, as Hernia Whittlebot, in London Calling, a show that opened at the Duke of York's Theatre on 4 September. Coward had the knack of Sitwell utterance: 'Life is essentially a curve and Art is an oblong within that curve. My brothers and I have been brought up on Rhythm as other children are brought up on Glaxo.'[16] The Whittlebots were briefly more famous than the Sitwells, as Coward introduced them into gossip columns and radio broadcasts. He put out a privately printed volume of Hernia's verses, followed by 'Chelsea Buns', clunking pastiches

Another caricature by Max Beerbohm of Osbert and Sacheverell Sitwell (1925)

of Edith Sitwell's. Sitwell was humiliated by an imputation that Hernia was a lesbian – there is, for example, a punning tribute 'To a Maidenhair Fern', as well as references to the groping of breasts and to 'virulent hermaphrodites'.[17] When Coward received an angry letter from Osbert, he thought it was a joke. Coward wrote an apology to Edith in late 1926. On the advice of Siegfried Sassoon, she sent a curt reply:

> Dear Mr. Coward,
> I accept your apology.
> Yours sincerely,
> Edith Sitwell[18]

She kept a close eye on him nonetheless. When he sought to reprint the 'indecent and offensive' verses in 1932, she had her solicitor send a letter to the publisher. She also obtained an opinion from counsel specialising in libel; he was ready to go to court, provided she could pay a retainer of one thousand pounds. She asked Sir George for the money, who must have balked,[19] but as it turned out the publisher was scared off. No reprint appeared. Until they were reconciled more than forty years later, Edith Sitwell very simply hated Noël Coward.

In 1923, Sitwell found an unlikely friend. John Freeman, a Georgian poet and winner of the Hawthornden Prize, struck up a correspondence with her in the spring. She was quick to say that she admired his work but had at first distrusted it because his name so often appeared in company with that of J. C. Squire and Edward Shanks.[20] A Methodist preacher, Freeman lived on a different planet from Sitwell, but they found common ground in the music halls. Sitwell asked: 'Have you ever seen Nellie Wallace? In her own way she is an extremely fine artist, – one of the only fine artists on the English stage. She is an extraordinary mime, has great personality, and has the most significant appearance I've seen in an English actress. Everything acts: her cheeks (which she flaps as though they were being blown by a wind, when she cries), her hands, her feet, her body. She is very tragic, though she is a low-comedy actress: the epitome of starvation.' Sitwell also wrote to Freeman about the brothers Fratellini:

> If you remember, they are the clowns whom Cocteau engaged to play in Shakespeare, and great French painters are always painting and drawing them . . . I saw them in a lovely shooting scene like something out of Stravinski's 'Chansons Plaisantes'. There was a twittering of birds, the clowns shot into the air, and down tumbled showers of carrots and turnips and onions, and one very large fish, – in fact everything countrified excepting a bird. – But one can't describe it; it has to be seen. I hope and believe you would like them as much as I did. For I, also, never go to the theatre, excepting to a Mozart opera, or certain Russian operas, or the Russian ballet. But music-halls delight me, and circuses still more.[21]

Sitwell spent much of the second half of 1923 on the continent, first in Paris, then in Amalfi, in both places working on *The Sleeping Beauty*, a long sequence of poems that must have owed something to

Diaghilev's production of *The Sleeping Princess* at the Alhambra in 1921.[22] Cyril Connolly thought this was Sitwell's best work and that it was indebted to Ravel, a suggestion Sitwell confirmed.[23] She said in *Taken Care Of* that the atmosphere of the poem was Londesborough; the dowager queen was modelled on her great-grandmother, the Dowager Duchess of Beaufort (since she could have had no recollection of this woman, Sitwell was probably thinking of her grandmother the Countess of Londesborough); the maid Malinn was based on a servant at Londesborough, and the cross housekeeper Poll Troy on Louisa Sitwell's servant Leckley.[24] There is even an appearance by one of Sitwell's childhood pets, a dog named Dido. However, the poem belongs as much to fantasy as to autobiography. It was partly inspired by Oriental art, especially the eighteenth-century Japanese artist Ogata Korin, who worked in paint and lacquer, and achieved a remarkably idealised style.[25] Sitwell quietly invites the reader to imagine the world of the poem as if rendered by this master:

> At Easter when red lacquer buds sound far slow
> Quarter-tones for the old dead Mikado,
>
> Through avenues of lime-trees, where the wind
> Sounds like a chapeau chinois, shrill, unkind –
>
> The Dowager Queen, a curling Korin wave
> That flows forever past a coral cave,
>
> With Dido, Queen of Carthage, slowly drives
> (Her griffin dog that has a thousand lives)
>
> Upon the flat-pearled and fantastic shore
> Where curled and turbaned waves sigh, 'Never more.'

At the time, Sitwell was seeing everything through Oriental art. In November she wrote to Graham Greene, sending him a section of *The Sleeping Beauty* to publish in a magazine he edited; she described Amalfi: 'It has been heavenly here, and this is the most beautiful place in the world, – very fantastic and Chinoiserie . . . Like a Korin painting.'[26]

In *The Sleeping Beauty*, Sitwell includes an unsettling lullaby:

> Do, do,
> Princess, do,
> The fairy Chatte Blanche rocks you slow.
> Like baskets of white fruit or pearls
> Are the fairy's tumbling curls –
> Or lattices of roses white
> Where-through the snows like doves take flight.
> Do, do,
> Princess, do,
> How furred and white is the fallen snow.[27]

The fairy reminds us of the governess Mademoiselle Blanchatte, who crushed Colonel Fantock. Here her job is to induce the sleep of adult consciousness. For Sitwell, the task of poetry is to awaken the reader from such a coma. Yet in the poem, the young woman at the age of sexual awakening pricks her finger on the spindle and enters a darkness from which, at the end of the sequence, she has not awoken; she has learnt caution.

Duckworth released the book in March. In a sign of Sitwell's new commercial heft, it was picked up by Alfred A. Knopf and published in the United States in August. The reviews were respectful. Robert Graves in the *Nation and Athenæum* described it as a visit to 'Looking-Glass-Land', observing that it 'has the inconsequent but powerful movement of a dream, and is strewn with memorable images'.[28] Writing in the *TLS*, Edgell Rickword found much to admire, but felt that there was a technical flaw in the repetition of certain images. He praised her thoughtfulness and intellectual awareness, and remarked: 'The considered audacity with which she de-animises nature in her imagery expresses very effectively the way in which the shades of the prison house close round the growing princess.'[29] E. M. Forster, whom she had not met, sent a letter praising the book. This was especially gratifying as she believed Forster was the best novelist of their generation.[30]

In late 1923 Sitwell was absorbed in *The Waste Land*, while its author, following a mental collapse in 1921 and sojourns at Lausanne and Margate, had disappeared from general view. On 21 March 1924, she reported to Graves that she had seen Tom Eliot for the first time in two years. Eliot told her that *The Waste Land* was a year's work. 'What a great poem it is . . . Tom says he considers the end of the book the best. It is wonderful – but then the whole poem is, I think, don't you?' Shortly after, she wrote: 'I'm longing to discuss "The Waste Land" almost line by line, as I want to know if you read the same meanings into it as I do; or what other meanings you read into it.'[31] John Freeman, on the other hand, thought the poem had no form; Sitwell tried to convince him by quoting a long stretch of Coleridge on the difference between organic and mechanic form, but in the end suggested that he talk to Robert Graves: 'Apart from his pleasure at the meeting, he can argue and I can't.'[32]

Sitwell spent the winter of 1923–4 in Paris, returning to London in March for the release of her book. About this time, Sir George was making another addition to the Sitwell properties. He obtained from the estate of a maternal aunt Weston Hall, the Northamptonshire house, unoccupied since 1911, where Louisa Sitwell had grown up. It came into the family in the early 1700s when a remote ancestor, Sir John Blencowe, gave it to his widowed daughter Susanna Jennens as a Valentine's Day present. In the 1740s, the poet Mary Leapor worked there as a kitchen-maid. For most of its history, it passed as a dower house along the female line, until Sir George decided it would be a good home for Sachie.[33] Edith visited Weston often in the years to come, and her grave is located there.

Edith found Weston's library intriguing. She told Graves on 10 September that she had been looking at books of travel from around 1690 and found in one this description of the dodo: 'He hath a mournful countenance and is much given to closing the eyes, as though he were in a Melancholy.' From *Sadducimus Triumphatus* (1682), on the trials of witches, she read that Queen Elizabeth had once been prevented from visiting Scotland when a witch baptised a cat. Sitwell was especially interested in how another witch caused the favourite horse of a Mr Justice Mompesson to get his hind leg stuck irremovably in his mouth.[34] She set about working some of these images into poems. One of them, about how the same Justice Mompesson was tortured by a demonic drumming noise in his house, provided the basis for 'The Drum', which opens later versions of *Façade*.

Through 1923 and 1924, Edith Sitwell was trying to decide what she made of Gertrude Stein. In the summer of 1923, she wrote a cautious review of *Geography and Plays*, but in another review in October 1924, she said that after a year of hard work on Stein she had decided she had been guilty of an injustice and could now declare her to be 'among the most important writers of the time'. Stein's style was 'strange, wild, fly-away; her words are like singing birds flying down upon a branch for a moment, together on the same bough, but to all appearance utter strangers to each other'. She believed that Stein could exercise a wide influence.[35] Many years later, she qualified this view; Stein remained for her an important writer who had 'revivified' language, but no young writer should take her work as a model.[36] Some would think the same thing true of Sitwell's work.

Duckworth released *Troy Park* in March 1925. It contained, among others, the autobiographical poems Sitwell had written after abandoning her memoir. Stephen Spender later judged this volume one of her most important.[37] Sitwell's own view of the book is captured in a letter to Robert Graves: 'In "Troy Park" I have found out definitely what I can and can't do in poetry. And that is a most useful discovery. Several of the quiet poems in the book I simply can't bear; and I now realise that (*apart* from "The Child who saw Midas," "Colonel Fantock," "An Old Woman Laments in Springtime," "Mademoiselle Richarde" and "The Pleasure Gardens," poems for which I cherish an affection), I am best when most swashbuckling.'[38] She was right. Some of the quieter poems in the collection are sleep-inducing, but it also contained plenty of swashbucklers, such as 'Four in the Morning':

> Cried the navy-blue ghost
> Of Mr. Belaker
> The allegro negro cocktail shaker . . .[39]

> And 'I do like to be beside the Seaside':
> When
> Don
> Pasquito arrived at the seaside
> Where the donkey's hide tide brayed, he
> Saw the banditto Jo in a black cape
> Whose slack shape waved like the sea . . .[40]

Yet there were other remarkable poems, in a different vein. Around the end of 1923, Graves was writing poems about ghosts – this gave Sitwell the idea for 'The Man with the Green Patch'.[41] She described it thus: 'Our Renishaw ghost is making its way into a new poem of mine. I'll send it you when it is finished . . . it is a concrete ghost, though. – I'm doing quite a new kind of work. No colours, no gaiety, ever so grey and bony; always, of course, slightly mad, because I am. These new poems will probably get me lynched. But who cares? It is all in a day's work.'[42] When Graves saw the poem, he liked it. Sitwell wrote:

You say that my 'ass-ear grass' and 'hairy sky' etc, terrify you, and you want to know what makes me do it. It is rather difficult to explain. I think it is that I have always been in two lives, – if you can understand what I mean. It's a queer somnambulistic floating back from my own perilous life to other people's safe one . . . and waking up with a scream. Perhaps subconsciously I wish I could get on friendly terms with the safe kind of life I hate, and am never able to do it. That is explaining badly, at once exaggeratedly and insufficiently, but you will see what I mean . . . a safe and material world.[43]

In later years, Sitwell could never understand why young poets of the 1930s were credited with social awareness, when she had been writing about poverty and injustice for years. Her own finances were tight, and she lived in a slum. Part of the problem was that she was so aristocratic. Also, her criticism of society was Christian rather than Marxist – and in the first years of the next decade that would hardly seem a sophisticated model of social understanding. Nonetheless, the thin skin that caused her to believe she was at times persecuted also enabled her to imagine in terrible detail the sufferings of others. She described herself to her editor Tom Balston as 'fundamentally kind, if you discount my conversation, which is very often not'.[44] One area in which *Troy Park* excels is the observation of women who have no money, such as the ancient governess, Mademoiselle Richarde, living by proxy:

A tiny spider in a gilded nut
She lived and rattled in the emptiness
Of other people's splendours; her rich dress
Had muffled her old loneliness of heart.
This was her life; to live another's part,
To come and go unheard, a ghost unseen
Among the courtly mirrors glacial green,
Placed just beyond her reach for fear that she
Forget her loneliness, her image see
Grown concrete, not a ghost by cold airs blown.
So each reflection blooms there but her own.
She sits at other people's tables, raises
Her hands at other people's joys and praises
Their cold amusements, drawing down the blinds
Over her face for others' griefs, – the winds
Her sole friends now . . .[45]

Sitwell was not really a feminist, but what she saw of the lives of
dependent women escaped the notice of most poets of her time, and
she had the skill to make something of it.

By March 1925, Sitwell had prevailed upon Dorothy Todd, the
editor of British *Vogue*, to arrange a meeting for her in Paris with
Gertrude Stein. She was then brought to Stein's house by the musician
Elmer Harden.[46] Sitwell described Stein for Violet Schiff: 'She is an
impressive oldish woman; her figure looks like that of a German hausfrau, or perhaps a head-mistress; but she has a superb face, with
sensitive modelling. And she seems full of rich, earthy, Schumannesque life, if you know what I mean.' They disagreed about the war, and
Sitwell found her views somewhat hard-minded:

She can't understand suffering; she is infinitely interested in the subtle-
ties of character. She is very dictatorial, and never listens to anything
anybody else may say; she merely interrupts them in the middle of
a sentence, says 'It isn't so, at all', or, 'It certainly is not for that
reason', and takes matters into her own hands. But I like her. She
lives surrounded by some of the most wonderful modern pictures I
have ever seen – superb Picassos, as well as many pictures by Juan

Gris, Matisse, etc. I think it was she and her brother who first found and helped Picasso.[47]

While Sitwell might admire Stein's taste in art, she deferred to no one where the piano was involved. She saw that Ezra Pound, 'who knows nothing of music', and Gertrude Stein were creating a cult figure out of the young pianist and composer George Antheil: 'Mr Antheil is tiny and round and flat, and talking to him . . . is very much like talking to a shut oyster that is being irritated by a pearl.' Antheil was known for a violent, percussive style, and the claims made for him struck her as absurd: 'I was assured by his admirers that he plays so loudly and so fast, and his own music is so difficult, that between the pieces he has to be carried out and slapped with wet towels like a boxer, and rubbed, and given smelling salts. I longed to ask if he wore boxing gloves, but didn't dare.'[48]

Sitwell started to write sketches for newspapers featuring the conversation of a Stein-like 'Madame X'; in one, a princess, who happens to be training pet tigers to appreciate music, invites Madame X to a party for a famous pianist named Barbados, reputed to demolish each instrument he plays: 'He smashes it utterly! It breaks down under him. And there he sits among the ruins like Nero when Rome was burning. So decadent! You must come!' An impressive-looking piano tuner accompanies Barbados at each performance 'to give first aid to the piano'.[49]

After an 'unpleasant operation' on her back, Edith Sitwell went to Spain in April. In Madrid, she received 'Sitwell Edith Sitwell', a word portrait of her written by Stein. She read it aloud at dinner to Osbert, Sachie, Willie Walton, and Richard Wyndham, who were travelling with her.[50] When she got back to London, she pressed a manuscript of Stein's work (probably *The Making of Americans*, even though she had not actually read the novel yet) on Tom Balston at Duckworth's, who turned it down. After that she tried to interest Virginia Woolf in it, for the Hogarth Press, but Woolf was not ready to take on Stein. The best Sitwell could do for her new friend was another salute in *Vogue* in October.[51]

Virginia Woolf had come to a new understanding of Edith Sitwell, thinking of her not as a pamphleteer or a protester but as something

more old-fashioned, a 'well born Victorian spinster' – a concept she
managed more delicately than did Harold Acton. After a dinner with
the Sitwells on 19 May, Woolf wrote: 'Edith is an old maid. I had never
conceived this. I thought she was severe, implacable & tremendous;
rigid in her own conception. Not a bit of it. She is, I guess, a little fussy,
very kind, beautifully mannered . . . She is elderly too, almost my age,
& timid, & admiring & easy & poor, & I liked her more than admired
or was frightened of her. Nevertheless I do admire her work, & thats
what I say of hardly anyone: She has an ear, & not a carpet broom; a
satiric vein and some beauty in her.'[52] At the end of October 1925, the
Hogarth Press released Sitwell's essay *Poetry and Criticism*.

That year, Sitwell attempted another modernist fairy tale, this time
Cinderella or 'Cendrillon' intertwined with a retelling of the story
of Venus and Psyche from which it is thought to derive. The myth of
Psyche would not be a surprising subject for a poet who had been
disappointed in her search for a husband. Some of the poem is playful, even flippant: 'And Cupid ran to Vulcan: "O papa! / Come quick!
For I have seen Mars kiss Mama!"'[53] Other parts are dream-like and
languid. The poem pursues a theme similar to *The Sleeping Beauty*:
'Sometimes the songs which may appear most strange / Are of the
growth of consciousness, – the range / Of consciousness awakening
from sleep.'[54] Sitwell wanted to account for how the evolving soul gradually separates itself from the material world and so becomes an
individual identity. The last section is largely built around Helen's
anthroposophical ideas – particularly a notion of Steiner's on waking
from a 'mineral sleep',[55] a kind of sleep which, owing to the accumu-
lations of salts in the body, 'lifts human beings wholly out of their
bodies and places them within the spiritual world. In this third stage
of sleep we live with the essential being of the spiritual world itself.'[56]

Sitwell invested an enormous effort in this sprawling poem, which
in some versions absorbed a good deal of *Elegy on Dead Fashion* (1926).
However, she separated them again in *Rustic Elegies*, released in March
1927, and called the Cendrillon poem 'Prelude to a Fairy Tale'. Even
so, she was not satisfied. She shortened the poem, and finally dropped
it from her later collections – salvaging from it only the playful 'Polka',
which she added to *Façade*: '"Tra la la – / See me dance the polka"'.[57]
Even though she came to regard Rudolf Steiner as 'otherwise tiresome',

his idea of awakening from a mineral sleep interested her as late as 1943: 'I once wrote a *very* bad poem based on that. One day I may write a good one.'[58] That day did not come.

The summer and autumn of 1925 were dominated by Sachie's plan to marry Georgia Doble, the beautiful daughter of a Canadian banker. Devoted to Sachie's genius, she was socially ambitious and hard-nosed. Although he did his best to welcome Georgia, Osbert felt that by marrying, Sachie was abandoning him. Within a few years Osbert decided that Georgia was a gold-digger, a view encouraged by his mischief-making friends, Christabel Aberconway and David Horner. However, in 1925 Osbert lamented not the appearance of a competitor for Sir George's money, but a rival for Sachie's affections. As is generally observed, Sacheverell's marriage began a gradual estrangement between the brothers, who by the 1960s were barely on speaking terms.

Greed was no part of Edith's character, and she could hope only for small inheritances – so she remained on the edges of these quarrels. In later years she privately took Osbert's side when there was trouble with Sachie and Georgia, assuming (unwisely) that he knew best about money, yet she managed to stay on good terms with all three. In July 1925, she wrote to Georgia about the engagement: 'I am *so* glad, dear, about this. It is lovely to think somebody is coming into the family whom one can care for, instead of somebody whom, quite possibly, one couldn't bear, – which is what so often happens. Congratulations sound such cold things. "I hope you will be very happy" is formal and silly. But we understand each other, you and I.'[59]

Edith nearly missed the wedding in Paris on 12 October. Coutts Bank demanded that she immediately repay sixty-eight pounds that she had run up in excess of her guaranteed overdraft; her arrangement with the bank left her no means of buying a ticket from London or clothes for the wedding. The best she could do was promise a phonograph as a wedding present.[60] Then, she tripped and fell in front of a bus and was lucky to escape with just a sprained ankle and some torn muscles. Nevertheless, money was found for a ticket and she was well enough to travel. At the last minute, Sir George and Lady Ida begged off, remaining in Florence. After the wedding, Edith and Osbert went on to Montegufoni. From there, Edith wrote to Georgia: 'your nature is just as lovely as your appearance, and it would be beyond words if one didn't value you at your real worth. Trust me implicitly. You can, you know.'[61]

The Gingers were always a trial. When someone left the house suddenly, Lady Ida told Edith: 'In future I shall think of myself. I shall be selfish in future. And see how people like that.'[62] The beauties of the castle had to be balanced against the uncongenial company. Edith wrote to Sydney Schiff: 'This is a most lovely and romantic place, at once grandiose and peaceful, in spite of a warlike history, with huge walls, plants growing in them, gigantic coats of arms, and a 13th century tower. The only disadvantage is a constant incursion of tarantulas, scorpions, Mrs. Hwfa Williams, and Mrs. George Keppel, these ancient and malevolent women are always here.'[63] At other times, Sitwell had kind words for Mrs Keppel, the former mistress of King Edward and the great-grandmother of the Duchess of Cornwall. Mrs Keppel was about Lady Ida's age, and they had a long friendship; on occasion she spoke up for Edith. Mrs Hwfa Williams was an Edwardian hostess and memoirist; there is no sign Edith Sitwell ever thought of her except as a tarantula or scorpion.

On her return to London at the beginning of November, she found waiting for her a copy of the French edition of Gertrude Stein's novel, *The Making of Americans*, which she described to Robert Graves as 'a most portentous book, so huge [925 pages] that it defies competition as to size. I haven't read it yet. It looks shrewd and rich in life, but not queer like "Geography and Plays," my favourite work of hers.'[64] Still, she wrote a warm review of it that Eliot published in the *New Criterion* in April – all part of her 'propaganda' for Stein.[65]

For the most part, winter in London was dreary, and conversation in the flat a bit earnest, as she told Georgia: 'Helen went away to lecture and came back suffering from diarrhoea and Sacred Glyphs and metaphysics.' The arrival of a clever young admirer offered relief from the weather and the anthroposophists. Allanah Harper was a 'bright young thing', a friend of Zita and Baby Jungman and of the future novelist Lady Eleanor Smith. Harper attended a poetry reading and fell a little in love with Sitwell: 'Here was the beauty of Pierro [sic] della Francesca. Her flat hair like that of a naiad, her hands as white as alabaster. On her long gothic fingers she wore huge rings, lumps of topaz and turquoise, on her wrists were coral and jet bracelets. She

Edith, Osbert, and Sacheverell Sitwell in early childhood.

Renishaw Hall, the ancestral home of the Sitwells in Derbyshire. Edith's father, Sir George Sitwell, made the design of its landscape his life's work.

Lady Ida and Sir George Sitwell: '. . . they *were* a pair, and the trail of what they have done is still all over everything'.

A curious masterpiece, Sir George Sitwell's short book *On the Making of Gardens* (1909) was based on his studies of two hundred Italian gardens.

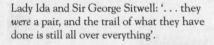

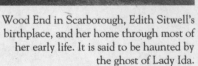

Wood End in Scarborough, Edith Sitwell's birthplace, and her home through most of her early life. It is said to be haunted by the ghost of Lady Ida.

Osbert, Sacheverell, and Edith, with their beloved nurse Eliza Davis (c. 1898).

John Singer Sargent's painting of the Sitwell family (1900): 'I was white with fury and contempt, and indignant that my father held me in what he thought was a tender paternal embrace.'

Edith Sitwell (centre) at art lessons in Scarborough – her dog can be seen on the mat beside her.

'Delightful but deleterious trio': Osbert, Sacheverell, and Edith Sitwell in 1924.

'People like me who are sex-mad have absolutely no obligation to their lovers.' The Russian painter Pavel Tchelitchew was hardly sane, but Sitwell loved him. Here they are in Toulon in 1931.

Façade at the New Chenil Galleries in 1926. From left, Osbert, Edith, and Sacheverell Sitwell, composer William Walton, and actor Neil Porter. Porter is holding a Sengerphone, a type of megaphone, through which he recited the poems.

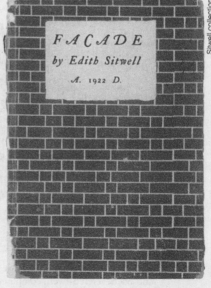

The 'party to end all parties' at the Gotham Book Store, 19 November 1948, in honour of the Sitwells' arrival in New York: Edith and Osbert in the centre, and at their feet is Charles Henri Ford. Seated at the left is William Rose Benet; behind him Stephen Spender; against the left bookshelves are Horace Gregory and his wife Marya Zaturenska. At the back of the picture are, from left, Tennessee Williams, Richard Eberhart, Gore Vidal, and José Garcia Villa; perched on a ladder, W. H. Auden; seated to Edith's left is Marianne Moore, with Elizabeth Bishop standing next to her; also on the right side Randall Jarrell is leaning his head back, with Delmore Schwartz in the foreground.

began to recite and a window opened on an enchanted world. Never had I heard a more beautifully modulated voice. Each vowel and consonant flowed, she seemed to weave poetry in the air.'[66]

At the end of the year Harper published an article on the three Sitwells, and Edith was happy to have won a new partisan, though she did question a reference in the article to Nancy Cunard, whose work was just 'a bad parody of Mr. Eliot'.[67] The twenty-one-year-old Harper was immediately invited to Pembridge Mansions, the poverty of which surprised her, and she was tempted to bring as a present for Sitwell a shade for the dangling bulb. Harper heard cross voices on the stairs. Sitwell said, 'That must be Tom.' When Eliot came in with Vivienne, Harper thought he looked like a young curate who would eventually become a bishop. Eliot sat next to Harper on the sofa and reached for a magazine containing an article in which Harper had complained of his obscurity. Harper grabbed it and sat on it. He tried to get at it, but Harper won the tussle. Vivienne's reaction is not recorded.

The following week, Harper returned and found among the guests Virginia Woolf, Edmund Blunden, William Walton, Arthur Waley, and Humbert Wolfe. Sitwell and Woolf were discussing Vita Sackville-West's new poem, *The Land*, later awarded the Hawthornden Prize. '"It is not poetry," Sitwell said, "it would be entirely suitable for the use of farmers to help them to count the ticks on their sheep."' Woolf asked: '"Edith, must one always tell the truth?"' Harper had spotted Woolf enjoying Edith's triumphs over Vita. In June, Woolf noted in her diary how at a dinner party Edith was 'tremulously pleased by Morgan's [E. M. Forster's] compliments (& he never praised Vita, who sat hurt, modest, silent, like a snubbed schoolboy).'[68]

Allanah Harper's devotion to Edith Sitwell amused her madcap friends. When they heard that Sitwell was coming to visit Harper's mother in St Leonard's Terrace, Lady Eleanor Smith and Enid Raphael (now remembered for the remark, 'I don't know why people talk about their private parts. Mine aren't private'[69]) laid an ambush. They enlarged a newspaper image of Wyndham Lewis's portrait of Sitwell to life size and nailed it above the mantelpiece in the sitting room. Harper found it just before Sitwell arrived and pried it off using an old sword of her father's. She covered up the nail holes by hanging a painting on the spot. Sitwell had no knowledge of the stunt; instead, she complimented Harper on her sense of poetry, then picked up a seashell from the mantelpiece and began reciting verses from John Keats.[70]

In the spring of 1926, Edith Sitwell and William Walton were again hard at work on *Façade*. The six-piece orchestra went through careful rehearsals. The performances of a version with seven new poems on 27 and 29 April at the Chenil Gallery in Chelsea[71] were exactly what they had hoped for. Ernest Newman, the biographer of Wagner and an influential critic, wrote in the *Sunday Times*: 'How much I enjoyed the fun may be estimated from the fact that I – a critic! – actually not only stayed to the end but added my voice and my umbrella to the clamour for encores of the best "items" long after the official proceedings were finished.' Sitwell herself read only a few of the slower poems. Constant Lambert seems to have recited some of the pieces, but most were performed by Neil Porter of the Old Vic.[72] Much as Sitwell prided herself on her reciting, this was a good decision. Newman wrote: 'The curious thing was the happiness of the correspondence between all factors of the affair; the music, the words, the megaphone, and the piquant phrasing of the lines by the reciter were as much bone of each other's bone and flesh of each other's flesh as the words and the music are of each other in "Tristan" or "Pelléas". At its best, "Façade" was the jolliest entertainment of the season.'

Newman's review appeared on 2 May, the day before the Trades Union Congress began a general strike in support of the coal miners, who were fighting against wage reductions and poor working conditions. Osbert felt that by giving no ground to workers the upper classes had brought a disaster upon themselves. Taking matters into their own hands, he and an overwrought Siegfried Sassoon met with the editor of the *Daily Express*, Beverley Baxter, and agreed, after some shouting, on a set of principles that might secure an agreement. Osbert then persuaded Alice Wimborne to press her husband, a former Cabinet minister and a cousin of the Chancellor of the Exchequer, Winston Churchill, to hold a meeting of labour leaders, politicians, and employers. This group had no influence on Stanley Baldwin's government – indeed, the strike collapsed by 12 May.[73] Nonetheless, the Wimborne House effort was an honourable one and might have taken on significance, had the strike continued.

Edith Sitwell's political views are difficult to tease out. In early 1924, she had encouraged Robert Graves to edit a political anthology: 'we'll show them what the Left Wing can produce.'[74] In 1926, Sitwell, though worn out by the inconvenience of the strike, took the side of the strikers. She wrote to Freeman: 'As for the strike, I feel we are assisting at a great landmark in history, a really great inner event, – but don't feel worthy of it, or anything but debilitated, harassed, and, if the truth were known, slightly bored.'[75]

Around the beginning of the General Strike, both Edith and Osbert received rambling letters from Vivienne Eliot, then in Rome, to the effect that they would soon hear of a scandal in which she had become involved. She felt that if she returned to Tom, he would be disgraced. She told them that she would remain abroad unless she heard from them by letter or cable and not to let Tom know she had written to them. They had no idea what to do. Osbert wrote later: 'Eventually, as it seemed to us that very probably he might not want her to go back to him, we decided not to answer her – in any case, from a practical point of view, owing to the General Strike, no letter or telegram from us could reach her.' Vivienne returned on her own and told her husband that when she had turned to the Sitwells for advice, they had ignored her. Relations with Tom Eliot turned cold and stayed so for a long time.[76]

Edith Sitwell had been trying for months to bring Gertrude Stein to England as a lecturer. The end of the strike allowed her to go ahead. According to *The Autobiography of Alice B. Toklas*, Stein wrote her lecture in a garage while waiting for repairs to her Ford, called 'Godiva' as it came to her stripped. She was terrified of lecturing, and sought advice from a professor of history who told her to read quickly and to keep her eyes fastened on her paper; this contradicted earlier advice to go slowly and never to look down. First came a party at Pembridge Mansions on 1 June, which Virginia Woolf described, snarlingly, to Vanessa Bell: 'a good deal of misery was endured. Jews swarmed. It was in honour of Miss Gertrude Stein who was throned on a broken settee (all Edith's furniture is derelict, to make up for which she is stuck about with jewels like a drowned mer-maiden). This resolute old lady inflicted great damage on all the youth.'[77] Then came the lectures on successive days at Jesus College, Cambridge, and at the Ordinary in Oxford (a literary society of which Harold Acton was president). Osbert helped Stein get past her nervousness by holding forth on all the kinds of stage fright it was possible to experience. She wrote of

Osbert: 'He had that pleasant kindly irresponsible agitated calm that an uncle of an english king must always have.'[78]

Stein put on a show at the universities, and for weeks afterwards Sachie chuckled at her crushing replies to silly questions. One of Edith's protégés, the young poet (later politician and memoirist) Tom Driberg, appealed to Virginia Woolf to publish the lecture,[79] which eventually appeared as *Composition as Explanation* in the Hogarth Essays series.

Through the early 1920s, Edith Sitwell's friendship with Siegfried Sassoon lagged a little behind Osbert's rows and reconciliations with him – even though Sassoon thought her the more interesting writer. On 1 May 1926, she thanked him for the gift of a book, but with faint praise. After working with Osbert on the Wimborne House talks, he came to Edith's party for Stein and afterwards wrote a warm letter. She responded on 4 June: 'You know what I've always felt about your poetry; it cuts right down to the bone, – the most rare and unusual thing in this muffled stifled age, – and moves one most profoundly.'[80] Before long Sassoon sent her manuscripts of Wilfred Owen that she had not known about, and she and Sassoon were often seen in company.

Edmund Gosse put it bluntly to Sassoon at dinner on 20 January 1927, 'Would you like to marry Edith Sitwell?'

Sassoon responded, 'I don't think poets ought to marry one another.'

'Perhaps I shouldn't have asked you that question. But don't let it deter you if you are really fond of her.'[81]

The problem for Sassoon was not that Sitwell was a poet, but that she was a woman. There were also differences of temperament; he always urged her to avoid publicity. He was both right and wrong: in her later career Sitwell probably damaged her reputation as a poet by seeking the limelight too much, while Sassoon damaged his by becoming a recluse.

From 1926, Sitwell began to rely chiefly on Sassoon for criticism of her new work. When he praised one of her poems, she wrote back: 'I was so particularly anxious that you should, because I've worked so frightfully hard digging for my poetry, – if you know what I mean, – and at last it seems to me as if, providing I dig hard enough, one of these days I may find something. One never knows.'[82] That kind of humility was not often on display, and she sometimes took Sassoon's remarks the wrong way. In March 1927, she wrote: 'My word, if it had been anyone but you who had told me to "consider and reconsider", and "sift" my poems, I *should have taken that person on a one-way journey!* Luckily, it *was* you. But the escape has been narrow . . . Do you suppose I write poems instead of singing in my bath? Or what? Do you suppose I toss these things off lightly, like yodelling? Or what?'[83] The diatribe ended in an invitation to tea.

Edith Sitwell bridled at criticism, but she did pay attention. As the years passed, she did sift her early work, folding some pieces into *Façade* and scrapping others entirely. She rejected one common criticism of her work, that she repeated lines and images, as a failure to understand the musical structure of her poems.

On 7 December 1926, Allanah Harper brought Edith Sitwell to meet Cecil Beaton, who had left Cambridge the year before, at his mother's house. On the strength of soft-focus pictures he had taken of her friends, Harper was urging him to become a professional photographer. Hugo Vickers observes that Beaton's originality lay in his use of unusual props or backgrounds. On this particular afternoon, Beaton was struck by Sitwell's Pre-Raphaelite garb and her medieval hands. He persuaded her to pose for photographs, among them one in which she appeared asphyxiated under a Victorian glass dome. Light got into the camera and ruined the film, but this was just the start of his experiments.[84]

Beaton had a range of interests, and in the late winter helped the memorably named director Widgey R. Newman to make two 'phonofilms', now lost, of Edith Sitwell reading poems at Clapham Studios. He conducted a number of sessions with the three Sitwells, taking photographs that were among the highlights of his exhibition at Coolings Galleries in November 1927. Beaton's best-known photograph from that year is of Edith Sitwell laid out as a regal corpse in a glittering fabric under a spray of lilies, with wooden cherubim on either side of her head.

His photographs of the Sitwells launched his career, and he always maintained that Edith was his favourite subject. There were times (for example, the 1940s) when she found Beaton annoying, but somehow they remained friends. Beaton told John Pearson: 'I was terribly impressed by Edith almost from the start. I loved her and thought her really beautiful. I wasn't interested in poetry, and hardly knew what to do with her poems which she used to insist on writing out for me. I found her sympathetic, sweet, loveable. Mind you, I was terribly shy at the time.'[85]

A friendship with D. H. Lawrence did not turn out so well. Sitwell admired his works, especially 'The Snake' and 'The Mountain Lion', which she called 'two beautiful and most moving poems'.[86] Osbert had grown very interested in him and made an effort to meet with him in Italy in 1926, but Lawrence and his wife went to Montegufoni at a time when only Sir George and Lady Ida were there. Lady Ida wrote to Osbert: 'A Mr. D. H. Lawrence came over the other day, a funny little petit-maitre of a man with flat features and a beard. He says he is a writer, and seems to know all of you. His wife is a large German. She went round the house with your father, and when he showed her anything, would look at him, lean against one of the gilded beds, and breathe heavily.'[87] Whatever Frieda's breathing signified, Lady Ida doubtless had a good time teasing her husband about it. In Sir George's version of the story, Frieda Lawrence jumped on all the mattresses to see if they were soft.[88] The Lawrences stopped at Renishaw in July, missing Edith and Osbert again.

Finally, at the end of May 1927, Edith and Osbert visited the Lawrences at Villa Merenda near Florence. Edith recalled that Lawrence looked like 'a plaster gnome on a stone toadstool in some suburban garden'. The two-hour visit passed amicably and courteously, but Lawrence could not figure them out: 'Osbert and Edith Sitwell came to tea the other day. They were really very nice, not a bit affected or bouncing: only absorbed in themselves and their parents. I never in my life saw such a strong, strange family complex: as if they were marooned on a desert island, and nobody in the world but their lost selves. Queer!'[89]

Edith Sitwell never forgave what happened next. There is no question that Lady Chatterley's Lover owes something to Lawrence's observation of the Sitwells. Clifford Chatterley, a writer of fiction, lives in an estate resembling Renishaw. He has an aunt like Lady Ida, and a sister, Emma, like Edith. Most importantly, Edith believed that, in the crippled and unsexed Clifford Chatterley, Lawrence had attempted a portrait of Osbert – all the crueller because Lawrence was delving into a hushed-up topic, Osbert's sexuality. John Pearson, however, points out that Lawrence's work on the novel was well advanced by the time the Sitwells made their visit. Chatterley's impotence is most likely modelled on Lawrence's own failures with Frieda. Nevertheless, when Lawrence wrote what was, in fact, the third version of the novel, he added the characteristics that led Sitwell to think the whole work modelled on her brother.[90] To the end of her days, Edith Sitwell regarded the novel as pornographic trash, and said she could describe it only 'with a five-letter word which, until Mr. Lawrence made a pet of it, was only allowed by our cricket-loving, golf-loving, tennis-loving compatriots to be used in connection with those games – not in connection with the game that interested Mr. Lawrence'.[91]

The 'strong, strange family complex' Lawrence wrote of was to take on a new dimension. On 15 April 1927, Georgia gave birth to her first child, Reresby. He eventually succeeded as seventh Baronet, after Osbert and Sachie, and he died just short of his eighty-second birthday in 2009. Predictably, Sir George became obsessed with his grandson. For her part, Edith made a fuss about the sensitive minds of children when she was talking about poetry, but otherwise they were, with the exception of her nephew, just noise-makers. After a visit to Weston she wrote to Georgia:

> The journey back was hell. Three children (travelling by themselves) got into my carriage and shrieked like parrots the whole way. They shrieked so loudly that it 'set off' the children in the next carriage, rather like something catching fire. The children in the next carriage started others in neighbouring carriages, and soon the whole train was a shrieking yelling hooting whistling mass of infant imbeciles. As you know, I haven't the unnatural love of children that afflicts some women (always excepting Reresby, for whom I have a real passion) and by the time I arrived I was longing for another Herod.[92]

With her fortieth birthday approaching, Edith seemed settled in her own way of life. No one could know, but she had reached a watershed when Virginia Woolf described her as

transparent like some white bone one picks up on a moor, with sea
water stones on her long frail hands which slide into yours much
narrower than one expects like a folded fan. She has pale gemlike
eyes; & is dressed, on a windy March day, in three decker skirts of
red spotted cotton. She half shuts her eyes; coos an odd little
laugh . . . All is very tapering & pointed, the nose running on like
a mole . . . She is a curious product, likable to me: sensitive, etio-
lated, affectionate, lonely, having to thread her way (there is
something ghostlike & angular about her) home to Bayswater to
help cook dinner. She said she would like to attach great bags & bal-
loons of psychology, people having dinner, &c, to her poems, but has
no knowledge of human nature, only these sudden intense poems –
which by the way she has sent me. In other ages she would have
been a cloistered nun; or an eccentric secluded country old maid. It
is the oddity of our time that has set her on the music hall stage.[93]

13

YOU ARE RUSSIAN, ARE YOU NOT?

'If I present Pavlik to you, it's your responsibility because his character is not my affair,' warned Gertrude Stein. 'Take care . . . find him customers.'[1] Edith Sitwell first glimpsed the painter Pavel Tchelitchew on 27 June 1927 at the opening in Paris of *The Triumph of Neptune*, the Diaghilev ballet for which Sacheverell wrote the scenario. Tchelitchew seemed to be looking for her: 'In the interval, I saw a very thin, desperately anxious looking young man staring straight at me as if he were staring at a ghost. I turned away, but in the second entr'acte, the same thing happened. Four days afterwards, I met him at a teaparty at Gertrude Stein's in the Rue Fleurus.'[2] Stein called him one of the greatest discoveries of the age.

Tchelitchew displayed a curious style of flirtation: 'Staring at me again as if he had seen a ghost, he said to me, "You are Russian, are you not?" "No, I am English." "But I am sure you are Russian." He then told me that I bore such an extraordinary resemblance to Father Zosimov, the saint in "The Brothers Karamazov," (who was his father's confessor and one of his greatest friends) that, hearing that Zosimov's granddaughter had escaped from Russia and was living in Paris, he was convinced that I was the woman in question.'[3]

Pavel Tchelitchew was born in 1898 to an aristocratic Russian family; he even boasted that his great-great-grandfather was the Sultan of Turkey. At the time of the Bolshevik Revolution, his family left Moscow for their estate in the village of Dubrovka. When they were expelled from it, they travelled by caravan to Ukraine, where at an art academy Tchelitchew became a Cubist. He served as a cartographer in a regiment of Uhlans during the Russo-Polish War, but caught typhus and was cut off from the White Army. Once he recovered, he made his

way to Constantinople. By 1922, he was working in Berlin, where he
had an exhibition, enjoyed his first success as a set painter, and made
the acquaintance of Diaghilev and Stravinsky. A bisexual, he took up
with a young pianist from Chicago, Allen Tanner, who shared his
fanatical devotion to horoscopes and lucky numbers. In August 1923,
they moved to Paris, and from 1924 they lived with Tchelitchew's
tubercular sister, Choura, in a flat at 150 Boulevard Montparnasse.[4]
Later, the three moved to 2 rue Jacques-Mawas.

During 1924, Tchelitchew shrugged off Cubism on the grounds that
it was disrespectful of human anatomy,[5] and in the following years he
became the leader of a fractious group that included Christian Bérard,
Eugene and Leonid Berman, Kristian Tonny, and others. Calling themselves 'neo-romantics', they eschewed not only Cubism but abstraction.
They produced sorrowfully figurative or allegorical work, owing its
inspiration partly to classical and Renaissance art, as well as to
nineteenth-century Symbolism. Most of the neo-romantics were set
designers too, so their work has a theatrical quality.[6] Tchelitchew,
in particular, was influenced by Doré and sought a visionary effect in
his images. Although they distrusted psychoanalysis, they had affinities with the Surrealists; Tchelitchew, for example, often blended
images of bodies and landscapes. Their reputation faded once Abstract
Expressionism became fashionable. A travelling exhibition in 2005–6
sought to revive interest in what one critic called 'the extraordinary
achievement of this until now woefully neglected group'.[7] Tchelitchew
himself remained just in view over the years, owing to the presence of
his large canvas *Hide and Seek* (1940–2) and many smaller pieces at the
Museum of Modern Art in New York. In 2008–9, a group of his works,
including *Hide and Seek*, was exhibited at the Museum of the City of
New York.[8]

In 1925, Gertrude Stein discovered his work and bought up a group
of his canvases, one of which she hung on the wall of her dining room,
mischievously seating Picasso where he would have to stare at it.[9]
Having broken with Hemingway, she took on Tchelitchew as her new
protégé, giving him and Tanner the run of her house. Stein's companion, Alice B. Toklas, immediately decided Tchelitchew was a piece of
work – malicious and ready to use Stein for his advantage. Although
Toklas's view of Tchelitchew cannot be taken at face value, others

thought much the same. The American novelist Glenway Wescott who knew the painter for thirty years spoke of 'his craziness – he has always been in a certain way insane, non-sane, psychopathological' – and he told John Pearson that the painter was 'a really *terrible* person'.[10] A reading of Tchelitchew's immense correspondence with Edith Sitwell reveals him as extravagant, visionary, superstitious, mad, and selfish.

That, however, was not how Edith Sitwell saw him. She fell wildly in love, and the two embarked on a mysterious and passionate relationship. It is unknown whether they slept together. Pavel, known to his friends as Pavlik, was mostly, but not strictly, interested in men. The painter's close friend and biographer, Parker Tyler – a man as dotty as himself – talks of the relationship with Sitwell as virginal, and of Tchelitchew feeling that every woman was a potential Circe against whom he must prepare counter-magic: 'Edith Sitwell (in his imagination) is the virgin who wishes to be deflowered and for this quasi-sacred purpose, *he*, Pavel Tchelitchew, *has been irrevocably elected* [Tyler's emphases]. His work is surely cut out for him. This Sibyl is just virginal enough, just erotic enough, to be (like any witch for that matter) subjugated – held in masculine thrall.' Whatever passed between them, he had, by around 1929, physically recoiled from Sitwell. As he exclaimed to Tanner, 'What – alone with *Sitvouka*? Non, mon cher! What do you want? *I should be raped!*'[11]

In the years that followed, Tchelitchew toyed with her expectations when he wanted her to buy a picture, to arrange exhibitions, or to find him commissions. He once remarked to Wescott: 'People like me who are sex-mad have absolutely no obligation to their lovers.'[12] There is no confirmation of it in their letters, but it is just possible that he and Sitwell had a brief sexual liaison, and that she remained hopeful ever after of it starting up again or resolving in marriage. This would make sense of her clinging to him and of her jealousy of his lovers. Her comments to Elizabeth Salter about never having had a passionate relationship do not exclude the possibility of a very brief sexual experience. It looked to others like an affair. Helen Rootham saw, or guessed, or feared that something was going on, so scolded Sitwell over the damage to her reputation. When Tchelitchew died thirty years later, Sitwell remained protective of his memory and pleaded with Tyler: 'Don't hand him over to the wolves.'[13]

What did she see in him? He could be affectionate and entertaining. Allanah Harper recalled him leaping and turning pirouettes for Sitwell's amusement outside Stein's house.[14] He had a knack of mimicry: apart from voices, he would imitate the sound of wind in an aspen tree or of paper blown from a table, and run through the subtle noises supposedly made by egrets, mice, butterflies in flight, mosquitoes, and fleas.[15] What Sitwell did not want was someone remote like her father or a brutish hunter like her mother's relatives. She looked for sensitive men and, perhaps naively, fell for bisexuals like Guevara, Sassoon, and Tchelitchew.

It is not certain that Sitwell really understood much about homosexuality, at least before 1932, when she asked her friend the art collector and author Edward James to explain some of the sex acts to her; he refused. Or perhaps she would not admit what she did know. For many years, she said nothing (at least in surviving letters) about Osbert's relationship, begun a few years earlier and amounting to marriage, with the socialite and occasional author David Horner. In the late 1920s she was jealous of Tanner's role in Tchelitchew's life and became sympathetic to him only when he was supplanted by the American poet Charles Henri Ford c.1933. Sitwell's perpetual complaint was that Tchelitchew could not tell who his real friends were, by which she meant he ought to see that she was the one who truly loved him. There was trouble here that had nothing to do with orientation. Tchelitchew was what we now call a child abuser. Charles Henri Ford's unpublished journals recount his own many seductions of pubescent boys – it is not at all unusual to read of him sleeping with fifteen-year-olds even when he himself was almost forty. He and Tchelitchew shared partners, and often engaged in threesomes. He described Tchelitchew as preferring sex with boys to sex with his male peers. On at least one occasion, Ford expected to be arrested along with Tchelitchew and another friend over their dealings with a minor, and wrote in his journal: 'Anyone who has sexual dalliance of any sort with children is looked upon, or at least called, a "degenerate" by the newspapers. *Quelle Cauchemar!*'[16] A nightmare indeed. Sitwell had no idea what she was involved in. Though she suffered on account of the rejection, she was probably never so fortunate as to be spared a marriage or a lengthy sexual relationship with Tchelitchew.

Still, her sexual frustration fuelled rows with Tchelitchew, who had a cruel temper. After the painter died of heart failure in 1957, his friend and supporter Lincoln Kirstein (founder of the New York City Ballet) claimed that Pavlik had died of anger.[17] In *Taken Care Of*, Sitwell describes sitting to Tchelitchew at a studio in London, with the door locked and the key in his pocket: 'he took to hurtling the armchair in which I sat across the slippery floor as if it were a perambulator, at the same time uttering shrieks of rage, and, at moments, hurling bare canvasses [sic] past my head, being careful, however, that they did not hurt that organ.' She puts a comic though unconvincing spin on his death threats: '"Yes, yes, I choos" (just) "*keel* you, you know! I choos keel you." "Very well old boy . . . if you must, you must! But kindly respect my amber!"' Eventually, Cecil Beaton appeared, heard the commotion, demanded that Pavlik open the door, and then joined them at tea. That was her story, and she stuck to it – Beaton was on the wrong side of the door to witness what actually happened.

Sitwell was forced, at least superficially, into the role of close friend or sister to Tchelitchew – she never made peace with this. She could, however, claim a role in his art. After meeting Tchelitchew briefly in June 1927, Sitwell returned to England. In October, she wrote to Tom Balston that she was going to be painted by a Russian: 'I tried to escape, but Gertrude put her sandal on me and pinned me to the ground, saying firmly: "He is going to be a very great man. I found Picasso, and I found Matisse (which is true) and I've never been deceived." – But oh, my poor face.' This portrait in gouache was followed almost immediately by another, finished before July 1928, when he held a one-man show at the Claridge Gallery in London.[18] He subsequently executed four more portraits and a wax sculpture of Sitwell. While he set great store by his large allegorical works *Phenomena* (1936–8) and *Hide and Seek* (1940–2), some of his most arresting images were portraits of Edith Sitwell, especially one done in pastel in 1935. Although she entered his opaque Symbolic system as a 'Sibyl', she wanted something more concrete: to be his wife.

A beginning with Tchelitchew was matched by an ending with Robert Graves. Although she had known of the plan for Graves to take a teaching job in Egypt, she was surprised when he, Nancy, and Laura Riding headed off in January 1926 without saying goodbye. Then, in

June 1927, she discovered an article by Riding in the journal *Transitions*, referring to a 'general flaw' in recent poetry, and claiming that Eliot, Sitwell, and other poets felt the need to caricature a tainted, ordinary language before they could communicate directly. Sitwell wrote to Sassoon: 'I don't quite know what poem Miss Riding has written which puts her in a position to be impertinent to Poe, Rimbaud, Eliot, or myself. The mere fact of having pinched Nancy's husband is not sufficient.' Since Sassoon had been urging her not to fight with critics, she promised to leave Riding alone if there was nothing further: 'I'm doing this not out of consideration for Robert's feelings, (he should have kept her in her place) – but simply because you have asked me not to.'[19]

The same criticism was made in *A Survey of Modernist Poetry*, published in November, in which Robert Graves now appeared as co-author. The book did observe that much of what she (and Eliot and cummings, but not William Carlos Williams) wrote was 'genuine poetry', but she sensed a defection. The publication of *Goodbye to All That*, with its distorted accounts of the soldiering of Sassoon and others, sealed the matter. Robert Graves was no longer considered a friend. When Sitwell found that Graves had sold a copy of her book *The Sleeping Beauty* that she had inscribed 'For Robert Graves and Nancy Nicholson in admiration from Edith Sitwell', she bought and resold it with a further note: 'I wrote this dedication at a time when Robert Graves was a tentative English nightingale and not an American loon or screech-owl. Though poor, I am happy to buy this book (from the shop to which he sold it) for the sum of 15s so that no one can accuse me of being a hoot-fan. Edith Sitwell.'[20]

In early October 1927, Edith Sitwell met Pablo Picasso at 27 rue de Fleurus. She liked him straight away: 'At the moment, he was extremely excited and over-joyed because his mother-in-law had just died. Also he was looking forward to the funeral, because, according to Gertrude, all Spaniards prefer funerals to circuses any day.'[21] Stein later remarked on something in Picasso's sensibility that became a touchstone for Sitwell. According to Stein, as a young man he had once rounded on 'the French version of the Bloomsburys': 'Yes, yes . . . your taste and intellect is so wonderful. *But who does the work?* Stupid, tasteless people like me.'[22]

Geniuses were sometimes difficult to manage. Around the end of 1927, Edith Sitwell invited Cecil Beaton to a tea party, where he would likely find Forster and the Eliots, along with W. B. Yeats: 'Oh bother, [Yeats] wants me to be a Rosicrucian. Such a strain, and so bad for the clothes, as it seems to lead to sandals and blue veils.'[23] On another occasion she told Sassoon about a lunch with Yeats at the Ivy, a restaurant surrounded by theatres:

The Manager, overcome with awe, practically threw away all the theatrical managers and originals and copies of Miss Tallulah Bankhead, and devoted himself, most respectfully, to Yeats, thereby calling the attention of the whole restaurant to us. I did not bless him, as Yeats . . . boomed out, in a bittern-like poet's voice, every now and then 'Come to Rapallo, and my wife and I will Lay Hands Upon You' . . . and 'Every time my wife and I put our hands in our pockets, we bring them out filled with the perfume of violets and lilies, – by purely mystical means.' And (archly) 'a friend of ours has a mother who might well be called a bit of a *Witch*' (shades of George Robey) and '[the composer Edmund] Dulac lit the candles with his fingers.' – The actor managers and the originals and copies of Miss Tallulah Bankhead couldn't get over it. Nor could I.[24]

Christmas came as a Sitwellian set-piece. Sir George and Lady Ida summoned Edith to the Curzon Hotel. She could not find a bus or taxi, so got soaked through her clothes and had to remain in them all day, most of it spent in conversation with the son and daughter of the Parsee High Priest of Bombay, who lobbed questions at her: 'What do *you* think about the New English Prayer Book, Miss Sitwell? Naturally, we are very interested.' Gnashing of teeth led to the breaking of a molar. When a dentist pulled it out a few days later, it came in three pieces. The procedure took an hour and ten minutes, by which time the novocaine had worn off: 'it made me wonder what sort of things are happening in China, if that kind of thing can happen here, – to somebody who hasn't even been particularly annoying.'[25]

Much worse things were on the horizon. Once a servant of the Londesboroughs, Edith Powell was Osbert's much loved cook.[26] Early in 1928, she was taken to the Royal Free Hospital for what she

understood to be preventive surgery, though she was really suffering
from breast cancer and had only two years to live. Part of her care fell
to Edith, who made the long bus ride to the hospital almost every day
for more than two months. There she saw a little girl of nine who had
lost a leg to tuberculosis. Coming from a family of seven children, the
girl was surprised at being given anything other than what she called
'bread and grease' to eat. She owned no warm clothes, so Sitwell and
the nurses knitted some for her. Sitwell told Sassoon that she had
started writing an outraged letter to 'Somebody' (she hadn't decided
whether this should be a politician or a newspaper) about children
lacking necessities: 'it is no good expecting anybody to understand anything – excepting just a few people, – I tore the letter up. It isn't
heartlessness, just stupidity.'27

Some months later, she made a scene at Arnold Bennett's house.
Lord Berners, a composer and polymath, 'giggled' about Mrs Powell's
condition: 'I should prefer a cook who didn't suffer from malignant dis-
eases.' Sitwell said as gently as she could: 'I suppose humanity has got
a dreadful way of cropping up in one, even if one is only a cook.'
Afterwards, Christabel Aberconway chided her for not being 'a woman
of the world'. Sitwell described all this later for Sassoon: 'I find being
a woman of the world so incompatible with being a lady – half the
time, – I mean what I consider a lady.'28

Illness was about to strike closer. Around the beginning of February
1928, Helen Rootham, then fifty-three, was exhausted, and she had
two suspicious lumps. Under local anaesthetic, a surgeon removed a
gland from under her arm; she waited, very ill, at Moscow Road, for the
pathology report, which showed that it was malignant and that more
surgery was necessary. Forbidding Sitwell to come because she would
'fuss', she hurried to Paris where Professor Henri Albert Hartmann,
who had treated Sitwell in 1905, removed the second lump, which may
have been in her breast. Once Sitwell received word from Paris, she
wrote to Gertrude Stein: 'Poor thing. She was really so wonderfully
brave, and behaved as though it were nothing.'29

Rootham's fiancé also behaved as though it were nothing. Sitwell
called Sassoon in to advise her on whether to confront 'one of the most
dangerous blackguards in London';30 she was afraid of stirring up
Helen's feelings about a man who had effectively dumped her. On

Sassoon's advice, she summoned the fiancé, then reported back: 'It has been perfectly awful, because the whole thing was simply brought on by misery over the cad to whom she has been engaged for the last eight or nine years ... he didn't even enquire if it was malignant or not, and she had to go to Paris, looking a dying woman, without one word from him. I sent for him, and had an interview with him which I imagine he didn't enjoy.' Edith compared him as a religious teacher to the recently deceased J. H. Smyth-Pigott – a defrocked clergyman who had led a sect called 'Agapemones' in Somerset; in 1902 he claimed to be the Messiah and over the years had bedded many of his female followers as 'soul-brides'.[31] She went on: 'I told H's fiancé that I had had to lie and say he had been ill, and that was why he had not been to see her. He replied "*Mystically* you were speaking the truth, Miss Sitwell." Gosh! "Mystically" is now going to be a catchword with me ... If I don't want to do a thing, I shall say: "Mystically, I will do it."'[32]

Sitwell made an impression on him: 'the little darling whisked over to Paris like a frightened rabbit. So now I suppose poor H. will be satisfied. It is something to know he can be frightened.'[33] Rootham wrote sad letters to Sitwell, remarking that her fiancé did everything late and that she felt like a ghost talking to Jack Straw.[34] Sitwell told Tom Balston that she was going to break up one of the man's meetings and expose him: 'I know a thing or two about him which would get him turned out of England if only I could tell the police.' What she knew about the man is hard to guess, but if he could be deported he must have been a foreigner – further evidence that the fiancé was indeed Dimitrije Mitrinović.

Helen's sister Evelyn, whose marriage to Truels Wiel was now over, had had nursing experience during the war, so Helen looked to her for care. However, in the year following Helen's surgery Evelyn required what Sitwell called, somewhat vaguely, 'the most appalling operation known', though it was not for cancer. Evelyn suffered from varicose veins, which made it difficult for her to walk. Both women turned to Sitwell as their protector.[35] Sitwell took the devastated Helen for a short holiday at a hotel in Bournemouth after Easter. Yet another blow came: they heard that Sir Edmund Gosse had undergone surgery. He died on 16 May 1928.[36] Sassoon, who had been particularly close to Gosse, was stricken.

For Edith Sitwell to get out of a funk, it was usually necessary for her to pick a fight. This happened in the pages of the *Daily Mail*, to which she had been contributing tart columns. A letter to the editor (23 June 1928) denounced her 'acid disposition and disagreeable mind'. Two days later Sitwell wrote that the letter-writer 'has taught me the value of birth-control for the masses'. The newspaper was then flooded with letters, so the editors sought the opinion of George Bernard Shaw, who was all for Sitwell: 'if a man hits Gene Tunney in the street he must put up with what he gets in return' (30 June 1928).[37]

Sitwell was happy to annoy other people, not many of whom took it as Shaw thought they should. A few months later, she told Sassoon: 'The Representative of the Gas Light and Coke Company is in a black passion with me. He could hardly speak, he was so annoyed. All because he brought me a document to sign, at the top of which was the heading, *Maker and Description*. And I wrote: God. Tall. Fair-haired. Not at all bad-looking. Grey eyes. He broke into a fury and said it was a legal document and I had defaced it!'

Her own face was a matter of concern to her, so she went to the Herbalists Association, asking for 'a message of hope for my dewlaps'. 'Yis, Modom,' said the assistant, and they consulted for some time over her dewlaps. Then Sitwell burst out, 'Do you realise that God has only relented about my hands and my ankles, and that if the joints in *them* enlarge, it will be the *River* for me?' 'Yis Modom.' The assistant paused. 'For *craggy* joints, use . . .' After this conversation, Edith put it to her sister-in-law, Georgia, 'Craggy joints . . . Now *have* I craggy joints?'

After 1928, Edith Sitwell wrote fewer and fewer playful poems. Her sense of humour ranged anarchically through her letters (she is one of her century's great letter writers) and through works like *The English Eccentrics* (1933). The poem 'Metamorphosis', first published in 1928, introduces images that are central to her work after 1940: Lazarus, the Arctic cold, transformations of the body out of death. These capture Sitwell's private sense – confided whimsically to herbalists – of a body growing older. The poem was largely completed before Helen's illness and so does not reflect the anxieties of the late winter of 1928.

She explained the origins of her next major poem, 'Gold Coast Customs', to the art historian Sir Kenneth Clark (later Lord Clark):

In the two years before I wrote the poem – I can't remember the exact date – there were terrible processions of Hunger-marchers, – the real thing, not a political demonstration. Three times I saw a figure walking beside these, as it were producing their music. I think he was mad. He was skeleton-thin, wore nothing but a suit, as shapeless and thin and shiny as mud – it looked as if it were made of mud. He had rouged the whole of his face as red as blood, and carried an empty food-tin, which he banged rhythmically with a large bone.[38]

This drummer is heard in the poem's pounding metres, which also owe something to 'The Congo' (1914), Vachel Lindsay's clumsy experiment with a drumming beat. In 1919, Sitwell told Robert Nichols that she admired Lindsay,[39] but later decided that Lindsay was a *'horrible'* poet and 'The Congo' his most awful work.[40]

Sitwell learned of a 'freak' party on a barge, at which the guests were dressed as beggars and had to step over the homeless people sleeping on the Embankment. In a newspaper article at the time, she described an Irish harvester who had recently died of starvation, a fearful contrast to the 'exceedingly vulgar and boring freak parties which have been held for the last year or two . . . These forms of modern behaviour create in me a violent passion for Queen Victoria, for the deans of the Victorian era, and for laws of conduct laid down by Lord Tennyson. I would rather have a dean than a divorcée any day, though I have been bored by specimens of both species; but at any rate deans are not vulgar.'[41]

What she saw seemed as cruel as cannibalism. To her, London was not unlike Ashantee in West Africa a hundred years earlier, where 'the death of any rich or important person was followed by several days of national ceremonies, during which the utmost licence prevailed, and slaves and poor persons were killed that the bones of the deceased might be washed with human blood. These ceremonies were called Customs.' Sitwell's poem, written in the summer and autumn of 1928, was titled in early drafts 'The Best Party', then 'Gold Coast Customs', and it reads as if a party in *Vile Bodies* had been crashed by Jonathan Swift:

One house like a rat-skin
Mask flaps fleet
In the sailor's tall
Ventriloquist street
Where the rag houses flap –
Hiding a gap.

Here tier on tier
Like a black box rear
In the flapping slum
Beside Death's docks.
I did not know this meaner Death
Meant this: that the bunches of nerves still dance
And caper among these slums, and prance.

'Mariners, put your bones to bed!'
But at Lady Bamburgher's parties each head,
Grinning, knew it had left its bones
In the mud with the white skulls . . . only the grin
Is left, strings of nerves, and the drum-taut skin.[42]

Sitwell explained to Allanah Harper: 'the 1¼ syllabled words "rear"
and "tier" make you feel that the houses are toppling over.' Elsewhere,
she relies on double rhymes for extra emphasis, and on assonance to
achieve a 'worm-like turning movement'. Underlining words for
emphasis, she said that moral chaos is suggested by lines made deliberately 'tuneless': '. . . dead / Grass creaks like a carrion-bird's voice,
rattles, / Squeaks like a wooden shuttle, battles . . .' Elsewhere, she allows
lines to 'lengthen themselves out, rear up, and come down with a crash
on one's head'.[43]

   In an early draft of the poem, she tried to versify Hegel's now derided
observation in The Philosophy of History: 'What we properly understand
by Africa, is Unhistorical Undeveloped Spirit, still involved in the
conditions of mere nature, and which had to be presented here only
as on the threshold of the World's History.'[44] As published, the poem
includes a long note from Hegel on 'the devouring of human flesh'
among Africans. Realising that this could be offensive, she commented

in later editions: 'It is needless to add that this refers only to a past age, and that, in quoting this passage, I intend no reflection whatever upon the African races of our time. This passage no more casts a reflection upon them than a passage referring to the cruelties of the Tudor age casts a reflection upon the English of our present age.'[45]

In 1951, Sitwell got into a row with the poet David Lutyens over whether the name Bamburgher in the poem is anti-Semitic.[46] About the same time, she defended the name to another correspondent as not anti-Semitic but international, as is the character of the crime the poem describes.[47] Geoffrey Elborn shrewdly proposes that the model for Lady Bamburgher is the Irish-American Emerald Cunard.[48] In early versions of the poem the hostess was named Hamburgher; the name was then changed to Bamburgher, which still served as a dactyl (a stressed syllable followed by two unstressed) but fitted in more tightly with the poem's patterns of alliteration and the underlying drumbeat. Either name would be Jewish. Lady Cunard's maiden name, Burke, is recognisable in both names. Still, in giving Jewish names to someone who represents amoral wealth, Sitwell does rely on a stereotype.

'Gold Coast Customs is my real joy, if you can call it a joy,'[49] Sitwell told Sassoon, who admired it and thought it frightening. Sitwell herself called it 'an absolute terror'[50] and said that writing it had left her 'shattered'.[51] The poem provided the title-piece of a new collection published on 24 January 1929, which included a Tchelitchew portrait of Sitwell as a frontispiece. In Osbert's view, Edith had 'broken through' in 'Gold Coast Customs' and fulfilled a prophecy made by Sir Edmund Gosse in 1926: 'I feel that she is a sort of chrysalis, in a silken web of imperfect expression, with great talents to display if only she can break out into a clear music of her own. There is no one I watch with more interest.'[52] Yeats himself was fascinated by the direction Sitwell's poetry had taken: 'Her language is the traditional language of literature, but twisted, torn, complicated, jerked here and there by strained resemblances, unnatural contacts, forced upon it by terror or by some violence beating in her blood, some primitive obsession that civilization can no longer exorcise.'[53]

After months of medical crises and the writing of such a violent work, Sitwell's visit to Renishaw in August 1928 was thankfully calm. She felt that her mother had forgiven her for existing – but only after an extended period of badgering her about her morals (perhaps Lady Ida had heard gossip about Edith and Pavel Tchelitchew). During a visit to Renishaw, Lady Ida called out in the night to her daughter, whose room was next door: 'Edith, have you ever been happy?'

'Yes, Mother. Haven't you?'

'Never bird-happy. Still, I have three very nice children.'

After this, she sighed and went to sleep again.[54]

Lady Ida was seldom well, and it often fell to the visiting Edith to entertain her. At some point she even suffered from aphasia, a brain disorder causing impairment of the ability to produce or comprehend language; it is hard to imagine a more difficult circumstance in which to make conversation.[55] In any event, the peace of the summer of 1928 was broken only when the two-year-old daughter of Osbert's servant John Robins pointed her finger at Lady Ida and told her to 'Bugger off.'[56] From Renishaw, the Sitwells moved straight on to Montegufoni. Edith was preparing for two performances of Façade at the International Festival of Modern Music at Siena on 14 September. Among their guests at the castello were Constant Lambert, Willie Walton, Christabel Aberconway, Arthur Waley, and Beryl de Zoete (Waley's companion and an expert on traditional dances). Lady Aberconway recalled that they stayed together for about three weeks and that on one evening the guests for dinner filled eight buses. A day or so before the performances, they watched the horse race, Il Palio, and then realised that Walton had contrived a small disaster. He had given Gino Severini's design for the new curtain to a set painter and had not asked his name or address. With the performance scheduled for the next day, they worked out that the painter's name might be Barone, so Lady Ida began canvassing all the Barones in the vicinity, saying enigmatically to each, 'Your son has done a curtain for my daughter.' Aberconway went to a restaurant the painter was thought to frequent, found him, and claimed the curtain.

By all accounts, the performances were a success.[57] Walton conducted and Lambert recited a version with twenty-two numbers, including for the first time 'Black Mrs Behemoth' and 'Popular Song', which were the last of a total of forty-three settings that Walton wrote for Façade.[58] However, the day was soured when Sassoon and his lover Stephen Tennant (the tubercular brother of Bimbo Tennant, who had

been killed in the war)[59] arrived too late to see *Façade*. Even though he
too was staying at Montegufoni, Sitwell avoided Sassoon for three days.
They finally met, by arrangement, in her bedroom, where she was
reclining under a mosquito net; he presented lilies, apologised, and was
forgiven. He recorded that it took seven minutes to win her over again
completely.[60]

Edith Sitwell's male friends tended to leave jilted women of their
acquaintance on her doorstep. In March, Sassoon and Blunden had
done just this with Aki Hayashi, who came to London after an affair
with Edmund Blunden in Japan.[61] Now Tchelitchew followed their
example. Stella Bowen was an Australian painter who lived with Ford
Madox Ford and had a daughter with him. In 1927, she set up
Tchelitchew and his ménage in two furnished houses at Guermantes,
a farming village east of Paris, where they stayed, paying little rent, in
the summers from 1927 to 1934.[62] When Ford and Bowen separated in
1928, Tchelitchew asked Sitwell to take her up. In a thoroughly characteristic sequence of events, Sitwell listened carefully to Bowen's
troubles, and wrote many compassionate and encouraging letters: 'you
can say anything to me without it hurting you. Because I see grief on
a large scale, and not on a small scale, it can never mean any loss of
pride on your part, if you show me that you are suffering. I only see you
finer.'[63] She also tried to find buyers for Bowen's art. However, she
wrote to Tom Balston: 'Why is it I have always to look after every
female bore who has got herself into a state of unpopularity? Siegfried's
Japanese and Pavlik's Australian, all in one year.'[64] Thus, she tried to
dismiss what had become for her a very important friendship and a serious emotional involvement.

In fact, the friendship flourished. Bowen, who was herself much
loved by a wide circle of friends, recalled nothing but kindness from
Sitwell: 'The English aristocrat, six feet tall, aquiline, haughty, dressed
in long robes and wearing barbaric ornaments, was a strange sight in
happy-go-lucky Montparnasse. But the sweet voice, the almost exaggerated courtesy and the extreme sensitiveness to other people's
feelings, were so immediately winning.' Bowen also observed Sitwell's
relationship with Tchelitchew: 'they were each of them a packet of
nerves, infusing therefrom a palpitating and sensuous life into their
respective work. The shape and texture of Edith's words were like

surfaces felt with the fingertips, and Pavlick's [sic] sombre paintings had
the organic, breathing kind of life, stilled but vital, of a fish whose gills
are just kept moving.'[65]

Adrian Allinson's cartoon from the late 1920s depicts the three Sitwells on what
appears to be a post-cubist camping holiday

At the end of 1928, Sitwell was in deeper financial trouble than
usual because she was covering expenses for Helen and for Pavlik. She
undertook for Duckworth *The Pleasures of Poetry*, a three-volume
anthology published between 1930 and 1932, and she accepted a commission from Faber to write a biography of Alexander Pope. Sitwell
identified with Pope, partly because of his spinal deformity but also
because she viewed him as a persecuted genius, not unlike herself. The
book appeared in March 1930, the product of shallow research, yet
vastly more entertaining than Maynard Mack's sober biography of
Pope, which is now regarded as definitive. She undertook to defend
Pope's life and poetry from all comers, portraying him as she would a
good modernist: as a master of 'rhetoric and formalism'. His adversaries
are just like the minor Georgians:

To these men, rhetoric and formalism were abhorrent . . . But in addition to this technical fault, we find in the verse of that time (as in

much contemporary verse) the fault of an exaggerated praise of worthy
home life, which alternated with swollen, inflated boomings and roar-
ings about the Soul of Man. These reigned triumphant, together with
healthy, manly, but rather raucous shouts for beer, and advertisements
of certain rustic parts of England, delivered to the accompaniment of
a general clumsy clodhopping with hobnailed boots.[66]

And with the hobnailed boots she is back to the problems of prosody.
While the book hardly presents a nuanced account of Pope's contemporaries, it makes a massive contribution to an undervalued subgenre,
the literary put-down: 'Addison was good-hearted, perhaps a little too
consciously so, was kind, but rather too deliberately open and just. He
might be described as the first of a long line of literary cricketers, for he
was always "playing the game" or being manly and above guile about
one thing or another.' Sitwell draws a self-portrait when she speaks of
Pope as the antithesis of Addison: 'although he spent a large part of his
life in doing kindnesses, and although he was the truest and loyalest of
friends, he had [an] unfortunate inhibition against speaking the truth.'[67]
    In one respect, the book did break new ground. Its last chapter
explained Pope's rhythms and versification; W. H. Auden thought it
'brilliantly displayed' the beauties of Pope's work. Half a century after
its publication, Donald Greene, a leading expert on Alexander Pope,
wrote that 'in spite of its flowery language, [it] should not be overlooked
by any beginning reader of Pope', and he agreed with Auden's observations.[68] Beyond an opening nonsense (perhaps derived from her
training on the piano) about how physical strength is necessary to write
some verse forms, she grows acute on Pope's use of the caesura, and on
his handling of the 'speed' of a line through the alternation of mono-
and polysyllabic words to achieve different effects. Although scholars
now take it for granted that Pope's heroic couplets are capable of huge
variety, in the 1920s they were often spoken of as monotonous and
inflexible. Sitwell made her case so convincingly that it entered the
common store of unfootnoted critical certainties.
    Sitwell's unusual expertise in poetic technique was honed by con-
versation with Sassoon, for whom she also had a strong affection. In
October 1928, hearing that he was ill, she urged him to drink raw eggs
beaten up in port and to take care over his meals. She even volunteered

to teach him to cook chops so that he would 'feel far more independent'.[69] However, after making a gift to him of a manuscript of 'Gold
Coast Customs' at the end of the year, she heard nothing more until
April, when Sassoon wrote asking why she was 'unfriendly'.[70] He sent
her a silk scarf and said he measured their friendship by years, not
weeks or months. Sitwell teased him, 'Did you mean us to measure it by
the years in which you *don't* speak to us, or the weeks when you do, or
the months when you do and don't, on and off? Kindly answer!'[71] Since
1927, their friendship had been made difficult by the presence of
Stephen Tennant. Sitwell did not like and was jealous of this 'daisy'.[72]
However, her antipathy did not preclude her introducing Tennant, an
art collector, to Tchelitchew. Tennant and the painter went on to form
a friendship and may even have been sleeping together. Sassoon was
briefly as jealous of Tchelitchew as Sitwell was of Tennant.[73]

Needing the money, Sitwell kept up her schedule of lectures, frequently refusing invitations on the grounds that she was terribly busy
but offering to squeeze them in if she was paid extra. Her lectures in
1929 often described D. H. Lawrence as king of the 'Jaeger school of literature'. In May, this came to the notice of Messrs Jaeger, who objected
to the comparison.[74] Recalling the episode about two years later,
Sitwell said she had explained to the clothing firm that her 'only reason
for comparing the works of Mr. Lawrence and those of Professor Jaeger
was this: that the works of both are hot, soft, and wooly; but that as the
works of Professor Jaeger are unshrinkable by time, and some of Mr.
Lawrence's, in my opinion, are not, I wished to apologise'. The firm
responded that owing to her 'courteous expression of regret, the matter
had been erased from their records, but they added: "We are soft, and
we are wooly, but we are never hot, owing to our system of slow conductivity . . ." How I wished that they would invent a system of slow
conductivity for "Lady C's Lover." Perhaps they did, for the new and
authorized edition has appeared, and . . . is soft and wooly, but not hot,
and is, as well, (again like the works of Messrs. Jaeger) in no need of a
depilatory.'[75]

A portion of Sitwell's earnings as a lecturer and writer went to
Tchelitchew, who required other kinds of help as well. As a stateless
person, he often had difficulty crossing borders. In the late spring of
1929, Sitwell turned to a 'Mr Gurney' in the Foreign Office to hurry

along the granting of a visa. This was probably Thomas Gurney, whose wife, a Scarborough friend of Lady Ida, had presented Edith at court in 1907.[76] From 1930, Sitwell looked to the politician Cecil Harmsworth (later first Baron Harmsworth) to secure Pavlik's visas.[77]

In May 1929, Pavlik arrived in London and set to work on a wax head of Sitwell. It appears that he stayed with the young anthropologist Geoffrey Gorer, whom Sitwell had first met at a literary society in Cambridge in 1924. Gorer knew Gertrude Stein's circle and had met Tchelitchew before Sitwell did. Although argumentative, Gorer became one of Sitwell's closest friends, as did his mother, Rée (or Rachel). Geoffrey Gorer told John Pearson that his mother and Edith Sitwell resembled each other. When they went to a show at Finsbury Park Empire in the Gorers' Daimler, Sitwell got out first, and the bystanders believed she was the comedian Nellie Wallace. However, when Rée got out, they changed their minds. '[Edith] was a very simple person underneath that most exotic of exteriors. A simple country girl, entirely self-educated. What she really liked was a schooner of beer and a plate of steak and onions.'[78]

Tchelitchew had come to London looking for people to buy his pictures and to commission portraits. Sitwell promoted him aggressively. On 6 June, she recounted for Sassoon the hardships of the painter's life and urged him to get Tennant to purchase something at an exhibition at the Galerie Pierre in Paris. She said that she had herself raised £45 against her biography of Pope to buy a picture. Six months later, she sent a cheque to Pavlik for £45 as half-payment for a painting. This seems to be a second purchase; if so, she paid him £135 for the two paintings. Even though her income increased that year by £50 owing to an inheritance from Blanche Sitwell, this was a huge amount for her to hand over to Pavlik. A patroness on tick, Sitwell constantly asked Tchelitchew about his finances and vowed to do everything she could for him: 'Vos tristesses sont mes tristesses; et vos espoirs sont mes espoirs.'[79] She bought his paintings because she thought them brilliant, but she also wanted to put money in his pocket. By purchase and gift, she acquired a collection – most of it hidden after 1939 in Evelyn Wiel's apartment in Paris. When at last Sitwell recovered most of the pictures in 1961, she had to auction off thirty-nine of them to pay debts.[80] A further group of works was subsequently found in the apartment.

Rounding up sitters for Pavlik had its comic side. At first, Sitwell

liked Diana Fitzherbert, the American wife of a baronet, but then
lumped her in with the 'cheap little sluts who arouse [Pavlik's]
chivalry'.[81] In October, when Sitwell needed to cancel an arrangement
to have tea with her, she took the occasion (so she claimed) to teach
a sixteen-year-old servant named Ethel not to be afraid of the telephone. Ethel girded her loins and made the call to Lady Fitzherbert: "'Is
that you, Bitch'erbal? Bitch'erbal *is that you*? This is Miss Sitwell speaking, and she won't see yer." Sensation. Curtain. "Ethel," I said sadly.
"Ethel," I said, "that is not the way to speak. You must not call Lady
Fitzherbert Bitch'erbal." "Why not, Miss?" enquired Ethel sullenly.
"Because Ethel," I said *rather* regretfully, "we have to try and remember old Mr. Manners.'"[82]

Tchelitchew's companion Allen Tanner played a bizarre trick on
Sitwell when she came to Paris in March 1930. He asked her to sell in
London a book that Thomas Jefferson had once given to the Marquis
de Lafayette. The book had come to Tanner from a man named
Semenoff who had stolen it from Count Louis de Lastérie.[83] Tanner
knew it was stolen property, but told Sitwell it had been purchased on
a quai in Germany. At the same time he asked her to keep the sale
secret from Pavlik and to say only that he had made the money from
writing a piano manual. When Sotheby's sold the book, the Count
claimed the proceeds. Fortunately, the auction house politely accepted
Sitwell's explanation. She could see that she had had a narrow escape,
as she explained to Stella Bowen:

> My poor mother has been in prison; but our characters as writers
> have made this almost forgotten. Allen, by his lying and lying, has
> not only risked my being prosecuted and perhaps imprisoned, but it
> is absolutely *certain* that *had* there been a case, or prosecution, – even
> with me only as Seller of Stolen Property (and I could probably have
> proved my innocence) the *newspapers* would have raked up the story
> of my mother, even if the *lawyers* did not. And in any case, it would
> have been the discussion of every Club and dinner party in London.[84]

In a series of letters Sitwell explained the matter to Tchelitchew and
warned him not to abuse her friendship. He took Allen's side and
accused her of being quarrelsome.[85]

A chill set in, but on 8 June 1930 Tchelitchew wrote:

Dear friend, you write to us very infrequently and I think that you
give us much less this year than last, for you know very well that if
I don't write it means that I am poisoned by my life, and prefer not
to speak of it for there is sometimes such a hell in my soul that it is
frightful to touch it and you know that there isn't a single person
who can understand and console me more than you, and your silence
and the rather hasty, reticent letters – letters which don't say even
the half of what they said last year – it makes me very sad and
unhappy – for I think that my best friend is withdrawing from me
gently but firmly.[86]

Unable to remain angry, Sitwell was soon calling him 'mon petit
Pavlik' and proposing that he, Stella and she go on an ocean voyage in
September, if such an idea did not seem too scandalous.[87] There was no
voyage, but the dispute was over.

Just after Easter 1930, there was a new spate of medical trouble. Mrs
Powell, who had had further surgery, was near death. Around 22 April,
Sitwell, expecting news, thought she heard the phone ringing in the
middle of night; she got out of bed, then fell badly and struck her head,
creating a tiny dent at her hairline and bruises on her face. In the
absence of her own doctor, Hal Lydiard Wilson, she went to Helen's
doctor, who failed to recognise concussion. Sitwell donned a veil and
continued visiting the hospital where Mrs Powell died in agony on 26
April. A few days later Helen travelled to Paris, where Evelyn had
undergone a second round of surgery herself, which left her an
'invalid'.[88]

Sitwell continued to suffer vertigo, headaches, and loss of memory
for more than six months. In August, Sir George inspected her forehead and urged her to consult another doctor. The matter of Edith's
dent created a sensation in the family; Lady Ida wrote to Sachie: 'I feel
much fussed about Edith. Mildred [Lady Ida's sister] wonders whether
there may be a bit of bone touching the brain and that it can easily be
moved without danger & that she ought to have that place X rayed.'[89]
It seems they jumped to the conclusion that it was a depressed fracture
of the skull, but it was merely concussion and got better over time.

Sitwell was very glad when at last she had something to laugh at. John Collier, a young man who had once attended her tea parties, had his first success in 1930 with the brutally funny novel *His Monkey-Wife; Or Married to a Chimp*. In it a schoolmaster named Fatigay returns from the Upper Congo with a chimpanzee named Emily, whom he gives to his cold-hearted and very modern fiancée Amy Flint. Emily falls in love with Fatigay and decides to educate herself to be worthy of him. She becomes a reader at the British Museum, where she wins the hearts of learned codgers, and then moves on to the London stage. The work concludes with inter-species matrimony. In its African imagery and its debunking of British 'civilisation', the book, though not so grim, has some things in common with 'Gold Coast Customs'. Sitwell invited Collier back to Pembridge Mansions, and wrote to him afterwards: 'The word "wit" has been debased from meaning Swift to meaning that wretched buffoon Noel Coward. But *you* have wit as Swift understood it . . . And I *know* that you have genius. And I never use that word lightly. I don't think anything is left to be said now either about men's attitude towards women, or about women's inmost thoughts. I have always liked you very much, but I think you are a most terrifying young man.'[90] Collier went on to achieve fame with his short stories, of which about thirty were published in the *New Yorker*.

Even more cheering was her own new book. On 27 May 1930, Balston sent her a copy of her *Collected Poems*, a summing-up of twenty years of work. She had done some, but not yet all, of the 'sifting' that Sassoon urged; at 288 pages, the book offered a fairly tough-minded account of what she felt she had accomplished. At least a third of her early work had been dropped. The idea was not to show development over time but to put strength on display, so the volume opened with 'The Sleeping Beauty' and ended with 'Gold Coast Customs'. The early work appeared in the middle, mostly absorbed into *Façade* and other sequences. She wrote to Balston, 'I need hardly say that I now loathe every poem I have ever written. That I can't imagine why I ever believed I was a poet, etc., etc. But if the *production* of the book has the effect it should have, and will have, my reputation is saved!'[91]

As always in the 1920s, her work polarised even the sympathetic critics. Blunden praised her 'particularity of genius and workmanship'.[92] W. R. Benet harrumphed in the *Saturday Review of Literature*: 'We prefer her "Gold Coast Customs" to yards and yards and yards of her satyrs, nymphs, fauns, Admirals, and high cockalorums of all sorts.'[93] The reviewer in the *Nation and Athenæum* wrote: 'Miss Sitwell is careless of lucidity . . . But even in this strange poetry there are human chords, which remain and echo in the memory when other sounds have ebbed away . . . At their approach, Miss Sitwell's style takes on a negative quality, a crystal blankness, from which the image looks up exquisitely clear; it fills the mind, not merely with delight but wonder, that a word here and there, so simple, should have this power of evocation.'[94]

Another of Siegfried Sassoon's caricatures of the Sitwells

14

ALL EARS FOR EDITH

Wyndham Lewis's biographer, Paul O'Keeffe, tells us that *The Apes of God* weighed three pounds and three ounces.¹ Lumbering, rancid, and self-congratulatory, this *roman-à-clef*, published on 3 June 1930, has a surprise ending – that is, the reader is agreeably surprised when it does, in fact, end. In the novel, Daniel Boleyn, a handsome poet based on Lewis's younger self, is led about literary and artistic London by an albino named Zagreus. From time to time they receive encyclicals and broadcasts from an unseen painter-turned-philosopher named Pierpoint. We learn that London is full of those who 'ape' the true, God-like artist. One of the leitmotifs is studio envy: for example, Lewis's sometime friend, the painter Richard Wyndham, portrayed as 'Dick Whittingdon', is said to have taken a block of studios that could be used by ten geniuses.² Past kindness is especially provoking: Sydney Schiff, who gave Lewis a good deal of money, is portrayed as 'Lionel Kein', a talentless 'pseudo-Proust'.³ Most of the Bloomsbury notables are identifiable among Lewis's apes and mountebanks.

The longest portion of the book, 'Lord Osmund's Lenten Party', portrays the Sitwells as Osmund, Phoebus, and Harriet Finnian Shaw. Georgia makes an appearance as the 'New Zealand Jewess' Babs Kennson.⁴ Sir George Sitwell is 'Cockeye' and Edith Powell becomes 'Mrs Bosun'. Edith Sitwell is presented, contradictorily, as both an old maid and a lesbian whose 'woman-mate' is Julia Dyott (Helen Rootham). With an extra touch of cruelty, Lewis added that for ten years the brothers had been trying to get Julia out of the family.⁵ Lewis wanted to make as much mischief as possible in the Sitwell camp.

The Apes of God got good reviews (although regard for the book evaporated before long) and in no time readers were putting names to its characters. Sitwell was embarrassed, uncertain, and angry. When she did not answer a letter, the Schiffs asked, by registered post, whether their old friendship was over. She apologised profusely and explained that there had been sicknesses, deaths, and hard work on an anthology, but the more likely reason for her not writing to them was Wyndham Lewis. She pretended that she had read only one page of the novel directed at herself and no part of the book relating to them, adding that Lewis had 'a mean personal reason for hating me, but I shall never tell anyone what that reason is'. She claimed that she was untouched by the remarks about her age and appearance: 'The things that hurt me are ethical things – lies about my life, etc. (though he *has* lied about that too, I believe).'

About two years later she decided to tell Pavlik about Lewis's grudge: he had wanted '*un "succès" avec moi (un succès de la sorte qu'il comprend) et je lui ai mis à sa place. Alas, il se venge en disant des mensonges de moi, d'une sorte très grossier.*'[6] It is important to note that in these letters about Lewis to the Schiffs and to Tchelitchew she denies that she is a lesbian. While Sitwell may have dissembled about certain matters, there is no substantial evidence to set against these denials.

Handling Wyndham Lewis carefully, W. B. Yeats wrapped a rebuke in high praise: 'Somebody tells me that you have satirized Edith Sitwell. If that is so, visionary excitement has in part benumbed your senses. When I read her *Gold Coast Customs* a year ago, I felt, as on first reading *The Apes of God*, that something absent from all literature for a generation was back again, and in a form rare in the literature of all generations, passion ennobled by intensity, by endurance, by wisdom. We had it in one man once [Swift]. He lies in St. Patrick's now under the greatest epitaph in history.'[7] Sitwell was comforted by 'this noble and unforgettable tribute . . . I've never been prouder of anything.'[8] Afterwards, Yeats lost interest in Lewis and his work, while continuing to admire Edith Sitwell.[9]

In August 1930, Cecil Beaton brought his tripod and lenses to Renishaw and took group portraits of the family. This provided Sitwell with an idea of how to tackle Lewis. Three months later she told the young poet Terence Fytton Armstrong (whose pseudonym was John Gawsworth) that she had begun a memoir, which she hoped would be 'rather good, excepting that everything of the most interest in my life will have to be left out till I'm dead!'[10] By this she meant chapters pertaining to Lady Ida, and to Osbert's 'sacrifice' in not testifying at her trial. Most of that memoir can be traced in Sitwell's manuscript notebooks, and a finished copy of the first chapter survives.[11]

In that first chapter, the family assembles for photographs in the ballroom. Sitwell says that her mother is as beautiful as an 'eternal statue' but moves with difficulty, and that 'little things, little waterdrops, or bee-wings, fret her away, and make her bitterly unhappy'. However, her conversation flashes with 'brilliance and insight'. Sir George is described as living partly in the Middle Ages, 'but his heart is invariably deeply warm and affectionate'. Her brothers are lovingly rendered, along with Georgia and the three-year-old Reresby.

Sitwell is unusually humble: she is 'plain' and learns things (apart from poetic technique) slowly. She recounts an incident in which she spoke dismissively of John Middleton Murry to Arnold Bennett, who responded with a short laugh: '"Spiritual pride is an awful thing – an awful thing," Pause, "and there's another awful thing! Remember this, Edith! God sees you, and me, and Middleton Murry as just the same. He sees no difference between us."' Poor Bennett was about to test the truth of this saying, as he died unexpectedly of typhoid at the end of March 1931.[12]

Sitwell decided to be 'charming' to almost every writer she described, apart from Lewis and Coward[13] – but this was by no means a work 'recollected in tranquillity'. Her treatment of Lewis was especially comical, dwelling on his lack of personal hygiene and his filthy living conditions. Yet as she wrote, often between fifteen hundred and two thousand words per day, she brooded on all the troubles of her early life, her frustration with Pavlik, her debts, and her fears for Helen. Sitwell was still bothered by the effects of the concussion at least until the end of October 1930. She also suffered from poisoned glands and received oxygen injections in her shoulder during the autumn.[14] In November, she fired off two letters to Sassoon, accusing him of deserting their friendship. He made the same accusation in return, and the two finally made peace again at the beginning of December. There were some pleasures – she went to Paris in November and spent time with Gertrude Stein. Tchelitchew designed some clothes for her and began another portrait: 'Very like a Piero della Francesca, though entirely per-

sonal to him. It has a strange eternity and peace about it; and by daylight the colour is luminous like mother of pearl. I am wearing a red
dress. It is only a head and shoulders portrait, but is almost over life
size.'[15]

Nevertheless, she was in a troubled state of mind. Earlier chapters
of this book have quoted sections from the memoir – for example, the
Bastille episode – that show her in a frenzy of rage against her family.
At the end of December, an event occurred that, more than any other,
explains this rage.

Her aunt, Florence Sitwell, died at seventy-two, and a legacy long
promised to Edith was given to someone else. Florence had heard how
Edith had handled an earlier bequest of three thousand pounds from
the estate of a great-aunt, giving Helen a thousand pounds and Evelyn
a hundred, then buying fur coats for them. Helen, for her part, squandered the money on her fiancé.[16]

Apparently at a time when her wits were diminished following
cancer surgery, Florence Sitwell changed her will in favour of Louisa
Sitwell's old retainer Sister Edith Woods, who had been describing
Edith Sitwell as 'undutiful' since she moved to Moscow Road. Indeed,
around 1914, Woods had urged Sir George to reduce Edith's allowance
and had had many years to work on Florence's feelings. Florence left
five thousand pounds to Woods for her lifetime, after which, reduced
by death duties, what remained would pass to Edith Sitwell.[17] When
she finally received her inheritance after Woods's death in 1953, it
brought her an annual sum of just £124.[18]

Around 1957, Raleigh Trevelyan was writing a biography of the
Essex hermit Jimmy Mason, a distant relative of Woods. He asked
Edith Sitwell to comment on Woods's death certificate, describing her
as 'a spinster of independent means'. Sitwell replied: 'She was *indeed* a
spinster of independent means – *my* independent means . . . It was, of
course, right that she should be provided for, but I was deprived of it
all.' In any event, Woods was happy with the bequest, and, according
to Trevelyan, she claimed until the end of her days that Sitwell blood
ran in her veins.[19]

The memoir was finished around March 1931, when it was to be
serialised in the *Daily Express*. At a breakfast with the sculptor Barbara
Hepworth, Geoffrey Gorer warned Sitwell that the newspaper would

drag up the story of Lady's Ida's trial to advertise the memoir.[20] In the summer she received a legal opinion that her book libelled Wyndham Lewis and should not be published. In the 1960s, when she was in an even deeper depression, she incorporated some episodes into *Taken Care Of*.

Helen was now a different woman. Although she still taught music, she was less able to fend for herself and made many demands. In June, Sitwell wrote to Sassoon, commiserating over how two years of his life had been spent caring for the tubercular Stephen Tennant:

> Invalids, poor things, don't realise how constant their claims on one's time become; they get immersed in a world of their own, and become (through no actual fault of their own) terribly selfish, – exerting, quite unconsciously, a kind of moral blackmail. One mustn't contradict them, or tell them the truth, or stop them doing anything they oughtn't to do, or have any existence of one's own, nor must one even have any worries, or look pale if one has had a sleepless night. And any joys one may feel impact on their nerves, and give them a shock, and make them worse. It's a grand life![21]

Nothing could help in this dark year but courage. Following one of Sitwell's returns from France, Sir George's butler, Henry Moat, came to Moscow Road. He heard that she had been ill and demanded, 'Miss Edith, it *wasn't* the *Sea*?!' She replied that it was not. 'Well that's all right then.' This was a standing joke between them, as she explained to Tchelitchew: 'He would have been so ashamed of me if it *had* been, I don't know what he would have done. When I was thirteen, I was on the sea with Henry in a violent storm, and had to lie down. Henry came up to me and said, roaring above the wind, "Miss *Edith*. If you lie there people will think the *Sea* is making you sick!! You must stand *up* to the Sea!" with which he hauled me to my feet and, with a proper sailor's roll, taught me my sea-legs.'[22]

Sitwell did have to rely on her sea legs in these months, but some good things happened too. For five years, there had been awkwardness between the Sitwells and T. S. Eliot – although it seems he did come to Moscow Road on occasion. Osbert finally spoke to Eliot about their decision not to respond to Vivienne's letters from Rome during the

General Strike of 1926. Eliot was satisfied, and Osbert was invited 'in token of reconciliation' to a dinner party on 3 July 1931 at the Eliots' flat in Clarence Gate Gardens, intended as a celebration of Vivienne's completion of a course of treatment at a nursing home. Also present were Geoffrey and Enid Faber, as well as James and Nora Joyce who, Osbert noted, were to be married at a register office in the morning – an important detail, as one biographer placed this dinner in the early summer of 1927, when Joyce was in Holland and France, but not in England.[23] When Vivienne came in, Osbert said, 'It is splendid to see you again, Vivienne.' Looking him in the eye, she replied slowly, 'I don't know about splendid: but it is strange, very strange.'

Renewed friendship with Vivienne produced difficult moments for Edith. Osbert recalled:

One day towards the end of Vivienne's life with Tom, an intimate friend of both of theirs met Vivienne walking in Oxford Street.

'Hullo Vivienne!', she called to her.

Vivienne looked at her suspiciously and sadly, and replied 'Who do you think you're addressing? I don't know you.'

'Don't be so silly, Vivienne: you know quite well who I am.'

Vivienne regarded her with profound melancholy for a moment, and then said 'No, no: you don't know me. You have mistaken me again for that terrible woman who is so like me . . . She is always getting me into trouble.'[24]

T. S. Eliot was by now well established as a director at Faber & Faber, which had published Sitwell's biography of Pope. However, most of her dealings at the firm were with another director, Richard de la Mare, the son of Walter de la Mare. At about this time she took on a new commission from the firm to write a popular history of Bath. At the end of August 1931, Sitwell wrote to Terence Fytton Armstrong from Paris that she was having an awful time with the book. She was working six hours a day 'at constructing it, writing it. I just hate writing it, – it bores me, but I must, because of money.'[25] What she produced was a pleasant, if decidedly minor, work.

Before the eighteenth century, the attractions of Bath were medical: its waters were believed to help the scrofulous, the leprous, and the gouty. As the book opens, in the reign of Queen Anne, the city is being elevated into one of England's most fashionable resorts. At the centre of the changes is Richard Nash, the city's uncrowned king; he came in 1702 as a gamester but soon rose to become Master of the Ceremonies and the arbiter of manners and fashion. In the supporting cast are Alexander Pope, Ralph Allen (the model for Fielding's Squire Allworthy), and Philip Thicknesse (a memoirist and man of quarrels who bequeathed his right hand to an estranged son as a reminder of duty).

Sitwell has no time for Pope's enemy, Lady Mary Wortley Montagu, but evinces an odd respect for Selina, Countess of Huntingdon, who made trouble for Nash by spreading Methodism in Bath. It is a lost world, embodied in Beau Nash, who grows old and impoverished, becoming a Colonel Fantock in the coffee houses, retelling anecdotes. At his death, his portrait is hung in the town hall, poems are written, and fifty guineas is spent on his funeral: 'In this manner was the light, glittering and warm dust that had been Beau Nash, blown away, out of the memories of men, to the sound of trumpets, eulogies, and lamentations.'[26] When the book came out in May 1932, she was proud of it but joked with Tchelitchew about what she called its horrible charm.[27]

While working on *Bath*, Sitwell was often in Paris, as was Allanah Harper who was usually in the company of the Anglo-Syrian painter Amy Nimr, with whom she shared a house and who was thought to be her lover. In 1932, Nimr married the diplomat Walter Smart and went on to establish a salon in Cairo, which attracted many British writers. Harper brought Sitwell to meet the Cubist Louis Marcoussis, but the two had an argument right away about the technical skills of Baudelaire and Rimbaud, and whenever they met thereafter, the debate started up again. Sitwell refused to sit in the disreputable cafés where she might come across avant garde poets, but was willing to go with Harper to literary salons, such as that of the Duchess de la Rochefoucauld, where she met Sir James Frazer, author of *The Golden Bough*. She discovered that his one unfailing topic of conversation was the complexity, dirt, and danger of the Paris Métro. Things went better with Paul Valéry, whom she also met at Rochefoucauld's house. Sitwell complained that no one cared for pure poetry any more, preferring poems to contain crude political or philosophical messages bundled up with displays of private emotion and messy love affairs. Laughing, Valéry remarked that thought in a poem should stay hidden like the nutritional qualities of fruit. He also claimed that form in verse was linked to repetition – a stance Sitwell had been taking for years in her arguments with British critics. At another salon, that of the Comtesse Marthe de Fels, she met Saint-John Perse, the French poet who would win the Nobel prize in 1960. Sitwell knew Eliot's translation of *Anabase* and delighted Saint-John Perse by quoting from memory lines on his childhood from *Éloges.*[28]

Harper often went with Sitwell to visit Tchelitchew. On one of their visits to his Paris residence and studio at 2 rue Jacques-Mawas, he was too busy to let them in and just closed the door. She describes a much happier visit to the painter at Guermantes, when they spent a Sunday afternoon lounging in hammocks hung between apple trees; Tchelitchew painted the scene in watercolours. The journey back to Paris took a sad twist. An Alsatian dog, dazzled by Harper's head-lamps, ran into her path. She struck him with a jolt that she compared to running over a tree trunk, but the dog was still alive. Amy Nimr ran to get a butcher to finish him off while Sitwell sat white-faced in the car. Harper said she could not forgive herself for killing such a beautiful animal, but Sitwell insisted that the accident was not Harper's fault. When they got under way again, Sitwell spoke with great animation about poets and composers, and she invited Harper to hear the Ninth Symphony with her. When she got out at rue Saint-Dominique, she told Nimr she had been trying to get Allanah's mind off the dog. 'Do you not think that my heart was not torn by what happened?'[29]

In England from October to December 1931, she worked to meet her deadline on the 'nightmare book',[30] but had time to see a little of John Collier and to hear William Walton's *Belshazzar's Feast*, which she described to Tchelitchew as '*énorme et superbe, terrible et rugissant*'.[31] Meanwhile, Sachie was writing what turned out to be his masterpiece, the long sequence *Canons of Giant Art* – including 'Agamemnon's Tomb', a piece particularly admired by Yeats. Sachie, who felt that he had been badly underrated by critics, was tempted not to publish the work at all. Edith praised the poems as some of the best in a century:

'I think it will be madness if you do not publish the Canons of Giant Art. *Please do so, immediately.*'[32] For the time being, he was willing to be ruled by her. It came out from Faber & Faber, with Eliot's implicit endorsement, in 1933, but Sachie persevered in the view that he was unappreciated. Though gloomy about his own situation, Sachie could be helpful to others. On 14 December he lent Edith eight hundred pounds that he had obtained from Sassoon, on which she repaid twenty pounds twice a year until May 1943, when she paid it off altogether.[33] She must have been in deep trouble with Coutts & Co. at the time, for she told him 'it has made, is making, and will make, the whole difference to my life'.[34]

Back in Paris in January, Sitwell asked Allanah Harper to bring her to meet Adrienne Monnier, the owner of La Maison des Amis des Livres, and Sylvia Beach, owner of Shakespeare and Company on the opposite side of rue de l'Odéon. Beach had become famous as the first publisher of Joyce's *Ulysses*. Looking through the window of her shop, Monnier saw them approaching and hurried out: 'I recognized you, Miss Sitwell, from T. S. Eliot's description. He also told me that you were the greatest living poetess and that your gift for recitation and the beauty of your voice are out of this world.'[35] Monnier dashed across the street to get Beach, who immediately invited Sitwell to give what Noel Riley Fitch says was the first poetry reading held at Shakespeare and Company.[36]

That reading led to a rift with Gertrude Stein, and Sylvia Beach left the event out of her history of the bookshop. Up to that point, Sitwell and Stein had had just one important quarrel that we know of: Stein once claimed that Stella Bowen had left Ford Madox Ford for another man, and Sitwell angrily insisted that it was a lie.[37] As late as November 1930, Sitwell was speaking of the pleasure she took in Stein's company. The real problem was Tchelitchew.

Early on, Alice B. Toklas had judged him an opportunist rather than a friend. Stein thought better of him for a while, but by the time she introduced him to Sitwell in 1927, she had come round to Toklas's view, so warned Sitwell about his character. Also, Stein decided she had at first overrated his talent. When Tchelitchew grumbled that his sister Choura was a poor hostess and refused to wear clothes of his choosing, Stein refused to comment until she heard the other side of the story. This led Tchelitchew to believe that Stein was meddling in his domestic affairs.[38] By August 1928, Tchelitchew was complaining to Sitwell of Stein's fickleness. In November, he claimed that Stein and Toklas were snakes, and that Stein especially was a creature of the devil who liked to torture people. On 31 December, he said that if he had lost a friend in Stein, he had gained one in Sitwell.[39] For the next three years, Sitwell was caught between Stein and Tchelitchew.

On short notice, Sylvia Beach rented chairs and printed invitations to the reading, while fearing no one would come. As it turned out, on 7 January 1932 most of literary Paris squeezed into Shakespeare and Company, including Valery Larbaud, Henri Michaux, Jules Romain, Stuart Gilbert, Jean Prévost, and Louis Gillet. James Joyce, declaring himself 'all ears for Edith',[40] could get only a chair in the back row. Tchelitchew must have been at least on speaking terms with Stein, as the two arrived in a group with Tanner and Bowen, and, according to the seating plan, were together in the front row.[41] Sitwell also wanted Harper there, as she was very nervous and planned to start by looking at her for encouragement.[42]

What happened next is a bit of a mystery. Sitwell read some passages of Shakespeare and other Elizabethans, and then began reading her own poetry. At least some of the audience expected Sitwell to read passages from Stein's work and discuss them. According to Natalie Barney, an American writer who lived for many years on the Left Bank and conducted a weekly salon, Stein 'sat bolt-upright, meditating, in spite of a twitch of her hands, a more gentlemanly reprisal than immediate exposure'.[43] This is just silly: all that Barney could see of Stein in a crowded room was the back of her head and no one knows what she was 'meditating'. She does not quote either Stein or Sitwell on their views of the reading. It is possible that Sitwell intended to snub Stein out of loyalty to Tchelitchew, but on that evening there was a cease-fire between Tchelitchew and Stein. It is more likely that in the rush to organise the reading, wires were crossed. Sitwell later resented Beach for letting the misunderstanding occur.[44] Immediately after the reading, Sitwell gave no sign of enjoying a malicious triumph, as Barney suggested, but was afraid that she had simply given a bad performance.[45] Sylvia Beach had no idea, at first, that anything was wrong. Sitwell signed books, gave Beach a copy of the Beaton photograph of her as an Angevin corpse, and inspected her collection of Whitman manuscripts.[46]

Allen Tanner said that some time later Stein sent a note to Sitwell, complaining obliquely about what had happened.[47] Sitwell wrote back, explaining her choices, and received a further note: 'You were so right not to read anything of mine the other night as Sylvia was your hostess. Thanks so much and love to you.'[48] Nevertheless, the two were never close again. Sitwell always wrote generously of her old friend, except in a few mildly ironic letters to Tchelitchew. In *The Autobiography of Alice B. Toklas* (1933), Stein wrote: 'This friendship like all friendships has had its difficulties but I am convinced that fundamentally Gertrude Stein and Edith Sitwell are friends and enjoy being friends.'[49] Years later Alice B. Toklas spoke of Sitwell with no sign of a grudge.[50] However, Tchelitchew's opinion of Stein and Toklas was worked into *Phenomena* (1938), a large canvas that presents his own autobiography in the light of Dante's Inferno. Here, Stein and Toklas become 'Sitting Bull' and 'The Knitting Maniac'; they are seated on a collection of canvases all turned face-down.[51]

Sitwell returned to London for an exhibition of Tchelitchew's work at Tooth's Gallery in February. Since Osbert had come to an understanding with Eliot, Edith saw a good deal more of Vivienne. It was a mixed blessing. She wrote to Sassoon on 16 March:

> The Eliots are coming to tea with me today, and I am terrified. Vivienne gets more and more possibilities into her conversation. Did you hear the story about the bees? – Smutch Hutchinson was having tea with her, in June, and Vivienne enquired if she was enjoying the honey, – (there being no honey). On Smutch replying, nervously, that she was enjoying it very much, Vivienne asked if she kept bees. Smutch said no. Whereupon V. replied, very dreamily: 'Neither do I. I keep *hornets. In my bed!*' Sensation. Curtain.[52]

There is a problem with the dating of letters, but there seems to have been another tea party the following week, to which Vivienne came without Tom. Sitwell also invited Georgia and her mother (Georgie Hyde Doble). When Vivienne entered, Sitwell (as she claimed) thought she smelt methylated spirits. Her servant at the time, named Nelly, knew better. She had been an attendant in a ward for drug addicts, and could detect a barbiturate. She called Sitwell out of the room and warned her, 'That's paraldehyde . . . They only give the Patients *that* if they are so violent nothing else has any effect. Don't you let her get near the windows or the mirror, and don't let her get *near* Mrs Doble! I can see she is going for *her*! If she tries anything on, don't wait to see what she is going to do! Knock her down, and sit on her face! . . . Often, it has taken six of us to hold one down.'[53] Going back into the sitting room, Sitwell braced herself for the sad duty of sitting on Vivienne Eliot's face, but it did not come to that: 'I found that Mrs. Doble had offered the lady a cigarette, and had been told that the lady *never* accepted anything from strangers. It was too dangerous. Poor Mrs D. was terrified, as she thought that the Patient was going to spring at her throat. Georgia was terrified too, and tea was undiluted hell.'[54]

Visitors, however, were not always hell. In April, she invited Ralph Hodgson to Moscow Road, describing him to Pavlik as '*très simple, excessivement gentil et modeste, très laid*'. She was impressed by his once having been a milkman; his colourful background also included time as a fairground boxer. He was a friend of Sassoon's and had gone to teach in Japan in 1924, at much the same time as Edmund Blunden did. From the beginning of her career, Sitwell venerated Hodgson's work, particularly 'The Song of Honour', and was glad to have his name associated with the Anglo-French Poetry Society while it lasted. Looking forward to this visit, she explained to Pavlik that Hodgson was one of the four superb poets in English, along with Yeats, Davies, and Eliot. In the same letter to Tchelitchew, she said that she had heard from Sassoon, who was coming to London after six months in the country. He wanted some gaiety and hoped she would go out with him. Perhaps trying to provoke jealousy, she added: '*je l'aime beaucoup*'.[55]

These were among the last visitors to the shabby salon in Moscow Road. Sitwell could no longer afford the rent. There was no concierge and the outside doors were left unlocked at night. Twice she encountered suspicious men in the stairwells. The local pub, she said, had a criminal clientele, and police often combed it for wanted men, including murderers. It was a dangerous spot and she had to go. In May 1932, she told Pavlik that from the autumn she would live in Evelyn Wiel's

flat in Paris, but he was to tell no one. Indeed, once Lady Ida worked
out in November that her daughter was settling in Paris rather than at
Montegufoni, her reaction was, according to Edith, to write daily letters
of abuse.

Her new home was at 129 rue Saint-Dominique between the
Avenue Bosquet and the Avenue de la Bourdonnais, not far from the
Eiffel Tower. The flat, the top right-hand one, was five flights up from
a bistro.[56] According to Allanah Harper, the apartment was dark and
dingy, and much worse than Pembridge Mansions.[57] Sitwell described
her bedroom as a 'box'.[58] As at Pembridge Mansions, there were a
number of naked light bulbs. She could not possibly re-establish her
salon here in Paris, where she had only a small sitting room, set aside
for her exclusive use just once a week, if plans did not go awry. For
three women, two of them ill, to squeeze into these cramped, dismal
quarters was a recipe for depression and rows. What began as a plan for
Sitwell to stay only two years stretched out finally to a miserable
seven.

For the time being, Sitwell was unlikely to find fault with the flat
while she had the hope of a new bolt-hole in England. She handed in
the key to 22 Pembridge Mansions at the end of July and went with
Sachie, Georgia, Sir George, and Lady Ida to visit the small house at
Long Itchington, near Rugby, where Florence Sitwell had lived at the
end of her life. She described it for Allen Tanner: 'This is a most exquisite, very tiny Elizabethan house, with a long low front, very pale
timbers, and whitewash, and latticed windows, and the front of the
house covered with jasmine, great hedges of sweetbriar, and everything
exquisite.' Although Edith thought she would be living in the house
'soonish', the hope evaporated as the family launched into new tussles
over money.[59]

Through the summer of 1932 Sitwell had worked on Tchelitchew's
behalf, organising a small exhibition at Gerald Duckworth's on 19 July,
which led to the sale of ten drawings. Among the buyers were Sam
Courtauld, Rebecca West's husband Henry Adams, Peter Watson (the
patron of the arts who later backed Horizon), and Inez Chandos-Pole.
The next day Sitwell sent Tchelitchew a cheque for eighty-one
pounds.[60] Shortly after, she was involved in a much larger plan for the
poet and art collector Edward James, best known as Salvador Dalí's

patron, to buy six paintings for five hundred pounds: 'I respect him more than I can say, and am becoming really fond of him.'[61] However, Sitwell's plan to move to Paris alarmed Tchelitchew, who thought she would make romantic demands of him. When he first heard, he waited six days before writing back to her. Then in October, when she had actually settled in at rue Saint-Dominique, he claimed that a letter about her arrival had been lost for a week. Sitwell found all this '*curieux*' it showed where things stood.[62] Not wanting to alienate her, he invited her to stay at the farmhouse in Guermantes.

In the autumn, Sitwell had a chance to train her guns on Wyndham Lewis's new novel, *The Snooty Baronet*: 'Mr. Percy Wyndham Lewis's new book disappoints me, and I think must disappoint the admirers of his earlier books.' In her comments on the main character, Sir Michael Kill-Imrie, she passes a private note to the author:

> Sir Michael is . . . bitter about the ladies, who are not attracted by him, and, to revenge himself, (though he does not admit the cause), he becomes a 'gossip-writer' of the Novel . . . Poor Sir Michael! He has, evidently, an uneasy vanity and a sad unrealized craving for affection. He must not be surprised, however, that ladies do not reply to his attacks upon them. He seems to have become rather déclassé, and he does not know, probably, that these unattainable beings do not take any action if a gutter-snipe spits in their faces, whilst the fact that he has escaped being horse-whipped proves only, that he is too dirty to touch.[63]

Lewis had made a fool of himself with his book *Hitler* (1931), praising the Führer-in-waiting. The Sitwells saw this as an opportunity for them to try to drive him mad. They sent him postcards in nonsensical German: 'Once I pricked my big toe and planted the mark on the p.c. and wrote "Rache" [revenge] on it.' And some of the mischief was more elaborate: 'L. hates being thought to be a Jew, and Osbert's secretary, finding out that a man called Sieff is organising an exhibition of Jewish artists, has written in the unfortunate Sieff's name to Lewis, asking him to exhibit, with the result that Lewis and Sieff are having a fearful row, and all the Jewish artists are vowing vengeance on Lewis for insulting their race.'[64]

Sitwell came to England early in 1933, spending most of February with Sachie and Georgia at Weston Hall. She cajoled Tchelitchew into staying there for a weekend, which appears to have been the occasion of an odd tantrum. Someone had left a book about Moscow in his bedroom, and he assumed the Sitwells were trying to upset him.[65] Tchelitchew was in England for what were becoming regular shows at Tooth's Gallery, which Edith promoted. Most of the eleven buyers were his regular supporters, Rée Gorer, Peter Watson, Sir Edward Marsh, and, as always, Edward James, who bought three.[66]

Through much of 1932, Sitwell had been engrossed in *The English Eccentrics*, which came out in May 1933. She had written *Bath* relying chiefly on volumes borrowed from the London Library, concentrating not on the architecture of Bath but on the extraordinary careers of Beau Nash and other eighteenth-century worthies. It was less a travel work than a book of characters.

In fact, both books belong to a once-popular genre; James Gregory tells us that between 1790 and 1901 there were more than sixty works of eccentric biography published in England. These ranged from magazine articles to such encyclopedias of quirks as Cyrus Reddings's *Memoirs of Remarkable Misers* (1863), John Timbs's *English Eccentrics and Eccentricities* (1866), and William Russell's *Eccentric Personages* (1868).[67] The passion for eccentrics can be seen in the novels of Dickens, and it is at work in *Left Hand, Right Hand!*, where Sir George Sitwell is presented as the sum of his oddities.

In 1932, Edith Sitwell decided that the Victorian books about eccentricity could be reworked into a smart, amusing volume, which made no claim to original research; she opens with an acknowledgment: 'The author would like to express her indebtedness to the biographers of her Eccentrics, and to those other collectors of Eccentricity whose works she has had an opportunity of consulting. Acknowledgments to the many titles have been made in the text wherever possible.'[68] Sitwell produced a hauntingly beautiful and amusing work that is so much better written than its sources that it belongs to a different order of literature.

Sitwell reaches behind the eccentric biographers to Isaac Disraeli's *Curiosities of Literature* (1791–1823) and, more importantly, to Robert Burton's *Anatomy of Melancholy* (1621), of which there were new editions in 1929 and 1932. The opening chapter of her book is called 'Goose Weather' – a time when spirits are low and winter clouds seem to her like battered stage properties: 'I thought of those medicines that were advised for Melancholy, in the Anatomy of this disease, of mummies made medicine, and of the profits of Dust-sifting.'[69] Relying on Pink's *History of Clerkenwell* (1865),[70] she goes on to describe the Battle Bridge Dust and Cinder Heap that covered many acres near what is now King's Cross from the time of the Great Fire of 1666 until the early nineteenth century, when it was shipped to Moscow and used in rebuilding the city after the French invasion. In this dust-heap, outcast dust-sifters found treasures and became wealthy: 'To go further in our search for some antidote against melancholy, we may seek in our dust-heap for some rigid, and even splendid, attitude of Death, some exaggeration of the attitudes common to Life. This attitude, rigidity, protest, or explanation, has been called eccentricity by those whose bones are too pliant.'

Like many of the earlier writers, Sitwell sees eccentricity as a very English phenomenon, 'because of that peculiar and satisfactory knowledge of infallibility that is the hallmark and birthright of the British nation'.[71] Sitwell saluted the refusal to conform of even the zaniest persons she described, among them the Countess of Desmond 'whose death at the age of one hundred and forty years, seems to have been . . . the result of climbing an apple tree – a strange occupation for a lady of her rank and years – and falling from this amidst a shower of glistening apples', and the hard-drinking Squire Jack Mytton who set fire to his nightshirt with a candle in order to scare himself out of the hiccups. There are sections on 'Caraboo', who posed as a princess from the South Seas and contributed to peace among nations by inducing Napoleon on St Helena to fall in love with her, and on Lord Rokeby, a fellow of Trinity College, Cambridge, as well as an ornamental hermit whose 'amphibious' life was spent primarily in the bath.[72]

Some reviewers were dismissive, but D. L. Murray in the *TLS* (18 May 1933) called *English Eccentrics* 'an amazing pell-mell, an entire D.U.B. or Dictionary of Unimportant Biography, most of it extremely entertaining'. E. M. Forster wrote in the *Spectator* (19 May 1933):

Where else in England, and where but in England, could one meet
such an adorable display of eccentricity? . . . Where, except in the
pages of Miss Sitwell? Not in the grand annual displays at Chelsea,
where the fashionable world turns out. Not in the full-dress
documented surveys of literature and life. But in pages such as hers,
where erudition is controlled by fantasy, and a slight wave of the
parasol performs a minor magic . . . The lesson to be drawn from it –
if so heavy a draught as a lesson be required – is that eccentricity
ranks as a national asset, and that so long as it is respected there is
some hope that our country will not go mad as a whole.'

Forster's opinion has been generally shared by three generations of
readers.

Good as it was, Sitwell wrote this book only because she needed money
to sustain her friends. In September 1931 Helen Rootham told Sitwell
that she thought the disease was returning, but her remission continued until 1933. Recognising the day and the time as a landmark,
Sitwell told Pavlik on Thursday, 13 July, 'Mon cher, je suis accablée
[overwhelmed] de misère. Aujourd'hui, à 2 ½, Helen a vue le grand
chirurgier Hartmann – Elle doit avoir une nouvelle operation.' Surgery
was set for Monday morning and Sitwell begged Pavlik to come, without fail, to the flat for breakfast as she would be alone and desolate as
she waited for news. It appears that at this time the cancer was in
Rootham's spine – it certainly reached there later. It is possible that
Helen's primary cancer was actually in the breast and that it metasta-
sised to the spine (a frequent occurrence), but Sitwell gives few details
about the illness. Rootham survived the surgery, spent some days in a
nursing home, and then returned to the flat exhausted and feeble.
Henceforth, Sitwell usually referred to her in her letters as 'poor Helen'
or 'pauvre Helen'.

For the next two or three weeks, Sitwell nursed her, and took care
of the house and the cooking, while Evelyn spent most of her days at
an office job, which she continued to hold despite being an 'invalid'
herself.[73] In mid-August, Helen was well enough to be left alone, so
Sitwell set out for England, where her mother met her at customs. Only
sixty-four, Lady Ida was now relying on a cane. Having just one lung,

she was lucky to have survived pneumonia and pleurisy eight months earlier.[74] Sitwell always marvelled at her mother's beauty. In an undated letter to Pavlik, she told him to enjoy Italy, which she saw as her country as much as England, and to seek out the treasures of the Uffizi, especially a series of Michelangelo's drawings of a young woman, 'superb with the kind of proud magnificent beauty that my mother had, more than any woman I've ever seen – staring at her image in old age, – equally beautiful in its own way, but with the immortality of the bone, not with the pride of summer'.[75]

Sitwell noticed now that her mother's memory was poor, and that she repeated herself as she described new troubles between Osbert, Sachie, and Sir George. When Lady Ida spoke of the boys' attempts to get money out of their father, she soon raised her own difficulties, and seemed to be lining up Edith as an ally in the troubles awaiting them in Derbyshire, while showing no interest in what her daughter had endured in the preceding month with Helen Rootham. Edith told Pavlik that she saw for the first time, 'complètement', to what degree her family had exploited her, and with what complete cynicism they accepted the difference between her financial state and their own.[76]

At Renishaw, Edith entered a maelstrom of accusations and complaints. Around 1925, Sir George had taken his capital from England to Switzerland and made over Renishaw to Osbert for life, after which it would pass down the male line. Sir George and Lady Ida planned to live out the rest of their lives at Montegufoni. Although Renishaw more or less supported itself, Osbert needed cash, so, according to one of the family solicitors, he obtained a ten-thousand-pound mortgage.[77] Sachie, too, was living far beyond his means and wanted to use capital to pay his debts. This was intolerable to Sir George, who believed that debts had killed his own father. Part of the dispute was whether provision should be made for Georgia, if she outlived Sachie and Reresby, or whether the money should pass only down the male line.[78] Apart from nasty scenes, the chief quality of these weeks was sheer boredom: 'Life is also enlivened by my father walking up and down the lawn, just outside the windows, dictating letters to his secretary: "Messrs. Humdinger, Humdinger and Humdinger. As I remarked in my last letter: Worm. Worm. Worm. Read what you've got."'

Edith was glad to leave Renishaw to spend a few days with Inez

Chandos-Pole at Radburne Hall near by. She went on to visit her
cousins the Beauforts at Badminton in Gloucestershire: 'The park has
a strange Tchaikowsky-like quality, with a mock-gothic gamekeeper's
house called Ragged Castle, and a pleasure house surrounded by
avenues, called Swan Park, and a walled orchard called Cherry
Gardens. The Beauforts are fearfully poor, so most of the house is shut
up.'[79]

After that, she stayed at nearby Nether Lypiatt, the house of the virtuoso harpsichordist, Violet Gordon Woodhouse, a modern English
Eccentric who had for a time lived happily with her husband and three
lovers in a 'ménage à cinq'. Her husband lost a good deal of money
during the Great War, so Violet became a professional musician. In
1926, her husband's two unmarried sisters were murdered by their
butler; they had intended to leave their money to a cousin but had not
signed their wills, so Violet's husband, as next of kin, inherited the
lot.[80] This freakish windfall allowed Violet to give up the concert circuit and to perform only at home for friends, such as the Sitwells.
Another 'old and reverenced friend', the poet W. H. Davies, came to
see Sitwell at Nether Lypiatt; they stayed up talking until 2 a.m. and
exhausted their hostess. Sitwell returned to London for dental surgery,
and rather than listen to Lady Ida's whining at a hotel, she retreated,
once it was done, to Renishaw, where she could nurse her four abscesses
in peace.[81]

A very characteristic shift was going on in Sitwell's sympathies.
Having once regarded Allen Tanner as her competition, and indeed a
crook, she now saw that he was being squeezed out of Tchelitchew's life.
In the midst of a family row, she wrote to Tanner:

My poor dear friend, I know what you have been through. You are
the most loyal and devoted of friends. But I beg of you not to do anything rash. You cannot part company – you can't do it. He is
absolutely devoted to you, and you are absolutely devoted to him.
You have great wisdom, and your wisdom will carry you through. I
too have known great sadness and bitterness, but I think I know it
no longer. Neither of you, Allen dearest, would be able, as I see it,
to endure life apart. Your lives have been too closely knit together,
in a great and noble friendship.[82]

Tchelitchew was involved with the twenty-five-year-old American writer, Charles Henri Ford, who had recently collaborated with Parker Tyler (Tchelitchew's future biographer) on a homoerotic novel, *The Young and Evil*. Sitwell was called upon to offer an opinion on the book. Trying to be objective, she asked Edward James to explain what exactly the men in the story were doing to each other; he said he thought the book indecent and would not explain the sexual acts because she would be shocked.[83] Apparently, Sitwell then assisted him in burning a copy of it.[84] She wrote to Ford: 'I think that there is much good writing, and that you have a strong visual sense, but I *do* get tired of the perpetual pillow fights. Frankly, don't either of you young men know *anybody* who is capable of getting into his own bed and stopping there? If you do, for goodness sake cultivate his acquaintance, and write about him next time for a change. Also, calling a spade a spade never made the spade interesting yet. Take my advice, leave spades alone, or if you must mention them, then mention the garden too.'[85]

Perhaps encouraged by Ford, Tchelitchew was considering a move to New York. On 21 September, his birthday, Sitwell sent him a horoscope clipped from a British newspaper, which included the warning: 'Guard against transport accidents.'[86] A true-believer in astrology, Tchelitchew was furious, convinced that Sitwell had hijacked the stars in her efforts to cling to him. Osbert proposed that Tchelitchew instead of Matisse do the sets for a Massine ballet; this, too, for some reason, Tchelitchew took as an insult. Edith responded that she had given him 'une grande amitie. Ne jetez pas cela!' She stood her ground, to a degree, and told Tchelitchew there was no money in America at the moment.[87] The row subsided and soon she was referring to him again, as she often did, as 'mon très aimé crosspatch'.[88] In another exchange of letters at about this time, Tchelitchew complained that he did not like visiting rue Saint-Dominique, because of 'l'influence et les lamentations' of the Roothams, but Edith could not afford her own flat, so she told him she had to stay where she was.[89] Tchelitchew's close friend Lincoln Kirstein told John Pearson that in 1933 the painter decided Sitwell had no real feeling for his work, and claimed he wanted to break with her altogether because of her possessiveness; in the end, he decided such a move would be bad for his career.[90]

In early November, Duckworth released *Five Variations on a Theme*, a slim volume of poems, some previously published. Taken together, they seem an oblique commentary on her love for the painter. The theme of the book is passion, death, and transformation. She had been working on the poem 'Romance' since 1931; it incorporates a poem published then as 'Epithalamium' (a poem written for a bride). Early drafts bore the title 'Dark Serenade'.[91] Towards the end, the poem becomes more erotic, hinting at a deflowering:

> When the green century of summer rains
> Lay on the leaves, then like the rose I wept.
> For I had dwelt in sorrow as the rose
> In the deep heaven of her leaves lies close.
> Then you, my gardener, with green fingers stroked my leaves
> Till all the gold drops turned to honey. Grieves
> This empire of green shade when honeyed rains
> And amber blood flush all the sharp green veins
> Of the rich rose?
>   So doth my rose-shaped heart
> Feel the first flush of summer; love's first smart
> Seemed no more sorrowful than the deep tears
> The rose wept in that green and honeyed clime.[92]

We cannot be sure whether Sitwell remembered such an experience or imagined it – her letters to Tchelitchew do not answer the question. Regardless, she was very proud of this poem. She told Balston in September: 'The joy of writing poetry again is almost too much for me.'[93] In fact, she did not complete another substantial poem to her satisfaction for six years. Most of the difficulty was that her poetry was choked by the circumstances of her daily life. It is also possible that having revealed so much of her secret life in this poem, she was fearful of what the next might require of her and so remained at an impasse.

Sitwell received a cheering letter about the book of poems from the novelist Charlotte Franken Haldane, who was then married to the geneticist J. B. S. Haldane. She remarked on the traditional character of the verse. Sitwell agreed: 'I myself think it traditional poetry, descended from Spenser, Milton, Marvell, and Dryden, and completely unrelated to the later poets. It is descended, too (as far as English poetry *could* be descended from French poetry) from Baudelaire.'[94] In another letter to her shortly after, Sitwell wrote:

> Someone, an owl called Philip Henderson, who has always been rude to me in the papers, wrote, the other day, saying that nothing roused any real feeling in me, as far as my poetry was concerned, but Love, Age, and Death! Can you beat it? And he went on to say that nobody knew *who* were the two people in love, in my 'Romance!' – Had I not received your letter and your essay on my poetry this morning, I should most certainly have written and said that the lady's name is Miss Perkins, but that I am pledged not, for the moment, to reveal that of the gentleman, because he is employed in a department of one of the West-London Stores! But I decided, after reading what you had written, to keep silence and my temper.[95]

Comical as this is, Sitwell was able to create in her later poetry a kind of tragic serenity that eluded her completely in her day-to-day life, which was tossed about on rip-tides of bad temper. She wanted her poetry not merely to record the frailties and trivialities of the world, but to oppose them and to remake them. Though a poet, Sitwell often couched her most important ideas about art in terms of music; she told Franken: 'I love Bach, too. But though I admire Mozart, I love him less, which is my fault, – preferring infinitely, Gluck, because he is less sweet. Bach is my god. He seems to have created a perfect world, in which there is no sin, and in which sorrow is holy and not ugly.'[96]

Sitwell's correspondence with Franken took another revealing turn on 5 December, when she wrote: 'I've been feeling terribly unhappy lately, and our correspondence is one thing which I look forward to. I've seen people behaving in such a dreadfully ugly way just lately. And I never can get used to it. I mean, in my personal life it has been very bad, oh very bad. And outside, these horrible lynchings in America, and the departure last week of the French convict ship for Devil's Island, have upset me terribly. – Nineteen hundred and thirty three years after Christ, and the "righteous" are still behaving like this!'[97] The phrasing, of course, anticipates her poem on the Blitz, 'Still Falls the Rain' (1940); her reaction to injustice was, as always, visceral rather than ideological and systematic. Lynchings in the American

South were widely reported in the British press in 1933, and Sitwell may have known of Arthur Raper's recently published book *The Tragedy of Lynching*, which tracked 3724 lynchings from 1889 to 1930.[98] Departures of convict ships for Devil's Island were a normal part of French life, even though most of those sent there would die. The penal colony had grown notorious after the publication in 1923 of Albert Londres's report *Au bagne*, which was followed by a series of books and articles revealing the brutality of the place.

Haldane responded that what terrified her personally was the emergence of Hitler, as she was Jewish. Sitwell wrote:

> My former letter to you was so inexpressive. Indeed you are right in speaking of the primal horror of Germany at present. It makes my blood boil. I did not know that you are a Jewess, but with the exception of one person, all my dearest friends (I have very few) are either Jewish or in part Jewish. So apart from the rage and horror I feel in the cruelty of the Nazis, I understand the crétinism of it. To ill-treat and turn out a gentle and faithful people, – certainly the most faithful of any I have ever known! But do not fear, dear Charlotte, that such outrages against decency and sense will ever occur in England. We know too well what our Jewish citizens have done for us. But I know the anguish you must feel in contemplating Germany.[99]

Revulsion against the Nazis was, sadly, not a universal sentiment in England or France in the early 1930s, Wyndham Lewis being an obvious example of someone praising their leader. Amazingly, Gertrude Stein did too: 'I say that Hitler ought to have the peace prize, because he is removing all elements of contest and struggle from Germany. By driving out the Jews and the democratic and Left elements, he is driving out everything that conduces to activity. That means peace' (*New York Times*, 6 May 1934). As Sitwell and Stein had disagreed about the First World War, it is likely that if their close friendship had continued through the 1930s, they would have argued over Hitler. Although Sachie and Osbert had some sympathy with Italian Fascism and were both for a time supportive of Oswald Mosley, there is no indication that Edith shared their views.

Her friendship with Franken was brief. Spending so much time in

Paris meant that her other important friendships in England would also wind down. Sitwell still cared about Sassoon and felt that she owed him a professional debt; she said that with the exception of Yeats's comments at the time of the publication of *The Apes of God*, 'you are the only person who has ever done anything at all for my poetry.'[100] He was certainly her best critic. When, around November, she learnt that Sassoon had become engaged to Hester Gatty, she wrote a letter of congratulation, but was privately jealous, and her contact with him would become rarer as he seldom emerged from his home at Heytesbury House in Wiltshire. Nevertheless, he and other friends continued to stand up for her work. Yeats threatened to withdraw from the Royal Society of Literature if Sitwell was not awarded its medal. He had his way.[101] Sitwell told Georgia in December that 'The Royal Society of Literature is behaving about the giving of the medal, as if they were Catherine of Braganza [the wife of Charles II] being "forced to receive" Lady Castlemaine [one of his mistresses].'[102] Sassoon delayed his honeymoon to serve as chairman[103] when Henry Newbolt presented the medal on 24 January 1934.

There was no letter or cable from Pavlik, Choura or Tanner, in honour of the day. Having leapt back and forth across the Channel to promote Pavlik's exhibitions, assumed unmanageable debts for him, and generally devoted herself to his happiness, Sitwell was upset. Switching (permanently, as it turned out) to English, she wrote: 'I know that you are very busy being "the cream in Miss [Djuna] Barnes' coffee" and Mr. Ford's Sugar Daddy; but I should have thought that you might have found a moment to spare from these people – so important intellectually, so important socially, – in which to remember me . . . I've been very poor and desperately unhappy for the last eighteen months, and during that time I have seen some strange spectacles. I am obliged to tell you this, otherwise I could not write to you, I am too hurt.'[104] Pavlik raged right back at her. Writing from Weston, she tried to close the subject around 12 February 1934: 'Pavlik dear, I think it is now time that you stopped quarrelling with me. It would be foolish for us to lose each other. I should miss you terribly, and I think, perhaps, one day, when you are able to see a little more clearly than you see at present, that you may miss me.'[105] She returned to Paris on 22 February and was soon trying to pick up the pieces:

Dearest Pavlik,

    Forgive me. For I am so unhappy, what should I do
without you? I have made myself ill, and now I am in bed.
Please write me a little word.

           With my love,

                Edith

I have my poem for you.

I'll try never to show jealousy or pain again.[106]

15

LET THE DEVILS HAVE IT

Just before Christmas 1933, Helen Rootham went through a crisis that Sitwell feared might kill her. She survived but was very weak. In the hope of building her strength up, Sitwell arranged to spend the late spring and early summer at the village of Levanto, south-west of Genoa. She wrote across the top of her letter of 5 May 1934 to Osbert, who was then travelling in China: *'Do not let the Gingers know I am here.'* Sir George and Lady Ida were, of course, lurking at Montegufoni. 'I came here a few days ago, because poor Helen has to have some sun. The sea is lovely, but the town is a triumph of ugliness, rather like the outskirts of Nottingham. However, the hotel is nice, the English people haven't found out who I am, – or if they have, they don't care, and I can work quietly. I am at work at (besides that bloody [biography of Queen] Victoria) a small book on modern poetry, in which I am simply going to "let the devils have it."'[1]

In the last two years, she had acquired significant new enemies. The Cambridge don, F. R. Leavis, senior editor of the journal *Scrutiny*, famously remarked in his *New Bearings in English Poetry* (1932): 'the Sitwells belong to the history of publicity rather than of poetry'[2] – a toxic quip with a long half-life. It is commonly observed that Leavis's idea of cultural centrality tended to boil down the literature of an age to a few names, an exclusive canon. In short, he was unable to deal with the strangeness and difference of literary accomplishments even within the same generation of writers.[3] His wisecrack helped to ensure that the one British woman of his time who briefly enjoyed status as a major poet was not merely pushed back into the second rank, but dismissed by many as a fraud. While he certainly promoted the understanding of some authors, notably D. H. Lawrence, his seriousness of mind concealed a Mariana Trench of priggishness. Sitwell was not far wrong when she said that summer to Balston: 'in his criticism he is like an ardent, tenderly ruthless young dentist probing a decayed molar.'[4]

Geoffrey Grigson, a Cornish poet who specialised in vituperative book reviews, was the editor of New Verse, an important journal that published and promoted the work of younger poets, especially W. H. Auden. With a decided preference for a poetry of close obser-vation, Grigson distrusted the large rhetoric to which Sitwell, as an admirer of Whitman and Swinburne, aspired. This honest difference of opinion was inflamed by loyalty to his good friend Wyndham Lewis, who, with obvious cynicism, encouraged him to see the Sitwells as 'useful enemies'.[5] A belligerent reviewer herself, Sitwell invited rough treatment from those who disagreed with her, but this point can be a distraction – it does not get us to a fair reading and valuation of her poetry.

In 1934, however, she was not worried about herself but about Sachie, who wilted in the face of hostile reviews. Writing in Leavis's Scrutiny, Grigson savaged Canons of Giant Art and reiterated a theme from The Apes of God: 'The Sitwells, in fact, reflect a society where dil-ettante art-worship is synonymous with culture.' He dismissed Sachie's language as 'bogus' and described his rhythms as vying with Hiawatha for monotony. 'Best leave these minimal creatures, these contemptible elvers, wriggling away in their dull habitat.'[6] Edith Sitwell had no idea how to wriggle away.

Having signed on with Faber & Faber to write a biography of Queen Victoria, she quietly asked Thomas Balston whether she could put out another volume of her Pleasures of Poetry anthology with an introduc-tion answering her critics. He thought that the permissions would cost too much, so she decided instead to write Aspects of Modern Poetry, a book of criticism to be ready by the end of July 1934. It was her last chance to work with a much loved editor. Balston's junior colleague, the novelist Anthony Powell, described an 'upheaval' at Duckworth's that summer:

At a meeting of the firm's directors to reconsider the still rickety condition of the business, there was a sudden explosion . . . Gerald

Duckworth's barely pent up rage over the years on the subject of the Sitwells, Waugh, Beaton, other modern abominations forced on him by Balston, broke out; while at the same instant Balston gave voice to his equally powerful resentment of what he had long regarded as Gerald Duckworth's obstruction and inertia.

Balston resigned.[7] Sitwell wrote from Paris: 'I cannot tell you what a frightful shock it has been, – actually I simply can't believe it, and only hope you will be able to reconsider it. Nothing will *ever* be the same for us, if we don't have you there. It was you who *made* the place.'[8] Balston, however, was finished as a publisher and, according to Powell, suffered a nervous breakdown upon leaving the firm. Sitwell had occasional contact with him in the years to come, when he led a scholar's life and haunted the Garrick Club.[9]

Research for the book took her in a new direction, as she explained to Tchelitchew: 'I have been reading some of the surréaliste manifestos, which are at once incredibly silly and very self-revealing. But on the whole, silly as these people are, they are not so hopelessly bad as most of the younger English and American poets, – none of whom have any sense of texture whatever.'[10] For a poet immersed in the Symbolists, there was some appeal in the Surrealists, though she objected, among other things, to their refusal to sift impressions and images. What to make of the movement was already an urgent question for Tchelitchew. Parker Tyler says: 'Though in a sense tangent to Surrealism, Neo-Romanticism crosses its territory wherever magical or metaphysical effects are suggested – both schools coalesce in (or rather out of) Chirico.'[11] Tchelitchew had in him something of the icon-painter's devotion to the other-worldly, which set him apart from Surrealists generally, although at the level of technique it is hard to make out a difference. Sitwell was cautiously absorbing this influence, too, in the mid-1930s, but since she was writing few poems the effects were not seen until 1940, when she reappeared as a religious poet who juxtaposed images, some culled directly from dreams, in a mysterious and occasionally shocking manner.

Apart from their 'silliness', Sitwell probably held back from a closer involvement with the Surrealist movement because of Tchelitchew's professional rivalries; he was always distressed when Edward James

bought one of Dalí's pictures. Another barrier between Tchelitchew
and the Surrealists may have been that André Breton had little time
for homosexuals, with the exception of the novelist René Crevel,[12]
who became Stein's friend and one of Tchelitchew's lovers. Indeed, he
also seems to have had a love affair with Choura Tchelitchew when the
two of them were treated for tuberculosis at the same sanatorium.[13]
Through Allanah Harper, Sitwell had at least a passing acquaintance
with the painter Max Ernst and the poet Tristan Tzara.[14] Visiting Spain
in June 1936, she missed the International Surrealist Exhibition at
London's New Burlington Gallery, which featured Dalí lecturing from
inside a diving suit and nearly suffocating. Over the years, however, she
responded readily to the works of individual Surrealists, among them
the poet David Gascoyne, whom she grouped in the 1940s with Dylan
Thomas and George Barker as the best of the younger poets.[15] In the
1930s, Sitwell was somewhat irritated by Herbert Read, but she probably watched his involvement with Surrealism from a distance. Sitwell
had no theoretical interest in Freud, telling Henry Treece of the New
Apocalypse movement in 1942 that he was wrong to think that 'the
poet should show in his images psychological symbols, his own disease,
and by uncovering them effect his cure' as this led to young people
equating malady with poetry. 'Oh, why won't people realise that poetry
is a specialist's job!'[16]

   In the spring of 1934, Sitwell read a book that she found at once
impressive and annoying – John Sparrow's Sense and Poetry. Only twenty-
seven, Sparrow was a barrister, a prize-fellow (and future warden) of
All Souls College, Oxford, the editor of several seventeenth-century
texts, and the author of a critical work on Virgil.[17] Sitwell drafted
and redrafted a letter to him, dated 14 May 1934, editing out anger
and adding praise, while disputing his claim that her most pleasing
poetry was 'purely decorative'. She urged him to consider not only
her early poems, but 'Gold Coast Customs', which could hardly be
described in such terms. She scolded him for misquotations: 'My dear
Sir, should you blame me for making an ugly sound when you have
made it for me?' In one case, the sense of a line as well as the sound
was altered: 'By the way, I didn't write "Emily-coloured hands", I said
"Emily-coloured primulas", to convey that they were like pink cheeks
of a country girl, – Emily being a country-sounding name.'[18]

Her own misquotations would soon be a problem. In August, Sitwell went to Brides-les-Bains near the Swiss border with Osbert, and Sparrow came to see her. The two sat and happily discussed prosody, cementing an alliance that Edith would need before the year was out.

Having missed her deadline, she was writing up to four thousand words per day (this likely included simple copying),[19] while trying to fend off bores. She told Pavlik that the Swiss 'have all the worst German faults: faithfulness when you don't want them to be faithful, stoutness, philoprogenitiveness, love of cakes, culture. Osbert is very angry because I have told one persistent lady that he is really Clemence Dane . . . She said, Are you not an actress? You *look* like one? I said I am. I act under the name of Sarah Siddons.'[20] But she couldn't laugh off her exhaustion, writing to Pavlik at the end of August: 'I had such a terrible dream last night. I dreamt I was in a low shallow grave, that I had had to dig with my own nails, and that I couldn't lie down because there were still a few drops of blood left in my heart, and so I wasn't allowed to be dead.'[21]

At the beginning of September, she had finished her essays on Hopkins, Yeats, Eliot, Pound, and Sacheverell Sitwell, then discovered at the last minute that Duckworth had advertised the book as containing an essay on W. H. Davies too, so she had to write one in just three days. The short volume that she intended ballooned to 264 printed pages. She had the first proofs back at the end of September but was too tired to inspect them properly.[22] The book, which came out on 15 November 1934, was bound to start a fight, if not the one she intended. It had real strengths, such as her discussion of Yeats's technique. Roy Foster writes in his biography of Yeats: 'Edith Sitwell noted that the early and late lyrics are united by the unearthly ability to fuse sound and sense, and perceptively analyzed WBY's vowel schemes, their relationship to the rhythmic plan of his poetry, and how they created a passionate and moving effect.'[23] It is hard to find before Sitwell's book so lucid and informative an account of the technical aspects of the poetry of Ezra Pound.[24] The volume is as entertaining as criticism can be: she proves early on, with crushing examples, that F. R. Leavis is often unable to hear the poetry he writes about.

However, G. W. Stonier, reviewing the book for the *New Statesman* (24 November), observed that, even as she dismissed Leavis, she made some arguments extraordinarily like his. In her defence, it should be noted that she makes many explicit references to Leavis's book, some dismissing his views, sometimes agreeing heartily with them. The verbal echoes that Stonier noticed were hardly the result of wilful theft of ideas; the reader knows from the outset that Sitwell has Leavis beside her as she writes. Over the next four issues, there were two letters from Grigson, one from Wyndham Lewis, and one from H. Sidney Pickering, asserting that aspects of the book were plagiarised. Edith wrote two let-ters and Osbert and John Sparrow one each in defence of it.

The dispute spilt over into other magazines. In a review not only unsigned but deliberately disguised to put off guesses as to its author-ship, Sparrow wrote in the TLS (13 December 1934), 'If ridicule can kill, Miss Sitwell has certainly achieved a handsome massacre.' He dis-puted her more extreme comments on Matthew Arnold and A. E. Housman, writing that some of her conclusions about the sound of lines were overworked, and perhaps imaginary, although on the whole the notice was favourable. Grigson dashed off another letter, published on 20 December, accusing the reviewer of being 'superficial, ill-informed and prejudiced', and listing many misquotations and mis-attributions as evidence that Sitwell was hardly doing justice to the texture of poetry. He quoted some phrases on the history of sprung rhythm from Herbert Read's Form in Modern Poetry that are similar to ones in Sitwell's chapter on Hopkins; he also pointed out that she quoted some of the same passages of Hopkins and of Coleridge that Read had cited.

Sparrow responded to Grigson's list of errors by saying that he had seen them too, but that they were incidental to the main argument and the result of careless proofreading. As for the alleged plagiarism, he had a simple response: 'It would have been for the most part impossible to omit mention of these matters or to express them very differently.'

A long letter from Sitwell appeared in January, asserting (truthfully) that she had been quoting the passages from Coleridge in her lectures for over a decade, and that she did not need Herbert Read's book to tell her about the history of sprung rhythm. This was a reasonable claim, since Hopkins's ideas on prosody had been widely known and discussed among poets and critics since Robert Bridges's edition of his works in 1918. As for Grigson's remarks on her 'queer debt' to Leavis, she said that in writing of Yeats and Eliot it was impossible not to refer to certain facts of common knowledge: 'I am unable to see why the fact that Dr. Leavis has read Mr. Yeats's *Autobiographies* and *Essays* should have made it incumbent upon me not to. And to take two passages from *The Waste Land*, I did not need Dr. Leavis's book to tell me that the title of this poem was taken from Miss Weston's *From Ritual to Romance*, or to tell me that a passage in *The Burial of the Dead* refers to the Tarot pack. Mr. Eliot's notes to the poem establish both these facts.'[25]

Sitwell had done herself no favours. *Aspects of Modern Poetry* was a sloppy production; her reputation as a critic who cared about the texture of poetry was undermined by her misquotations. Although she had a general defence against the charge of plagiarism, she could have signalled more clearly where her book overlapped with others in the field. She failed to give proper attribution and was technically guilty of a degree of plagiarism. The whole episode gave encouragement to the view that the Sitwells were not writers of greater or lesser merit, but 'apes' and mountebanks. Oddly enough, sixteen years later, F. R. Leavis claimed Geoffrey Grigson had plagiarised his book *The Great Tradition* for a series of radio talks on the English novel.[26] Had she known of it, Sitwell would have been gleeful to see her accuser accused.

Aspects of Modern Poetry revealed her discomfort with the younger poets. In 1933, she had dismissed Stephen Spender as 'over-rated' and impertinent for his negative comments on Sachie's work, though she thought Auden respectful and gifted.[27] In her book, she compared Britain's younger poets to the Surrealists in their wish to become recording machines and never to filter impressions, and she argued, in effect, that their words remain abstract: the sense of sight is almost 'non-existent' and the words never become incarnate, things of flesh and blood: 'We find in several of these young men, in Mr. Auden and Mr. Bottrall especially, considerable technical achievement, as far as rhythmical impetus and the suitability of the rhythm to the theme is concerned, but no tactile sense whatever. The line, in consequence, has neither height nor depth. An intellectual apprehension of words, this they have, but no sensual feeling, no tactile apprehension of them.' In 1934, Auden had not yet written the poetry that would make a nonsense of these claims. In fact, Sitwell was not far off in another observation: 'All, or nearly all, of these poets present surface difficulties, because they suppress intermediary processes of thought, or else they give so many that the reader is bewildered. This surface difficulty gives the impression that the poems conceal great depths. This is rarely so.'[28] Sitwell excluded C. Day Lewis from her strictures, as a poet who is 'truthful, bare and austere',[29] but she could summon up little of the encouragement she had usually lavished on rising talents and, in general, treated them to a lecture from the headmistress. She was threatened by their sudden prominence, and she did not like that Auden and his friends were, as she put it in a letter, 'being taken up by the Communists'.[30] She was, after all, in love with a man made homeless by Lenin.

Sitwell was blind-sided by Sachie's reaction to the book. Her chapter on him contained ample praise, but it dwelt more on his sequence *Dr Donne and Gargantua* than on the *Canons of Giant Art*, and so, in his view, compounded the neglect of his best poetry. Worse still, she had actually identified defects in his work. In reference to one passage, she wrote: 'Mr. Sitwell suddenly changes his scale, dwarfs it, and allows artificialities of an unreal kind, the sort that were used by the minor Elizabethans, to creep in (these two habits are amongst his worst dangers).'[31] She wrote to him:

I cannot conceive how you can *so* have misunderstood my essay on you. The book was largely written so as to include that essay . . . I could not *call* you a poet of genius because you are my brother, and it would have let loose a million little hounds at your throat. But I think I have *proved* you to be a poet of genius . . . I picked two points of contention with you, because I was determined that nobody should say 'here is a sister carried away by the fact of the poet being her brother'. I have, I think, combated and *absolutely* disproved *all* the charges which fools may bring against you.[32]

Sachie apologised and withdrew his complaint.

In late November 1934, Sitwell went back to Levanto to work on her 'suetty book' about Queen Victoria, which was supposed to be finished by May.[33] Having spent the summer in Spain painting bullfighters, Pavlik sailed in November with Ford and Tanner to New York. They went on to Chicago, where Tanner stayed when the others returned to New York; this marked their final separation. Sitwell missed having Christmas dinner with Pavlik, as they had done for several years. She wrote: 'the sensations of being in a new country must be wonderful, – the feeling of an entirely new air, an entirely new civilisation.'[34] Pavlik's exhibitions in Chicago and New York won good reviews, but he was disappointed with the country, so Sitwell suggested he come back and henceforth regard France as his home and England as his market: 'I believe most truthfully that in a way Fortune is like a bird in a wood. If we know how to whistle to her, as a bird-fowler whistles, she will come to us. One must not lose faith in that power, for if one loses faith, the power goes.' She went on: 'Your letter has made me terribly sad. I always think of you really, you know, as if you were rather a sad little boy, not as if you were grown up at all. And that is one way in which I love you, amongst other ways. You are not only a great painter, you are a little boy. I long to have you safe home again.'[35]

In Levanto, she was struck by the beauty of the sunsets and the sense of physical space. She told Pavlik that her room in Paris was just large enough to hold a bed, her books, and a chair: 'I feel cramped and shut in there.' By January 1935, she had changed her mind about Victoria, which she now believed would be a 'really satisfactory' book,[36] especially as it allowed her to write on topics dear to her heart, such as the Tolpuddle Martyrs, but, needing money, she broke off to write several articles and reviews, among them 'Some Notes on my Own Poetry' for the *London Mercury* (March 1935). This essay can reasonably be seen as a fugitive chapter from *Aspects of Modern Poetry*. She describes the kind of sound she was trying to create in her poetry, and the techniques she used to achieve it, including her management of vowels and consonants, assonance, dissonance, end-rhyme, and internal rhyme to affect the speed at which a line can be read. Since her biography of Pope, she had pulled the language of prosody in new directions, but she seemed not to have grasped the limits of explanation: at some level, what happened in her ear was idiosyncratic and inexplicable, just as the reader's ability to share that experience was also mysterious. A good deal of what she presented as objective and certain was rooted in the impressions of an unusually refined sensibility. W. H. Auden and Stephen Spender thought Sitwell no intellectual, although Auden thought she wrote ravishing lines, and Spender said to John Pearson

246 EDITH SITWELL

that her work was 'very very beautiful' and her forms were 'wholly original – and very good'.[37] Others went further. Denise Levertov wrote at
the time of Sitwell's death (*New York Times*, 10 December 1964):
'Perhaps no one has ever lived who had a more highly developed
understanding of the relation in poetry of meaning and aural values' –
a wild claim, but a sign of how Sitwell's technique could excite other
poets. However, the essay Sitwell produced in 1935 sets up to reveal
things about her own work and about poetry in general that may
remain out of reach. The essay underwent great revisions and was used
as an introduction to her *Selected Poems* (1936) as well as some later
volumes, including her *Collected Poems* (1957), where it assumes an
unhelpful importance; its one certain effect is to leave new readers in
a muddle.

'I'm literally dead of overwork,' she wrote to Cecil Beaton when she
got back to Paris in March. 'By May, I shall have written 130,000 words
in one year.'[38] Even so, she was planning another book – again, for the
sake of the advance. She was convinced that Faber & Faber was not
promoting her prose works as they deserved, so she took a commission
from Victor Gollancz to write an eighty-thousand-word novel based on
the life of Jonathan Swift to be delivered in the autumn of 1936.[39]
With the biography to be finished in the early summer, she would have
no rest between projects. Some months later, she wrote to Pavlik: 'The
truth is, that nobody, – and certainly no woman, – can write one book
a year, of the sort of size I have to produce. It is like having a baby every
nine months.'[40] Now forty-seven, Sitwell had passed the age at which
she could hope ever to have a child, and her letters contain occasional
hints of sadness on this point.

In March 1935, Edith Sitwell discovered the novels of Walter
Greenwood, a young writer who captured the scrabbling life of a slum
in Salford. Sitwell read *Love on the Dole* (1933) and *His Worship the
Mayor* (1934), declaring him 'a Dickens of our Time' in the *Sunday
Referee* (24 March 1935). She then sent him what amounts to a fan
letter: 'I feel impelled to tell you that I know you to be, not only a born
writer, but a great writer (and I never use the word great lightly). I do
not know when I have been so deeply, so terribly moved and so strongly
impressed as I have been by these two superb novels.'[41]

With Pavlik set to arrive in Paris around 11 May, Sitwell took up an old theme: 'Rabbits are naturally flattered at being accepted on terms of equality by tigers – but in the long run this does not lead to their happiness. They would be much happier with rabbits.'[42] He was no sooner in Paris than her jealousy of his friends and lovers boiled over again, reducing her to an apology and a promise to be his devoted friend. Nevertheless, tensions remained for some time. On 18 June, René Crevel, faced with worsening tuberculosis and embroiled in a dispute at a literary congress, gassed himself. Sitwell was heading off to London and her letter of consolation to Tchelitchew got lost in a manuscript book, or so she said; almost a month passed before she realised her mistake. She apologised abjectly and begged him not to cut her off.[43] It is just possible that she could not bring herself to console him for the death of one of his lovers.

That July, Sitwell stayed at the Sesame, Imperial and Pioneer Club at 49 Grosvenor Street in Mayfair, one of a small number of 'cock-and-hen' clubs where women could entertain men. An amalgamation of three clubs founded in the late nineteenth century, it had a background in the suffragist movement, with low subscriptions originally intended to appeal to teachers and other professional women.[44] This club served as her residence in London for twenty-six years, and her dinner parties, luncheons, and cocktail parties there attracted writers, musicians and artists, much as her old tea parties had at Pembridge Mansions. She found much to complain of at the club – busybodies, meddlers, 'old trouts', and people who spread their colds – but she became a fixture there.

She went to Renishaw in August, where among the guests was the crime novelist Marie Belloc Lowndes, elder sister of Hilaire Belloc. Sitwell wrote to her afterwards: 'I, too, *very* rarely make friends now; I have only made two new ones in the last ten years or so, and when you came to stay here, I felt, indeed knew, that I had found a third one. It is the rarest and the happiest thing.'[45] They continued a friendly correspondence for several years. Later, during a visit to Renishaw, Belloc Lowndes described Edith and Osbert to her daughter as 'kind-hearted, but extremely censorious, with violent feelings of hate against many writers, and especially "poets who are puffed". I understand that, for she is really very, very good. Were she a man, this would be recognised.'[46]

In honour of Pavlik's opening at Tooth's Gallery on 23 October,

Sitwell hosted a small cocktail party at the Sesame. Among those invited was Stephen Spender, with whom she had already had at least one pleasant meeting. She had avoided discussing his work in *Aspects of Modern Poetry*, as it seemed to belong to a different genre than that of most of the other young poets. Spender had admired Sitwell's poetry when he was a schoolboy and, at sixteen, published a sonnet dedicated to her in his school magazine, but in the early 1930s he had recoiled somewhat from the Sitwell phenomenon. By the mid-1930s he had returned to a cautious admiration, which grew warmer in the 1940s.

Noise was Sitwell's great enemy. In search of quiet in which she could work, she went at the end of the year to Gerona on the coast of Catalonia. 'The sea is just opposite my window, and makes a noise like the sound of a bible being opened, and quantities of pages being turned over all at once,' she wrote to Pavlik, who was setting out again for the United States. The Spanish city was lovely, but Sitwell had to contend with voices from a café beneath her bedroom: 'Male Spaniards seem never to go to bed – females sometimes, but, if one may judge from appearances, only in order to give birth to children.'[47]

While in Gerona, she wrote an important review for the *London Mercury* (February 1936) of four younger poets, Ronald Bottrall, Archibald MacLeish, William Empson, and Dylan Thomas. Bottrall, who disliked Grigson and was not a member of Auden's circle, had written Sitwell a 'charming' letter about *Aspects of Modern Poetry*, but he made clear how unhappy he was with her comments. She promised to clarify them in a review of his next book.[48] She was much more generous in the *London Mercury*, and also found a good deal to praise in Empson: 'His language is full, intense and charged with meaning.' She thought MacLeish capable of good lines and passages, but added that in him 'the great British Public have been sold another pup'. Dylan Thomas proved a revelation to her. She had scorned 'Our eunuch dreams' without naming its author in *Aspects of Modern Poetry*, a book Thomas characterised as her 'latest piece of virgin dung'.[49] Now, however, in 'A grief ago' and *Eighteen Poems*, she found what she had been hoping for in a young poet: 'He has very great gifts, though they are not as yet completely resolved. He is, at moments, a prey to his subconscious self, and consequently to obscurity; but from that subconscious self rise, time after time, lines which are transmuted by his conscious self into really great poetry.'

T. S. Eliot and Stephen Spender had already encouraged Thomas, but it is generally agreed that Edith Sitwell was the chief architect of his fame. For the next few years, she wrote to him and about him, found money for his family, and bore with his drunken pranks. Her attitude was proprietorial. She wrote to Pavlik on 10 February that she was travelling from Paris to London, partly to meet Dylan Thomas:

> It is absolutely beyond doubt that that boy is going to be a very great poet indeed: his poems are on a huge scale, are ferociously individual, and very strange, – his form is miraculous. And, being very young, his poems have not the awful glibness one fears in the young. They are like rock matrix, or else are enclosed, like young buds. His is certainly the one *genius* for poetry that has arisen in the younger generation. And I'll thank all the silly people there are about, waiting to ruin genius, to keep their hands off him.[50]

Although for Dylan Thomas a trip to London usually meant a bender, he arrived sober at the Sesame Club on 20 February and made a great impression on Edith Sitwell, who remembered that he behaved 'Beautifully . . . He always behaved with me like a son with his mother.' Thomas characterised the party as 'more dukes than drinks' and went out afterwards to get properly tight.[51]

The other reason for Sitwell's visit to London was the release of *Victoria of England* on 13 February. Intended for a popular market, this book played to some of her strengths – the ability to evoke atmosphere and to render the character of an autocratic woman (she had inside information on that subject). Relying on Engels, she vividly recounted the horrors of poverty and labour in the mid-nineteenth century. The book had few claims to originality, and Sitwell acknowledged a considerable debt to Lytton Strachey. Still, it was very readable. She wrote to Osbert from Weston on 5 March: 'Victoria is having a violent success; I couldn't have believed it possible, but there we are! When I left London a week today, it was selling at the rate of 150 copies a day, and ten days after publication, although the 1st edition had been a very big one, (4,500 copies) they started printing a second edition. America is printing *separately*, too, so with any sort of luck, I may perhaps make some money.'[52] While writing the book, she seems to have been briefly swept up in her subject, rhapsodising over Victoria's 'eagle'-like greatness in old age. However, once the book was out, she moderated her opinion, as she told Sassoon: 'It was of course a great time, owing to social reform, etc, but she was *not* a great woman, and it is no use anybody telling me she was.'[53] In November, one of her agents, Nancy Pearn, suggested that she write a poem about Victoria, but Sitwell refused: 'I've had enough of the old girl to last me.'[54]

Edith Sitwell loved being celebrated, but she did not care to be taken up and dropped and then taken up again. At some point, apparently in the 1930s, she composed a letter to a woman whom Osbert names 'Mrs Almer' in *Left Hand, Right Hand!*:

> Dear Mrs. Almer,
>   After five years, you have again been kind enough to ask me to luncheon. The reason for this is that I have just published a successful book: the reason I have had a successful book is that I do not go out and waste my time and energy, but work hard, morning and afternoon. If I accept your kind invitation, I shall have to leave off earlier in the morning, and shall be too tired to work in the afternoon. Then my next book will not be such a success, and you will not ask me to luncheon; or, at best, less often. So that, under these circumstances, I am sure you will agree it is wiser for me not to accept your present kind invitation.
>   Yours sincerely,
>   Edith Sitwell[55]

It is possible that there was no Mrs Almer and that this letter was written as a party-piece.

Fame brought other queer demands on Sitwell's time. In 1935, her friend John Beevers, a religious writer, and his wife Marjorie had asked her to help find work as a publisher's reader for 'a wretched deformed semi-dwarf' named Douglas Burton, whom she met and tried to help. On 14 February 1936, Burton struck an author named Douglas Bose on the head with a sculptor's hammer, angry because Bose had recently thrown a brazil nut at a woman, giving her a black eye. Having a thin skull, Bose died of his injuries. The Beevers urged Sitwell to go into the witness box and describe Burton as mad, while Burton's brother wanted her to raise a thousand pounds for a defence against the murder charge. Though afraid of scandal, Sitwell was willing to testify if it would save the man, but John Sparrow, after consulting another barrister and Burton's solicitor, advised her to stay away from the trial; it would be squalid and her testimony could not affect the outcome. As it was, the medical evidence was sufficient, and Burton was found 'guilty but insane' on 30 April.[56]

Meanwhile, a very different kind of insanity was suddenly abroad in Europe, and Tchelitchew, still in New York, had to decide where his future lay. On 7 March 1936, Hitler overthrew the Locarno Pact and sent forces into the demilitarised Rhineland, confident that the French and the British lacked either the money or the stomach to drive him out of it. He was right, but Europe was brought near to war. Tchelitchew did not want to go back into uniform, and as a Russian refugee he had no idea what might become of him if France was over-run. Sitwell returned to Paris on 30 March and wrote to him the next day: 'Do *not* worry about war, dear. I am told by everybody in England that there will not be one. Nobody wants one, and unless the French land us in one through sheer fright, I am sure – at least I hope to God – there will be peace. If war should break out, you must be a conscientious objector. On no account must you fight. The thought is too dreadful for anything.'[57] Two weeks later, she suggested that in the event of conflict England would be safe for him. Nevertheless, she believed that unless 'that pin-head Eden' did something new about Italy, there was no immediate danger of war. 'I *know* the English don't want it, and I do *not* believe that the Germans do. But you must run no risks.'[58]

At that moment, the threat of war was not her main worry. She wrote to Georgia: 'I am feeling dreadfully sad. Poor Helen, poor poor thing. She has started something under her other arm, – *and* Hartmann has found something under the skin of her neck on the side on which she was operated. He says the thing under the arm is a little better, and so he is not going to operate yet, because both the places may go down.'[59] As she recalled later, Helen's piety made her absent-minded:

'Poor darling, knowing she had had cancer, she yet would not look
where she was going, because she was thinking about some silly mystical book, some ridiculous old priest's helpless sermon – and would fall
downstairs! She would go out in the pouring rain to Communion at 6
in the morning! It was impossible to look after her.'[60]

At the beginning of May, she took Helen and Evelyn to Gerona for
another holiday, hoping that sunlight and fresh air might help. This
time she avoided the hotel and rented a small house with 'palms, a
nutmeg tree, a pomegranate tree, a medlar tree, crowds of the most
beautiful roses I have ever seen, and nightingales and a pair of crested
grebes, who are nesting here. There are also swarms of frogs.'[61]

She came to Gerona intending to work on her novel about Jonathan
Swift:

> I have crowds of notes for it, but it is not actually started yet. The
> principal theme is the story of Swift and Stella, but put into modern
> clothes. And then there is the secondary theme of the girl who loves
> the unfortunate man who killed her lover [in war], – because it gives
> me the chance of showing the wickedness and blindness of hatred
> between nations. I have done, – though I say it as shouldn't – a really
> terrific description of the dead man's mother receiving the news of
> his death in battle. And I am going to have huge street scenes, with
> hunger-marchers, etc. It is all very difficult, as I have never done any-
> thing of the sort before.[62]

While Sitwell was conjuring street scenes on the page, real ones
were taking place in France, where the election of a leftist government
under Léon Blum had set off a wave of strikes involving about two million workers hopeful of winning better wages and hours. Sitwell read
of this in Spain and wrote to Pavlik on 9 June: 'I think everything looks
very dangerous everywhere except in England, at present. I sympathise
very strongly with the strikers in their demands. The shop-people, for
instance, work for far too long hours. In a dairy where we buy butter,
the women arrive at 6 in the morning, and do not leave before 10 at
night, – but I do hope there will not be riots, which always terrify me.
I do implore you to keep away from any places where there is likely to
be trouble.'[63]

Spain was more unstable than France. On 16 February, the Popular Front won a national election. In June, the country was convulsed with strikes, and by 18 July there were insurrections in Spanish Morocco and Seville; the Civil War had begun. Fortunately, Edith Sitwell had left Catalonia around 15 July, but Helen and Evelyn stayed on. The small house had a plate-glass window, giving anyone on the hill opposite a good view of what was going on inside. When the killing started, Helen, in a superbly courageous act, hid a priest there, disguised as a countryman: 'the Reds came and dragged him out, and he would have been shot then and there, if the local doctor hadn't saved him by saying he was mad. Which terrified her.'[64]

'To-day the deliberate increase in the chances of death, / The conscious acceptance of guilt in the necessary murder,'[65] wrote W. H. Auden about the war when it still seemed a pure cause; he later came to regret his glibness. During the war, the Nationalists' acts of repression were more numerous, although there were large-scale atrocities on both sides. Particularly offensive to Sitwell and Helen Rootham was the Loyalist assault on the Catholic Church – the murders of 4184 secular priests, 2365 monks, and 283 nuns – most of them occurring in these first weeks of the conflict.[66] Until disillusionment set in about such massacres and about the role of the Soviet Union in the war, the Loyalists were a fashionable cause, but Edith Sitwell wanted nothing to do with it.

It took her some time to get word of Helen and Evelyn. On her way to Renishaw around the beginning of August, she wrote to Pavlik:

I have received news at last – (all the postal arrangements have broken down) – a letter from a patient but very irritated Lieutenant of an English Man-of-War, saying the Man-of-War had called at San Feliu to rescue British [subjects], and H. and E. had refused to leave (although told by the captain they ought to do so) because they say they feel perfectly safe. They always have known better than everybody about everything, and I expect this chance of being a really thorough nuisance is too much of a temptation to be resisted.[67]

It is possible that Helen delayed because she was still trying to provide shelter for the priest. She failed to register with the consul, putting

herself in danger of being stranded. With the assistance of the same
doctor who had protected the priest, the two women managed, at
short notice, to get passage on a steamer. Sitwell wrote to Christabel
Aberconway on 21 August: '[Helen] was marooned for four days in
Cadiz harbour, on an English ship; and whilst there was told by a man
(who was no. 5 on the list) that the British Consul at Cadiz was no. 36
on a list of 137 put down by the Communists to be hanged and *burned*
if they got possession of the town. She says the terror of their last six
days before she and her sister got on to the British boat had to be
endured to be believed.'[68] In a similar account for Pavlik, Sitwell added,
'You who know the horrors of revolution will understand all this.'[69]

16

TWO NATIONS

'Pavlik is painting a new portrait of me,' Sitwell wrote to David Horner
from Paris on 26 October 1936. 'When I sat to him last he uttered a
long plaint, and for some time I was unable to discover the gist of it.
But when boiled down, it transpired to be the fact that he *cannot* work
properly in Paris, on account of his brother-in-law's pince-nez. These
flash, when he comes in to meals, tired from working; and they are, in
addition, very large and round as to the lens, very thick, too, which
gives him an owl-like appearance disturbing to a painter.' This is one
of the rare times that Sitwell made fun of Tchelitchew behind his back,
but she *was* pleased with the painting. In this portrait of her as a sibyl,
she wears a plain dress; her hair is almost unkempt and her broad forehead exposed; in the background is a blue curtain. She holds a quill pen
and a sheet of paper, and the veins in her long hands are emphasised.
On a board hanging beside her are two hands forming E and S in sign
language.

For months there had been trouble between Tchelitchew and
Edward James over Salvador Dalí. That summer James had entered a
contract to pay Dalí a regular sum and to assume ownership of the art
works he produced during a two-year period. Dalí blithely cheated on
their arrangements, and James could not get all the works he was owed.
Tchelitchew felt neglected, and in the background there was another
odd situation: James had fallen unrequitedly in love with Ruth Ford,
the sister of Charles Henri whom he thought despicable and depraved.[1]
Sitwell had urged Tchelitchew not to throw away real friends like
Edward James (and, by implication, herself) for people like 'little
bamboo tables, very dry and strengthless on which you can place no
reliance. You *did* do that you know, and this is the result.'[2] Happily,

Edward James bought the 'Sibyl' portrait, and Tchelitchew was able to sail to the United States in November with money in his pocket and no further need to worry about his brother-in-law's pince-nez. Meanwhile, James came to read his poetry to Edith Sitwell, who grew 'fonder and fonder' of him.[3]

W. B. Yeats's *Oxford Book of Modern Verse* came out in November 1936 – a strange selection, in which the most represented poet was Oliver St John Gogarty, with a huge amount of space given to Yeats's Irish friends. He left out Owen and Rosenberg altogether, allotting just two pages to Sassoon. Eliot was there but represented by minor work. However, the Sitwells had no reason to complain: Sachie's poem 'Agamemnon's Tomb' was included, as was an eighteen-page selection of Edith's works. Roy Foster observes that, for Yeats, Edith Sitwell's intensity of vision made up for a technique he did not admire. Yeats's introduction with its salute to her 'high style of "perpetual metamorphosis", with "a nightmare vision like that of Webster" coiled beneath, is a compelling and intelligent defence of a writer already dividing critical opinion down the middle'.[4] Michael Roberts's *The Faber Book of Modern Verse*, published in the same year, offered a more sensible representation especially to younger poets, but Edith Sitwell was allowed just four pages. Sachie was permitted ten for 'The Farnese Hercules' – an excellent choice as that poem is both well wrought and representative of him. However, as the editor of anthologies that had to compete with Roberts's book, Edith Sitwell regarded it as 'one of the worst anthologies I have ever seen',[5] although almost no one agreed with her.

Helen Rootham returned from Spain in August in a dire condition: 'Poor soul, I am so sorry for her, sorry with all my heart.'[6] She revived enough to go to England and deal with a family crisis – a nephew was himself dying of cancer, and her sister Ethel had relapsed into mental illness. Helen was trying to translate 'Of the Doctrine of Divine Love' by the Abbé Coste and needed a publisher, so Marie Belloc Lowndes, a Catholic, gave her an introduction to Burns, Oates & Washbourne. However, morphia made it impossible for her to finish the manuscript.[7] In February, she underwent a light-ray treatment in Paris,[8] after which Sitwell took her in the first week of March to Levanto for another extended holiday. By the end of the month, however, she was immobilised with back pain. On one of the few occasions she was able to leave the hotel, they were nearly killed; Sitwell wrote: 'It was up in the mountains, and another motor dashed round a corner, straight into us, and as nearly as possible pushed us over a ravine.' They were saved by their chauffeur, an ex-racing driver, who managed to keep the car on the road.[9]

While in Levanto, Sitwell was finishing her novel, but with distractions, as she told Richard Jennings: 'most awful people with legs like flies, who come in to lunch in bathing costume, flies, centipedes, an idiot boy who has been given charge of the church bell, which he rings *literally* all day on Sundays, barking dogs, people who bang doors, and an incessant wireless. They also tore up the road just outside our bedroom windows.' She told Jennings that Dylan Thomas was 'rapidly heading for having his ears boxed. I can feel the tips of my fingers tingling to come into contact with the lobes of his ears. And it would do him a lot of good, for he was evidently insufficiently corrected as a child. *What* a tiresome boy that is, though a very gifted one.'[10]

She had followed up her earlier praise with a review of *Twenty-Five Poems*, claiming that he 'showed every promise of greatness' (*Sunday Times*, 15 November 1936). This was the review that launched his fame. She set him up with her own agent and gave him introductions to various writers, editors, and publishers. When he missed the appointments, these people wrote reproachfully to Sitwell. Later in the summer, when Thomas was working on a fishing boat, she sent money from an anonymous donor that allowed Dylan and Caitlin to buy knives and towels, to go to a Garbo film, and to pay off the 'clamourers'. She was trying to find him suitable work, and he asked her help in getting him into the BBC, where, among other things, he would like to broadcast Sachie's poems: 'it's great and grand aloud, isn't it? pillars and columns and great striding figures through a microphone'.[11] However, Dylan Thomas's speciality was a disappearing act, driving Sitwell to the observation that he should join Maskelyne and Devant, the magicians, illusionists and plate-spinners.[12] Finally exasperated at his failure to answer letters, she stopped writing. When *The Map of Love* came out in August 1939, she thought it 'ghastly', but continued to hope that in time he would make something of an incomparable talent.[13]

In Levanto, Sitwell generally got up at 5.30 a.m. when it was certain to be quiet, and she would write up to four thousand words per day (some of it copying). Helen was not fit to travel until the end of June, and when they reached Paris she immediately took to her bed in pain. Sitwell wrote to Christabel Aberconway: 'Life has been hell for four months, excepting that I'm under the impression that I've written the book I've been waiting twenty years to write. It's *nearly*, but not quite, finished.'[14] She told Pavlik that she thought it 'a second Gold Coast Customs'.[15]

In a letter of 8 July 1937 from the Sesame Club, she remarks almost as an aside: 'Everything is very tiresome here. My mother is supposed to be dying. It won't, I imagine, be immediately. I am sorry for her, but she has always been terribly unkind to me, and I can't pretend to feel anything personally, that I don't feel.'[16] Lady Ida had travelled to London from Montegufoni a week earlier in fair health but was soon taken to a nursing home in London with pneumonia. She died there on 12 July. Her obituary in *The Times* (13 July 1937) called her 'A Great Lady of Yorkshire', described her beauty and her ability to talk to fishermen about their problems, and just hinted at her scandal: 'she was unversed in practical affairs'. Her funeral took place at Lois Weedon church near Weston Hall two days later. According to *The Times* (15 July 1937), Edith attended the funeral, along with Osbert, Sachie, and Georgia, but 'Sir George Sitwell was unable to be present through illness' – he was distraught.

Edith remained in England until October for a joint presentation with Osbert and Sachie of the University of London's Northcliffe Lectures, published the following year as *Trio*. They attracted crowds of thirteen hundred per lecture, a reassuring sign that the Sitwells still mattered in the literary world, as Edith waited for the reviews of *I Live Under a Black Sun*. The novel was dedicated to John Sparrow, which seems to have irked Tchelitchew. She addressed him in the third person: 'I *have* a very great friend, one who has my most devoted and tender affection. I did not dedicate my book "I Live Under a Black Sun" to him, because the book is about a man of genius who lived in darkness, – and *he* is a man of genius. I felt that if I had, it would have drawn down darkness of one kind or another upon our world.'[17] That Tchelitchew might expect a dedication goes to the heart of the story. Only Jonathan Hare, Sitwell's twentieth-century Swift, possesses the genius to describe in tales of big men and small men, in the conversation of wise horses, and in modest proposals for the eating of flesh the madness that Sitwell's generation had lived through. Yet Hare is himself touched by a selfishness that grows to insanity: 'I *must* have someone who believes in me, who is ready to give up her will to me.'[18] He destroys the lives of three women who love him, each of whom seems to represent a mood of Sitwell's spurned devotion to Tchelitchew, although her main interest is in Anna, a character based on Swift's 'Stella'. Not dedicating the book to Tchelitchew was either superstitious (a fear that he would end up like Swift) or a small gesture of independence.

The novel is as strange as any later work of Magic Realism, as it collapses the boundaries between one age and another. The poet Richard Church wrote in the *Christian Science Monitor* (17 November 1937) that the novel needed a more restrictive intellectual frame, prompting Sitwell to explain to him: 'I took Swift and those two [three?] women and put them into the present time, because they don't live in time, they live in eternity and theirs is a story which recurs and recurs again (I've seen it happen in my own experience), and because I wanted to show the individual madness against the universal madness.' About a year later, she wrote to the journalist Raymond Marriott: 'It is an allegory, in a sense, as you will see. The reason I put Swift into modern clothes is because the spirit of the modern world is power gone mad. And Swift is power gone mad. I have tried to show the futility and barrenness of hatred. It is a terrible book, I think. I felt as if I had been through an earthquake, after I had written it.'[19] The book is extremely hard-minded: the only artist able to represent the insanity of the age is at the same time the embodiment of the private madness. The path to redemption (or revolution) winds back on itself, and the novel specifically defies the hope of moral progress. It is a work of Christian belief insofar as it gazes into hell.

I Live Under a Black Sun is Sitwell's answer to the Marxism of the 1930s. One of the epigraphs is taken from Nadezhda Krupskaya's memoir of her husband Vladimir Ilyich Lenin (a work Allanah Harper introduced her to): 'And observing these howling contrasts in richness and poverty, Ilyich would mutter through clenched teeth . . . "Two nations."' Early in the novel, a revolutionary's bomb succeeds in killing a governor, but it also kills a child and sparks a war:

the fronds of his hair were all dabbled and stiff as if they had lain in
some dreadful rain. His body was so broken that, little as he was, his
mother could scarcely gather him in her arms. Yet sitting there
through many hours, huddled ape-like with her long maternal arms
sheltering her ruins, in the broken sunlight, she could feel his small
hands squeezing her heart, knocking at it as he had done in the long
months of waiting before he was born . . . And far away in the cities,
the newspapers of Europe contained the news of the murder, all the
newsboys in the capitals were shouting it along the streets: 'Murder
of a Governor! Bomb thrown at a procession!' – a sensation, but
unimportant and to be discussed idly for a moment and then forgotten. For there were plans to be made for to-morrow and the days to
follow, houses and big businesses to be built, credits to be established,
schemes to be begun, marriages to be celebrated. But in the darkness
under the trees in the great cities, the young girls held the hands of
dead men, pressed lips to lips that were already cold. For the two
nations that alone inhabit the earth, the rich and the poor, walking
to their death in opposed hordes, had found the only force that could
bind them together, a cannibalistic greed, hatred, and fear. No longer
need they fear each other, for both nations will be swept away.[20]

While Sitwell thought Lenin right to 'howl' at poverty, at the same
time the promises of his revolution were debunked by mothers and
widows in their grief.

Sitwell said to Tchelitchew that the book 'varies between lyricism
and savagery' – that is, between a private lament for lost love and the
'howl' of the battlefield, as well as that of the penniless migrants whom
she had observed for so many years in Bayswater. As always in her
work, much of her meaning is worked out in the sounds of language.
Different sections of the book operate in different rhetorical registers –
a quality that discourages most readers until they have got through
about fifty pages. Much of the book, of course, is written in a middle
register, satirising domestic life and courtship. However, other sections
attempt to render extreme emotional states. When she writes of longing, there are echoes of Swinburne, and when she describes beggars
huddling in the cold, or battle scenes, or Swift's mind finally collaps-
ing, her prose becomes, as above, rhapsodic, even visionary.

Sitwell expected to take a battering with this book – and some critics did believe she was overreaching; the reviewer in the *New Statesman* (2 October 1937) remarked: 'Miss Sitwell is a delightful poet, but she is decidedly not a novelist.' At first the reviews bothered her; 'all the Pipsqueakery are after me in full squeak'.[21] Nevertheless, the good reviews took her by surprise, as she told Tchelitchew: 'The News Chronicle – a very important paper, – published a review by Ellis Roberts, – a very important critic, – saying it could only have been written by a spiritual child of Turgenieff and Emily Bronte, that it is a book of almost unbearable beauty and terrific power. The Manchester Guardian [Wilfrid Gibson] is half off its head about it, and says only "Wuthering Heights" compares with it.'

In fact, Gibson went further: 'I hesitate to use that much bandied and shop-soiled word "genius"; it would be so much more politic, so much safer, to apply the inevitable epithet "brilliant"; yet if this novel has not a touch of genius I must admit that I do not know what genius is' (5 October 1937). William Soskin in the *New York Herald Tribune* (27 February 1938) remarked: 'There are no adjectives to describe the darkness of this novel, its pity and its terror. Miss Sitwell proves that her icy delicacy can achieve more than the violent onslaughts, the tumult and shouting of the large-scale propaganda novelists.' Evelyn Waugh remarked that Sitwell, always good at such things, could easily have provided background detail and atmosphere for an ordinary historical novel:

But the tragedy and the mystery of Swift were too potent for such a treatment; she seems to have seen deep into his tortured soul, to horror lurking beneath horror, into a world where costume and decor become meaningless. It is a terrifying book . . . Miss Sitwell's book, or so it seems to me, is like a magnesium flame in a cavern, immediately and abundantly beautiful at first sight, provoking further boundless investigation. It is a book that must be read patiently, more than once and it must be read.[22]

I Live Under a Black Sun is indeed a masterpiece, one of the great novels of its time, yet until Peter Owen republished it in 2007 it had been out of print for almost fifty years.

Writing on an ostensibly historical subject allowed Sitwell to cast a veil over autobiography. Tchelitchew apparently did not guess that Jonathan Hare was based partly on him. She was not sued by Wyndham Lewis, though he was the model for a villain named Debenham.[23] Evidently, Sir George did not notice that he was the model for the gloomy and introverted Sir Henry Rotherham, or that aspects of Lady Ida are to be found in Mrs Linden. The Rootham sisters are reflected in the character of Becky Mintley – a woman of stocky appearance, like Evelyn, and inclined, like Helen, to both charity and scolding.

In the autumn of 1937, Sitwell wrote to Pavlik from Paris:

I returned back here to unspeakable sadness, – to find that – as we now fear – the cancer has attacked the poor unhappy Helen's *spine* and one *hip*. She has such pain as is unimaginable, and sometimes moans and weeps all day. When she is not doing that, she lies with her wretched discoloured face thrown back over her pillow, her eyes shut, her mouth pinched. Her face, when she is asleep, has the terrible owl-like wisdom that people's faces have when they are dying. They are giving her increased doses of morphia and that is all she looks forward to. She says terrible things: 'I suppose this day will pass like all the other days I have to bear.' And it may go on for *ages*. Yes. Ages.[24]

Sitwell was thinking about a new novel to be called 'To the Dark Tower Came'; although she assembled notes and made newspaper clippings about circuses, flea circuses, animal cruelty, and stupid bishops, she was not ready to start on it.[25] Instead, she wrote a radio play about Beau Brummel called *The Last Party*, broadcast on the BBC on 3 April.[26] Work became a secondary consideration as Helen's condition worsened. In February 1938, Edith wrote to Sachie: 'No news excepting that Helen seems a little stronger. But she is absolutely helpless. She can't move one leg at all. And she has to have morphia twice a day. She cried this morning when I took her in her early morning tea, because she said she wondered if she would ever walk again. And I said of course she would. But the doctor told Evelyn he thought she would *never* walk again. We have to keep that from her at all costs. He says the poor thing is not dying. Life here is absolute hell, and that is all there is about it.'[27]

Now that music lessons and translations were out of the question, Helen had almost no money of her own. Some years earlier Evelyn had been making about ninety pounds per year from office work,[28] barely enough to cover her expenses. Now, at sixty-one, she was hobbled by varicose veins, and her annual earnings, it seems, were reduced to about sixty pounds.[29] The cost of the household and of Helen's care fell squarely on Sitwell. In December 1935, her overdraft had stood at £516. On 27 February 1937, Percy Haddock of Coutts & Co. sent a chivvying letter – her overdraft was £935 and he looked forward to it being reduced.[30] By June 1938, it had reached £1031. Sitwell's investments returned about five to six hundred pounds per year, out of which she paid Helen an annual allowance of £270 (divided into quarterly payments).[31] Nursing care alone, Sitwell told Pavlik, cost three hundred pounds per year. Between March and June 1938, Sitwell cashed an unusual series of fifteen cheques totalling £138. She had one place to turn for help, but she knew there was a trap. She wrote to Pavlik on 14 March: 'That sunny-natured old cannibal (Ginger) is trying to get me to go to Florence. Apparently he thinks I am going to spend my life between the horrors of this flat, and looking after him! It is utterly impossible, of course, to do any serious work, because I feel nothing: I am utterly numb.'[32] While she harboured resentments, Sitwell seldom quarrelled with her father, and she was probably correct in thinking that he wanted her to be the prop of his old age.

Edith had already borrowed £150 from Sir George, and he sent a separate cheque for some champagne to cheer Helen, but the doctor forbade her to drink it; she was allowed only a teaspoon of brandy in a tisane. Edith thanked her father, then added: 'But the dreadful thing is, darling, that I am forced to *beg* you to lend me, as an advance from mother's money which you are so generously handing over to us, another £150. I know only too well what a large sum it is to borrow, and how much it is asking of you. But that wretched woman now *has* to have three injections of heroin a day. The morphia no longer works, and she has to have the stronger drug.'[33] Sir George sent the cheque by 24 March, when he remarked in a letter to Georgia that Edith 'never came down on me before'.[34] However, accepting money from

Sir George meant that she could not avoid him, so on 5 April she went to Montegufoni intent on getting more help.

Ten days later she wrote to Helen: 'I had a long talk with Father yesterday, who fully understands how *very* ill you have been, and *will* need building up for ages. He says I am never to *hesitate* to ask him for more money the moment it is needed for you. And that you are on *no* account to spare expenses . . . So please, dear, bear that in mind. There is no conceivable money worry for you, and anything you could possibly want, you are to have at once.' At the same time, she found a small gift for Helen: 'Oh, how I do hope you will like the Crucifix I am bringing to you. It really does seem to me to be lovely. One of the arms of the Cross is, unhappily, damaged, but it is so ancient one can't wonder.'[35] It was the sort of gift you might give to someone who is losing everything.

Sitwell returned around 25 April to find Helen often delirious. Even an intended kindness added to her sorrow: 'Three days before she died, some good religious friend of hers came and sat beside her, and called her. She seemed to be dying at the moment. But she revived, because of that. Afterwards, she said to me, with a frightful despair, with infinite bitterness: "You know, Edith, I was in such peace. I was just going. And that *poor good fool* brought me back."'[36] On the following day Helen went 'raving mad' with pain and would shriek when lifted because the drugs were failing.[37] She died, at last, on Sunday, 8 May 1938,[38] and was buried in Paris.

After Helen Rootham's death, Sitwell fell silent. It appears that she went to Weston on 19 May and then to the Sesame. She returned to Paris in July, moving on to Renishaw in August. Her financial records show one significant item. In June, she made her first quarterly payment of £67 10s to Evelyn Wiel – the amount she had given to Rootham over the years – representing about half her income apart from writing.[39] On her deathbed, Rootham had pleaded with Sitwell to take care of her sister and to continue to live in the flat with her. Sitwell made the promise.

After almost a year's stay in the United States, Pavlik was in London that summer to design a ballet, as well as for an exhibition at Tooth's Gallery of *Phenomena* and other works. He made little time to see the distraught Sitwell, although at some point he remarked of her mourning dress: 'It makes you look like a giant orphan.'[40] He visited many friends but seemed to be dodging her. Even in Paris, he held back, and on 25 July she received a *pneumatique* from him that he was leaving again. She congratulated him on his successes but then spoke her mind:

> This year, two friends have left me. One, a most noble-minded woman, loyal, invincibly, to her beliefs, invincibly loyal in her friendships, left me against her will. She left me because she had to die. She suffered during six months, – an illness which was one ghastly nightmare, not only for her, but for her sister and me. Then she died, a death which was so unspeakably frightful, so appalling, that I am now, after my long self-control, completely broken down by it, and am ill. The other friend left me, utterly heartlessly, utterly callously, because he wished to. For no reason. Or for a reason so base, so mean, and so petty that it is completely unworthy of the great artist that he is, and I am ashamed for him.

They exchanged a few more letters and met amicably in Paris on 3 September. 'Let us forget our silly trouble this summer,' she wrote shortly after. Pavlik sailed for New York in the middle of September, but she did not write to him again for six months.

For a long time her attention had been fixed on a private world, but in September 1938, with Hitler demanding the Sudetenland, she could see Paris preparing for war. She wrote to David Horner: 'In the future (if things go on like this) I should think children will grow gas-shelters on their backs as snails grow shells. Sometimes, I suppose, a head will peer out, as it does with snails. Otherwise, all you will see will be gas-shelter. I don't know why one doesn't go quite mad.' She was gradually reviving from her ordeal, and her sense of humour was coming back:

> Just as, in England, no one must beg a dog not to bark, or breathe a word against an aspidistra, so, here, no one must ask a child not to be every qualified little kind of nuisance. The darling little children of the district have chosen this moment, when we are all nearly crazy with worry, and they are on holiday, to whirl round and round the fountain which is just underneath the windows, on four wooden

sledges which seem to have as many iron wheels as a centipede has legs, – shrieking at the tops of their voices as they go. At least most of them shriek. Others have whistles. They do this practically all day. And nobody must ask them not to.[41]

In the autumn of 1938, Sitwell settled down to work on an anthology for Victor Gollancz, which she hoped to have ready by Christmas. It took until the next summer. She also wrote a radio play about Romeo Coates, one of her English Eccentrics, which was broadcast on 23 February 1939.[42] She submitted a dutiful review (*Sunday Times*, 2 October 1938) of David Horner's travel book *Through French Windows*, attributing to it 'charm and wit and perception' and 'admirable writing'.[43] However, she was tired and ill. Her physician in England was Lord Dawson of Penn (physician-in-ordinary to the King, he is now remembered for the technically treasonous act of hastening the death of George V in 1936 with an injection of morphine and cocaine[44]). During the summer he told Sitwell that she was exhausted, and he later performed a gynaecological procedure: 'I became like the Woman in the Bible, and remained like it for a whole month.'[45] Then she caught a chill at the end of October visiting Helen's grave. She arrived at the Sesame on 12 November with Evelyn in tow, and appears to have stayed on in England until after Christmas.

Largely to get away from Evelyn, Sitwell decided to act on a suggestion Tchelitchew had made before his departure. She tried to set up an American lecture tour, in which she expected to be able to read from a script, while the agent thought she should work from memory. She wrote to Rée Gorer: 'I am having a protracted argument with the agent, Mr. Colston Leigh, on the subject of whether I am, or alternatively am not, a trick cyclist. As far as I can make out, he would like me to bicycle round and round the platform on the tip of my nose, with my feet in the air, intoning at the same time on the effect that texture has on the caesura.'[46] Leigh wanted to bring her to the United States, but with war on the horizon, their plans fell through and she would not cross the ocean for another decade.

Around March 1939, Tchelitchew reappeared in Paris for a *vernissage*, as Sitwell told Gorer: 'He is looking very thin and ill. He is furious with me for not having written to him for six months, and hints that I have broken his faith in human nature by deserting him when he was ill. He will never be the same again, he says, never. Either to me, or in general. I think he must have forgotten last summer.' She added, as an afterthought: 'Pavlik says the doctors tested him to see if he was getting cancer, which upset me horribly.'[47] Unable to hold out any longer, she finally wrote to him:

> My dearest Pavlik,
>   This is only a little note, just to send you my unchanged affection, and my unchanged friendship. It made me terribly unhappy seeing you so white and thin. Everything made me terribly unhappy.
>   I had to recover from the pain I had been caused last year, before I could write. But never for one moment did I mean to leave you for always. I couldn't.
>   When shall I see you?
>   Best love
>   Your friend
>   Edith

She intended to go to Montegufoni in early April to spend a fortnight with Sachie and Georgia and to check on Sir George who had suffered internal bleeding. That trip was cancelled when Mussolini, trying to match Hitler's territorial gains in the Sudetenland and Austria, marched his troops into Albania on 7 April. As it turned out, she would never see Sir George again. Edith went instead to London, where she needed to correct proofs against a 1623 First Folio of Shakespeare.

On 18 May, Tchelitchew thanked her for her help at a *vernissage* in Paris; he was unhappy that the critics took no notice of his work, and he knew who the culprits were: 'But the Jews are very very against me, and I feel and know it! What an awful race after all.'[48] The remark was not just harsh but obtuse. Since Kristallnacht on 9–10 November 1938 most of the world had been aware of the persecution of Jews under Hitler. Some refugee ships had already sailed, notably the *St Louis* from Hamburg on 13 May; its voyage soon caused a furore when Cuba and then the United States refused to accept its 937 refugees. The ship returned to Europe, some of its passengers finding safety in England, but

532 were trapped on the continent during the war and 254 eventually died in the Holocaust.[49]

Yeats had died in January so was spared the summer of 1939 when, indeed, the worst were full of passionate intensity. Edith Sitwell, like everyone else in Europe, watched as war came nearer. In mid-August, she received a telegram from Osbert, urging her to get back to England. She left behind books, paintings, manuscripts, and a beloved cat at rue Saint-Dominique, arriving in London on the 18th. Evelyn Wiel hunkered down in Paris and hoped that the trouble would pass. Tchelitchew had been staying at Saint-Jorioz on Lac d'Annecy; luckier than most of the Jewish refugees, he got himself on the SS *Champlain* to the United States on 29 August,[50] where he remained in safety for the duration of the war.

On 27 August, Sitwell wrote Tchelitchew a letter from Renishaw, sending copies of it to Paris, Guermantes, and Saint-Jorioz: 'I think now nothing but a miracle can save us. If it *does* break, it may be years before we meet again. But no matter how long the years may be, you will always be in my heart, held warm there, and in my thoughts. I shall write to you every week, unless some accident happens to prevent it, and I beg of you to write to me, when you have time . . . I am too sad, too wretched, too horror-stricken to write more.'[51]

17

AND WITH THE APE THOU ART ALONE

Joseph Goebbels was the right opponent for Edith Sitwell. For twenty years she had been climbing into the ring with the likes of Squire, Lewis, Leavis, and Grigson, and she often wound up punching shadows. Through the summer of 1939, Stephen King-Hall, a naval officer who became a successful dramatist, journalist, and politician, produced five newsletters that were at first mailed, then smuggled, into Germany in an attempt to counter the 'encirclement' theory that the Nazis were using to persuade the German public of the need for more territory. Goebbels railed against these newsletters in his 'Antwort an England' (*Völkischer Beobachter*, 14 July 1939), and he quoted from *Victoria of England* about Britain's colonial interference with other races and nations.

Sitwell was having none of that. She composed a letter, which was vetted by Rab Butler, then Under-Minister for Foreign Affairs, and it appeared in *The Times* (11 October 1939):

Sir,

Some weeks before the present war broke out Dr. Goebbels, in a diatribe against Britain addressed to Commander King-Hall, was good enough to drag in my name as a witness to the truth of his accusations.

Dr. Goebbels quotes me as having written: 'Unhappily, side by side with this increasing enlightenment on the part of the governing classes, grew a wish to interfere with all nations possessing a different pigmentation of the skin – purely, of course, for their own good, and because Britain had been appointed to this work by Heaven.' This quotation is correct; but he omits to say that I was writing of the years between 1833 and 1843.

It is understandable that Dr. Goebbels finds it difficult to believe that a nation can improve, and can become more humane, in 100 years. But it is a fact. All nations have, I am afraid, been guilty of great cruelties and injustices in the past (some of the deeds in the years of which I wrote are indefensible): but I am unable to agree with Dr. Goebbels that this makes it right and advisable that any nation should commit cruelties and injustices in this age.

Dr. Goebbels is shocked, I presume (one can do no more than guess at his meaning owing to his rather turgid and over-emotional style of expression), at the idea that, in the benighted years of which I wrote, the British should have wished to 'interfere' with other nations. Let me point out to him that side by side with this 'interference' has come a great amelioration of conditions among the people interfered with. Can the German Minister of Propaganda claim that the German 'interference' with people of another race, the wretched, stricken Jews, has resulted in any amelioration of their conditions?

It must astonish Dr. Goebbels that when this war was forced upon us, the Indian native rulers, without one exception, made offers of help and of treasure to the King Emperor. It must astonish Dr. Goebbels that the whole of the Empire, and the Dominions, have declared themselves as standing by our side. But this may no doubt be the result of the horrible cruelties and persecutions to which they are subjected by Britain. Just as the rising of the valiant Czecho-Slovak nation against their German 'protectors' may be a tribute to one year's experience of the gentle loving kindness of these.

I am, Sir, yours faithfully,
Edith Sitwell
P.S. This letter will, of course, be represented as part of a new Jewish plot, although I am 100 per cent Aryan; or else as an attempt to encircle Dr. Goebbels and the Beloved Leader.[1]

In later years, Edith Sitwell would be quick to remind people that this letter would have been her death warrant, had the Germans crossed the Channel, but at the time she enjoyed slapping down Goebbels as another pipsqueak with a bad prose style.

'It is a bore having no home,' Sitwell wrote to Tchelitchew.[2] At the end of August 1940, she went as Osbert's guest to Renishaw, but told Tchelitchew that she could not stay there indefinitely nor could she go back to France: 'Everything is going wrong with all my affairs, but then it is so with everybody.'[3] At the end of November, she still thought she would have to rent a room somewhere. In fact, she spent four months with Sachie and Georgia at Weston in 1940, in addition to other shorter visits there, and made some brief trips to London, but otherwise remained at Renishaw for the duration of the war. She continued to regard it as her home until about 1960, when poor health and quarrels made it impossible to stay longer. For generations, the Sitwells had used the house only in the summer, yet it made no sense to remain in London and become, as she had put it for Sir Edmund Gosse twenty years earlier, an 'Aunt Sally for the Germans'.

At Renishaw, Edith generally had the company of Osbert, his sec-retary Lorna Andrade, the cantankerous butler John Robins, and his wife Susan, and whichever servants John Robins had not driven away. In August 1940, David Horner joined the RAF but was at first posted near by.[4] Through the war years, many of their friends came north to what must have seemed an island of safety and comfort, at least in con-trast to London. Still the house was cold, and there was no electricity. Andrade told John Pearson that it was lighted by kerosene-burning 'Aladdin's Lamps', and at night they would all pick up candles in the hall to light their way to bed. The Duke's Landing and other ghostly parts of the house remained shut off.[5] In due course, Osbert provided billets for ten officers at Renishaw Hall and for their batmen in an adjoining cottage.[6]

Tchelitchew settled in Weston, Connecticut, and he and Sitwell exchanged weekly letters, though they were often delayed and some dis-appeared in transit. Tchelitchew's early reports were glum: 'I am sad all inside me. I have no pleasure of seeing people, talk to them and be forced to listen to their [illegible] of egoism and dullness. I am dull myself. I can hardly do any work.' Yet for the most part through these years he was effusive, encouraging and generous towards her. He even offered an oblique apology for abandoning her after Helen's death, claiming he had been ill and mad at the time.[7] He was soon supplying gossip from the art world, observing that Dalí was borrowing ideas from Buñuel, and, more importantly, from himself: 'I know that Dalí has stolen plenty of my ideas,

but I don't care. One day I will say it in print, in papers, but not now.'[8]
He even sent back word of a small triumph for Sitwell: Wyndham Lewis
had praised Tchelitchew's work to both Peter Watson and Edward James,
and had asked James whether they had any common friend. James said
his great friend was Lewis's great enemy, Miss Edith Sitwell. 'Mr. Lewis
looked rather confused after this.'[9] Sitwell wrote back that one should
'never underrate one's enemies'; he should remember that Wyndham
Lewis has a 'really great brain' and that he was bound to admire
Tchelitchew 'in his secret heart' – but she was surprised that Lewis, who
was not generous, admitted the quality of Pavlik's work.[10]

The troubles of the war brought one great compensation – Sitwell
was able to work all the time. In the autumn of 1939, she was briefly
distracted and embarrassed when it was discovered that Evelyn, in
typing up the anthology some months earlier, had left out whole
pages.[11] The book had to be reset and publication was delayed until the
end of January 1940. On 2 October, Sitwell told Tchelitchew that she
had an idea for a two-part poem inspired by an odd phrase from Ben
Jonson's Epigram CXXX 'To Mime': 'Out dance the babioun'. She had
a sense that her long drought in poetry was ending, 'But first I must
practice my technique like a pianist.'[12] On 29 November, she wrote:
'One must find a mental refuge somewhere, so I am beginning, or trying
to begin, to write poetry. It has a completely new winter atmosphere,
is very cold and, I think, strange. I am helped, tremendously, by listening, on the gramophone, to a strangely beautiful symphony of
Prokofiev's.'[13] At about the same time she was studying what she called
discords in the speeches of Lady Macbeth. By the end of December
1939 she had produced two poems, 'Lullaby' and the closely linked
'Serenade: Any Man to Any Woman'; these are among her best poems
and among the best poems written in English during the war.

LULLABY

Though the world has slipped and gone,
Sounds my loud discordant cry
Like the steel birds' song on high:
'Still one thing is left – the Bone!'
Then out danced the Babioun.

She sat in the hollow of the sea –
A socket whence the eye's put out –
She sang to the child a lullaby
(The steel birds' nest was thereabout.)

Do, do, do, do –
Thy mother's hied to the vaster race:
The Pterodactyl made its nest
And laid a steel egg in her breast –
Under the Judas-coloured sun.
She'll work no more, nor dance, nor moan,
And I am come to take her place.
Do, do.

There's nothing left but earth's low bed –
(The pterodactyl fouls its nest):
But steel wings fan thee to thy rest,
And wingless truth and larvae lie
And eyeless hope and handless fear –
All these for thee as toys are spread,
Do – do –

Red is the bed of Poland, Spain,
And thy mother's breast, who has grown wise
In that fouled nest. If she could rise,
Give birth again,

In wolfish pelt she'd hide thy bones
To shield thee from the world's long cold,
And down on all fours shouldst thou crawl
For thus from no height canst thou fall –
Do, do.

She'd give no hands: there's naught to hold
And naught to make: there's dust to sift,
But no food for the hands to lift.
Do, do.

Heed my ragged lullaby,
Fear not living, fear not chance,
All is equal – blindness, sight,
There is no depth, there is no height:
Do, do.

The Judas-coloured sun is gone,
And with the Ape thou art alone –
Do, do.[14]

Sitwell later said that in this poem one hears 'the voice of materialism from the heart of despair, singing a lullaby for the dying world'.[15] She had written an ironic lullaby in The Sleeping Beauty,[16] and the image of sifting dust takes her back to the opening of The English Eccentrics. However, as with many of her war poems, the imagery here has most of its roots in I Live Under a Black Sun, where the grief of a mother stands as a rebuttal to bombs, but here the mother dies and a beast mimes motherhood. The war returns humanity to a state where it has no moral advantages over the ape, and humanity becomes the steel-winged pterodactyl. The lines are short and the rhymes closely spaced to hint at a lullaby, but in fact the rhythms refuse to settle into a soothing pattern. The ambiguously consoling 'Do – do' doubles for a 'discordant cry' and finally beckons one to nightmare.

The companion poem, 'Serenade: Any Man to Any Woman', dissolves another natural love into a battlefield. Even in late drafts Sitwell indicates that she was writing about the siege of Warsaw,[17] but the poem was finally altered to refer to all of Europe:

Dark angel who art clear and straight
As cannon shining in the air,
Your blackness doth invade my mind
And thunderous as the armoured wind
That rained on Europe is your hair;

And so I love you till I die –
(Unfaithful I, the cannon's mate):
Forgive my love such brief span,

But fickle is the flesh of man,
And death's cold puts the passion out.

I'll woo you with a serenade –
The wolfish howls the starving made;
And lies shall be your canopy
To shield you from the freezing sky.

Yet when I clasp you in my arms –
Who are my sleep, the zero hour
That clothes instead of flesh, my heart, –
You in my heaven have no part,
For you, my mirage broken in flower,

Can never see what dead men know!
Then die with me and be my love:
The grave shall be your shady grove
And in your pleasaunce rivers flow

(To ripen this new Paradise)
From a more universal Flood
Than Noah knew: but yours is blood.

Yet still you will imperfect be
That in my heart like death's chill grows,
– A rainbow shining in the night,
Born of my tears . . . your lips, the bright
Summer-old folly of the rose.

Not many serenades involve wolfish howls, starvation, and cities burning like rainbows – and yet Sitwell thought of these poems as providing
'mental refuge'. She told Tchelitchew on 1 January 1940, 'I am still tin-
kering about with them. They are extremely direct, and have a hard
shrieking sound, very discordant in the lullaby.'[18] Sitwell was immersed
in the poetry of the First World War, but when she writes, however
ironically, of death in war as an embrace, she may be thinking more of
Walt Whitman, in whose Civil War poems the deaths of soldiers are

treated many times as an erotic desolation, as in his 'Vigil for boy of responding kisses, (never again on earth responding).'[19] However, Sitwell's metaphors are more savage than Whitman's. As well, 'Lullaby' and 'Serenade: Any Man to Any Woman' are plainly written in response to the prophecies of Yeats and Eliot about the destruction of Europe; she treats those prophecies as fulfilled in the events of 1939.

In the second half of the Great War, there had been a common belief, however flawed it now appears, that the men in the trenches were betrayed, that the conflict was being prolonged by politicians and prof-iteers – Sassoon and others raged against the whole enterprise. In 1939, there could be no doubt that Chamberlain's government wanted peace and that the war was brought on by Hitler. Sitwell applauded, for exam-ple, how British planes dropped pamphlets on Germany rather than explosives in the early days of the war, but she could see that it was nec-essary to fight. As she put it to Tchelitchew on 29 November 1940:

> It is terribly difficult to work here, in the centre, as it were, of the
> misery and menace. It is terrible for a convinced pacifist like myself.
> But I do not see *what* else we could have done. The menace was
> unceasing, the bullying and lying shameless. The English are an
> extraordinary people. Nothing could surpass the calm and resolution
> of the general behaviour, and (with the exception of one paper)
> there is none of the undignified and blatant yelling of threats and
> abuse that disfigured the last war. The Germans, on the other hand,
> are indefatigable in their abuse.[20]

Sitwell accepted that for the British this was an honourable war.

Sitwell made a foray to London in December, and at the end of January she spent another ten days there, but found the city deserted. In January, she read Cecil Beaton's *My Royal Past* (1939), a fictitious memoir of Baroness von Bülop; she found it vulgar and effeminate and thought that Beaton would do better if he enlisted: '*That* young man, together with certain others, ought to hang out his chiffons on the Maginot Line.'[21] Back at Renishaw, she settled in to a reading of Wagner's prose works, which she found dull, but she was struck by his comments on the effects of consonants on vowels, and thought that something he said of music in his book on Beethoven, a comment derived from Schopenhauer, was true of all the arts: 'Music is not an image of phenomena, or more correctly, of the adequate objectivity of the will, but an immediate image of the will itself, and represents accordingly the metaphysics of all that is physical in the world, the thing per se, which lies beyond all appearance.'[22] It was a key point for her: whether poetry was obliged to render the details of the physical world or whether it must reach after more elusive realities – a point that would put her at odds with the next two generations, who generally preferred poetry that was 'closely observed'.

Sitwell told Tchelitchew that he might find Renishaw a calm place to work: 'Also, I am more peaceable now, the war having taught me a terrible lesson. I am peaceable and placid.'[23] With the Phoney War stretching out, she thought that he might be able to visit. She decided also that she should herself go to Paris to check on Evelyn and to recover some of her possessions.

Sitwell went first to Weston on 20 April and came down with measles, so she postponed her trip. On 10 May, the Nazis began their Western offensive. Within a matter of days, the French position was desperate. Sitwell wrote on 6 June, immediately after the evacuation of three hundred thousand troops from Dunkirk: 'The last fortnight has been on such a gigantic scale, that everything in history since the Crucifixion seems dwarfed – only Shakespeare could do justice to it. First, that monstrous betrayal by the King of the Belgians, – that unspeakably disgraced eternally shamed traitor, – then the wonderful heroism of the allied armies, – and their saving by the sea . . . that description of the ships, the small boats, everyone belonging to the sea going down to save our men, the French, the English.'[24] On 14 June, Paris fell. Sitwell remarked afterwards: 'if I hadn't had measles, I should have been in Paris now!!! And I should probably have been shot, as I imagine the Gestapo are after me, – I teased Hitler and Goebbels most horribly, in the Times, just after war started.'[25]

Sitwell and Tchelitchew had a common anxiety after the fall of France. Sitwell lost touch with Evelyn Wiel, and Tchelitchew with his sister Choura. At the same time, Sir George was stranded in Italy; he was eighty-one and had recently had an operation. Through the Board of Trade, Osbert was able to send him just thirteen pounds per month,[26] and with letters routed through Portugal contact became sporadic.

Edith stayed at Weston Hall until the end of July. She made trips to London, and at one point remarked to David Horner how active cross-dressers were at the Sesame Club. The actress and romantic novelist Naomi Jacob appeared uniformed as a major and became 'the centre of one Lizzie scene after another. (I wonder why they make such appalling scenes?)' Whenever Jacob approached her, Sitwell pretended to have lost her voice, and she refused to have anything to do with another lesbian member of the club who was raging against Jacob to the porter.[27] Sitwell grew tolerant of Jacob: upon meeting her in the 1950s she would address her as 'Field-Marshal', and Jacob, having stood to attention, would ceremoniously bow and kiss her hand.[28]

At Weston, things were tamer. Sitwell was knitting for the troops and declared herself 'the Pull-Over Queen'.[29] She received as a visitor Alec Guinness, whose wife Merula was a very distant cousin of the Sitwells through Joan Wake's family.[30] Sitwell had seen him performing in December at a small London theatre with Martita Hunt and decided he was the 'greatest Hamlet' she had ever seen.[31] At Weston, they read poetry to each other. She thought of writing a play for him, and in the following year he made a private recording for her of 'Lullaby' and 'Serenade: Any Man to Any Woman'. It was, however, a gruelling time for Sachie and Georgia as they sent their younger son, Francis (b.1935), to Georgia's relatives in Montreal on 25 June. Sachie was now serving, resignedly, as an officer in the Home Guard.[32] Tchelitchew begged Edith to come to America and earn her living as a lecturer, but she refused, since regulations forbade women under sixty to leave, and in any event she felt she must remain in England while it was threatened. She thought that the Germans had forgotten what the English were like: 'I pity them if they *do* come over. We have got our teeth and jaws well set, and our fists clenched.'[33] *Henry V* was ringing in her ears.

Sitwell thought the departure of Auden and Isherwood for America at the beginning of the war cowardly, yet she admired Auden's poetry more and more. She wrote in August about his collection *Another Time*, which contained 'In Memory of W. B. Yeats', 'September 1, 1939', 'In Memory of Sigmund Freud', 'Musée des Beaux Arts', and 'Dover': 'Auden's new book has some really fine poetry in it. He has been grossly over-praised, and for all the wrong reasons, by people who know nothing about verse, but in this book he really has produced some beautiful poetry.'[34]

Sitwell's 'Lullaby' had appeared in the *TLS* (16 March 1940) and 'Serenade: Any Man to Any Woman' in *Life and Letters To-day* (April 1940), where they created a sensation. T.S. Eliot published her *Poems New and Old* in October, and the volume was immediately acclaimed. For example, when Harold Hannyngton Child reviewed her career in the *TLS* (16 November 1940), he declared that she could not help but create beauty. He found in 'Romance' lines 'positively Tennysonian in their pure beauty of sound' and in the new poems 'a sad or a terrible beauty'. Sitwell wrote to Tchelitchew: 'It is the first time I have been really judged as the kind of poet I, in reality, am.'[35]

In the autumn of 1940, the back pain that had afflicted her on and off since childhood became constant. She told Tchelitchew on 27 September: 'I had very bad curvature as a child, and indeed, spent most of my childhood encased in surgical instruments, or on my back. I am now in almost perpetual pain with my spine and right hip, and can hardly walk.'[36] She received daily massage and heat treatments in Chesterfield, and told Tchelitchew on 4 December that after her treatments she could only go to bed and stay there until dinner: 'I am still *very* lame indeed, and am still in a good deal of pain, but not in frightful pain. It used to come on in waves of an hour at a time, like toothache when a nerve is exposed!' In the midst of a February blizzard, she wrote again of sciatica and neuralgia of the spine, 'these are like a pack of wolves eating me alive'. Among the terrible experiences of that year, the question of Sitwell's health may seem minor, but it becomes a crucial theme in her story. From 1940 to 1964, Edith Sitwell was almost always in physical pain, sometimes immobilised by it, and for the last few years of her life she was restricted to a wheelchair. A bad temper was made infinitely worse. Her obsession with Grigson, Leavis, and other reviewers would take on mind-filling proportions as she lay, curled and wretched, on her bed. It is not known whether she received strong medications for the pain, but she came to rely on large martinis and white wine for comfort, and was undoubtedly an alcoholic by the mid-1940s.

Nevertheless, she tried to bear up, as she told Tchelitchew: 'in the face of the gigantic heroism one sees round one every day, one must not think of oneself at all. I would like, if possible, to be worthy of my noble and heroic race. The English are maddening in many ways, but by God, they are brave!'[37] On 7 September 1940, the Germans began their run of fifty-seven consecutive nights of bombing London. Sitwell was struck by the steadiness shown by people like her agents, Pearn, Pollinger and Higham, whose office in Covent Garden was hit in one of the early raids yet they were up and running three days later. Robert Herring operated Life and Letters Today from an office just below Higham's. It was demolished at the same time, so he came as a refugee to Renishaw and continued publishing the magazine from a house in Station Road almost without interruption.[38]

Herring's backer was the historical novelist 'Bryher', Winifred Ellerman, who had inherited a shipping fortune. At the end of September, she made a perilous journey from Switzerland to England via Portugal, after which she too came for a brief visit to Renishaw. Although Sitwell had met Bryher on two earlier occasions, and had long been acquainted with her lover the Imagist poet 'H.D.' (Hilda Doolittle), this was the beginning of a very important friendship. Bryher became, in effect, Sitwell's patron and the 'anonymous donor' behind many of the gifts to writers and artists that Sitwell arranged. On this visit, she offered to attempt to contact Evelyn Wiel. Sitwell wrote: 'I can't even begin to say what I think of your great kindness, and I can't even begin to thank you.'[39]

After the initial battering of London, bombing spread to other ports and industrial cities, including Coventry, devastated on 14 November. Sheffield was an obvious target. On 21 August, Osbert wrote to David Horner: 'The night before last there was a tremendous raid, though only by one airplane, at 11.15 and at midnight – I thought every window in the house would be blown in. And the rooms shook as though in an earthquake. The bomb fell about 1½ miles away.'[40] Eight days later, he wrote that Sheffield had been badly hit and that several bombs had fallen on the Sitwells' property.[41] By early November, the village began to receive refugees.[42] On the night of 12 December 1940 came the terrible raid in which the Marples Hotel and many other buildings were destroyed. Other raids followed, and although Renishaw was on the outskirts of Sheffield, Edith Sitwell could hear the explosions and see distant flames.

As seen in the opening paragraphs of this book, the raids on Sheffield made a deep impression on Sitwell. She ventured into the city, saw the wreckage, the scenes of death, the suffering and gallantry of the survivors. There was nothing she could do but write about it. Robert Herring published a group of her new poems in January 1941, among them 'Street Song', with its arresting final phrase 'the burden of Atlas falling?'[43] This poem, which took up again the imagery of the separate nations of rich and poor, was part of a draft composition first titled 'I Walk in City Ways' and later 'The Crucified'. This same piece also contained the early workings of 'Still Falls the Rain', which took somewhat longer to complete.[44] These poems arose from a sense that she had looked directly at evil. She wrote during the summer of 1941: 'I used not to believe in hell, but how, now, can one believe that there is not a hell awaiting the ghastly monster who has inaugurated this world-wide ruin?'[45]

While the war seemed to fill her imagination, Sitwell became involved in an odd literary fracas. For about a year, she and Osbert had been pursuing the journalist Hamilton Fyfe over a review in *Reynolds News* (18 February 1940) of *Edith Sitwell's Anthology*, in which he claimed that the Sitwells' pursuit of publicity in the 1920s had won them a position beyond their merits: 'Now oblivion has claimed them, and they are remembered with a kindly, if slightly cynical, smile.' As for the anthology itself, his main observation was that it was a bit heavy to hold. Most authors would regard a snide and lazy review as an occupational hazard. Osbert and Edith believed that it was time to set an example to malicious reviewers. Their pugnacious solicitor Philip Frere consulted expert counsel and brought back news that the passage was indeed libellous. Sachie was doubtful but was eventually cajoled into joining the action. The newspaper tried to settle for fifty pounds, but the Sitwells held out for five hundred each.

With the trial approaching, Edith spent almost three weeks in London getting ready for her testimony, which was carefully scripted; she prepared written answers defending her own harshest comments as a reviewer. For example, if asked whether her statement that Rupert Brooke had been 'eclipsed' did not amount to much the same thing as Fyfe's comment about 'oblivion', she was prepared to say 'eclipse is not oblivion. It is, of its nature, temporary. And a temporary eclipse frequently follows about five years after the death of an author. Then, in time, he regains his position in the hearts of the public.'[46] Under cross-examination, she fended off a question on whether she had once said Alfred Noyes's poetry was like cheap linoleum by saying she thought cheap linoleum *very useful* and that she admired Noyes for the fact that his work sold well. The judge interjected, 'So does cheap linoleum.' She said that she had not sued Wyndham Lewis because he was an old acquaintance and nobody paid attention to his comments on other people's work anyway. Osbert was pressed on whether the case was a publicity stunt – a possibility suggested by the Sitwells posing out-side the court for a press photograph – but he maintained that they were merely looking for a taxi. They called as witnesses the publisher Daniel Macmillan, the novelist Charles Morgan, and others to testify that the Sitwells were still important writers. The defendants called no witnesses but argued fair comment. On 10 February 1941 the Sitwells won £350 each in damages.[47]

Stephen Spender thought the *Reynolds* case came close to censor-ing reviewers, just as George Bernard Shaw and Sir Hugh Walpole applauded the Sitwells' actions. For all her rancour and paranoia, Edith Sitwell thought she had no choice but to stand up for her work. She said once to Lorna Andrade: 'If you want to make yourself a name you must dig and dig and never let up.'[48] And in fairness, a woman writer faced the problem of prejudiced or malicious reviewing dispropor-tionately – the idea of suffering it in silence did not appeal to Edith Sitwell.

The Sitwells were not the only authors or artists of their time to rely on legal action or the threat of it. In 1932, J. B. Priestley had threat-ened Graham Greene and the publisher William Heinemann with a libel suit over a thinly disguised portrait of himself appearing in *Stamboul Train*. As a result, thirteen thousand copies already printed and bound had to be unstitched and new pages inserted. Greene was successfully sued by Shirley Temple's managers in 1938 over a review in *Night and Day* in which he claimed that her little body was being peddled to the pederastic tastes of middle-aged men and the clergy. In 1956, Greene got himself on the other side of a statement of claim when he joined Evelyn Waugh in a successful suit against Rebecca West and the Beaverbrook press over West's book *The Meaning of*

Treason. The *Observer* later settled a case with Greene out of court.[49] In a year when she lost three-quarters of her income, the *Reynolds News* case brought Edith Sitwell about as much money as she was used to getting for a book advance, just as the satisfaction of trouncing a critic made up for a good deal of back pain. But it lacked the dignity and usefulness of lashing Goebbels.

And strange new griefs were at hand. On 28 March 1941, Virginia Woolf put stones in her pockets and drowned herself in the River Ouse at Rodmell in Sussex. Although her body was not found for three weeks, she was presumed dead. Through her years in Paris, Sitwell had drifted away from Virginia Woolf, but on 4 April she wrote to Leonard Woolf: 'No words can express our feelings at this dreadful heartrending thing. We are absolutely overcome. All our thoughts are with you. What can you, and Mrs. [Vanessa] Bell, be enduring, with the pain and the grief and the shock . . . But all my life I shall remember the feeling of light, and of happiness, that she gave one. As a person, as well as in her art. Everything seemed worthwhile, important, and beautiful.'[50]

The death of Virginia Woolf was a sign that the world Sitwell had once inhabited was disappearing. Another came on 17–18 April, when a parachute landmine carrying a ton of explosives came down in Moscow Road. Pembridge Mansions was destroyed, and twelve people killed.[51] Sitwell wrote about a year later: 'the flat exists no more . . . Everyone is dead. I am told the horror was unendurable. It seems strange to think of those poor, commonplace people. The people in the flat next mine, the old Jewess [Emily Hirsch?] and the fortune teller on the bottom floor. The Jewess was never found.'[52]

Once in a while, Sitwell laid aside her resentments and learnt to like a foe. She had written to Edward James in 1939: 'Any mention of any member of the Ford family gives me severe intestinal disturbances. The son ought never to have been introduced to me, – but he was. As for the mother and the daughter, when I want a sponge, I'll buy one. In any case, I don't propose to make sponges part of my social life.'[53] Nevertheless, as had once happened with Allen Tanner, Edith Sitwell came, by 1941, to regard Charles Henri Ford as a friend. She admired his most recent book of poems, and, for his part, he promoted Sitwell's work in New York. Tchelitchew wrote to her: 'Yes my dear, we going to do everything we can to make your name more and more well known here, because you are a great poet and a great person and I do hope that no bomb will ever destroy the portrait I painted of you, because it is yourself in every sens [sic] but unseen by eyes of saps. You going [sic] to be a legendary person, don't worry you will be and I know that, I don't know why I know things like that, but I know.'[54] Ford had set up the avant-garde *View* magazine, but his work on it was delayed by enlistment in the army in 1942; some of Sitwell's works appeared there from 1943.

It was also a good time for Sitwell's friendship with Tchelitchew himself. There were occasional eruptions when Edith expressed jealousy over his friends in New York or when letters got lost and he believed she was ignoring him. In spite of this, Tchelitchew made great claims for their friendship: 'I miss you too very very very much, but strangely to say I feel your presence more than any one. I think because of your thoughts and your work – our thoughts work like wireless all the time.'[55] Tchelitchew believed in telepathy and clairvoyance, and when he claimed mental connection with Sitwell, he probably meant it literally – though this does make it difficult to fathom his rage over lost letters. About a year later, Sitwell explained her views on this subject to him: 'I am not in the least surprised, psychologically, that you often hear people asking you questions. It sounds a strange thing to say, but I think there is a leakage in time. Both you, and Osbert, Sachie and I are, not exactly clairvoyant, but the kind of "sensitives" that make clairvoyants. Osbert and I both dream things, – though they are only minor things, that come true.'[56] It is possible that Edith Sitwell (or Helen Rootham) had read not only Steiner on the spiritual possibilities of sleep, but J.W. Dunne's *An Experiment with Time* (1927), a popular book that convinced Graham Greene and many others that the sleeping mind may travel through time.[57]

In the early years of the war, Sitwell suffered frequent nightmares about Helen's death, the flat in Paris, the dangers faced by Evelyn, and even the privations of the cat she had left behind. In April 1941 she told Tchelitchew: 'My letters must seem unreal, because I feel as if I were walking in some sad dream, bound hand and foot, so that I can only walk at a very slow pace, and with no sense of direction.' Since only beauty and truth were, at the moment, beyond the touch of beasts, she took 'unearthly comfort' in reading Chaucer.[58] On 22 May, she wrote: 'I have been near death, and I have seen terrible things. I saw what the human body can come to, when I nursed Helen. I have seen wrecked streets, with the houses broken down to the ground like broken teeth, and a few rags of what were once beds, where people lay who now are dead, broken into pieces, like the houses.'[59]

On 9 June, she wrote again of the ruined houses of Sheffield and added, 'I never pray now, excepting mutely, but my thoughts are full of anxiety and of hope for you, and of will that all may be better. When I say that I do not pray, I do not mean that I do not believe in God. It is only that I have been too numb.'[60] On 18 July, almost a month after the invasion of the Soviet Union, she wrote: 'When I think of those monsters who have brought this horror upon the world, announcing, as if it was something to be proud of, that nine million men are now engaged in battle, I think heaven protects one by numbing one's imagination at such a time, or one would never sleep or eat again. But why should one be protected when those nine million men are undergoing this unspeakable ghastly horror. I do not dare to dream.'[61]

18

AN ABBESS

'My vinegary spinster aunt' was how Vita Sackville-West described Amalia Martin.[1] Edith Sitwell had known Martin all her life as one of Lady Ida's more pleasant friends. The bloodlines in the Sackville family are more complicated even than those of the Sitwells. Martin was one of five illegitimate children of the diplomat Lionel Sackville-West (second Baron Sackville) and Josefa Durán, a Spanish dancer known as Pepita. Vita Sackville-West's *Pepita*, a book about their family history, came out in 1937. In a family riven by litigation, Martin took offence. She wanted her own story told and asked Edith Sitwell to do it. Sitwell signed a contract for a novel with Gollancz and offered Martin a share of the proceeds. The heart of the book would be a revelation of who had murdered Pepita's first husband in Granada.[2]

As early as December 1938, Sitwell saw that the story, however fictionalised, could set off lawsuits, but she went on to write a good deal of it under the working title 'Spring Torrents' – a borrowing from Turgenev.[3] In the summer of 1941, she consulted the solicitor Philip Frere about the risk of libel. His answer was that the book could not be published. Martin was furious, insisting that a contract existed between them for the completion of the book. She wanted Sitwell to consult another lawyer, or, failing that, to hand over the manuscript. Sitwell remained conciliatory as letters and cables multiplied in the autumn but eventually told Martin in December to direct her letters on the subject to Frere.[4] Sitwell herself was upset at abandoning the work, and marked on one draft, 'Retain in Jewel Box. Notes for novel. Very Important.'[5]

In one of the novel's plot-lines, Sitwell describes her own life and draws portraits of Sir George and Lady Ida. There is also a description of a boarding house, which was eventually incorporated into *Taken Care Of* as a scene from her childhood. Notes in her manuscript books identify the owner of the boarding house, Madame Baker, as Evelyn Wiel.[6] This supposed recollection of childhood is, in fact, an expertly turned short story based on life with the Roothams in the 1920s and 1930s. Armoured against her sorrows by make-up, Madame Baker is a big woman, full of conceit about a past in which she moved in diplomatic circles and drank champagne from a slipper, but now she bears up to poverty and solitude. Another character in the boarding house is the falsely humble 'oracle', who announces he is going to turn his back on the world. Dicky Wilkins in *Taken Care Of*, he is called 'Mytton Dicksee' or 'Mitty' in a draft[7] – a name that suggests Dimitrije Mitrinović. He encourages a new generation towards war and annihilation, while he drinks tea. At the end, he is terrified at night by a mouse biting through the wainscot and scampering to its hole.

For the war effort, Sitwell took on a short, morale-boosting book, *English Women*, with character sketches of notables from Elizabeth Tudor to Virginia Woolf. Part of the beautifully produced 'Britain in Pictures' series, edited by W. J. Turner and published by Collins, it appeared in June 1942 and marked the beginning of her research for *Fanfare for Elizabeth* (1946). She was disappointed with Gollancz's delays over *Look! The Sun*, an anthology of poems that she had assembled for children, as well as with the firm's failure to publicise her works. On the other side, Victor Gollancz cannot have been happy with Sitwell's failure to produce her second novel. The Canadian Rache Lovat Dickson was courting her for Macmillan, of which he was a director and general editor. He stayed at Renishaw in July 1941 and reached an agreement with Sitwell to publish a volume of her new poems. As she told Pavlik, 'They are written, purposely, with the utmost simplicity, and are almost devoid of images.'[8]

Street Songs came out on 20 January 1942. The book opened with 'Still Falls the Rain', which had already created a stir when published in the *Times Literary Supplement* (6 September 1941). The editor, D. L. Murray, had written to David Higham: 'It is a really great poem: such it must be called.'[9] The book closed with the hitherto unpublished 'An Old Woman', which now claimed almost as much attention from reviewers. The poem is easily misread as Sitwell presenting herself as a seer – the sort of misreading that led to later claims that her vision-ary images are 'unearned'. The old woman is not Sitwell herself although she 'has seen too much, looked on too many sorrows'. Sitwell imagines a growth, which she herself has not achieved, from grief into benediction. The labouring woman would be no stranger to the kitchen gardens of Sitwell's poetry in the 1920s. She is also that mythic figure in her work, the bereft mother, 'nurse of the unreturning'. Sitwell gestures to W. B. Yeats when she writes of the woman's body as 'mortal dress'. The poem is a spiritual experiment – Sitwell proposes a hypo-thetical state of heart in which suffering opens into vision and forgiveness:

> . . . creeds grow old
> And change, – man's heart, that sun,
> Outlives all terrors shaking the old night:
> The world's huge fevers burn and shine, turn cold,
> Yet the heavenly bodies and young lovers burn and shine,
> The golden lovers walk in the holy fields
> Where the Abraham-bearded sun, the father of all things,
> Is shouting of ripeness, and the whole world of dews and
> > splendours are singing
> To the cradles of earth, of men, beasts, harvests, swinging
> In the peace of God's heart. And I, the primeval clay
> That has known earth's grief and harvest's happiness,
> Seeing mankind's dark seed-time, come to bless,
> Forgive and bless all men like the holy light.[10]

In a TLS review (7 February 1942), Harold Hannyngton Child (who had reviewed Poems New and Old) observed that in this new collec-tion Sitwell placed enormous strains on her technique as she moved suddenly from terrifying images of war to passages of pure beauty about the grief of love, but that her risk-taking paid off in poem after poem. As a critic, he too was engaged in risk-taking, as he now embarked on the sort of claims that a critic may make only once or twice in a lifetime:

Her 'Old Woman' absorbs and surpasses Villon's Heaulmière and Ronsard's old spinner by candlelight. She is 'an old woman in the light of the sun'. She has known the whole of life; and she affirms her faith in the 'holy' light of the sun. Comfort ye my people – perhaps comfort is not a bad name for this majestic assurance. It is not argument; it offers no proof; it is an act of faith. It lives entirely by the poetry in it. And if we are not carried away by its poetic beauty, this poet, so brilliant, so wilful, so capricious, has here achieved a poem in which manifold strains of thought and feeling are woven in a noble and unassailable simplicity. Bits of it are unmistakably Miss Sitwell's. The whole shows her poetic art in its true greatness.

The book received many rave reviews, but one of the most interesting responses was unpublished. Marianne Moore wrote to Bryher:

I have been carrying it round with me since I came and forcing people to listen. I do not know which I like best for I like each one as I read it – they are rich and various, and deep. And act on many *levels* (that is something I miss in much modern poetry – it seems flat, one-dimensional, a painted scene.) But this is first a beautiful rich design, rich and heavy with gold and embroidery, and one can stay there and just taste the words and follow the design, and then you realize that this design lives and breathes and speaks as a living being might, and you are penetrated with the meaning – as if Yeats' golden bird of Byzance suddenly actually *sang*, stood in the middle of his poem and sang.[11]

At the same time, Sitwell's earlier work was still holding public attention. For William Walton, as much as for Sitwell, *Façade* kept evolving. At the Aeolian Hall on 29 May 1942, Walton conducted a twenty-one-piece version, which, in a different order, became the one usually associated with the title.[12] In 1977, eight unpublished numbers were brought forward at a concert in honour of Walton's seventy-fifth birthday, but while reading proofs a few months later Walton dropped three numbers and replaced them with three others, then substantially reworked and reordered the music in what became known as *Façade 2*.[13]

At the Aeolian performance of 1942, Constant Lambert recited, and
the orchestra consisted of flute (and piccolo), clarinet (and bass clarinet), trumpet, alto saxophone, cello, and percussion.[14] Sitwell went to
London for the concert and basked in the reviews: 'I am told it has
every virtue of a gay kind, – beauty, wit, brilliance, light-heartedness,
technical virtuosity, etc. The people have now discovered that I was
not pretending in that work to put forward a new theory of the universe, but was just doing technical feats of an extreme difficulty, making
technical experiments, and having fun!'[15]

While in London, she met Stephen Spender's new wife Natasha
(née Litvin), a pianist. They came to the Sesame Club on a day when
Grosvenor Street was full of military officers. Stephen Spender was
wearing the blue uniform of the Fire Brigade and had just come off two
full days of duty. With the younger members involved in the war effort,
the club was left to the elderly, with Edith Sitwell a conspicuous presence. Once the three of them were seated, Sitwell began to giggle and
asked what it might be like to cast Macbeth from the old ladies at the
other tables. Then she and Stephen Spender launched into an intense
discussion of poetry.

Natasha Spender became one of Edith Sitwell's most loyal and
understanding friends. In her opinion, the image of Edith as a queen,
ever ready to slap down impertinence, obscured how 'her soul was fired
by devotion to friends and to unfortunates: her famous solitude was less
that of a queen than of an abbess, even, at times, a hermit'. In her
sketch of Sitwell (Telegraph, 20 June 2008) she recounts as an example
of her kindness a luncheon at the Sesame with the mentally ill David
Gascoyne, who was being persecuted by imaginary beings behind his
chair. Sitwell asked what was the matter; he explained; and she urged
him to ignore them as they were only trying to annoy him. A psychiatrist would hardly see this as a treatment for hallucinations, but her
words bought Gascoyne a few minutes of peace and he rejoined the
conversation.

At fifty-four, Edith Sitwell had cast a good deal of bread on the
water. At the end of 1941, some of it returned to her. 'Out of The
Blue' in December, as Osbert put it, Bryher gave Edith, David Horner
and himself each a cheque for five hundred pounds.[16] From her new
money, Edith bought two Ascot hats, and when Georgia showed up

in uniform, Osbert told the two women that they looked like
'Diligence and Dissipation'.[17] A little later, Osbert wrote to David:
'Edith has bought a new fur coat, and then cried, poor darling,
because she thought it so awful to be extravagant at this time. I told
her she was the only one of the family who had ever let a thing like
that worry her.'[18]

This was early days for Bryher's kindness. In the spring of 1942 she
gave Edith about three thousand pounds to buy a house at 8 Gay Street
in Bath, which Violet Gordon Woodhouse had recommended.[19] It had
once been owned by Samuel Johnson's friend Hester Thrale. Sitwell
rented it out, believing she would inherit enough money upon Sir
George's death to set up a small household. However, Bath was the
wrong city for her work, broadcasting and lecturing, after the war.
Bryher helpfully bought the house back from her in 1949 – so that
Sitwell kept the original sum.[20]

'Renishaw is just as you saw it,' wrote Evelyn to Laura Waugh on 20
June 1942.

> Shabbier outside with the lawns grown long & the hedges ragged so
> that you might think the house deserted till you come inside. There
> everything is open; no evacuees or billeted soldiers; no dust sheets
> except in the ball room. Banks of potted plants & bowls of roses;
> piles of new & old books & delicious cooking . . . There is an
> extremely charming artist called Piper staying here making a series
> of drawings of the house. Osbert bland & genial; Edith alternating
> between extremes of venom and compassion. They have done what
> I most hoped they would do – left me alone for the afternoon.[21]

This was probably a good weekend for the English novel. Spending
time with John Piper undoubtedly gave Waugh ideas for the character
of Charles Ryder in *Brideshead Revisited*, whose *métier* was the painting
of great houses as they awaited demolition. Indeed, Piper was the only
architectural painter that Waugh knew, and he later drew the illustrations for the novel but did not submit them to Waugh because he
was not satisfied with them.[22] That same weekend Waugh handed over
to Osbert a short character-sketch of Sir George Sitwell, later included
as an appendix to *Laughter in the Next Room* (the fourth volume of *Left*

Hand, Right Hand). It was based on a single meeting with Sir George
at Renishaw in the late 1920s: 'I had noted with fascination during my
stay how his beard would assume new shapes with his change of mood,
like the supple felt hat on an impersonator. Sometimes he would appear
as King Lear on Dover cliffs, sometimes as Edward Lear on Athos,
sometimes as Mr. Pooter at Margate. Tonight he was Robinson Crusoe.'[23]
That is a great deal to deduce from a single meeting, but Osbert and
Edith had treated Waugh to many anecdotes about 'Ginger'. Waugh
often combined the features of several real people to create a fictional
character, so there is a possibility that Charles Ryder's father owes some
characteristics to Sir George. An aloof collector of antiquities and a
leg-puller, his power of mind is revealed in sly jokes. Most importantly,
Ned Ryder sees his son's debts as an occasion for irony rather than assistance: 'In Queer Street? Let us say you are in Queer Street and leave
it at that.'[24]

In English literature from 1920 to 1950, Sir George Sitwell is rather
like Woody Allen's Zelig, in that he appears unexpectedly at historic
moments. Huxley, Lewis, and Edith herself inserted him into novels –
Waugh can probably be added to that list. Since early 1941, Osbert had
been working on memoirs in which the centrepiece is a sprawling caricature of his father. The confused remnants of the actual man had
appealed to Osbert in 1941 to come and get him out of Italy; according to Edith, he believed that Osbert's failure to do so was a kind of
revenge.[25] In fact, despite the mockery and rancour, the Sitwells were
anxious that their father should be safe and comfortable. In April 1942,
he had crossed the border into Switzerland with his nurse and moved
in with distant relatives, Olga and Bernard Woog, at the Villa Fontanelle
in Porto Ronco near Locarno. Osbert wrote to David Horner: 'Edith
and I expect him to arrive here any day now in a glider, as a sort of footnote to invasion.'[26]

Letters from his hosts suggested Sir George was being pampered. In
December, Edith described the situation to Rée Gorer:

> The wife is the daughter of that world-scourge, Inez Chandos-Pole,
> the husband is a charming, practical, quiet Swiss. The old gentleman
> simply descended on them like a blight. He inhabits their house; he
> has changed all their modes of existence. He won't let them go to

bed at night, because he wishes them to sit up with him; he insists
on having a hot meal of roast chicken at 4 o'clock in the morning,
so that the cook has to sit up too; and when he wants anything
expensive and they say that they have no money, he makes a cluck-
ing sound, puts his head on one side, tossing it irritably, and says, 'I'm
afraid I can't help that!'.[27]

Inez had died in 1941; however, Edith had known Olga 'intimately' for
years and trusted her.[28] Sir George wanted to marry his German nurse,
and, even worse, from Osbert's point of view, to give her an annuity of
five hundred pounds. Bernard Woog managed to get rid of her, so Sir
George transferred his love to another nurse.[29] Through all of this,
Edith's and Osbert's sympathy was with the Woogs, but that would
change as events unfolded.

With no sign of the war ending, Edith wanted to put her own affairs
in order. In 1932, Helen Rootham had placed most of the contents of
the Moscow Road flat in a warehouse under her own name, and Edith
could not get at them until her will was proved. The will made in 1931
was simple – Helen's few assets were left to Evelyn for her lifetime with
the remainder to Edith. The estate was handled by the Roothams'
brother Ernest, a seventy-eight-year-old solicitor in Barnstaple; Edith
found the effort of making him do anything 'like poking a dead
mule'.[30] In June 1942, the boxes reached her: 'Things belonging to
poor Helen, records of her past terrible sadness while she was gradually facing the fact that her engagement was drifting into nothing, that
the man had drifted away. Records of the beginning of my career as a
poet. All these, and books that I had once liked and that now I am
going to give for salvage. – Oh dear! It is very strange to look in the
glass afterwards.'[31] Through that summer she was haunted by memories of rue Saint-Dominique, and she told Pavlik she could never live
there again: 'It is a horror to me. When I think of all that has happened there.'[32]

Evelyn was still out of touch. At the beginning of 1941, Edith had
received permission from the Board of Trade to send her ten pounds per
month – the maximum permitted for a person of sixty-five under rules
for trade with the enemy. In August, a telegram about Evelyn signed by
a stranger named Herlain reached Coutts Bank: 'Tell Edith Sitwell send

money situation désespérée.'[33] Osbert was in the bank when it arrived and, as Edith reports it, he burst into tears. In late October 1942, one of Evelyn's letters finally got through to England. No money had reached her, and she was supporting herself by knitting. Edith was horrified: 'Darling, I *never* would desert you. *Never*. I cannot conceive why the monthly allowance has not reached you . . . I think of you unceasingly, and long to see you. I think of you going about your daily life with such noble-mindedness. How well I see the rooms in the flat. I dream, continually, sometimes every night, for weeks on end, that I am back in the flat. And then I wake up in an agony of mind, wondering how you are, and how my darling little angel [the cat], whom you did not mention, is.' Shortly afterwards, the Foreign Office mistakenly cancelled Sitwell's permission to send funds, and she was forced to plague the Red Cross for assistance, but when she was allowed to send money again, it, too, went astray.

Sitwell had not seen her old friend Walter Sickert in a long time when he died in January 1942, but her memories of him were revived by the young Denton Welch's article 'A Visit to Sickert at St Peter's', in the September number of Cyril Connolly's *Horizon*. In his last years, Sickert was standing on the outer ramparts of eccentricity. Welch wrote of his own terror and amusement at the painter's singing, dancing, and other shenanigans at a tea party where they met. Sitwell wrote to Welch: 'I cannot tell you how much my brother Osbert, with whom I am staying, and I, enjoyed your alarming experience with Mr. Sickert. We laughed till we cried – though really in some ways it was no laughing matter. But one thing came out very clearly, and that is, that you are a *born writer*!'[34] Welch had wanted to become a painter, but while he was attending Goldsmith's College School of Art, a car struck him as he rode his bicycle. His spine was fractured and he suffered other terrible injuries that led to his death in 1948 at the age of thirty-three. When he received her letter, Welch wrote in his diary how thrilling it was to have praise from 'a great genius',[35] but Edith Sitwell went further than praise: she provided a foreword to his autobiographical novel *Maiden Voyage*, which he dedicated to her.

In the autumn of 1942, Pavlik managed to get some news of his family on the continent. Even though her husband had recently died of tuberculosis and she was herself very ill, his sister Choura gave shelter to a woman and her Jewish husband, an act Edith described as 'Wonderful, brave, and really holy'.[36] In December, there were many press reports about the persecution of Jews. The Polish government in exile sent a note to the Allied governments, confirming that the Germans had now killed about a third of Poland's 3,130,000 Jews (*The Times*, 11 December 1942). Edith wrote: 'Oh Pavlik, I am *sick* with horror when I read what is happening to the Polish Jews. One's heart bursts to read it. What *can* the souls be of the men who have ordered such things to be? . . . We shall punish them, of course. But as I say, no earthly punishment could suffice.'[37] In March, she spoke of the Jews as 'a warm-hearted, fundamentally *good* people! It makes me literally ill to think what is happening to them under this monstrous reign of terror and cruelty.'[38]

In the early months of 1943, Osbert was often ill with what was diagnosed as a form of heart disease. Then, around the beginning of April, David Horner's brother was murdered in London. Horner seldom saw his brother but was nonetheless devastated.[39] These concerns naturally took Osbert's attention away from a poetry reading that he and Edith were organising for the 'French in Great Britain Fund', sponsored by the Marchioness of Crewe, so Edith took care of most of the details. Held on 14 April at the Aeolian Hall, it was attended by the Queen and both princesses. After a rehearsal, Edith wrote to Pavlik: 'Tom Eliot is reading the last section of The Waste Land at our reading . . . I cannot tell you what an impression it makes on one, hearing that great – that very great – poet read that work of fire and passion and prophecy. I felt choked, and could hardly speak after he had finished. I had not seen him for years. Like myself, he looks much older after the terrible experiences we have been through, but he has still that look of a tiger or puma that he used to have when he was a young man.'[40]

The glory of the rehearsal gave way on the night to backstage farce. The performance opened smoothly. D. L. Murray gave an address. The Poet Laureate, John Masefield, paid tribute to the recently deceased Laurence Binyon, reading some of Binyon's poems as well as some of his own. The other readers, apart from Eliot and Sitwell, were Edmund Blunden, Gordon Bottomley, 'H.D.', Wilfrid Gibson, Walter de la Mare, Vita Sackville-West, W. J. Turner, and Arthur Waley.[41] Dorothy

Wellesley (Lady Gerald Wellesley) was expected to read but when she did not appear on stage, Sackville-West and her husband Harold Nicolson hurried out to track her down. They found her in a stupor. Later, Wellesley telephoned Sackville-West repeatedly, denying that she had been drunk and threatening to commit suicide. For once, Edith saluted Vita unreservedly: 'Osbert and I will never cease being grateful to you both for averting a frightful scene. (It was pretty bad, as it was . . . but my goodness, what it *might* have been – if the platform had been reached! . . .) It was you and your husband who saved any situation that *could* be saved; you both were really wonderful in dealing with it.'[42]

This visit to London gave Sitwell a chance to have luncheon with Denton Welch, who came to the Sesame on 19 April. It was a tame affair but Welch wrote a hypnotic sketch about it that gave an edge even to the maid's comment, 'The tongue is very good today, madam.' He described Sitwell herself: 'Black hat, black cloak and black dress to the ground. The draft from the floor swept the folds of the cloak against her, and a powder white hand held the hem at her throat. Two enormous rings glittered on her fingers. The lovely palest reservoir blue stones reached from the first to the second joints. They flashed and flashed again.' Sitwell urged him to try something 'violent and vulgar' next in his writing: 'I will tell you what your danger is; it is, as it were, your ingrowing toenail. Everything in, in, in.'[43] Sitwell gestured as though pulling on a rope. Good advice, but with only five years left to him, Welch hardly had time to broaden his range or turn his gaze outward.

For years, Sitwell had been collecting aphorisms about poetry, art and music. Now she assembled them, with her own remarks interspersed, in *A Poet's Notebook*, published by Macmillan on 30 April 1943 (a different collection with the same title came out in the United States in 1950). It was a characteristic sort of book for her; she preferred pithy utterances to sequential arguments. Heavily represented were Plato, Blake, Wagner, Emerson, Whitman, Schopenhauer, Baudelaire, Rimbaud, Mallarmé, and Cocteau. There were sections on Chaucer and his contemporaries, on Ben Jonson, and on Christopher Smart and Gerard Manley Hopkins. The book ended with two of Sitwell's new poems, 'A Mother to her Dead Child' and 'Green

Song' – practical demonstrations of how she tried to live up to the values of her masters. In the following year, she put out a similar common-place book, entitled *Planet and Glow-Worm*, which was intended to soothe the minds of the sleepless and the anxious. This quirky anthology eventually became a favourite of the young Bruce Chatwin, and when, towards the end of his life, he was trying to assemble his many note-books on travel through Australia into a single book, he relied, at least to a degree, on Sitwell's book as a model for organisation. The book that resulted, *The Songlines* (1987), is generally taken to be his masterpiece.[44]

Stephen Spender seemed to be under Sitwell's influence when in May 1943 he sent her his 'Sketches for Sonnets', exalted meditations on time and mortality with the stripped-down imagery that Sitwell favoured. She wrote to him: 'The identity of the sonnets is grave and splendid, and the poems have the magnificence that a sonnet should have, – and they have a deep life that is one with the sonority. Thank God the small way, "the close and observant small kind of poetry," will never be *your* way.'[45] In a draft of his review of *Street Songs*, Spender had said that 'religious poetry is literal statement' and that 'the poems of the mystics are reportage of poetically experienced lives'. He was obliquely asking a complicated question. Modern poetry is expected to be ironic, or, in William Empson's term, ambiguous, but religious poetry affirms a single order or meaning in human experience. How, then, was Sitwell's most recent poetry properly modern? Spender was probably exaggerating the role of 'literal statement' in Sitwell's poetry, much of which was written on the borders of Surrealism, as she told another new friend, the Oxford don Maurice Bowra: 'It is a danger-ous thing to say, but I can say it to you. Sometimes, when I begin a poem, it is almost like automatic writing. Then I use my mind on it afterwards. It was so here ['Street Song']. For that reason, partly, it means several things to me, whilst being deeply experienced.'[46] And given Sitwell's immersion in Symbolist poetry, she counted on suggestions or overtones to complicate any literal statement she might make.

Sitwell was moving towards a sacramental sense of art, believing that the change rendered by craft upon the raw material of life is analogous to the change of bread and wine in the Eucharist. This was

a helpful way for a Christian poet to address the expectation that the
language of poetry should hold meanings in tension. Sitwell dedicated to Spender the poem 'Harvest' (of which an earlier version had
been published as 'Bread of Angels'). It draws on Aquinas's 'Sermon
of the Body of Our Lord' and suggests how the body of a poem
becomes joined to its meaning in 'The universal language of the
Bread'.[47]

Oddly enough, Sitwell's poetry was converted to Rome long before
she was. At this time, she avoided churches, and while in Renishaw
attended the 'sleepy' Anglican services only because the tenants
expected to see her there.[48] When Georgia's father died in January
1942, Edith's letter of consolation gave a glimpse of her underlying religious beliefs and her view of the afterlife: 'I am sure, when people die,
they do just feel they want to rest; and they know, which we don't, until
we too come to die, that it is only for a time. They feel that, of that I
am as certain as I can be of anything, and I don't mean that it applies
only to people who are religious.'[49] However, she felt the churches had
missed the point of recent history, as she told Pavlik in 1945:

> Oh is it not sad to think that when a faith is so deeply needed to save
> the world, a faith did arise: the black and appalling creed of the Nazis.
> That and that only. What hideous mockery. Because it was not only
> self-seeking that brought this horror about, – it was a black and
> hideous religion, like the religion of Baal or of Moloch. They were
> willing, these people, to die for their Anti-Christ. How pitifully have
> the churches of Christ failed to deal with this: there is no fire in the
> faith – none. Many good men, much hard work – but not the fire of
> the saint. That is left to a few – a very few outside the church.[50]

In the early summer of 1943, strange letters and telegrams began
arriving from Switzerland, leading Edith to believe that Bernard Woog
was drunk when he wrote them. Finally, in the first week of July came
a telegram: 'Father sends blessings. State far worse. Doctors pes-
simistic.'[51] Sir George apparently spent three days in prayer and two
under morphine before dying quietly on 9 July.[52] His remains were cre-
mated in Switzerland and a small memorial service was held for him at
Eckington church near Renishaw on 17 July.

Upon her father's death, Edith expected to receive about five thousand pounds. By 13 July, she learned that she had been left just a thousand pounds.[53] But then another will appeared, which removed her control of that amount and gave her instead an annuity of sixty pounds, which, she remarked, would become just thirty pounds after taxes.[54] Sir George had, in fact, written a number of contradictory wills in an effort to tie down money for Reresby and Francis, as well as (male) children not yet born. A will that came to light at the end of the month laid out different annuities: first claim for Reresby £600, for Francis £300, and for an American cousin £250; after those, £1200 for Osbert, £700 for Sachie, and £200 for Edith. Eventually, the lawyers worked out that only two wills mattered: one in England mainly concerned with property, and one in Switzerland dealing with money. However the estate was resolved, the entailed English properties with self-supporting rents were already in Osbert's hands. Sachie had Weston, and was about to receive £5000 from Lady Ida's marriage settlement, so both men were certain of comfort.[55]

Edith had allowed herself to dream of a future in which Bryher's gift and a legacy from her father would together allow her the independence to live in Bath and devote herself solely to poetry. In her anger, she now told Pavlik that her father had tried to force her to earn a living by writing prose: 'He has tried to murder my poetry. He will not succeed. For nearly ten years I did not write poetry, because of my ghastly worries. He shall never do that to me again.'[56] By 8 August, she had calmed down somewhat and wrote to Sybil Colefax:

> I am glad he died peacefully in his sleep, without pain, and without (I think) knowing he was dying. He was frightened to die. I shall remember about him that he was truly kind to my poor friend Helen and indeed behaved like a human being to her; and that he did *not* prosecute two employees who each embezzled £200 from him. I shall remember these things, and I shall try and think that he could not help certain things which grew in his nature. But – he remained to the last what he has been for the last thirty years. He had, of course, a miserable married life. But then, so did my mother. Poor old man! But they *were* a pair, and the trail of what they have done is still all over everything.[57]

Without open disagreement with Sachie, Edith very unwisely took Osbert's view of the estate and thought the worst of Georgia for her complaints about money: 'Smash and grab raiders are not in it!'[58] Osbert was sometimes generous: in May, he had bought Edith four hundred pounds' worth of defence bonds so as to free her own money to pay off a loan at Coutts.[59] Presumably such acts blinded her to other aspects of his conduct: '[Father] has long tried to ruin Osbert's life: he has not succeeded, because Osbert is a very great soul, and has a kind of saint-like comprehension of and pity for such beings.'[60] A stickler for loyalty, Edith often referred to Cain in her poetry, but it seems she remained unaware of one of the worst betrayals in her life.

Already living beyond the dreams of most people, Osbert had hopes of an even finer life. He described the baronetcy to David Horner as a 'new toy' and proposed to have a gramophone record made that sang, 'Sir O, Sir O, Sir O', for when he was depressed.[61] He had long since tired of Sachie's whining over money and was going to take a hard line:

The wish to behave especially badly to me and to Edith was, of course, present in S's mind, but I made up my mind a long time ago to try not to quarrel irrevocably with him until I was provided for; and I have paid more attention to my affairs than has Sachie. In any case, primogeniture, rightly or wrongly, [illegible] to protect me, and at Father's death, under the Marriage Settlement, I had to get the estates I now hold for life . . . But I do feel very sorry for Sachie – if the figures are correct. On the other hand, he has far more capital than I have.[62]

For a time, the bequests appeared moot. Most of Sir George's money had been placed in a *Stiftung* (endowment or private foundation), but a great deal of it had disappeared. His children initially believed that Sir George had just squandered it on gardens, renovations, bad pictures, and chairs that must not be sat on. However, by the first months of 1944, Osbert could see that Woog, who had once worked at the bank where Sir George did business and who had obtained a power of attorney, had stolen all but ten or twelve thousand of what had once been at least sixty-five thousand pounds.[63]

Moreover, Woog and his wife had been named as heirs to what was left in the *Stiftung*. Osbert began to think that his father's death was not natural, and Edith, an avid reader of Agatha Christie, agreed, writing to Sachie in February 1944: 'I should think a whole lot can be proved against [Woog]: and if you ask me, I should think it quite probable that there were strange incidents surrounding the end. Do you take me?'[64] She told Horner: 'I think we shall find that sulphonal played its part in gathering the old gentleman to his forefathers . . . not self-administered.'[65]

Even though the consul, à lawyer, and a chartered accountant were pursuing the matter in Switzerland, more help seemed necessary. At Edith's suggestion, Osbert sent Lorna Andrade to Eleanor Lucie-Smith, known professionally as Nell St John Montague, a medium and psychometrist who was a friend of their cousin Irene Carisbrooke. They asked Montague to examine the handwriting of Woog and of Sir George and also to gaze into crystal. The medium suspected that something terrible had happened to Sir George, but held out little hope of getting the money back.[66] Apart from spiritual vibrations and glimpses in the ball, there was not a scrap of earthly evidence to support the charge of murder. The fortune-teller was wrong on all counts, and her gift of foresight did not save her from being killed by a bomb six months later.[67]

After long wrangling, the bank paid restitution, and Osbert made sure that the final benefit of the estate fell to him. It is necessary here to look many years into the future – albeit without the aid of crystal. In 1965 (just after Edith's death), Philip Frere's younger colleague Hugo Southern took over the Sitwell file and wrote a letter to Osbert, reviewing the history of the estate: 'you know virtually all of what I will have to say in this letter.' Southern described how Sir George Sitwell had made many *Stiftungs*, and the one that was currently operating was dated 20 August 1935. It paid out annuities of £1200 to Osbert, £100 each to Edith and Sachie, and a total of £150 to two cousins. The validity of this (and any other of the *Stiftungs*) could be successfully challenged, and under either Italian or Swiss law the estate would then be divided equally among the three children. In a subsequent letter Southern placed the value of each share at that time at about fifty to sixty thousand pounds.[68]

It is evident from these letters that for many years Osbert knowingly profited at the expense of his brother and sister. There was no reason for the *Stiftung* to continue operating, except that it put money in Osbert's pocket. Some of his annuity was tied to the upkeep of Montegufoni, but, then, he also had the enjoyment of living for much of the year in a castle. An acute businessman, Sir Reresby Sitwell later observed to John Pearson that Osbert 'snitched' money that belonged to Edith and Sacheverell, and that this probably required the acquiescence of the 'eminence noir' Philip Frere.[69] Hugo Southern was disgusted by his dealings with Osbert and later described him to Pearson as 'utterly, completely selfish'.[70] Edith spent most of the late 1940s and 1950s in crushing anxiety over her debts, when she ought to have had a comfortable life. Osbert told Lorna Andrade that he did not help Edith because she was as extravagant as Lady Ida and that money given to her was wasted.[71] It is often said that Osbert did not know about Edith's money problems, but Andrade's recollections indicate precisely the opposite. In any event, the money was not his either to give or to withhold.

Believing what Osbert told her about money, Edith had constantly to hold her tongue in dealings with Sachie, since much of what he said implied doubt of Osbert's judgment or goodwill. For their part, Sachie and Georgia failed to grasp that the person most injured by Sir George's will-making was Edith. The tension mounted through the autumn of 1943 and flashed out over an apparently unrelated question. Ten years younger and a boy, Sachie had not witnessed Edith's childhood. It was easier for him to look on his early years with generosity and forgiveness – he had less to forgive. His book *Splendours and Miseries*, published in December, contained a description of Lady Ida's qualities as a mother that appalled Edith. She described the book to David Horner:

> I really haven't any words to say what he has done to *me* by that
> chapter. I do not need to tell you that by this, he has succeeded in
> leaving me alone with the hell of my childhood, (he was never in
> it) – has succeeded in conveying that it was all *my* fault (I suppose
> *I* ill-treated *her*, when I was a child of eight and nine, a child of
> thirteen!) *Why* do you suppose he has stuck a knife into my back in

this way? Out of mawkish sentimentality – and because like his
father before him, he cannot see anyone else's life, or his own life,
honestly.[72]

The last sentence contains the essence of her rage. Sir George had
never accepted that his wife had abused Edith, nor that Edith needed
the means to have a separate life, so had in desperation thrown in her
lot with the Roothams. Now Sachie, whom she loved and admired,
was guilty of the same disregard for her emotions and her material
needs.

For about two weeks she mulled over her response. She praised the
book handsomely, then addressed the issue of the last chapter: 'It is not
how I see the situation.' She recounted for him the psychological
injuries she had suffered at Lady Ida's hands, and what she believed was
the damage done to Osbert by the fraud trial. Then she demanded in
all kindness that Sachie – who gave up poetry after the reviews of
Canons of Giant Art – show a little courage:

> I realise, my darling, only too well from this chapter, that you have
> been suffering from great unhappiness. Many things have gone to
> make this up: loneliness at school; the first war coming while you
> were yet so young; your young friends being killed; the dreadful 1915
> incident; *this* war; and, I think, too, the extraordinary wave of idiocy
> that has swept over the country on the subject of poetry . . . You are
> surrounded by people *devoted* to you. You are at the height of your
> powers. Don't take refuge in some dream of childhood. Don't allow
> yourself to pulled down by imbecile publishers, either. Go straight
> ahead, and leave these dreams behind. Now is the time to write more
> poetry. You owe it to us that you should.
> And the tide is turning.[73]

At the end of the war, he did start writing verse again – and it doubtless owed something to Edith's mixture of encouragement and
badgering.

The exchange with Sachie forced her to think about whether recent
experience had changed her. Although she speaks in the language of
neurasthenia, she had recognised some truths about herself. She wrote

to Pavlik: 'I, for one thing, have become much wiser. Although my terrible childhood has left its mark, and I shall always be nervous, and have sudden outbursts brought on by my wrecked nervous system, and the fear of people that has been instilled into me.' It was an accurate assessment. Childhood had trained her to expect sudden cruelties. Serenity might be *imaginable* in her poetry, but she knew that she would live and die a woman of extremes.

19

THE DANCING MADNESS

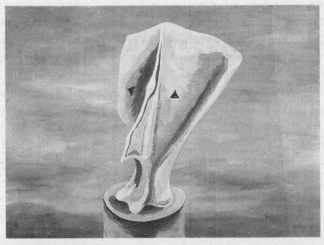

John Banting's whimsical pseudo-portrait of Edith Sitwell (1943) was based on a propped-up bone and some bits of glass

'I am much more intelligent than when I saw you last, because I have used my mind much more profoundly, and because I have read *and understood* very great and wonderful works. So when you speak to me of painting now, although *I* shall always remain silent out of reverence for you, and out of a proper humility and knowledge of my ignorance, I shall at least absorb *everything* that you are saying. I can be a better companion [for] you. I have real *hunger* to learn.'[1] Sitwell found Tchelitchew's intuitive and chaotic mind intimidating. She wanted to make herself more pleasing to him when they met again after the war. At the same time, she wanted to kindle new poems. She put it to

Stephen Spender, 'I've got very much the night-school nature, and try to educate myself.'[2]

Her programme of reading from 1943 was offbeat and sometimes esoteric. While the subject would bear an interesting book for specialists, here it is possible to offer only a short summary. At Tchelitchew's suggestion, she took up Paracelsus, the sixteenth-century alchemist and hermeticist. She struggled with him but kept trying: 'It is certain that until one begins to understand that there are Secrets in nature, one will get nowhere. And every great artist is, as you say, in some sense a Magician.'[3] Perhaps as a result of her reading in this area (and the influence of Tchelitchew himself), she often depicts sudden transformations in her later poems; the words 'become' and 'change' take on an enormous weight in her poetry. However, this may have been just a further development of the impulse that led to her poem 'Metamorphosis' back in 1928.

She grew fascinated with works that had inspired Blake and Novalis, leading her to re-read the shoemaker-mystic Jacob Boehme, drawing from his *Aurora* (1612) imagery of precious stones.[4] She wrote later that she found Kierkegaard 'tepid and damp . . . I really hate him. Hate him as much as I love Boehme and Blake and Whitman, who are love.'[5] In the autumn of 1943, she took up John Livingston Lowes's *The Road to Xanadu* (1927) – an account of Coleridge's reading and how it bore fruit in 'The Rime of the Ancient Mariner' and 'Kubla Khan'. Here, she learnt of Thomas Burnet's *The Theory of the Earth* (1681–90) with its visions of deluge and apocalypse: 'The description of the bottom of the sea after all the waters had been drained from it, is so tremendous that one gasps – and so is the description of the mountains when the earth is being destroyed by fire on the Last Day, – and the description of the sun at the time of an earthquake.'[6]

Two years later, Burnet makes an appearance in Sitwell's 'The Shadow of Cain'. Probably from a reading of Coleridge's letters, Sitwell discovered the German philosopher Lorenz Oken[7] (1779–1851), whom she regarded as mad but visionary, and to whom she returned again and again until she wrote 'The Shadow of Cain', in which she quotes him on the nature of 'zero'.[8] Sitwell was attracted to Plato and to that 'great and derided heart and intelligence' Ralph Waldo Emerson.[9] Through these years, she continued reading the sources behind Shakespeare, becoming absorbed in several of them, notably the Greek travel writer Pausanias. Essentially, Sitwell was trying to understand the intellectual formation and the inspirations of a handful of authors who inspired *her*. This reading was an approach to the minds of Shakespeare, the Romantics, and Walt Whitman.

Coleridge coloured her view of almost everything in the late months of 1943. She wrote to Colin Hampton, cellist of the Griller Quartet, which performed privately at Renishaw Hall programmes that included an important new composer: 'I'm not sure that [Benjamin] Britten hasn't been, spiritually, where Coleridge went before he wrote *The Ancient Mariner* – to those polar regions . . . Only Britten saw it, I think, from a freezing height, like a bird – very, very high up. And Coleridge saw it from the sea.' In the years to come, she would have a close friendship with Britten, who would set to music a number of her poems. As for Coleridge, his grip on Edith Sitwell extended even to her sense of humour as two years later she described for T.S. Eliot her dealings with visiting bores: 'I am the Wedding Guest to every Ancient Mariner, and am now bent permanently sideways, with my right ear almost touching the ground.'[10]

Sitwell needed also to keep in touch with new developments in contemporary writing and for this she turned to the poet and editor John Lehmann. In 1936, he founded *New Writing*, which became *Penguin New Writing* in 1940 – a best-selling anthology packaged as a magazine. He also founded *Daylight, New Writing and Daylight*, and in 1954 the *London Magazine*. At Cambridge he had been a close friend of the poet Julian Bell, Clive and Vanessa Bell's son who was killed in Spain. Lehmann worked at the Hogarth Press and in 1938 purchased Virginia Woolf's share of the firm.[11] He moved in leftist circles in the 1930s, and even though he admired *Street Songs*, he expected a cool reception from Edith Sitwell when they met at the Sesame Club probably in the spring of 1943. They were introduced by a common friend, Demetrios Capetanakis. Lehmann recalled: 'I was struck at once by the sculptural beauty of [Edith's] oval face . . . I recognized at that earliest tea-party what was in fact perfectly clear from her poetry, and could not be concealed even by the shower of shafts of satiric wit that sometimes filled the air around her: that her response to any genuine emotion was immediate and that she was extremely sensitive, especially to all forms of suffering, human or animal.'[12]

It was the suffering of Capetanakis that cemented the bond between Sitwell and Lehmann. Himself an able poet and a friend of George Seferis, Capetanakis was doing propaganda work for the Greek government in exile when he was found to have leukaemia. He died on 9 March 1944 at the age of thirty-two, and Lehmann was crushed. Sitwell wrote to Lehmann at great length about grief – lessons she had learnt after Helen's Rootham's death:

How well I know that feeling that one must deaden the pain somehow, temporarily. I think you are an extremely courageous person – otherwise I would warn you: 'don't try to deaden it: for if you do, you will never be the same person again: for if one deadens anguish, some part of one remains numb.' But I do not think that will be so with you: I do not dread it for *you*, in the very least. How thankful I am that you were spared that last afternoon: it would only have been an anguishing memory for you. Osbert, who has seen a great many men die, says he believes *all* people want, at that moment, is, not to be surrounded. No human contact can appear to them real, and it is only an added cruelty.[13]

At Lehmann's request, Sitwell wrote an essay on Demetrios Capetanakis for *New Writing and Daylight* (Autumn 1944), reprinted in 1947 in Lehmann's commemorative volume *Demetrios Capetanakis: A Greek Poet in England*. From 1944, John Lehmann became Sitwell's main literary adviser (apart from Osbert and Sachie) and one of her most trusted friends. The Sitwell name added lustre to his publications, even if their tastes sometimes differed. On one of her appearances at his office, she asked the secretary, 'Has Mr Lehmann found some more mousy geniuses for me to approve?'[14]

That Sitwell should be friends with Spender, Lehmann, and, soon, Louis MacNeice, indicated a softening in her views – at least towards individual writers – but her beliefs about the relation of politics to poetry were unchanged. She wrote to Pavlik:

a poet is not made great or otherwise by his politics. Naturally the *spirit* of a poet could be shown by certain adherences. I mean, a poet who cringed to the Germans would be a mean skunk, and worse than a mean skunk. But it does *not* make a poet great or otherwise, to be left-wing or right-wing. Yeats was not left-wing. He wasted a lot of time by such politics as he did indulge in. I remember once, in my presence, someone asked Mr. Shaw if Yeats had a great deal of influence over the Irish. 'Immense' replied G.B.S. 'He has only to say a thing should be done, for the Irish to do the exact opposite.'[15]

Sitwell's remarks amplify an earlier comment on her old friend: 'Yeats? A *very* great poet, but not always wise otherwise. He could be, and was, deceived in life, but never in poetry. That happens.'[16]

There was no lasting improvement in Sitwell's health. In the autumn a doctor had remarked on her low pulse rate. Back pain continued, and in the spring of 1944 she was receiving daily treatments from a masseur who tried to entertain her with riddles about Donald Duck.[17] Her own problems, however, were eclipsed by those of the people around her. She wrote to Lehmann in June:

My young maid (a village girl from here), who came when she was 16, and left at 21 to go into the WRNS, got married here, three days after Demetrios [Capetanakis] died, to a boy of her own age in the Air Force. They had three weeks leave for their wedding and honeymoon, and a week after they went back to duty, he was posted missing. It is simply frightful to see that poor child, to whom I am devoted, and who is devoted to me. She was given compassionate leave, most of which she spent in my room, not speaking excepting to say from time to time, 'Oh Miss Edith, Miss Edith.'[18]

Sitwell received the news of the D-Day invasion with a mixture of rejoicing and pity, as she told Pavlik: 'I was going to write to you yesterday; but the tremendous event which is in everybody's mind and heart, made it impossible to do anything, to settle to anything. Oh, the feeling of pride, and the deep sadness for the young lives that must go. Both are overwhelming. And I feel my eyes filling with tears, at all moments of the day.'[19] As the Allies approached Paris in August, Lieutenant David Gilliat, only son of Edith's favourite cousin Veronica, was killed in action on the day before his twenty-third birthday: 'She is exactly the kind of mother who may die or go mad.'[20] Even though Paris was liberated on 25 August, many more weeks passed before Sitwell could contact Evelyn Wiel. Since 1940, Sitwell's love of the French had evaporated: 'I am rejoiced that France is free. But I shall find it extremely difficult ever to speak to a Frenchman again. We have died in hundreds and thousands because of their shameful cowardice . . . I can pity cowards, but I do not like them when they boast.'[21]

Sitwell's *Green Song* came out from Macmillan on 15 August 1944. At forty pages, it was a slim volume, but it contained a number of important poems. In 'Invocation' and 'Harvest' she added depth to the persona of the old labouring woman – now connecting her with a 'corn goddess'. Throughout the book images of emeralds multiply, partly from her reading of Jacob Boehme and even John Donne's sermons, but more in an effort to evoke the imaginative world of 'The Rime of the Ancient Mariner': 'And ice, mast-high, came floating by, / As green as emerald.' At the heart of the volume is a dream of peace:

> On this great holiday
> Dives and Lazarus are brothers again:
> They seem of gold as they come up from the city
> Casting aside the grave-clothes of their lives
> Where the ragged dust is nobly born as the Sun.
> Now Atlas lays aside his dying world,
> The clerk, the papers in his dusty office . . .[22]

In a period when much of her verse was inspired by the war, it is striking that (arguably) the most impressive single poem in the collection is 'Heart and Mind' – a piece devoted to the 'timeless' themes of love, Eros and mortality:

> Said the Lion to the Lioness – 'When you are amber dust, –
> No more a raging fire like the heat of the Sun
> (No liking but all lust) –
> Remember still the flowering of the amber blood and bone,
> The rippling of bright muscles like a sea,
> Remember the rose-prickles of bright paws

Though we shall mate no more
Till the fire of that sun the heart and the moon-cold bone are
    one.'
Said the Skeleton lying upon the sands of Time –
'The great gold planet that is the mourning heat of the Sun
Is greater than all gold, more powerful
Than the tawny body of a Lion that fire consumes
Like all that grows or leaps . . . so is the heart
More powerful than all dust. Once I was Hercules
Or Samson, strong as the pillars of the seas:
But the flames of the heart consumed me, and the mind
Is but a foolish wind.'

Said the Sun to the Moon – 'When you are but a lone white
    crone,
And I, a dead King in my golden armour somewhere in a dark
    wood,
Remember only this of our hopeless love
That never till Time is done
Will the fire of the heart and the fire of the mind be one.'

With several lines approaching fifteen syllables and one stretching to seventeen, Sitwell was here declaring herself Whitman's daughter.

Her engagement with the literary traditions of the United States was deeper than that of any British-born poet of her generation, and the fragility of her posthumous reputation owes partly to her work being difficult to assimilate within a British literary tradition. This poem is a farewell to erotic love, and it doubtless draws, at some level, from her disappointments with Tchelitchew. Yet because she relies on allegorical figures – the lion and lioness, the skeleton, the sun and moon – the poem preserves its secrets. Gordon Bottomley wrote of 'Heart and Mind': 'I have more than once cast back my mind over the poetic achievement of the century, and each time I realize more surely – in my conception – that no other poem so fine has appeared in our country throughout this period.'[23]

At the *TLS*, Edith Sitwell was the property of Harold Hannyngton Child, who wrote yet another adulatory review (2 September 1944):

'The reader who adventures for himself may find, perhaps, that the spirit of Abt Vogler is not altogether a Victorian affectation.' In the reference to 'Abt Vogler', Robert Browning's poem about organ music, Child was saying that in Sitwell's poetry he could hear the voice of God. This was fortunate for him, as he died the following year.[24]

While most reviews were full of praise, a few were negative, including one by Julian Symons, a young poet (now remembered as a crime writer) and friend of Wyndham Lewis, who gave her a savaging in *Our Time*. She wrote to Pavlik: 'There is a sort of tug-of-war going on here. The principal poets and men of letters saying I am now where Yeats was as an old man, – the dregs of the literary population insulting me for all they are worth. I have no heart, I know nothing of life, I am a damned aristo, etc. The damned aristo, like the damned aristo to whom she is writing, knows more about life and has a stronger vision of it than any of which they could conceive.'[25]

More flattering than the best review, the Spenders asked Edith Sitwell to be a godmother to the child they were expecting – their first, Matthew, born in March 1945: 'I shall *love* the little creature, with warmth and tenderness. It will be most wonderful to see it grow in mind and spirit and body. I shall feel it a great responsibility of love, on my side, never to fail the child, and to help bring it to its own vision of the greatness of life, to help open its eyes and let it see for itself.' Employing the phrase she would later apply to Virginia Woolf, she asked: 'would you like me to *knit* for the baby? I may tell you that I am the Knitting Queen . . . ("a beautiful little knitter," I am told by experts. Why "little"? I think it is an expression of approbation.)'[26]

Paradoxically, Edith Sitwell could be distressed by the threat of an 'impertinent' review or terrified by a bank manager, but in the face of real danger she was unflappable. She described for Pavlik a reading she and her brothers gave at the Churchill Club in London on 25 October 1944, in the days of the V-1 rockets:

> There were a great many officers of the various services. Suddenly, the air-raid warning went. I had just stood up to read my poem about the Raids, 'Still Falls the Rain'. I waited till the noise of the warning had stopped, and then began the poem. No sooner had I begun the poem, than the *whistle* went. That means 'Imminent Danger' – that the

doodle-bug is coming down!!!! I continued to read, with the doodle-bug flying *immediately* over our heads, very low over the roof. I hope and think I showed no sign of fright. The thing was over our heads, immediately over, the *whole* time, until I came to the last three lines. Then it went over, and some other poor miserable wretches got it. Sir Kenneth Clark was in the audience. One is supposed to fall on one's face when the whistle goes, but I remained standing and reading, and the audience with great courage remained in their seats.

Lady Spender recalled that the buzz-bomb cut out right overhead – a sign that they would be hit. When praised for her courage, Edith said that no one saw her knees knocking under her long skirt (*Telegraph*, 20 June 2008). Of course, Sitwell was not always reckless during raids. On Christmas Eve, seven V-1s flew over Renishaw, landing near enough to blow open the back door, while she sat, very sensibly, under the kitchen table.[27]

In October 1944, Sitwell received the first collected edition in England of *Four Quartets*. She wrote to Eliot in October 1944: 'I thought I knew each of the *Four Quartets* as well as it would be possible for anyone excepting yourself to know them. I have often read them together. But seeing them together in a book is a very great experience. At this time when horror has taken the place of awe, – I feel awe return to me, with this work.'[28] Like Sitwell (though he suffered less criticism for it), Eliot had become an intensely visionary and theological poet. She was certain that, of all her contemporaries, he was the one who could enlarge her technique and deepen her vision, so her reading of his works was more or less constant.

It appears that Eliot came to the Sesame on 24 October and that he then helped mend some fences. His close friend, the editor and critic John Hayward, with whom he shared a flat in Chelsea from the following year, had once had a pleasant acquaintance with Edith Sitwell. However, in 1935 he had written what she called a 'cheap and unworthy' article on *Aspects of Modern Poetry* for an American newspaper (presumably he had not reckoned on her 'Argus-eyed press cuttings agency'[29]), so she had broken with him.[30] In November 1944, Hayward wrote a conciliatory letter, which Eliot had probably encouraged, and Sitwell was delighted to see him again.[31] Muscular dystrophy kept the acerbic Hayward in a wheelchair, and, like Sitwell, he remained 'a little outside life'. Within a few years, she was closer to him than she was to Eliot, and when the friendship between the two men splintered over Eliot's marriage to Valerie Fletcher in 1957, she unquestioningly took Hayward's side.

At last, a letter from Evelyn Wiel dated 12 November 1944 reached Renishaw on 15 December. It was Sitwell's first contact with her in more than two years, and her letter contained, or implied, a reproach. Sitwell wrote: 'it just made me feel like crying. If you *ever* talk again, as you talked in this letter, about money, *I do not know what I shall do. I simply can't bear it.*' She told Evelyn that fifty pounds had already been sent, that her allowance would be paid as soon as the bank could arrange it, and that she hoped to be allowed to send sixteen pounds per month. Then she described her unceasing efforts to send money since the fall of Paris four years earlier, and volunteered to show her the letters and documents. She begged Evelyn to come and visit England so that she could meet her new friends, especially John Lehmann, the Spenders, 'Bryher' and 'H.D.'.[32]

Among those new friends was one female poet, who, like Sitwell, had written some of the outstanding poetry of the Second World War. Sitwell was rather defensive of her position as England's leading woman poet, and found it easier to honour Americans, especially Gertrude Stein, Marianne Moore, and 'H.D.', but there was more to it than just defending turf. She did not believe that women poets in Britain had lived up to the challenges of modernism and that instead they had tended to weep like minor Victorians. She put it to Maurice Bowra: 'any woman learning to write, if she is going to be any good at all, would, until she had made a technique for herself (and one has to forge it for oneself, there is no help to be got) write in as hard and glittering a manner as possible, and with as strange images as possible (strange, but believed in). Anything to avoid that ghastly wallowing.'[33] One of the first Imagists, Hilda Doolittle did write in a hard and glittering manner. Sitwell believed that her three war sequences – poems that intertwined images of the bombing with Egyptian archaeology, feminised versions of Christianity and other faiths, together with the teachings of Sigmund Freud – were the work of a master. When one of the sequences, *Tribute to the Angels*, was published in April 1945,

Sitwell declared: 'I say you are a lucky woman, because you did have your hand guided. It really is the flowering of the rood . . . Yours is the supreme apple tree, the flowering apple . . . I am walking *entirely* in a spell. And that perhaps is the ultimate thing to be said for any poem.'[34]

It had been a long time since Sitwell had heard anything from Graham Greene, but she followed his career. In January 1945, he asked her to contribute a poem to a publication of Eyre & Spottiswoode, the publishing firm where he was now a director. She wrote to him on 22 January:

> By an odd coincidence, I was, at the moment, trying to overcome my natural shyness to write to you. I had just been re-reading 'The Power and the Glory' and also 'Brighton Rock', and wanted to say that, leaving everything else aside (if one could) the fact they are very great novels, you bring home to one, more than anyone except-ing the greatest of priests could do, and as much as he could do, the horror, the very smell of sin, and the wonder and the hope of redemption . . . I have so often wanted to write to you, and am very glad this opportunity has arisen, though my letter to you doesn't in the least express what I feel about your great novels.[35]

Flying bombs or not, the end of the war was in sight, and when Sitwell went to London at the end of December 1944, she received many visitors, among them Herbert Read, who, she told Pavlik, was once a great friend, but he had drifted away owing to his first wife's atti-tude, and there had been a breach: 'But I have always liked him, and was glad when he came to see me.' After two weeks, she returned to Renishaw with a plan to get back something of the life she had known at Pembridge Mansions: 'if the war *ever* ends, I am going to be one of the London *hostesses*!! But people will have to earn their entry, because if they are not interesting, they won't be allowed in.' Osbert thought that Edith's 'lame dogs' would spoil her salon, but she intended to have 'special bore days' when they could cancel each other out.[36]

Sitwell's threat never again to speak to a Frenchman proved hollow when the composer Francis Poulenc visited her in London and again in March at Renishaw. He and the singer Pierre Bernac came over from Sheffield where they had a concert. A friend of one of the neo-romantic

painters, Christian Bérard, Poulenc bore news of Tchelitchew's triumphs
in the United States. The Sitwells discovered that their visitors had no
idea what had happened in England during the war, so Osbert took
Poulenc and Bernac on a tour of bomb-sites in Sheffield, which, as
Edith observed, 'gave them something to think about'.[37]

In most of what the Sitwells wrote about Renishaw, the reader
would seldom be aware that it was on the outskirts of a great industrial city. Sachie called it 'the house of tragic memories' – a place of
beauty, solitude, and despair. Edith's letters during the war certainly
change that impression. In the preceding four years, she and Osbert
had spent almost as much time there as all the Sitwells taken together
since the death of their grandfather eighty years earlier. It was a shift
in perspective; they discovered day by day how their house of ghosts
was welded to the world of the living. Edith had lived in slums most
of her adult life, so it did not take much for her to become impassioned about the people of Sheffield and their courage under the
bombardment.

On the other hand, the 'poetic' Renishaw continued to impress itself
upon Sitwell. She still referred to it only half jokingly as 'Wuthering
Heights', and she saw the Derbyshire sky as a tableau of mysteries:

> we are having what is known as a Sheffield Blight. This is just as
> individual and strange as a London fog, and I have never seen it any-
> where else. The sky is suddenly filled with lurid, Judgment-Day
> clouds, the day turns quite dark, then the actual clouds are cleared
> away, and the whole air suddenly becomes of a strange lurid threat-
> ening clear brown. There was one day this winter when that
> happened and a great tree outside my window, covered with frost,
> was illumined by an unseen ray. The tree looked as if it were made
> of huge diamonds. There was no light elsewhere – all was brown and
> yet lurid and strange like a poem by Dante.[38]

Sheffield is surrounded by hills, so the strange effect, which could cause
sudden darkness in the afternoon, was probably caused by smoke
trapped under clouds, especially as wartime industries burned great
quantities of the sulphurous local coal. The shaft of light may have
come from the massive ironworks near by.[39]

Nevertheless, after four years at Renishaw, Edith was anxious to get to London as often as she could. In April, she held a large party at the Sesame, attended by both T. S. Eliot and Herbert Read. She went to the first night of *The Duchess of Malfi* with John Gielgud as Duke Ferdinand: 'He was utterly and supremely magnificent – what fire! What passion! What beauty of voice.' Her time in London, however, was 'darkened' by revelations about the concentration camps. Tom Driberg, she learnt, had gone as a Member of Parliament to Buchenwald and was given a piece of tattooed skin that was to have been made into a lampshade. She suggested to Tchelitchew that the Nazis' ability to look on such sufferings without pity, even with pleasure, was bound up with some sexual vice.[40] In her next letter, she wrote: 'I do think the Germans had among themselves an infectious madness. Think of the dancing madness, the religious mania of the middle ages – and how it spread like a plague.'[41] Sitwell was referring to frenzies such as occurred in Strasbourg in 1518, where about four hundred people danced, hopped and leapt into the air for days or even weeks, until many of them dropped dead.[42]

After VE Day, she asked, 'Is it possible that this devilment and hell is at an end?' She noted with sadness that the war in the Pacific continued and that her nephew Reresby, now eighteen, was about to go into the Guards as a private. Nonetheless, there was something wonderful about the costers (street vendors) of the East End of London, who, as Osbert told her, had turned out in their 'pearlies' (pearl-button finery) to salute the King at Buckingham Palace. She told Pavlik: 'Those men and the women are the real London people. The war for them has been nightly and daily bombing, in narrow streets, daily and nightly risk of death and appalling mutilation and the loss of all they possess. These they bore unflinchingly, and this has been their day, as well as the day of the Armies and Navies and Air Forces. What an unconquerable spirit.'[43]

That summer Sachie was a burden to Edith; easily depressed about money, he was positively pining for the *Stiftungs*. He also told Edith several times that he could not face reviewers and that he might never write poetry again. At a glance, this seems emotional blackmail – a way of drawing Edith to his side in quarrels with Osbert over money. Yet Sachie was in genuine turmoil. Edith was kind but unwavering: 'just look at your poor sister: has anyone ever been more torn to pieces? But I am going strong . . . *I know what we are. And I'm damned if I am going to watch you throwing yourself away.*' Soon, Sachie found a solution he could live with: he began to write poetry again but left it for the most part unpublished. When Edith died in 1964, he decided out of duty to her memory to publish his verse. By that time, reaction against the Sitwells had set in, and, unable to find a major publisher willing to take on his poems, he had no choice but to circulate them privately in pamphlets and chap-books. Astonishingly, no major selection of his later poetry appeared until 1982, when he was eighty-five. This was the poet of whom T. S. Eliot wrote in 1918: 'We have attributed more to Mr. Sitwell than to any poet of his generation.'[44]

On 10 September 1945, Edith and Osbert Sitwell were sitting in a train carriage on their way to a reading in Brighton. An article in *The Times* captured Osbert's attention and he passed it to Edith. It contained the observations, published the day before in the *New York Times*, of William Laurence, a journalist who watched the bombing of Nagasaki from an observation plane. He described the flames rising at fearful speed: 'It was no longer smoke or dust or even a cloud of fire, it was a living thing, a new species of being, born right before our incredulous eyes. At one stage of its evolution, covering millions of years in terms of seconds, the entity assumed the form of a giant square totem pole, which at its base was about three miles long, tapering off to a mile at the top. Its bottom was brown, its center was amber, its top, white. But it was a living totem pole, carved with many grotesque masks grimacing at the earth.'

Like most of the world, Edith Sitwell was still trying to understand what had happened on 6 and 9 August: 'We were sitting – ordinary human beings – doing our ordinary tasks when perhaps *the most gigantic event since the Crucifixion took place*.' She believed that to harness the power of the sun for war was blasphemy. 'But if it *would* end war, then even that horror would be in the end beneficent. How can one tell? How is one's puny mind to seize the implications?' She was contemptuous of the claim that atomic energy could create a world of leisure: 'It will only mean a non-stop hideous noise of crooning from the wireless, fresh vulgarities from the cinema, cruder and weaker and worse books. Above all, it will mean non-stop revolutions. For revolutions in many cases have sprung not only from discontent with poverty, misery and injustice, but from sheer *boredom*. And the People are going to be *bored*.'[45] She believed that the end of meaningful work (as opposed to drudgery) would be a spiritual calamity. It is on a point like this that Sitwell, the 'convinced pacifist' who thought Lenin right to speak of the separate nations of rich and poor, shows herself in some respects a Tory. What she feared in the materialism of the left was an equality of diminishment: 'How strange is the point of view that makes people believe Democracy should flatten people down, instead of pulling people up. That was *not* the point of view of Whitman, the most noble and inspired of all Democrats.'[46] And, in a theme that is usually associated with R. S. Thomas, she believed that that other materialism, science (especially atomic science), had the power to grind away at human identity, leaving a civilisation of 'grubs'.[47]

Sitwell's belief that the bomb was a blasphemy against the light derives from the Gospel of John and from her recent reading of John Donne's Sermon CXVII on Christ as light. That same sermon (mingled with passages of Coleridge and Boehme, and some lingering notions from Mitrinović) seems to have given her the idea for 'A Song of the Cold'. Donne wrote: 'To end all, we have no warmth in ourselves; it is true, but Christ came even in winter; we have no light in ourselves; it is true, but he came even in the night.'[48] Sitwell's poem is about homelessness, and so reaches back to 'Gold Coast Customs' and *I Live Under a Black Sun*:

> Here in the fashionable quarters of the city
> Cold as the universal blackness of Hell's day
> The two opposing brotherhoods are swept
> Down the black marble pavements, Lethe's river.
> First come the worlds of Misery, the small and tall Rag-Castles,
> Shut off from every other. These have no name,
> Nor friend to utter it . . . these of the extinct faces
> Are a lost civilisation, and have no possession
> But the night and day, those centuries of cold.
> Even their tears are changed now to the old
> Eternal nights of ice round the loveless head
> Of these who are lone and sexless as the Dead.[49]

First published by Lehmann in *Penguin New Writing*, 'A Song of the Cold' was the title-piece of a large selection of Sitwell's work published by Macmillan on 27 November 1945. Containing just a few poems from *Façade* and *The Sleeping Beauty*, the volume reflected Sitwell's desire to be valued for her most recent work. Generally, the critics approved; for example, Basil Taylor wrote in the *TLS* (26 January 1946): 'In the poems written during the war years has come the major poetry of which she has always seemed capable. Her technique has matured, until she is now in command of all those intricacies of language with which she formerly experimented. The result is a music, not so immediately exciting, perhaps, but in fact infinitely more subtle and flexible.'

Sitwell had deliberately not sent a copy of her new book to the *Listener* because of earlier negative reviews; nonetheless, a review was published, dwelling on several faults in her poetry before offering an extraordinary assessment: 'But after all, one must admit that only one other woman [Sappho] has written poems of such technical variety and imaginative depth.' She then heard on the grapevine that, in Oxford, C. S. Lewis, whom she had never met, was also comparing her work to Sappho's – as had Capetanakis and Bowra before him.[50] The comparison to a poet dead for 2500 years suggests that even the most sympathetic critics did not know what to make of the fact that a woman was arguably the outstanding English-born poet of her day. Sitwell lapped it up. She did not have a classical education, so had read Sappho in translation before the First World War, but her sense of that poet would always be refracted through a passage of Swinburne's *Anactoria*, which influenced much of her later work, particularly 'The Shadow of Cain':

> on each high hill
> Clear air and wind, and under in clamorous vales
> Fierce noises of the fiery nightingales,
> Buds burning in the sudden spring like fire,
> The wan washed sand and the waves' vain desire,
> Sails seen like blown white flowers at sea, and words
> That bring tears swiftest, and long notes of birds
> Violently singing till the whole world sings –
> I Sappho shall be one with all these things . . .[51]

This particular passage was very much on her mind in the last months of 1945.

The horrors of the peace almost equalled those of war, and Sitwell was looking for terms in which to describe them. She followed the trial of Josef Kramer, the man who operated the gas chambers at Auschwitz and had been made commandant of Bergen-Belsen when the as yet unknown Anne Frank died there in March 1945. British forces, entering the camp in April, found thirteen thousand corpses on the ground, of which one in ten had been partly cannibalised. Mass burials had been going on for days, so the thirteen thousand represented only a fraction of the deaths. The living existed in a state of misery beyond imagining. Kramer's picture appeared in *The Times* on 21 April, but his cruelties became most widely known after he went on trial in September at Lüneburg with forty-four other men and women who served as guards and administrators. He and ten others were hanged on 13 December 1945.[52]

Sitwell's first approach to these events came in the uncompleted 'A Song of the Time', which in her manuscript book is marked 'Josef Kramer Monster of Belsen'. Here she returned to 'Gold Coast Customs' for imagery of the cannibal mart, which then opens into an apocalyptic vision derived from photographs from the camps:

> But see, see how like Christ the sun comes again,
> Over the Babel of the bought and sold,
> Over the cannibal mart
> To Belsen, Buchenwald, Dachau . . . Even the agony of gold
> Is silent seeing them . . . But He who walked the wave now
>   walks once more
> On the Sea of Blood – to the devastated shore
> Where the parti-coloured garments of Christ, the bodies of
>   men
> Are torn and divided . . . With their blood, their stripes, for dye.
> See how those darkened tatters lie
> Together, as if in love.[53]

Sitwell returned to this passage and made it the climax of 'The Shadow of Cain', completed around May 1946. By then, she had reshaped it, added weight to the individual lines, and made its reference to the camps (and the atomic bomb) something for readers to judge for themselves:

> . . . And the fires of your Hell shall not be quenched by the rain
> From those torn and parti-coloured garments of Christ, those rags
> That once were Men. Each wound, each stripe,
> Cries out more loudly than the voice of Cain –
> Saying 'Am I my brother's keeper?' Think! When the last
>   clamour of the Bought and Sold
> The agony of Gold
> Is hushed . . . When the last Judas-kiss
> Has died upon the cheek of the Starved Man Christ, those
>   ashes that were men
> Will rise again
> To be our Fires upon the Judgment Day!
> And yet – who dreamed that Christ has died in vain?
> He walks again on the Seas of Blood, He comes in the terrible
>   Rain.[54]

A passage of this sort brings the problem of Sitwell's achievement sharply into focus. Many of the best poets of her time agreed that she had an astounding technical skill. She was never more deft, line by line, than in 'The Shadow of Cain'. For example, in the passage above, the fifth line has twenty syllables and it should sag in the middle, but Sitwell pivots on the word 'Think!' and inserts three internal rhymes – so the line holds. Something like it occurs three lines down in the phrase 'Starved Man Christ' where three stresses secure the centre of a seventeen-syllable line. The lulling effects of the long lines are immediately offset by short lines.

Nowadays, the default opinion of Sitwell's later work (read or, more often, unread) is that she is guilty of fatal overreach. Yet in her lifetime, readers who grappled with the work often came to a very different opinion. Sir Kenneth Clark included 'The Shadow of Cain' among the fifteen to twenty poems of hers that, he claimed, stand among the century's finest,[55] just as Allen Tate undoubtedly had it in mind when he called her 'one of the great poets of the twentieth century' (New York Times, 10 December 1964).

The question is whether she would have been a better poet if she had attempted less. Her own view was that modesty and small horizons were death for a woman poet. She told Stephen Spender in March 1946: 'a woman's problem in writing poetry is different to a man's. That is why I have been such a hell of a time learning to get out my poetry. There was no one to point the way. I had to learn everything – learn, amongst other things, not to be timid. And that was one of the most difficult things of all. And I think that if I started getting the thing into very strict limits it might bear the marks of a return to timidity.'[56]

Sitwell never attempted more in a poem than she did in 'The Shadow of Cain', and it occupied her, on and off, for almost nine months. She believed quite literally that man's relation to nature had been changed by the bomb in a 'world-reversing event'[57] and that history must now be re-narrated. In a new matricide, humanity had ripped open the womb of nature, or, as she put it in a passage echoing William Laurence's account of the bomb at Nagasaki:

> We did not heed the Cloud in the Heavens shaped like the
> hand
> Of Man . . . But there came a roar as if the Sun and Earth had
> come together –
> The Sun descending and the Earth ascending
> To take its place above . . . the Primal Matter
> Was broken, the womb from which all life began.
> Then to the murdered Sun a totem pole of dust arose in
> memory of Man.[58]

It is impossible in this book to trace all the interlaced allusions in this poem, but the central narrative can be summarised briefly. It opens with a description of the world's emergence out of nothing, from Lorenz Oken's 'zero', a world that oscillates between great heat and great cold. The Biblical Fall is associated with the ice ages, when life is torn between hot-blooded and cold-blooded creatures, possessed of 'opposing famines', as reflected later in the poem in the pairings of Cain and Abel, Lazarus and Dives. Time in the poem is mythic or, in Laurence's phrase, 'covering millions of years in terms of seconds'; thus, the animal nature of earliest times looks towards August 1945:

And now the Earth lies flat beneath the shade of an iron wing.
And of what does the Pterodactyl sing –
Of what red buds in what tremendous spring?[59]

The red buds take us back to the passage from Swinburne's *Anactoria* quoted above. Sitwell describes a deluge with effects like the bomb, and it sweeps away the comfortable but heedless city of Cain. The oceans of the world are left as a hollow place where Lazarus appears. He represents, among other things, 'Life's lepers', those born with physical and mental deformity and those with a predisposition to crime. Sitwell echoes Paracelsus on how gold may cure leprosy – 'A quintessence of the disease for remedy'.[60] But then a newly sprung wheat-ear, also gold, threatens Dives with his fate: '"The same as Adam, the same as Cain, the same as Sodom, the same as Judas."' And, as we have seen, the poem ends with a vision of Christ coming in vengeance, coming 'in the terrible Rain'.[61]

In a strange contrast to the largeness of her poetry, Sitwell now dreaded a return to confinement in her private life. Throughout 1945, she had been putting off a reunion with Evelyn Wiel, fearing the request that she come and live in rue Saint-Dominique again. When John Lehmann went to Paris in August 1945, she asked him to check on Evelyn and explained some of the situation to him:

> having had to leave home owing to my mother's conduct and habits, I had great charges of honour and gratitude, and so have had, in the past, and still have, to pay out a part of my income. But I have the house in Bath, (a present) and I have an allowance, and I can earn money. And I never, never mention the charges I have spoken of, because it is so terribly painful to the helpless, generous and noble-minded person concerned, – and was to the one who is now dead. I should have been lost if it had not been for them . . . Evelyn Wiel is one of the most wonderful women I know. (I lived in the flat before the war, and she looked after me like a mother. She is the sister of my dear Helen Rootham, who brought me up, and who is now dead.) . . . She has no brain in particular, but a heart of gold, and one of the most lovely natures I have ever known.[62]

Despite her cruel tongue, excessive kindness was a trap that Edith Sitwell often fell into. She told Pavlik: 'Oh, what a fool I have made of myself in the past: oddly enough, in every single case because I really tried to live a truly Christian life, helping where I could help. I never refused help, where I could give it.'[63] In late December, Evelyn Wiel came to England and stayed with Sitwell first in London and then, in January, at a hotel in Bournemouth. They had a talk about money, and Evelyn agreed to ask her brother, the solicitor Ernest Rootham, to take part of the burden from Sitwell. Having sent some money during the war, he told her he could do little more. Evelyn wrote a blistering letter, to which he responded, '"Don't write nasty letters to me. I am not quite so bad as you appear to think."'[64] Sitwell believed Ernest Rootham was a selfish swine who was perfectly happy for Evelyn's problems to fall on her. He made occasional efforts to help Evelyn, but Sitwell carried the bulk of her expenses and grew increasingly angry about the arrangement.

Evelyn's mind was wandering, and she needed attention through the day. It was a glimpse of the future. Edith wrote to Pavlik:

> What between the agony of heart and the knowledge that if I give way, and go back to the life I had before the war, *I shall never write poetry again* – I am utterly exhausted and worn out. It is horrible. She is so good – one of the best and most golden-hearted of people. And she is so devoted to me. I wouldn't hurt her for anything. But I *have* to write. . . . I *have* to be free. You see, I never was, in all my life, until the war came. Is not that a terrible thing to say? I was bound hand and foot. First by my frightful mother, and then afterwards by affection, pity, and duty. I really am in some ways a very bad nature, and I feel I have been sacrificed enough. And then, having said that, I feel cruel.[65]

Sitwell's guilt over Evelyn Wiel was then compounded by a train ride to Southampton with three badly burnt airmen, one of whom had lost his nose and lips and yet did not complain: 'What woman could ever be worthy to love him?'[66]

Sitwell was annoyed that Lincoln Kirstein had tried to bring Choura to the United States to live with Pavlik. She saw it as a case of a good person doing an 'appallingly wicked' thing while remaining certain of his own virtue – as the dying Helen had done in making Edith promise to go on living in the flat with Evelyn. Pavlik's case was hardly parallel to Edith's, but she believed it was: 'And in the past someone who was truly fond of me, and who examined the conscience *most* carefully, did that same thing to me, – but no doubt under the semi-belief it was doing me a kindness. So only the *thing* is wicked – not the intention. And only the intention counts with God, I am sure. But the act, sometimes, is pretty hard to bear if we are only human.'[67]

Knowing of her worries about Evelyn, Pavlik decided to be encouraging so he launched into a broken rhapsody over her achievements. He said he detected mystery and a 'note of joy' in her writings of the last year,

> not earthly one, but universal joy of having joined the road that goes straight to eternity. It is a final overtaking of all other thoughts of all feelings by the one of unearthly heavenly love and tenderness and goodness . . . After many years of long hard road for your fragile supersensitif heart, supersensitif brain – a golden door had appear itself slowly but definitly. When one reaches that door – it means eternity, it means the one thing doing[?] in the church – eternal glory, glory to person, but impersonal glory in itself . . . I am so glad that you see that door getting more and more oppen and the wonders it will revel to you are beyond guessing and beyond description.[68]

The biographer can add nothing to this, except, perhaps, *sic*.

Sitwell was undoubtedly touched by what he said, but his cheerful talk about a door may have taken on a nightmarish quality in her mind, or the image may have reappeared simply by coincidence. In one of her notebooks, we find this passage:

> When they reached the open door,
> The Fate said 'My feet ache . . .'
> The Wanderers said 'Our hearts ache . . .'

There was great lightning
In flashes coming over the floor . . .
The whiteness of Bread, the whiteness of the Dead,
The whiteness of the Claw –
All this coming to us in lightning through the open door . . .

It is marked 'Note: written on the very verge of sleep'.[69] With slight modifications it was incorporated into 'The Shadow of Cain'. Pavlik thought that the visionary door was golden and would open to glory. What Sitwell saw through the door was the light of destruction.

20

AN OLD MAD FACE

I think that, in some way, I offended you, through some thoughtless, irresponsible written or spoken word, on some occasion, those nine or ten years back . . . May I say, now, as I know I should have said many years before, how sorry and, inarticulately, more than that, I am . . . If my apology, true as my love of your Song of the Cold, reads to you as stiltedly as, quickly writing, it sounds to me, I'm sorry again and can only say how hard I find it to move naturally into the long silence between now and nine beautiful, dreadful years ago.[1]

Dylan Thomas had just read Edith Sitwell's review of his *Deaths and Entrances*. Not long after Helen's death in 1938, she gave up on him because of his disappearing acts. She did not like the poetry he produced in the late 1930s, but she continued to hope that he would mature. Now, especially in 'Fern Hill', his poem about a Welsh childhood, she could see that he was living up to his promise. He came to luncheon at the Sesame on 11 April 1946 and seems to have maintained the demeanour of a penitent. The other guests were Louis MacNeice and his wife Hedli (an actress and singer). Louis MacNeice's first book *Blind Fireworks* (1929) was influenced by Edith Sitwell, and he made no secret of the fact – even to Geoffrey Grigson.[2] Thomas appears to have allowed MacNeice to carry the conversation, as Sitwell pressed for information on yet another 'scientific horror', the lobotomising of the mentally ill.[3] It was at this luncheon, or one soon after, that Dylan Thomas expressed a strong preference for her recent work: 'You have only been a great poet during the last six years.'[4]

All three took part in a poetry recital at the Wigmore Hall on the afternoon of 14 May. John Masefield presided in a programme that also included T. S. Eliot, Edith Evans, John Gielgud, C. Day Lewis, Walter de la Mare, and Flora Robson. The Queen, Princess Elizabeth, and Princess Margaret were in the audience, and the whole affair was, in Sitwell's view, elegant and dull:

> Then, suddenly, on to the stage tramped – there is no other word for it – Dylan. A strange figure – short, powerful looking, and as broad as he is high, dressed in highly unsuitable clothes four sizes too large for him: violently checked trousers which looked as if they were done up with string, a bright turquoise blue coat and a collar and tie that were springing from their moorings . . . Dylan then, slowly and in a dark voice that seemed to come from the very centre of the earth and the beginnings of life, recited The Tyger. His short figure and ugly inspired face with its eyes like pebbles, short thick nose, thick lips, were forgotten. I think everyone knew that they were listening to one of the greatest works of Man, spoken by a very great poet. He might have been Blake himself.[5]

His wife Caitlin made a rather different impression. According to Denys Kilham Roberts (a solicitor who ran the Society of Authors), she somehow got behind the Queen and, unpresented, asked, 'I say, – do *you* like this? I don't. I think I shall ask for my money back,' and then dropped cigarette ash on the Queen's dress. Back at the Sesame, where Sitwell held a dinner party for a group of fifteen, Caitlin needed the help of Sitwell and Betty Kilham Roberts to get up the stairs: 'Mother of God, dear, *must* we be moving?' As the dinner was about to start, Georgia Sitwell said to the guests: 'Oh there is a woman in the cloak-room more *roaringly* drunk than anyone I have ever seen in my life.' Dylan Thomas answered grimly, 'That will be my wife.'

Thomas went on to castigate Eliot for allowing F. R. Leavis to talk about 'Dislodging Milton' from the canon. Then he asked about his work at Faber & Faber: 'why does a poet like you publish such *awful* poetry. *You know* it is bad.'

Caitlin took a fancy to Sacheverell, but when she spilt some ice cream on her bare arm she demanded that John Hayward, whom she had never met before, lick it off. He refused, so she repeated her demand. Hayward said he would lick it off any part of her body anywhere else, but *not* in the dining room of the Sesame Club. Caitlin answered, 'The insults of Men! You great pansy. What for are you sitting in that throne, and twisting your arms like that?' They made some sort of truce, and at the end of the meal she sat stroking his wrist and calling him 'Old Ugly'. Other guests were not amused. Sitwell felt herself 'suddenly transfixed by two blue *lightnings* from John Lehmann's eyes . . . I am sure lightnings on Judgment Day will be just like that.'[6]

That summer Sitwell was exchanging transatlantic favours with Charles Henri Ford. He appointed her an advisory editor of his magazine *View*, and under its imprint he was set to publish the American edition of *Green Song*. In London, she began hawking around his manuscript 'Sleep in a Nest of Flames', but her agent David Higham thought that with paper shortages no publisher would want a long collection of poems from a little-known author, so she gently persuaded Ford to make cuts.[7] Even so, the manuscript went from firm to firm for over a year, until she had to tell him it could not be published in England.[8] The book, with a foreword by Sitwell, was eventually published in the United States by James Laughlin of New Directions in 1949.

As she was always a performer in letters and conversation, it was part of Edith Sitwell's schtick to lament the number of unpublished writers who sent their manuscripts to her. In fact, she regarded the search for talent as part of her own vocation as a poet, and there turned out to be some of it in the village. The novelist and poet Paul West (b.1930), who went on to great success in the United States, grew up in Renishaw, and around 1946 he sought out Edith Sitwell to judge a poetry competition. He had heard in the village that she slept in a coffin, talked to ghosts, and could burn your eyes out with her stare.[9] She tackled him about his plans for university:

> At once she engaged the future for me, spelling out answers to questions I had never intended asking. She read my superego like a book, insisting that of course I should try for Oxford, where they trained prime ministers and taught you how to drink brandy and get plump, whereas Cambridge was for those awful scientists or boffins, backroom boys, who wanted to blow the world up. She mentioned *The Shadow of Cain*, which I had actually read. 'Oxford,' she said

mesmerizingly, 'will make you reach beyond yourself and be something in this world, the other place will stand you, dear boy, at a microscope and send you blind. I never attended a university myself. My nose was so hideous they decided to keep me out of sight in the hall cupboard. At least until some doctor, not a Nazi, made me presentable and straightened my dear old Plantagenet schnoz. You take those exams, and don't let me catch you not doing well. Tell them you know me and that I have taught you to appreciate poetry.'

'Well, you have, Miss.' I had read her extraordinary patient look at the texture of Alexander Pope, a most unusual book for its period, with all the virtues of F. R. Leavis's close reading without his moral bigotry.

She was shocked, yet stubbornly gratified.

'No science, young you.'

'No, ma'am. I promise. I can't count anyway.'

'*Oxford.*'

'Oxford, ma'am, if I can.'

'Of course you can. If you don't, they'll hear from me. There are some awfully nasty people in the literary profession, young you, and they are going to hear from *me*, vulgarly known as getting it in the neck.'[10]

At the risk of stating the obvious, West's encounter with Sitwell is entirely typical of her; her snobbery was real but extremely porous. A person of talent could walk right through it.

At the beginning of September 1946, Edith Sitwell went to London for the release of *Fanfare for Elizabeth*, a short book for a popular audience about the early life of Elizabeth I. The subject resonated for her: Elizabeth was an unwanted child who achieved greatness, if not love. Sitwell had worked on it from time to time for about five years. Back in 1942, she had written to Tchelitchew about her research:

One can get no *personal* comfort, but I do get a kind of *world* comfort, – I mean, hope for the world's future, from reading the history of the time of Henry the Eighth. I realise from this, that humanity has always been subject to these appalling and gigantic moral illnesses and fevers. In the time of Henry VIII, definitely, nobody was

quite sane. Then it was a religious malady, now it is the insanity of
political creeds, which will go to any length, and sacrifice anything,
just as the two religious maladies of the time of Henry, sacrificed
everything . . . at that time it must have been natural to think the
whole world was sinking into chaos, with the appalling disasters
which were sweeping Europe . . . But then everything passed, and the
world became, for a time, comparatively sane again.[11]

The book sold nineteen thousand copies within three weeks of its
release,[12] and by January 1947 she had begun a sequel.

After hearing Constant Lambert recite *Façade* on 9 September 1946
at the Lyric Theatre, Hammersmith, Sitwell went with Evelyn Wiel for
a fortnight to the Branksome Towers Hotel in Bournemouth. A pattern
was being established that allowed her to spend time with Evelyn two
or three times each year without going to the flat in Paris. Against all
the odds, Evelyn had been trying to pull her weight by teaching
English, but she was in no shape to work: 'She registers *nothing*, is very
deaf, and has lost her memory entirely. She has the nature of a saint –
all the old tiresomeness and inferiority complex has gone.'[13]

Having been effectively released from her promise to live in Paris,
Sitwell was able to press on with her career, which now included broadcasting. The BBC's Third Programme was launched on 29 September
1946 with a mission to broadcast the classical repertoire in music and
drama and, insofar as possible, literature and the other arts.[14] It later
became Radio 3. A natural choice, Edith Sitwell was the subject of
three broadcasts in October and November, with Dylan Thomas reciting some of her work. In the first two broadcasts, the poet and critic
Henry Reed, now remembered mainly for the sequence 'Lessons of the
War', and 'Chard Whitlow', his parody of T. S. Eliot, discussed her
poetry. The first broadcast on 26 October consisted of readings and
observations on her early and late manners. In the second broadcast,
on 16 November, Reed said that he wanted to provide 'a balanced esti-
mate of her work. It has, I think, incomparable virtues; it has also some
limitations. I want to look at both these things.' He found the early
poems amusing, if sometimes over-decorated: 'You have to be rather a
dull dog never to enjoy them. But one is always waiting for them to
stop and for the real poem to begin.'

Reed then quoted one of Sitwell's odd remarks (doubtless arising from her years as a pianist) on the relation between women's physical strength and the acquisition of technique in poetry. Surprisingly, Reed did not disagree with her: 'I should be the last to suggest that a man poet was by nature, automatically, and without effort, a good technician; I'd dare to say, however, that a woman poet was by nature a worse technician; just as women prose writers tend to be less grammatical than men. Women's sensitiveness lies elsewhere; to divert part of it to the acquisition of formal excellence is one of the tasks which women writers have to face.' He then posed a question about her later poems: 'Here is a poet, you say, who has every sign of being on a large scale . . . Lyrical, rhapsodical, at times cryptic and sibylline, the music pours out, praising or lamenting. And then, a certain doubt . . . The great music seems to be repeating itself too often and at too long a stretch.' He suggested that she was one of those romantic writers 'who don't know their own strength'.[15]

In her response broadcast on 2 December, Sitwell said that she had changed her view somewhat over the years: 'Technique *is* very largely a matter of physique. But I no longer speak of "men poets" and "women poets" . . . and, although I have a profound dislike of masculinity in women, in private life, I am at the same time extremely displeased if anyone refers to me as a woman poet.' She was expressing the same discomfort that Graham Greene later claimed when called a 'Catholic novelist' rather than a novelist who happened to be a Catholic. As for whether she was repeating herself, she could say only that she believed otherwise and that she was her own sternest critic: 'I throw away reams of verse.'[16]

In January 1945, Sitwell had said to Tchelitchew that she was hoping to write 'a new kind of poetry, soon. One with practically no images, very "muscled".'[17] By this she meant a poetry that worked chiefly by sound, texture, syntax, and rhythm – an experiment in something near to pure form. In the early 1940s, she had stripped her imagery down to a handful of symbols such as wheat, sunlight, bone, deluge, precious stones, leprosy, and gold, and she made repeated use of the figures of Cain, Dives, Lazarus, and the returning Christ. The problem was that these could appear in only so many permutations before they became predictable – an effect she tried to offset by quoting or echoing offbeat works, usually of a visionary character. Sitwell's poetry after 'The Shadow of Cain' continues to explore possibilities of sound and texture, but the reader has a more distracting sense of images and phrases being repeated. Some poems do break new ground, but more rarely than in the 1920s and the early 1940s.

Meanwhile, Geoffrey Grigson broke new ground in critical vituperation: he wrote in *Polemic* of the 'idiot romance' of Sitwell's work, and hinted that her success was the work of a 'black militia' of reviewers. Sixty-five years later, what stands out in Grigson's article is his repeated use of the word 'frigidities' to characterise lines of her poetry. Although the term had appeared occasionally in earlier criticism, it was a misogynistic cheap shot when applied to a woman poet. Grigson also seized on one of Sitwell's descriptions of an unborn child and called it 'the horrible embryo (which could only have been contrived by a poet who had never experienced pregnancy)'. He faulted her for 'untruths to nature' and insinuated that her supposed failure as a poet proceeded from sexual inadequacy and childlessness.[18] Although Grigson is often regarded as a tough-minded truth-teller, it seems that in this article he inadvertently revealed something about his own thinking. His kind of close observation stands, partly, on a hidden foundation of ideas about sex, gender, and perception. Indeed, the 'nature' that the poet was meant to observe was, at least to a degree, a masculine imagining that posed as plain fact. That Grigson supported some women poets who wrote as he preferred does not really answer this objection to his criticism, especially as he was one of those most responsible for the eventual demolition of the reputation of the outstanding woman poet of the time.

Sitwell did not say what among all this most offended her, but she was prepared to launch a libel suit – and on this occasion it might have been a useful gesture on behalf of women writers generally.[19] John Piper, a friend of both writers, tried to broker a truce. Sitwell resented Piper's meddling but had to submit since Osbert needed him to illustrate his memoirs. Holding her nose, she exchanged letters with Grigson in December, agreeing that they should not criticise each other in print. Before long Grigson was criticising her work again without actually naming her.

In the midst of this tangle, she listened on 2 December to the third broadcast about her work, in which Dylan Thomas recited 'The Shadow of Cain'. She told Pavlik: 'His reading is one of the most transcendentally great things imaginable, and last night he exceeded himself. It was terrible, and it was great. Every possible means was used. And hearing it, I felt – well, perhaps I need not bother, really, about all the little Grigsons and worms of that sort.'[20] Sitwell was now calling Dylan Thomas her 'spiritual son'.[21]

With the war over, Sitwell spent a good deal of time in London, and was steadily making new friends. Peace also made it possible to travel abroad, so in January 1947 she obtained a new passport. It described her eyes as grey and her hair as brown. Although she was often said to be considerably over six feet tall, her height was given as five feet, eleven inches.[22] Her first journey was mainly for business. Osbert had to see lawyers and accountants in Switzerland in order to settle Sir George's estate. Travelling with David Horner, they arrived at the Grand Hotel in Locarno on 19 January and stayed until 7 March; they went on to Lausanne for a week before returning to London on 15 March. While in Switzerland, Edith composed a lecture to be delivered on her return, as well as her presidential address to the League Against Cruel Sports.

In Switzerland, she read some works by Jean-Paul Sartre. She admired the play *Huis-clos* (*No Exit*), but found that Sartre lacked the visionary depth she looked for in a writer: 'He is *cleverness* itself: but there is *not one* drop of genius in the whole of his composition. He has an enormous inventive power. But there seems to be no connection between the real world or the world of the spirit, and that invention.'[23] More important for her was a reading of Carl Gustav Jung's *The Psychology of the Unconscious*. She wrote to Pavlik:

I think Jung is a writer, often, of great nobility and beauty, although all psycho-analysts seem to me slightly cuckoo. I think it was H. G. Wells who said in conversation that all that might be true about Viennese Jews, but it wasn't true about him. And I thoroughly agree with him. But Freud and Jung seem to have had most unpleasant patients, and personally I don't think it was much use curing them on the outside. They would continue hopelessly and crawlingly unwholesome inside. And all these insinuations upset every human

relation. I don't believe little girls have sexual feelings about their
fathers, or little boys about their mothers. But that, of course, is more
Freud's way of seeing things than Jung's.[24]

It is not surprising that she became more and more enthusiastic about
Jung, whose views on archetypes dovetailed with her own approach to
poetic imagery.

Sitwell and Tchelitchew had been writing to each other now for
about twenty years, and Tchelitchew was wondering what should
become of their correspondence. He declared in September 1946 that
their letters must remain private and never be printed, but by January
he had changed his mind, telling Sitwell he would write in his will that
they might be published thirty-five years after his death. Sitwell was a
bit startled by his decision, but eventually agreed with it. In April, he
wrote: 'I wish I could see and talk to you – but frankly to say your letters are of such value to my mind to myself that I really couldn't have
more physical sensation even when I will see you, so much of you is in
every line – free frank and simply stated.'[25] At the risk of over-analysing
a compliment, it seems that Tchelitchew saw the letters as erotic but
safe; Sitwell's language was naked yet it made no claims on his own
body. Nearly sixty, Sitwell might well have married him if asked, and she
told him again and again that she was easier to get along with than she
had been back in Paris: 'I shall never get the wisdom I long for, but I am
not, perhaps, the fool I was.'[26] These hints played on his mind and soon
caused a great deal of trouble. In May, she suggested that Tchelitchew
go to Zurich to be analysed by Jung, and it is a pity that he did not do
so, as he was on the verge of one of his periods of deep irrationality.

As Edith Sitwell's reputation grew in the 1940s, there was interest
in her relationship with Yeats. His widow, Georgie Yeats, wrote to her:
'I remember the great stimulus he got from his deep admiration of your
work and the affection he felt for yourself personally. Perhaps you did
not know that. When he had met you he always talked for days about
you and your own exciting conversation. By "exciting" I mean exciting in his own sense. You encouraged him and gave him new ideas and
approaches. Your chapter in "Aspects of Modern Poetry" especially.'[27]
It is strange to think that Yeats, who so influenced Sitwell, was also
influenced by her.

At Georgie Yeats's suggestion, Sitwell met in December 1946 with Richard Ellmann who was writing his biography of Yeats. Although Sitwell could see that Ellmann was a man of ability, she felt that Mrs Yeats did not understand what he was doing; she thought it 'disgusting' that he was so concerned with whether or not Yeats had had sex with Maud Gonne. Indeed, at this point she reveals her ambivalence about Jews. She was ferociously opposed to any persecution of or discrimination against Jews, but on a personal level found Jewishness inscrutable: '[Ellmann] is a Jew and therefore has a kind of *mental* sexual mania (Freud, after all, was a Jew. And I am certain that some Jews *do* have those odd kinks – manias for their mothers, and so forth. But I *don't* think it is normal in races which are not Jewish, – that sort of in-turning mania). They – the Jews – always fuss more about sex than anybody else.'[28]

In June 1946, Sir Kenneth Clark had asked Edith Sitwell for a chronology of her poems. She wrote to him at length and with typical inaccuracies about time and place, but it gave him something to work with.[29] His article was published a year later, and it made much of the connection with Yeats. She responded:

> It was so strange, reading what you said about 'The Poet Laments the Coming of Old Age', – the phrase 'It is almost impossible to read the last two lines except in an Irish accent.' – Actually, when I wrote the poem, I had been thinking about Mr. Yeats, and things he had said to me once about a foolish wisdom – not particularly significant in themselves, but opening out on to a horizon. The 'Poor Young Simpleton' poem was a come-back to Vanessa and Stella – only a boy was speaking instead of a woman, in order to fit the second part of the poem. *Through* 'I Live Under a Black Sun' I exteriorised, and learnt everything, almost, that I could learn, excepting technically.[30]

Clark's essay appeared in an issue of *Horizon* (July 1947) dedicated to the Sitwells. The editor Cyril Connolly wrote that 'during the darkest years of the war they managed not only to produce their best work, to grow enormously in stature but to find time to be of immense help to others . . . and so this number . . . is wholeheartedly dedicated to them.' Of course, Connolly praised Edith Sitwell's work in the most

extraordinary ways while she lived but after her death reduced his esti-
mate sharply. Sachie thought this a piece of trimming.[31]

Edith Sitwell spent the summer of 1947 at Renishaw. For a poet who
created fantastical worlds and symbolic landscapes, the preceding seven
years had deepened her attachment to the actual but no less mysterious terrain of Derbyshire and Yorkshire. She wrote to Pavlik at the end
of August:

> Last night I went for a motor drive, with Osbert, over the wonderful
> moors. I cannot tell you the beauty of the shape of those infinite
> spaces, infinite stretches, long lines of calm and of distance. The
> moon was very strange, like a veiled weeping woman. In Wilde's
> awful work 'Salome' somebody or other said 'The Moon is like a
> veiled woman.' And when I was seventeen, I thought, 'This is impres-
> sive, but it isn't true.' But last night, I saw it for myself. A mist had
> gathered in a long line beneath the Moon, faintly over it, and above
> it . . . so that it was like a veiled woman with outstretched arms.[32]

A few days later, she went south to spend five weeks with Evelyn,
and they split their time, as usual, between London and Bournemouth.
In London, Sitwell discussed with the American poet Diana Reeve the
possibility of a reading and lecture tour of the United States, to be organised by the Colston Leigh Agency. Reeve contacted her cousin the
philanthropist Ralph Lowell, who invited Edith and Osbert to give the
Lowell Lectures in Boston. Pavlik was delighted by the idea of the tour,
but Edith hesitated on the grounds that she could take only five pounds
out of the country and would need a new wardrobe. An expert at finding patrons, Pavlik went to one of New York's most philanthropic
families and had everything arranged by the late winter. Vincent Astor's
wife Minnie and his sister Alice Pleydell-Bouverie agreed to bankroll a
visit by Edith and Osbert Sitwell. They could provide accommodation
at the St Regis Hotel and deduct any losses from income tax as a dona-
tion for 'cultural relations'. The Astors had had contact with Sachie a
few years earlier, and were evidently interested in the Sitwells.[33] On 8
January 1948, Edith sent a cable to Pavlik confirming that she, Osbert,
and David Horner were coming for several weeks in October, and asking
him to 'prepare the ground' for readings at the Museum of Modern Art.

She contacted Professor Theodore Spencer to set up appearances at Harvard and Wellesley College. Sachie was not included in the plan, which led to a new quarrel, with Georgia complaining that Osbert and Edith were 'skimming the cream off the milk'.[34]

Through the autumn of 1947, Edith Sitwell was putting together a selection of the writings of William Blake. However, she abandoned the book because she felt overmatched by Northrop Frye, the Canadian scholar whose *Fearful Symmetry: A Study of William Blake* she reviewed for the *Spectator* in October. She wrote a fan letter to Frye and sent him a copy of 'The Shadow of Cain'. He wrote back:

> Thank you very much for *The Shadow of Cain*, a very lovely, haunting, and almost unbelievably suggestive poem. The apparently effortless way in which a contemporary situation expands, by way of certain human archetypes, into its ultimate values of primeval cold and unquenchable life, makes the poem a kind of miniature epic. I know by this time what to look for in major poetry, and I always find it. Reversing the axiom, when I find what satisfies me in a poem I know that it is major, and *The Shadow of Cain* belongs to the restricted canon of major poetry. The close connection between your mind and Blake's, which has become so striking in recent years, is an additional and personal reason for my liking it, not because I want all poetry to be 'Blakean', but because you are one of the few poets who confirm the authenticity of the experience I went through in submitting myself to Blake's influence.[35]

Like Jung, Frye offered Sitwell a theoretical justification for a poetry that was visionary and archetypal, and through 1948 Sitwell recommended Frye's work to almost every writer she knew.

Jack Lindsay, although hardly in Northrop Frye's league, was an influential Marxist critic from Australia. He became absorbed in Sitwell's work, and she regarded him, at least for a time, as a 'seer' in criticism.[36] She invited him and his wife Ann to lunch at the Sesame on 24 March 1948, and was astounded by the number of craters in his face, 'as though he had once been a volcano!' But she liked him immediately.[37] In July, he sent her his essay 'The Latest Poems of Edith Sitwell', which gave a leftward spin to her writing.[38] She wrote to him:

'Your understanding is the most extraordinary I know. I am amazed always by its depth, its sweep, and its comprehensiveness. Because every overtone is seized – not only the foundations and what Jung (I think) called "the suns from below the horizon" . . . this great illumination and belief is as much needed by my creative self, as water is by a plant, and sun is by a plant.' She paid him the extraordinary compliment of asking permission to read from his essay in one of her broadcasts as a better account of the meaning of 'The Shadow of Cain' than she could give herself.[39] Lindsay thought that for Sitwell there was no great contradiction between Christianity and Marxism,[40] but she may have led him on somewhat and told him what he wanted to hear. In any event, they became friends, despite Sitwell's occasional outbursts over his requests that she read books and manuscripts that excited him but caused eye-strain for her.

Perhaps prompted by her exchanges with Frye and Lindsay, Sitwell wrote to Tchelitchew on 15 May: 'People pay no heed to symbols. If they *did*, they would regard them as warnings, as lights, as signposts, and men would be wiser.' She went on to describe a symbol that her poetry shared with Sachie's:

A Gold Man occurs frequently in my poetry. And a great many people talk a great deal of nonsense about this. Actually, in a field somewhere near Sachie's house, a man clothed in gold armour was dug up (when we were children). He had obviously been killed in battle. Would not that haunt the memory of anyone? Both Sachie and I are haunted by it. And to this is added the memory of the finding of the Tombs of the Atridae – and of how for one moment the finder – a dull German – saw the face of Agamemnon and the gold by which he was surrounded – and then everything vanished – into dust – into air.[41]

Sitwell's longing for symbols with an ultimate validity was drawing her closer to Catholicism. That spring she read a number of novels and essays by François Mauriac and Léon Bloy. She found somewhat vulgar Bloy's notion that it is better to suffer with the poor than to create great art. She later described him for a new protégé, the Catholic poet and novelist Tom Clarkson, as 'A furious man of genius, loving God but hating his fellow men'.[42] Alec Guinness recalled that for a time she was

Sitwell meets Marilyn Monroe in Hollywood in January 1953: 'her face was . . . strangely, prophetically, tragic, like the face of a beautiful ghost . . .'

Eyes that do not meet: Edith, Sacheverell, and Osbert Sitwell photographed by 'Baron', c.1937. By this time the brothers were becoming estranged.

Sitwell trusted Siegfried Sassoon to criticise her new poetry in the 1920s and 1930s: 'you are the only person who has ever done anything at all for my poetry'.

A boozing, brawling South African poet, Roy Campbell became Sitwell's godfather when she entered the Catholic Church in 1955.

Dylan Thomas: Sitwell was his first great promoter and called him her 'spiritual son'.

Stephen Spender believed Sitwell a brilliant and original poet, and he became a close friend from 1942. He is seen here in a portrait by Robert Buhler (1939).

The painter Walter Sickert befriended Sitwell c.1906. They shared an interest in serial killers.

Virginia Woolf was a close friend, but Sitwell gradually lost interest in her work and dubbed her 'a beautiful little knitter'.

'Come to Rapallo, and my wife and I will Lay Hands Upon You': Sitwell thought Yeats the greatest of modern poets, but found his religious ideas bizarre.

Gertrude Stein: '. . . her figure looks like that of a German hausfrau, or perhaps a head-mistress; but she has a superb face, with sensitive modelling. And she seems full of rich, earthy, Schumannesque life . . .'

Marianne Moore believed that Sitwell's war poetry spoke 'as a living being might, and you are penetrated with the meaning – as if Yeats' golden bird of Byzance suddenly actually *sang*, stood in the middle of his poem and sang'.

Edith Sitwell wrote her best poetry at Renishaw Hall during the Second World War. Here she sits in the chilly drawing room in 1945.

© Bill Brandt Archive

Sitwell stopped sitting for Wyndham Lewis when he made a pass at her, so her famous portrait (1923–35) has no hands. He took revenge on her in his *roman-à-clef*, *The Apes of God* (1930), which portrayed her as a lesbian.

The genial but absent-minded Roger Fry was one of Sitwell's early friends among the Bloomsbury circle. He painted this portrait of her in 1918.

From the 1920s Edith Sitwell adopted 'gothic' dress. In this 1927 portrait by C. R. W. Nevinson, she wears a veiled hat resembling a wimple.

An Australian painter living in France, Stella Bowen became a close friend of both Sitwell and Tchelitchew, executing this portrait of Sitwell between 1927 and 1929.

Tchelitchew's pastel of Sitwell (1935) was lost in Paris for almost thirty years. After it had been recovered and exhibited in 1964, the dying Sitwell had it hung opposite her bed, where she could see it at all times.

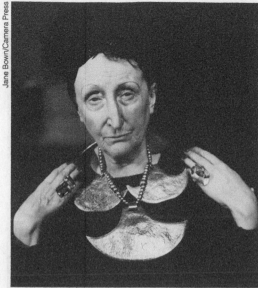

Sitwell's 'Aztec' collar, designed by Millicent Rogers, often clanked as she moved.

A photograph from Sitwell's last session with Cecil Beaton in 1962. Note the rings: Sitwell had a passion for amethysts, aquamarines and amber.

Edith Sitwell was Cecil Beaton's favourite subject. In 1927 he photographed her as a regal corpse, laid out under a spray of lilies.

'obsessed' and gave him as a birthday present a book about Bloy. In Guinness's view, this author touched Sitwell's compassionate nature.[43] Closer to home was Graham Greene; in 1945, she had written to him: 'I said before, but I repeat it, what a great priest you would have made. But you are better as you are.'[44] In May 1948, she read *The Heart of the Matter* and wrote to David Horner (himself a convert to Catholicism): 'Have you read Graham Greene's new book? It may prevent me from committing suicide!!'[45]

At the centre of a new group of friendships was the South African poet William Plomer. Sitwell had known him since 1929, but the two had grown closer during the war as they were both friends of Lehmann and Capetanakis. Plomer visited Renishaw at the beginning of September 1944, and became a frequent guest at the Sesame. When suffering from neuritis in April 1945, Sitwell was comforted to receive a letter from him: 'It arrived at a moment when I was considering cutting my throat with my left hand because I couldn't use my right hand sufficiently to do any work. But I changed my mind immediately, though I still write with an uncertain hand, as you can see.'[46]

Plomer introduced Sitwell to Lilian Bowes Lyon, whom he had once thought of marrying. She suffered from diabetes and Buerger's disease, an autoimmune condition that damages the circulatory system. Sitwell described her for Pavlik on 21 May 1948: 'I have to go and see a poor woman who was kicked by a hysteric in the slums (where she was working) during one of the air raids – and who, as a result has had to have both legs taken off – and *may* have to have both arms off!! It gave her an exceedingly rare disease. Her name is Lilian Bowes Lyon: she is a cousin of the Queen. She is a saint, and writes, for a woman, quite fair poetry. (I *don't* consider myself a woman when I write poetry).'[47] Peter Alexander tells us that the sequence of amputations owing to gangrene was toes, feet, legs below the knee and then below the hip.[48] Allergies made it impossible for her to take painkillers. Sitwell wrote letters of comfort to both Plomer and Bowes Lyon through the next year. One of Bowes Lyon's last letters was to Sitwell on 12 July 1949: 'So Edith, I did try hard to die, three times I had to put off *in case* someone's feelings got hurt, & even now I am tethered by tiny dim little threads I haven't fully honoured until now the question arises, of whether to break them & at last stop being racked – but *hurt* the dim "others" or

to let the grey little threads hold me & let the pain increase.'[49] Two
weeks later, she died at the age of fifty-three (*The Times*, 26 July 1949).

Another of Plomer's friends, Ian Fleming, the Bond creator, made a
clumsy entrance into Edith Sitwell's world in December 1947. At a
luncheon for Osbert who had just won the *Sunday Times* book prize for
Laughter in the Next Room, Fleming told Sitwell that he was amused at
Plomer placing 'The Shadow of Cain' first on a list of admired contemporary works. Sitwell bit her tongue but then complained to Plomer,[50]
who persuaded him to write a letter of apology. An improbable friendship developed between Sitwell and Fleming, centred on their shared
interest in Jung and Paracelsus. By June, they were talking of collabo-
rating on a book (never actually written) about poets and mystics.
Fleming sent her a translation he had made of Jung's speech at the birthplace of Paracelsus; Sitwell copied out sections of it and sent them to
Pavlik. She was seized by Jung's comments on modern science's approach
to the 'Paracelsian concept of spiritually animated matter', and she found
Jung's remarks on Paracelsus 'enthralling': '"As, unprejudiced, he accu-
mulated the kernels of surface experience, so did he create the
philosophic basis of his work from amongst the primitive shadows of the
soul." (Is that not what we should do? Indeed, what we *do*?)'[51]

Greene, Plomer, Bowes Lyon, and Fleming belonged to Sitwell's net-
work of friends in London. She was also developing new connections
across the ocean. Among the younger poets Edith Sitwell most admired
was the Filipino, José Garcia Villa, who spent much of his life in New
York. In the late summer of 1944, he sent her a copy of his collection
Have Come, Am Here. Not knowing the author, she approached it with
a sinking feeling but soon decided she liked his work very much. He
had a cummings-like taste for verbal experiments, such as inserting a
comma after each word. This was not what interested Sitwell, as she
told John Lehmann: 'You know I think José Villa a really fine poet. I,
too, think his *experiments* are bosh, – especially the comma one.'[52] She
encouraged Villa, and around 1945 he decided to dedicate an issue of
his journal *Viva* to her. He solicited essays from various critics but first
found himself stymied by the paper shortage, then simply mislaid some
of the contributions. Finally, Charlie Ford intervened and brought in
James Laughlin to publish *A Celebration for Edith Sitwell* in advance of
the reading and lecture tour. For some time, Sitwell had distrusted

Laughlin. Dylan Thomas had reported back to her Laughlin's gossip about her supposed lesbianism. He visited her at Renishaw in mid-July, spoke well of Charlie's poetry, and conducted himself pleasantly. Sitwell decided that Thomas was simply wrong. To her mind, Laughlin was 'a perfectly decent and honourable person'.[53]

Sitwell's growing reputation in Britain was contributing to a problem that would greet her when she arrived in New York. At the end of 1947, she wrote to Pavlik, 'Did I tell you that on the 7th of May, I shall be no longer *Miss* Sitwell, but *Doctor* Sitwell? I am being given an honorary degree of Doctor of Letters (Litt.D.) and shall from then onwards call myself and be called Dr. Sitwell, in order to keep the nasty little boys who are still attacking me in order.'[54] The degree from Leeds was organised by the critic and anthologist, Professor Bonamy Dobrée, a friend of Herbert Read's. In February, she learnt of a second doctorate coming her way, this one from Durham, which would make her 'Dr. Dr. Sitwell' or 'Double Doctor Sitwell'.[55] She decided to style herself 'Miss Edith Sitwell, D. Litt., Litt. D.', but also used 'Miss Edith Sitwell, D. Litt., D. Litt.', and after a further award from Oxford in 1951, 'Miss Edith Sitwell, D. Litt., D. Litt., D.Litt.'. Always regretting her odd education, she was thrilled by this recognition from the universities, but she knew what she was doing was funny. William Plomer said in early 1948 that if she was to become a doctor he would register with her under the National Health Service, and she answered: 'Yes, do become one of my patients. The great thing would be, I should always advise my patients to do exactly as they like – which would result in an almost immediate cure.'[56] She brandished her doctorates at the pipsqueakery, but her last two, from Sheffield in 1955 and Hull in 1963, did not matter so much as she was by then Dame Edith Sitwell.

At first, Pavlik was pleased for Sitwell, and addressed her as 'My dearest futur [sic] doctor',[57] and he continued to congratulate her through the spring. However, he was brooding, complaining about his state of mind and of a lack of recognition – he was at the time one of the more fashionable artists in New York. Sitwell could see that the doctorates were beginning to bother him, so she wrote that it was sad there was no doctor of painting as there was a doctor of letters, as he should surely be awarded such a degree: 'But are the crowds – the huge crowds – that pass by your pictures – not *more* honouring than a Doctorate? I think so.'[58]

Edith Sitwell in the 1950s: one dame and several doctors

Tchelitchew was envious and perhaps a little bored by Sitwell's doctoral glee, although the problem lay deeper than that.

With Sitwell's arrival in New York now fixed for October 1948, Tchelitchew was spooked by her expectations of him and by the approach of his fiftieth birthday on 21 September. These pressures contributed to a new episode of what several of his friends believed was mental illness. In his journal, Charlie Ford noted at the time that Pavlik was in a continual panic over money; he claimed there was no friendship in America and called Charlie a 'parasite'. On another occasion he looked in a mirror and was terrified of a face that was mad and old.[59] Early in the summer, he protested to Edith that while visiting New York John Lehmann had not gone to see his large canvas *Hide and Seek* – his usual touchiness was growing more acute.[60] He spoke of a veil of melancholy over his mind, and there were signs of paranoia.

She did her best to console him but failed to see the danger on the horizon: 'Dear Pavlik, how wonderful it is to think that in only just over four months, I shall be seeing you, sitting beside you and talking, and seeing your pictures . . . The excitement and happiness will be almost too much.'[61] By 25 September, she was clearly aware that something was wrong: 'But oh me! You *are* not pursued by mocking laughter, any longer. You are a great painter! . . . Keep absolutely firm, in your heart.'[62]

21

THE OTHER SIDE OF THE WORLD

'Women are happier when they're fucked,' mused Pavel Tchelitchew one evening shortly before Edith Sitwell's arrival in New York. Charles Henri Ford replied, 'So are men.'[1] Pavlik did not want to break down the wall between his rackety world and that other world of myths and symbols where he and Edith were courtly lovers. After years of paper and ink, he would now have to deal with her bodily presence, and he supposed she would pressure him for sex. And he was not pleased that the critics thought more of her than they did of him.

Twelve hours late because of a rough crossing, the *Queen Elizabeth*, with its 2246 passengers, docked in New York at 7.50 p.m. on 21 October 1948 (*New York Times*, 22 October 1948). Minnie Astor's chauffeur brought Pavlik and Charlie to Pier 90, West 50th Street, and gave them dock passes indicating they were to meet 'Mr. Oscar Sitwell and daughter'. After much confusion they found Edith, who was by now relying on a walking stick. They embraced and kissed her, and gathered up the sixteen pieces of luggage she and Osbert had brought – among them extra copies of her new book *A Notebook on William Shakespeare*, for which an officious customs inspector demanded eighty-five cents in duty. A dockside reporter lobbed questions at Osbert, who offered up bland comments on how the last twenty or thirty years had been a great time for his country's writers.

The next night, Alice Pleydell-Bouverie gave a dinner for the Sitwells at the St Regis. Among the guests were Tchelitchew and Ford, Lady Ribblesdale (Pleydell-Bouverie's mother), Monroe Wheeler of the Museum of Modern Art, Mary Rockefeller (first wife of Nelson Rockefeller), and Lincoln and Fidelma Kirstein. Edith Sitwell was wearing a dress made of black and white material that Tchelitchew had sent to her in advance of the visit. The cloth symbolised the bee-priestess who figures in some of Sitwell's poems, and he had advised her that her wardrobe should follow a medieval theme. However, when he saw the dress, he thought the tailoring was awful and could not conceal his annoyance. When they said goodnight, Sitwell was crying because she had had little chance to speak with him.

The next day he went to the St Regis for lunch with the Sitwells prior to taking them to see his great work *Hide and Seek* (or *Cache-Cache*). As often happened after the mid-1940s, Sitwell was suffering from lumbago; she could not make the outing to the Museum of Modern Art. She appeared at lunch in a red turban. Tchelitchew thought that it was too 'fixed' and that the ones she used to make herself were better – but he did not say this to her. Elizabeth Bowen once famously referred to Edith Sitwell as a high altar on the move; that effect was largely contrived by Tchelitchew who designed much of Sitwell's wardrobe and regarded her appearance as one of his artworks. Trying to be cheerful, Sitwell gave him and Charlie a dozen Liberty silk ties before the two men took Osbert to see the picture.[2]

As soon as she was well, she went with Pavlik to see *Hide and Seek*. Painted between 1940 and 1942, Pavlik had often written to her about it, and he sent her one of the preparatory sketches, which she treasured. Yet no small sketch or photograph can convey the strange complexity of this 6'6" x 7'1" oil painting. Beginning with *Phenomena* as his Inferno, Tchelitchew planned to work through the cycle of Dante; *Hide and Seek* was his Purgatorio; he did not produce a Paradiso. *Hide and Seek* follows his usual technique of melding bodies and landscapes. Here, the central image is a tree, composed mainly of the bodies of many infants, whose eyes are generally turned towards some point within or beyond the tree. Most of them are gazing into a cave or a vagina, at the front of which stands a small figure with its arms spread and a butterfly to its right. The tree is phallic, and the whole work is a labyrinth, from which, Parker Tyler tells us, escape is symbolised by birds in the upper left-hand corner.[3]

Tchelitchew expected an immediate outpouring of wonder, but Sitwell stood silent before this painting. Whatever she eventually said was insufficient, and he took offence. When she spoke of this picture in future, it was always as a masterpiece, but it is possible that, at first, she was bothered by it. For example, the puzzle aspect, not evident in small reproductions, can strike one, straight off, as too clever. When it was displayed at the City Museum of New York in 2009, one visitor took her first look at all the small crowded bodies and asked, 'Where's Wally?'[4] The painting has an extraordinary inner life, but that becomes evident only after one has looked at it for some time. Sitwell wrote to Tchelitchew on the day following her visit: 'It is happy, to me, to be writing to you, because, writing being my natural form of expression, I can produce what I want to say more naturally than by speaking. I speak badly and inadequately.' Her praise of the work was unstinting: 'The beauty, the *light* in matter, is incredible. It makes everything I passed – I mean all pictures – on coming away from it, look trivial and petty, with no vision behind. I *reverence* you. How wonderful that seeking child with her companion butterfly are, plunging forward into that mysterious luminous darkness.' She continued in this vein for four pages and then asked: 'Dearest Pavlik, please let me come and sit and talk to you quite quietly, soon. What is the use of meeting amongst fools?'[5] Apparently, Pavlik was touched by this letter.[6]

But he did not want to be alone with her, and he told Ford that her admiration for his art was muddled by sexual attraction to him. He scoffed at telephone messages left by 'Dr' Sitwell. There were other scenes. In Cecil Beaton's presence he spoke of how at his studio rose-coloured light fell on the pavement below the train track, and he asked whether she thought it beautiful. Sitwell said she would need to think about it, so Pavlik began to stamp with rage.[7] Privately, he complained to Ford about the pretentiousness of her conversation and the title 'Dr Sitwell'. Parker Tyler, who witnessed some of these events, guessed that Tchelitchew was envious of her acclaim and wanted to bring her down when the rest of America seemed to be rejoicing over her.[8] He was lashing out at Ford too, comparing them both to vampires.

One evening he said to Ford, 'I don't love anybody.'

Ford asked, 'Not even me?'

'Not even myself.'

He had come to an impasse in his work, and he and Ford were soon considering a break-up.[9]

Edith and Pavlik had a dinner by themselves on 15 November, after which he told Ford that Edith regarded him only as 'a living cock in front of her'. He said that she had sat like 'a big white worm', and that she was entirely selfish.[10] Pavlik wrote to her the next day: 'I know you think a lot of bitter things of myself and my behaviour. Are you sure that in your life I myself am really an idea, instead of a reality?'[11] – doubtless a fair question, one he might have also asked of himself about his view of Sitwell. He explained to Ford a little later that by 'selfish' he meant seeking glory for herself – he was plainly not used to Edith upstaging him. He then compared the two Sitwells to 'piles of shit'.[12] Nevertheless, he was conscious of his mind not being right; he described his depression to Sitwell and sought her comfort. She wrote on 21 November: 'I was so happy to get your letter – to know, at least, that a part of that terrible darkness that was over you on the night when I dined with you is, though not dissipated, at least less possessive. I have thought of nothing else.'[13] However, she had to watch her step. It appears that on 8 December someone claimed that Tchelitchew's work was morbid, and he blamed Sitwell for not speaking up. She wrote: 'I was too overcome, yesterday, to try to speak . . . I write with the utmost humility to the sublime artist who has shown those secrets [of life]. Why, nobody should be afraid of death, seeing this persistence of life, this transcendental flowering, this lily-stem of the bone, ineffably strong and undying.'[14]

And yet, apart from her Russian problems, Edith Sitwell's visit to the United States was a triumph. *A Celebration for Edith Sitwell* came out on the day of her arrival, followed shortly by the Vanguard Press edition of *The Song of the Cold*, which included the companion poems to 'The Shadow of Cain': 'Dirge for the New Sunrise' and 'The Canticle of the Rose'. On 25 October, she and Osbert held a press conference for twenty reporters at Colston Leigh's office on Fifth Avenue. About the early performances of *Façade*, she said, 'Even when I make a joke it is from a deep conviction. Who would purposely try to annoy the public?' Osbert cut in, 'I would . . . Frequently.' He said he was afraid to enter the shops in New York because there would be no stopping him. He needed some good fountain pens but had discovered that it was not necessary to buy them since after a day of book-signing he usually had two more than when he began (*New York Times*, 26 October 1948). Wyndham Lewis saw press photographs of the Sitwells on tour and remarked: 'She has changed since the days when I painted her portrait. She now has become a Van Eyck.'[15]

When the novelist Glenway Wescott (Wheeler's lover and an acquaintance of Edith Sitwell since 1923) remarked on her patience with reporters, photographers, and socialites, she said, 'Walt Whitman is my patron saint. I took a vow not to lose my temper in this country.'[16] However, on other occasions, he saw that she was 'hypersensitive and irritable'. He told John Pearson that when he saw her one morning at the St Regis, she said, 'I can't stand myself. I'm so ugly. All I want is for somebody to put his head in my mouth and I will bite it off.'[17]

On 8 November, Edith and Osbert held a joint reading at the Town Hall. Edith appeared in a black dress and red cape, wearing what she called her 'Lady Macbeths' – her silver necklace and bracelets. She read clearly and dramatically, and afterwards Pavlik went backstage to congratulate her. She remarked glumly that she would probably not see him again as he was avoiding her.[18] The reading was followed by a luncheon in the Sitwells' honour attended by five hundred people at the Waldorf-Astoria, at which there was a formal debate among various writers and artists including James Michener, the novelist, and Edward Weeks, editor of the *Atlantic Monthly*, on whether 'something valuable and lasting would come out of the confusion of the contemporary age'. At the end, Edith Sitwell proposed that it was time once again for the poet to walk hand in hand with the priest (*New York Times*, 9 and 21 November 1948).

The Song of the Cold was released on 9 November, and was the occasion of 'the party to end all parties', as the proprietor Frances Stelloff described it, at the Gotham Book Mart: 'the darndest assortment of celebrities, freaks, refugees from Park Lane, "and the lifted-pinkie set" crowded the shop so I couldn't make my way from the tea table to the alcove where Miss Sitwell sat – pining for a cup of tea'.[19] The picture appeared in a celebratory article on the Sitwells in *Life* magazine in December.

On their tour, the Sitwells ranged north to Buffalo, Toronto, and Hamilton, south to Washington and Lynchburg, and west to Kansas City – with sell-outs at every stop. On 20 December in Boston, she was, as she told Minnie Astor, confronted after a reading by a psychiatrist who wondered why she wrote about Christ rather than the dignity of man: 'I said "Isn't Christ good enough for you? Surely he *is* the dignity of man. And what do you want me to put my trust in, – the atomic bomb?" I then bowed from the waist, and said I feared I was keeping him from his friends.'[20] For Sitwell, the Second World War had shown that secular humanism was a dead-end and that the real human narrative was of sin and redemption. Over Christmas, Edith and Osbert remained in Boston, which she thought like an 'English Cathedral city'. Harvard was 'beautiful' even though everything was closed. Christmas morning brought a curious tableau: 'A large owl has gone to live in a courtyard, and in the morning, the courtyard is one huge graveyard of the bones of mice.'[21]

Just before Christmas, Sitwell received a copy of Denton Welch's new book *Brave and Cruel, and Other Stories*, which she thought his 'infinitely best' work, but then heard from Welch's friend, the philosopher and biographer Maurice Cranston, that he had died on 30 December. Sitwell wrote back: 'I shall never forget him. Dear, living young creature, who would have done so much.'[22]

Sitwell was back in New York on 2 January for a dinner with Pavlik, who afterwards told Charlie that he had delivered a lecture on the subject of humility.[23] On a couple of occasions, Sitwell met with Marianne Moore, laying the groundwork for a pleasant friendship. The Sitwells were Igor Stravinsky's guests at a concert he conducted at the Town Hall.[24] Through Alice Pleydell-Bouverie, Sitwell met Truman Capote; the following August he wrote to Sitwell from Tangier where he was 'writing a novel with one hand and fanning myself with the other' and recalled their meeting as 'fun'. He then asked her to be a referee for his application for a Guggenheim fellowship.[25]

On 5 January 1950, Charlie Ford brought Jean Cocteau, who was also staying at the St Regis, to have lunch with her. Tchelitchew was there, as was Monroe Wheeler, who told John Pearson that Sitwell did not enjoy sharing public attention with Cocteau while in New York. Cocteau dominated the conversation until it turned to the film of *Joan of Arc*, then in production. He remarked that the French did not really like Joan of Arc. Sitwell piped up that her ancestors had been responsible for burning her.[26]

The climax of the tour was a performance of *Façade* at the Museum of Modern Art on 19 January. The event was organised by Wheeler with the encouragement of Josephine Crane, a trustee of the museum

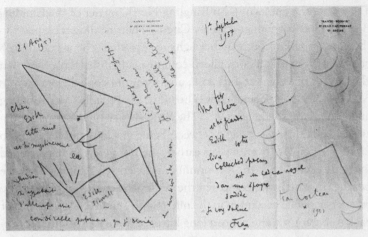

For many years a friend and admirer, Jean Cocteau sent these drawings to Sitwell in the summer of 1957. The second paid tribute to her recently published *Collected Poems*

who took a particular interest in the Sitwells. Tchelitchew disliked Crane, a senator's widow, and it is said that one of Sitwell's quarrels with Tchelitchew occurred at her apartment at 820 Fifth Avenue.[27] Still, *Façade* was another sell-out. Frederick Prausnitz conducted a six-piece orchestra drawn from the Juilliard School. Edith Sitwell was the main reciter, leaving one poem for David Horner to read. The musicians and reciters remained in the fourth-floor projection room, speaking into microphones. In the auditorium the crowd saw two projected images, switched for the second half of the programme, of hair, bone, and open mouths – these were designed by Esteban Frances, a Spanish artist recommended by Tchelitchew.[28] According to Philip Hamburger of the *New Yorker*, Sitwell appeared at the end of the performance, 'looking just about the most elegant woman of our time. She was wearing a great, golden something over her shoulders – a perfect complement to that monumental face, which is certainly one of the marvels of the world.'[29] Columbia Records followed up the performance with two records released in May. After the concert, one woman told Osbert, 'I feel so happy. Just like a bird in a cage.'[30]

At the end of January, the Sitwells went to the resort town of Sarasota in south-west Florida, a place recommended by Charlie Ford.

They were the guests of John Ringling North, owner of the Ringling
Brothers and Barnum and Bailey Circus. Their reading took place in
the Ringling Mansion, which sought to reproduce the air of a doge's
palace, with marble floors, gilded columns, a high balcony, Venetian
glass, acres of velvet and damask, and furniture copied from various
periods and styles. Someone was heard to say proudly, 'Mrs Ringling
made that lampshade herself.'[31] The Sitwells were given a tour of the
circus, and Edith was caught between being gracious and speaking up
for her principles. Twenty years earlier, she had given an impassioned
speech in support of the Performing and Captive Animals Defence
League, in which she compared the treatment of the animals to the
practice of public execution in the nineteenth century.[32] When she got
back to New York, she wrote a long letter of thanks to North, promising to try to return to Sarasota every year, but she also put in a plea for
a huge gorilla who was the star of the circus:

> I do beg of you to stop an imitation snake being put into Gargantua's
> cage. I really beg you to. It is terrible to think of that poor creature
> being terrified, and you have such kindness to all the animals that they
> obviously are devoted to you, and I *know* you would never allow
> Gargantua to be frightened. Only one gets so used to a thing if one is
> near it every day, that one sometimes doesn't realize it. It is dreadful
> to think of what those moments must mean to him. I felt so sad about
> the state of gorillas. I think nature punishes them for being born.[33]

Glenway Wescott organised Edith Sitwell's election as an honorary associate of the National Institute of Arts and Letters; an obvious
choice, she received 116 of a possible 125 votes.[34] The other foreign-
ers elected were the artists Pablo Picasso and Yasuo Kuniyoshi, and the
composers Ralph Vaughan Williams and Gian Francesco Malipiero.
Sitwell and Kuniyoshi were fêted at a dinner party at the Knicker-
bocker Club on 19 February. Apparently in a panic over an address
she had to make there, she suddenly felt inspired at 4.30 a.m. the day
before, and was able to write a talk on Blake and Whitman, which
opened with the remark that she and her brother had been so well
received in America that 'for the remainder of our lives we shall think
of this country as our second home'.[35]

Tchelitchew watched Sitwell's triumphs with increasing irritation, and his comments in mid-February reveal a strange mingling of appetites for domination and for sex. He said that Edith was a great poet, but often an unpleasant person and an idiot: 'She wants a cock in her cunt.' Evidently he gave some thought to this question, as shortly afterwards he found it necessary to explain to Ford that he was physically disgusted by her heavy body – she had been slim when he met her.[36] He told Ford that she was not sufficiently feminine, by which, according to Parker Tyler, he meant she should be more passive. He said on 18 February that she had been ungrateful to him: 'she has neither intelligence nor heart. I'd like to tell her so and slap her face and have her kneel at my feet and kiss my hand and crawl like a worm.'[37]

There followed a large farewell dinner at Voisin's restaurant, attended by Kirstein, Auden, and others. Tchelitchew delivered a public scolding, declaring that whatever she said about his genius, she did not really look at his pictures.

Before leaving New York, she tried to talk with Pavlik about his anger, but succeeded only in provoking him further. She wrote from the *Queen Elizabeth* on 15 March 1949: 'This is just to send you my love, and to tell you I shall be, all my life, the devoted and loyal friend I have been to you for over twenty years – twenty years in which your troubles have been my troubles, and your happiness and triumph my happiness and triumph . . . I would not, for worlds, have done anything to annoy you, that last day. All I tried to do was to put something right between us. Instead of which, by some foolish clumsiness, I made everything askew.' At the end of the letter, she said she would not disturb him by writing to him.[38]

In a letter of 24 March, Pavlik observed that she promised always to be his friend, yet would no longer write to him. He told her, 'you expect more than I can give', and 'don't be surprised to know that people equally laughed at your work here.' He told her she had ignored his female friends, among them the novelist Mary McCarthy and the harpsichordist Sylvia Marlowe. He claimed that her recording of *Façade* came about because he had put her in touch with an executive of Columbia Records – although it was actually organised by Monroe Wheeler. In a sweeping way, he accused her of putting her interest before his.[39]

She received the letter on the afternoon of 28 March, and took
seven days to draft and redraft her reply, trying to find a dignified tone.
She answered his various claims and asked:

> Do you really think I do not realise what you and Charlie have done
> for my work? I do not know how else I am to express my gratitude
> than in the way I have expressed it, over and over again. Osbert and
> I know that we owe it entirely to you that we came to America. Do
> you think we should ever forget that? . . . Would it really give you so
> much pleasure if my next book got bad reviews in America? Would
> it really? Never once, have I put myself before you, or thought of
> myself first.
>
> Lastly, you are wrong in thinking you have to make our personal
> relations clear to me. It is quite unnecessary. I have neither the right
> nor the wish to make any claims upon your time. I have made no
> claims of any kind at all. I have no wish to intrude upon, or disturb,
> either you or your great work.
>
> It was quite unnecessary, as well as a little unkind, to tell me that
> 'You have no idea what I went through while you were in New York.'
>
> I had indeed!
>
> Well, I have gone away now, to the other side of the world. I still
> send you my love, although you did not send yours to me.
>
> Edith[40]

Edith Sitwell had not particularly liked Mary McCarthy when introduced to her, but the younger writer did her a favour. Unprompted, she
took Tchelitchew to task for his treatment of Sitwell. His next letter
was amicable – or perhaps just less bloody-minded – and he mentioned
his conversation with McCarthy. On 22 April, Sitwell wrote, 'We will
most certainly *never*, after this letter, refer again to what has happened.'
She wanted an end of quarrels and spoke of McCarthy as 'a woman
possessing a real heart and kindness'. In that letter, she praised her
new friend the engineer and writer Lancelot Law Whyte, whom she
believed had 'one of the most important minds of any man alive'. She
was reading his book, *The Unitary Principle in Physics and Biology*, and
she believed it could be of use to Pavlik's work: 'He is wonderful on
the subject of the development of form and its relation to mental

processes.'[41] She was trying to steer the conversation back to the sort of topics she and Pavlik had always had in common.

Why bother? A reasonable person would say she should have nothing more to do with him, but Tchelitchew was Sitwell's great love and, despite the abuse, she was going to hang on to the relationship. Moreover, she felt an obligation to his genius. Perhaps she also recognised a point that her biographer and readers of this book must affirm: if Tchelitchew was suffering a flare-up of mental illness, he was not entirely responsible for what he said and did. He certainly deserves a new biography himself, and such a book would need to consider this question carefully. Nevertheless, the American journey left Sitwell with wounds that did not heal and marks the beginning of her own psychological decline. She explained to Rosamond Lehmann on 18 June what she had been going through: 'the days drifted on in a kind of mist, hopelessly. If people dug me out, wrote to me, or telephoned, I would drift towards them. But my own feeling made it appear to me that if they didn't, it meant they didn't want to see me. All my confidence in the possibility of gaining affection and friendship had gone. And I didn't want to inflict my own deadness on other people; they have troubles of their own.'[42]

Charlie Ford's father had died recently, so both he and Pavlik needed a change of scene. They decided to go to Paris to see Choura, and to Italy to see the Argentine painter Leonor Fini. Sitwell maintained the polite fiction that Pavlik's problems were chiefly physical and that a holiday would do him good. Although he suffered from colitis and a gall-bladder condition, he really needed the care of a psychiatrist. According to his letter of 14 May, he was looking to voodoo and witchcraft: 'I wish to see a very good soothsayer or fortune-teller to tell me what is the matter with me', and added that he had no love left for anyone.[43] By June, he was talking of dying. Edith wrote: 'Dearest Pavlik don't – don't – speak about that longer journey. No. You are wanted too much, and are too dear to everyone.'[44]

It took an effort for her to go to London on 11 May for rehearsals of Humphrey Searle's setting of 'Gold Coast Customs', with a performance at Broadcasting House the following week. Two reciters were required: Edith Sitwell took the female part and Constant Lambert the male. The music was performed by a full orchestra and a male choir.[45]

Sitwell thought the work itself 'sublime' and described Searle as 'an odd young man, exceedingly shy, and with an occasional really terrifying twitch. It doesn't come on all the time, but only sometimes, and when it does I jump violently. He is very nice and courteous, and quite mute. The latter I think a good thing, as he may be left in peace to get on with his work.'[46]

Anything American could cheer her up. She was editing *The American Genius*, an anthology published by John Lehmann in February 1951. Captivated by the writing of Robert Lowell, she singled out 'The Ghost' from *Lord Weary's Castle* (1946) as having 'a force, a despair, a wretchedness that is really great'.[47] That summer she was visited by Alice Pleydell-Bouverie, Minnie Astor, and Minnie's sister, Betsey Whitney, whose husband Jock became American ambassador to the Court of St James's. They all urged her to waste no time getting back to the United States. Osbert told Edith that there was every chance of arranging another tour in the autumn of 1950. This was great news, not least because the first tour had brought her a net profit of £1332.[48] She asked him to take Sachie and Georgia too, but he refused, saying: 'How *like* them, to get at you when I was away!'[49] While she understood that they could not go about like 'a troupe of acrobats', as she put it for Geoffrey Gorer, she was nevertheless anxious for Sachie at least to make a separate tour of the United States, something he finally did in late 1952.[50] However, there were several rows about his being left behind in 1950.

The Canticle of the Rose, a 288-page selection of Sitwell's poems, came out on 20 September. At sixty-two, she was widely regarded as one of the best poets writing in English. All her life, Sitwell had been touchy about reviews, but private humiliation now sharpened the need for public praise. Good reviews were rarely good enough, and even mild criticisms were devastating. She was annoyed when the *Times Literary Supplement* (30 September 1949) gave a joint review to her book of poems and Villa's book of essays, so that her poems got about a third of a page of discussion – an unreasonable complaint since Villa's book was about her poems. The unsigned review was written by Alan Pryce-Jones, a thoughtful critic of Sitwell's work, who observed: 'It is the peculiar strength of Dr. Sitwell to convince [us] that . . . extreme statements are valid. Absence, loneliness, heartache – the ordinary sources of poetic tears – count less for her than the plight of man.' He was making the point, pursued elsewhere in the review, that Sitwell, for all her emotional force, is never sentimental. Sitwell commented in her journal: 'The critic ought not to spoil me.'[51]

Wanting a warrior on her side, she soon found one. Sitwell had known the hard-drinking South African poet Roy Campbell since about 1920, when she met him in the company of William Walton, but she later came to distrust him as a friend of Wyndham Lewis. Peter Alexander tells us that, in the Spanish Civil War, Campbell toured the Front by car on 1 July 1937 and afterwards claimed to have fought for Franco.[52] His sequence *The Flowering Rifle* (1939) is the best-known English work taking the Nationalist side. In 1946, Faber & Faber published his *Talking Bronco*, which included satiric poems about 'MacSpaunday', a composite of MacNeice, Spender, Auden, and Day Lewis. As his publisher, T. S. Eliot suggested softening aspects of the book but made this revealing remark: 'Of course I have the additional reason for never expressing an opinion about any modern poetry, that I am a publisher, and therefore not in a position to do so: but even if I wasn't, I should think twice about it, because if I said exactly what I think about a good deal of it, it would simply be put about that I was jealous and didn't want any younger men to be successful.'[53] Evidently, despite publishing some of their most important works, Eliot's private view of the 1930s poets was not far off Campbell's – or Sitwell's, for that matter. Edith Sitwell was now friends with three of those younger poets; Auden himself still annoyed her, but she behaved pleasantly towards him for tactical reasons. When *Talking Bronco* came out, she wrote to Natasha Spender that she thought it an 'outrage', underlining the word four times.[54]

In April 1949, Roy Campbell went to a poetry reading where he punched Stephen Spender lightly on the nose. With blood trickling, Spender urged the crowd to be calm: 'He is a great poet; he is a great poet. We must try to understand.' Spender had spoken of him repeatedly as a Fascist, although, according to Peter Alexander, Campbell did not have strong political views, just a distaste for leftist humbug and a desire for comradeship.[55] That summer, he went on a new campaign against the Auden group, writing 'Moo, Moo or Ye Olde New Awarenesse', a review of Geoffrey Grigson's anthology *Poetry of the*

Present, in which he said that Grigson's relation to the muses was that 'of a cuckold at his own key-hole'. As soon as Sitwell heard that it was being published in *Poetry Review*, she sent a telegram – 'very urgent' – to its editor, her old protégé and Campbell's sidekick, John Gawsworth (Terence Fytton Armstrong), ordering three dozen copies.[56] By virtue of a fist fight in 1946, Campbell and Louis MacNeice had become friends and drinking companions. However, many of Sitwell's other friends loathed Campbell, among them Rosamond Lehmann who was then in a relationship with C. Day-Lewis. Undeterred, Sitwell invited Roy and Mary Campbell to the Sesame in August. At another party that year, Alexander tells us, 'he knelt at her feet, kissed her hand, and announced solemnly, "Edith my darling, you are a great lady! I will be your knight and fight your battles for you!"'[57]

Battles were at hand. Sitwell wrote to Tchelitchew on 23 September:

There has been a fracas. Roy Campbell, having begged Grigson to try hitting him (but Mr. G somehow didn't feel quite like it) sighted Grigson outside Broadcasting House (where they are both producers) went up to him, took him by the sleeve, called two of the commissionaires as witnesses, led Grigson into the tea-room where the B.B.C. boys have their morning coffee (it was crowded), took off Grigson's spectacles, put them in his pocket, shook him violently, and then slapped his face over and over again.[58]

When reprimanded by the head of the BBC, Campbell said he had done it 'from a chivalrous motive'. While this was the version of the story that Sitwell liked, it is more probable that Campbell only menaced Grigson with his walking stick.[59] She denied asking Campbell to fight Grigson, but when reproached by William Plomer, she said, 'I am sorry that you are not pleased that this man was slapped for insulting me.'[60] She was certainly egging Campbell on.[61] However, she did have to rein him in over Stephen Spender, prompting him to write back: 'I am very sorry indeed about having gone too far in my feud with Spender . . . My acrimony was partly due to being reduced to earn my living by waiting and the fact that my agents tell me that the impossibility of getting my work published in U.S.A. is due to unceasing propaganda against me in all S.S.'s lectures. But I agree that it is unchristian to go on badgering him.'[62]

Despite being a pacifist, Edith had always liked the idea of a man who could fight; it had been part of her attraction to the gallant Siegfried Sassoon and the 'champion of all weights' Álvaro de Guevara. After her troubles with Tchelitchew, she was pining for a little chivalry. Above all, she thought Campbell a superb poet and particularly admired his poem 'To a Pet Cobra'. He became one of her closest friends and eventually her godfather.

Away from this quirky Camelot, Sitwell worked with Peter Watson through the summer of 1949 to organise an exhibition for Tchelitchew at the Hanover Gallery. He was to arrive on 3 October but finally decided he was too ill to leave Paris. For the first three weeks of September, Sitwell was pinned down by a visit from Evelyn Wiel, but still she sent out a three-line whip among her friends to fill the gallery. She was helped by Sachie, who 'is in a very sweet and good mood, more sweet than I have seen him for years, because he is happy, writing poetry again'. Five paintings were sold on the first day, and she judged it a success.[63]

An exhibition for Tchelitchew was bound to attract attention and support, yet, at the same time, Sitwell took on a harder challenge by promoting the works of someone entirely unknown. Lewis Thompson was born in Fulham in 1909 and as an adolescent fell in love with the mystical writings of the East. In 1932, he went to India and lived for years as a mendicant, carrying all he owned in a box. From 1944 to 1947, he worked as librarian and writer-in-residence at a school in Benares, of which the nominal head was Krishnamurti. Then for two years he was supported by one of Gandhi's friends. Always in poor health, he suffered sunstroke in June 1949 and was found wandering by the Ganges. He developed a high fever, and one of the last things he did was to write a letter to Edith Sitwell before dying on 24 June 1949. That letter was lost, but the Swiss explorer Ella Maillart, who described herself as Thompson's best friend, sought Sitwell's advice about his manuscripts around the beginning of October.[64]

Knowing nothing of this poetical holy man, Sitwell agreed, out of politeness, to read the poems that another of Thompson's friends, the translator Deben Bhattacharya, sent to her in November. She wrote to

Sachie: 'poor Mr Lewis Thompson – (whose poems I was swearing about having to read) – is a magnificent poet! I couldn't believe my eyes!! It is the first time that has ever happened. He is unequal. But my goodness, good when at his best!'[65] She wrote of him to Pavlik: 'How strange and tragic and fatalistic it is that he should have died of sun-stroke. It has almost a mythological quality. I was sent his photograph – with black staring eyes.'[66] She tried to interest Daniel Macmillan (and doubtless others) in publishing a book of Thompson's work but failed.[67] The best she could do was to include some of his work in *The Atlantic Book of British and American Poetry* (1958), including 'Black Angel', which opens:

> One day that black and shining angel who
> Haunted my nights in Arles and at Ajmeer,
> Monster of beauty loud with cruel gems,
> I shall encounter in some lane at noon
> Where painted demons have struck dumb the walls.[68]

It was presumably in Sitwell's anthology that Lawrence Durrell found this poem: 'I have read "The Black Angel" and would give five years of my life to have written it. If Thompson wrote other poems as explosive and majestic as this one, he would rank amongst the greatest spiritual poets in English. And not just of this Godforsaken century, either.'[69] A mixture of the visionary and the homoerotic, most of Thompson's poems remained unpublished for half a century, until Richard Lannoy edited a collection in 2001 and gave it the title *Black Sun*.

The American edition of *The Canticle of the Rose* came out in December and was greeted by a twenty-one-gun salute in the *New York Herald Tribune* (18 December 1949). Under the headline, 'Edith Sitwell's Steady Growth to Great Poetic Art', Katherine Anne Porter wrote that Sitwell's work was 'the true flowering branch springing fresh from the old, unkillable roots of English poetry, with the range, variety, depth, fearlessness, the passion and elegance of great art'. Sitwell wrote to thank Porter and to praise her most famous work set in the influenza outbreak of 1918: 'There is no living prose writer for whom I have a greater admiration and living feeling . . . I shall never forget the first time I read 'Pale Horse, Pale Rider' – to me one of the greatest of short stories, as it must be to everyone. It was an extraordinary experience, living through that strange hallucination . . . I had just been nursing a dying friend, going through her deliriums with her, and I know the appalling exactitude of fever that you produced.'[70] The two met later in New York, and Porter remained a friend for the rest of Sitwell's life.

Edith Sitwell's political opinions seem to sprawl over the ideological spectrum. Her writing can be seen as symbolic, ethical, mythological, and theological, but it does not openly endorse any particular platform, nor do we know much about how she voted. Jack Lindsay made an effort to read her works as consistent with Marxism, but he probably gave too little weight to Sitwell's sense that the materialism of the left sought equality by diminishment. The post-war nationalisation of coal mines erased a portion of the Sitwells' family history, yet Osbert was paid compensation.[71] Edith thought the ensuing coal shortage of 1947 a sign of the incompetence of Manny Shinwell, the Minister of Fuel and Power.[72] Although Osbert had often spoken ill of Churchill, he was now disgusted that Attlee had decided to develop an English hydrogen bomb,[73] an opinion Edith must have shared. In the election of 23 February 1950, Labour's majority was sharply reduced; they lost power altogether in the election of 1951. As the results were announced in 1950 she kept seven pages of tallies in her notebook (beside a draft of 'A Song of the Dust') and concluded: 'Anyhow they have lost 81 seats and we have gained 65.' This means that she voted Tory.

That winter Sitwell suffered from synovitis – a painful condition of the joints, for which she continued to receive massage in Chesterfield. She was plagued by insomnia and a permanent headache, and her oculist considered but did not perform operations on both eyelids to relieve eye-strain. In the meantime, she fussed endlessly over Tchelitchew's health. For example, she sent him a gift of three hot-water bottles, which sorted oddly with another gift at the same time of a multivolume set of the works of the Swedish scientist, philosopher, and mystic Emanuel Swedenborg.

In mid-April 1950, Edith Sitwell made her first journey to Montegufoni in a dozen years. The *castello* had had a remarkable war. From 1942, it became the main storehouse of pictures from the Uffizi and Pitti galleries and from churches and museums in Tuscany. It was chosen because it was remote and because it had doors and windows tall enough for the larger paintings to pass through. Uccello's *Battle of San Romano*, Cimabue's *Virgin Enthroned*, Giotto's great *Madonna*, and Botticelli's *Primavera* were all stored there. At one point, the *castello* also housed two thousand refugees, and at other times had garrisoned soldiers of various armies, including a group of Germans who used a circular Ghirlandaio from the Uffizi, face upwards, as a table-top.[74]

Pavlik and Charlie were then in Rome. After repeated invitations, they came on 20 May for two days. In a phrase added later to his journal account of this visit, Charlie wrote: 'All of Edith's highly plumaged, witty early poetry was like a mating call – which was never answered.'[75] Wearing a black dress and coat and a straw hat, she greeted them in the courtyard. As they drank tea in the garden, Charlie observed how her forehead was still smooth and unlined. Osbert told Charlie about a well in the castle, where a woman had drowned herself. Her husband was lowered by ropes to retrieve the body, but while her corpse was being pulled up it came loose, fell on the husband, and killed him. Charlie asked Osbert not to tell that story to Pavlik as he would fear ghosts.

Edith, trying to keep things pleasant, told them the story of her difficult trip from England to Italy. Perhaps nervous, she told the story again at dinner, adding that she was known in Pisa for the way she walked up and down wringing her hands. Afterwards, everyone went for a stroll on the terrace, but Edith slipped away. Charlie thought she was uneasy because of the way the conversation was going, or was perhaps drunk or ill. That night, Pavlik was afraid, presumably of ghosts, but may have fancied Edith might come to his bedroom. Given her personality and their recent troubles, it is hard to imagine her attempting it. Even so, he demanded that Charlie sleep in his bed. On their second day Osbert took them on a tour of the castle, including the chapel with its reliquaries full of the skulls and bones of forgotten saints – a sight that cannot have calmed Pavlik. He insisted that Charlie come to his bed for a second night. The weekend passed without Edith and Pavlik having a row.

Lincoln Kirstein was one of the very few people to whom Sitwell could talk about Tchelitchew. In a letter of 17 May 1950, he suggested

that the painter had always been insane: 'I have been submerged in letters from Pavlik; read one way, they sound like an insane megalomania,
schizophrenia, and persecution obsession. Read another way, they are
like all the letters we have always gotten from him.' He thought that
Tchelitchew's recent, very lonely, interior landscapes were exceptional.
'He seems to pay for his visions with his peace of mind, and we pay for
them indirectly by his madness, but I am inclined to think it is worth
it.'[76] To James Soby, the author of a book on Tchelitchew's art, Kirstein
expressed the gloomier view that the painter's 'megalomania has developed past most people supporting it' and that he was headed perhaps
for a schizophrenic break.[77] Hoping to relieve some of the painter's
worries, Kirstein and Sitwell set up a fund for Tchelitchew, canvassing
for donations of a thousand dollars annually from Minnie Astor,
Edward James, and others. It took a year to arrange and most of the
work was done by Kirstein, but by 1951, Tchelitchew was financially
secure.[78]

When Edith and Osbert returned to England in June 1950, Osbert's
left hand was trembling with a circular motion. A specialist told him
that he was suffering from Parkinson's disease. He was seen by a second
specialist in August who offered the more optimistic opinion that it
was merely a Parkinsonian condition and that he might be largely
unaffected for ten to fifteen years. In fact, he deteriorated quickly
and within a few years was helpless. Edith heard of the first diagnosis
just before heading to Aldeburgh for the festival recently founded by
Benjamin Britten and Peter Pears. She and William Walton performed
Façade on 22 June, and she stayed on to give a lecture (*The Times*, 24
June 1950). However, she found her appearances very difficult as she
was stricken by the news about Osbert.

Sitwell spent most of July in London with Evelyn Wiel, returning
there from Renishaw on 6 September before sailing to the United
States on the 13th. Just before boarding the ship, she received a letter
from Sachie, reproaching her and Osbert for going without him: 'I
don't know what I have ever done to let either of you down.' Edith was
irate, writing to Pavlik:

I have *never*, until I came to live at Renishaw had *anything* in my life
excepting what I made for myself, and my friendships. I was poor, I

lived in a poor cheap flat. I had to look after one old woman after
another. My holidays were always at some cheap hotel in the bleak
north of France – (or, and that was better, at Levanto). What darling Helen was *preparing* for me was, that I should have to support,
not only her and Evelyn, but also her eldest sister, whom I had seen
three times in my life, and who suffered from attacks of homicidal
mania. (Twice another sister had woken up in the middle of the
night, to find Ethel R. with her hands round her throat, trying to
strangle her!) We were all to live in a cathedral city in the north of
France, where H could show off to the priests and nuns. I was to
write bad prose books and no poetry, in order to support the household, and I was – of course – never to see anyone like myself. *That*
was the life prepared for me, and only stopped by poor H's mortal illness, and by her finding priests in Spain. S. is not rich; but he has a
most beautiful house with wonderful things in it. He and G. have
always done *everything* they wanted, – travelled, had fun. Do you
think they need grudge me this?[79]

Pavlik's abuse, Sachie's moaning, Georgia's quarrelling, Osbert's illness, Evelyn's demands, her own physical pain, tight finances, and a
steady intake of wine and gin were taking their toll. She now felt certain that most of the people she loved had either ignored her needs or
actively exploited her. Sitwell was coming to believe that life had
cheated her – that she had been 'taken care of'. She described her
voyage to the United States that September as if it were a parable of
her own survival over the years. Apparently, a hurricane blew open the
porthole of her cabin and water poured in. When it was finally closed,
a steward of thirty-seven years' experience remarked, 'By all the laws
of the sea, the whole sea ought to have been in your cabin, and everything in it washed away – including you. I can't make out why that
didn't happen.'[80]

FALLEN MAN DREAMS HE IS
FALLING UPWARD

Lincoln Kirstein could see that Edith Sitwell had star power. While he did not care for her poetry, he thought her a natural performer and wanted her to put on a show with the New York City Ballet, which he and George Balanchine had founded. Dressed as Queen Elizabeth, she would sit on a throne under a canopy and speak 'dramatic verse in a dramatic frame'. There would be a dance scene called 'The Great Seal' involving heraldic beasts, such as the lion and the unicorn. If it went ahead, Sitwell would appear four to seven times a week during the ballet season.[1]

It was important for Sitwell to try a more limited performance first. She had been reciting Shakespeare for at least twenty years – for example, at the Shakespeare and Company reading in 1932 – so Kirstein proposed that she do some scenes from *Macbeth* at the Museum of Modern Art, where she had enjoyed such a success with *Façade*. The other readers were Glenway Wescott as Macbeth, the actress Gertrude Flynn as a gentlewoman, and Bernard Savage as the doctor. Sitwell had been working on her lines since April, but her rehearsals in New York were interrupted by bronchitis. She then anxiously insisted on six full rehearsals, with lights. The performance on 16 November 1950, for the benefit of the Museum's Program Fund, pleased a friendly audience but not the critics. Wescott himself thought the visual aspect of the show more impressive than the acting; he wrote in his journal: 'George Lynes has taken a photograph of Edith Sitwell as Lady Macbeth – wearing a crown of gilt paper (cut in sharpnesses), looking down her famous nose, and frowning, with both her incomparable hands held up before his, all ten fingers pointing – which seems to me to characterize Lady Macbeth better than most of her reading (except the sleepwalking scene).'[2]

John Mason Brown wrote in the *Saturday Review* (2 December 1950): 'A lecture is one thing, a play another. The two do not mix.' From his point of view, it was 'overintellectualized': 'That Dr. Edith has an arresting voice, no one can deny. But that she has scant knowledge of how to use it dramatically seems equally incontestable. Reading with an ear for assonance rather than an eye for character, she succeeded chiefly in reducing Lady Macbeth to a lesson in prosody.' Brown's review must have stung. Since the days of the Anglo-French Poetry Society, Sitwell had prided herself on her ability to recite, and actors took her opinions seriously. John Gielgud sought her views on the interpretation of Shakespeare's plays, while Alec Guinness turned to her in April 1951 for advice on how to speak his lines in *Hamlet*: 'I do want to be reassured – about pausing at the end of each line. With a fractional pause on every line I find it all so much more insistent and firm.'[3] Nonetheless, Sitwell was not a professional actress and her experiment with *Macbeth* failed. In the end, Kirstein abandoned hope of a larger show.

In New York, Sitwell found a great friend in the thirty-three-year-old novelist Carson McCullers, whose regard for her was nothing short of worshipful. They met on 31 October at a party given by Tennessee Williams, another writer whom Sitwell liked and admired. After reading two of McCullers's books, Sitwell wrote on 21 November: 'The *Heart is a Lonely Hunter* stabbed my heart and my conscience, as nothing has done for many years . . . As for *The Member of the Wedding* the beauty of it is so great that I am living in the summer of that book.' Having suffered rheumatic fever when young, then a series of strokes, McCullers was frail, as well as unstable. Her drinking and emotional breakdowns placed some burden on Sitwell in the years that followed, as on several occasions she showed up muddled at the Sesame Club, but Sitwell seemed not to grudge her involvement in McCullers's world. The novelist saw Sitwell's work through the lens of great affection, but her regard for Sitwell's poetry preceded any acquaintance with her: 'I know well "The Canticle of the Rose" and as a poet you have no contemporary peer. The amazing thing is the synthesis of youthful lyricism with the maturity of a great intellect. I wish T.S. Eliot had been capable of such development – but this is a churlish thought, because he has given so much.'[4] She soon turned to Sitwell's prose: 'Why did you not tell me about *I Live Under a Black Sun*? I read it yesterday and again today . . . This book has the remorseless and hallucinated power of Dostoyevski (sp?) . . . the language is that of a great poet.'[5]

Sitwell also met the poet Theodore Roethke, who was manic depressive. Kirstein told John Pearson that Roethke was stoned when he came to see Sitwell at the St Regis and began to remove his trousers so they could have sex; Sitwell supposedly told him to stop or she would have to call her brother.[6] If this actually happened, Sitwell made no mention of it. Roethke, she said in a letter to Kenneth Clark's wife Jane, was going to be a very good poet: 'He came to see me. He is like a very nice, large German bear – unwieldy and kindly.'[7] A few months later, he sent Sitwell a manuscript of his poems, with a letter in which he remarked: 'Our meeting meant a great deal to me. I felt we could have gone on laughing and talking interminably.'[8]

Pavlik was on his way to New York. Edith described her worries about him to Evelyn Wiel, who wrote back: 'What a fool Pavlik is! & what a dog in the manger. He says he is not in love with you, but he expects you to behave as a little lap-dog, to be taken up or put down as the mood moves him.'[9] He arrived in New York, apparently on 24 November. Edith was unable to greet him properly as she had a meeting with Columbia Records that day. This made him unhappy. On 28 November, she and Osbert set out on a three-month lecture and reading tour, which meant she could not attend Tchelitchew's exhibition, opening on 1 January 1951. He brooded on her absence and was unmoved by her explanation that the itinerary had been contractually agreed long before the exhibition was arranged. Best wishes would not do.

Edith Sitwell inaugurated the year's reading series at the 92nd Street YMHA Poetry Center, run by John Malcolm Brinnin, now best known as Dylan Thomas's friend. Her reading was a success and she was immediately invited back. With David Horner heading separately to Chicago, Edith and Osbert went by train to sell-out events in Cleveland, Columbus, Chicago, and Kansas City. From 10 to 17 December they were in Texas, going first to Austin, then to Houston, where they met the tragically named patron of the arts Ima Hogg in her mansion on Lazy Lane. After San Antonio, they took a two-week break in Mexico City, where Edith picked up amoebic dysentery and spent most of Christmas 'writhing'.[10] On 4 January 1951, they reached El Paso and, two days later, California where she suffered more bronchitis and coughed through her readings. However, she told John Lehmann that she liked Hollywood: 'Lots of film stars, including Harpo Marx, came. And during my reading of the *Macbeth* sleep-walking scene, I was just announcing that Hell is murky, when a poor gentleman in the audience uttered the most piercing shrieks and was carried out by four men, foaming at the mouth. As one of the spectators said to me, "You ought to be awfully pleased. It was one of the most flattering things I have ever seen."' If only that had been the reaction at the Museum of Modern Art!

The Sitwells saw Aldous Huxley for whom Edith's affection was undimmed. She endured forty-five minutes of the conversation of Mary Pickford who 'discoursed to me of her role as Little Lord Fauntleroy, and said she always regarded herself as a Spiritual Beacon'. Ethel Barrymore was 'delightful', but Osbert blamed Edith's bronchitis on the actress's heavy breathing. The waiters were casual, laughing loudly and joining in the Sitwells' conversation during meals, so Edith judged they must have been smoking marijuana.[11]

On 11 February, they arrived in New Orleans, and went on for a stay of ten days with the Ringlings in Sarasota, where she was back with her friends the gorillas. One named Vicki kissed her hand: 'It has made me very vain, for I can't believe many people can boast of this. The gorilla fondled my hand (going over each finger in turn) and then kissed the palm over and over again. She then flung her arms round my neck and pressed her cheek against mine.'[12] They spent five days at West Palm Beach and returned to New York on 2 March. Apart from readings of her own work, Edith gave recitations from Shakespeare or other Elizabethan poets at most of the stops, and when she returned to New York she made recordings of Shakespeare for Columbia Records. The last important event was a benefit reading in New York on 10 March for the poet Kenneth Patchen; Sitwell had been in correspondence with him and his wife for about six months. He had had back surgery and was unable to afford, among other things, cortisone treatments for his arthritis.[13] In a programme probably organised by his friend and publisher James Laughlin, the Sitwells joined forces with W. H. Auden, e. e. cummings, Archibald MacLeish, and William Carlos Williams (*New York Times*, 28 February 1951).

Sitwell had not heard from Tchelitchew in some time. On 18 March, two days before sailing to England on the *Queen Elizabeth*, she suggested that perhaps a letter from him had been lost. A month later she was back at Renishaw and could see that he was ignoring her letters.[14] Many months would go by before she heard from him again. Tchelitchew would pop in and out Sitwell's life in future, reviving old claims of affection, but she could hardly trust him. While she continued to honour his art, she must have known that he was not the man she had imagined him.

Not surprisingly, Sitwell's poetry at this time focuses often on a sense of human diminishment. Her work on Shakespeare seems to have planted in her mind 'The Great Chain of Being', at least as the form of a question to be asked of modern life. Her 'Gardeners and Astronomers', published that summer in the *TLS*, yearns for greatness in human beings. Old men, like Yeats's in 'Lapis Lazuli', pose the questions:

> Then why are we less than the astronomers?
> Than Hipparchus, who saw a comet that foretold
> The birth of Mithridates and began
> To form his catalogue of stars that are no more
> Than the long-leaved planets in our garden-shed.

> And men of emeralds walking through the night
> Of early Chinese annals, Emperor Hwan-Té
> Whose pleasure-dome was an observatory, Chien-Ké
> Who shook a branch and all the stars together glittered
>   bright:
> Now are they but the dust of lilies on our garden-bed.

> And why are we less than these?
> Does not each dark root hold a world of gold?
> And was not Aristophanes,
> Who gave the world green laughter, son of the garden-goddess?

The problem, she believes, lies in a material conception of humanity. She describes next a flat, geometrical world in which human beings are differentiated by dimension or colour, not by essence or by inwardness. Science mistakes the shadow of the human being for the reality, and the age gives power to that shadow:

> Some dream that all are equal,
> As in the gardener's world of growth, the plant and planet,
> 		King and beggar;
> And Fallen Man dreams he is falling upward. And the eyeless
> Horizontal Man, the Black Man, who in the Day's blazing
> 		diamond-mine, follows the footsteps
> Of Vertical Man, is ever cast by him
> Across all growth, all stone – he, great as Man's ambition,
> And like to Man's ambition, with no body
> To act ambition – he, the sole horizon,
> Epitome of our age, now rules the world.

The myth of material progress, Sitwell believes, begins in abstraction and ends in illusion. She contrasts all that with a more fertile darkness and with the natural processes of an orange tree like Marvell's:[15]

> And in the gardens the airs sing of growth:
> The orange-tree still sighs,
> 'I am the Dark that changed to water and to air,
> The water and the air that changed to gold –
> The gold that turned into a plant. From the cool wave of the
> 		air grows a smooth
> Stem, and from this the gold, cold orange-tree.
>
> And happy as the Sun, the gardeners
> See all miasmas from the human filth but as the dung
> In which to sow great flowers,
> Tall moons and mornings, seeds, and sires, and suns.

In a period when her imagery tended to repeat itself in distracting ways, 'Gardeners and Astronomers' managed to strike a new note, and it may be the finest poem she wrote in the 1950s.

*

Over the years, Sitwell had never been comfortable with W. H. Auden, though she claimed otherwise. The visits to the United States were changing that – she saw a good deal of him and he treated her pleasantly. On 17 May he came to Renishaw for the night, where, as Sitwell told Natasha Spender, he was 'great fun, and told us about a novelist living in South America, who has been writing a novel for the last 20 years from which the letter E is excluded. We thought it would limit the work if it was literary criticism, as practically the only poets who could be mentioned would be Wyatt, Wordsworth, and Dylan.'[16]

Maurice Bowra was now vice-chancellor of Oxford University, and he arranged for Sitwell and Arthur Waley to be among those granted honorary doctorates at the Encaenia of 20 June 1951. She thanked Bowra 'for the two days which have been the most wonderful days of my life (which has had many days of wonder, but of a different and remote wonder)'.[17] When John Gielgud later received the same honour, Sitwell wrote: 'Fools are made knights and dames – and anyhow, who would want to walk through doors in Heaven ahead of William Shakespeare? – Fools are made doctors by other fools in other universities, but no fool has ever been given an Hon. D. Litt. by Oxford.'[18]

After receiving her degree Sitwell went to the Sesame Club. Just as some other poets founded journals or publishing imprints to advance their art, Sitwell intended her salon at the Sesame to bring writers, musicians, and artists together to inspire each other by conversation. Given the collapse of her private world, Sitwell looked more and more to these gatherings as a substitute for intimacy. Her trips to the United States gave her more money than she was used to, and she poured it into entertaining. As she told Gore Vidal, whom she had met through Alice Pleydell-Bouverie, 'I have no money, you know. It all goes for lunch here.'[19] She often held luncheons for up to twenty guests and tea parties for a hundred.[20] She ran to infinitely greater expense than she had done at Moscow Road, where crowds were smaller and the fare was sticky buns. Also, she found herself with more pests, among them Alice Hunt, a wealthy American who wanted to marry Osbert. In Sitwell's letters, she becomes 'la chasseresse' – the huntress. Waley's companion, Beryl de Zoete, an expert on ethnic dances, was another regular.

Although she liked Beryl, Sitwell made fun of the seventy-two-year-old's tireless pursuit of young men.

How to deal with bores became a perennial concern. David Higham's younger colleague, Bruce Hunter, recalls a story told by Higham's wife Nell: 'They lived in Keats Grove in Hampstead where Edith came to tea one day. Later, her car, returning, pulled into the drive and their small son, Matthew, dashed out to see who it was, returning to announce, "Dame Edith, there's a man here who says you have to leave now." Nell was greatly embarrassed, "You mustn't say that, Matthew." But Edith laughed and said, "Matthew, I must engage you for one of my parties, to get rid of gluebottoms."'[21]

However, Sitwell lost the company of some friends far too soon. Less than a month after the publication of the definitive score of *Façade: An Entertainment*, Constant Lambert died on 21 August at the age of forty-six, of pneumonia and diabetes.[22] Lambert was a good friend of the Sitwells, and Edith trusted him more than anyone else to perform *Façade*. The tenor Peter Pears, Benjamin Britten's companion and collaborator, tried his hand at recitation when *Façade* was put on in Liverpool at the beginning of August 1951; she thought his performance a 'triumph',[23] and afterwards Pears took Lambert's place as her favourite reciter of the poems.

Sitwell remained gloomy over Tchelitchew's continued silence, and it affected her work. While struggling with an encyclopedia article on poetry, she wrote to David Horner on 7 October: 'I am having *hell* with my essay, and have never felt less like writing anything. My poetry seems to have deserted me entirely.'[24] She began to resent Tchelitchew's having given her letters to Yale University. In November, Geoffrey Gorer urged her not to post an angry letter: 'let sleeping Pavlik lie . . . If you really want to place restrictions on your letters write to the Librarian at Yale & and send him a copy – but it is no use arguing with a Russian about treachery . . . Pavlik is very Russian: when he says "You (E.S.) are not interested in my work" he means "I am not interested in your work" – just like Vishinsky in the U.N.'[25] She did write a letter to Tchelitchew on 16 November, defending her conduct through the long years of their friendship, but it went unanswered.

She joined Osbert and David in Italy at the end of November. Most of her time was spent in Montegufoni, but in January 1952 she stayed at Taormina in Sicily, and in February at Amalfi. Her sojourn in Italy lasted until 5 April – much longer than expected, partly because, on Christmas Eve, they heard that Susan Robins had inoperable cancer. She had been employed by the Sitwells for thirty-five years, and, despite rows, they valued her friendship. They decided to stay away from Renishaw so that her husband could nurse her in peace. She died on 21 March.

While at Amalfi at the beginning of February, Sitwell received a letter from Zosia Kochanski, one of her friends in the United States. The widow of the violinist Paul Kochanski, she had been a friend of Sitwell's cousin Elsie Swinton before the First World War, but it is not certain whether Sitwell had met her at that time. Kochanski later came into Tchelitchew's circle in New York. In 1951, she was urging Tchelitchew to be reconciled with Sitwell. Edith wrote on 4 February: 'I am deeply touched that you should have spoken to Pavlik again. Perhaps he *will* write to me again some day – but it will be too late . . . I never think of him now, as it is bad for the soul to think of such conduct.' It seems, rather, that she could think of little else.

Sitwell believed that Tchelitchew had been poisoned against her by the painter Leonor Fini, who, by a fluke, was also in Amalfi: 'I was able to avoid the disgust of having her introduced to me, but unfortunately her presence in the hotel where only two other people were staying, did bring all Pavlik's conduct back to me. She is a *horrible* looking woman – looks as horrible as she is. I was going to say that she looks like an epitome of the Seven Sins. But that would be paying her a compliment – imputing to her a certain greatness. There is no greatness. She is just an open slum.'[26]

At Montegufoni, the Sitwells had a pleasant visit from E. M. Forster on 21 March. She was also receiving gossip from the other side of the Atlantic, which she passed on to Jack Lindsay:

I hear our dearest Dylan has been painting New York (literally) red. The centre of his activities being the Literary Salon of Mrs. Murray Crane, – the watchwords of the Salon being Decorum, Bonne Tenue, and the milder and more restrained forms of Evening Dress. At one of the interminable evenings of Culture to which one is doomed there, Dylan suddenly sprang at Caitlin, and (according to

my informant) 'kicked, punched, and bloodily beat' her. Mrs. Crane
shrieked and fainted, – being revived with difficulty. There is then
a gap in the narrative. I *think* Dylan was sent home, but do not know
what happened to Caitlin. However Dylan soon reappeared, and
demanded the money for his taxi. My informant wrote, gloomily: 'I
don't suppose he will be asked again.'!!27

Edith Sitwell had heard almost nothing from Siegfried Sassoon in
about ten years. His marriage had ended in 1944, and he lived in near-
seclusion in Heytesbury. In April 1952, he sent Sitwell a copy of
Emblems of Experience, a pamphlet of poems, along with a diffident
letter. Sitwell wrote back: 'But what *do* you mean by this phrase in your
letter about "reviving" my "former liking" for your poems? How could
I possibly ever cease to admire and have the strongest feeling for a
poetry that has, in reality, the "blood and fire" that poor Robert
Nichols was always talking about in his phoney way, and that he, poor
soul, never achieved. These new poems have all that same life.' Sitwell
and Sassoon had a strange, durable friendship that survived rows and
silences. She asked: 'Why do we never see you now? I can't say I blame
you for keeping away from the literary world, which is sheer hell, with
all those thousands of geniuses. But we don't belong to it.' She invited
Sassoon and his son George to lunch, but he refused on the grounds
that he was now living a very solitary existence. Despite her public persona, Sitwell had an (accurate) sense of herself as 'a little outside life'.
She could understand Sassoon's estrangement from things and wrote on
28 April: 'Like you, I have never really got on with the universe.'28

The highlight of the summer was her recitation of *Façade* on 8 July
at the Festival Hall, in a programme sponsored by the Society for
Twentieth Century Music, of which William Walton was president.
George Weldon conducted, and the musicians were drawn from the
London Symphony Orchestra. The audience filled the seats and boxes,
and many people stood in the aisle, chiefly to hear Edith Sitwell recite
(*The Times*, 9 September 1952).

Humphrey Searle's setting of 'The Shadow of Cain' was performed
on 16 November. Edith Sitwell and Dylan Thomas recited, while
Searle conducted the London Symphony Orchestra, and Gordon
Watson played the piano. As the *Times* reviewer observed, the music

was not meant to obtrude on the words, but to underline the form of the poem, and to illuminate its meaning and images. To this end it relied on 'shattering noise, dead silence, and instrumental monotone or held chords' (*The Times*, 17 November 1952). Sitwell admired Searle's music intensely, but this concert had a distressing aftermath.

Searle and his wife Gillen had contacted many of Sitwell's friends to act as guarantors for the concert, which, in the event, lost £430, so they asked the guarantors to pay up – apparently something close to ten pounds each.[29] Sitwell was horrified that her friends were being imposed on in this way, and she felt betrayed, indeed swindled, by the Searles, writing a cheque herself to cover the whole amount. After a discussion with Philip Frere, Humphrey Searle came away 'worried and perplexed': 'Why did you not write to us? And why do you wish to undertake the entire responsibility yourself? The guarantors have co-operated most enthusiastically, and some have offered more than they promised in the first place.' He added that guarantees are normal for concerts.[30] However, Sitwell was not won over by this, nor by Gillen's postscript to one of her husband's letters: 'A big hug and kiss for the New Year for Edith from Gillen. NOT TO WORRY!'[31] At least one of the guarantors, Geoffrey Gorer, refused her money. He believed that Searle and Gordon Watson did well out of the concert, and that the guarantors knew what they were doing when they signed up.[32] Sitwell decided she would have nothing more to do with the Searles, 'after their monstrous conduct'.[33]

Sitwell was mishandling her finances, so the loss associated with the concert caused her more trouble than it should have. That year, despite substantial income from British and American royalties, she declared a net loss of £1053, much of it owing to transportation costs and hotel bills. It is not clear whether that figure includes her hundred-pound annuity and the returns on about ten thousand pounds cautiously invested in companies such as the Canadian Pacific Railroad. Bryher was helping her out with a covenant that paid her annually another £275.[34] Nevertheless, her overdraft was barely manageable; by 1955, it exceeded five thousand pounds secured against an equal value of Defence Bonds.[35] Edith was evidently paying rent to Osbert for the time she spent in his properties, and she was sending a direct payment of two hundred pounds per annum to Evelyn, while trying unsuccessfully to induce Ernest Rootham to match this.[36] Evelyn complained of being 'hard up',[37] but when she came to the Sesame she contributed to a more serious problem: Edith was operating a free bar and dining room for her friends, most of whom had no idea that she was not a wealthy woman.

By the end of 1952, however, she had found a new source of income. On her last visit to the United States, between bouts of bronchitis and dysentery, she had been writing sections of dialogue for a film of *Fanfare for Elizabeth*. In a long, confidential negotiation, David Higham secured a contract for her to write the screenplay for Columbia Studios. She would be paid five thousand dollars – equivalent to a little under £1800 – which was to include her transportation and living costs in California. If the studio decided to go ahead with the film, she would get another twenty-five thousand dollars,[38] the kind of payday to which, for example, Graham Greene was accustomed.

Of course, a journey to the United States was simpler for Sitwell than it was for Graham Greene, who had tried to execute a piece of mischief against the American government. He revealed in a *Time* magazine cover story (29 October 1951) that he had been a member of the Communist Party for six weeks while a student at Oxford. This put him, as a religious and literary celebrity, on the wrong side of the McCarran Act, intended to keep Communists and other subversives out of the United States. In early 1952 he was denied the usual twelve-month visa and given instead a three-month one. In the United States he spoke to various newspapers about the danger of McCarthyism.[39] At the American consulate in Florence on 14 October, Edith Sitwell made the standard declaration: 'I, Edith Louisa Sitwell, born at Scarborough, England, on September 7, 1887, hereby declare under oath that I am not and have never been a member of or affiliated with a Communist, Fascist, Nazi, or other totalitarian party or organization in any country, or any section, subsidiary, branch, affiliate, or subdivision of any such party or organization.'[40] Unlike Greene or Waugh, she actually liked Americans, and, having missed out on an Oxbridge education, had no memberships either to hide or to reveal.

The Sitwells reached New York on 26 November after a voyage in which Osbert reduced an attendant to exhaustion by repeatedly falling asleep with his head pressed against a bell-button.[41] They stayed as usual at the St Regis. Evelyn Waugh's laudatory profile of Osbert appeared in the *New York Times* four days after their arrival. Edith gave a reading of her poetry on 18 December, and shortly afterwards they made the train journey to Los Angeles, where she was dazzled by mid-winter greenery: 'On our way from the station, we drove between long lines of gigantic palms in the wide boulevards . . . Great golden stars of dew were falling from the tall mimosa trees, the oleander, the giant tree-fern and the other tropical vegetation. (Although the month was January, the heat was almost tropical.)' After a week at the Hotel Bel-Air, Columbia Studios set her up in an apartment at Sunset Towers – an enclave of stars, starlets, gangsters, and millionaires on Sunset Boulevard.

In Hollywood she worked under the eye of George Cukor, a prolific director best known for *A Star is Born* (1954) and *My Fair Lady* (1964). Osbert thought that Groucho Marx had modelled his movements on Cukor, 'placing one foot on the ground, when sitting, in such a way that he can spring to his feet and escape at a moment's notice'. Cukor had great hopes of landing Laurence Olivier and Vivien Leigh to play the leads in *Fanfare for Elizabeth*. He set Sitwell to collaborate with the Hungarian Walter Reisch, a veteran screenwriter who had worked with Cukor on other films including *Gaslight* (1944). His sense of humour ran to funny voices: 'That is the scene where you have those Cardinal-guys threaten the King with eternal damnation, and you have the King say, "That's O.K. by me, boys! I am the King of England, and you can tell your boss the Pope to hell with his damnation."'[42] Though he remained friendly, Sitwell's and Reisch's collaboration was vexed: she wanted to preserve the book's rich language and atmospheric detail, while he wanted to reduce the work to its 'girders'. Sitwell also believed he was vulgarising the script.

Hollywood provided Edith Sitwell with a very satisfying enemy. The gossip columnist Hedda Hopper was, as Sitwell put it, syndicated 'in every village "Mortician's Do-It-Yourself Home Gazette"'. Hopper had no idea what she was taking on when she wrote: 'Before leaving London, [Sitwell] said, "I love horror," then posed for a picture to prove it' (*Los Angeles Times*, 20 December 1952). She later wrote of how Harry Cohn, who ran Columbia Pictures, approached Sitwell at a party: 'She was gracious, and said "Who are you?" "I'm the man who sends your checks each week," replied Harry. "Oh," said Miss Sitwell, "goodnight." Cohn fled' (*Los Angeles Times*, 18 February 1953). Sitwell described this last episode as fiction, and asked for a retraction. When none came, she later wrote: 'I should hate to see her disgraced, I, here and now, withdraw her statement on her behalf.' That winter, Los Angeles suffered an outbreak of rabies: 'I was told on good authority that this was due to the fact that Miss Hedda Hopper had pursued the dogs and succeeded in biting them – but I doubt this. After all, they run very fast.'[43]

By 21 February 1953, Osbert had moved on to Palm Beach. Edith spent some time with 'dear Aldous and Maria Huxley – two of my oldest and greatest friends'. They took her to see Forest Lawn Cemetery, the inspiration for Waugh's novel *The Loved One*, and also arranged a meeting for Sitwell with the astronomer Edwin Hubble. During the car ride Aldous Huxley kept up a long grumble about Coleridge and Wordsworth:

> Really, Edith, that any man reputed to be sane should have written, quite deliberately,
>
> 'I need not say, Louisa dear,
> How glad we are to have you here,
> A lovely convalescent . . .'

The lines were from Coleridge's 'To a Young Lady On her Recovering from a Fever'.[44]

Edwin Hubble, who came up with the theory of an expanding universe, had worked for many years at Mount Wilson and Mount Palomar observatories; he would die just a few months later. He showed Sitwell slides of galaxies many light years away. Sitwell remarked, 'How terrifying!' He answered, 'Only when you are not used to them. When you are used to them, they are comforting. For then you know that there is nothing to worry about – nothing at all!'[45]

In her visits to New York, Sitwell had become attached to a group of servants at the St Regis Hotel: Rose Haughton and Mary Rohan, and two waiters named Max and Charlie.[46] Sitwell actually sent money to the Irish Rohan to help bury her husband in 1949.[47] However, she spent most of her days in the world of artists and writers and their patrons. That changed, to a degree, in Hollywood, of all places, where she came to know a group of black people:

> Once, feeling sad, I felt a dark hand placed on my arm, and a gentle voice asked 'What is the matter, Madam Sitwell – don't you believe in God?' Some talked with me of their ideals, and of their feeling that all is hopeless because their skins are black. I asked 'Do you really think that God is pink and white as if He has just come from Miss Elizabeth Arden's or Madame Helena Rubinstein's salons? When you get to Heaven, perhaps you may find God is – a coloured man?'[48]

The hand she referred to was probably that of her maid Velma Leroy, with whom she developed a friendship. Given her age and generation, Sitwell was bound to see her in terms of certain stereotypes, but her affection was sincere. She wrote that Leroy had

> a face like a large yellow hothouse begonia, enormous rolling black eyes, hair which had been straightened, but ending at the back with a little curling black drake's tail, and wrists and ankles of an extreme delicacy amongst the best I have ever seen. She was a creature of such gentle warmth and kindness that I think of her as one of the few saints I have ever known. She was to me like Blake's Little Black Boy. She loved everything that lived. I was deeply touched to learn that after I left Hollywood, she attended night-classes in order to be worthy of my friendship. (It was I who should have striven to be worthy of hers).[49]

Life magazine commissioned Sitwell to write an article about Hollywood – presumably looking for a mix of glamour and waspishness. What they got was closer to *I Live Under a Black Sun*. She saw Los Angeles as an 'Enormous city of wild hopes, of Jacob's ladders, of terrible depths into which those who had once such high hopes may sink'. She did her best to find out about Hispanic gangs and about the life of the poor in Los Angeles. Guided by Velma Leroy and the police detective Alfred Branch, and with photographers in tow, she set out for skid row, where she saw 'those poor wretches who had been "damned by the rainbow"'. Everywhere were the homeless: 'Some were young, and these had nothing between their one outer covering of rags and their skins, so that it seemed they had early been made ready for the grave.'

This was *not* what *Life* wanted. That afternoon, she went on to a meeting with Marilyn Monroe. Sitwell supposed that this encounter was contrived by the editors so that the two would exchange splendid insults. Generally, Sitwell despised the sex-kittens of Hollywood: 'Though I did not meet Miss Gabor, I saw her in action during luncheon in the famous Romanoff restaurant. She was doing a kind of deep-sea diving act into the eyes of a gentleman who looked like a button-manufacturer.'[50] Monroe struck Sitwell as a different case, and she pitied her: 'I understand she is in trouble for having a beautiful figure; but I do not think this can be regarded as a crime. I understand also that she was in trouble for allowing this to be photographed for a calendar. But there have always been models for painters and for photographers. Perhaps the people who blamed her have never been hungry, with no money to pay for a meal – have never been in fear of having no roof over their heads.'[51] Having just come from skid row, Sitwell believed she saw indelible marks of sorrow on this actress, too: 'On the occasion of our meeting she wore a green dress, and, with her yellow hair, looked like a daffodil . . . In repose her face was at moments strangely, prophetically, tragic, like the face of a beautiful ghost – a little Spring-ghost, an innocent fertility-daemon, the vegetation spirit that was Ophelia.'[52] They spoke of Rudolf Steiner, whose works Monroe was reading, and Sitwell came away thinking her intelligent and well mannered. *Life* rejected Sitwell's article, so she later reworked it as the last chapter of *Taken Care Of*. Sitwell had subsequent meetings with Monroe and her husband Arthur Miller, in New York and at the Sesame Club.

During these ten weeks in Hollywood, the sixty-five-year-old Sitwell suffered badly from sciatica; the pain limited her movement and caused her to sleep poorly. Apart from poetry readings at the universities, she made few public appearances. One journalist, Edwin Schallert, found her habit of entertaining with cocktails at noon impressive even by the alcoholic standards of the movie business. He also made the common mistake of overestimating Sitwell's height at six feet, three inches. As

she boarded the train at Pasadena at the end of March, she asked not
to be photographed as she was feeling 'wretched', but finally consented:
'Please understand, I don't want to seem uncooperative' (*Los Angeles
Times*, 29 March 1953).

She had completed a script, which Walter Reisch kept working at,
cutting and compressing. Sitwell was very disappointed with the new
version that reached her in England. George Cukor arranged for an
extension of the delivery date, urging Sitwell to rework the script as she
judged best. She had assumed that her work on this part of the project
was done, but it would soon be necessary for her to return to California.

Edward Weeks of the *Atlantic Monthly*, now Sitwell's publisher in the
United States, thought Sitwell should undertake a great new anthology of English and American poetry: 'Now is the time to shoot for the
moon: 2000 pages,' he wrote on 12 June 1953. He paid her an advance
of two thousand dollars, drawn down during 1953 and 1954. Although
Sitwell had relied on the historian Dorothy Marshall as a researcher
and typist, for this new project a full-time secretary was needed, so she
hired Mary Fraser, whose salary was paid by Weeks. Fraser remained
with Sitwell until 1957, when she took a teaching job in Sweden and
had to deny the claim in a newspaper there that she was Sitwell's ghost-
writer.[53] Weeks had great ambitions for this anthology, investing about
forty thousand dollars and aiming for an initial print run of at least fifteen thousand copies.[54]

Sitwell spent most of the summer of 1953 at Renishaw, before going
to Switzerland to visit Bryher on 7 September, but her mind was on the
United States, to which she would sail in early November. While at
sea, she received a telegram from John Malcolm Brinnin of the YMHA
Poetry Center that Dylan Thomas had died in New York on 9
November. Arriving on the 12th, she was immediately drawn into the
mêlée surrounding Thomas's death. She wrote to Sachie:

Oh, it has been so *awful* about Dylan. Tell Georgia this, but nobody
else, and ask her on no account to repeat it. We were met by John
Brinnin, who had looked after him, and another man, at the boat,
in tears. (John had cabled to me on the ship, telling me Dylan was
dead). D loved nobody but Caitlin, but had got involved with
another woman. Apparently, money sent by D to Caitlin in England

had not reached her, and she sent him this appalling cable, ten days before he died: 'You have left me no alternative but suicide or the streets. Hate. Caitlin.' From that minute, D never looked back, but just drank and drank. He then fell into a coma from which he never emerged. *We are going to say he died of diabetes. Don't forget.*

Edith went on to describe how after Caitlin arrived,

That * * Oscar Williams telephoned telling her about the other woman!! Can you imagine? She threw herself on the dying Dylan's body, preventing him from breathing and smashing the oxygen tent (he was unconscious.) She was pulled off him and then flew at John Brinnin and tried to strangle him. (Williams had told her the other woman was an ex-secretary of John's.) It took four men to pull her away from John, (who, I may say, was *wonderful* with Dylan). She then tore the habits off two nursing nuns, and the two doctors present ordered her to be sent to Bellevue (the lunatic asylum.) This was prevented, and she was sent, instead, to an inebriates' home from which she was rescued, after three or four days, by the British Consul. Everybody accused everybody else of God knows what, and everybody tried to lay their accusations against each other before me. O. Williams, whom I do not know, rang me up 19 times in two days, in an effort to involve me in a row.[55]

The fighting that occurred around Thomas's deathbed has been well documented; his friends split into two groups, each accusing the other of failing him in his need. There is no confirmation that the telegram that Sitwell says Caitlin sent to Dylan Thomas ever existed. Andrew Lycett, one of Thomas's biographers, believes that Sitwell misunderstood something Brinnin may have told her: Caitlin had sent an angry letter to Dylan, care of Brinnin, that never actually reached Dylan himself.[56] Since Sitwell is very clear about the text of the telegram, it is also possible that she picked up some accurate information. It is not the sort of question that can be resolved.

For many years it was commonly believed that Thomas's drinking spree caused 'a severe insult to the brain' leading directly to his death,[57] but it is now thought that medical error also played a role. One of

Thomas's doctors tried to sedate him with half a grain of morphine sulphate; given Thomas's drunken state and other illnesses, the morphine likely depressed his breathing and put him into a coma. However, as Paul Ferris reminds us, years of drinking put Thomas in a position where such a disaster could occur.[58] At one point, the doctors at St Vincent's Hospital suspected diabetes to be the cause of Thomas's coma, but the theory was discounted, and an effort by some researchers to revive it in 1997 was not well received.[59] In any event, Sitwell and some others wanted to conceal the squalor of his death, seizing on diabetes as an explanation. However, the story got out, largely through Brinnin's memoir *Dylan Thomas in America* (1955) – a book Sitwell thought 'awful'.[60]

Louis MacNeice wrote to Sitwell on 7 December, conveying an offer from the *Sunday Times* that she should fly back to London briefly in January at their expense to make the first of the personal tributes to Dylan Thomas at a memorial programme.[61] Sitwell refused since she was obliged to work on the script in California. She wrote to Maurice Bowra: 'That poor, most dear, and most wonderful poet! I still feel absolutely numb, which was the state I fell into after the first dreadful knowledge both of that death and the manner of it. What young poet can begin to compare with him?'[62]

23

FROST ON THE WINDOW

Edith Sitwell's collection *Gardeners and Astronomers* brought together poems she had written over the past four years. Reactions were more mixed than she had been used to in the 1940s. A crop of poets younger than Dylan Thomas and George Barker was coming into its own, and, for many, the apocalyptic poetry of the war years seemed remote and overdone. Many younger poets argued for focus, common sense, clarity, modesty of intention, and plain language. These were the virtues of 'The Movement', a loose group that included Kingsley Amis, Robert Conquest, Donald Davie, D. J. Enright, Thom Gunn, Elizabeth Jennings, Philip Larkin, and John Wain. This shift of taste reflected the austere tone of the post-war years, and a revival of some of the neglected qualities of the best Georgian verse.

It was also affected by the cultures of the leading universities. At Cambridge, Leavis was imparting his kind of seriousness, as well as a distrust of dilettantes, to students in the English School. At Oxford, there was a vogue of logical positivism associated with A. J. Ayer and others, encouraging a distrust of things beyond the empirical.[1] While a later generation might think the logical positivists' trust in facts and in 'experience' was grounded in its own hidden leaps of faith, they contributed to a literary mood that preferred observation to vision – and that was bad news for Edith Sitwell.

It is necessary to be careful in characterising the reaction of poets of the 1950s to Edith Sitwell's work. It was not simply a matter of literary munchkins dancing and singing, 'Ding-dong, the witch is dead.' She had her admirers, among them John Heath-Stubbs and Charles Causley. In 1956, John Lehmann published some of Ted Hughes's work in the *London Magazine*, and she was very struck by it: 'One has great hopes of him.'[2] In 1995, I asked Hughes whether Sitwell had ever reached out to him, as she so often did with young poets: 'No, I never had any communication with Edith Sitwell, and wasn't aware of her opinions about my verse. Perhaps because I came through Cambridge, she felt wary of me – though I was as sceptical of Leavis and his destructive temperament as she was. My general feeling for her was always – liking, with an inclination to defend her.'[3] As Professor Marsha Bryant tells us, the hard-to-please Sylvia Plath had an unqualified admiration for Edith Sitwell's work and spoke of Sitwell and Marianne Moore as 'ageing giantesses and poetic Godmothers'.[4]

Nevertheless, *Gardeners and Astronomers* encountered a good deal of scolding, of which L. F. Duchene's was fairly typical: 'In short passages one becomes aware of Dr. Sitwell's power. But in large doses, her continuous over-emphasis, her "superbe", her symbolism in capital letters – derived from literature rather than life – her clotted rhythms, all conspire to an over-dressed monotony and a certain hollowness. In the shade of Dr. Sitwell's enormous will to grandeur her true shoots of poetry have been starved of the light they need if they are to grow' (*Manchester Guardian*, 2 March 1954). Note that this reviewer thinks it fairly straightforward to experience 'life' without too much literature fogging the windscreen.

The *New Statesman* (23 January 1954) ran a mildly satirical piece under the title 'Queen Edith' and there followed a predictable back-and-forth of letters to the editor. Writing in the *Spectator* (8 January 1954), Anthony Hartley fastened on the closing lines of 'A Song of the Dust':

> If every grain of my dust should be a Satan,
> If every atom of my heart were Lucifer –
> If every drop of my blood were an Abaddon,
>   – Yet should I love.

Hartley thought this bordered on bathos. 'The imagery has taken over and developed itself into extravagance, affecting the meanings communicated to the reader. One image leads to the next, but the ideas behind them do not follow. Quite the reverse. They are destroyed and made ridiculous.' Among other things he complained about her comparison of sap to peridots and beryls.

Sitwell sent a cable to the editor: 'Please have Anthony Hartley

stuffed and put in a glass case with mothballs at my expense. The finest
of all your collection.' As she explained to David Pleydell-Bouverie:
'many years ago I sent the Editor, when he was being tiresome, a stuffed
owl, suggesting he should give it reviewing as it had recently been
combed for moths.'[5] She then wrote a letter for publication (22 January
1954): 'It is good of Mr. Hartley to teach, not only me, but the late
John Donne, Dean of St. Paul's, how to write . . . the passage of which
this gentleman complains with such vehemence, is an adaptation from
one of Donne's sermons.' She added: 'I shall, no doubt, be told that
little Mr. Tomkins (or whatever his name may be), this week's new
great poet, does not incorporate in his work, phrases from the past,
giving them a twist, and importing new meaning. That is so. But more
than one great poet does. And it is useless to deny it.' As for peridots
and beryls, she wrote: 'one day in spring Mr. Hartley should try breaking off a twig from its branch.'[6] There followed more letters pro and con
on the merits of Sitwell's allusions and echoes. One whimsical letter
(29 January 1954), signed 'Little Mr. Tomkins', claimed that 'the sap
of a tree is more like Double Diamond than peridots and beryls'.

Meanwhile, the recently published *Lucky Jim* reached Sitwell in
Hollywood at the end of January 1954. She read it, read it again, then
wrote to its author, Kingsley Amis: 'You are a born writer. Your natural gifts, your observation, your insight, are exceedingly remarkable,
and your handling of language is nothing short of brilliant . . . I shall
watch your career with the greatest interest: it will be, I am convinced,
of very high distinction.'[7] She also wrote to the *Spectator* (19 February
1954) that she and Anthony Hartley could at least agree about the
merits of this new novel. Amis was in a sticky position: *he* had written the 'Little Mr. Tomkins' letter; there was no way out, so he
copped to it in the next issue and thanked her for her praise (26
February 1954). After a short delay to make him squirm, she wrote on
8 March: 'Do not feel the slightest discomfort. When you come to the
luncheon party I shall give for you, you will find me completely oblivious that this has ever happened.'[8] Amis and his wife came to the
Sesame in late June, and he wrote afterwards with perfect grace: 'It
was delightful to meet you and to talk to you – such a privilege and
a pleasure.'[9]

During the *Spectator* tussle, Sitwell was in California, where work on the script was slow. She described for Minnie Fosburgh (now divorced from Vincent Astor and married to an artist, James Fosburgh) an evening of work at George Cukor's house: 'The enormous black poodle – the size of a large cart-horse (I adore him) – was chasing one of the dachshunds across the sofa, over my lap (trampling on my appendix) backwards and forwards.' Cukor mentioned the actress Jean Simmons; Reisch began yelling about how awful she was.

> After about five minutes of this, the dachshund suddenly turned, just as it was being chased over my lap, and put its head into the poodle's mouth, where it became fixed – I thought irrevocably. The poodle's eyes were distended with fear and suffocation. Walter stopped yelling and pulled, violently, at the dachshund's back legs. The dachshund, thinking Walter was trying to tear it in two, as its head was held as in a vice, shrieked down the poodle's throat – making the poodle's fear and suffocation far worse . . . I *still* cannot think how the dachshund was dislodged, but it was, at last. George said, rather huffily, when I expressed wonderment and condolence, that it is always happening.[10]

Matters did not improve. She told Osbert on 8 February:

> Tomorrow, George and the second in command at the Studio are coming round here to listen to Walter yelling. Walter has discovered that the name of Lot's wife was Edith; he has also found that Savonarola's last words, as he was about to be burnt, were 'I am in love with fire.' Therefore, the other day, yelling because I had told him we couldn't use the word 'décolletage', but must say 'bosom' – hanging head downwards over the sofa, he shrieked 'Oh, Dr. Stillwell! Oh, Miss Atkin! Oh, Mrs. Lot! Oh, Signorina Savonarola! Oh, you bosom-fetichist ("bosom" twice in three pages)! Oh, shades of the Hay office! Oh, shades of Harry Cohn! Oh, what shall I do?' (Straightening himself, suddenly) 'What are you laughing at?'[11]

Walter Reisch's comic rant probably owed something to talking with Sitwell about her poems, especially this passage from 'The Night Wind':

Now in the streets great airs the colour of the vines
Drift to the noctuas, veiled women, to the faceless ones, the
    nameless ones –
To Lot's wife staring across the desert of her life.[12]

Under the guise of Lot's wife, Sitwell probably did consider her own life a desert. In the meantime there were things to be laughed at – among them Walter Reisch.

Back in New York, Sitwell wrote on 3 April to Geoffrey Gorer that Cukor had been preoccupied with the shooting of A Star is Born and with Judy Garland, 'who screams and cries and hits people with her shoe all the time'. Without Cukor to keep Reisch in line, Sitwell felt the script had been 'wrecked' again. The studio wanted her to come back in July, but she refused. Columbia still wanted to produce the film, although no date was ever fixed. As late as 1962, George Cukor was still talking about it, but like many other promising scripts Fanfare for Elizabeth was lost in 'development hell'. Sitwell's book never came close to the screen, except indirectly. Trying to understand her role in the BBC series Elizabeth R (1971), Glenda Jackson found that academic historians contradicted each other, yet a reading of Fanfare for Elizabeth made all the difference: 'Edith Sitwell's intuitions – that gave me the clues I needed.'[13]

Meanwhile, Tchelitchew hove into view. In her letter to Gorer, Sitwell wrote: 'Pavlik is now trying to make it up with me – via Minnie Astor-that-was, Fosburgh-that-is. He wrote to her, "Please tell Edith I often dream of her – not have forgotten her – hope she hasn't forgotten me. Give her please, my love and when I see her all will be all right again."!!!'[14] None of Sitwell's letters to Tchelitchew after 1951 has come to light, so her full reaction is hard to gauge. It appears that he contacted her directly in June when her name was again in the news.

She was named in the Birthday Honours List as a Dame Commander of the Order of the British Empire (The Times, 10 June 1954). Equivalent to a knighthood, the honour was granted largely on the recommendation of Denys Kilham Roberts and the Board of the Society of Authors.[15] Sitwell was gleeful, recognising how useful it would be in dealing with the pipsqueakery, but she told Jane Clark that she dreaded curtsying to the Queen owing to arthritis in her knees: 'I shall fall at the Queen's feet, or else (being of immense strength) I shall bring her down with me in a kind of death-grapple!!!'[16]

Congratulations poured in. Sassoon, in his disconnected way, delayed for almost a year, before sending a letter with another book of poems. Edith told him: 'like Persephone, I am frequently out of circulation as far as my friends are concerned, for six months or so out of the year.' She thanked him for his good wishes: '*You were* one of the very first poets, as you were one of the very first people, who upheld me. And you don't know – or perhaps you do, what I feel about that . . . It may amuse you to hear that when I went to the Palace to get my decorations, the military band, which was at the moment hotly engaged in "Chu-Chin-Chow" stopped in the middle of a phrase, and changed to "Annie Get your Gun".'[17]

Sitwell herself probably thought about getting a gun as she was still trying to make Ernest Rootham assist with Evelyn's expenses; he was more generous with suggestions than with money. Evelyn wrote to Edith on 8 June:

> I have been trying to puzzle out what he exactly means by an annuity, I looked the word up in the dictionary but it did not help me much . . . Does he want to put me into a home for women in reduced circumstances? Perhaps it would be a good idea, but I would rather not accept any suggestion coming from him as I do not trust him. Also he has no right to suggest anything as he never does a thing for me. The only person who can arrange my future for me is you, and whatever you suggested I would always gladly accept. I owe my life to you & you have the ordering of it.[18]

Evelyn came for her visit in August, and the two discussed how Edith should negotiate with him, but it was all moot as Ernest Rootham died a few weeks later (*The Times*, 21 September 1954). Sitwell worked herself into a frenzy about his skinflint will, and Philip Frere teased her a few months later over a vicious letter she wrote to the solicitors for the estate. Taking the view that she might have committed that impossible thing, a criminal libel against a dead man, he urged her to hightail it to Persia while he put a stop to any possible prosecution.[19] Silly and peripheral as this episode seems, it provides a first glimpse of the general fury that would overtake Dame Edith Sitwell in the coming months.

For now, there was the matter of Pavlik. His letters were friendly and dealt with safe topics such as his veneration for the philosopher Gaston Bachelard, who was the only man of substance he could find in Paris apart from Picasso whom he thought 'sort of gaga'.[20] Bachelard admired Tchelitchew's paintings and had written the preface to the catalogue of his exhibition that summer at the Galerie Rive Gauche.[21] Although Tchelitchew hurt Sitwell many times and was often bizarre in his thinking, he led her, very occasionally, in good directions. In 1950, he had introduced her to Bachelard's writings; she had read with fascination *La terre et les rêveries de la volonté* and some other works.[22] Indeed, for a time she was absorbed in Bachelard, as she ordered four more books in 1951: *La psychanalyse du feu, Le pluralisme cohérent de la chimie moderne, La valeur inductive*, and *La formation de l'esprit*.[23]

In his account of science, Bachelard insisted on an awareness of mental structure and interior process – the sort of thing Sitwell was also grasping after in the writings of Lancelot Law Whyte. Given what science had produced at Hiroshima, Sitwell believed the claims of positivists to be smug and dangerous. This particular stance had implications for what she wrote and what she praised. To her mind, the poetry of close observation – advocated by both Grigson and The Movement – was often morally and spiritually evasive. For her, such poets founded their technique on a naive confidence about the intelligibility of the material world. Even though she rejected Surrealism because of its ultimate disorder of thought and form, she took seriously its efforts to confront the interior life. Though not a philosopher, Sitwell felt that no poetry could be truly great that fell into the gap between subject and object, self and other, which had blighted Western thought since the time of Descartes.

Sitwell was 'nearly driven bats' in the summer of 1954, trying to write an 'An Elegy for Dylan Thomas' that had been commissioned by the American journal *Poetry*.[24] Finished at the end of September, it reflects her preoccupation with Bachelard. She claims that a true poet must bring a new creation myth to a world trapped by its materialist ways of thinking:

to the Minotaur in the city office
Crying to the dunghill in the soul, 'See, it is morning!'

And seeing all glory hidden in small forms,
The planetary system in the atom, the great suns
Hid in a speck of dust.
     So, for his sake,
More proudly will that Sisyphus, the heart of Man,
Roll the Sun up the steep of heaven, and in the street
Two old blind men seem Homer and Galileo, blind
Old men that tap their way through worlds of dust
To find Man's path near the Sun.[25]

The friendship of Homer and Galileo is Sitwell's metaphor for a consciousness that unites science and poetry; each by itself is blind, but they can be brought together in a conception like William Blake's of the glory of forms.

Pavlik announced on 20 September that he was coming to London for an exhibition of his work at the Hanover Gallery, and he asked Edith to help with the opening. She told Sachie: 'His Lordship has written to me about this, and seems to think nothing has happened – the last 4 years having, apparently, slipped his memory.'[26] Sachie was angry for her sake. Writing from Montegufoni where she remained until about 19 October, Edith cautioned Georgia: 'In re Pavlik. I beg of Sachie not to show anything, as the whole thing is going to be a fearful strain and *most* painful for me, and I don't want anything to happen which would be an extra strain. I have been asked to *open* his exhibition, on the 26th. What I am doing, I am doing simply because he is a very great artist – for no other reason. I am afraid I do not feel the same. I shall be very amiable to him, but, as I say, I do not feel the same.'[27] She heard soon after that Tchelitchew's doctor had forbidden him to travel to England.[28] On 22 October, he told Edith that she was 'first' of all his friends, but in the rest of the letter he seemed more concerned with missing the show than with not seeing her.[29] In the following months, his letters went on in their self-regarding way – recounting, for example, how Bachelard had praised his work and how a psychic had told him he had 50 per cent more brain than other men.[30]

As Sitwell pondered the problems of materialism, her bank was considering her overdraft. A reading tour was laid on for November, but Coutts & Co. were reluctant to extend Sitwell more credit to make the trip. In what must have been an embarrassing request, she asked her American publisher Edward Weeks to write a letter to the bank. He explained for one of the directors, Charles Musk, how much his firm had invested in her project: 'we undertook it in the belief that the Anthology will have a wide reading and a long life. Anything that you can do to facilitate the length of Dame Edith's stay in New York will be deeply appreciated.'[31] The bank acquiesced, and Edith joined Osbert and David on the ocean liner.

Her new *Collected Poems* was released by Vanguard in New York that month, and the reviews were celebratory. In the *New York Herald Tribune* (23 January 1955), Gene Baro saluted her 'technical brilliance'. Richard Eberhart wrote in *Poetry*: 'Edith Sitwell reaches up to a great paradox, wondrous simplicity, direct intuitive power, gained through precise, accurate, intellectual judgments surpassed in a unity of positive praise available to any ear. Sublimity of utterance and a deep truth come directly through her flowing means and all her artful balances. This is the power of the concrete, a massive presence of reality, a passionate experience of truth.'[32] In one of the most important of all reviews of her work, Kenneth Rexroth, the San Francisco poet who launched the Beats, saw through to her struggle with the Symbolists and Surrealists:

> Edith Sitwell is the nearest thing to a major poet that the British Isles have produced since Hardy, Lawrence, and Yeats. With the possible exception of Hugh MacDiarmid she is now the only British Poet who possesses that special accent of both individuality and scope which makes a writer a member of world literature . . . Her later poems have absorbed the systematically deranged world of Rimbaud, the madness of Lautréamont, the ghoulish, rebus-picture fables of the surrealists, all the insanity and agony of the modern world . . . In addition, they have a solemn music . . . Behind the vision, behind the new virtuosity, is something rare in modern verse, so artistic and so neutral: the moral earnestness that makes English poetry great . . . these are good words for the human race to hear. (*New York Times*, 23 January 1955)

There was plenty to celebrate, and Sitwell got on with it. A story reached Lincoln Kirstein that one night in New York Sitwell was so drunk that when she heard the pipes rattling at 3 a.m. she demanded that the hotel manager break down the wall because a nun was trapped inside.[33] The same story reached the magazine writer and diarist Leo Lerman, who threw a birthday party for Osbert on 6 December 1954, at which an unwilling W. H. Auden wound up playing butler to Lerman's guests. When the cake appeared, Auden led the singing and Osbert wept. Edith fell into an intense, hand-holding, and presumably bibulous conversation with Marlene Dietrich. Sitwell declared, 'You are the great revelation of my life' and promised to send her a copy of *Collected Poems*. The bisexual Dietrich liked the looks of Sitwell and remarked, 'A great woman, that one.'[34]

The tour included Boston, Washington, and other cities, but the highlight that year came in Chicago. Karl Shapiro, then editor of *Poetry*, was delighted to follow up 'An Elegy for Dylan Thomas' with an appearance by Sitwell on 26 January. On a snowy night, she sold out Fullerton Hall at the Art Institute of Chicago. She also gave a reading sponsored by the *Chicago Review* at the University of Chicago, where she was introduced to another large crowd by the poet and critic Elder Olson, whose wife Jerri Hays Olson wrote an account of the evening. After dinner at the faculty club, Dame Edith was told that it was time to go out the back door and across the street to Mandel Hall where the reading would take place. She sank into the nearest sofa, saying, 'My dear, I can't walk.' A car was brought to the front door and it took her through a tangle of one-way streets till they reached the other building. 'After what must have seemed to her a very long ride, Dame Edith looked at me triumphantly and said, "See, my dear, I told you I could not have walked."'[35] Funny as this is, it also tells us that by 1955 Dame Edith Sitwell was not so much lazy as lame.

Before another reading at Northwestern University, Dame Edith gave an interview to the radio journalist Mary Merryfield, who reported:

We were amused yesterday when this poet had the same difficulty all women seem to have – finding something in her handbag. She insisted we were her guests for tea and when the waiter came with the check, she started through the cluttered interior of a round black velvet purse, pawing handkerchief, spectacle case, and all sorts of trivia to the surface including a handful of bills – not in a billfold – some of which she seemed to seize at random and thrust into the surprised hand of the waiter, murmuring, 'thank you, thank you so much. Thank you. Thank you.' She then pushed the bills et cetera back into the bag, clicked it shut and declared, 'I never know whether they'll let me sign one of those bills, whether they want you to pay when things come or whether they're going to hover nearby and confuse you.'

During the interview, Sitwell praised two Midwestern poets, Marianne Moore and Isabella Gardner. Merryfield asked pointedly how in troubled times Sitwell found the serenity to write poetry: 'She tossed her head and answered us: "Yes. I believe. I believe in people – and I believe. Anyway, it's better with all banners flying – isn't it?"'[36]

In fact, Sitwell had reached the end of what had always been a limited serenity. Osbert's disease was progressing, making life undoubtedly difficult for David Horner, who left New York to continue an affair begun earlier with the painter Brian Connelly.[37] On 17 January, Edith scribbled across a letter to Sachie, *Private and Confidential / Destroy / Let Silence be / the Watchword*' in which she recounted that

> Dear little Lord Fauntleroy has *not* been in New York during the whole of our stay, but has been staying with a friend in the Country. (He did lunch once with O). *Nor* has he gone with O to Florida . . . I am afraid I really let myself go to O on the subject of the little Lord's behaviour, and this has not made me popular. To have chosen this moment to let O be looked after by strangers!!! I did not tell you until I could control myself, because it is dangerous for us if we fall into rages over it, because he will come back when there is something to be got out of it.[38]

Edith did indeed speak her mind to Osbert, and he was extremely angry. It appears that he told her then that he and Horner had been lovers for many years and that he could not do without him. In London, it was said that Osbert had had to explain to Edith for the first time in her life what homosexuality was. That story is not credible.

Sachie knew of and was embarrassed by Osbert's sexuality. Even Sir George had referred to Horner as Osbert's 'boy-friend',[39] though perhaps not in front of Edith. Since the First World War she had been constantly in the company of homosexuals. She undoubtedly received reconnaissance about Tchelitchew's lifestyle, and Charles Henri Ford believed she knew that Tchelitchew was a homosexual.[40] In 1934, she had been able to frame a question for Edward James about what, specifically, the men were doing with each other in *The Young and Evil*, and Geoffrey Gorer recalled that she was shocked not by the homosexuality in that book but by the promiscuity.[41] On the other hand, it is likely that she simply chose not to think about Osbert and David as lovers, pretending that their connection was much as hers had been with Helen Rootham.

In the midst of her rage against Horner, she became interested in the number of murders in New York. She told Sachie she was 'cross' with the police for killing August Robles, described by the *New York Times* (21 February 1955) as a 'squint-eyed killer'; he was shot during a siege by hundreds of police at an apartment in East Harlem after a running gun battle and a three-day manhunt. She said she had been hoping to contact him: 'Very reliable, and dirt-cheap! Only 250 dollars for "air-conditioning" someone! I can think of someone who could do with it!'[42]

In the absence of a hitman, Sitwell turned to the clergy. Her anger was an overpowering experience – and Osbert's demand that she control herself was beyond her strength. It would not be true to say that bad temper caused Edith Sitwell to become a Catholic. As we have seen, she had pondered the step since 1918 when she told Robert Nichols: 'one day I shall become a Roman Catholic. (It is the only creed for someone like myself, I do feel that more and more.)'[43] She had been exposed to more than thirty years of Helen Rootham's devotions. As a literary formalist, Sitwell found the Catholic idea of transubstantiation of bread and wine attractive as a symbol; it provided the key image for her poem 'Harvest'. She told the novelist and music critic Edward Sackville-West, himself a Catholic, about her reasons for delay: 'You say it took twelve years to bring you to your resolution. It must have taken about the same time to bring me to mine.' However, her hesitation in the last few years had been because

she did not want to distance herself from her brother: 'Because Osbert
is so ghastly ill, and I felt, so to speak, that I could not leave him.
Then one day in New York this winter, he told me that I must
become a Catholic. And he said, "How do you know that I may not
become one too." And so I hope he will.'⁴⁴ The period of twelve years
would take her back roughly to David Horner's reception into the
Church; she congratulated him at the time.⁴⁵ In a very strange twist,
it is possible that over the years his conversation and example had led
her closer to conversion, yet it took rage against him in 1955 for her
to make the final leap.

   The first people she turned to were the Campbells, asking them to
be her godparents. Mary Campbell responded on 3 March: 'Dear Edith
there is nothing that would give us greater joy – We are both absolutely
delighted & honoured. Roy had tears of joy in his eyes as he read your
letter.'⁴⁶ Before leaving the United States on 9 April, Sitwell wrote to
Father Martin D'Arcy, a Jesuit priest who specialised in converting
writers, among them Evelyn Waugh. In Muriel Spark's *The Girls of
Slender Means* (1963), one character can 'never make up his mind
between suicide and an equally drastic course of action known as
Father D'Arcy'.⁴⁷ He wrote to Sitwell on 14 April: 'Your letter reached
me this morning. I cannot say how happy it made me. I had felt such
love moving in your last volumes of poetry. I am anxious to help in
every way I possibly can.'⁴⁸ However, he was at Notre Dame University
in Indiana, and Sitwell was back in London. He recommended that she
see the historian, Father Philip Caraman, a Jesuit who edited the
Month. Caraman was a close friend of Waugh, and it was he who said
Mass for him in Latin on Easter Sunday 1966, after which Waugh collapsed and died in the toilet at Combe Florey. For a time, Caraman was
also a friend of Graham Greene but they fell out over Greene's relationship with Catherine Walston.

   Caraman told Sitwell on 1 May: 'I am convinced that the Holy
Spirit has so worked already in your heart and mind, that there is little
left for a priest to do, save take you systematically through the principal articles of Catholic belief.'⁴⁹ Sitwell was excited about what lay
ahead; she wrote to him from Montegufoni: 'I believe, and trust with
all my heart, that I am on the threshold of a new life. But I shall have
to be born again. And I have a whole world to see, as it were for the

first time, and to understand as far as my capacities will let me.' Prayer, however, had always been a problem for her: 'I feel very far away, as if I were speaking into the darkness.'[50] He suggested that she had out-grown old ways of praying and should pass on to new ones: 'Try simply resting in the presence of God, and, as it were, taking God in: quietly kneeling down, trying to do nothing except love him.'[51]

Edith Sitwell was no mystic, although at times her artistic experi-ences took on such a tone. On 23 April she attended a performance at the Wigmore Hall of Benjamin Britten's *Canticle III: Still Falls the Rain*. She wrote to Britten on the 26th:

> I am so haunted and so alone with that wonderful music and its wonderful performance that I was incapable of writing before. I had no sleep at all on the night of the performance. And I can think of nothing else . . . During the performance, I felt as if I were dead – killed in the raid – yet with all my powers of feeling still alive. Most terrible and most moving – the appalling loneliness, for all that it was a communal experience one was alone, each being was alone, with space and eternity and the terror of death, and then God.[52]

Sitwell's experience of God was bound up with her sense of the glory hidden in forms – just as she had described in 'An Elegy for Dylan Thomas'. At Caraman's suggestion, she read more of Aquinas, as well as Martin D'Arcy's *The Nature of Belief*, in which she fastened on this sentence: 'The evil of unbelief is that it must shut its eye to the forms and patterns of truth inscribed in the universe, and retire to the inner sanctuary of the mind, there to rest in uncertainty, in the presence of a fugitive self and the broken idols of its hopes.' Sitwell had her own way of saying this: 'When I was a very small child, I began to see the patterns of the world, the images of wonder. And I asked myself why those patterns should be repeated – the feather and the fern and rose and acorn in patterns of frost on the window – pattern after pattern repeated again and again. And even then I knew that this was telling us something. I founded my poetry upon it.'[53]

Caraman made several trips to Renishaw in July, and they decided

to go ahead with her reception into the Church on 6 August, the Feast
of the Transfiguration, which Caraman thought fitting as 'a revelation
of the blinding beauty of the soul in God's grace'.[54] Perhaps by way of
an apology, she invited Alec Guinness. They had not had much contact for about four years. Sitwell tended to be dictatorial at her
dinner parties, pronouncing judgments on writers and artists, and she
expected her guests to agree with her. On one occasion, she declared
that Beethoven was a bore, and asked her guests whether she was not
right. Dylan Thomas and Stephen Spender agreed in turn. Guinness
tried to evade the question, but Sitwell asked again whether he
agreed, so he said, 'Not at all. I imagine Beethoven will be played
and loved long after everyone at this table has been entirely forgotten.' Invitations to the Sesame stopped coming. Responding to this
very different invitation, Guinness told her his own news: 'I am
receiving instruction from a Roman priest. I only tell you that as I
know you won't despise it. And anyway you gave me the Leon Bloy
books!'[55]

Since the Campbells lived in Portugal and could not attend the ceremony, Sitwell asked Evelyn Waugh to serve as an additional godfather.
He wrote to Caraman, 'I am an old friend of Edith's & love her. She is
liable to make herself a little conspicuous at times.' He urged them to
avoid publicity: 'What I fear is that the popular papers may take her up
as a kind of Garbo-Queen-Christina . . . There are so many malicious
people out to make a booby of a Sitwell.' On 7 August, he wrote to
Nancy Mitford: 'Yesterday I went to London to stand godfather to
Edith Sitwell who has submitted to the Pope of Rome. She looked
fine – like a 16th century infanta – and spoke her renunciation of heresy
in silver bell tones.' A new protégé, the poet Quentin Stevenson, afterwards an actor, served the Mass and told Victoria Glendinning that
Sitwell made her renunciations with great emphasis.[56]

Waugh wrote to Sitwell on the 9th:

It is 25 years all but a few weeks since Fr. D'Arcy received me into
the Church. I am aghast now when I think how frivolously I
approached . . . You have come with much deeper insight. Should I
as Godfather warn you of probable shocks in the human aspect of
Catholicism? Not all priests are as clever and kind as Fr. D'Arcy and

Fr. Caraman . . . But I am sure you know the world well enough to expect Catholic bores and prigs and crooks and cads. I always think of myself: 'I know I am awful. But how much more awful I should be without the Faith'. One of the joys of Catholic life is to recognize the little sparks of good everywhere, as well as the fires of the saints.

He expressed some hope for Sitwell's moral character: 'I heard a rousing sermon on Sunday against the danger of immodest bathing-dresses and thought that you and I were innocent of that offence at least.'[57]

While she was laying up treasure in heaven, Sitwell faced an income tax problem on earth. That July, a bill became due for £1038. Since this would go directly on to her overdraft, Charles Musk at Coutts wanted her to put off paying it until she could meet with him and go over her whole situation. Noting ominously that expenditures had exceeded receipts for some time, he wondered whether her agents would be collecting considerable funds soon. She replied, in effect, that it was impossible to ignore the demands of the Inland Revenue. He then suggested a temporary extension of credit to pay half the amount, with a plan to clear up the remainder when she received a payment from Columbia Pictures in January.[58] The Inland Revenue was not satisfied, but in September her accountant counselled her to delay payment further in view of her 'extremely embarrassing' overdraft.[59] The problem was not resolved, and in March 1956 she had to ask for a loan of £1468. The bank agreed for the amount to remain temporarily on the books, even though this raised her net indebtedness to nine hundred pounds above securities: 'In the circumstances, we trust that you will restrict your drawings upon us as much as possible.'[60] Through the 1950s, the Inspector of Taxes repeatedly queried Sitwell's expense claims and accepted them only after long wrangling with her accountants.

Sitwell seems not to have considered shutting down the parties at the Sesame or cutting back on entertainment while abroad. Instead, she dwelt on how she had been cheated in various ways – by her parents, by Sister Edith Woods, by Humphrey Searle, and by Ernest Rootham. She began to believe that Helen and Evelyn had exploited her financially over the years. She had, indeed, given away a lot of money and continued to do so. However, in another way, she was making excuses for her way of life. Her commitment to Catholicism could not provide an easy cure for the unhappiness of a person who, for all her virtues, drank so much. Nor could an accountant sort out her business affairs when she was making key decisions on the basis of such an addiction. The parties continued. Sitwell was desperately counting on a best-seller to fix the money problem, so through the summer of 1955 at Renishaw, and from October to the beginning of March at Montegufoni, she worked on her anthology and on her delayed sequel to *Fanfare for Elizabeth*.

Italy's winter that year was cold. With her thoughts full of snow and ice, Sitwell retold in her letters a story she had heard about a group of polar bears, walruses, seals, and sea-elephants who had supposedly floated with the currents all the way from the North Pole to Rio de Janeiro: 'I expect there was a good deal of quarrelling en route.' At the end of their journey they were placed in a zoo: 'Such a sad end to a lovely outing.'[61] On 18 February, she told Benjamin Britten that the temperature at Montegufoni was thirteen degrees below zero: 'It is said that the wolves are out in the mountains. I have suggested that the Priest's step-mother, a very fat woman and a great trial to him and his parishioners, should be exposed, tied to a tree. This suggestion was greeted with enthusiasm.'[62]

She would doubtless have liked to tie David Horner to the same tree. She believed that Osbert declined over the winter, and that Horner was the cause of it. Back in England, she consulted with Philip Frere and with Osbert's physician, Armando Child, to whom she wrote on 20 May 1956: 'Something *has* to be done to protect Osbert. He is being made much worse by a situation that is horrible, grotesque, and vile. He is too ill, too shocked, and too despondent, to do anything himself, so I am going to do it for him. We *cannot* go on like this.'[63] In her opinion, Osbert should be placed in a nursing home, while David Horner was to be turned out of Renishaw. It was a tough-minded plan, but nothing came of it; Osbert was not so biddable. Meanwhile, according to Quentin Stevenson, Edith's homophobic talk about Horner was giving offence to guests at the Sesame.[64]

Knowing of the tax problem and Edith's need to work steadily, Evelyn decided to stay in Paris that summer, and, instead, Edith later made one of her now rare visits to Paris, staying at rue Saint-Dominique for two nights in October.[65] The anthology appeared ready for copy-editing at the end of August, but many errors were found in the text. It would be two more years before the volume came out. There was a greater problem with her treatment of Elizabeth I, *The Queens and the Hive*. She delivered the first twenty-four chapters that summer,[66] but as her health declined, the book ground to a stop. It did not finally appear until 1962. A sign of her anxiety about this book can be found on the contract with the American publisher: she drew five vertical lines beside the clause requiring delivery on 1 September 1956, with the publisher having the right eventually to terminate the contract and recover its money.[67]

Her circle at the Sesame attracted new members. Alberto de Lacerda was born in Mozambique in 1928 and became one of the most important Portuguese poets of the twentieth century. He arrived in London in 1951 and worked with the Portuguese Service of the BBC, meeting Sitwell through Roy Campbell and Arthur Waley.[68] Sitwell called de Lacerda 'one of the most intelligent and subtle people I have ever known'.[69] Quentin Stevenson became a regular from 1954, and she often spoke of him, to his embarrassment, as the next great poet. For several years, Sitwell and Stevenson had a warm friendship; she helped him find work, while he tried to interest her in some of the Movement poets, especially his friend Elizabeth Jennings, but, with Sitwell, that argument was unwinnable.

Stevenson also introduced her to the work of another of his friends, Geoffrey Hill, about whom Sitwell had no doubts: she repeatedly praised his work in her lectures of the late 1950s as 'outstanding'.[70] Joe Ackerley advised Stevenson that Sitwell was overpraising him. Indeed, Stevenson found Sitwell's praise an unbearable pressure and stopped seeing her later in the decade. However, she was not unique in being dazzled by his abilities. His book *The Succession* (1957) drew some remarkable reviews. For example, Peter Levi, himself a first-rate poet, later to be elected Professor of Poetry at Oxford, mused: 'Is this embodiment of an intimate personal passion in almost showily brilliant technique not what we were waiting for, we with our little magazines and our movements to keep poetry half-alive?'[71] Going about his acting career, Stevenson published practically nothing else, but sent Levi a sheaf of new poems in 1999, which led Levi to

confirm his opinion that Stevenson was the best poet of their generation.[72] And yet, as late as 2011, Stevenson's later work has had only a
private printing.[73]

Marilyn Monroe and her new husband Arthur Miller came in the
late summer of 1956 to London, where Monroe was filming *The
Sleeping Prince*, while Peter Brook was putting on a production of
Miller's play *A View from the Bridge*. Natasha Spender had no idea she
was walking into a media event as Sitwell had merely invited her to
lunch with a couple called Miller. She arrived to discover maids clus-
tered in the windows and other staff at the door waiting for the movie
star to appear.[74] Monroe recited some of Dylan Thomas's poems and a
sonnet by Hopkins: 'I wake and feel the fell of dark, not day.' Sitwell
stuck to her guns about Monroe and declared her 'quite remarkable'.[75]

That summer James Purdy, then living in Allentown, Pennsylvania,
had his first collection of stories, *Don't Call Me By My Right Name*, published by a small press. He sent copies to various writers he admired,
hoping to be noticed: 'A kind of psychic impulse caused me to mail a
copy to Dame Edith Sitwell, to the Castello di Montegufoni, Italy. I
never expected Dame Edith (whom I did not know) to set eyes on the
book, let alone read it.' Yet she did. On 20 October, she wrote that she
thought several of the stories were 'masterpieces. They have a terrible,
heart-breaking quality.'[76] He then sent her *63: Dream Palace*, a short
novel. She wrote back on 26 November: 'What a *wonderful* book! It is
a masterpiece from every point of view. There can't be the slightest
doubt that you are a really great writer, and I can only say that I am
quite overcome.'[77] These letters left him 'unhinged'.[78] She pressed the
books on Victor Gollancz, who published them as a single volume in
1957; to Purdy's and Sitwell's dismay, he altered some sexual passages
to avoid prosecution. In 1961, Sitwell contributed an introduction to
Purdy's *Color of Darkness*. He went on to have a distinguished career
and was saluted by Gore Vidal in 2005 as an 'outlaw' of American literature (*New York Times*, 27 February 2005).

Purdy never forgot his debt to Edith Sitwell. In 1991, Val Clark,
then his agent at Curtis Brown, brought a new colleague to meet him
at his home in a brownstone in Brooklyn Heights, New York. While
he made Turkish coffee, they looked around his flat. On the walls
were hand-coloured engravings of boxers: 'Off to the side, a little

lower near his bed stand, perhaps above his head when he lay asleep or just off to the side so he could see her there from where he lay, was a framed photograph of Edith Sitwell. When . . . he saw us gazing upon that image, he told us how she, Dame Edith Sitwell, was his guardian angel.'[79]

24

THE EMPRESS PENGUIN

'The housemaids will wax the floors, and I slipped and crashed on to my face, waking to find myself lying in a pool of blood, with my head on Miss Fraser's knee, she holding towel after towel to my face, and the butler putting ice on my forehead. I cannot think how I escaped breaking my nose and both cheek bones.'[1] This accident happened at Montegufoni around the beginning of December 1956. Sitwell was always clumsy, and her letters since the 1920s describe many falls, but now they were becoming dangerous. In October 1954 she had tumbled into an old-fashioned lift that stopped, as she maintained, three feet below the floor, leaving her with injuries to her ribs and right hand.[2] In February 1956, she told Benjamin Britten: 'I got influenza twice – or rather it returned to me, this being a habit of the new kind. And then, just as I had recovered, and was walking about with legs made of cotton wool, I crashed onto the stone passage. Why I didn't kill myself, I can't think. But I bruised, strained, and tore every muscle and tendon that could be bruised, strained, or torn!'[3] Osbert's secretary, Lorna Andrade, attributed Edith's falls to liquor.[4]

Sitwell's general physical condition was poor. When Stephen Spender asked her to join a group of writers and artists going to Hungary to show solidarity with the revolution against the Stalinists, she refused, despite sympathy with the cause:

I should only be a liability to the rest of the party if we did get visas. I shall be seventy on my next birthday, and am now extremely lame. I have arthritis in both knees, acute rheumatism in both feet, and often am only able to walk – and slowly at that – with the aid of a stick. In addition, I get attacks of sciatica in its most acute form. I had it for over a year, and it returns, so that when I travelled back from Aldeburgh Festival, I could not put my feet to the ground when I reached Liverpool Station, and had to be carried out of the train, wheeled along the platform in a truck, and carried into my club.[5]

Sitwell gave John Lehmann a long account of all the illnesses suffered that winter in Montegufoni by members of the household, including boils and paratyphoid. One person alone was untouched: 'D.H. is radiantly well, and his pretty golden curls are like sunlight in the house and in my heart!!!!'[6] Disgust with Horner shaped her reaction to the news that, early on the morning of 10 January 1957, T. S. Eliot had married his secretary Valerie Fletcher, and that he had given John Hayward no notice that he was going to move out. Most friends, including Natasha Spender, could see that after ten years of caring for Hayward, Eliot, himself in bad health, was entitled to some happiness. However, Sitwell took Hayward's side completely, writing to Lehmann: 'Oh! What a beast Tom is!!! No, no, what you tell me is really too much! You wait! I'll take it out of that young woman! I'll frighten her out of her wits before I've done. As for Tom – he will, of course, be punished. He will never write anything worth while again. And indeed, hasn't for a very long time now. The Four Quartets are, to my mind, infinitely inferior to his earlier work – completely bloodless and spiritless.'[7] Lorna Andrade told John Pearson that, after hearing about Eliot's marriage Sitwell took to her bed for three days.[8]

Sitwell returned to England on 4 February and set out for the United States two weeks later. She was looking forward to reciting poetry again, as she told Sachie: 'I have been like a dead person now, for two years, with no poetry excepting my anthology.' David Horner had his own plans: 'As soon as we got on to the boat, O came to my cabin and told me that animal was going off again (for the duration) with the same animal as before. O said it was "a very good thing, as we need a little holiday." I must not refuse to speak to the second animal, as if I did, the other would "make a scene!" The impudence! The blackmail! The sickening, horrible creature! And they simply aren't house-trained! If you could have seen them on the dock!' Soon she was calling him 'little Jackal Horner'.[9] After her arrival on 24 February, she spent time with Minnie Fosburgh and Betsey Whitney who encouraged her in her outrage, as did their friend, Edith's American physician Connie Guion. As the wife of the ambassador, Whitney was adamant that if Horner came back to England there would 'be no queening it at the American Embassy'.[10] Homophobia was the order of the day.

The Sitwells were still filling auditoriums, but no longer merited the detailed press coverage that had been given to their first visits. Several itineraries for the tour survive. While it is not clear which was the final one, the Sitwells certainly gave readings at Manhattanville College and the YMHA Poetry Center in New York, and at Dartmouth College in New Hampshire. They spent a week in Washington, where she recited *Façade*, and appeared as well in Chicago, Detroit, Chapel Hill, Minneapolis, and Birmingham. They may also have appeared at South Bend (Notre Dame University), and in Montreal and Pittsburgh. The Sitwells were in Austin from 5 to 7 April; according to one observer at a reading at the University of Texas, 'she startled her audience by producing an alarm clock from her large reticule and in a menacing rasp demanding the time from a terrified young man in the front row.' The tour finished up back in New York on 16 April. Edith thought it had gone very well, but judged herself a 'stretcher case'.[13]

These American tours were essential to her finances. The gross revenues were high: most appearances brought in five hundred dollars each and the one in Texas brought in a thousand, to be split with Osbert after the agent's commission.[14] However, a good deal of the money was scattered in expenses: for example, avoiding aeroplanes, her first-class passage on the ocean liner was £443.[15] At a glance this seems extravagant, but by now both she and Osbert were disabled and they could not travel without the constant attention of stewards. It appears that she had to use a wheelchair most of the time she was in the United States.[16] That summer Coutts told her that her net indebtedness stood at £4586, exceeding her security by £1300 (the gross figure for her overdraft was about £13,000).[17] Lorna Andrade recalls that one night in 1957, Sitwell stood in the doorway of her bedroom at Renishaw and asked whether people were still sent to gaol for debt.[18]

Shortly before leaving the United States, Sitwell gave a press conference where an 'oaf' of a reporter sought her reaction to the death of Roy Campbell. She knew nothing of it and was devastated. On 23 April, Roy and Mary Campbell had been driving home from Holy

Week celebrations in Seville, when a tyre blew out and the car struck a tree. Mary was badly injured, and Roy's neck was broken.[19] Edith wrote to Georgia on 2 May, the day before sailing: 'Roy's death has been a dreadful shock to me, and a grief. He was so chivalrous to me, and one of my greatest friends . . . When I think that a noble, chivalrous man who was a great poet is dead – and what we have left!'[20]

Early on Christmas Day 1956, Pavel Tchelitchew, then in Rome, began spitting up blood and his nails turned blue. At the hospital, he was told that he had had a heart attack. He also learned that his heart was greatly enlarged and it had no regular rhythm. A cardiologist described his condition as grave. Tchelitchew believed he was dying and saw himself as a little bird sitting on his own shoulder.[21] His lungs bore old tuberculosis scars, and in recent years he had suffered from a tapeworm. He remained in hospital until 7 March, having picked up an infection of the lungs that took a hundred antibiotic injections to clear. He wrote to Sitwell on 12 March: 'Life is sometimes very strange indeed. The good sisters tryed [sic] to convert me into Catholicism – but I told them that a man of my kind can not be pinned to what an ordinary man can be. If I would be protestant naturally I would become Catholic – but Greek Orthodox is very lovely – very philosophical pythagorean.'[22] He later confessed to a Russian Orthodox priest. By April, he was spitting blood again and was back in hospital with episodes of syncope (fainting) as he struggled to breathe. As late as July 1957, Charlie Ford found it hard to accept what was happening and failed to communicate to Tchelitchew's friends how very ill he was.[23]

That summer Sitwell was at the Sesame, keeping an eye on Evelyn Wiel and awaiting reviews of the British edition of her *Collected Poems*. Among her guests was Beryl de Zoete, who brought her own irritations: 'She now raises her left hand above her head, and with her right hand twangs at my knee as though it were some archaic musical instrument. It is very painful, and I should like to hit her!'[24] Sitwell was receiving kind letters from James Purdy, who wrote that 'John Cowper [Powys], as I told you, is one of your deepest admirers, and does not lose track of you!' Purdy urged her to ignore the critics, and declared that 'The person who should win the Nobel Prize, dear Edith, is *you*! So many poets not fit to tie your shoe laces have won it.'[25] Sitwell wrote to

Waugh on 28 July, praising his tale of hallucinations, *The Ordeal of Gilbert Pinfold*: 'Leaving everything else aside, it seems to me the book must be highly valuable to every nervously constituted person. I, for one, always think "they" are persecuting me. And very often they are, but not always, and seldom as badly as I think!'[26]

A protégée of both Evelyn Waugh and Graham Greene and a friend and admirer of Roy Campbell, Muriel Spark had recently published her first novel, *The Comforters*, to acclaim, but she too was feeling persecuted when she came to visit Dame Edith Sitwell at the Sesame. That morning she had discussed the manuscript of her second novel with her agent Paul Scott, who is now remembered as the author of the *Raj Quartet*. He was not impressed and flicked the manuscript across the desk towards Spark using his third finger and thumb. Although he was willing to continue representing her, she left his office irate. She was nervous of meeting Sitwell, since she had once said in a review that Yeats was the greater poet – Sitwell seemed not to remember the review. This 'wonderful woman' told Spark how she admired the mysterious qualities in her writing. When Spark told the story of her dealings with Paul Scott, Dame Edith offered her a sabre-toothed consolation: '"My dear," she said, "you must acquire a pair of lorgnettes, make an occasion to see that man again, focus the glasses on him and sit looking at him through them as if he was an insect. Just look and look."' Dame Edith demonstrated with her own eyeglasses which hung from a chain around her neck.[27] It was a master's class in the art of the putdown, and Sitwell could not have had a student more apt than Muriel Spark.

Sitwell was enjoying herself again and so was entirely unprepared for the telegram that reached her on 1 August: 'Dearest Edith This message brings tragic news but also our dearest love last evening at eight Pavlik's great heart beat no more love again Choura Charlie.'[28] She wrote to Sachie on 6 August: 'Yes, it was a dreadful shock; so much so that I have been quite numb. One can only say that he was so ill, I doubt if he could ever have painted again, and that would have made life a hell to him. I think somebody might have told me he was dying. I knew he was very ill, but he had been so since January. If I had known I should have written to him . . . It has been an awful year. First, dear Roy's death, and now Pavlik's.'[29]

Sitwell's public tribute to Tchelitchew appeared in *The Times* on 20 August:

It is difficult for his friends to realize that they will never see him again. Nobody ever lived with more vehemence than this man, who was one of the greatest painters of the age. I have known several men of genius. Pavel Tchelitchew was perhaps the greatest I have known well . . . In Lorca's 'A Poet in New York' occurs a sentence about persons who wished 'not for form but for the marrow of form'. Tchelitchew gave both the marrow and the form. He seemed to capture the quintessence of light, and the first study for his great picture 'Hide and Seek' fills a room at Renishaw with that quintessence on the darkest day. Thinking of him, I see him, a desperately thin, anxious-looking young man, jumping for joy and clapping his large painter's hands, because there was snow on the ground, and it reminded him of his childhood – before the sufferings began, and the greatness.

That summer, *Collected Poems* was launched into heavy waters. It did receive some fine reviews. Although he later back-pedalled, Cyril Connolly wrote in the *Sunday Times* (28 July 1957): 'When we come to compare the collected poems of Dame Edith Sitwell with those of Yeats, or Mr. Eliot or Professor Auden, it will be found that hers have the purest poetical content of them all.' In the *Manchester Guardian* (20 August 1957), Anne Ridler called the book 'superb'. A reviewer in *The Times* (25 July 1957) wrote: 'If Dame Edith's appeal was once a rather private one, she is to-day a poet of the public gesture, large, generous, outgoing. Her habit of repeating favourite phrases and images, if it sometimes becomes a mannerism, at the same time does help to give the later poems their simplicity and sweep.' There were others in this vein.

However, there were also a good many negative reviews, of which the most influential was that of A. Alvarez (*Observer*, 28 July 1957). He thought the early poems had about them the air of a Christmas panto, and asked, somewhat solemnly: 'for adults, does it really *matter?*' Despite Alvarez's subsequent achievement as a critic and poet, one glimpses beyond that phrase a severe, donnish, even puritanical account of what poetry ought to be. He went on: 'Do the tricks of rhythm and rhyme, the exotic, improbable, nursery-tale objects make the early poems into anything more than delicious games? Was, in fact, Dame Edith, for all her inventions, ever "modern" in any significant sense? I would suggest, instead, that she used the new taste for difficulty as an excuse to free herself not from outworn conventions of feeling and expression . . . but from the perennial convention that a poem should mean something.' He went on to complain that Sitwell invited readers to engage in 'free-association – a kind of "do-it-yourself" verse'.

Heaven forbid that the author of *The Savage God* should tolerate 'delicious games' in literature, but this is not just po-faced; it is actually a false description of Sitwell's early poems. On one level, almost any of Sitwell's early poems can be shown to have significant paraphrasable content. On another level, we have seen in this book how the musical techniques of her work are themselves extraordinarily meaningful. One is left, then, to ask whether Alvarez has not himself a surprisingly limited conception of how the modern poem must operate. As for the later poetry, he says it is 'noisy and uncertain. She is so used to backing gracefully out of any definite commitment that she hasn't the means to handle full statements.' This sounds magisterial – an empress-with-no-clothes judgment. Yet in the course of this book we have seen again and again that fairly straightforward readings of her poems reveal structures of thought and feeling that are original, serious, and unified.

Sitwell was not able to see all this as an interesting difference of opinion – a necessary tangle with a gifted mind. Forgetting what she had said to Waugh about her supposed persecutors, Sitwell told Connolly that she thought Alvarez 'seething with hatred'. She watched her opportunities and later wrote a negative review of his book *The Shaping Spirit: Studies in Modern English and American Poets*. Having told Sachie that the bad reviews of her book were being organised by Grigson, she then wrote to a friend from the 1920s, the physician Hal Lydiard Wilson, 'the whole of the gutter press rose as one man and insulted me.'[30] In the absence of a promised review, she suspected a personal slight from Alan Pryce-Jones, the editor of the *Times Literary Supplement*. When one finally appeared on 20 September, she thought it perfunctory and hidden away.

In fact, Pryce-Jones wrote the unsigned review himself, and it stands with Rexroth's in 1955 as one of the most insightful readings of

Sitwell's poetry. He is one of the few critics alert to her work's affinities with modern music:

> Very early, Dame Edith laid down her *Grundgestalt*, a tone-row upon which she has spent a lifetime composing inversions, crab-inversions, contrapuntal movements of every kind. 'King', 'Rag', 'Gold', 'Ass', the notes of the row can be extended to considerably more than the twelve tones of the scale. By choosing some degree of limitation, however, Dame Edith has gained power through a method with which Schönberg would have experienced a practical sympathy. Like him, she has abolished the distinction between major and minor as an emotive factor . . . Having shown prodigies of virtuosity in variations on the scherzo, she has moved on to explore the possibilities of the long line – an adagio music which is particularly hard to sustain at concert pitch. These achievements alone must suffice to place her among the most consistently interesting of modern English poets. And in these 400 pages there is plenty to show that the word 'interesting' is only the lowest common factor of an outstanding collection of poetry.

Sitwell swore she would never talk to Pryce-Jones again – an oath she eventually had to break.[31]

This was the same old stuff: Sitwell always took reviews personally. But the death of Tchelitchew had made a difference. Grief, physical pain, anger with David Horner, panic about debts, liquor, and simple loneliness were breaking her down. In the coming years, there would be occasions when those around her feared for her sanity.

In that hard summer of 1957, one very good thing happened. After four years of able service, Mary Fraser was moving to Sweden, so Sitwell needed a new secretary. The pianist Gordon Watson proposed his friend Elizabeth Salter. Born in Angaston, South Australia, in 1918, she came to England in 1952. By 1957, she had a detective novel to her credit and would later become a biographer. Watson arranged for her to come to the Aldeburgh Festival in mid-June, where Sitwell and Day-Lewis were reading Blake's poems in the church. That initial meeting was frosty, and Salter assumed the job was a non-starter: 'How could one become secretary to a legend?' Nevertheless, Sitwell changed her mind and telephoned to hire her. On a July evening, Salter came to the Sesame to have drinks with Sitwell, Watson, and de Lacerda. Evelyn Wiel appeared a little late; Salter noticed that she had only two teeth left in her mouth and that a collection of noisy gold bangles ran up to her elbows. The evening passed happily, and Salter settled into the job that lasted until Sitwell's death.[32]

Sitwell's seventieth birthday fell on 7 September and the newspapers swarmed. Treating such interest as morbid, she told the *Evening Standard*: 'I am lying down for a little rest, covered by lots of bouquets of flowers.' The *Sunday Times* ran a friendly discussion with Sitwell conducted by John Lehmann, William Plomer, Frederick Ashton, and John Raymond. Even so, there was little comfort for her. She apologised to her 'dear Godmother' Mary Campbell for a late letter: 'ever since the early summer, griefs and disasters have been heaped on my head . . . The only thing to do, at such a time, is to be *silent* to those who are suffering more deeply than oneself – not to heap one's sorrows and troubles onto their greater ones, which is the height of selfishness. But now I realise that I must be being taught some lesson.'[33]

There was also work to get done. The proofs for her anthology filled a whole postbag, and she had to enlist Salter and de Lacerda to help her through them. She suffered from eye-strain and often wore dark glasses. By 23 September, she was in Montegufoni with various jobs to finish, most importantly *The Queens and the Hive*. Through these months Sitwell wrote regular letters to her secretary, asking her to type up manuscripts and to answer certain letters that did not merit a direct response. One instruction that Salter received from time to time, and always disobeyed, was to send out a form[34] that Edith and Osbert had composed for pests.

Another way to deal with pests and lunatics was to redirect their enquiries to F. R. Leavis. In this enterprise, Sitwell had the help of C. Day-Lewis, who had wondered a couple of years earlier whether it might soon be time to stop: 'I'm just planting picador's darts. I feel no animosity against Leavis. He's a valuable bull. If we kept him running around until he dropped, we should have the S.P.C.A. after us.'[35] Sitwell was also looking for pranks to play on F. W. Bateson, editor of *Essays in Criticism*, another critic with whom she had a feud. In her lectures, she often mocked his pronouncements that 'Poetry has a more honourable function than the titillation of the aesthetic sense', that poetry is 'no

A.   Name in full (Block letters as throughout)
....

B.   Specimen of usual signature ....

C.   Passport number .... (This must be accompanied by
     six photographs 2¼ inches by 4, and these must be signed both
     by a clergyman and by a Justice of the Peace. They must, also,
     have been taken within the last six months. Old photographs
     cannot be accepted.

D.   Finger Prints number (if any) ....

E.   When were you born ....

F.   Where were you born ....

G.   How were you born ....

H.   If not, why not ....

I.   For what purpose are you going there ....
     ....

J.   And if so, where ....

K.   Of what sex are you ....

L.   Age, sex and weight of your wife ....
     ....

M.   Father's name in full ....

N.   Mother's maiden name in full ....

O.   Has any relative of yours ever been confined in a mental home
     ....

P.   If not, why not ....

Q.   If so, give full details, with accompanying photograph ....
     ....

R.   Did you ever meet Burgess and Maclean, or anyone who ever
     knew them ? This last must be accompanied by an attestation
     taken in the presence of a Commissioner of Oaths ....
     ....

A form compiled by Edith and Osbert Sitwell in the 1950s, to be filled out by correspondents and visitors they judged to be lunatics

more useful, strictly speaking, than any other human activity', and that poetry is essentially a political act like voting. According to Sitwell, if Bateson had his way, we would have to get rid of a great many poets, starting with Keats (*The Times*, 16 May 1957).

While in Montegufoni, Sitwell tried, unsuccessfully, to organise another tour for the spring. She told Sachie that she hoped to do three lectures per week at a thousand dollars each.[36] This was an impossibility, as only the oil-rich University of Texas had been able to pay so much on her last tour. She returned to England around 14 February and six days later gave the address at a memorial service for the novelist Charles Morgan (*The Times*, 20 February 1958). On 12 March, she was

presented with the William Foyle Poetry Prize for *Collected Poems*; at
the luncheon, John Lehmann saluted her as 'a great poet, who has
found new words, new forms to fit the emotions, feelings, and thoughts
of her time . . . She is a pythoness poised in deadly attack against all
enemies of literature' (*The Times*, 12 March 1958).

Even if she was a pythoness, she feared attack from many directions, and counted on strict loyalty from her friends. In March, Alec
Guinness won an Oscar for *The Bridge on the River Kwai*, which was
followed by a cover-story on him in *Time* (21 April 1958). When he
received his copy, Guinness saw that it attributed to him an anecdote
about Sitwell's reception into the Church: 'Can you imagine Dame
Edith being borne majestically down the aisle on a little satin pillow?'

He rang up Sitwell at the Sesame and asked to see her urgently. She
invited him to lunch, but he said that she might not want him there
after she heard what he had to say: 'I found her sitting, alone and forlorn, on a dingy sofa in an ante-room.' He gave her the magazine and
disowned the quotation. Sitwell read it and flushed before laying it
aside. 'Stay to lunch,' she said. Guinness refused. 'It doesn't matter
about this,' she said, tapping the magazine. 'I am fortified against the
press.' De Lacerda appeared with his copy of the magazine, but she said
she had already seen it. After lunch, Guinness kissed Edith, and she
whispered, 'Light a candle for me in Farm Street one day.' Many years
later, he said that he had remembered once or twice to do so: 'When
I pass the chapel where she was baptized I can still conjure up her tall
figure, swathed in black, looking like some strange, eccentric bird and
Father Caraman pouring water over her forehead in the ancient rite.
She seemed like an ageing princess come home from exile.'[37]

In these months, Sitwell was working on one of the best poems of
her old age. 'His Blood Colours My Cheek', dedicated to D'Arcy and
published by Caraman in the *Month*, was based on a saying of St Agnes.
It is reminiscent of Yeats in its depiction of a soul fastened to a dying
animal, but it is also fastened to the animal's million years of evolution.
The poem contrasts two visions of ascent – the small ambitions of the
insect and the longing of the human heart for light:

[. . .]
I, an old dying woman, tied

To the winter's hopelessness
And to a wisp of bone
Clothed in the old world's outworn foolishness
– A poor Ape-cerement
With all its rags of songs, loves, rages, lusts, and flags of death,
Say this to you,
My father Pithecanthropus Erectus, your head once filled with
    primal night,
You who stood at last after the long centuries
Of the anguish of the bone
Reaching upward towards the loving, the all-understanding sun –
To you, who no more walk on all fours like the first
Gardener and grave-digger, yet are listening
Where, born from zero, little childish leaves and lives begin!
I hear from the dust the small ambitions rise.
The White Ant whispers: 'Could I be Man's size,

My cylinders would stretch three hundred feet
In air, and Man would look at me with different eyes!'
And there the Brazilian insect all day long
Challenges the heat with its heavy noise:
'Were I as great as Man, my puny voice
Would stretch from Pole to Pole, no other sound
Be audible. By this dictatorship the round
World would be challenged – from my uproar would a new
Civilisation of the dust be born, the old world die like dew.'
[. . .]
But I see the sun, large as the journeying foot of Man, see the
    great traveller
Fearing no setting, going straight to his destination,
So I am not dismayed.
His Blood colours my cheek; –
No more eroded by the seas of the world's passions and greeds, I
    rise
As if I never had been ape, to look in the compassionate, the
    all-seeing Eyes.[38]

This poem was followed in the summer of 1958 by 'The Outsiders' – a much slighter piece occasioned by Sitwell's anger at the government's failure to remove the criminal ban on private homosexual acts, as recommended by the Wolfenden Report of 1957. This poem was probably inspired by her worries about Osbert. In the absence of mercy, the supposedly 'Damned' crawl away to

> the Dead Sea shore. Their bliss,
> Their love, they knew now was a Pillar of Salt,
> From whom they had hoped to win Oblivion's Kiss.[39]

The phrase 'Pillar of Salt' was the old play on her own name Edith – the wife of Lot. The passage seems to say that because of the law homosexuals were condemned to the same desert of rejection that she herself had long inhabited.

In May, Sitwell recited *Façade* at Oxford, where she had a long talk with Salter and told her much of the story of her early life. The performance itself took place in the Town Hall with Peter Stadlen conducting. At the rehearsal the John Piper screen and its wooden frame fell, passing within inches of where Sitwell was seated at the front of the stage. It was caught by Stadlen's wife who fell to her knees and held the frame for a moment in a posture Sitwell compared to Christ carrying his cross.[40]

In Oxford, Sitwell met two of the Beat poets, Allen Ginsberg and Gregory Corso. Corso told her he was compiling an anthology to be illustrated with photographs of the poets in the nude; Sitwell declined his invitation to contribute. They were in town to give readings, including one at New College, a hotbed for the Campaign for Nuclear Disarmament. Corso read out his poem: 'O bomb I love you / I want to kiss your clank, eat your boom.' Members of the college poetry society called him a Fascist and threw shoes. He retaliated by calling them a bunch of creeps. Ginsberg tried to explain the poem, but ran into a wall of political orthodoxy, so he called them a bunch of assholes. Then both men walked out.[41]

Sitwell invited them to luncheon at the Sesame Club. They were several hours late. Quentin Stevenson went out to the street to look for them. Appearing at last, they announced that they were high.[42] Corso had brought a copy of his book *Gasoline*, with the inscription: 'For Sitwell . . . paeans, lyric hats, fennels, all for assured company . . . There's the Empress penguin, the King penguin, and the Ringed-neck penguin . . . Only penguin to have for pet is Ringed-neck because all other penguins must be refrigerated. I had a dream last night that I had a tall regnant Emperor penguin, but no refrigerator . . . anyway with love . . . Gregory Corso 1958.'[43]

In roll-neck sweaters and jeans, they sat on either side of Sitwell and traded stories with her about the horrors of childhood. Perhaps in recognition of their recent adventure, the menu included an ice-cream dish, 'bombe à l'américaine'.[44] Sitwell wrote to James Purdy:

> They behaved with great courtesy. The poor boy with the sweet expression [Corso] had, he told me, been sent to prison *at the age of 17 for three years* for organising a bank robbery! If ever, in my life, I saw anyone who had obviously been sweetened and in a way re-formed, by such a terrible experience, it was that boy. I am sure he is a kind of haunted saint, – a saint who has lost his way. For he *has* lost it. The other looked like a famished wolf . . . In an interview given to [the *New York Times*] the poor boy who had been in prison said that at a recital he gave of his poems in Paris, he had removed all his clothes, and recited as he was when he was born.[45]

According to Salter, the conversation moved from the worth of Aldous Huxley's experiments with mescaline to the three younger poets' use of marijuana to heighten sensibility. This surprised Sitwell who suggested that poets naturally had extreme sensibility as part of their equipment. When they left, they declared her an 'angel' and she told them that they were the hope of poetry. She later wrote of Ginsberg that there was 'no more important young poet, no young poet of greater gifts writing at this time'.[46]

The day after their luncheon, Sitwell received a letter from an Oxford don, probably Bowra, detailing the antics of Corso and Ginsberg: 'I took to my bed, and lay there with my mouth open pondering!'[47] A story went around Oxford that the Beats had offered Sitwell heroin but that she turned it down because it made her come out in spots. In late 1959, *Life* magazine included the tale in an article on the Beats, bringing down a savage letter from Sitwell: 'This is the most vulgar attack, actuated by an almost insane malice . . . You had better apologize, publicly, both to Mr Ginsberg and me immediately.' Ginsberg, too, denied the heroin story and, knowing what was best for them, the magazine printed an apology on 8 February 1960. The experience confirmed the opinion of the press that she had expressed to Graham Greene: 'Really it is the lowest profession: or do you think that drug-trafficking is lower? I doubt it!'[48]

On 16 May 1958, Sitwell received a distressing letter from Charles Musk about her overdraft, which now stood at £2400 above security: 'We feel sure you will appreciate that we could not agree to allow such a position to continue indefinitely, and in the circumstances we shall be glad to learn, at your convenience, whether you are in a position to deposit any further approved security with us.' In a desperate move, Sitwell offered to lay aside for the bank half the money from the anthology and *The Queens and the Hive*. She also offered the manuscript of an autobiography that she said she was writing. Unless she was able to repay the debt, the bank could hold the manuscript as its property to be published after her death and the deaths of her brothers. Musk responded gently to her proposal saying that the bank would be 'honoured' to receive her manuscripts when they were ready.[49] In 1951, Lehmann had suggested she write a memoir, but she had refused, largely because she did not want to trespass on Osbert's ground.[50] In 1958, she had various autobiographical fragments lying about from earlier attempts and had written a magazine article on 'Coming to London' about her years at Pembridge Mansions, yet was too absorbed in other work to get the new memoir properly started.

That summer, Sitwell was elected a vice-president of the Royal Society of Literature, along with Sir Winston Churchill, Somerset Maugham, C. Day-Lewis, and the translator E. V. Rieu. However, it was also a summer of migraines as she worked her way through a last pile of proofs for the anthology. Ted Weeks set her another task, as she explained to Sachie: 'He has sent me over, in two detachments, 8000 *sheets for me to sign with my name*. Yes, eight thousand! This isn't a joke, it is true. I have had fearful trouble with the Customs, who naturally think, either that the sheets bear invisible tracings of the latest atomic weapons, or else conceal some new way of smuggling cocaine. However they are now rescued, and my life is one long hell signing them.'[51]

Little, Brown released *The Atlantic Book of British and American Poetry* on 12 November 1958. Sitwell had been given essentially a free hand to compile a book of whatever she thought good or important. In the course of 1092 pages she did just that. David Daiches's review in the *New York Times* (16 November 1958) described it as 'generous, exciting, original, disorganized, unequal and sometimes acutely exasperating'; most other reviewers said much the same thing. Daiches simply could not understand, among much else, her exclusion of Johnson, Crabbe, Landor, and Edwin Arlington Robinson, as well as her devoting sixteen pages to the Welsh poet David Jones. Sitwell was plainly declaring war on received opinion – her poets were the visionaries, rhapsodists, and metrical innovators. Thinning out the mid-eighteenth century, she gave most space (twelve pages) there to Christopher Smart. The Romantics are massively represented. An eminent Victorian bore is poked in the eye: Matthew Arnold gets a single page, but Tennyson, Whitman, and Hopkins about fifteen each. She wrote a long letter to the newspaper (11 January 1959) justifying her choices, especially with regard to Jones (who was also a great favourite of T. S. Eliot's). Although devoted to Johnson's prose, she felt it was impossible to cut a passage out of 'The Vanity of Human Wishes', adding, memorably, that she did not include George Crabbe because she was not a sadist. She ended her letter asking for pity not blame: 'It is terrible to find oneself a solitary, highly unpopular electric eel in a pool peopled by worthy, slightly somnolent flat-fish.'

Victor Gollancz published the anthology in England a year later; again, most reviewers thought the book quirky, brilliant, eccentric, and often wrong. G. S. Fraser, in the *TLS* (1 January 1960), took just this position, but he also observed that while Sitwell's introductions to the poets were historically simplistic, her technical observations were very subtle. He added: 'Lots of theoretical critics, for instance, have jibbed at Dame Edith's notion of "texture"; nearly every competent practising reviewer of poetry uses it.' Actually, the idea had gained currency in the rarefied world of critical theorists, among them John Crowe Ransom, who defined a poem as 'a *logical structure* having a *local texture*' (his emphasis).[52] Sitwell's admirer, Northrop Frye, discussed the idea in his

Anatomy of Criticism,[53] as did W. K. Wimsatt and Monroe C. Beardsley in their famous essay 'The Affective Fallacy'.[54] Following Sitwell's own example of avoiding sadism, I cannot dwell on this point, except to say that Sitwell – often taken, even by such friends as Spender, Auden, and Connolly, to be a person of no ideas – contributed more to our under-standing of literature than she is given credit for.

Sitwell still had to finish her book on Queen Elizabeth, but her time was being eaten up, oddly enough, by leprosy. In November 1958, she heard that Graham Greene was making plans to research his novel, eventually entitled *A Burnt-Out Case*, at a *léproserie* in the Congo. She wrote to him from Montegufoni: 'Osbert and I are horrified to hear of your proposed sojourn among the lepers. But we feel you ought to have a little preliminary experience, think of us as moral lepers, and come here on your way.' She recommended that he read a book she had once encouraged John Lehmann to publish, *Miracle at Carville* (1952), by a Catholic of 'beautiful, touching faith' named Betty Martin who under-went an experimental sulphone treatment for leprosy and was cured.[55]

Nowadays, the term leper is thought offensive. In his history of the disease in modern times, Tony Gould calls it the 'odious L-word'.[56] Still, there is no telling this part of the story without it. When Sitwell returned to London in March, she fell 'into the iron *grip* of a Leper's Stepmother', something she likened to an instrument of torture:

> It is all, really, Graham Greene's fault that I got involved. Graham
> Greene came to luncheon with me two days after his return from a
> Leper Hospital in Belgian East Africa, where he had spent – I think –
> two months. So leprosy was much in my thoughts. A few days after
> this, I got *lumbago*, and the *Evening Standard* (which, I think, hires
> spies on the telephone exchange,) rang me up, *pestering* me, asking
> what was *really* the matter, and enquiring if one of their young ladies
> could come and see me. 'Better not,' I replied, 'for I have *everything*
> infectious excepting leprosy.'

This comment appeared in print and caused the stepmother of a man who had been infected in India to write and tell Sitwell that the dis-ease was not infectious, and that her words were humiliating to patients in the two English leprosariums. Having no idea that there were such places in England, Sitwell apologised immediately and discovered that the stepmother herself was poor and strangely afflicted. Salter tells how, for many months, Sitwell sent the woman a weekly hamper of groceries worth five pounds, but its recipient was beyond helping.

About a year later Sitwell explained it all to Benjamin Britten's friend Princess Margaret of Hesse: 'she took to *writing* to me, literally *every* day – and sometimes twice a day, with a list of grievances – amongst which are the facts that – apart from her stepson being a Leper, her husband, who is 78, suffers from Lolita-trouble, (so that, as the police disapprove of this, he is always being *snatched* away from her and incarcerated either in *jail or in a lunatic asylum*,) and that *clergymen fly like the wind when they see her*.'[57] On one occasion, Sitwell instituted a search in her room for a lost envelope from a leprosarium. It is impossible to catch leprosy from such an object, but Sitwell was convinced that all sorts of germs could travel in envelopes. Around November 1959, Sitwell had her doctor write to the woman and say that she was too sick to correspond further.

After about a year of working for Sitwell, Elizabeth Salter noticed that her employer was becoming more and more irritable. On 5 September 1959, Sitwell told her she was 'horribly depressed'.[58] As often happened at such moments, she wrote a cranky letter – in this case to the editor of the *Daily Mirror* on 9 September about 'the horrible story of George Chrobruk, of Hadylane, Chesterfield, who poked a cat out of a tree, and allowed his two Alsatian dogs to tear it to pieces – a process which lasted for *seven minutes*. This Monster was – fined £3. When will it be possible for a proper punishment to be inflicted for cruelty? My own feeling is that a revival of the stocks would be the only way in which to put a stop to this.' Since Sitwell was seldom cheerful in the years that remained, letters like this proliferated.

She also began to complain about Evelyn Wiel. The owners of the house in rue Saint-Dominique were trying to sell it and wanted her out, and it seems that Evelyn hoped Edith would set her up somewhere else. In the end, she was able to stay, but her rent increased, and she complained about debts. Though eighty-one, she mentioned that she was still giving English lessons to bring in money. Although her need was real, and she had no one else to help her, she did try to work on Edith's emotions. It was not a good time for this, as Edith's accountants had had to file appeals over her taxes.

Edith wrote to Salter from Montegufoni around November 1958: 'For three days I couldn't keep any food down, and got no sleep at all. The nights were an absolute nightmare of retching, and a kind of mental horror. This was simply brought on by the Income Tax badgering me to send them details I have not got here, and by poor darling Evelyn's plaints.' She explained to Salter how a third of her inherited income had gone to the Rootham sisters: '[Evelyn] has got nearly all my pictures, and now won't come over to England although I pay for *everything*, because she says she would "have to get so many things." She really behaves as if she were Garbo or Monroe. (She had £50 out of my prize last year). That family is a damned nuisance, and of no interest. Oh dear, I had not meant to go in for this long diatribe.'[59]

Sitwell's diatribes need to be taken with caution; though now very cantankerous, she continued to care about Evelyn, to send over three hundred pounds annually in a quarterly allowance and gifts, and to exchange warm letters that gave pleasure to both. On 20 January 1959, Edith wrote to Evelyn, 'I hate to bother you. But there is going to be a Memorial Exhibition of Pavlik's work. So please, darling, will you *bring over* the *four* he painted for me, and the *large drawing* of *a woman sitting on the sand*, and also that of *a child lying yelling under a flag, with an old woman bending over it*.' Evelyn decided against an early visit because of the expense, so Salter and de Lacerda were sent to collect them. Around 9 May, they visited the flat in Paris, to find Evelyn waiting for them amid cobwebs and peeling wallpaper. On the mantel were stacks of Edith's books and in a back room her paintings and drawings – many more than they had expected. Driving back to England with the pictures that Sitwell had asked her to fetch, Salter realised that the sale of the whole Tchelitchew collection could get her employer out of debt.[60] Evelyn delayed about the rest of the canvases, saying that to send them would cost a small fortune[61] – presumably in duty – but she also liked having the artworks in her flat. Quick to see herself as Sitwell's sole friend and protector, Salter thought Evelyn charming but 'unscrupulously mercenary'.[62] That is a hard phrase. Edith herself was probably closer to the truth in the 1930s and 1940s when she wrote of Evelyn as clinging to the outward signs of a vanished dignity.

The demands on Sitwell's time were unrelenting. The founder of Christian Action, Canon John Collins, wanted to involve her in his

work against apartheid, and his wife Diana Collins (later Dame Diana
Collins) wanted her help for the Campaign for Nuclear Disarmament.
These causes were close to Sitwell's heart, but Caraman thought she
should hold back: 'Your poetry can change the world more effectively
and you must devote yourself to that without any fears or worries that
you are or might be discourteous to cranks or enthusiasts.'[63] *The Queens
and the Hive*, though nearly finished, was at a standstill. Quite apart
from the effects of liquor, her legs were now atrophying, and she collapsed twice at a reading in Florence in February.[64] Aspiring writers
made their usual demands; she received on average two unsolicited
manuscripts per day: 'I never read manuscripts in any case though I
always *glance* at them.'[65] The Inland Revenue prodded her with 'unan-
swerable questions', including, bizarrely, whether she had given
satisfaction in her last situation: 'I think I shall reply that I was last
employed in a menial capacity by Miss Imregard A. Potter, of 8 The
Grove, Leamington Spa, in 1911, but that I did not give satisfaction.
There was some small unpleasantness, and I was dismissed without a
character.'[66]

25

I PREFER CHANEL NUMBER 5

'Great in far greater ways, Dame Edith Sitwell is a virtuoso of rhythm and accent,' said Marianne Moore in a lecture at the Johns Hopkins Poetry Festival in November 1958.[1] Higher praise was hard to come by, and most poets would simply bask in it. Instead, Sitwell chose to fight another odd rearguard action in the spring, when she returned to England. She went after an article that praised Christopher Logue for 'Jazzetry' – combining poetry and jazz: 'I am all for Mr. Logue and his friends continuing to recite their verses to jazz if it amuses them. But I shall be grateful if their efforts are not hailed as a new experimental art-form, and if they do not claim that they are its inventors' (*The Times*, 30 April 1959). Sitwell wanted it known that she and William Walton had been there first – thirty-seven years earlier.

Logue sent in a letter (5 May), explaining what he thought were differences between their inspirations and remarking that this particular sentence was hurtful and unworthy of a famous poet. On it went, with even Allen Tate writing from All Souls (12 May) to scold Logue for not admitting Sitwell's originality. The argument spread to *Encounter* and the *Daily Mail*. For once, however, Sitwell felt foolish and regretful over her letters to the editor. She decided that she had done him an 'injustice', that he had not stolen her idea, and that he was indeed an able poet. Later, she saw his translations from the *Iliad* and wrote: 'I regret having had any dispute with you. It grieves me that I was not one of the first to praise you.'[2]

Sitwell's appearance, quick wit, and supply of anecdotes made her a natural for television. On 6 May 1959, she was interviewed by the former politician John Freeman on his new programme *Face to Face*. Other guests wilted under Freeman's questioning, and when Evelyn

Waugh appeared a year later he resorted to grim stonewalling. Sitwell, however, was at her ease, defending her manner of dress and her taste for honours, describing her parents' marriage, and finally declaring that her poetry grew out of the fire of love for God and man. She appeared from time to time on other programmes, such as *The Brains Trust*, but the questioning was too restrictive for her to get proper mileage out of her anecdotes.[3]

At Benjamin Britten's request, she composed a poem that spring titled 'Praise We Great Men' and read it on 10 June at a concert in the Festival Hall, as part of the Purcell–Handel Festival. Intended to be recited rather than read on the page, the poem repeats the word 'Praise' in an effort to evoke Christopher Smart's poems, while it also tries to take up the tradition of poems for music on St Cecilia's Day. Dryden and Pope had written such poems, and Purcell and Handel had set them to music.[4] While not an important poem in Sitwell's canon, it had a curious afterlife. For years, Britten wanted to compose music for it, and it was the last thing he turned his hand to in 1976, but he died without having completed the score.[5]

Praising God in verse came easily for Sitwell, although not other-wise. The previous summer she had told Father Caraman that she was still unable to pray. He wrote back: 'You are really praying all the time you are thinking about God (in any way) and about all his creation. Any kind of contact with the mind or heart with God is prayer so you need not worry, dear Edith.'[6] The two of them conspired to find new converts. For many years, Caraman hoped, in vain, to win over Osbert, so that he might feel 'at home in the universe'.[7] Sachie, a resolute unbeliever, was never a candidate for conversion. In 1958–9, Caraman had his eye on Rosamond Lehmann and was upset when she decided not to convert because she hoped to remarry.[8] Caraman's main advice to Sitwell herself was that she slow down and get rest – and he urged her to skip Mass if she was suffering from migraines.[9]

Apart from a few public appearances, Sitwell remained at Renishaw from 16 May to 5 October. She told Salter: 'I am trying to avoid a very bad breakdown. My last three years have been appalling.'[10] At the beginning of August she told Salter to refuse all invitations to read or lecture during the autumn and winter.[11] At the beginning of September, she told Evelyn Wiel that she was not long for this world.[12]

Still, Sitwell made an adventure out of her reading at the Edinburgh Festival on 9 September. She and Salter set out in a chauffeured car from Sheffield with a supply of egg sandwiches, ham, liver sausages, smoked salmon, and chipolatas, which were to serve as a travelling lunch and then as supper once they arrived. In fact, Sitwell now only toyed with her food. She probably had more of a zest for the bottle each of white wine and gin that also went north with them. The matinée reading at the Lyceum Theatre nearly turned into a riot; the audience complained that they could not hear her, so she told them to pay more attention. The complaints continued, so she told them to get hearing aids. Salter ran backstage to have the curtain lowered, but by the time she got there the crowd had calmed down. Sitwell continued to read her own poems, some of Osbert's, and her old standby, the sleepwalking speech from *Macbeth*. She was annoyed when she heard of Salter's attempt to lower the curtain.[13] She did not want to be pulled out of a good brawl.

However rambunctious, she was growing more frail and soon took one of her worst tumbles. At the Sesame Club, she usually occupied a double room on the top floor,[14] where her bed, in great disrepair, was propped up on telephone directories. On 17 November, she reported to Georgia:

> At about 1 in the morning on Friday week, I, unable to sleep, was reaching out to find my lamp, (which had been put as far away from me on the table as possible) in order to read. I must have got too near the edge of this exquisite bed (which I think must have been one on which Burke and Hare despatched their victims, hired specially from Madame Tussaud's for me) when the whole thing gave way, and I was precipitated with my face against the iron part of the other bed. By the grace of heaven, I'd knocked over the telephone, in crashing, and the night porter rang up and said 'Are you all right?' I said 'No.'

The next thing she remembered was that she came to in bed with the staff of the club hovering around her. She had a blackened right eye and bruises going down her neck.[15]

Shortly after, Sitwell made the two-day journey to Montegufoni. She had handed the manuscript of *The Queens and the Hive* to the novelist Michael Stapleton, an editor with the Oxford University Press, and

a friend of Salter and Gordon Watson. He had earlier done research on
Queen Elizabeth I for Sitwell, so Macmillan commissioned him to
bring the nearly complete manuscript into publishable form.[16] Sitwell
turned her attention to a selection of the poetry of Swinburne, but her
plans were interrupted by another injury, which she described for
Sachie on 18 December:

> Ever since I had that accident in London, I have been terrified of
> complete darkness, so when the light went out, and I had a candle
> but no matches, I got out of bed to try to find another switch –
> couldn't, so felt my way back to my bed – caught hold of what I
> thought was the foot of the bed, but it wasn't; it was a very flimsy
> chair, which gave way, hurling me on to my spine onto the floor,
> where I lay in agony for about 5 hours, till I was called, when I was
> picked up and put on my bed really screaming with pain. I couldn't
> stand, or turn in bed, and am only now, after a fortnight, able to sit
> up without acute pain.[17]

She was bedridden through most of the winter. At times she had to
be carried downstairs by the butler. When making plans for a return
journey on 10 March 1960, she asked to be met by a wheelchair at
Calais, Dover, and London, as it was now impossible for her to walk any
distance.[18]

In what seems to have been a pleasant and somewhat recuperative
period, she stayed at the Sesame until 28 May. There was one troubling
event: on 19 May, J.W. Nicholson, a collector of taxes, threatened proceedings for arrears of £364 3s.[19] This was prevented by the usual
juggling, but she had almost no room to manoeuvre. At the same time,
Pavlik's old friend Parker Tyler pressed her for information for his biography of the painter. Some months earlier, she had heard from Tyler
and told him that she and Tchelitchew had had 'the same kind of
friendship that existed between Michelangelo and Princess Colonna'.
Tyler came to visit her at the Sesame in late May, and although she
wanted to be helpful, her dealings with him were unsettling.[20]

Sitwell's depression and drinking were at their worst at Montegufoni
or at Renishaw, where she watched Osbert shaking and she had to contend with David Horner, who, as Lorna Andrade told Geoffrey Elborn,

spoke cuttingly and treated Edith unpleasantly. Edith advised Andrade, as the other woman in the house, that the two of them must keep quiet.[21] Horner was himself a drinker though he held it better than Edith did.[22] Undoubtedly, he had heard about some of her remarks on his sexual adventures and so regarded her as an enemy.

That summer Sitwell suffered an emotional collapse, partly owing to Tyler's book and partly owing to the atmosphere of the house. She wept about Pavlik and took his paintings down from the wall, offering one to Andrade, who thought she was talking and behaving madly.[23] At other times, she claimed that Osbert had obstructed several of her marriage proposals because of the young men's quarterings. She also provoked David Horner by speaking, he thought incoherently, about Oscar Wilde's arrest and the Cleveland Street Affair of 1889 (a rent-boy scandal in which Lady Ida's cousin, Lord Somerset, had been involved). Turning the tables on her for her earlier attempts to get rid of him, Horner now wanted her out of the house. He thought she had 'persecution mania and paranoia with frustrated sex thrown in',[24] and declared that she belonged in a mental hospital.

By the end of July, she had been admitted to Claremont Nursing Home in Sheffield, where, as Geoffrey Elborn notes, it was discovered that she was suffering from a kidney infection related to long-untreated cystitis, a condition that the doctors thought was probably responsible for her rage, malice, and other mental aberrations.[25] She revived quickly, and charmed the doctors and nurses, but they had still to reduce her intake of alcohol, get her to eat more food, and begin walking again. In the meantime, her patience was sorely tried. She was pestered by nuns who came to peer at her and by priests wanting to hear her confession.[26]

The question of Edith Sitwell's future was being fought out between David Horner and Georgia Sitwell. Horner was adamant that Edith should not come back to Renishaw, even for a week to gather up her things since she might get around Osbert and settle in again. Edith had spoken harshly of Georgia many times, but now it was Georgia who insisted that such treatment would be cruel.[27] Edith's stay at the Claremont stretched well into August. She did return to Renishaw, but almost immediately fell in her room and broke her left wrist. She stayed then for a month in the Royal Hospital in Sheffield, at the end of which she was wrapped in blankets and carried by car to London. Her family had arranged for her to go to another nursing home. Instead, she went to the Sesame Club on 18 September and took up her old life. She told Benjamin Britten in October: 'The Great Reaper undoubtedly made a dead set at me, but I intend to resist him!'[28]

She was returning to London in a time of controversy. The *Lady Chatterley* trial took place in late October 1960. Following the lead of Alfred Knopf in the United States, Allen Lane, the founder of Penguin Books, decided to put out an unexpurgated version of Lawrence's novel in Britain. In a test case for the Obscene Publications Act of 1959, the main prosecutor Mervyn Griffith-Jones famously asked: 'Is it a book you would have lying around in your own house? Is it a book you would even wish your wife or your servants to read?' After testimony from a string of cultural luminaries, the jury returned an acquittal and marked a new era in the publishing business and in British culture.[29]

While the case was going on, Edith Sitwell had luncheon with Gore Vidal, during which she declared that her family had never forgiven Lawrence for the book. Vidal told her that Lawrence had never written it, and that the style and the dates confirmed that it was really the work of Truman Capote. Sitwell thought it was stupid of her not to have noticed, since the clues were there. Announcing that they had to move quickly before the case was decided, she called for paper and pen, and prepared to write to the judge. Vidal insisted that it should be a letter to *The Times*, so Sitwell began: 'Dear sir, I am a little girl of seventy-four and I have it, on the best authority, that the actual author of "Lady Chatterley's Lover" . . .' Sadly, the rest of the letter did not survive the luncheon. Writing in the 1990s, Vidal added: 'I remember her best like that, in a pool of light in a corner of the Sesame Club dining room.'[30]

Sitwell was now writing the autobiography that she had promised to the bank. Indeed, back in April her agents had sold serial rights to the *Observer*, which on 13 November published her suddenly topical sketch of D. H. Lawrence and a shorter one of Aldous Huxley. This was followed on 20 November by her sanitised accounts of Dylan Thomas and Roy Campbell, and on 27 November by sketches of Wyndham Lewis and Pavel Tchelitchew. Since Lewis had died in 1957, there was no longer any fear of lawsuits. She brought out her anecdotes about the rats in his studio and his hunt for a filthy collar. She concluded that, despite considerable gifts, Lewis had never produced a wholly satisfactory picture or book.

A rebuke came on 18 December. In a letter to the editor, T. S. Eliot dismissed her description of sitting to Lewis as having no resemblance to his own. In fact, their experiences *were* very different. Lewis would hardly have pressed Eliot to have sex with him. In her sketch Sitwell did not refer to sexual advances, but they still shaped her attitude towards him. Eliot went on to claim that Lewis was one of the most important writers of his generation. He also described the sketch as 'gossipy'; this is odd since Sitwell's account of Lewis, though exaggerated, is first-hand. Sitwell's comments on Eliot's marriage and his treatment of Hayward had circulated in London, so perhaps it was payback time.

Sitwell wrote to Graham Greene:

I am in a fearful temper with the late Mr. T. S. Eliot – who wrote a very priggish letter about me to The Observer. (He always was very priggish!) I have not read his Book of Practical Cats. Can you tell me if it is true that he is the author of these lines,

'I tort I taw a Puddy-Tat a-creeping up on me!'
'You did. You taw a Puddy-Tat.
The Puddy-Tat was me!'

I wonder who put it into my head that he is the author![31]

Sitwell's work on the autobiography was hampered by noise. She wrote to Georgia in November: 'there is an electric drill in the house next door, which is attached to my bedroom wall, and goes on all day from 8.30 to 5.30.'[32] The publisher Longman Green was converting into offices the building adjacent to the Sesame Club on Grosvenor Street. The noise was unbearable but, in the spirit of resisting the Great Reaper, she refused to switch rooms. Instead, she wrote letters of complaint to everyone she could think of – including her former publisher now ensconced at 10 Downing Street. She proposed to buy vipers at Harrods, fatten them up, and then mail them in parcels to the builders.

She telephoned Scotland Yard and said she was going to slap the faces of the workmen; the officer who took the call said that if she did they would be obliged to restrain her. In January 1961, she became vice-president of the Mayfair branch of the Noise Abatement Society, and on behalf of that organisation conducted an enormous press conference at the club. A new friend, the novelist Henry Cecil, eventually spoke to one of the firm's directors who happened to be a warden at his church; they came up with a plan to stop the noise at certain hours, but this did not help much. She simply had to wait till it was over.[33]

Salter believed that the battle over noise, silly as it was, took a toll on Sitwell's morale and on her health. She developed a disease of the middle ear, and her diet was reduced to smoked salmon and champagne, which she shared with the two nurses required to tend her at the club. Around the beginning of June, she developed a fever of 105°, and one of her nurses thought it time to call a priest from Farm Street. Sitwell pulled through that crisis, but, according to Salter, she realised through these months that she must die soon, prompting her to write 'A Girl's Song in Winter':

> That lovely dying white swan the singing sun
> Will soon be gone. But seeing the snow falling, who could tell
> one
> From the other? The snow, that swan-plumaged circling
> creature, said,
> 'Young girl, soon the tracing of Time's bird-feet and the bird-
> feet of snow
> Will be seen upon your smooth cheek. Oh soon you will be
> Colder, my sweet, than me!'[34]

The Sesame Club was the wrong place for a woman in Sitwell's condition, and with its seasonal closure coming in August something else had to be arranged. After consulting with Sachie and Georgia, Salter rented a flat at 42 Greenhill in Hampstead, which had the right features: it was large enough to receive guests, was centrally heated, and had no stairs to impede a wheelchair. The transition was not easy. During the autumn, Salter herself had to go into hospital. When she came out, she discovered that Sitwell's resident nurse was quarrelling with the chef hired for parties, and that the housekeeper had hung Edith's underwear in the sitting room. By December there was a more sinister development: the nurse was drugging Sitwell into a compliant and incoherent state. With Sachie's backing, Salter took over direct management of the household, sacked the nurse, and hired the more diligent and humane Sister Doris Farquhar.[35] Sitwell liked and trusted Farquhar but described her for Lady Snow (the novelist Pamela Hansford Johnson) as a constant interrupter of work: 'She always bounds in saying, "I know you hate it, but it has to be done." I never know what. She then turns the Hoover on, because she says what will People think of Her if she doesn't.'[36]

Although absorbed in her own problems, Sitwell was distressed to hear of the suffering of her friends. 'H.D.' had been living since 1946 in a hotel-cum-sanatorium in Switzerland but was evicted with the other residents in the spring of 1961. She died on 27 September. Sitwell was saddened but also angry, declaring that she would like to 'strangle' the people behind the eviction, which she believed had hastened the poet's death. She wrote to Bryher: 'Well, we have lost someone you loved, and who was loved by many, and one of the best poets of our time.'[37]

Since 1958, Osbert had been considering brain surgery as a treatment for his Parkinson's disease. He finally underwent the procedure on 4 October 1960. On 15 October, Edith reported to Hal Lydiard Wilson that he could now use his right leg, and that they believed his right hand would soon cease trembling (it did, to a degree). These improvements came as a great relief to her. However, the benefits were temporary, and Philip Ziegler tells us that by mid-1963 Osbert slipped back into his old condition.[38]

But the news was not all bad. Robert Covington (the accountant) and Charles Musk were trying to clean up her debts. In the summer of 1961 she accepted the advice of friends to sell off her manuscripts and letters. A dodgy private collector managed to see Sitwell alone and purchased one of her notebooks cheaply, so Salter put the matter in the hands of Sotheby's. At the same time, Salter finally proposed a sale of the Tchelitchews. Sitwell accepted that this painful measure might encourage the art world to take a new look at Pavlik's work. Salter made two trips to Paris that autumn to get paintings and papers out of the flat at rue Saint-Dominique; a third was necessary later. It was a difficult job, as Evelyn could not remember where things were hidden, and she did not like giving up the artworks when they were found.[39] Doubtless she felt as if a part of her meagre world was being taken from her.

The sale of manuscripts took place at Sotheby's on 12 December 1960 and 19 June 1961. The chief item was a long series of ledgers that contained the drafts of many of her works going back to about 1910. The ultimate purchaser was the University of Texas, and Sitwell came away with about fifteen thousand pounds. Thirty-nine Tchelitchews were sold in an auction on 13 December – many for several hundred pounds apiece, the wax mask of Sitwell for a thousand pounds, and a portrait for twelve hundred.[40] John Lehmann understood that the sale of the pictures brought in a little over ten thousand pounds in total.[41] In a princely act, Kenneth Clark and Minnie (Astor) Fosburgh bought some of the Tchelitchews and returned them to her; she was delighted to have again 'the lovely pictures which have been so much of my life. You have filled a gap which would have been otherwise entirely empty. And I can never be grateful enough to you.'[42] Her debts were settled; while the sales did not make her rich, she had nothing more to fear from the Inland Revenue or the bank.

That winter, Osbert and David were at Montegufoni. On the night of 7 March, David tumbled down a flight of stairs into a cellar, and Luigi Pestelli, the butler, found him there unconscious in the morning. His skull was fractured and he had suffered a cerebral haemorrhage, along with a broken right arm and other injuries. The cause of his fall is unclear: Christabel Aberconway told John Pearson that David had been chasing a young cook, but there is no direct evidence that David's fall was caused by anything other than drinking.[43] Two days after it happened, Lorna Andrade wrote to Georgia that he kept repeating the word 'obviously' and was unaware that he had lost most of his power to communicate. Edith went through the motions but could not summon her usual sympathy for a suffering person. Despite a gradual recovery, David Horner had no role in what remained of her life.

Since they were both in such poor shape, Edith and Osbert now saw each other only occasionally. Sachie and Georgia became more involved in her affairs, as did their younger son Francis (1935–2004),

who had spent most of the 1950s abroad. After his National Service in
the Navy, he joined the Shell Corporation. Among other postings with
the company, Francis spent two years in Kenya, where his houseboy
dubbed him 'Father Tum-Tum'. Back in England, he went into adver-
tising and public relations. For years Osbert had pressed Edith to make
David Horner the beneficiary of her will, but she sympathised with
Francis, who stood to inherit little of Osbert's wealth, so she made him
her chief heir. As her literary executor until his death in 2004, he was
tireless in promoting her works. His most imaginative move was allowing Alannah Currie, late of the Thompson Twins, to record *Façade* to
club music.[44]

Amid trumpets, Dame Edith Sitwell turned seventy-five on
7 September 1962. She was so inundated with cards, messages and
flowers that she had to put a notice in *The Times* (12 September 1962)
thanking the senders and promising to reply as she was able. Macmillan
capitalised by bringing out two new books: *The Outsiders*, a slim volume
of poems written since 1957, and, at last, *The Queens and the Hive*. At
the same time, they reissued *Fanfare for Elizabeth*. Within two weeks *The
Queens and the Hive*, the size of which Sitwell compared to a telephone
book, went into a fourth printing and was at the top of the bestseller
lists. Reporters were beating on her door; she told Sir John Gielgud that
Sister Farquhar spent much of her time throwing them downstairs.[45]

The coverage often dwelt on Sitwell's affinities with the Virgin
Queen, something she herself took seriously. While writing the book,
she had had an astrologer do a detailed comparison of their charts: 'To
get away from astrological jargon, I should say that both mentally and
emotionally you are akin to the great Queen. True, the mental side of
your Horoscope is a great deal more inventive and artistic than was
hers, while you lack the wonderful Mars link that she had with the
common people.' The astrologer also hinted that she was the reincarnation of Elizabeth[46] – a point that came up from time to time in her
conversations and interviews. Reincarnation is a slippery business.
Years later, Francis Sitwell invited the Spenders' son-in-law Barry
Humphries to open a horticultural show at Weston Hall, and in the
character of Dame Edna Everage, he announced rhymingly: 'As for me,
I'm no ordinary mother and wife, / I was Dame Edith Sitwell in a
previous life.'[47]

The Queens and the Hive was dedicated to George Cukor, who still hoped to put a film of *Fanfare for Elizabeth* into production. He had not noticed the dedication until Noël Coward called him about it. Somewhat earlier Coward had tried to make peace with Osbert, who told him he must hold back until Coward had sorted things out with Edith. Cukor was heading to England to meet with her, so Coward asked him to convey how much he had enjoyed the new book. Cukor urged him to write a letter to her.[48]

When she met with Cukor, Sitwell could see immediately that her old enemy, now 'dear Mr Coward', had done her a favour by stirring up the producer's interest in her work and wrote of this to Osbert, who strongly favoured burying the hatchet.[49] After receiving Coward's kind-hearted letter, she sent him a cable on 21 September: 'Delighted Stop Friendship never too late', and she invited him to a concert being held in honour of her birthday.[50] He could not attend, but visited her on 18 November. According to Salter, he apologised for the Whittlebot episode, and Sitwell accepted without hesitation. Coward wrote in his diary: 'I must say I found her completely charming, very amusing and rather touching. How strange that a forty-year feud should finish so gracefully and so suddenly. I am awfully glad. She gave me her new slim volume of poems. I am fairly unrepentant about her poetry. I really think that three-quarters of it is gibberish. However, I must crush down these thoughts otherwise the dove of peace will shit on me.'[51] A few days later, Coward sent Sitwell a copy of his collected short stories, and she said she liked them very much.[52] In the following year he gave her one of his own paintings; it could not bear comparison with her Tchelitchews, but she was touched by the gesture.

Hedda Hopper got word of the rapprochement and wrote of it in a syndicated column.[53] Sitwell warned Hopper she would punish her: 'when I do, you won't know what has hit you! I do not know how to address you. I cannot call you a goose, as geese saved the capitol of Rome, and no amount of cackling on your part would awaken anybody! Nor can I call you an ass. Since Balaam's constant companion saw an angel, and recognized it. I can only imagine that you belong to the vegetable tribe, and that all the fizzing and spurting of yours is the result of a vegetable decaying.'[54]

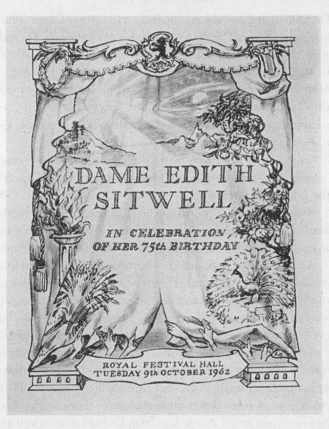

Hopper was just one of the journalists interested in Sitwell that autumn. 'Never before, I think, has anyone attended their own Memorial Service,' Sitwell wrote to Coward of the concert planned for 9 October at the Festival Hall: 'The Press is madly excited at my being 75, and is looking forward avidly to my funeral.'[55] At other times, she referred to the event as her centenary – but she loved it. Francis Sitwell and the violinist John Woolf organised the concert in cooperation with the Park Lane Group, which promoted young musicians. Having been transported to the hall by ambulance, Edith was wheeled on stage by Francis; she read some of her own recent poems. Peter Pears sang *Canticle III: Still Falls the Rain*, and Sebastian Shaw and Irene Worth performed *Façade*, with William Walton conducting. The programme also included selections from Rossini and Mozart. Britten had been expected to perform, but he was too ill, so his place was taken by the twenty-two-year-old virtuoso pianist Stephen Bishop (now known as Stephen Kovacevich); Britten's friend Neill Sanders played the horn.[56] Sitwell joked about Shaw's growling recitation, but raved over Pears's performance of the *Canticle*; she wrote to Britten: 'What a great artist! I invariably have to wear black spectacles when I hear that work. I never get over it. My words, and the suffering, seem to have been born with the music.'

After the concert, there was a supper party at the hall; among the guests (apart from family and performers) were Sir Malcolm Bullock, Sir Frederick Ashton, the Clarks, the Snows, Harold Acton, Cecil Beaton, Cyril Connolly, Sir John Gielgud, Victor Gollancz, Graham Greene, John Lehmann, and Carson McCullers.[57] Edith had organised the seating carefully, but Georgia moved people about, separating McCullers from her nurse. McCullers's illnesses had by now affected her mind. Sitwell told Maurice Bowra: 'she will get up suddenly and kiss people and say "May I touch you." I thought that she would respect Father Caraman's cloth, so put her next to him. Not a bit of it! She kept on getting up and asking if she could touch him.'[58]

It was one of the last great nights of Sitwell's life. She wrote to Francis: 'I didn't get to sleep till past 6. I was so excited.' She thanked him profusely: 'You are a superb organiser and a born impresario. Kenneth Clark says there has been nothing like it in our time.'[59] There was, however, one last event in her seventy-fifth birthday celebrations. Francis had booked her on to *This is Your Life*. Given that she had a heart murmur, Eamonn Andrews could not spring his usual surprise, as it might simply kill her – in which case the programme would need a different title. She was inclined to say no to the planned programme until she heard that her old maid Velma Leroy was making the journey from California. Broadcast on 6 November, the show brought together Osbert and Sachie, her cousin Veronica Gilliat, Cecil Beaton, Arthur Waley, Geoffrey Gorer, George Cukor, and others. The sentimental climax was Velma Leroy's declaration that Edith was 'the world's most marvellous woman'.[60]

Salter recalled that the following months were a falling back to earth and that Sitwell slipped into a depression. Indeed, a doctor judged then that she had suffered from depression throughout her life –

not a surprising diagnosis.[61] Her spirits were briefly lifted at the end of November by a luncheon with Cecil Beaton and the Queen Mother.[62] A little more good news came on New Year's Day: the University of Hull would grant her an honorary doctorate in June.[63] In January 1963, however, an infection threatened to become pneumonia, so Farquhar urged that Sitwell be moved out of London and if possible out of England. When Salter described how she had once seen extraordinary gems for sale in Colombo, Sitwell herself proposed that they go on a round-the-world voyage.[64] Both Salter and Francis Sitwell were uneasy about this idea, but as Dame Edith told Jane Clark, 'the whole of Harley Street' was telling her to go.[65]

Transported to Tilbury in an ambulance, Dame Edith was carried aboard the SS *Arcadia*, where she found flowers from Graham Greene, Sherman and Jeanne Stonor, and other friends waiting in her stateroom.[66] For the first few days she had the company of Sachie and Georgia on their way to Gibraltar. After that, she was in the hands of Farquhar and Salter. During the voyage Sitwell worked on the early chapters of her memoir,[67] reshaping a good deal of old material, eliminating nuances and adding ferocity. Though Sitwell was still capable of pleasant conversation, treated those around her with courtesy, and could tell a good story, her writing had lapsed into rancour. The memoir is, at times, less a record of her life than of her moods while writing it.

When they reached Colombo, Salter went ashore and brought back a selection of gems. Sitwell picked out a large aquamarine for purchase, and returned the rest. Salter soon discovered that she had broken the law in bringing unbought stones to the ship, and it was only by luck that she and Sitwell were not imprisoned for smuggling. The ship then sailed on to Australia, where reporters came to Sitwell's cabin at Melbourne and Adelaide. The ship reached Sydney on 3 April, where Sitwell was to disembark. She was too worn out to deal with another gaggle of journalists, so Elizabeth Salter took her place, describing what it was like to work for Sitwell and recounting her experiences as a crime writer in Britain.[68] As an Australian success story, she had some star power of her own. However, she had to promise a press conference with Dame Edith Sitwell.

Sitwell was taken off the ship in secret when the crowds dispersed.

She settled in at the Fernleigh Castle in the suburb of Rose Bay. This hotel had a hilltop view of the harbour and the bridge. As the *Arcadia* sailed away, it came as close to the shore as the captain dared and in front of the Fernleigh Castle blew its horn three times in salute to Sitwell.[69] On 16 April, she gave one of her classic press conferences, this time lying back on her bed and wearing a wide hat. Owing to her illness, she asked the reporters to photograph only her hands. She said she had just one face but that if she had a dozen they could have them – then she gave in and allowed the photographs. She declared herself 'mad about Australians'. The reporters wanted her opinion of the Australian accent, so she asked, 'Isn't it the same as the English accent?' The reporters took great interest in the photographs she had laid out of her three cats, Shadow, Leo and Belaker: 'They never say anything silly, you see, and that's something.' When asked whether she had been a handful for her parents, she responded, 'My parents were a handful for me. They weren't parents I would recommend to anybody.'[70]

She gave a private interview to Audrey Armitage of the *Sydney Morning Herald*: 'Poems have parents. Those parents are ideas. I start with one idea – or a scene – like the old Roman road that runs through my brother's property in Derbyshire. I wanted to write a poem about that. Behind the road stands a field of ripe wheat. That was the beginning of one poem, then another idea was added and worked on . . . I don't have a complete idea when I start writing, nor do I know how it will be worked out.' She seems to have been talking about 'The Little Ghost Who Died for Love'.[71] Unknown to Sitwell, Armitage was one of the country's most prolific pulp novelists, specialising in cheap sex and cadavers, yet she had loved Sitwell's poetry since her student days. In her article, she noted with sadness the wheelchair pushed against a wall – the implications were obvious. The article appeared under the headline 'Farewell to a Genius'.[72]

They sailed out of Sydney on 17 April in the Dutch ship *Willem Ruys*, but their passage across the Pacific was turbulent. Some passengers wandered about in life-vests, claiming the ship was doomed – provoking contempt from Sitwell when she heard of it. Yet even though Henry Moat had trained her to stand up to the sea, she was herself very ill when they reached Panama City. On the morning after they docked in

Miami, Farquhar sent Salter to find a priest. Sitwell had started to haemorrhage during the night. A doctor considered her well enough to travel on to Bermuda, where another doctor thought her bleeding might be fatal. She was taken ashore in a little tossing boat, and, for the first time in her experience of Edith Sitwell, Salter heard 'sounds of fear' from her. Despite her own anxiety, Salter had to sail back alone to England with their luggage. Farquhar remained with Sitwell in Bermuda. Once tests proved that the bleeding – caused by a varicose vein at the base of her neck – was not lethal, she was flown home. This was one of the very few times in her life that she boarded an aeroplane.

Back at the Greenhill flat, she stabilised and the threat of pneumonia receded. Nevertheless, she was too fragile to attend a dinner of the Royal Society of Literature on 25 June, so sent Sachie to receive her scroll as a Companion of Literature (C.Lit.).[73] She was also obliged to miss the degree ceremony in Hull three days later where she was to have received her fifth honorary doctorate.[74] Late in July, pneumonia finally took hold. She wrote to Evelyn on 12 August: 'I am only just come out of hospital. I was picked up unconscious, and rushed to hospital, where the doctors thought I was dying, and told Elizabeth that if I survived the night I had a 50-50 chance of surviving. I had very bad pneumonia, and was delirious.'

Evelyn was now fairly senile. Edith addressed her as 'My darling' and gave the only answer she could to her concerns: 'I have written straight off to Mr. Musk, asking him to send you through some money.'[75] That autumn, Evelyn fell and broke her hip and was never again able to leave the hospital. To avoid distressing Edith, who for all her complaints about Evelyn continued to care about her, Salter held back the news until mid-December. After Christmas, Salter was sent to Paris again to negotiate financial arrangements for Evelyn. Edith would continue the allowance, but the French authorities would have to cover medical expenses. Salter also went to the flat. With the help of a neighbour, she found in Edith's old bedroom a further group of Tchelitchews hidden behind a bookcase, among them the pastel of Sitwell in profile that many regard as the finest of all his portraits. They also discovered a cupboard that had been wallpapered over. In it were fifty-six more of Sitwell's large notebooks, including the manuscript of *I Live Under a Black Sun*.[76]

Sitwell lent the portrait and other pictures to the now defunct Gallery of Modern Art at Columbus Circle in New York to be part of a retrospective of 350 works of Pavel Tchelitchew from 21 March to 19 April 1964. The Museum of Modern Art lent *Hide and Seek*, and, after much diplomacy, the Soviet government lent *Phenomena*, which Tchelitchew had willed to the Russian people. The show was the main attraction on the opening day of the new gallery, drawing 3358 visitors, some of them merely curious about the building's marble architecture. It was nonetheless a hugely successful exhibition, with Tchelitchew lauded by critics, among them John Canaday of the *New York Times*: 'As a straight draftsman, Tchelitchew was as expert and graceful an artist as recent decades have produced.'[77] There was no question of Dame Edith Sitwell travelling across the Atlantic, but she followed all the reviews, and heard from an excited Monroe Wheeler that her portrait was generally thought to be the best in the exhibition. Sitwell had the satisfaction of seeing Tchelitchew's reputation higher than it had been for many years. It faded, of course, but not in the months she had left to her. Despite all the grief Pavlik had caused her, she could go to her grave believing that with him she had been involved in greatness.

Through that winter the Australian composer Malcolm Williamson, later Master of the Queen's Music, visited Sitwell on a number of occasions. A friend of Salter and Gordon Watson, he had recently completed an opera of Graham Greene's *Our Man in Havana*. Now, with the encouragement of Benjamin Britten, he was writing another based on *The English Eccentrics*, to be performed at the Aldeburgh Festival in June. Sitwell was thrilled by his work, and despite extreme pain attended its first London performance at the City Temple Hall on 14 July.

Although her memory was slipping in matters of detail, Sitwell retained her wit, but whatever she had of good judgment deserted her. She experienced unremitting pain from sciatica, fibrositis in her arm, a lingering infection in her finger, eye-strain, and migraines. And she was still drinking far too much. She continued to rain letters upon the editors of newspapers and literary journals. Some of the letters were well crafted. For example, she saw in the *TLS* (14 November 1963) a review entitled 'Ugh', which compared reading various books by

William Burroughs, including *The Naked Lunch*, to 'wading upstream through the drains of a big city'. Her response appeared on the 28th:

> Sir,
>
> I was delighted to see, in your issue of the 14th instant, the very rightminded review of a novel by a Mr. Burroughs (whoever he may be) published by a Mr. John Calder (whoever he may be).
>
> The public canonisation of that insignificant, dirty little book *Lady Chatterley's Lover* was a signal to persons who wish to unload the filth in their minds on the British public.
>
> As the author of *Gold Coast Customs* I can scarcely be accused of shirking reality, but I do not wish to spend the rest of my life with my nose nailed to other people's lavatories.
>
> I prefer Chanel Number 5.
>
>   Edith Sitwell, C.L.

This was great fun for readers, but it was erasing the sense that she had been a considerable, perhaps an outstanding poet, and replacing it with the belief that she was an amusing reactionary and an irritable crank.

She became unhappy with the noise at Greenhill – children playing, the lift door banging, the loud talk of other tenants. Suspecting that a leak from upstairs had been the cause of her recent illness, she told Waugh that she lived in 'an odious small flat under one occupied by the son of the local undertaker, who succeeded in giving me pneumonia – in an effort, I suppose, to be of use to his Dad'.[78] She also thought the place too small to receive her guests in and too small for the cats, of which there were now four. Salter looked for better accommodation in central London, but was refused by landlords who would not tolerate so many pets. Finally, in May 1964, she found a cottage in Hampstead, at 20 Keats Grove, across from what had once been the home of John Keats. David Higham would be one of her new neighbours. Best of all, the landlady liked cats. While Salter set up the new house and Farquhar took a holiday, Dame Edith went to Bournemouth with another nurse. Francis stayed with her there and, as he told Victoria Glendinning, watched her drink a double martini at breakfast.[79] It was about this time that she was asked by a journalist how she felt: 'Dying, but apart from that I'm all right.'[80]

Upon her return to what she called 'Bryher House', Sitwell found all her books assembled in one place for the first time in decades. Her Third Folio of Shakespeare was displayed in a glass case. Her Tchelitchews were hung throughout the house, and the lost portrait from Paris was placed on the wall opposite her bed. Since she seldom stirred from bed, that painting was in her sight most of the time until she died. Sitwell declined in the early summer, but rallied under treatment from a new doctor. When Julian Symonds tried to start a row with her in the pages of the *London Magazine* – a clever piece of geriatric bear-baiting – she had to delegate her side of the argument to John Lehmann.

In September, she received a visit from Marianne Moore, who wrote to Osbert on 13 September:

> Edith – She seemed to me, firm and resolute, – was in bed, waited on by ardent Sister Farquhar; and presently Miss Salter came in – so encouraging and beautifully dressed. Sister Farquhar made tea despite my protest and Edith let her delay my Taxi, for I was just leaving, so fearful of doing Edith harm. In fact I had written to her, a little detailed news of our London experiences and plans – so I would not be tempted to elaborate and stay too long. Edith's left forefinger was bandaged – very trying for her – an infection following pneumonia . . . Hoping in spite of all, that I may see you and Edith, somehow, some sunny day – in New York, valiant Osbert.[81]

Father Caraman visited her and expected on one occasion to hear her last confession, but as Edith told one of her last visitors John Freeman, 'I routed him.' She said she did not feel like a pious conversation with the priest so pretended to be asleep, but she opened one eye and glimpsed him in a chair beside her bed, 'surreptitiously helping himself to the cat's biscuits'.[82]

Salter stitched together the fragmentary chapters of the memoir, and on 8 December, Graham Nicol, an editor at Hutchinson, came with illustrations for the book. Sitwell grumpily rejected some photographs of her parents. He told her that her work on it was now finished and that there would be proofs soon. She said, 'Thank the lord for that.'[83]

That night she suffered a haemorrhage and was taken to St Thomas's

Hospital for a blood transfusion. Francis saw her briefly. Sachie and Georgia hurried to London and were waiting in a corridor with Reresby when a doctor told them that she had died of heart failure.[84] On 14 December, a Requiem Mass was celebrated by Father Martin D'Arcy at Farm Street and her funeral took place later in the day at Lois Weedon church near Weston Hall.[85] Osbert was too ill to leave Montegufoni.

Georgia wrote to Evelyn Waugh that Edith was the first Catholic to be buried in the church cemetery since the Reformation.[86] By mistake, she was actually buried in the plot beside Lady Ida. Knowing that his sister had spent most of her life trying to get away from her mother, Sachie obtained the permission of the Home Secretary to have her moved (*The Times*, 5 April 1965). Dame Edith Sitwell's grave now overlooks a pleasant valley where sheep graze immediately beyond, and the grass slopes down to some quiet fish ponds. On her gravestone is a bronze plaque by Henry Moore of a child's hand in that of an old man to signify the continuance of life through the generations.[87] Engraved below it are lines from 'The Wind of Early Spring':

> The past and present are as one –
> Accordant and discordant, youth and age,
> And death and birth. For out of one came all –
> From all comes one.

Abbreviations

Persons:

DH	David Horner
ES	Dame Edith Sitwell
GRS	Sir George Sitwell, 4th Baronet
GS	Georgia Sitwell (Lady Sitwell)
HR	Helen Rootham
IS	Lady Ida Sitwell
OS	Sir Osbert Sitwell, 5th Baronet
PT	Pavel Tchelitchew
SS	Sir Sacheverell Sitwell, 6th Baronet

Publications:

Bradford	Sarah Bradford, *Splendours and Miseries: A Life of Sacheverell Sitwell* (London: Sinclair-Stevenson, 1993).
CP	Edith Sitwell, *Collected Poems* (London: Macmillan, 1957).
Craggs	Stewart Craggs, Preface, v–xii, in *William Walton Edition*, gen. ed. David Lloyd-Jones, consultant Stewart Craggs (Oxford: OUP, 1998–), vol. 7: *Façade Entertainments*, ed. David Lloyd-Jones (2000).
Elborn	Geoffrey Elborn, *Edith Sitwell: A Biography* (New York: Doubleday, 1981)
Fifoot	Richard Fifoot, *A Bibliography of Edith, Osbert and Sacheverell Sitwell* (1963; 2nd edition, revised, London: Archon Books, 1971).
Ford	Charles Henri Ford, *Water From a Bucket: A Diary 1948–1957* (New York: Turtle Point Press, 2001).
FWGC	Sacheverell Sitwell, *For Want of the Golden City* (London: Thames and Hudson, 1973).
Glendinning	Victoria Glendinning, *Edith Sitwell: A Lion among Unicorns* (London: George Weidenfeld & Nicolson, 1981).
LHRH	Osbert Sitwell, *Left Hand, Right Hand!*, 5 vols (London: Macmillan, 1945–50).
ODNB	*Oxford Dictionary of National Biography* (online).

Pearson   John Pearson, *Façades: Edith, Osbert and Sacheverell Sitwell* (London: Macmillan, 1978).

Salter   Elizabeth Salter, *The Last Years of a Rebel: A Memoir of Edith Sitwell* (London: Bodley Head, 1967).

SL   Edith Sitwell, *Selected Letters*, ed. John Lehmann and Derek Parker (London: Macmillan, 1970).

SLES   Edith Sitwell, *Selected Letters of Edith Sitwell*, ed. Richard Greene (London: Virago, 1997; revised edn, 1998).

TCO   Edith Sitwell, *Taken Care Of* (London: Hutchinson, 1965).

TG   Osbert Sitwell, ed., *Two Generations* (London: Macmillan, 1940).

Tyler   Parker Tyler, *The Divine Comedy of Pavel Tchelitchew* (New York: Fleet, 1967).

Ziegler   Philip Ziegler, *Osbert Sitwell: A Biography* (London: Chatto & Windus, 1998).

Institutions:
BL   British Library

HRC   Harry Ransom Humanities Research Center, University of Texas at Austin

NYPL   New York Public Library

PRO   Public Record Office

WSU   Washington State University, Pullman, Washington

Letters between Sitwell and Tchelitchew are from the Edith Sitwell–Pavel Tchelitchew Correspondence, Yale Collection of American Literature, Beinecke Rare Book and Manuscript Library, unless otherwise stated.

Notes

PROLOGUE: WHY?

1 ES to SS, 24 December 1940, ES Collection, HRC.

2 ES to PT, 30 December 1940.

3 ES to PT, 6 June 1940.

4 ES to PT, 27 May 1941.

5 *SLES*, 14–15.

6 Unidentified newspaper interview, c.1962, in SS Collection, 5:2, HRC

7 Glendinning, 4.

8 See, for example, Spender's interview with John Pearson, Sitwell Collection, McFarlin Library, University of Tulsa.

9 *New York Times*, 11 January 1959. Sitwell repeated the quip many times.

CHAPTER 1: FACTS OF LIFE

1 *LHRH* 2, 192.

2 *LHRH* 2, 142.

3 ES to Lady Colefax, Bodleian Library, Colefax Collection, Ms. Eng. C. 3169, ff. 67–8.

4 ES to Bryher, 26 December 1941. Bryher Papers, Beinecke Library, Yale University.

5 ES to PT, 26 December 1945.

6 TCO, 20.

7 Fragment of journal, Works 179, ES Collection, HRC. This passage contains several deletions and interlineations. I have quoted the version that is most coherent.

8 *LHRH* 1, 57–63.

9 *LHRH* 1, 146–9.

10 TCO, 28.

11 ES, 'Why I Look as I do', Works U-V-W, ES Collection, HRC.

12 ES, unpublished autobiography, Works 42, ES Collection, HRC.

13 SS, *Splendours and Miseries*, 242.

14 Obituary of Lady Ida Sitwell, *The Times*, 13 July 1937.

15 FWGC, 298.

16 LHRH 1, 138.

17 TG, xx.

18 TCO, 41.

19 TCO, 30.

20 LHRH 1, 77.

21 ES, autobiographical fragment, Works 42, ES Collection, HRC.

22 ES, autobiographical fragment, Works 12, ES Collection, HRC.

23 TCO, 27.

24 TCO, 29.

25 Draft of *LHRH* 1, OS Collection, 3.9, HRC.

26 This and the preceding paragraph are based on ES, autobiographical fragment, Works 42, ES Collection, HRC.

27 LHRH 1, 244.

28 ES, 'Christmas Past and Present', Works 42, ES Collection, HRC.

29 An extended account of Christmas at Blankney may be found in *LHRH* 2, 179–208.

30 TCO, 26.

31 SL, 198.

32 Reresby Sitwell, *Renishaw Hall and the Sitwells*, 3–5.

33 Evelyn Waugh, *The Diaries of Evelyn Waugh*, 780.

34 Reresby Sitwell, op. cit., 4–5.

35 TG, xvii; *LHRH* 1, 20.

36 Reresby Sitwell, op. cit., 5.

37 Pearson, 21.

38 Archbishop Davidson's letters to Blanche Sitwell may be found in the Lambeth Palace Library.

39 SS, Foreword, *Hortus Sitwellianus* (Wilton: Michael Russell, 1984), 9–10.

40 ES to Lady Colefax, n.d., Colefax Collection, Bodleian Library, MS. Eng. c. 3169, f. 105.

41 TCO, 66–7.

42 TG, xxxiii.

43 TG, 170–1.

44 TCO, 69.

45 GRS, *Idle Fancies in Prose and Verse*, 69.

46 SS, Foreword, *Hortus Sitwellianus*, 9–10.

47 I am grateful to the college archivist, P. Hatfield, for information on Sir George's time at Eton.

48 *LHRH* 2, 159.

49 Christ Church Tutor's Book and Collections Book. I am grateful to the college archivist, Mrs Judith Curthoys, for information on Sir George's time at Christ Church.

50 GRS and Carl Von Buch, letter to the editor, *The Times*, 12 January 1880.

51 Ibid. See also *Daily Telegraph*, 13 January 1880, *Evening Standard*, 12 January 1880, and *LHRH* 1, 256–7.

52 *LHRH* 1, 61n.

53 GRS, Preface (unpaginated), *The Barons of Pulford*.

54 Pearson, 22.

55 Muriel Spark, 'A Drink with Dame Edith', *Literary Review*.

56 TCO, 22.

57 TCO, 26–7.

CHAPTER 2: A SENSE OF PLACE

1 'Shipwrecks and Storms', http://www2.northyorks.gov.uk/unnetie/storyboards/east_coast/the_sea.cfm. Further information from Mark Vesey of the Scarborough Maritime Heritage Centre, relying on research by Arthur Godfrey. See: www.scarboroughsmaritimeheritage.org.uk.

2 ES, autobiographical fragment, Works 42, ES Collection, HRC.

3 ES, 'Eccentricities of Fashion', Works 206, ES Collection, HRC.

4 'Waltz', CP, 144.

5 *LHRH* 1, 120–5.

6 Ibid., 85–7.

7 ES, autobiographical fragment, Works 42, ES Collection, HRC.

8 Ibid.

9 *LHRH* 3, 299–300.

10 Andrew Clay, e-mail to Richard Greene, 22 December 2009.

11 ES, 'Readers and Writers', *The New Age*, 1562, n.s., 31: 16 (17 August 1922), 196.

12 'No More', *An Indian Summer* (London: Macmillan, 1982), 20.

13 *LHRH* 1, 19.

14 Ibid. 2, 36–9.

15 SS, *All Summer in a Day*, 79.

16 *LHRH* 2, 36–7.

17 Ibid. 1, 104.

18 SS, *All Summer in a Day*, 27.

19 ES, autobiographical fragment, Works 271, ES Collection, HRC.

20 SS, Foreword, *Hortus Sitwellianus* (Wilton: Michael Russell, 1984), 9.

21 OS, *Tales My Father Told Me*, 20.

22 Reresby Sitwell, *Renishaw Hall and the Sitwells*, 13.

23 GRS, *On the Making of Gardens*, 46–7.

24 SS, *The Homing of the Winds*, 10.

25 *LHRH* 1, 254.

26 *TCO*, 32–3.

CHAPTER 3: SERVANTS AND SURGEONS

1 Evelyn Waugh, *Men at Arms* (Harmondsworth: Penguin, 1964), 173.

2 *LHRH* 1, viii.

3 Comments by Peter Dixon Knagg in OS file of Rache Lovat Dixon collection, National Library of Canada.

4 See *LHRH* 1, esp. 94–107. The following discussion draws from these pages.

5 Rose Ellen Hepwell to ES, n.d., ES Collection, HRC.

6 *TCO*, 28, and *LHRH* 1, 126.

7 *LHRH* 1, 100n.

8 Ibid. 1, 99.

9 *TCO*, 28.

10 *LHRH* 1, 101–2.

11 Online Register of Births, PRO.

12 1901 Census Online, PRO; *LHRH* 1, 95 and 127.

13 *LHRH* 1, 89.

14 Ibid. 1, 96.

15 Ibid.

16 Ibid. 1, 172.

17 OS, *Before the Bombardment*, 144.

18 *TCO*, 27.

19 *LHRH* 2, 6–7.

20 Davis to OS, 11 December [1912?], OS Collection, HRC.

21 ES, autobiographical fragment, Works 12, ES Collection, HRC. See also ES's poem 'Mademoiselle Richarde', first published in the *Spectator*, 31 May 1924, but omitted from her *Collected Poems* of 1957.

22 Online Register of Births, PRO. Death notice, *The Times*, 3 April 1963.

23 Lydia King-Church to GRS, 1 April 1903, Renishaw Papers, Box 36.

24 *LHRH* 2, 97.

25 ES to GRS, 17 March 1903, Renishaw Papers, Box 36.

26 ES, 'Notes on my Childhood', Works 92, ES Collection, HRC.

27 *TCO*, 42–3.

28 Ibid., 39.

29 ES to GRS, 12 February 1903, Renishaw Papers, Box 36.

30 *SLES*, 248.

31 ES, draft of speech, Works 166, ES Collection, HRC.

32 Renishaw Papers, Box 37 and 577:9.

33 ES to PT, draft, Works 246, ES Collection, HRC.

34 Jessie Bradley to Geoffrey Elborn, 1 July 1977, Sitwell Collection, McFarlin Library, University of Tulsa.

35 *LHRH* 2, 21–2.

36 SS interview with Geoffrey Elborn, Sitwell Collection, McFarlin Library, University of Tulsa. For information on Dawson, see Fiona Richards, 'William Baines and his Circle', *Musical Times*, vol. 130, no. 1758 (August 1989), 460–3.

37 SS interview with John Pearson, 18–19 December 1974, Sitwell Collection, McFarlin Library, University of Tulsa. *LHRH* 1, 204–8, contains an extended portrait of Rubio.

38 Renishaw Papers, Box 36.

39 ES, 'Notes on My Childhood', Works 92, ES Collection, HRC.

40 This corrects the suggestion in Glendinning, 27–8, that the specialist was Heather Bigg.

41 A. H. Tubby, *Deformities*, 133.

42 For a brief overview of scoliosis, see the website of the American Academy of Orthopedic Surgeons: www.aaos.org.

43 A. H. Tubby, op. cit., 122–3.

44 Ibid., 163.

45 *TCO*, 53.

46 A.H. Tubby, op. cit., 166–7.

47 Ibid., 517, and F. Gustav Ernst, *A Guide to the Selection and Adaptation of Orthopædic Apparatus*, 40–1.

48 See ES, 'Notes on My Childhood', Works 92, ES Collection, HRC.

49 See Elborn, 84.

50 ES, *Alexander Pope* (London: Faber & Faber, 1930), 22.

51 ES to GRS, 8 January 1903, Renishaw Papers, Box 36.

52 *TCO*, 40.

53 F. Gustav Ernst, op. cit., 15–19.
54 *TCO*, 42.
55 Lydia King-Church to GRS, 1 April 1903, Renishaw Papers, Box 36.
56 *LHRH*, 2, 152.
57 1901 Census Online, PRO.
58 'Butt, Dame Clara' and 'Rootham, Cyril (Bradley)', www.groveonline.com.
59 1891 and 1911 Censuses Online, PRO.
60 *Who Was Who*.
61 ES to PT, 22 September 1950.
62 *LHRH* 2, 153.
63 SS interview with John Pearson, 18–19 December 1974, Sitwell Collection, McFarlin Library, University of Tulsa.
64 ES refers to such a translation in 'What Do We Mean by Liberty', *Sunday Referee*, 5 May 1935; reprinted in Salter and Harper (eds), *Edith Sitwell: The Fire of the Mind: An Anthology*. (New York: Vanguard Press, 1976), 174. Another reference occurs in a letter from ES to PT, 5 December 1935. I have not found that this translation was ever published.

CHAPTER 4: GROWING EYEBROWS

1 *LHRH* 1, 225. The date of Sargent's visit is drawn from David Greer, *A Numerous and Fashionable Audience*, 58.
2 Reresby Sitwell, *Renishaw Hall and the Sitwells*, 4 and 10; and *The Sitwells and the Arts of the 1920s and 1930s*, 21.
3 *LHRH* 1, 229.
4 *TCO*, 51.
5 Ibid., 50–1.
6 *LHRH* 1, 232.
7 David Greer, op. cit., 59.
8 *LHRH* 2, 6.
9 Ibid. 2, 113.
10 GRS, *On the Making of Gardens*, vii.
11 SS interview with John Pearson, Sitwell Collection, McFarlin Library, University of Tulsa.
12 Renishaw Papers, Box 36.
13 Ibid., Box 546:7.
14 Louisa, Lady Sitwell's diary, Renishaw Papers, Box 30.
15 Ibid.

16 ES to PT, 16 September 1942.

17 Renishaw Papers, Box 36.

18 Ibid.

19 *This Is Your Life: Dame Edith Sitwell*, BBC, 6 November 1962.

20 HR to IS, 4 November 1904, Renishaw Papers, Box 36.

21 ES to GRS, 6 October 1904, Renishaw Papers, Box 36.

22 *SLES*, 277–8.

23 ES to Florence Sitwell, 25 February 1905, Renishaw Papers, 546:7.

24 *LHRH* 2, 153.

25 Ibid. 2, 243.

26 ES to Florence Sitwell, 25 February 1905, Renishaw Papers, 546:7.

27 See Princess Salm-Salm's memoir, *Ten Years of My Life* (London, 1876); Robert N. White, *The Prince and the Yankee* (London and New York: I. B. Tauris, 2003).

28 HR to GRS, 25 January 1905, Renishaw Papers, Box 36.

29 HR to GRS, 2 February 1905, Renishaw Papers, Box 36.

30 What follows is closely based on David G. Schuster, 'Personalizing Illness and Modernity: S. Weir Mitchell, Literary Women, and Neurasthenia, 1870–1914', *Bulletin of the History of Medicine*.

31 Charlotte Perkins Gilman, *The Living of Charlotte Perkins Gilman: An Autobiography* (1935; reprinted, New York: Harper Colophon, 1975), 91–6. Cited by Schuster, 718.

32 *SLES*, 251–2.

33 ES to GRS, 27 January 1904, Renishaw Papers, Box 36.

34 ES to GRS, 4 March 1905, Renishaw Papers, Box 36.

35 ES to GRS, 10 May 1905, Renishaw Papers, Box 36.

36 HR to GRS, 15 May 1905, Renishaw Papers, Box 36.

37 ES to Florence Sitwell, 25 February 1905, Renishaw Papers, 546:7.

38 ES to Florence Sitwell, 21 April 1905, Renishaw Papers, 546:7.

39 HR to GRS, 6 February 1905, Renishaw Papers, Box 36.

40 ES to GRS, 17 June 1905, Renishaw Papers, Box 36.

41 ES to Florence Sitwell, 5 September 1905, Renishaw Papers, 546:7.

42 ES to GRS, 4 November 1905, Renishaw Papers, Box 36.

43 HR to GRS, 29 September [1906], Renishaw Papers, Box 36.

44 HR to GRS, 14 October [1906], Renishaw Papers, Box 36.

45 ES to GRS, 18 October 1906, Renishaw Papers, Box 36.

46 ES to GRS, 7 November 1906, Renishaw Papers, Box 36.

CHAPTER 5: BRINGING OUT

1 *ODNB.*

2 *LHRH* 5, 13–24.

3 Nicola Shulman, A *Rage for Rock Gardening*, 42–7.

4 *ODNB.*

5 IS to GRS, n.d., Renishaw Papers, Box 36. Lady Ida's penmanship is extremely illegible; transcriptions of it are frequently tentative.

6 IS to GRS, 16 May 1907, Renishaw Papers, Box 36.

7 IS to GRS, 22 May 1907, Renishaw Papers, Box 36.

8 1911 Census.

9 Constance Lane, *The Three Rectories*, 121.

10 ES to Denys Kilham Roberts, n.d. [c.1942], Holland Library, WSU.

11 ES to GRS, 19 June 1907, Renishaw Papers, Box 36.

12 Constance Lane, op. cit., 122.

13 ES to GRS, 19 June 1907, Renishaw Papers, Box 36.

14 *The Times*, 8 July 1907.

15 ES to GRS, 19 June 1907, Renishaw Papers, Box 36.

16 Constance Lane, op. cit., 121.

17 Ibid., 121–2.

18 Constance Sitwell, *Frolic Youth*, 8. Note: the author assigns events to 1905, which, because of internal references to political events such as the Hague conference, must have occurred in 1907.

19 Ibid., 18.

20 'A Self-Developed Person', *Yorkshire Weekly Post*, 1936: *Edith Sitwell: The Fire of the Mind: An Anthology*, ed. Elizabeth Salter and Allanah Harper (New York: Vanguard Press, 1976), 68.

21 *LHRH* 2, 298–9.

22 Adela Lane to Lady Sitwell, 17 February 1908, Renishaw Papers, Box 36.

23 These letters are in the private collection of Neil Ritchie.

24 Constance Sitwell, *Bounteous Days*, 33.

25 A.H. Tubby, *Deformities*, 166–7.

26 ES to Florence Sitwell, n.d. [June 1908], Renishaw Papers, Box 546:7.

27 The description of the party is drawn from *LHRH* 2, 294–300.

28 Recollections of Veronica Gilliat (née Codrington) on *This Is Your Life: Dame Edith Sitwell*, BBC, 6 November 1962.

29 IS to OS, 28 October 1908, Renishaw Papers, Box 501. Cited in Ziegler, 32.

30 Constance Sitwell, *Bounteous Days*, 123.

31 Constance Sitwell, *Bright Morning*, 56–7.

32 *LHRH* 3, 73–6.

CHAPTER 6: BECOMING A POET

1 *LHRH* 3, 46.

2 SL, 104 and 252; *LHRH* 3, 45–6; Elizabeth Salter, *The Last Years of a Rebel*, 20–1.

3 Lady Sitwell to GRS[?], 6 January 1907, Renishaw Papers, Box 36.

4 ES, Introduction, *Swinburne: A Selection* (London: Weidenfeld & Nicolson, 1960), 47.

5 Ibid., 50–1.

6 Salter, 20.

7 See David Greer, *A Numerous and Fashionable Audience*, 1, 80, and 108–14. I am also indebted to David Greer for entertaining my queries about Swinton and Edith Sitwell.

8 Draft of 'Coming to London', Works 259, ES Collection, HRC; printed in *London Magazine* 4:4 April 57, 39–44.

9 ES, autobiographical draft, Works 273, ES Collection, HRC.

10 David Greer, op. cit., 36–7.

11 Ibid., 77–80 and *passim*.

12 Matthew Sturgis, *Walter Sickert*, esp. 345–59. This section and the rest of the chapter owe a considerable debt to Sturgis's work, as well as Greer's.

13 David Greer, op. cit., 71; Matthew Sturgis, op. cit., 355.

14 Autobiographical draft, Works 273, ES Collection, HRC.

15 *ODNB*.

16 Pearson, 50.

17 TCO, 88.

18 Matthew Sturgis, op. cit., 385.

19 *LHRH* 5, 163. OS's account of the Sitwells' forty-year friendship with the painter is found on 163–206. See also the long memoir OS provides in Walter Sickert, *A Free House! Or the Artist as Craftsman*, xiii–liv.

20 David Greer, op. cit., 76–107.

21 *ODNB*; Valerie Langfield, *Roger Quilter, His Life and Music*, 34.

22 Transcriptions in Works 329, ES Collection, HRC.

23 David Greer, op. cit., 114–15, 123.

24 Walter Sickert, 'Idealism', *Art News*, 12 May 1910, 208.

25 Matthew Sturgis, op. cit., 362.

26 *The Scotsman*, 6 March 2004.

27 Salter, 67.

28 Walter Sickert, 'Post-Impressionists', *Fortnightly Review*, January 1911, 107.

29 *SLES*, 96.

30 Barbara Cassell, Foreword to Constance Lane, *The Three Rectories*, vii.

31 SS interviewed by John Pearson, 18–19 December 1974, Sitwell Collection, McFarlin Library, University of Tulsa.

32 Matthew Sturgis, op. cit., 374–96.

33 Fragment of letter to OS [c. June 1913] in Works, 40:1, ES collection, HRC.

34 *ODNB*.

35 Michael Holroyd, *Lytton Strachey: A Biography* (revised edn, London: Penguin, 1979), 452n, 590n. Further information from Ana Monrabal of the National Gallery.

36 Matthew Sturgis, op. cit., 421.

37 Walter Sickert, 'The Post-Impressionists', op. cit., 102.

38 Works 328, ES Collection, HRC.

39 A thorough account of Sitwell's debt to the Symbolist movement may be found in Patricia Clements, *Baudelaire & The English Tradition*, 218–59.

40 SS, *Apologia in Prose*, *Dodecameron*, unpag.

41 *ODNB*.

42 Joan Wake, 'My First Meeting with Edith Sitwell', in *The Early Unpublished Poems of Edith Sitwell*, ed. Gerald W. Morton and Karen P. Hegelson (New York: Peter Lang, 1994), 71–2.

43 ES, 'Nocturne', Works 329, ES Collection, HRC.

44 CP, 3.

CHAPTER 7: THE GREAT WARS

1 *SLES*, 277.

2 SS interview with Geoffrey Elborn, Sitwell Collection, McFarlin Library, University of Tulsa.

3 *The Times*, 5 November 1914 and 15 March 1915.

4 A letter read out in court and quoted in *Daily Mail*, 13 March 1915.

5 *LHRH* 3, 82–90.

6 *SLES*, 5.

7 Ibid., 8.

8 Ibid., 7–8. The date of the letter should be corrected to 8 May 1911.

9 *LHRH* 1, 175–7.

10 Ibid. 3, 110.

11 SS to OS, 2 March 1912, OS Collection, 24:12, HRC.

12 SS to OS, n.d., OS Collection, 24:12, HRC.

13 *Who Was Who, 1929–40*.

14 SS to OS, n.d., OS Collection, 24:5, HRC.

15 Ziegler, 34.

16 *LHRH* 3, 161.

17 *The Times*, 5 November 1914.

18 *LHRH* 3, 166.

19 *The Times*, 5 November 1914.

20 *LHRH* 3, 166.

21 *Daily Mail*, 15 October 1913. A number of the newspaper sources used in this chapter were first identified by Bradford, whose detailed account of the court cases has been very helpful to me.

22 *Daily Mail*, 11 March 1915.

23 Ziegler, 39.

24 *LHRH* 3, 164.

25 Willie [Martin] to OS, OS Collection, 24:7 (unidentified correspondence), HRC.

26 John J. Withers to OS, 20 November 1912, OS Collection, 24: 11, HRC.

27 SS to OS, 26 December 1912, OS Collection, recip. files, HRC.

28 ES, autobiographical draft, Works 282, HRC.

29 *TCO*, 79.

30 SS to OS, 20 February 1913, OS Collection, HRC.

31 IS to SS, 6 June 1913, Weston Papers. Cited by Bradford, 51.

32 *Daily Mail*, 12 March 1915.

33 *Daily Mail*, 15 and 16 October 1913.

34 HR to OS, OS Collection, Correspondence, 24.2, HRC.

35 *SLES*, 11.

36 *Kelly's Directory of Paddington and Bayswater for 1918*.

37 *SLES*, 67.

38 GRS to ES, 8 June 1914, ES Collection, HRC.

39 Archbishop Davidson to Blanche Sitwell, 18 February 1915, Lambeth Palace Library.

40 *SLES*, 277.

41 Ibid., 18.

42 *LHRH* 3, 282–3.

43 *TCO*, 75.

44 SS to OS, 18 August 1914, OS Collection, 24:5, HRC.

45 SS to OS, 12 September 1914, OS Collection, 24:5, HRC.

46 *The Times*, 5 November 1914.

47 Sir George Lewis to OS, 6 November 1914, OS Collection, 24:11, HRC.

48 Archbishop Davidson to Blanche Sitwell, 24 November 1914, Lambeth Palace Library.

49 Information from the website of the Scarborough Maritime Heritage Centre: www.scarboroughsmaritimeheritage.org.uk.

50 *LHRH* 4, 75.

51 *Daily Mail*, 16 January 1915.

52 *Daily Mail*, 23 January 1915.

53 *Daily Mail*, 13 February 1915.

54 Archbishop Davidson to Blanche Sitwell, 8 February 1915, Lambeth Palace Library.

55 *ODNB*.

56 *Daily Mail*, 15 March 1915.

57 *ODNB*.

58 *Daily Mail*, 9 and 10 March 1915.

59 *Daily Mail*, 10 and 11 March 1915; *The Times*, 10 and 11 March.

60 *Daily Mail*, 12 March 1915.

61 *The Times*, 11 March 1915.

62 *Daily Mail*, 13 March 1915. *The Times* for the same date reports the amount as £125. For Moat's departure see *LHRH* 3, 188.

63 *SLES*, 19.

64 *Daily Mail*, 13 March 1915. *The Times* for the same date has a slightly different transcription of the exchange, which gives the judge a greater tone of exasperation.

65 *The Times*, 15 March 1915.

66 *LHRH* 3, 166.

67 Bradford, 63.

68 *TCO*, 78.

69 Archbishop Davidson to Blanche Sitwell, 17 May 1915, Lambeth Palace Library.

70 Wake's note to a letter from Davidson to Blanche Sitwell, 17 March 1915, Lambeth Palace Library.

71 Letter to Joan Wake [May 1915], *The Early Unpublished Poems of Edith Sitwell*, ed. Gerald W. Morton and Karen P. Hegelson (New York: Peter Lang, 1994), 69.

72 *SLES*, 20.

CHAPTER 8: I DO HOPE IT ISN'T LADYLIKE

1 SS to OS, 17 March 1913, OS Collection, 24:5, HRC.

2 SS to OS, 30 March 1913, OS Collection, 24:5, HRC.

3 Information on Jennings is chiefly taken from Hugh Cudlipp, *Publish and Be Damned!*, 125–30. See also Maurice Edelman, *The Mirror*, 27–8.

4 *SLES*, 10.

5 *The Early Unpublished Poems of Edith Sitwell*, ed. Gerald W. Morton and Karen P. Hegelson, 2.

6 *SLES*, 191.

7 Ibid., 15.

8 Ibid., 14–15.

9 ES, *The Mother and Other Poems* (Oxford: p.p. by B. H. Blackwell, 1915), 18.

10 *SLES*, 18.

11 Allanah Harper interview with Geoffrey Elborn, Sitwell Collection, McFarlin Library, University of Tulsa.

12 Works 259, ES Collection, HRC.

13 TCO, 79–81; drafts of TCO in Works 259, 277, and 278, ES Collection, HRC.

14 Draft of TCO, Works 278, ES Collection, HRC.

15 SS interview with Geoffrey Elborn, Sitwell Collection, McFarlin Library, University of Tulsa.

16 A search for confirming evidence at the PRO has come up empty.

17 *LHRH* 3, 47.

18 Draft of TCO, Works 277, ES Collection, HRC.

19 SS interview with Geoffrey Elborn, Sitwell Collection, McFarlin Library, University of Tulsa.

20 Salter, 56.

21 TCO, 80.

22 'Aubade', CP, 16.

23 Census Online, PRO. Jane Fenwick's place of birth is given as Yorkshire.

24 Fifoot, 19; *SLES*, 234; the recent price was advertised on www.bertram-rota.co.uk

25 *SLES*, 20–1.

26 See *TLS Centenary Archive*.

27 ES to Denys Kilham Roberts, n.d. [c.1942], Holland Library, WSU.

28 *The Times*, 15 July 1937.

29 *SLES*, 22.

30 SS to OS, n.d. [c. March 1912?], OS Collection, 24:5, HRC.

31 *SLES*, 23.

32 Helena Blavatsky, *Isis Unveiled*, 1, 311.

33 See OS, 'Night', *Wheels*, First Cycle, December 1916, 18.

34 Draft of article c.1926, Works 11, ES Collection, HRC.

35 Philip Warner, *The Battle of Loos*, 1.

36 For what follows see especially Ziegler, 55–7; *LHRH* 4, 93–6.

37 *LHRH* 4, 94.

38 ES to DH, 18 January 1943, OS Collection, HRC.

39 See, for instance, the anthology *Scars Upon My Heart*, ed. Catherine
   Reilly.

40 ES, 'The Dancers', *Clowns' Houses* (Oxford: Basil Blackwell, 1918), 25.

41 *SLES*, 24.

42 *LHRH* 4, 116.

43 *SLES*, 14–15.

44 'Clowns' Houses', *Twentieth Century Harlequinade and Other Poems*, 11–14.

45 'Some Forms of Expression in Modern Poetry', lecture c.1923, Works 15,
   ES Collection, HRC.

46 Nina Hamnett, *Laughing Torso*, 105.

47 *TCO*, 85.

48 Denise Hooker, *Nina Hamnett*, 106.

49 *TCO*, 83.

50 *LHRH* 5, 238–9.

51 Ibid. 5, 229.

52 This portrait draws from *LHRH* 5, 207–44; *ODNB*.

53 Lecture c.1922, Works 9, ES Collection, HRC.

54 *ODNB*.

55 *LHRH* 5, 238.

56 ES, 'Wheels', *Wheels*, First Cycle (Oxford: B. H. Blackwell, 1916), viii.

57 Lois Gordon, *Nancy Cunard*, 63.

58 Fifoot, 81.

59 Iris Tree, '1', *Wheels*, First Cycle, 57.

60 Quoted in *Wheels*, Third Cycle, (Oxford: B. H. Blackwell, 1919), 102.

CHAPTER 9: THE TANGO

1 *ODNB*. What follows relies heavily on Diana Holman-Hunt, *Latin
  Among Lions*.

2 Diana Holman-Hunt, op. cit., 20.

3 Ibid., 69.

4 *ODNB*.

5 Harold Acton interview with John Pearson, 8 April 1973, Sitwell Collection, McFarlin Library, University of Tulsa.

6 Elizabeth Salter interview with Victoria Glendinning, April 1978, Sitwell Collection, McFarlin Library, University of Tulsa.

7 Diana Holman-Hunt, op. cit., 166.

8 Ibid., 185.

9 Bradford, 182.

10 Lois Gordon, *Nancy Cunard*, 62.

11 *SLES*, 78.

12 *TCO*, 89–90.

13 Aldous Huxley, *Letters of Aldous Huxley*, ed. Grover Smith, 132.

14 Siegfried Sassoon, *Memoirs of an Infantry Officer*, 218.

15 Jean Moorcroft Wilson, *Siegfried Sassoon*, 386.

16 *SLES*, 26–7.

17 Siegfried Sassoon, *Siegfried Sassoon Diaries 1915–1918*, ed. Rupert Hart-Davis, 197; cited in Jean Moorcroft Wilson, op. cit., 15.

18 *LHRH* 3, 268.

19 Richard Greene (ed.), *Graham Greene*, 398–9.

20 ES, 'Plutocracy at Play', *Clowns' Houses* (Oxford: Blackwell, 1918), 27–8.

21 *LHRH* 5, 35–67, is an extended portrait of Gosse.

22 *TCO*, 95–6.

23 *LHRH* 5, 63.

24 Ibid. 5, 56.

25 *TCO*, 93.

26 *LHRH* 5, 54.

27 Ibid. 5, 41.

28 Quoted in Ann Thwaite, *Edmund Gosse*, 472.

29 T. S. Eliot, *The Letters of T. S. Eliot*, ed. Valerie Eliot and Hugh Haughton, 1, 206.

30 *LHRH* 4, 32–3.

31 Aldous Huxley, op. cit, 141

32 Hubert Nicholson, 'Glimpses of Edith Sitwell', unpublished MS in Glendinning files of Sitwell Collection, McFarlin Library, University of Tulsa.

33 Geoffrey Gorer interview with John Pearson, Sitwell Collection, McFarlin Library, University of Tulsa.

34 Lyndall Gordon, *T. S. Eliot*, 107–8.

35 Lyndall Gordon e-mail to Richard Greene, 17 March 2008.

36 ES, *Clowns' Houses* (Oxford: Blackwell, 1918), 7.

37 Ibid., 14.

38 Ibid., 26.

39 Siegfried Sassoon to OS, 3 July [1918], Southern Illinois University Carbondale.

40 *LHRH* 5, 103. OS's account of Owen includes pp. 89–109.

41 Quoted in *LHRH* 5, 106.

42 *SL*, 19.

43 Ibid.

44 Ibid., 20.

45 *SLES*, 31–2.

46 *SL*, 23.

47 Wilfred Owen, *Poems*, intro. Siegfried Sassoon (London: Chatto & Windus, 1921), ii.

48 *LHRH* 5, 232.

49 Sitwell's letters to Nichols are quoted in Anne and William Charlton, *Putting Poetry First*, 74–7.

50 Ibid., 77.

51 Ibid., 186–7.

CHAPTER 10: ALICE IN HELL

1 Ethel Grant to ES, 22 August 1964, recipient file, ES Collection, HRC.

2 Nina Hamnett, *Laughing Torso*, 114.

3 Ibid.

4 Osbert's description of Armistice Day can be found in *LHRH*.

5 *SLES*, 29.

6 'Recent Poetry', *The Sackbut*, II:4 (October 1921), 38.

7 ES to Elizabeth Salter, 1 September 1958, Holland Library, WSU.

8 Virginia Woolf, *A Moment's Liberty*, ed. Anne Olivier Bell, 57.

9 *TCO*, 85–6.

10 Ibid., 86.

11 *SL*, 199.

12 ES to Robert Graves, n.d., Robert Graves Papers, Southern Illinois University Carbondale.

13 *SL*, 40.

14 Draft of newspaper article, Works 211, ES Collection, HRC.

15 Draft of review of *Men Without Art* by Wyndham Lewis, Works 235, ES Collection, HRC.

16 Denton Welch, *The Journals of Denton Welch*, ed. Michael De-La-Noy, 15.

17 James King, *The Last Modern*, 64 and 122.

18 John Skeaping, *Drawn from Life*, 85.

19 'Herbert Read', Works 232, ES Collection, HRC.

20 ES to Marguerite Bennett, n.d., ES Collection, HRC.

21 Form letter for Anglo-French Poetry Society, n.d., ES Collection, HRC.

22 Preliminary list of members, Anglo-French Poetry Society, n.d., ES Collection, HRC.

23 'Lecture', Works 332, ES Collection, HRC.

24 Arnold Bennett, 'Concerning James Joyce's "Ulysses"', *Outlook*, XLIX (29 April 1922), 337–9.

25 Draft of *TCO*, Works 258, ES Collection, HRC.

26 *Musical Times*, 1 May 1914, 331.

27 *Musical Times*, 1 December 1916, 554.

28 *SLES*, 240.

29 *Musical Times*, 1 June 1920, 422.

30 T. S. Eliot, *The Letters of T. S. Eliot*, ed. Valerie Eliot and Hugh Haughton, 1, 487–9.

31 ES to Robert Graves, n.d., Robert Graves Papers, Southern Illinois University Carbondale.

32 Harold Acton interview with John Pearson, 5 March 1975, Sitwell Collection, McFarlin Library, University of Tulsa.

33 *TCO*, 183.

34 Quoted in ES to Elizabeth Salter, 28 November 1957, Holland Library, WSU.

35 Elizabeth Clegg, 'Meštrović, England and the Great War', *Burlington Magazine*, 740–51.

36 Helen Rootham (trans.), *Kosovo*. I am grateful for Neil Ritchie's observations on Lavrin's possible role in the translation.

37 Quoted in Andrew Rigby, *Initiation and Initiative*, 22.

38 Edwin Muir, *An Autobiography*, 174.

39 See, for example, his poem 'Stanzas on Painting' in H. C. Rutherford (ed.), *Certainly, Future*, 51–2.

40 The copy is in the New Atlantis Archive, Special Collections, University of Bradford Library. An undated letter from ES to Mitrinović in the same archive also uses the word 'pupil'.

41 Andrew Rigby, op. cit., 12–15 and *passim*.

42 *ODNB*.

43 His inscribed copy of Helen Rootham's *Fundamentals of Music and their Relation to Modern Life* is in the New Atlantis Archive, Special Collections, University of Bradford Library.

44 Andrew Rigby, op. cit., 85–109 and *passim*.

45 Dimitrije Mitrinović, 'Aesthetic Contemplations', Rutherford, *Certainly, Future*, op. cit., 36–7.

46 Geoffrey Gorer interview with John Pearson, Sitwell Collection, McFarlin Library, University of Tulsa.

47 See 'Creaking Sarah and Laughing Sal', *Nation*, 13 October 1923, reprinted in *The Best British Short Stories of 1924*, ed. Edward J. O'Brien and John Cournos (Small, Maynard, 1924), 221–5. This anthology also includes Edith Sitwell's 'Undergrowth', 230–43.

48 These translations appeared in the Pastiche column of the *New Age*, 27:22 (30 September 1920), 324, and 28:18 (3 March 1921), 216; her translation of the traditional 'Song of the Building of Skadar' appeared in 24:8 (22 May 1919), 71–2.

49 'Music', *New Age* 30:21 (23 March 1922), 276–7.

50 'Music', *New Age* 30:8 (22 December 1921), 93.

51 Edwin Muir, 'Recent Verse', *New Age* 28:24 (14 April 1921), 284.

52 Wallace Martin, *The New Age Under Orage*, 282.

53 Edwin Muir, review of *The Hundred and One Harlequins* by Sacheverell Sitwell, *New Age* 31:17 (24 August 1922), 211.

54 Helen Rootham, *Fundamentals of Music and their Relation to Modern Life*, 2.

55 CP, 296.

CHAPTER 11: TOO FANTASTIC FOR FAT-HEADS

1 ES, 'Stopping Place', *The Wooden Pegasus* (Oxford: Basil Blackwell, 1920), 82.

2 ES, 'The Ape Sees the Fat Woman', *The Wooden Pegasus*, 46.

3 ES, 'The King of China's Daughter', *The Wooden Pegasus*, 57.

4 Geoffrey Grigson interview with John Pearson, Sitwell Collection, McFarlin Library, University of Tulsa.

5 ES, 'Solo for Ear-Trumpet', *The Wooden Pegasus*, 105.

6 Salter, 57.

7 ES, *Children's Tales (From the Russian Ballet)* (London: Duckworth, 1920), 7–8.

8 Ibid., 12–13.

9 'Igor Stravinski and the Modern World', *New Age* 19:8 (23 June 1921), 92–3. The article is continued in 19:10 (7 July 1921), 118. I am grateful to Neil Ritchie for drawing my attention to this article, which is not recorded in Fifoot.

10 The development of the sequence can be seen in Fifoot.

11 SS, 'The Octogenarian', *An Indian Summer*, 16–19.

12 ES, 'Some Notes on my Own Poetry', CP, xvi.

13 SS, *Liszt*, 30–1.

14 *LHRH* 4, 180–1; Craggs, vi.

15 William Walton interview with John Pearson, Sitwell Collection, McFarlin Library, Tulsa.

16 *LHRH* 4, 184–5.

17 See William Walton interview with John Pearson, Sitwell Collection, McFarlin Library, Tulsa; Neil Ritchie, 'Footnote to Façade', *The Book Collector*; SLES, 38.

18 Craggs, vi.

19 Salter, 166.

20 SLES, 34–5.

21 ES to Valery Larbaud, 10 March 1922, Médiathèque Municipale Valery Larbaud, Vichy.

22 Paul O'Keeffe, *Some Sort of Genius*, 214.

23 *TCO*, 99–106; *LHRH* 4, 30–1; Paul O'Keeffe, op. cit., 238–40.

24 Autobiographical fragment, Works 345, ES Collection, HRC.

25 'Hazards of Sitting for My Portrait', *Observer*, 27 November 1960.

26 Paul O'Keéffe, op. cit., 249–50.

27 Salter, 61.

28 ES, review of *Poems* by Marianne Moore, *The Sackbut* II:6 (December 1921), 38.

29 ES, 'Readers and Writers', *New Age* 31:13 (27 July 1922), 161.

30 ES, 'Readers and Writers', *New Age* 31:15 (10 August 1922), 184–5.

31 See autobiographical fragment, Works 12, ES Collection, HRC.

32 ES to Robert Graves, n.d., Robert Graves Papers, Southern Illinois University Carbondale.

33 *Gloucestershire Notes and Queries* (Oxford, 1879), 35.

34 *Notes and Queries*, series 4, vol. 5 (January–June 1870), 121.

35 W. H. Matthews, *Mazes and Labyrinths*, 156–63; Thomas M. Greene, 'Labyrinth Dances in the French and English Renaissance', *Renaissance Quarterly*.

36 ES, 'Readers and Writers', *New Age* 31:10 (6 July 1922), 119–20.

37 ES to Robert Graves, n.d., Robert Graves Papers, Southern Illinois University Carbondale.

38 ES, 'Colonel Fantock', *CP*, 174–7.

39 A draft of Sitwell's letter is in Works 326, ES Collection, HRC.

40 Robert Graves, *Goodbye to All That*, 294.

41 Autobiographical fragments, Works 37, ES Collection, HRC.

42 ES to Robert Graves, n.d., Robert Graves Papers, Southern Illinois University Carbondale.

CHAPTER 12: GERTRUDE

1 ES to Graham Greene, 25 April 1923, Graham Greene Papers, Lauinger Library, Georgetown University.

2 Norman Sherry, *The Life of Graham Greene*, 1, 141–2.

3 ES to Graham Greene, 15 June 1923, Graham Greene Papers, Lauinger Library, Georgetown University.

4 David Higham, *Literary Gent*, 125, 154–5 and *passim*.

5 Notes for *Reynolds News* Libel Case, Works 120, ES Collection, HRC.

6 ES's account of the debate may be found in Works 120, ES Collection, HRC. Noyes's account is in *Two Worlds for Memory*, 185. The published text of Sitwell's lecture appears to have been revised from the one she delivered on the day; see 'Lecture IV: Poetry and Modern Poetry', *Yea and Nay: A Series of Lectures and Counter Lectures Given at the London School of Economics in Aid of the Hospitals of London* (London: Brentano's, 1923), 76–88.

7 Craggs, vii.

8 *LHRH* 4, 187–91.

9 ES interview with Elizabeth Salter, Sitwell Collection, McFarlin Library, University of Tulsa.

10 William Walton interview with John Pearson, Sitwell Collection, McFarlin Library, University of Tulsa.

11 Angus Morrison interview with John Pearson, Sitwell Collection, McFarlin Library, University of Tulsa.

12 William Walton interview with John Pearson, Sitwell Collection, McFarlin Library, University of Tulsa.

13 Virginia Woolf, *The Diary of Virginia Woolf*, ed. Anne Olivier Bell, 2, 246.

14 *LHRH* 4, 187–91.

15 Review of *Façade*, *Vogue* (July 1923).

16 Noël Coward, *The Letters of Noël Coward*, ed. Barry Day, 82.

17 Noël Coward, 'Chelsea Buns', *A Withered Nosegay*, 143 and *passim*.

18 *SLES*, 72.

19 Draft of letter, ES to GRS, Works 230, ES Collection, HRC.

20 *SLES*, 42.

21 Ibid., 45–6.

22 John Drummond, *Speaking of Diaghilev*, 366.

23 *SLES*, 400.

24 *TCO*, 30, 60–2 and 65.

25 See 'Ogata Korin', www.oxfordartonline.com.

26 ES to Graham Greene, 7 November 1923, Graham Greene Papers, Lauinger Library, Georgetown University.

27 *CP*, 62.

28 *Nation and Athenæum*, 19 April 1924.

29 Review of *The Sleeping Beauty*, *TLS*, 3 April 1924.

30 ES to Thomas Balston, n.d. [c. March 1925], Holland Library, WSU.

31 ES to Robert Graves, 21 March 1924, Robert Graves Papers, Southern Illinois University Carbondale.

32 *SLES*, 47–8.

33 Sir George Sitwell, *A Brief History of Weston Hall*.

34 ES to Robert Graves, 10 September 1924, Robert Graves Papers, Southern Illinois University Carbondale.

35 Draft of review in Works 7, ES Collection, HRC; the review appeared in *Vogue*, 64:12 (early October 1924), 81 and 114.

36 *TCO*, 136–7.

37 Stephen Spender interview with Geoffrey Elborn, Sitwell Collection, McFarlin Library, University of Tulsa.

38 ES to Robert Graves, n.d., Robert Graves Papers, Southern Illinois University Carbondale.

39 ES, 'Four in the Morning', *Troy Park* (London: Duckworth, 1925), 81.

40 ES, '"I do like to be beside the Seaside"', *Troy Park*, 83.

41 Autobiographical fragments, Works 37, ES Collection, HRC.

42 ES to Robert Graves, n.d., Robert Graves Papers, Southern Illinois University Carbondale.

43 ES to Robert Graves, 21 March 1924, Robert Graves Papers, Southern Illinois University Carbondale.

44 ES to Thomas Balston, 17 August 1926, Holland Library, WSU.

45 ES, 'Mademoiselle Richarde', *Troy Park*, 99–100.

46 Alice B. Toklas, *What is Remembered*, 118.

47 *SLES*, 54.

48 Ibid., 52.

49 Draft of 'A Party in Honour', Works 17, ES Collection, HRC. These sketches of Paris are not recorded in Fifoot.

50 *SLES*, 54–5.

51 ES, 'The Work of Gertrude Stein', *Vogue* 66:7 (early October 1925), 73 and 98.

52 Virginia Woolf, *The Diary of Virginia Woolf*, ed. Anne Olivier Bell, 3, 24.

53 ES, 'Prelude to a Fairy Tale', *Rustic Elegies* (London: Duckworth, 1927), 49.

54 *Rustic Elegies*, 83.

55 See notes for this poem in Works 3, 18, and 16, ES Collection, HRC.

56 Rudolf Steiner, 'The Three Stages of Sleep', http://wn.rsarchive.org/Lectures/19220324p01.html.

57 CP, 136.

58 ES to PT, 22 June 1943.

59 *SLES*, 56.

60 Ibid., 58.

61 Ibid., 59.

62 Ibid., 60.

63 Ibid.

64 ES to Robert Graves, c. November 1925, Robert Graves Papers, Southern Illinois University Carbondale.

65 *SLES*, 64.

66 Allanah Harper, 'Memory of Dame Edith Sitwell', unpublished MS, Sitwell Collection, McFarlin Library, University of Tulsa.

67 *SLES*, 63.

68 Virginia Woolf, *The Diary of Virginia Woolf*, ed. Anne Olivier Bell, 3, 28.

69 Richard Vinen, *A History in Fragments: Europe in the Twentieth Century* (Cambridge, MA: Da Capo Press, 2001), 89.

70 Allanah Harper, 'Memory of Dame Edith Sitwell', unpublished MS, Sitwell Collection, McFarlin Library, University of Tulsa.

71 Craggs, viii.

72 Ibid.

73 *LHRH* 195–238; Ziegler, 151–2.

74 ES to Robert Graves, 3 January 1924, Robert Graves Papers, Southern Illinois University Carbondale.

75 ES to John Freeman, Thursday [6 May 1926], McCormick Library of Special Collections, Northwestern University, Evanston, Illinois.

76 OS, unpublished memoir of T. S. Eliot, OS Collection, HRC.

77 Virginia Woolf, *The Letters of Virginia Woolf*, ed. Nigel Nicolson and J. Trautmann, vol. 3, 269–70.

78 Gertrude Stein, *The Autobiography of Alice B. Toklas*, 232–5.

79 *SLES*, 67–8.

80 ES to Siegfried Sassoon, 4 June 1926, Holland Library, WSU.

81 Max Egremont, *Siegfried Sassoon*, 300.

82 ES to Siegfried Sassoon, 9 November 1926, Holland Library, WSU.

83 ES to Siegfried Sassoon, 22 March 1927, Holland Library, WSU.

84 *The Sitwells and the Arts of the 1920s and 1930s*, 111–12. See also Hugo Vickers, *Cecil Beaton*, 68–101 and *passim*.

85 Cecil Beaton interview with John Pearson, McFarlin Library, University of Tulsa.

86 *TCO*, 108.

87 *LHRH* 4, 272.

88 *TCO*, 107.

89 D. H. Lawrence, *Collected Letters*, ed. Harry T. Moore, 2, 979. Cited by Pearson, 226.

90 Pearson, 224–32.

91 *TCO*, 110.

92 *SLES*, 105.

93 Virginia Woolf, *The Diary of Virginia Woolf*, ed. Anne Olivier Bell, 3, 132–3.

CHAPTER 13: YOU ARE RUSSIAN, ARE YOU NOT?

1 Tyler, 220–1.

2 Notes for article on Tchelitchew, Works 171, ES Collection, HRC.

3 ES, draft of 'Pavel Tchelitchew', Works 88, ES Collection, HRC.

4 Tyler, *passim*.

5 Ibid., 298.

6 See David Ebony, 'The Melancholy Gang: Eugene Berman and his Circle', *Art in America*.

7 Ibid.; see also David Duncan, *Pavel Tchelitchew: The Landscape of the Body*.

8 See Kenneth E. Silver, 'Neo-Romantics', *Paris/New York: Design/Fashion/ Culture*.

9 Tyler, 310.

10 Glenway Wescott, *Continual Lessons*, ed. Robert Phelps with Jerry Rosco; see also Glenway Wescott interview with John Pearson, Sitwell Collection, McFarlin Library, University of Tulsa.

11 Tyler, 340.

12 Glenway Wescott, op. cit.; see also Glenway Wescott interview with Pearson, Sitwell Collection, McFarlin Library, Tulsa.

13 Tyler, 7.

14 Allanah Harper, 'Memory of Dame Edith Sitwell', unpublished MS, Sitwell Collection, McFarlin Library, University of Tulsa.

15 Tyler, 220–1.

16 C. H. Ford, entries for 9 May 1949 and following days, unpublished journal, C. H. Ford Papers, 23:3, HRC. Note: Ford's published journals do not reveal the full extent of these activities.

17 Tyler, 20.

18 Ibid., 348.

19 ES to Sassoon, n.d., Holland Library, WSU.

20 Quoted in Martin Seymour-Smith, *Robert Graves: His Life and Work*, 135–6.

21 *SLES*, 81.

22 Ibid., 96.

23 Ibid., 82.

24 ES to Siegfried Sassoon, n.d., Holland Library, WSU.

25 ES to Tom Balston, two undated letters, Holland Library, WSU.

26 *LHRH* 4, 53.

27 ES to Siegfried Sassoon, 9 March 1928, Holland Library, WSU.

28 ES to Siegfried Sassoon, 9 June 1929, Holland Library, WSU.

29 *SLES*, 88–9.

30 ES to Siegfried Sassoon, n.d., Holland Library, WSU.

31 *ODNB*.

32 ES to Siegfried Sassoon, n.d., Holland Library, WSU.

33 ES to Siegfried Sassoon, n.d., Holland Library, WSU.

34 ES to Sassoon, 13 March 1928, Holland Library, WSU.

35 Draft of letter, ES to Sir Harold Satow, 1 January 1942, recip. file, ES Collection, HRC; ES to Sassoon, n.d., Holland Library, WSU.

36 *ODNB*.

37 *SLES*, 91–2.

38 ES to Kenneth Clark, 25 May 1949, Morgan Library and Museum, New York.

39 *SLES*, 28.

40 *SL*, 200.

41 Draft of 'A World I Would Like to Live In', Works 29, ES Collection, HRC.

42 *CP*, 238.

43 *SLES*, 97–9.

44 Manuscript notebook, Balston Collection, Holland Library, WSU.

45 *CP*, 426.

46 *SLES*, 344–5.

47 ES to Robert [Herring?], c.1951, recip. file, ES Collection, HRC.

48 Elborn, 69.

49 ES to Siegfried Sassoon, n.d. [November 1928], Holland Library, WSU.

50 ES to Thomas Balston, n.d. [November 1928], Holland Library, WSU.

51 ES to Sydney Schiff, 27 December 1928, BL.

52 *LHRH* 4, 289–90, citing Evan Charteris, *The Life and Letters of Sir Edmund Gosse*, 496.

53 W. B. Yeats, 'Modern Poetry: A Broadcast', *Essays and Introductions* (New York: Macmillan, 1961), 501.

54 *TCO*, 20.

55 ES to 'H.D.', c.1943, 'H.D.' Papers, Beinecke Library, Yale University.

56 ES to Thomas Balston, 5 August 1928 and n.d. [August 1928], Holland Library, WSU.

57 ES to Thomas Balston, n.d. [October 1928], Holland Library, WSU; *LHRH* 4, 289; Christabel Aberconway, *A Wiser Woman?*, 90–2.

58 Ibid.

59 Craggs, ix.

60 John Stuart Roberts, *Siegfried Sassoon*, 225.

61 ES to Siegfried Sassoon, 13 March 1928, Holland Library, WSU.

62 Allen Tanner, 'The Early Tchelitchew', unpublished MS, McFarlin Library, University of Tulsa.

63 *SLES*, 94.

64 ES to Thomas Balston, 28 November 1928, Holland Library, WSU.

65 Stella Bowen, *Drawn from Life*, 172–3.

66 ES, *Alexander Pope* (London: Faber & Faber, 1930), 3–5.

67 Ibid., 84–5.

68 Donald Greene, 'An Anatomy of Pope-bashing', *The Enduring Legacy: Alexander Pope Tercentenary Essays*, ed. G. S. Rousseau and Pat Rogers (Cambridge: Cambridge University Press, 1988), 250. Auden's remarks are found in 'Pope (1688–1744)', *From Anne to Victoria*, ed. Bonamy Dobrée (London: Cassell, 1937), 103. For a general discussion of Sitwell's sense of the eighteenth century, see Richard Greene, 'Sir Beelzebub's Syllabub: Or, Edith Sitwell's Eighteenth Century', *Lumen*.

69 ES to Siegfried Sassoon, 25 October 1928, Holland Library, WSU.

70 ES to Siegfried Sassoon, Good Friday 1929, Holland Library, WSU.

71 ES to Siegfried Sassoon, 18 May 1929, Holland Library, WSU.

72 ES to Thomas Balston, c. November 1928, Holland Library, WSU.

73 John Stuart Roberts, op. cit., 221.

74 ES to Siegfried Sassoon, 18 May 1929, Holland Library, WSU.

75 Draft of 'Decency and Censorship', Works 34, ES Collection, HRC.

76 ES to PT, 10 February 1930.

77 Letters from ES to Harmsworth are in the private collection of Neil Ritchie.

78 Geoffrey Gorer interview with John Pearson, Sitwell Collection, McFarlin Library, University of Tulsa.

79 ES to PT, 2 June 1930, Beinecke Library, Yale University.

80 Catalogue of the Collection of Works by Pavel Tchelitchew, the property of Dame Edith Sitwell, Wednesday, 13 December 1961, HRC.

81 *SLES*, 108.

82 ES to Thomas Balston, c. October 1929, Holland Library, WSU.

83 See Glendinning, 135–7, and Elborn, 73–7.

84 *SLES*, 107–8.

85 ES to PT, 3 April 1930 and 12 May 1930, Beinecke Library, Yale University.

86 Translation by an unknown hand (possibly Lorna Andrade) of a letter from PT to ES, 8 June 1930, Sitwell Collection, McFarlin Library, University of Tulsa.

87 ES to PT, 13 June 1930, Beinecke Library, Yale University.

88 ES to Siegfried Sassoon, 3 October 1933, Holland Library, WSU.

89 IS to SS, 9 September 1930, SS Collection, HRC.

90 *SLES*, 129.

91 ES to Thomas Balston, 27 May 1930, Holland Library, WSU.

92 *Fortnightly Review*, n.s., 128 (August 1930), 271–2.

93 *Saturday Review of Literature*, 7 (11 October 1930), 212.

94 *Nation and Athenæum*, 47 (9 August 1930), 596.

CHAPTER 14: ALL EARS FOR EDITH

1 See Paul O'Keeffe, *Some Sort of Genius*, 290–1.

2 Wyndham Lewis, *The Apes of God*, 189.

3 Ibid., 122.

4 Ibid., 394.

5 Ibid., 501–2.

6 ES to PT, c. May 1932, Beinecke Library, Yale University.

7 W. B. Yeats, *The Letters of W. B. Yeats*, ed. Alan Wade (London: Hart-Davis, 1954), 776.

8 ES to Thomas Balston, c. 23 September 1930, Holland Library, WSU.

9 R. F. Foster, *W. B. Yeats*, 2, 435.

10 ES to Terence Fytton Armstrong, 21 November 1930, Berg Collection, NYPL.

11 See Works 37, 42, 212, 271, ES Collection, HRC. The finished first chapter may be found in the Sitwell Collection, McFarlin Library, University of Tulsa.

12 *ODNB*.

13 ES to Thomas Balston, 8 October 1930, Holland Library, WSU.

14 *SLES*, 121.

15 ES to Terence Fytton Armstrong, 21 November 1930, Berg Collection, NYPL.

16 Salter, 52.

17 GRS to SS, 6 January 1931, SS Collection, HRC.

18 In a fragmentary draft of a letter, possibly to Raleigh Trevelyan, ES Collection, HRC, the amount is given as just £24. Presumably, this should be £124, the amount given by the Public Trustee in a supplemental statement of account of Florence Sitwell's estate (1955), ES Collection, HRC.

19 Raleigh Trevelyan published, with names changed, a letter Sitwell had written to him about Edith Woods in *A Hermit Disclosed*, 263–5. See his article, 'Two Ediths and a Hermit', *London Review of Books*. I am grateful to Mr Trevelyan for information on this episode.

20 ES to PT, c. 31 March 1931, Beinecke Library, Yale University.

21 ES to Siegfried Sassoon, June 1931, Holland Library, WSU.

22 ES to PT, c. April 1931?, Beinecke Library, Yale University.

23 Richard Ellmann, *James Joyce*, 650–1. This corrects Pearson, 242.

24 OS, unpublished memoir of T. S. Eliot, OS Collection, HRC.

25 ES to Terence Fytton Armstrong, 27 August 1931, Berg Collection, NYPL.

26 ES, *Bath* (London: Faber & Faber, 1932), 184.

27 ES to PT, c. May 1932, Beinecke Library, Yale University.

28 Allanah Harper, 'Memory of Dame Edith Sitwell', unpublished MS, McFarlin Library, University of Tulsa.

29 Ibid.

30 ES to SS, 14 December 1931, ES Collection, HRC.

31 ES to PT, 7 December 1931, Beinecke Library, Yale University.

32 *SLES*, 131–2.

33 Promissory note, OS Collection 24:2, HRC; Bank books, misc. file, ES Collection, HRC.

34 ES to SS, 14 December 1931, ES Collection, HRC.

35 Allanah Harper, op. cit.

36 Noel Riley Fitch, *Sylvia Beach and the Lost Generation*, 311.

37 ES to Thomas Balston, 23 October 1930, Holland Library, WSU.

38 Tyler, 317.

39 PT to ES, 15 August 1928, 17 November 1928, n.d. [c. November 1928], and 31 December 1928, Berg Collection, NYPL.

40 James Joyce, *Letters of James Joyce*, ed. Stuart Gilbert, 300.

41 Noel Riley Fitch, op. cit., 311.

42 Allanah Harper, op. cit.

43 Natalie Clifford Barney, 'When Poets Meet', *A Perilous Advantage*, 177–8.

44 Salter, 114.

45 Tyler, 339.

46 Noel Riley Fitch, op. cit., 311.

47 Tyler, 339.

48 Gertrude Stein to ES, n.d., ES Collection, HRC.

49 Gertrude Stein, *The Autobiography of Alice B. Toklas*, 232.

50 Salter, 114.

51 See Tyler, 308 and *passim*.

52 ES to Siegfried Sassoon, 16 March 1932, Holland Library, WSU.

53 ES to Siegfried Sassoon, 22 March 1932, Holland Library, WSU.

54 *SLES*, 134.

55 ES to PT, c. 28 April 1932, Beinecke Library, Yale University.

56 *SLES*, 277.

57 Allanah Harper interview with Geoffrey Elborn, Sitwell Collection, McFarlin Library, University of Tulsa.

58 ES to PT, c. 4 June 1933, Beinecke Library, Yale University.

59 *SLES*, 140.

60 ES to PT, 20 July 1932, Beinecke Library, Yale University.

61 ES to PT, n.d., Beinecke Library, Yale University.

62 ES to PT, 16 October 1932, Beinecke Library, Yale University.

63 Draft of review of *The Snooty Baronet*, Works 231, ES Collection, HRC. Fifoot does not record its publication. In general, the notebooks indicate that Sitwell wrote many more reviews and newspaper articles in the 1920s and 1930s than are recorded in the bibliography.

64 *SL*, 43.

65 SS interview with Geoffrey Pearson, Sitwell Collection, McFarlin Library, University of Tulsa.

66 ES, Works 141, ES Collection, HRC.

67 James Gregory, 'Eccentric Biography and the Victorians', *Biography*, 342.

68 ES, *The English Eccentrics* (London: Faber & Faber, 1933), 13.

69 Ibid., 17.

70 ES to Allanah Harper, c. 1 January 1933, McFarlin Library, University of Tulsa.

71 ES, *The English Eccentrics*, 20–1.

72 Ibid., 55.

73 ES to Siegfried Sassoon, 3 October 1933, Holland Library, WSU.

74 IS to SS, 27 December 1932, SS Collection, HRC.

75 ES to PT, n.d.

76 ES to PT, c. 25 August 1933, Beinecke Library, Yale University.

77 Hugo Southern interview with John Pearson, Sitwell Collection, McFarlin Library, University of Tulsa.

78 Ziegler, 187–90.

79 *SLES*, 148.

80 Jessica Douglas-Home, *Violet, passim*; *ODNB*.

81 *SLES*, 149.

82 Ibid., 146.

83 Edward James, *Swans Reflecting Elephants*, 169–71.

84 Charles Henri Ford, 'Flesh and Marble', unpublished MS, C. H. Ford Papers, 21:2, HRC.

85 *SLES*, 145.

86 Clipping included with ES to PT, 21 September 1933, Beinecke Library,

Yale University.

87 ES to PT, 10 October 1933, Beinecke Library, Yale University.

88 ES to PT, 14 October 1933, Beinecke Library, Yale University.

89 ES to PT, c. September 1933, Beinecke Library, Yale University.

90 Lincoln Kirstein interview with John Pearson, McFarlin Library, University of Tulsa.

91 Works 33, 227, 228, and 232, ES Collection, HRC.

92 CP, 230.

93 ES to Thomas Balston, c. September 1933, Holland Library, WSU.

94 SLES, 151.

95 Ibid., 153–4.

96 Ibid., 152–3.

97 Ibid., 152.

98 Arthur Raper, The Tragedy of Lynching, 1.

99 SLES, 154.

100 ES to Siegfried Sassoon, 3 October 1933, Holland Library, WSU.

101 ES to PT, 11 July 1944, Beinecke Library, Yale University.

102 SLES, 158.

103 ES to PT, n.d., Beinecke Library, Yale University.

104 ES to PT, n.d., Beinecke Library, Yale University.

105 ES to PT, c. 12 February 1934, Beinecke Library, Yale University.

106 ES to PT, early 1934, Beinecke Library, Yale University.

CHAPTER 15: LET THE DEVILS HAVE IT

1 SLES, 161.

2 F. R. Leavis, New Bearings in English Poetry, 73.

3 See, for example, Claudia L. Johnson, 'F. R. Leavis: The "Great Tradition" of the English Novel and the Jewish Part', Nineteenth-Century Literature.

4 ES to Thomas Balston, c. June 1934, Holland Library, WSU.

5 Geoffrey Grigson interview with John Pearson, Sitwell Collection, McFarlin Library, University of Tulsa.

6 Scrutiny, vol. 2, 201–2; for the context of this review, see Bradford, 239–41.

7 Anthony Powell, To Keep the Ball Rolling, 2, 197–8.

8 ES to Thomas Balston, n.d. [summer 1934], Holland Library, WSU.

9 Anthony Powell, op. cit., 197–8.

10 ES to PT, 10 June 1934.

11 Tyler, 350.

12 See, for example, Lawrence Schehr, *Alcibiades at the Door, passim.*

13 Alice B. Toklas, *What is Remembered*, 127–8.

14 Allanah Harper, 'Memory of Dame Edith Sitwell', unpublished MS, McFarlin Library, University of Tulsa.

15 Lecture on Poetry, c.1948, Works 97, ES Collection, HRC.

16 *SLES*, 232–3.

17 *ODNB*.

18 ES to John Sparrow, draft, Works 234, ES Collection, HRC. The final draft is quoted in John Lowe, *The Warden*, 77–9.

19 ES to SS, 26 September 1934, ES Collection, HRC.

20 ES to PT, 24 August 1934.

21 ES to PT, 31 August 1934.

22 ES to SS, 26 September 1934, ES Collection, HRC.

23 Roy Foster, *W. B. Yeats*, 494.

24 I am grateful to Professor Fred Flahiff for this observation.

25 *SLES*, 168–9.

26 Ian MacKillop, *F. R. Leavis*, 267–8; cited by Claudia L. Johnson, 198.

27 *SLES*, 155.

28 ES, *Aspects of Modern Poetry* (London: Gerald Duckworth, 1934), 228–31.

29 Ibid., 246.

30 ES to PT, 4 January 1935.

31 ES, *Aspects of Modern Poetry*, 174.

32 *SLES*, 165–6.

33 ES to PT, 26 November 1934.

34 ES to PT, 25 December 1934.

35 ES to PT, 29 December 1939.

36 ES to PT, 12 January 1935.

37 Stephen Spender interview with John Pearson, Sitwell Collection, McFarlin Library, University of Tulsa.

38 *SLES*, 173.

39 Draft of letter to Norman Collins, c. spring 1935, Works 224, ES Collection, HRC.

40 ES to PT, 4 January 1936. ES mistakenly dated this letter 1935.

41 *SLES*, 173–4.

42 ES to PT, 12 April 1935.

43 ES to PT, 18 July 1935.

44 Elizabeth Crawford, *The Women's Suffrage Movement*, 126–7. See also Geoffrey Gorer interview with Geoffrey Elborn, Sitwell Collection, McFarlin Library, University of Tulsa.

45 *SLES*, 179–80.

46 Marie Belloc Lowndes, *Diaries and Letters of Marie Belloc Lowndes 1911–1947*, ed. Susan Lowndes, 228.

47 ES to PT, c. December 1935.

48 *SLES*, 176–8.

49 Dylan Thomas, *The Collected Letters*, ed. Paul Ferris, 206.

50 ES to PT, 10 February 1936.

51 Dylan Thomas, op. cit., 242–4; Constantine Fitzgibbon, *The Life of Dylan Thomas*, 201.

52 *SLES*, 184–5.

53 ES to Sassoon.

54 *SLES*, 190.

55 *LHRH* 4, 126; *SLES*, 180.

56 *The Times*, 1 May 1936.

57 ES to PT, 31 March 1936.

58 ES to PT, 13 April 1936.

59 *SLES*, 187.

60 ES to PT, 28 September 1942.

61 ES to PT, 20 May 1936.

62 ES to PT, 21 April 1936.

63 ES to PT, 9 June 1936.

64 ES to PT, 3 December 1946. See also draft of TCO, Works 257, ES Collection, HRC.

65 W. H. Auden, 'Spain', in *Poetry of the Thirties*, ed. Robin Skelton (Harmondsworth: Penguin, 1964), 136.

66 These are commonly accepted figures derived from Antonio Montero Marino, *Historia de la persecución religiosa en España, 1936–1939*. For comment on them, see Bruce Lincoln, 'Revolutionary Exhumations in Spain, July 1936', *Comparative Studies in Society and History*, 241.

67 ES to PT, c. August 1936.

68 ES to Christabel Aberconway, 21 August 1936, British Library.

69 ES to PT, 22 August 1936.

CHAPTER 16: TWO NATIONS

1 John Lowe, *Edward James*, 113–15 and 133.

2 ES to PT, c. 27 August 1936.

3 ES to PT, 24 November 1936.

4 R. F. Foster, *W. B. Yeats*, 2, 557.

5 *SLES*, 351.

6 ES to PT, 17 September 1936.

7 ES to Lord Clonmore, draft letter, Works 214, ES Collection, HRC.

8 Percy G. Haddock to ES, 27 February 1937, McFarlin Library, University of Tulsa.

9 ES to PT, 10 April 1937.

10 *SLES*, 198.

11 Dylan Thomas, *The Collected Letters*, ed. Paul Ferris, 297.

12 *SLES*, 198.

13 ES to PT, 16 August 1939.

14 ES to Christabel Aberconway, c. July 1937, BL.

15 ES to PT, 8 July 1937.

16 ES to PT, 8 July 1937.

17 ES to PT, c. October 1937.

18 ES, *I Live Under a Black Sun* (London: Victor Gollancz, 1937), 16.

19 *SLES*, 208.

20 ES, *I Live Under a Black Sun*, 40–1.

21 ES to DH, 3 October 1937, ES Collection, HRC.

22 *Night and Day*, 21 October 1937, 208–9.

23 See Glendinning, 211.

24 ES to PT, c. October 1937.

25 Works 236, ES Collection, HRC.

26 Information from Rachel Lawson, BBC Written Archives Centre. The play was published in *Twelve Modern Plays*, ed. John Hampden (London: Gerald Duckworth, 1938), 287–312.

27 *SLES*, 203.

28 ES to Sassoon, n.d. [c.1930], Holland Library, WSU.

29 *SLES*, 277.

30 Percy G. Haddock to ES, 27 February 1937, McFarlin Library, University of Tulsa.

31 Bank books, ES Collection, HRC.

32 ES to PT, 14 March 1938.

33 *SLES*, 204.

34 GRS to GS, 24 March 1938, SS Collection, HRC.

35 *SLES*, 205–6.

36 *SL*, 120.

37 ES to Hal Lydiard Wilson, 3 October 1962, ES Collection, HRC.

38 *The Times*, 18 May 1938. This corrects Glendinning, 213, and *SLES*, 479n.

39 Bank books, ES Collection, HRC.

40 Tyler, 413.

41 ES to DH, 23 September 1938, OS Collection, HRC.

42 Information from Rachel Lawson, BBC Written Archives Centre. The final script has not survived, but drafts may be found in Works 49, 205, 223, 236, 238, and 253, ES Collection, HRC.

43 I am grateful to Neil Ritchie for drawing this review to my attention.

44 *ODNB*.

45 ES to GS, c. November 1938, ES Collection, HRC.

46 *SLES*, 209.

47 Ibid., 210.

48 PT to ES, 18 May 1939.

49 Figures from United States Holocaust Memorial Museum, www.ushmm.org.

50 C. H. Ford, Journal, Ford Papers, 20:2, HRC.

51 ES to PT, 27 August 1939.

CHAPTER 17: AND WITH THE APE THOU ART ALONE

1 *SLES*, 213–15; see also Stephen King-Hall, *Total Victory*.

2 ES to PT, 29 November 1939.

3 ES to PT, 27 September 1939.

4 Ziegler, 249.

5 Lorna Andrade interview with John Pearson, Sitwell Collection, McFarlin Library, University of Tulsa.

6 ES to Bryher, 11 July 1942, Bryher Papers, Beinecke Library, Yale University.

7 PT to ES, 23 October 1939.

8 PT to ES, 15 January 1940.

9 Ibid.

10 ES to PT, 1 February 1940.

11 ES to PT, 10 November 1939.

12 ES to PT, 2 October 1939.

13 ES to PT, 29 November 1939.

14 ES, 'Lullaby', *CP*, 274–5.

15 Blurb for *Street Songs*, Works 59, ES Collection, HRC.

16 *CP*, 62.

17 See drafts in Works 54, ES Collection, HRC.

18 ES to PT, 1 January 1940.

19 'Vigil Strange I Kept on the Field One Evening', Walt Whitman, *Selected Poems*, ed. Christopher Moore, 192–3.

20 ES to PT, 29 November 1940.

21 ES to PT, 1 February 1940.

22 ES to PT, 28 February 1940.

23 Ibid.

24 ES to PT, 6 June 1940.

25 ES to PT, 1 August 1940.

26 ES to PT, 12 October 1940.

27 ES to DH, 6 May 1940, ES Collection, HRC.

28 Salter, 33.

29 ES to PT, 10 July 1940.

30 Obituary of Lady Guinness, *Telegraph*, 23 August 2001.

31 ES to PT, 14 December 1939.

32 See Bradford, 290.

33 ES to PT, 1 August 1940.

34 ES to PT, 20 August 1940.

35 ES to PT, 6 January 1941.

36 ES to PT, 27 September 1940.

37 ES to PT, 12 October 1940.

38 ES to PT, 27 September 1940. See also Paul West, *I, Said the Sparrow*, 87.

39 *SLES*, 216–17.

40 OS to DH, 21 August 1940, OS Collection, HRC.

41 OS to DH, 29 August 1940, OS Collection, HRC.

43 OS to DH, 5 November 1940, OS Collection, HRC.

43 *CP*, 278.

44 See Works 54 and 58, ES Collection, HRC.

45 ES to PT, 23 August 1941.

46 See Works 84, ES Collection, HRC.

47 Law Reports, *The Times*, 6–11 February 1941.

48 Lorna Andrade interview with John Pearson, Sitwell Collection, McFarlin Library, University of Tulsa.

49 Richard Greene (ed.), *Graham Greene, passim*.

50 *SLES*, 224.

51 Geoffrey Green, 'Bayswater and the New West End Synagogue during World War Two'. www.newwestend.org.uk. I am grateful to Mr Green for answering my e-mailed queries.

52 ES to PT, 14 June 1942.

53 ES to Edward James, draft, Works 238, ES Collection, HRC.

54 PT to ES, 5 March 1941.

55 PT to ES, 26 May 1941.

56 ES to PT, 11 July 1942.

57 Richard Greene (ed.), op. cit., 419.

58 ES to PT, 16 April 1941.

59 ES to PT, 22 May 1941.

60 ES to PT, 9 June 1941.

61 ES to PT, 18 July 1941.

CHAPTER 18: AN ABBESS

1 Information from the late Nigel Nicolson.

2 ES to PT, 29 April 1940.

3 ES to GS, c. November 1938, ES Collection, HRC.

4 *SLES*, 227–8. See also drafts of letters to Martin in Works 47 and 84, ES Collection, HRC; notes from Amalia's correspondence are in Works 46.

5 Works 305, ES Collection, HRC; see also Works 48, 65, 71, 138, 214, 238, 262, 289.

6 See Works 262 and 289, ES Collection, HRC.

7 Works 305, ES Collection, HRC.

8 ES to PT, 5 January 1942.

9 ES to PT, 11 September 1941.

10 CP, 261–3.

11 Marianne Moore to Bryher, 1 March [1942?], recip. file, ES Collection, HRC.

12 Craggs, x.

13 ES, note, *Façade 2: Facsimile* (Oxford: Oxford University Press, 1979), unpag.; Craggs, xi.

14 *The Times*, 23 May 1942.

15 ES to PT, 9 June 1942.

16 OS to DH, 11 December 1941, OS Collection, HRC.

17 OS to DH, 19 December 1941, OS Collection, HRC.

18 OS to DH, 18 February 1942, OS Collection, HRC.

19 OS to DH, early 1942 and 13 March 1942, OS Collection, HRC; Jessica Douglas-Home, *Violet*, 264–5.

20 Letter from Coutts Bank, 9 March 1950, recip. file, ES Collection, HRC.

21 Evelyn Waugh, *The Letters of Evelyn Waugh*, ed. Mark Amory, 163.

22 Ibid., 207–8.

23 *LHRH* 4, 269–70.

24 Evelyn Waugh, *Brideshead Revisited* (London: Chapman and Hall, 1945), 63. I am grateful to Selina Hastings and Robert Murray Davis for advice on the connection of GRS and Edward Ryder.

25 ES to PT, 3 April 1941.

26 OS to DH, 5 April 1942, OS Collection, HRC.

27 *SLES*, 236.

28 *The Times*, 3 February 1941; ES to PT, 24 July 1944.

29 OS to DH, 30 September 1942 and 20 November 1942, OS Collection, HRC.

30 ES to PT, 16 February 1942.

31 ES to PT, 21 June 1942.

32 ES to PT, 27 July 1942.

33 *SL*, 84.

34 Ibid., 90.

35 Denton Welch, *The Journals of Denton Welch*, ed. Michael De-La-Noy, 9.

36 ES to PT, 9 December 1942.

37 ES to PT, 14 December 1942.

38 ES to PT, 16 March 1943.

39 ES to PT, 20 January 1943 and 7 April 1943.

40 ES to PT, 14 April 1943.

41 *The Times*, 15 April 1943; Victoria Glendinning, *Vita*, 323.

42 *SLES*, 238–9.

43 Denton Welch, *A Lunch Appointment*; see also *The Journals of Denton Welch*, 67–76.

44 Information from Nicholas Shakespeare.

45 *SLES*, 241.

46 Ibid., 254.

47 *CP*, 266.

48 ES to PT, 10 January 1942.

49 ES to GS, January 1942, private collection of Neil Ritchie.

50 ES to PT, 25 June 1945.

51 Quoted in ES to PT, 6 July 1943.

52 ES to PT, 4 February 1944; OS to DH, 24 July 1943, OS Collection, HRC.

53 OS to DH, 13 July 1943, OS Collection, HRC.

54 ES to PT, 19 July 1943.

55 OS to DH, 28 July 1943 and 31 July 1943, OS Collection, HRC.

56 ES to PT, 28 July 1943.

57 *SLES*, 249.

58 ES to PT, 28 July 1943.

59 OS to DH, 2 May 1943, OS Collection, HRC.

60 ES to PT, 28 July 1943.

61 OS to DH, 15 July 1943, OS Collection, HRC.

62 OS to DH, n.d. [1943], OS Collection, HRC.

63 OS to Lorna Andrade, n.d. [1944], OS Collection, HRC.

64 *SLES*, 256.

65 ES to DH, c. 27 February 1944, ES Collection, HRC.

66 OS to Lorna Andrade, 13 March 1944, 18 March 1944, and n.d. 1944, OS Collection, HRC.

67 *The Times*, 26 August 1944; ES to PT, 7 October 1945.

68 Hugo Southern to OS, 15 April 1965 and 1 July 1965, OS Collection, HRC.

69 Reresby Sitwell interview with John Pearson, Sitwell Collection, McFarlin Library, University of Tulsa.

70 Hugo Southern interview with John Pearson, Sitwell Collection, McFarlin Library, University of Tulsa.

71 Lorna Andrade interview with John Pearson, Sitwell Collection, McFarlin Library, University of Tulsa.

72 *SLES*, 250.

73 Ibid., 251–2.

CHAPTER 19: THE DANCING MADNESS

1 ES to PT, 21 March 1944.

2 *SL*, 115.

3 ES to PT, 14 August 1944.

4 ES to PT, 14 December 1943.

5 ES to PT, 30 April 1946.

6 ES to PT, 4 February 1944.

7 For information on Coleridge's reading and annotation of Oken's works, I am grateful to Professor Heather Jackson.

8 ES to PT, 8 February 1945; *CP*, 370 and 433.

9 ES to PT, 10 August 1943.

10 *SL*, 132.

11 Adrian Wright, *John Lehmann, passim*; ODNB.

12 John Lehmann, *In My Own Time*, 326–7.

13 *SLES*, 258.

14 Eugene Walter (as told to Katherine Clark), *Milking the Moon*, 108.

15 ES to PT, 21 March 1944.

16 ES to PT, 21 April 1943.

17 ES to PT, 21 March 1944.

18 *SLES*, 261.

19 ES to PT, 7 June 1944.

20 ES to PT, 24 August 1944.

21 ES to PT, 14 September 1944.

22 ES, 'Holiday', *CP*, 308.

23 Gordon Bottomley to ES, 24 January 1944, recip. file, ES Collection, HRC.

24 *ODNB*.

25 ES to PT, 29 November 1944.

26 *SLES*, 269–70.

27 ES to PT, 28 March 1945.

28 *SLES*, 270.

29 ES to John Crosby, draft, 7 September 1962, Works 266, ES Collection, HRC.

30 *SLES*, 175.

31 Ibid., 270–1.

32 Ibid., 271–3.

33 Ibid., 253–4.

34 Ibid., 274.

35 ES to Graham Greene, 22 January 1945, private collection of Neil Ritchie.

36 ES to PT, 25 January 1945.

37 ES to PT, 16 March 1945.

38 Ibid.

39 I am grateful to Chris Hobbs and other local historians for information on this subject.

40 ES to PT, 26 April 1945.

41 ES to PT, 4 May 1945.

42 See John C. Waller, 'In a Spin: The Mysterious Dancing Epidemic of 1518', *Endeavour*.

43 ES to PT, 11 May 1945.

44 T. S. Eliot, review of *Tarr* by Wyndham Lewis, and of *The People's Palace* by Sacheverell Sitwell, *Egoist* 6 (June/July 1918), 84–5.

45 ES, 10 August 1945.

46 ES to PT, 21 July 1945.

47 ES to PT, 3 February 1946.

48 See notes in Works 79, ES Collection, HRC.

49 *CP*, 292.

50 ES to PT, fragment 1946.

51 Algernon Charles Swinburne, excerpt from *Anactoria*, *Edith Sitwell's Anthology* (London: Victor Gollancz, 1940), 597.

52 See *The Times*, 17, 18, 24 September; 3, 8, 9, 10 October; and 15 December 1945.

53 Works 77, ES Collection, HRC.

54 *CP*, 376.

55 Lord Clark interview with John Pearson, Sitwell Collection, McFarlin Library, University of Tulsa.

56 *SLES*, 280.

57 ES to PT, 10 August 1945.

58 *CP*, 373.

59 Ibid., 371.

60 Ibid., 375 and 434n.

61 Ibid., 376.

62 *SLES*, 277–8.

63 ES to PT, 5 November 1945.

64 Evelyn Wiel to ES, 23 January 1946, recip. file, ES Collection, HRC.

65 ES to PT, 26 December 1945.

66 ES to PT, 3 February 1946.

67 ES to PT, 20 February 1946.

68 PT to ES, 30 December 1945.

69 Works 62, ES Collection, HRC.

CHAPTER 20: AN OLD MAD FACE

1 Dylan Thomas, *The Collected Letters*, ed. Paul Ferris, 652–3.

2 Geoffrey Grigson interview with John Pearson, Sitwell Collection, McFarlin Library, University of Tulsa.

3 ES to PT, 12 April 1946.

4 ES to PT, 16 May 1946.

5 Ibid.

6 *SLES*, 281–6.

7 Ibid., 287.

8 ES to PT, 3 November 1947.

9 Paul West, *I, Said the Sparrow*, 86.

10 Paul West, *Oxford Days*, 15–17.

11 ES to PT, 2 February 1948.

12 ES to PT, 26 September 1946.

13 ES to PT, 5 October 1946.

14 *Radio Times*, 29 September 1946; see also http://www.bbc.co.uk/radio3/classical/thirdprogramme/gallery/gallery.shtml?1

15 Transcripts of Reed's broadcasts, misc. file, ES Collection, HRC.

16 ES, 'Response to Henry Reed', Works 340, ES Collection, HRC; I am grateful to Rachel Lawson of the BBC Written Archives Centre for further information.

17 ES to PT, 25 January 1945.

18 Geoffrey Grigson, 'How Much Me Now Your Acrobatics Amaze', *Polemic*. An expanded version of the essay may be found in his *The Harp of Aeolus*, 151–60.

19 ES to PT, 19 July 1946.

20 ES to PT, 3 December 1946.

21 ES to PT, 5 October 1946.

22 Passport, misc. file, ES Collection, HRC.

23 ES to PT, 1 March 1947.

24 ES to PT, 29 January 1947.

25 PT to ES, 14 April 1947.

26 ES to PT, 3 May 1947.

27 Quoted in ES to PT, 26 July 1946.

28 ES to PT, 9 December 1946.

29 ES to Sir Kenneth Clark, 3 June 1946, Morgan Library and Museum, New York.

30 ES to Sir Kenneth Clark, 24 July 1947, Morgan Library and Museum, New York.

31 SS interview with John Pearson, Sitwell Collection, McFarlin Library, University of Tulsa.

32 ES to PT, 30 August 1947.

33 Neil Ritchie owns a copy of Sacheverell Sitwell's *British Architects and Craftsmen*, inscribed to Mrs Vincent Astor on 18 December 1945.

34 ES to PT, 21 May 1948.

35 Northrop Frye to ES, 12 April 1948, recip. file, ES Collection, HRC.

36 ES to PT, 26 July 1948.

37 ES to PT, 27 March 1948.

38 See Jack Lindsay, 'The Latest Poems of Edith Sitwell' in José Garcia Villa (ed.), *A Celebration for Edith Sitwell*, 44–53.

39 *SLES*, 308–9.

40 Jack Lindsay interview with Victoria Glendinning, Sitwell Collection, McFarlin Library, University of Tulsa.

41 ES to PT, 15 May 1948.

42 ES to Tom Clarkson, 25 January 1949, collection of Neil Ritchie.

43 Alec Guinness, *Blessings in Disguise*, 151.

44 ES to Graham Greene, n.d. [1945], Graham Greene Collection, Georgetown University.

45 ES to DH, 1 June 1948, OS Collection, HRC.

46 *SL*, 129.

47 ES to PT, 21 May 1948.

48 Peter Alexander, *William Plomer*, 237–8 and *passim*; this book is my main source of information on Sitwell's relations with Plomer and Bowes Lyon. I am also grateful to Professor Alexander for answering other queries by e-mail.

49 Lilian Bowes Lyon to ES, 12 July 1948, recip. file, ES Collection, HRC.

50 *SL*, 154–5.

51 ES to PT, 20 June 1940; see Pearson, 394–5.

52 *SL*, 169.

53 ES to PT, 19 July 1948.

54 ES to PT, 29 December 1947.

55 ES to PT, 16 February 1948.

56 *SL*, 159.

57 PT to ES, 7 January 1948.

58 ES to PT, 9 May 1948.

59 Charles Henri Ford, *Water from a Bucket*, 3–14.

60 ES to PT, 15 May 1948.

61 ES to PT, 5 June 1948.

62 ES to PT, 25 September 1948.

CHAPTER 21: THE OTHER SIDE OF THE WORLD

1 Ford, 12.

2 The account of the initial days of Sitwell's visit owes a great deal to Tyler, 461–4, and Ford, 14–17.

3 Tyler, 433 and *passim*.

4 Marianne Marusic to Richard Greene, 7 December 2008.

5 ES to PT, c. 27 October–2 November 1948.

6 Charles Henri Ford, journal, Ford Papers, 22.3, HRC.

7 Cecil Beaton told different versions of this story in his interviews with John Pearson and Victoria Glendinning, Sitwell Collection, McFarlin Library, University of Tulsa.

8 Tyler, 463–4.

9 Ford, 20–1, 33–4.

10 Charles Henri Ford, journal, Ford Papers, 22:3, HRC.

11 PT to ES, 16 November 1948, Berg Collection, NYPL.

12 Charles Henri Ford, journal, Ford Papers, 22:3, HRC.

13 ES to PT, 21 November 1948.

14 ES to PT, 8 December 1948.

15 Wyndham Lewis, *The Letters of Wyndham Lewis*, ed. W. K. Rose, 475.

16 Glenway Wescott, *Continual Lessons*, ed. Robert Phelps with Jerry Rosco, 217.

17 Glenway Wescott interview with John Pearson, McFarlin Library, University of Tulsa.

18 Ford, 19.

19 Francis Steloff, 'Some Gotham Party Lines', quoted in Elizabeth Salter, *Edith Sitwell*, 78; see also W. G. Rogers, *Wise Men Fish Here*, 224.

20 ES to Minnie Astor, 21 December 1948, Holland Library, WSU.

21 ES to PT, 26 December 1948.

22 ES to Maurice Cranston, 10 January 1949, ES Collection, HRC.

23 Charles Henri Ford, journal, Ford Papers, 22:4, HRC.

24 W. G. Rogers, op. cit., 167–8.

25 Truman Capote to ES, 21 August 1949, recip. file, ES Collection, HRC.

26 *SLES*, 318–19; Ford, 27–8; Monroe Wheeler, interview with John Pearson, Sitwell Collection, McFarlin Library, University of Tulsa.

27 Monroe Wheeler interview with John Pearson, Sitwell Collection, McFarlin Library, University of Tulsa.

28 Charles Henri Ford, journal, Ford Papers, 22:4, HRC.

29 Philip Hamburger, 'Musical Events: Cheers for Sitwell–Walton', *New Yorker*, 29 January 1949, 46.

30 Dorothy Norman, 'Two Lions Rampant: The Sitwells in the Same Room', MS, misc. file, ES Collection, HRC.

31 Dorothy Norman, 'Two Lions Rampant: The Sitwells in the Same Room', MS, misc. file, ES Collection, HRC.

32 See draft of speech, Works 10, ES Collection, HRC.

33 ES to John Ringling North, draft letter, Works 179, ES Collection, HRC.

34 Glenway Wescott, op. cit., 216–17.

35 ES, draft of talk on Whitman and Blake, Works 179, ES Collection, HRC.

36 Charles Henri Ford, journal, Ford Papers, 22:4, HRC.

37 Tyler, 464.

38 ES to PT, 15 March 1949.

39 PT to ES, 24 March 1949, Berg Collection, NYPL.

40 ES to PT, 3 April 1949; see earlier drafts of this letter in *SLES*, 316–19.

41 ES to PT, 22 April 1949.

42 *SLES*, 324.

43 PT to ES, 14 May 1949, Berg Collection, NYPL.

44 ES to PT, c. June 1949.

45 ES to PT, 10 May 1949.

46 ES to PT, 24 June 1949.

47 *SLES*, 320.

48 Statement of expenses for American tour, October 1948 to March 1949, misc. file, ES Collection, HRC.

49 *SLES*, 325.

50 Ibid., 325; Bradford, 361.

51 Journal entry, Works 179, ES Collection, HRC. ES kept a journal in the 1950s, but I have not been able to locate the rest of it – she may have destroyed it.

52 Peter Alexander, *Roy Campbell*, 173. I am also indebted to Professor Alexander for answering my e-mailed queries.

53 Quoted in Peter Alexander, op. cit., 206.

54 ES to Natasha Spender, 11 June 1946. This letter is in the private collection of Lady Spender.

55 Peter Alexander, op. cit., 143–4, 213–14, and *passim*.

56 ES to John Gawsworth (Terence Fytton Armstrong), 5 August 1949, Berg Collection, NYPL.

57 Peter Alexander, op. cit., 211–15.

58 ES to PT, 23 September 1949.

59 Peter Alexander, op. cit., 215.

60 *SLES*, 327.

61 Peter Alexander, op. cit., 215.

62 Roy Campbell to ES, n.d. [c. 1949], recip. file, ES Collection, HRC.

63 ES to PT, 2 October 1949; ES to PT, Wednesday [5 October 1949].

64 Maillart approached Sitwell through a woman named Irene (possibly the Marchioness of Carisbrooke, a cousin of Sitwell's on the Denison side), to whom she addressed a letter now in the recip. file, ES Collection, HRC.

65 ES to SS, c. December 1949, ES Collection, HRC.

66 ES to PT, 17 December 1948.

67 See Daniel Macmillan to ES, 23 June 1950, recip. file, ES Collection, HRC.

68 Lewis Thompson, 'Black Angel', *Black Sun*, ed. Richard Lannoy, 64. I have drawn biographical information from Lannoy's introduction, xi–xxi. See ES (ed.), *The Atlantic Book of British and American Poetry*, 2 vols (Boston: Little, Brown, 1958; London: Victor Gollancz, 1959), 869–73.

69 Quoted in Andrew Harvey, Foreword, Thompson, *Black Sun*, ix.

70 *SLES*, 331–2.

71 Ziegler, 322.

72 *SLES*, 294.

73 Ziegler, 320–2.

74 *LHRH* 4, 371–90.

75 Ford, 83–5; the manuscript journal is in the Ford Papers, 24:3, HRC. The details of their visit are drawn from this source.

76 Lincoln Kirstein to ES, 17 May 1950, recip. file, ES Collection, HRC.

77 Martin Duberman, *The Worlds of Lincoln Kirstein*, 482–3.

78 Tyler, 482.

79 ES to PT, 22 September 1950.

80 Ibid.

CHAPTER 22: FALLEN MAN DREAMS HE IS FALLING UPWARD

1 Lincoln Kirstein to ES, 27 August 1950, recip. file, ES Collection, HRC.

2 Glenway Wescott, *Continual Lessons*, ed. Robert Phelps with Jerry Rosco, 286. See also *New York Times*, 4 and 26 November 1950.

3 Alec Guinness to ES, 8 April 1951, recip. file, ES Collection, HRC. Gielgud's letters may be found in the same file.

4 Carson McCullers to ES, 26 November 1950, recip. file, ES Collection, HRC.

5 Carson McCullers to ES, n.d., recip. file, ES Collection. This letter is not attributed to McCullers in the collection, but is certainly written by her.

6 Lincoln Kirstein interview with John Pearson, Sitwell Collection, McFarlin Library, University of Tulsa.

7 ES to Jane Clark, 23 April 1951, Morgan Library and Museum, New York.

8 ES, 'Younger American Poets', Sitwell Collection, McFarlin Library, University of Tulsa.

9 Evelyn Wiel to ES, 29 October 1950, recip. file, ES Collection, HRC.

10 ES to Dorothy Marshall, 31 January 1951, Holland Library, WSU.

11 *SL*, 173.

12 Ibid., 174.

13 Kenneth and Miriam Patchen's letters are in the recip. file, ES Collection, HRC.

14 ES to PT, 18 March 1951 and 20 April 1951.

15 For a discussion of allusions to Marvell in Sitwell's poetry, see James Brophy, *Edith Sitwell*, 125–32.

16 ES to Natasha Spender, 20 May 1951, Berg Collection, NYPL.

17 *SL*, 176; *The Times*, 21 June 1951.

18 *SL*, 183.

19 Gore Vidal, 'How I Survived the Fifties', *New Yorker*, 66.

20 Salter, 15.

21 I am grateful to Bruce Hunter for this anecdote.

22 *ODNB*; Craggs x.

23 ES to Peter Pears, 7 August 1951, Britten–Pears Library, Aldeburgh.

24 ES to DH, 7 October 1951, OS Collection, HRC.

25 Geoffrey Gorer to ES, 13 November 1951, recip. file, ES Collection, HRC.

26 *SLES*, 348–9.

27 Ibid., 346.

28 ES to Siegfried Sassoon, 19 and 28 April 1952, Holland Library, WSU.

29 Humphrey Searle to ES, 17 December 1952, recip. file, ES Collection, HRC.

30 Humphrey Searle to ES, n.d., recip. file, ES Collection, HRC.

31 Humphrey Searle, 1 January 1953, recip. file, ES Collection, HRC.

32 Geoffrey Gorer to ES, 19 January 1953, recip. file, ES Collection, HRC.

33 *SLES*, 355.

34 Financial papers in misc. file, ES Collection, HRC.

35 Coutts & Co. to ES, 1 July 1955, recip. file, ES Collection, HRC.

36 Philip Frere to ES, 17 August 1953, recip. file, ES Collection, HRC.

37 Evelyn Wiel to ES, 4 February 1953, recip. file, ES Collection, HRC.

38 David Higham to ES, 17 November 1952, recip. file, ES Collection, HRC.

39 See Richard Greene (ed.), *Graham Greene*, 198; and Norman Sherry, *The Life of Graham Greene*, 2, 437–46.

40 McCarran form, misc. file, ES Collection, HRC.

41 *SLES*, 352.

42 Ibid., 353.

43 Draft of 'Hollywood', Works 156, ES Collection, HRC.

44 *SLES*, 353–4.

45 Ibid., 379.

46 ES to Minnie Astor, 29 December 1949, Holland Library, WSU.

47 Three letters of Rohan's from late 1949 are in the recip. file, ES Collection, HRC.

48 Draft of 'Hollywood', Works 156, ES Collection, HRC.

49 Draft of 'Hollywood', Works 89, ES Collection, HRC.

50 Draft of 'Hollywood', Works 156, ES Collection, HRC.

51 Ibid.

52 *TCO*, 183.

53 Mary Fraser to ES, 16 August 1957, recip. file, ES Collection, HRC.

54 Edward Weeks to ES, 12 June 1953, recip. file, ES Collection, HRC. See also Edward Weeks to A. C. E. Musk (Coutts & Co.), 29 October 1954, recip. file, ES Collection, HRC.

55 ES to SS, 10 December 1953, ES Collection, HRC.

56 Andrew Lycett, *Dylan Thomas*, 369.

57 See John Malcolm Brinnin, *Dylan Thomas in America*, 277 ff.

58 See Paul Ferris, *Dylan Thomas*, 315–26.

59 See James Nashold and George Tremlett, *The Death of Dylan Thomas*.

60 *SLES*, 386.

61 Louis MacNeice to ES, 7 December 1953, ES Collection, HRC.

62 SL, 187.

CHAPTER 23: FROST ON THE WINDOW

1 See, for example, Tijana Stojkovi , 'Unnoticed in the casual light of day', 65–7.

2 SLES, 406.

3 Ted Hughes to Richard Greene, 8 July 1995.

4 Information from Professor Marsha Bryant, who cites The Unabridged Journals of Sylvia Plath 1950–1962, ed. Karen V. Kukil (New York: Anchor Books, 2000) and other works.

5 ES to David Pleydell-Bouverie, 30 January 1954, Morgan Library and Museum, New York.

6 SLES, 358–9.

7 Ibid., 360.

8 Ibid., 362.

9 Kingsley Amis to ES, 25 June 1954, recip. file, ES Collection, HRC.

10 SLES, 357–8.

11 Ibid., 361.

12 ES, 'The Night Wind', CP, 387.

13 Jackson is quoted in Leo Lerman, The Grand Surprise, ed. Stephen Pascal, 348.

14 SLES, 363.

15 ES to Denys Kilham Roberts, 27 June 1954, Holland Library, WSU.

16 ES to Jane Clark, 26 June 1954, Morgan Library and Museum, New York.

17 ES to Siegfried Sassoon, 3 May 1955, Holland Library, WSU.

18 Evelyn Wiel, 8 June 1954, recip. file, ES Collection, HRC.

19 Philip Frere to ES, 28 March 1955, ES Collection, HRC.

20 PT to ES, 20 September 1954.

21 Note in Works 191, ES Collection, HRC.

22 ES to Jane Clark, 12 May 1950, Morgan Library and Museum, New York.

23 Anglo-French Literary Services, receipt, 14 June 1951, recip. file, ES Collection, HRC.

24 SLES, 366.

25 CP, 424.

26 ES to SS, 2 October 1954, SS Collection, HRC.

27 SLES, 368–9.

28 PT to ES, 14 October 1954.

29 PT to ES, 22 October 1954.

30 PT to ES, 6 November 1954 and 1 January 1954.

31 Edward Weeks to A. C. E. Musk, 29 October 1954, recip. file, ES Collection, HRC.

32 Richard Eberhart, review of *Collected Poems* by Edith Sitwell, *Poetry*, v. 87 (October 1955), 48.

33 Lincoln Kirstein interview with John Pearson, Sitwell Collection, McFarlin Library, University of Tulsa.

34 Leo Lerman, op. cit., 175–6 and 395.

35 Jerri Hays Olson, unpublished MS, Sitwell Collection, McFarlin Library, University of Tulsa.

36 Transcript of Mary Merryfield's Radio Journal, WMAQ – NBC, 28 January 1955, misc. file, ES Collection, HRC.

37 See Pearson, 428–38.

38 *SLES*, 370.

39 OS to DH, n.d. [c. 1930], OS Collection, HRC.

40 C. H. Ford interview with Geoffrey Elborn, Sitwell Collection, McFarlin Library, University of Tulsa.

41 Geoffrey Gorer interview with Geoffrey Elborn, Sitwell Collection, McFarlin Library, University of Tulsa.

42 *SLES*, 373.

43 Quoted in Anne and William Charlton, *Putting Poetry First*, 77.

44 *SLES*, 380.

45 ES to DH, 2 April 1944, OS Collection, HRC.

46 Mary Campbell to ES, 3 March 1955, ES Collection, HRC.

47 Muriel Spark, *The Girls of Slender Means* (London: Macmillan, 1963), 63; quoted in ODNB.

48 Martin D'Arcy, SJ, to ES, 14 April 1955, ES Collection, HRC.

49 Philip Caraman, SJ, to ES, 1 May 1955, ES Collection, HRC.

50 *SLES*, 378.

51 Philip Caraman, SJ, to ES, 15 May 1955, ES Collection, HRC.

52 *SLES*, 376.

53 Ibid., 378–9. See also Martin D'Arcy, SJ, *The Nature of Belief*, 261.

54 Philip Caraman, SJ, to ES, 5 August 1955, ES Collection, HRC.

55 Alec Guinness to ES, 18 July 1955, ES Collection, HRC. See also his *Blessings in Disguise*, 151–2.

56 Quentin Stevenson interview with Victoria Glendinning, Sitwell

Collection, McFarlin Library, University of Tulsa.

57 Evelyn Waugh, *The Letters of Evelyn Waugh*, ed. Mark Amory, 447–8 and 450–1.

58 Coutts & Co to ES, 1 and 21 July 1955, ES Collection, HRC.

59 R. R. Nash to ES, 19 September 1955, ES Collection, HRC.

60 Coutts & Co. to ES, 26 March 1956, ES Collection, HRC.

61 *SLES*, 382.

62 Ibid., 384.

63 Ibid., 385.

64 Quentin Stevenson to Richard Greene, 10 and 26 June 2009.

65 ES to Bryher, 20 October 1956, Bryher Papers, Beinecke Library, Yale University.

66 Edward Weeks to ES, 28 August 1956, ES Collection, HRC.

67 Contract with Little, Brown, 22 May 1956, ES Collection, HRC.

68 John McEwan, obituary, *Independent*, 4 September 2007.

69 *SLES*, 392.

70 Lecture on Poetry, Works 73, ES Collection, HRC.

71 Peter Levi, review of *The Succession* by Quentin Stevenson, *The Isis*, 30 October 1957, 23.

72 Peter Levi to Quentin Stevenson, 28 January 1999. Mr Stevenson has kindly sent me a photocopy of Levi's letters on the subject.

73 Quentin Stevenson, *The Making of Them* (2000).

74 'Lady Natasha Spender Remembers Edith Sitwell', *Daily Telegraph*, 20 June 2008.

75 Donald Spoto, *Marilyn Monroe: The Biography* (New York: HarperCollins, 1993), 376.

76 *SL*, 206–7.

77 *SLES*, 390.

78 James Purdy, 'An Autobiographical Sketch', James Purdy Society website, http://www.wright.edu/~martin.kich/PurdySoc/Autobio.htm; *SL*, 207; *SLES*, 390–2.

79 Val Clark, e-mail to Richard Greene, 21 May 2002.

CHAPTER 24: THE EMPRESS PENGUIN

1 *SLES*, 392–3. In some accounts of her fall, Sitwell names Andrade rather than Fraser.

2 ES to Lady Aberconway, 10 October 1954, BL.

3 *SLES*, 384.

4 Lorna Andrade interview with Geoffrey Elborn, Sitwell Collection, McFarlin Library, University of Tulsa.

5 *SLES*, 389.

6 Ibid., 395–6.

7 Ibid., 396.

8 Lorna Andrade interview with John Pearson, Sitwell Collection, McFarlin Library, University of Tulsa.

9 *SLES*, 397–8.

10 ES to SS, 14 March 1957, SS Collection, HRC.

11 Itineraries, ES Collection, HRC.

12 Brian Parker, e-mail to Richard Greene, 7 May 2009. Professor Parker is a member of the English Department at the University of Toronto.

13 *SLES*, 401.

14 Elizabeth Kray (YMHA Poetry Center), report on earnings 1957, ES Collection, HRC.

15 Account of Literary Earnings and Expenses 1956/57, misc. files, ES Collection, HRC.

16 Burke, Covington and Nash to Inspector of Taxes, 25 February 1959, ES Collection, HRC.

17 Coutts & Co. to ES, 30 July 1956 and 15 August 1957, ES Collection, HRC.

18 Lorna Andrade, 'Jottings', unpublished MS, Sitwell Collection, McFarlin Library, University of Tulsa; see also her interviews with Geoffrey Elborn and John Pearson at the same repository.

19 Peter Alexander, *Roy Campbell*, 240.

20 *SLES*, 398.

21 Charles Henri Ford, *Water from a Bucket*, 224–45.

22 PT to ES, 12 March 1957.

23 Further information on Tchelitchew's death is drawn from Tyler, 32–52.

24 *SLES*, 399.

25 James Purdy to ES, 26 July 1957, ES Collection, HRC.

26 ES to Evelyn Waugh, 28 July 1957, BL.

27 Muriel Spark, 'A Drink with Dame Edith', *Literary Review*, 31–2.

28 Charles Henri Ford and Choura Zoussailoff to ES, telegram, 1 August 1957, ES Collection, HRC.

29 *SLES*, 400.

30 Ibid., 400–1.

31 Ibid., 403–4.

32 Salter, 13–23.

33 *SL*, 216–17.

34 An original of this questionnaire may be found in ES Collection, HRC. It is transcribed in Salter, 49.

35 C. Day-Lewis to ES, 30 September 1955, ES Collection, HRC.

36 ES to SS, 8 November 1957, SS Collection, HRC.

37 Alec Guinness, *Blessings in Disguise*, 152–3.

38 ES, 'His Blood Colours My Cheek', *The Outcasts* (London: Macmillan, 1962), 21–2.

39 ES. 'The Outcasts', *The Outcasts*, 15.

40 The Oxford performance and the Beat luncheon are described in Salter, 48–70.

41 Barry Miles, *Allen Ginsberg: A Biography* (New York: Simon & Schuster, 1989), 246–8.

42 Quentin Stevenson interview with Victoria Glendinning, Sitwell Collection, McFarlin Library, University of Tulsa.

43 This presentation copy is now at the HRC. I am grateful to Patrice Fox for transcribing the inscription.

44 Barry Miles, op. cit., 246–8.

45 *SL*, 223–4.

46 Draft of *TCO*, Works 273, ES Collection, HRC.

47 *SL*, 224.

48 ES to Graham Greene, 17 April 1958, Lauinger Library, Georgetown University.

49 A. C. E. Musk to ES, 16 and 21 May 1958, ES Collection, HRC.

50 *SL*, 174–5.

51 *SLES*, 409.

52 John Crowe Ransom, 'Criticism as Pure Speculation', *Critical Theory Since Plato*, ed. Hazard Adams (New York: HBJ, 1971), 886

53 Northrop Frye, *The Anatomy of Criticism* (Princeton: Princeton University Press, 1957), 82.

54 W. K. Wimsatt and Monroe C. Beardsley, 'The Affective Fallacy', Hazard Adams (ed.), *Critical Theory Since Plato*, 1030.

55 ES to Graham Greene, 15 November 1958, Lauinger Library, Georgetown University.

56 Tony Gould, *Don't Fence Me In*, 20.

57 *SLES*, 424–5; Salter, 73–5.

58 ES to Salter, 5 September 1959, Holland Library, WSU; Salter, 75.

59 *SLES*, 409–10.

60 Salter, 104; Evelyn Wiel to ES, 9 May 1959, ES Collection, HRC. Note: de Lacerda is left out of Salter's version, but mentioned in Wiel's letter.

61 Evelyn Wiel to ES, 5 September 1959, ES Collection, HRC.

62 Salter, 104.

63 Philip Caraman, SJ, to ES, 20 January 1959, ES Collection, HRC.

64 ES to Elizabeth Salter, 16 February 1959, Holland Library, WSU.

65 ES to Elizabeth Salter, 23 June and 17 August 1959, Holland Library, WSU.

66 ES to Elizabeth Salter, 26 January and 21 May 1959, Holland Library, WSU.

CHAPTER 25: I PREFER CHANEL NUMBER 5

1 Marianne Moore, 'Dame Edith Sitwell', *Four Poets on Poetry*, ed. Don Cameron Allen, 76.

2 ES to Christopher Logue, drafts, Works 72, 266 and 300, ES Collection, HRC.

3 See Salter, 118–21.

4 *SLES*, 415–16.

5 Humphrey Carpenter, *Benjamin Britten*, 581.

6 Philip Caraman, SJ, to ES, 13 July 1958, ES Collection, HRC.

7 Philip Caraman, SJ, to ES, 3 December 1958, ES Collection, HRC.

8 Philip Caraman, SJ, to ES, 6 May 1959, ES Collection, HRC.

9 Philip Caraman, SJ, to ES, 23 September 1959, ES Collection, HRC.

10 ES to Elizabeth Salter, 29 June 1959, Holland Library, WSU.

11 ES to Elizabeth Salter, 5 August 1959, Holland Library, WSU.

12 Evelyn Wiel to ES, 5 September 1959, ES Collection, HRC.

13 ES to Salter, 20 August 1959, Holland Library, WSU; Salter, 93–5; *The Times*, 10 September 1959.

14 Miss Sutton and Miss Wright interview with John Pearson, Sitwell Collection, McFarlin Library, University of Tulsa.

15 *SLES*, 421.

16 Michael Stapleton, autobiographical statement, ES Collection, HRC.

17 ES to SS, 18 December 1959, SS Collection, HRC.

18 ES to Elizabeth Salter, 27 January 1960, Holland Library, WSU.

19 J. W. Nicholson to ES, 19 May 1960, ES Collection, HRC.

20 *SLES*, 422 and 427.

21 Lorna Andrade interview with Geoffrey Elborn, Sitwell Collection,

McFarlin Library, University of Tulsa.

22 Lorna Andrade interview with John Pearson, Sitwell Collection, McFarlin Library, University of Tulsa.

23 Lorna Andrade, 'Jottings', Sitwell Collection, McFarlin Library, University of Tulsa.

24 DH to GS, n.d. [1960]; quoted by Elborn, 250. I am here following Elborn, 249–52, as he had unique access to SS and GS in his research.

25 Elborn, 251.

26 *SLES*, 434.

27 Elborn, 252.

28 *SLES*, 428.

29 See Jeremy Lewis, *Penguin Special*, 315–33.

30 Gore Vidal, 'How I Survived the Fifties', *New Yorker*, 66. Vidal answered a further query in a letter to me of 25 October 1995.

31 ES to Graham Greene, 9 January 1961, Lauinger Library, Georgetown University.

32 *SLES*, 430.

33 Salter 130–3; *The Times*, 3 January 1961.

34 ES, 'A Girl's Song in Winter', *The Outcasts* (London: Macmillan, 1962) 26; the wording of line four is corrected as indicated by *SLES*, 438. See Salter, 134–5.

35 Salter, 139–47.

36 *SLES*, 436–7.

37 Ibid., 433.

38 Ziegler, 361–3.

39 Salter, 137–8.

40 *The Times*, 13 and 14 December 1961 and 20 June 1962. See also a draft of a press release on the sales of MSs in Works 290, ES Collection, HRC. A copy of the Tchelitchew auction catalogue with Sitwell's essay on the painter is also in the ES Collection, HRC. The figure of £1200 derives from an unidentified newspaper clipping in the ES Collection, HRC.

41 John Lehmann, *A Nest of Tigers*, 270.

42 ES to Kenneth Clark, 21 January 1961, Morgan Library and Museum, New York.

43 Lady Aberconway interview with John Pearson, Sitwell Collection, McFarlin Library, University of Tulsa.

44 William Sitwell, obituary of Francis Sitwell, *Independent*, 12 February 2004.

45 *SLES*, 440–2.

46 P. I. H. Doyle to ES, 25 April 1956, ES Collection, HRC.

47 William Sitwell, obituary of Francis Sitwell, *Independent*, 12 February 2004.

48 Noël Coward, *The Letters of Noël Coward*, ed. Barry Day, 83–7; Salter, 155–60.

49 *SLES*, 440.

50 *SL*, 245.

51 Noël Coward, *The Noël Coward Diaries*, ed. Graham Payn and Sheridan Morley, 518.

52 *SLES*, 448–9.

53 For example, *Los Angeles Times*, 9 October 1962.

54 *TCO*, 180.

55 *SL*, 346.

56 John Lehmann, op. cit., 272–4; Salter, 171–6.

57 *The Times*, 10 October 1962.

58 *SLES*, 451.

59 Ibid., 449.

60 See Salter, 167–8.

61 Ibid., 169.

62 *SLES*, 450.

63 *The Times*, 1 January 1963.

64 *SLES*, 169–70.

65 ES to Jane Clark, 2 March 1963, Morgan Library and Museum, New York.

66 *SL*, 250.

67 Salter, 171–9. I rely heavily on this source for my account of the voyage.

68 *Sydney Morning Herald*, 4 April 1963.

69 *Sydney Morning Herald*, 20 April 1963.

70 *Sydney Morning Herald*, 17 April 1963.

71 Salter, 91.

72 *Sydney Morning Herald*, 20 April 1963.

73 *The Times*, 26 June 1963.

74 *The Times*, 25 May 1963. Further information from Judy Burg, University Archivist, University of Hull.

75 *SLES*, 454.

76 Salter, 187–9.

77 *New York Times*, 22 March 1964.

78 ES to Evelyn Waugh, September 1964, BL.

79 Francis Sitwell interview with Victoria Glendinning, Sitwell Collection, McFarlin Library, University of Tulsa.

80 *Sun*, 10 December 1964.

81 Marianne Moore to OS, 13 September 1964, OS Collection, HRC.

82 Freeman is quoted in Tom Driberg, 'Edith Sitwell at Home', *Encounter*, XXVI:5 (May 1966), 55.

83 Salter, 201.

84 Elborn, 275–6.

85 *The Times*, 15 December 1964.

86 GS to Evelyn Waugh, 20 January 1965, BL.

87 Elizabeth Salter, *Edith Sitwell*, 101.

Further Reading

Aberconway, Christabel, A Wiser Woman? (London: Hutchinson, 1966).

Acton, Harold, Memoirs of an Aesthete (London: Methuen, 1948).

——————, More Memoirs of an Aesthete (London: Methuen, 1970).

Alexander, Peter, Roy Campbell: A Critical Biography (Oxford: Oxford University Press, 1982).

——————, William Plomer: A Biography (Oxford and New York: Oxford University Press, 1989).

Barney, Natalie Clifford, A Perilous Advantage: The Best of Natalie Clifford Barney, ed. and trans. Anna Livia (Norwich, VT: New Victoria Publishers, 1992).

Bowen, Stella, Drawn from Life (1940; 2nd edn, Maidstone: George Mann, 1974).

Bowra, C. M., Edith Sitwell (Monaco: Lyrebird, 1947).

Bradford, Sarah, Splendours and Miseries: A Life of Sacheverell Sitwell (London: Sinclair-Stevenson, 1993).

Brinnin, John Malcolm, Dylan Thomas in America (Boston: Little, Brown, 1955).

Brophy, James, Edith Sitwell: The Symbolist Order (Carbondale and Edwardsville: Southern Illinois University Press, 1968).

Blavatsky, Helena, Isis Unveiled, 2 vols (1877; Theosophical University Press Online Edition).

Carpenter, Humphrey, Benjamin Britten: A Biography (London: Faber & Faber, 1992).

Cevasco, G. A., The Sitwells: Edith, Osbert, and Sacheverell (Boston: Twayne, 1987).

Charlton, Anne, and William Charlton, Putting Poetry First: A Life of Robert Nichols 1893–1944 (Norwich: Michael Russell, 2003).

Charteris, Evan, *The Life and Letters of Sir Edmund Gosse* (London: Heinemann, 1931).

Clegg, Elizabeth, 'Meštrović, England and the Great War', *Burlington Magazine*, vol. 144, no. 1197 (December 2002), 740–51.

Clements, Patricia, *Baudelaire & The English Tradition* (Princeton, NJ: Princeton University Press, 1985).

Coward, Noël, *The Letters of Noël Coward*, ed. Barry Day (New York: Alfred A. Knopf, 2007).

——————, *The Noël Coward Diaries*, ed. Graham Payn and Sheridan Morley (London: Macmillan, 1983).

——————, *A Withered Nosegay* (London: Methuen, 1984).

Craggs, Stewart, Preface, v–xii in *William Walton Edition*, gen. ed. David Lloyd-Jones, consultant Stewart Craggs (Oxford: Oxford University Press, 1998–), vol. 7: *Façade Entertainments*, ed. David Lloyd-Jones (2000).

Crawford, Elizabeth, *The Women's Suffrage Movement: A Reference Guide 1966–1928* (London: UCL Press, 1999).

Cudlipp, Hugh, *Publish and Be Damned! The Astonishing Story of the Daily Mirror* (London: Andrew Dakers, 1953).

D'Arcy, Martin, SJ, *The Nature of Belief* (London: Sheed & Ward, 1931).

Douglas-Home, Jessica, *Violet: The Life and Loves of Violet Gordon Woodhouse* (London: The Harvill Press, 1996).

Driberg, Tom, 'Edith Sitwell at Home', *Encounter* XXVI:5 (May 1966), 55.

Drummond, John, *Speaking of Diaghilev* (London: Faber & Faber, 1997).

Duberman, Martin, *The Worlds of Lincoln Kirstein* (New York: Knopf, 2007).

Duncan, David, *Pavel Tchelitchew: The Landscape of the Body*, Katonah Museum of Art Catalog no. 27 (1998).

Ebony, David 'The Melancholy Gang: Eugene Berman and his Circle', *Art in America* (March 2006), www.artinamericamagazine.com.

Edelman, Maurice, *The Mirror: A Political History* (London: Hamish Hamilton, 1966).

Egremont, Max, *Siegfried Sassoon: A Biography* (London: Picador, 2005).

Elborn, Geoffrey, *Edith Sitwell: A Biography* (New York: Doubleday, 1981).

Eliot, T. S., *The Letters of T. S. Eliot*, ed. Valerie Eliot and Hugh Haughton, 2 vols to date (London: Faber & Faber, 1988–).

——————, review of *Tarr* by Wyndham Lewis and *The People's Palace* by Sacheverell Sitwell, *Egoist*, 6 (June/ July 1918), 84–5.

Ellmann, Richard, *James Joyce* (New York: Oxford University Press, 1965).

Ernst, F. Gustav, *A Guide to the Selection and Adaptation of Orthopædic Apparatus* (London, 1889).

Ferris, Paul, *Dylan Thomas: The Biography* (1977; new edn, London: Hodder and Stoughton, 1999; Washington: Counterpoint, 2000).

Fifoot, Richard, *A Bibliography of Edith, Osbert and Sacheverell Sitwell* (1963; 2nd edn, revised, London: Archon Books, 1971).

Fitch, Noel Riley, *Sylvia Beach and the Lost Generation: A History of Literary Paris in the Twenties and Thirties* (New York: W. W. Norton, 1983).

Fitzgibbon, Constantine, *The Life of Dylan Thomas* (London: J. M. Dent, 1965).

Ford, Charles Henri, *Water from a Bucket: A Diary 1948–1957* (New York: Turtle Point Press, 2001).

—————, *The Young and Evil* (Paris: Obelisk Press, 1933).

Foster, R. F., *W. B. Yeats: A Life*, 2 vols (Oxford: Oxford University Press, 1997–2003).

Glendinning, Victoria, *Edith Sitwell: A Lion among Unicorns* (London: George Weidenfeld & Nicolson, 1981).

—————, *Vita: The Life of Vita Sackville-West* (London, 1983).

Gordon, Lois, *Nancy Cunard: Heiress, Muse, Political Idealist* (New York: Columbia University Press, 2007).

Gordon, Lyndall, *T. S. Eliot: An Imperfect Life* (New York and London: W. W. Norton, 1998).

Gould, Tony, *Don't Fence Me In: From Curse to Cure Leprosy in Modern Times* (London: Bloomsbury, 2005).

Graves, Robert, *Goodbye to All That* (1929; Oxford and Providence, RI: Berghahn Books, 1995).

Green, Geoffrey, 'Bayswater and the New West End Synagogue during World War Two', www.newwestend.org.uk.

Greene, Richard (ed.), *Graham Greene: A Life in Letters* (London: Little, Brown, 2007; New York: W.W. Norton, 2008).

—————, 'Sir Beelzebub's Syllabub: Or, Edith Sitwell's Eighteenth Century', *Lumen*, 20 (2001), 101–9.

Greene, Thomas M., 'Labyrinth Dances in the French and English Renaissance', *Renaissance Quarterly*, 54:4, part 2 (winter 2001), 1403–66.

Greer, David, *A Numerous and Fashionable Audience: The Story of Elsie Swinton* (London: Thames Publishing, 1997).

Gregory, James, 'Eccentric Biography and the Victorians', *Biography*, 30.3 (summer 2007), 342–76.

Grigson, Geoffrey, *The Harp of Aeolus* (London: George Routledge & Sons, 1947).

——, 'How Much Me Now Your Acrobatics Amaze', *Polemic*, 3 (May 1946), 8–13.

Guinness, Alec, *Blessings in Disguise* (London: Hamish Hamilton, 1985).

Hamnett, Nina, *Laughing Torso* (London: Constable, 1932).

Higham, David, *Literary Gent* (London: Jonathan Cape, 1978).

Holman-Hunt, Diana, *Latin Among Lions: Alvaro Guevara* (London: Michael Joseph, 1974).

Hooker, Denise, *Nina Hamnett: Queen of Bohemia* (London: Constable, 1986).

Huxley, Aldous, *Letters of Aldous Huxley*, ed. Grover Smith (London: Chatto & Windus, 1969).

James, Edward, *Swans Reflecting Elephants: My Early Years* (London: Weidenfeld & Nicolson, 1982).

Johnson, Claudia L., 'F. R. Leavis: The "Great Tradition" of the English Novel and the Jewish Part', *Nineteenth-Century Literature*, 56:2 (September 2001), 198–227.

Joyce, James, *Letters of James Joyce*, ed. Stuart Gilbert (New York: Viking Press, 1957).

Kennedy, Michael, *Portrait of Walton* (Oxford: Oxford University Press, 1989).

King, James, *The Last Modern: A Life of Herbert Read* (London: Weidenfeld & Nicolson, 1990).

King-Hall, Stephen, *Total Victory* (London: Faber & Faber, 1941).

Lane, Constance, *The Three Rectories: Withington – Kennington – Little Gaddesden* (Chichester: Phillimore, 2004).

Langfield, Valerie, *Roger Quilter, His Life and Music* (Woodridge: Boydell Press, 2002).

Lawrence, D. H., *Collected Letters*, ed. Harry T. Moore, 2 vols (London: Heinemann, 1962).

Leavis, F. R., *New Bearings in English Poetry* (London: Chatto & Windus, 1932).

Lehmann, John, *Edith Sitwell* (London: British Council and National Book League, 1952; revised edn, 1970).

—————, *In My Own Time: Memoirs of a Literary Life* (Boston: Little, Brown, 1969).

—————, *A Nest of Tigers: Edith, Osbert, and Sacheverell Sitwell in their Times* (London: Macmillan, 1968).

Lerman, Leo, *The Grand Surprise: The Journals of Leo Lerman*, ed. Stephen Pascal (New York: Alfred A. Knopf, 2007).

Lewis, Jeremy, *Penguin Special: The Life and Times of Allen Lane* (London: Penguin, 2006).

Lewis, Wyndham, *The Apes of God* (1930; Santa Barbara: Black Sparrow Press, 1981).

—————, *The Letters of Wyndham Lewis*, ed. W. K. Rose (London: Methuen, 1963).

Lincoln, Bruce, 'Revolutionary Exhumations in Spain, July 1936', *Comparative Studies in Society and History*, 27:2 (April 1985), 241–60.

Lindsay, Jack, *Meetings with Poets* (London: Frederick Muller, 1968).

Lowe, John, *Edward James: A Surrealist Life* (London: William Collins, 1991).

—————, *The Warden: A Portrait of John Sparrow* (London: HarperCollins, 1998).

Lowndes, Marie Belloc, *Diaries and Letters of Marie Belloc Lowndes 1911–1947*, ed. Susan Lowndes (London: Chatto & Windus, 1971).

Lycett, Andrew, *Dylan Thomas: A New Life* (London: Weidenfeld & Nicolson, 2003).

MacKillop, Ian, *F. R. Leavis: A Life in Criticism* (London: Allen Lane, 1995).

Marino, Antonio Montero, *Historia de la persecución religiosa en España, 1936–1939* (Madrid, 1961).

Martin, Wallace, *The New Age Under Orage: Chapters in English Cultural History* (Manchester: Manchester University Press, 1967).

Matthews, W. H., *Mazes and Labyrinths* (London: Longmans, Green, 1922).

Mégroz, R. L., *The Three Sitwells: A Biographical and Critical Study* (London: Richards Press, 1927).

Mitchell, L. G., *Maurice Bowra: A Life* (Oxford: Oxford University Press, 2009).

Moore, Marianne, 'Dame Edith Sitwell', *Four Poets on Poetry*, ed. Don Cameron Allen (Baltimore: Johns Hopkins Press, 1959).

Muir, Edwin, *An Autobiography* (London: Hogarth Press, 1954).

Nashold, James, and George Tremlett, *The Death of Dylan Thomas* (Edinburgh: Mainstream Publishing, 1997).

Noyes, Alfred, *Two Worlds for Memory* (Philadelphia and New York: J. B. Lippincott, 1953).

O'Keeffe, Paul, *Some Sort of Genius: A Life of Wyndham Lewis* (London: Jonathan Cape, 2000).

Pearson, John, *Façades: Edith, Osbert and Sacheverell Sitwell* (London: Macmillan, 1978).

Powell, Anthony, *To Keep the Ball Rolling*, 4 vols (London: Heinemann, 1976–82).

Raper, Arthur, *The Tragedy of Lynching* (Chapel Hill: University of North Carolina Press, 1933).

Reilly, Catherine (ed.), *Scars Upon My Heart* (London: Virago, 1993).

Riding, Laura, and Robert Graves, *A Survey of Modernist Poetry* (London: Heinemann, 1927).

Rigby, Andrew, *Initiation and Initiative: An Exploration of the Life and Ideas of Dimitrije Mitrinović* (Boulder: East European Monographs, CLXIV, 1984).

Ritchie, Neil, 'Footnote to Façade', *The Book Collector* (Summer 1996), 261–2.

Roberts, John Stuart, *Siegfried Sassoon* (London: Richard Cohen Books, 1999).

Rogers, W. G., *Wise Men Fish Here: The Story of Frances Steloff and the Gotham Book Mart* (New York: Harcourt, Brace & World, 1965).

Rootham, Helen, *Fundamentals of Music and their Relation to Modern Life* (London; Burns, Oates & Washbourne, 1925).

———— (trans.), *Kosovo: Heroic Songs of the Serbs*, intro. Maurice Baring, historical preface Janko Lavrin (Oxford: B. H. Blackwell, 1920).

———— (trans.), *Prose Poems from Les Illuminations*, intro. Edith Sitwell (London: Faber & Faber, 1932).

Rutherford, H. C. (ed.), *Certainly, Future: Selected Writings by Dimitrije Mitrinović* (New York: Columbia University Press, 1987).

Salter, Elizabeth, *Edith Sitwell* (London: Jupiter Books, 1979)

————, *The Last Years of a Rebel: A Memoir of Edith Sitwell* (London: Bodley Head, 1967).

Sassoon, Siegfried, *Memoirs of an Infantry Officer* (1930; London: Faber & Faber, 1965).

————, *Siegfried Sassoon Diaries 1915–1918*, ed. Rupert Hart-Davis (London: Faber & Faber, 1983).

Schehr, Lawrence, *Alcibiades at the Door: Gay Discourses on French Literature* (Palo Alto: Stanford University Press, 1995).

Schuster, David G., 'Personalizing Illness and Modernity: S. Weir Mitchell, Literary Women, and Neurasthenia, 1870–1914', *Bulletin of the History of Medicine*, 79.4 (2005), 695–722.

Seymour-Smith, Martin, *Robert Graves: His Life and Work* (London: Hutchinson, 1982).

Sherry, Norman, *The Life of Graham Greene*, 3 vols (London: Jonathan Cape, 1989–2004).

Shulman, Nicola, *A Rage for Rock Gardening: The Story of Reginald Farrer Gardener, Writer & Plant-Collector* (Boston: David R. Godine, 2004).

Sickert, Walter, *A Free House! Or the Artist as Craftsman*, ed. Osbert Sitwell (London: Macmillan, 1947).

Silver, Kenneth E., 'Neo-Romantics', in Donald Albrecht (ed.), *Paris/New York: Design/Fashion/Culture 1925–1940* (New York: The Monacelli Press, 2008), 216–29.

Sitwell, Constance, *Bounteous Days* (London: Cecil Woolf, 1976).

—————, *Bright Morning* (London: Jonathan Cape, 1942).

—————, *Frolic Youth* (London, 1964).

Sitwell, George R., *The Barons of Pulford* (p.p., 1889).

—————, *A Brief History of Weston Hall, Northamptonshire, and of the Families that Possessed It* (London: p.p., 1927).

—————, *Idle Fancies in Prose and Verse* (Oxford: p.p., 1939).

—————, *On the Making of Gardens* (London: John Murray, 1909).

Sitwell, Osbert, *Before the Bombardment* (London: Duckworth, 1926; reprinted 1974).

—————, *Left Hand, Right Hand!*, 5 vols (London: Macmillan, 1945–50).

—————, *Tales My Father Told Me* (London: Hutchinson, 1962).

————— (ed.), *Two Generations* (London: Macmillan, 1940).

Sitwell, Reresby, *Renishaw Hall and the Sitwells* (p.p., n.d.).

Sitwell, Sacheverell, *All Summer in a Day* (London: Duckworth, 1931).

—————, *Apologia in Prose, Dodecameron* (Brackley: p.p., 1977).

—————, *For Want of the Golden City* (London: Thames & Hudson, 1973).

—————, *The Homing of the Winds* (London: Faber & Faber, 1942).

—————, *An Indian Summer* (London: Macmillan, 1982).

—————, *Liszt* (1934; London: Columbus Books, 1988).

—————, *Splendours and Miseries* (London: Faber & Faber, 1943).

The Sitwells and the Arts of the 1920s and 1930s (London: NPG, 1994).

Skeaping, John, *Drawn from Life: An Autobiography* (London: Collins, 1977).

Spark, Muriel, 'A Drink with Dame Edith', *Literary Review* (February 1999), 32.

Sparrow, John, *Sense and Poetry* (London: Constable, 1934).

Spender, Natasha, 'Lady Natasha Spender Remembers Edith Sitwell', *Daily Telegraph* (8 June 2008).

Stein, Gertrude, *The Autobiography of Alice B. Toklas* (1933; New York: Vintage Books, 1960).

Stojkovi, Tijana, *'Unnoticed in the casual light of day': Philip Larkin and the Plain Style* (London: CRC Press, 2006).

Sturgis, Matthew, *Walter Sickert: A Life* (London: HarperCollins, 2005).

Thomas, Dylan, *The Collected Letters*, ed. Paul Ferris (London: J. M. Dent, 1985; 2nd edn 2000).

Thompson, Lewis, *Black Sun: The Collected Poems of Lewis Thompson*, ed. Richard Lannoy (Prescott, Arizona: Hohm Press, 2001).

Thwaite, Ann, *Edmund Gosse: A Literary Landscape 1849–1928* (London: Secker & Warburg, 1984).

Toklas, Alice B., *What is Remembered* (New York: Holt, Rinehart & Winston, 1963).

Trevelyan, Raleigh, *A Hermit Disclosed* (London: Longman's, 1960).

—————, 'Two Ediths and a Hermit', *London Review of Books* (5 September 1985).

Tubby, A. H., *Deformities: A Treatise on Orthopædic Surgery* (London, 1896; 2nd edn 1912).

Tyler, Parker, *The Divine Comedy of Pavel Tchelitchew* (New York: Fleet, 1967).

Vickers, Hugo, *Cecil Beaton: The Authorized Biography* (London: Weidenfeld & Nicolson, 1985).

Vidal, Gore, 'How I Survived the Fifties', *New Yorker* (2 October 1995), 62–76.

Villa, José Garcia (ed.), *A Celebration for Edith Sitwell* (New York: New Directions, 1948).

Waller, John C., 'In a Spin: The Mysterious Dancing Epidemic of 1518', *Endeavour*, 32:3 (September 2008), 117–21.

Walter, Eugene (as told to Katherine Clark), *Milking the Moon: A Southerner's Story of Life on This Planet* (New York: Crown Publishers, 2001).

Walton, William, *Façade 2: Facsimile* (Oxford: Oxford University Press, 1979).

Warner, Philip, *The Battle of Loos* (London: Kimber, 1976).

Waugh, Evelyn, *The Diaries of Evelyn Waugh*, ed. Michael Davie (London: Weidenfeld & Nicolson; Boston: Little, Brown, 1976).

——————, *The Letters of Evelyn Waugh*, ed. Mark Amory (London: Weidenfeld & Nicolson, 1980).

Welch, Denton, *A Lunch Appointment* (North Pomfret, VT: Elysium Press, 1993).

——————, *The Journals of Denton Welch*, ed. Michael De-La-Noy (London: Allison & Busby, 1984).

Wescott, Glenway, *Continual Lessons: The Journals of Glenway Wescott 1937-1955*, ed. Robert Phelps with Jerry Rosco (New York: Farrar Straus Giroux, 1990).

West, Paul, *I, Said the Sparrow* (London: Hutchinson, 1963).

——————, *Oxford Days: An Inclination* (Latham, New York: British American Publishing, 2002).

Whitman, Walt, *Selected Poems*, ed. Christopher Moore (New York: Gramercy Books, 1992).

Wilson, Jean Moorcroft, *Siegfried Sassoon: The Making of a War Poet* (London: Duckworth, 1998).

Woolf, Virginia, *The Diary of Virginia Woolf*, ed. Anne Olivier Bell, asst. Andrew McNeillie, 5 vols (London: The Hogarth Press, 1977–84).

——————, *The Letters of Virginia Woolf*, ed. Nigel Nicolson and J. Trautmann, 6 vols (London: The Hogarth Press, 1975–80).

——————, *A Moment's Liberty: The Shorter Diary*, ed. Anne Olivier Bell (London: Hogarth Press, 1990).

Wright, Adrian, *John Lehmann: A Pagan Adventure* (London: Gerald Duckworth, 1998).

Ziegler, Philip, *Osbert Sitwell: A Biography* (London: Chatto & Windus, 1998).

List of Illustrations

Acknowledgements

In the writing of this book, I have benefited from the generosity of many people. My greatest debt is to the late Francis Sitwell and to Susanna Sitwell, who encouraged my research over many years. I am also grateful to the late Sir Reresby Sitwell and to Lady Sitwell, to William Sitwell and to other members of the Sitwell family. For twenty-three years I have had the good advice of Bruce Hunter of David Higham Associates; he is the best and most patient of literary agents. I have had the guidance of expert publishers and editors at Little, Brown UK: Alan Samson, Richard Beswick, Lennie Goodings, Zoe Gullen and their colleagues. I have had the help of an expert research assistant, Marybeth Curtin. I am under very great obligations to many other people: Rev. William Adams, Peter Alexander, Sidney Aster, John Barham, James Beechey, Andrew Biswell, Barbara Cassel, Anne Charlton, Andrew Clay, HRH the Duchess of Cornwall, Melba Cuddy-Keane, Robert Murray Davis, Barry Day, Kildare Dobbs, Geoffrey Elborn, Roy Foster, Patrice Fox, Fred Flahiff, Isaac Gewirtz, the late Sir John Gielgud, Lyndall Gordon, Edward Greene, Geoffrey Green, Francis Greene, Sarah Greene, Samuel Greene, the late Sir Alec Guinness, John Haffenden, Jonathan Harris, Selina Hastings, Chris Hobbs, the late Ted Hughes, Heather Jackson, Sir Patrick Leigh Fermor, the late Peter Levi, Jeremy Lewis, John MacDermot, Marianne Marusic, Rev. Gilles Mongeau, SJ, The Rt Hon the Lord Monteagle, Barbara Newman, Richard Oram, Karl Orend, Brian Parker, Derek Parker, David Pearce, John Pearson, Andrew Rigby, Neil Ritchie, Jane St. Aubyn, Amanda Saunders, Mary Savigny, Nicholas Scheetz, Rabbi Geoffrey L. Shisler, James Sexton, Nicholas Shakespeare, Lady (Natasha) Spender, Sam Solecki, Thomas Staley, Quentin Stevenson, The Hon. Julia Camoys Stonor, Elizabeth Swarbrick, Nicholas Swarbrick, Margaret Swarbrick, Leslie Thomson, Raleigh Trevelyan, Gore Vidal, James Watson, Alexander Waugh, Paul West, and Philip Ziegler. The research for this book was funded by a Fleur Cowles Research Fellowship and a Mellon Foundation Research Fellowship, both of which were granted by the Harry Ransom Center at the University of Texas at Austin, and by a Standard Research Grant of the Social Sciences and Humanities Research Council of Canada.

Index